CLASSIC STAR WARS

THE EARLY ADVENTURES

writer & artist
Russ Manning

cover artist
Al Williamson

cover colorist
Tom Roberts

colorist
Ray Murtaugh

art retouch
Rick Hoberg
Brian Snoddy

introduction
Mike Royer

art assist
Rick Hoberg
Dave Stevens
Alfredo Alcala

---

publisher
Mike Richardson

series editors
Peet Janes
Bob Cooper

collection editor
Suzanne Taylor

production design
Harald Graham

collection design manager
Brian Gogolin

special thanks to
Lucy Autrey Wilson and **Allan Kausch**
at Lucasfilm Licensing,
Barry Short, Roger Manning,
David Seidman, and **Mike Royer.**

CLASSIC STAR WARS

THE EARLY ADVENTURES

by

Russ Manning

DARK HORSE COMICS®

MIKE RICHARDSON
publisher

NEIL HANKERSON
executive vp

DAVID SCROGGY
vp of publishing

LOU BANK
vp of sales & marketing

ANDY KARABATSOS
vp of finance

MARK ANDERSON
general counsel

MELONEY C. CHADWICK
director of editorial adm.

RANDY STRADLEY
creative director

CINDY MARKS
director of production & design

MARK COX
art director

SEAN TIERNEY
computer graphics director

MICHAEL MARTENS
director of sales & marketing

TOD BORLESKE
director of licensing

DALE LAFOUNTAIN
director of m.i.s.

KIM HAINES
director of human resources

CLASSIC STAR WARS® THE EARLY ADVENTURES VOLUME FOUR

This book collects issues 1-9 of the Dark Horse comic-book series *Classic Star Wars®: The Early Adventures*.

Published by
Dark Horse Comics, Inc.
10956 SE Main Street
Milwaukie, OR 97222

May 1997
First edition
ISBN: 1-56971-178-X

2 4 6 8 10 9 7 5 3 1

Printed in Canada

A Master Storyteller

by Mike Royer

To say that Russ Manning was an influence on me and my career is an understatement. Simply put, I would not have spent the last 31 years doing what I love, supporting family, home, and hobbies with the product of my hand and mind if not for the encouragement and tutelage of Russ Manning, my mentor. I am a member of what I consider a select group of artists who worked with and were influenced by Russ Manning . . . such illustrious talents as Bill Stout, Dave Stevens, and Rick Hoberg.

I was born in 1941, and, as a youngster, I fell in love with comic strips . . . old, yellowed pages of Foster and Hogarth's "Tarzan," Raymond's "Flash Gordon," and Caniff's "Terry and the Pirates" discovered in my grandmother's attic as well as the contemporary Tufts's "Casey Ruggles and Lance," Foster's "Prince Valiant," Caniff's "Steve Canyon," and Hamlin's "Alley Oop." The comic books I bought were usually those reprinting the aforementioned titles. Most "new material" impressed me

Russ Manning

little, with the exception of Kirby (that's another story) and the artist doing back-up stories in *Tarzan*, and then full titles such as *Dale Evans, Sea Hunt*, etc. With the early '60s publication of *Magnus, Robot Fighter* I finally learned that artist's name: Russ Manning. I held in my hands the finest example of comic-strip art created exclusively for comic books. It was then that I decided the direction my life should take — the world of comic art.

Somehow, I discovered Russ's interest in Burroughs fandom, and I naively assumed he would attend the Dum-Dum at the upcoming World Science Fiction Convention. After securing permission from Hulbert Burroughs, another

Burroughs fan and I produced a 36-page *Wizard of Venus* comic book, which we took to Oakland for the '64 World Con. My goal was to meet Russ, show him my attempt at comic art, and see what would then transpire. However, he did not attend.

Undaunted, I returned home to Oregon. I drew up new sample pages and sent them to Russ's home outside Orange, California. In early '65, Russ responded saying that the samples showed some promise, and "If I ever needed any help, I don't see why you wouldn't be capable of it." That was all the encouragement I needed. Within three months, my family and I were residents of Southern California.

Russ Manning, perhaps remembering the help and encouragement given to him at the beginning of his career by Jesse Marsh, really didn't need help with his comic-book assignments. However, he found work for me to do, a kindness for which I will always be grateful. For about a year, my evenings and weekends were spent circling balloons, finishing rough pencils, completing partially inked figures, etc. I was "assisting" and learning from a master.

The second year, as a result of Russ's recommendation, I went from working days for Sherwin-Williams Paint to the limited animation *Marvel Super Heroes* television series and continued to assist and learn from Russ Manning's Gold Key comic-book assignments. As Russ's popularity grew with comic-book buyers, Gold Key wanted more work from him. Russ informed his editor that the only way he could produce more work would be if I worked with him more than I already was. The only way I could do that and give up the animation business would be by having full-time employment in comic books.

Thanks to Russ, I was now working full-time in the comics industry, assisting him and pulling assignments from Gold Key comics. It transpired that Russ's efforts on the *Tarzan* comic book (the "more" Gold Key wanted) resulted in Edgar Rice Burroughs, Inc. offering him the "Tarzan" syndicated comic strip. Russ left Gold Key/Western Publishing to do what he'd always wanted to do — a syndicated comics feature — and I now had my foot firmly planted in the door of the comic-book business.

In a few months, I was assisting on the "Tarzan" daily and Sunday strips, working with and learning from the most dynamic syndicated strip artist of the decade. Russ found new ways to do wonderful panel breakdowns within the mechanical restrictions of the Sunday strip that have never been equaled for sheer beauty and execution . . . it was an ability he would bring to his next assignment. As I began inking almost full–time for Jack Kirby, the talented Bill Stout joined Russ's team. Benefiting from Stout's color experience, Russ utilized the time saved in coloring the Sunday release to do even greater work on his "Tarzan" graphics.

One day in mid-1978, Russ telephoned to say he was going to be writing and drawing the "Star Wars" daily and Sunday strip and would be continuing to produce the Sunday "Tarzan." He asked if I would be interested in doing all the inking and lettering. Russ would be trusting me with *all* the inking! Talk about intimidating! It turned out to be an exciting 17 weeks. Then Disney called, but that's yet another story.

Russ Manning was the consummate cartoonist/illustrator. He rightfully took great pride in his work, both the art and the written word. He was the kind of creator who, I believe, felt that the work should all come from his hand to be truly his. With the amount of work he had to produce, there was just no way he could do it all himself, and I feel very privileged that, as a "necessary evil," Russ selected me.

I've spoken little of Russ's work on "Star Wars" because you hold in your hands a collection of some of the greatest daily comic-strip art and writing done in the last quarter of the 20th century. It speaks for itself. Within prescribed guidelines of continuity length, separate daily and Sunday adventures, and instructions to not involve the complete cast in both continuities, Russ drew on his love of science fiction, his admiration of the cinematic achievements of *Star Wars*, and his years of experience as a master of graphic storytelling and poured himself completely into his challenging new assignment.

It's all here . . . the great design sense, the masterful use of black, the "framing" of set-ups so we see just what the master storyteller wants us to see, and, above all, "The line defines the form."

Russ Manning was a unique talent. As an artist he believed one should strive to do what movies and television couldn't do . . . make the impossible "work." As a human being, he believed in putting family and community above all else. When a member of his family entered his studio, the work waited. Since most of the residents of his canyon community were away during the daytime, he became a volunteer fireman. Many a time his studio alarm would go off and he'd leap for the door with "It's a fire or rescue . . . see you later!" We worked many late hours because, in Russ Manning's world, real life took priority over "make believe." Fortunately for us, the product of his "make believe" remains to be enjoyed again, or to be discovered for the first time.

To me, Russ Manning is not really gone. Occasionally, in my dreams, I'm driving up to Russ's studio in the canyon. He's sitting at this drawing board while an operatic aria is wafting through the room . . . a pile of strips are in his outstretched hand, and he smiles and says, "We've got lots to do."

Enjoy these adventures.

Mike Royer

—Mike Royer
January 1997

CLASSIC

STAR WARS

THE EARLY ADVENTURES

PART ONE

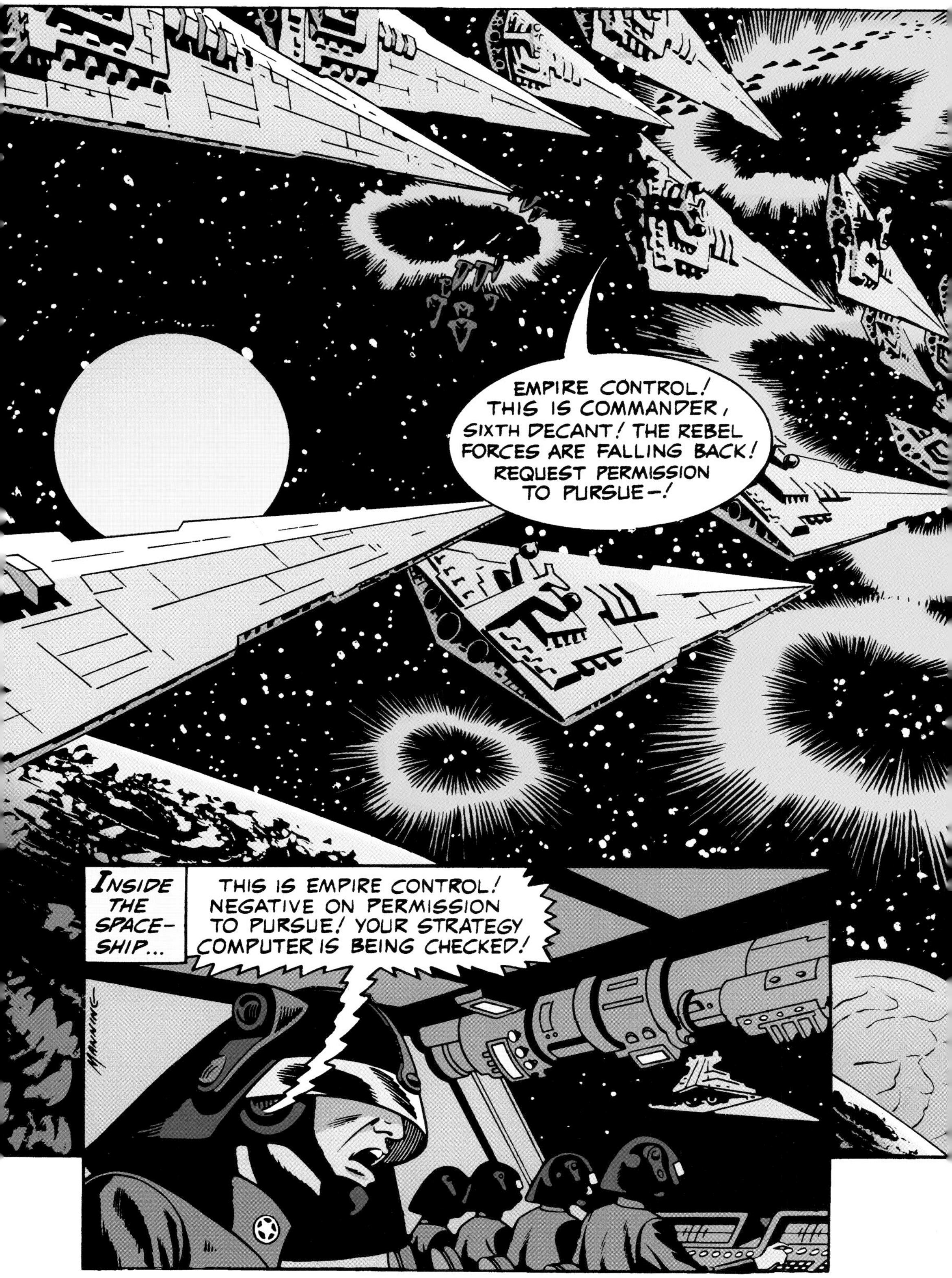
EMPIRE CONTROL! THIS IS COMMANDER, SIXTH DECANT! THE REBEL FORCES ARE FALLING BACK! REQUEST PERMISSION TO PURSUE--!
INSIDE THE SPACE-SHIP...
THIS IS EMPIRE CONTROL! NEGATIVE ON PERMISSION TO PURSUE! YOUR STRATEGY COMPUTER IS BEING CHECKED!

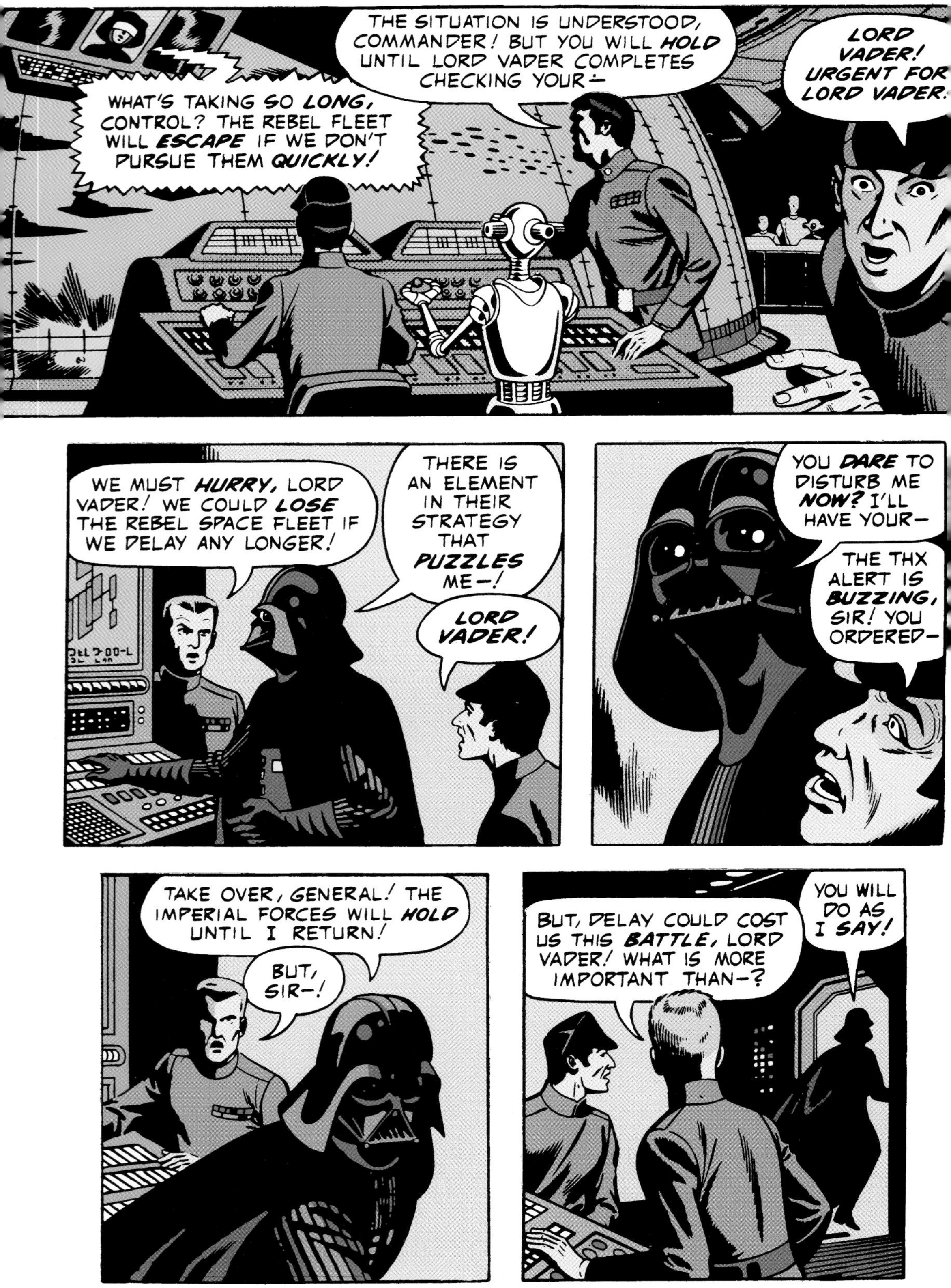

WHAT'S TAKING SO LONG, CONTROL? THE REBEL FLEET WILL ESCAPE IF WE DON'T PURSUE THEM QUICKLY!
THE SITUATION IS UNDERSTOOD, COMMANDER! BUT YOU WILL HOLD UNTIL LORD VADER COMPLETES CHECKING YOUR—
LORD VADER! URGENT FOR LORD VADER!
WE MUST HURRY, LORD VADER! WE COULD LOSE THE REBEL SPACE FLEET IF WE DELAY ANY LONGER!
THERE IS AN ELEMENT IN THEIR STRATEGY THAT PUZZLES ME—!
LORD VADER!
YOU DARE TO DISTURB ME NOW? I'LL HAVE YOUR—
THE THX ALERT IS BUZZING, SIR! YOU ORDERED—
TAKE OVER, GENERAL! THE IMPERIAL FORCES WILL HOLD UNTIL I RETURN!
BUT, SIR—!
BUT, DELAY COULD COST US THIS BATTLE, LORD VADER! WHAT IS MORE IMPORTANT THAN—?
YOU WILL DO AS I SAY!

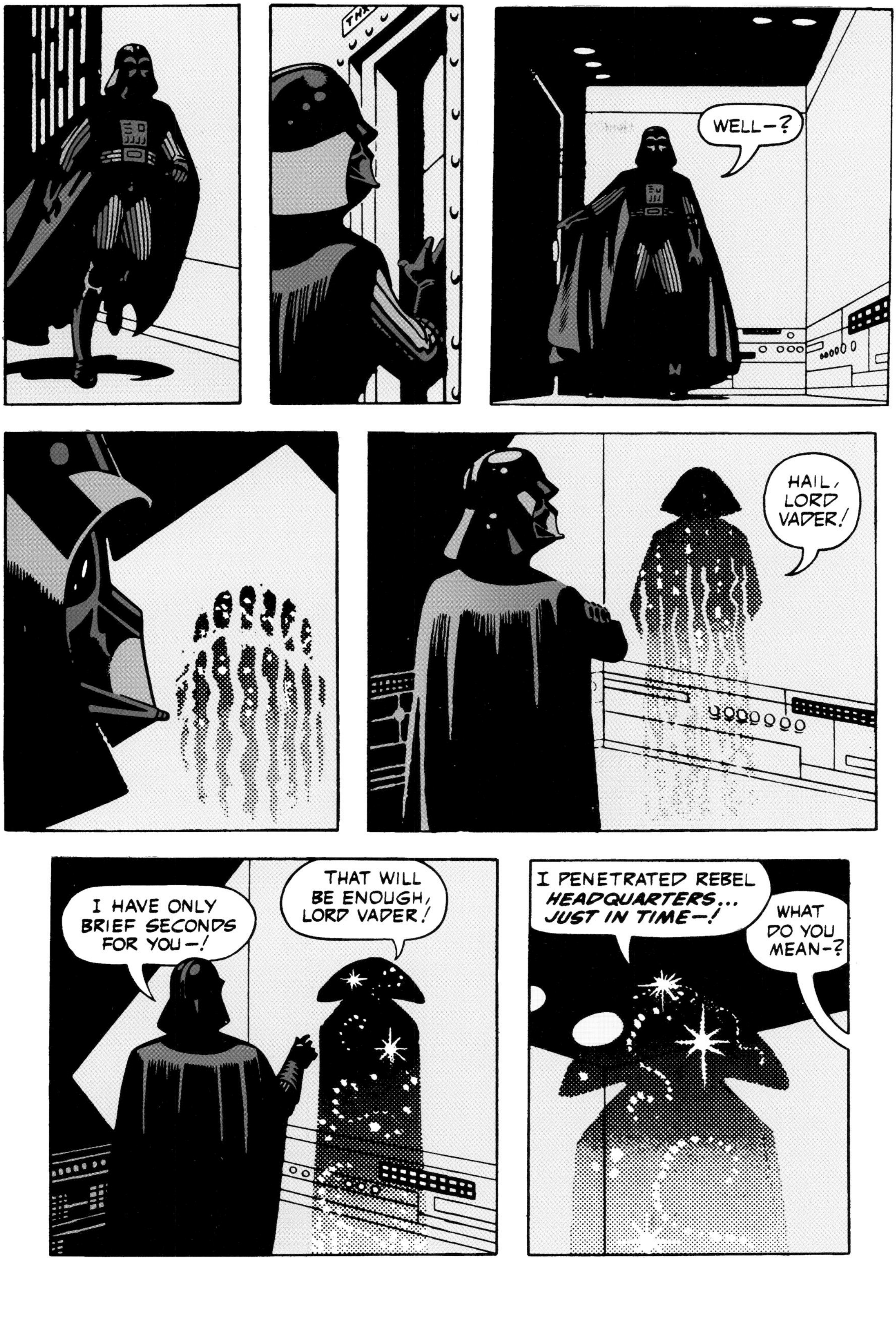
WELL—?
HAIL, LORD VADER!
I HAVE ONLY BRIEF SECONDS FOR YOU—!
THAT WILL BE ENOUGH, LORD VADER!
I PENETRATED REBEL HEADQUARTERS... JUST IN TIME—!
WHAT DO YOU MEAN—?

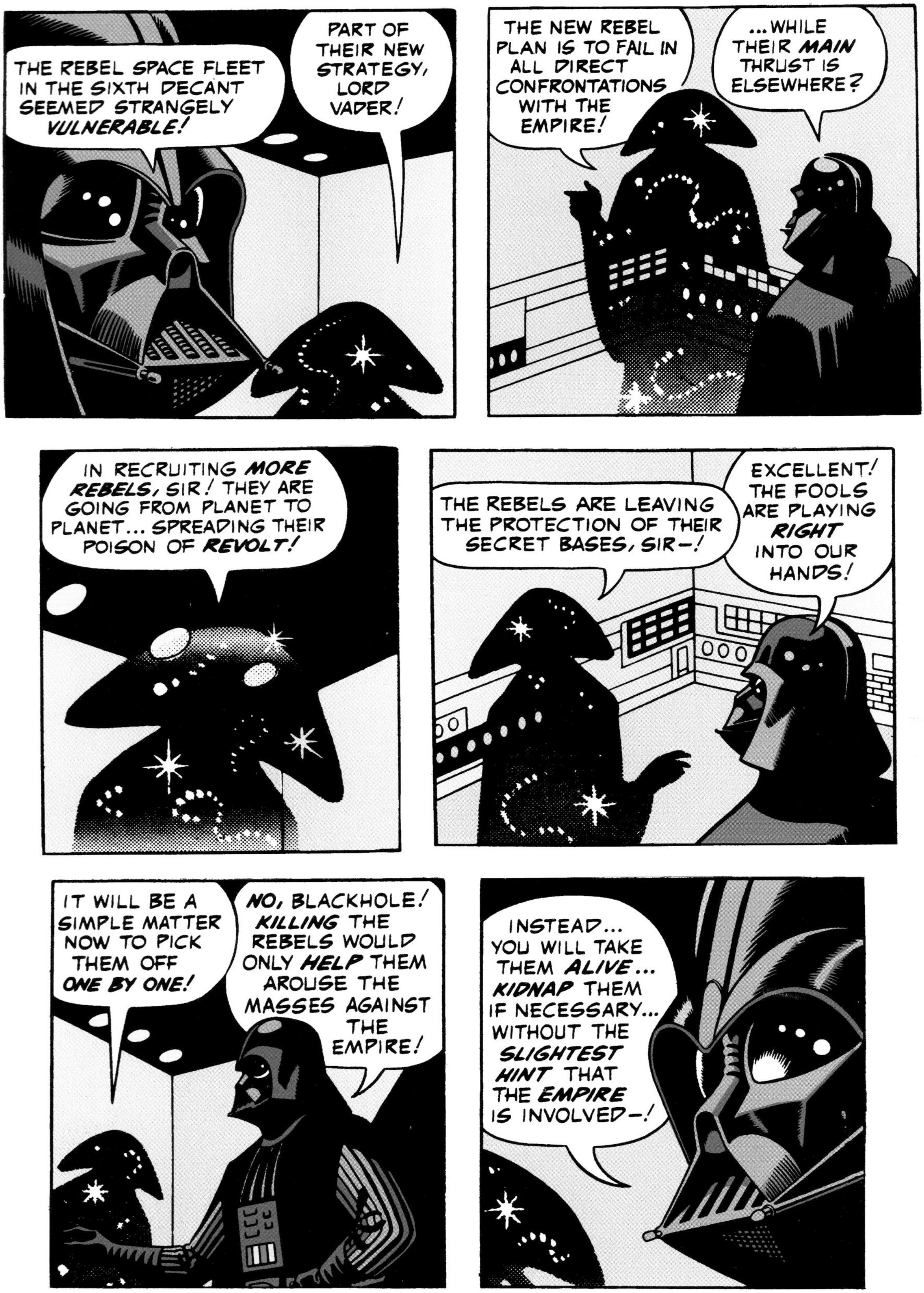
THE REBEL SPACE FLEET IN THE SIXTH DECANT SEEMED STRANGELY VULNERABLE!
PART OF THEIR NEW STRATEGY, LORD VADER!
THE NEW REBEL PLAN IS TO FAIL IN ALL DIRECT CONFRONTATIONS WITH THE EMPIRE!
...WHILE THEIR MAIN THRUST IS ELSEWHERE?
IN RECRUITING MORE REBELS, SIR! THEY ARE GOING FROM PLANET TO PLANET... SPREADING THEIR POISON OF REVOLT!
THE REBELS ARE LEAVING THE PROTECTION OF THEIR SECRET BASES, SIR--!
EXCELLENT! THE FOOLS ARE PLAYING RIGHT INTO OUR HANDS!
IT WILL BE A SIMPLE MATTER NOW TO PICK THEM OFF ONE BY ONE!
NO, BLACKHOLE! KILLING THE REBELS WOULD ONLY HELP THEM AROUSE THE MASSES AGAINST THE EMPIRE!
INSTEAD... YOU WILL TAKE THEM ALIVE... KIDNAP THEM IF NECESSARY... WITHOUT THE SLIGHTEST HINT THAT THE EMPIRE IS INVOLVED--!

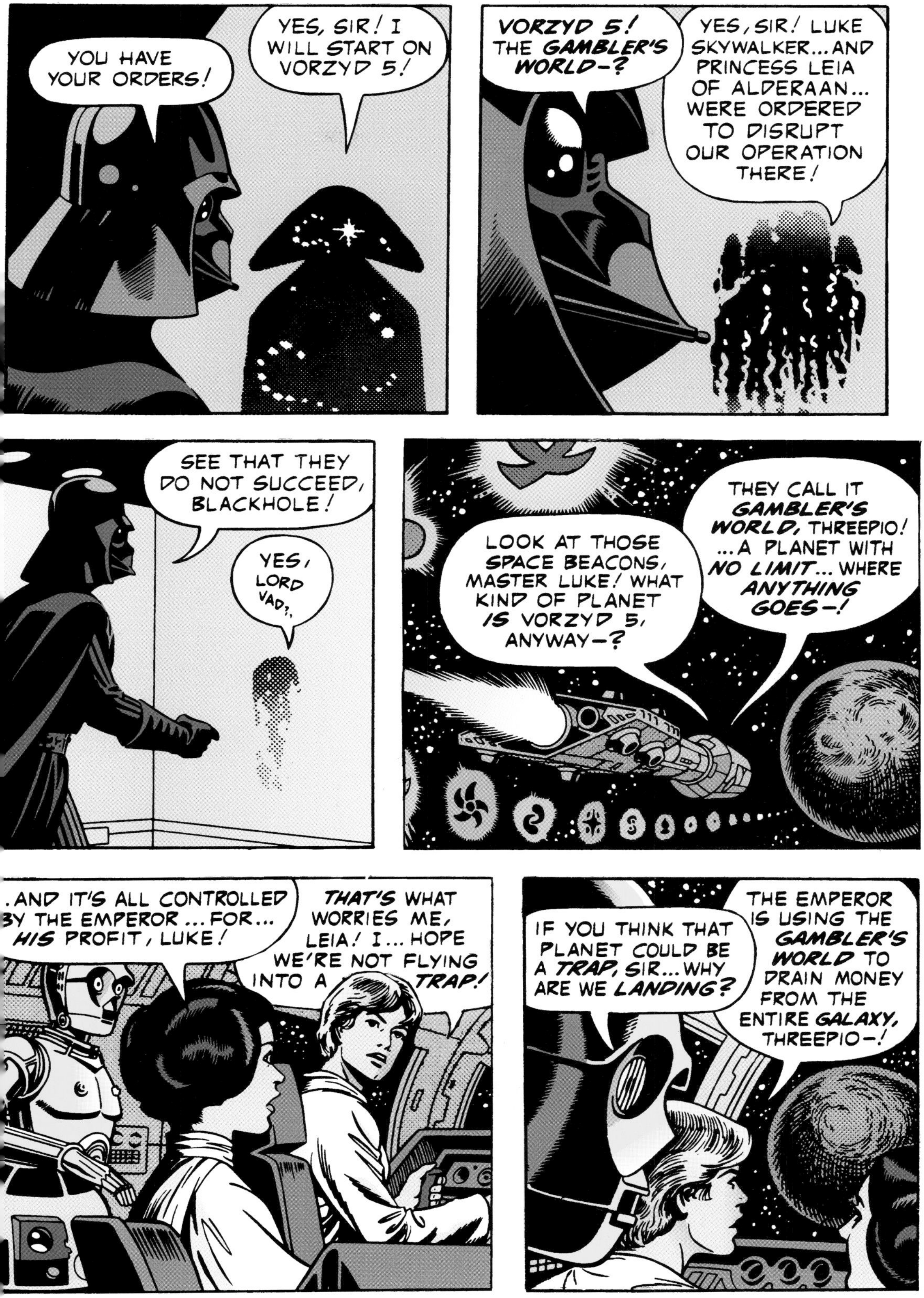
YOU HAVE YOUR ORDERS!
YES, SIR! I WILL START ON VORZYD 5!
VORZYD 5! THE GAMBLER'S WORLD–?
YES, SIR! LUKE SKYWALKER...AND PRINCESS LEIA OF ALDERAAN... WERE ORDERED TO DISRUPT OUR OPERATION THERE!
SEE THAT THEY DO NOT SUCCEED, BLACKHOLE!
YES, LORD VAD?,,
LOOK AT THOSE SPACE BEACONS, MASTER LUKE! WHAT KIND OF PLANET IS VORZYD 5, ANYWAY–?
THEY CALL IT GAMBLER'S WORLD, THREEPIO! ...A PLANET WITH NO LIMIT... WHERE ANYTHING GOES–!
.AND IT'S ALL CONTROLLED BY THE EMPEROR ... FOR... HIS PROFIT, LUKE!
THAT'S WHAT WORRIES ME, LEIA! I... HOPE WE'RE NOT FLYING INTO A TRAP!
IF YOU THINK THAT PLANET COULD BE A TRAP, SIR... WHY ARE WE LANDING?
THE EMPEROR IS USING THE GAMBLER'S WORLD TO DRAIN MONEY FROM THE ENTIRE GALAXY, THREEPIO–!

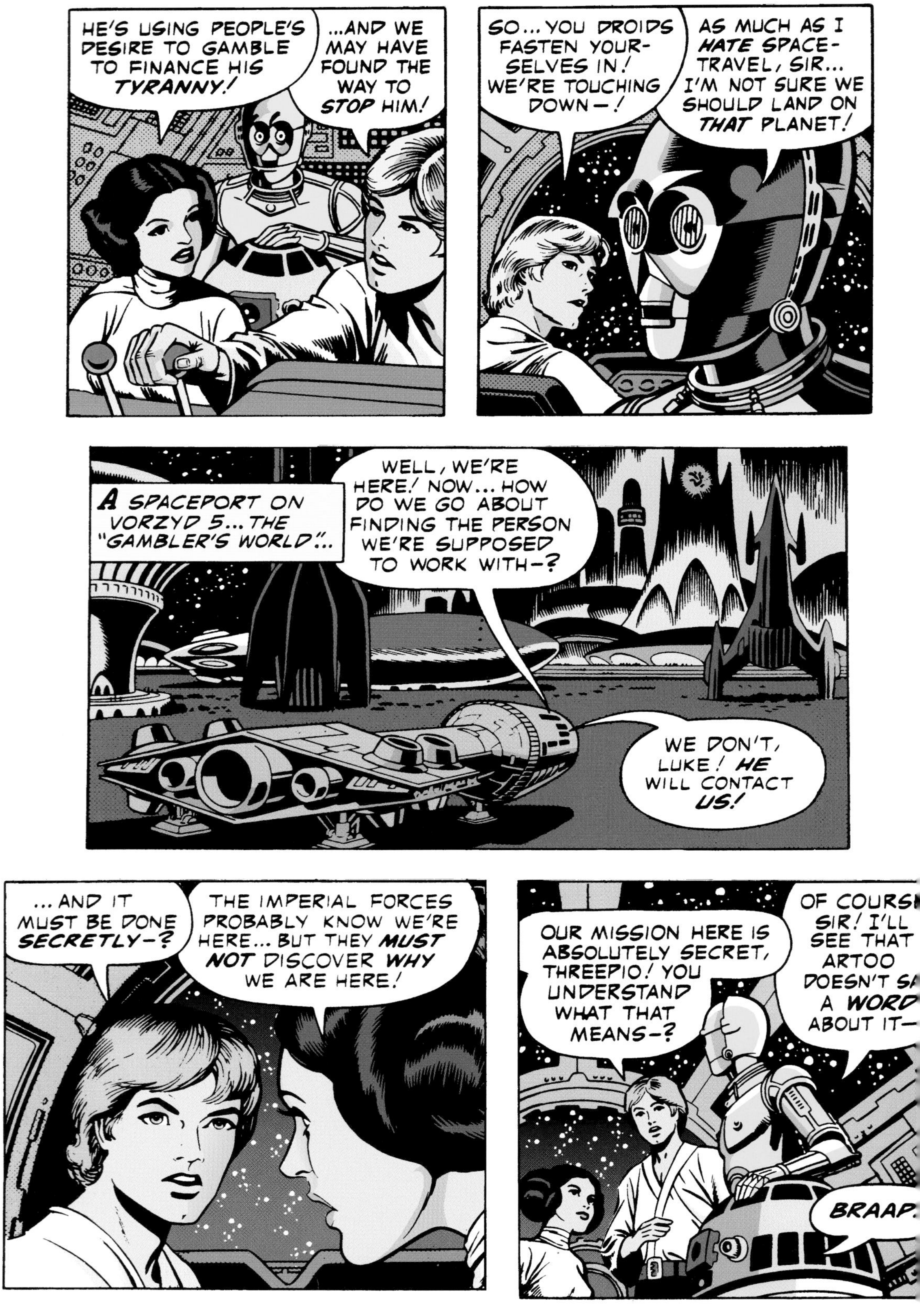

HE'S USING PEOPLE'S DESIRE TO GAMBLE TO FINANCE HIS *TYRANNY*!
...AND WE MAY HAVE FOUND THE WAY TO *STOP* HIM!
SO... YOU DROIDS FASTEN YOURSELVES IN! WE'RE TOUCHING DOWN—!
AS MUCH AS I *HATE* SPACE-TRAVEL, SIR... I'M NOT SURE WE SHOULD LAND ON *THAT* PLANET!
A SPACEPORT ON VORZYD 5... THE "GAMBLER'S WORLD"...
WELL, WE'RE HERE! NOW... HOW DO WE GO ABOUT FINDING THE PERSON WE'RE SUPPOSED TO WORK WITH—?
WE DON'T, LUKE! *HE* WILL CONTACT *US!*
... AND IT MUST BE DONE *SECRETLY*—?
THE IMPERIAL FORCES PROBABLY KNOW WE'RE HERE... BUT THEY *MUST NOT* DISCOVER *WHY* WE ARE HERE!
OUR MISSION HERE IS ABSOLUTELY SECRET, THREEPIO! YOU UNDERSTAND WHAT THAT MEANS—?
OF COURS
SIR! I'LL
SEE THAT
ARTOO
DOESN'T S
A *WORD*
ABOUT IT—
BRAAP

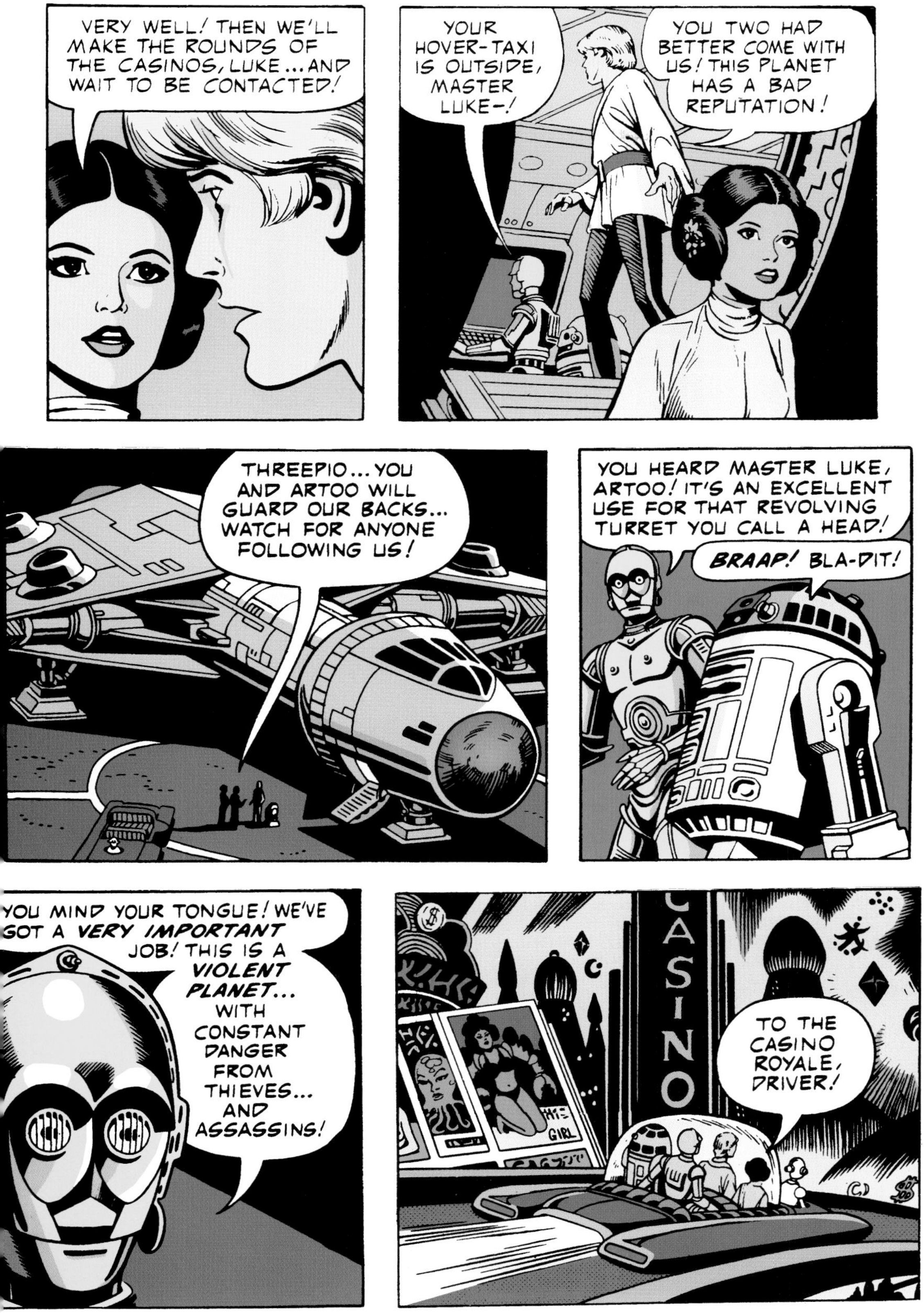
VERY WELL! THEN WE'LL MAKE THE ROUNDS OF THE CASINOS, LUKE... AND WAIT TO BE CONTACTED!
YOUR HOVER-TAXI IS OUTSIDE, MASTER LUKE-!
YOU TWO HAD BETTER COME WITH US! THIS PLANET HAS A BAD REPUTATION!
THREEPIO... YOU AND ARTOO WILL GUARD OUR BACKS... WATCH FOR ANYONE FOLLOWING US!
YOU HEARD MASTER LUKE, ARTOO! IT'S AN EXCELLENT USE FOR THAT REVOLVING TURRET YOU CALL A HEAD!
BRAAP! BLA-DIT!
YOU MIND YOUR TONGUE! WE'VE GOT A VERY IMPORTANT JOB! THIS IS A VIOLENT PLANET... WITH CONSTANT DANGER FROM THIEVES... AND ASSASSINS!
CASINO
TO THE CASINO ROYALE, DRIVER!

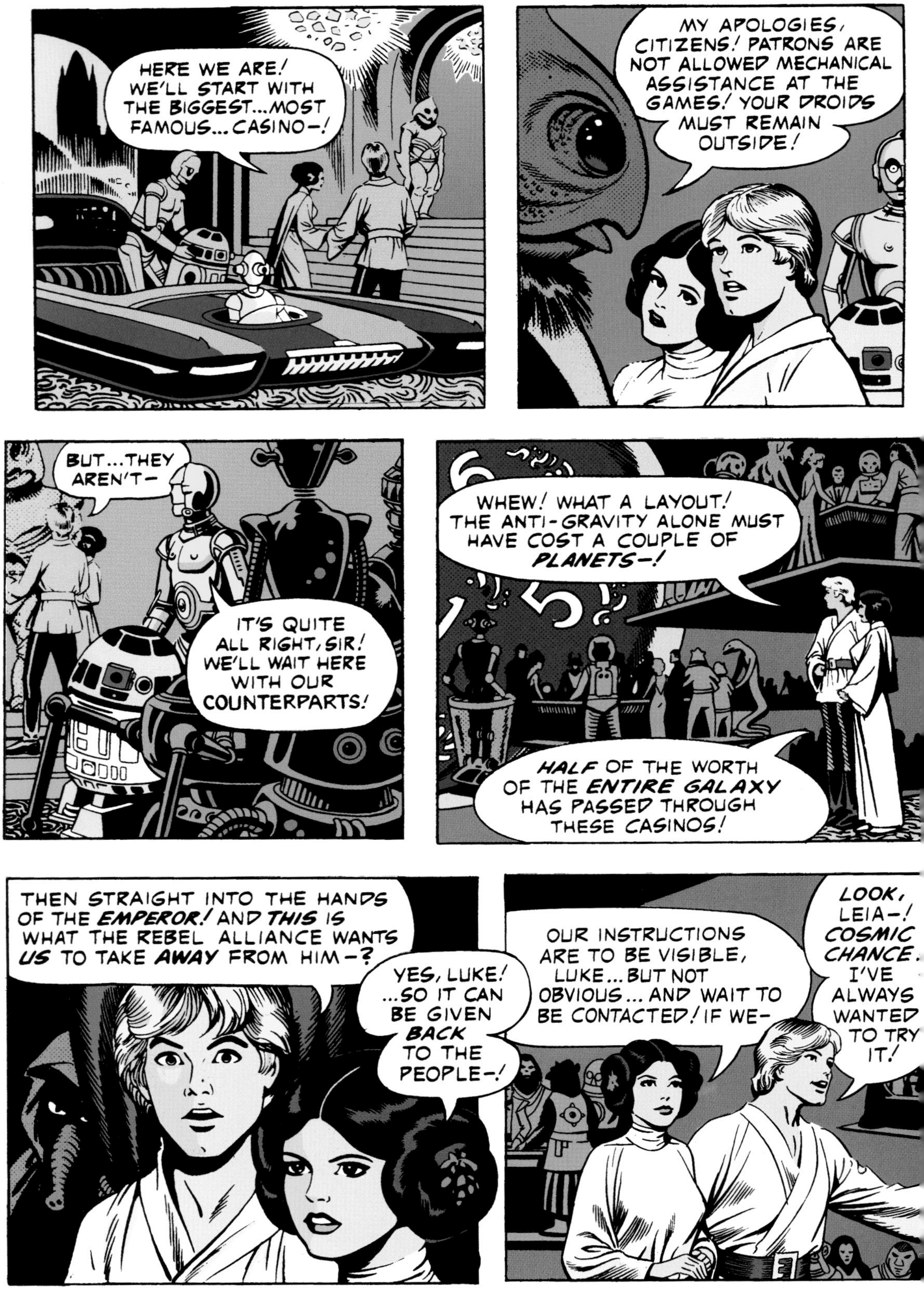
HERE WE ARE! WE'LL START WITH THE BIGGEST...MOST FAMOUS...CASINO-!
MY APOLOGIES, CITIZENS! PATRONS ARE NOT ALLOWED MECHANICAL ASSISTANCE AT THE GAMES! YOUR DROIDS MUST REMAIN OUTSIDE!
BUT...THEY AREN'T-
IT'S QUITE ALL RIGHT, SIR! WE'LL WAIT HERE WITH OUR COUNTERPARTS!
WHEW! WHAT A LAYOUT! THE ANTI-GRAVITY ALONE MUST HAVE COST A COUPLE OF PLANETS-!
HALF OF THE WORTH OF THE ENTIRE GALAXY HAS PASSED THROUGH THESE CASINOS!
THEN STRAIGHT INTO THE HANDS OF THE EMPEROR! AND THIS IS WHAT THE REBEL ALLIANCE WANTS US TO TAKE AWAY FROM HIM-?
YES, LUKE! ...SO IT CAN BE GIVEN BACK TO THE PEOPLE-!
OUR INSTRUCTIONS ARE TO BE VISIBLE, LUKE...BUT NOT OBVIOUS...AND WAIT TO BE CONTACTED! IF WE-
LOOK, LEIA-! COSMIC CHANCE. I'VE ALWAYS WANTED TO TRY IT!

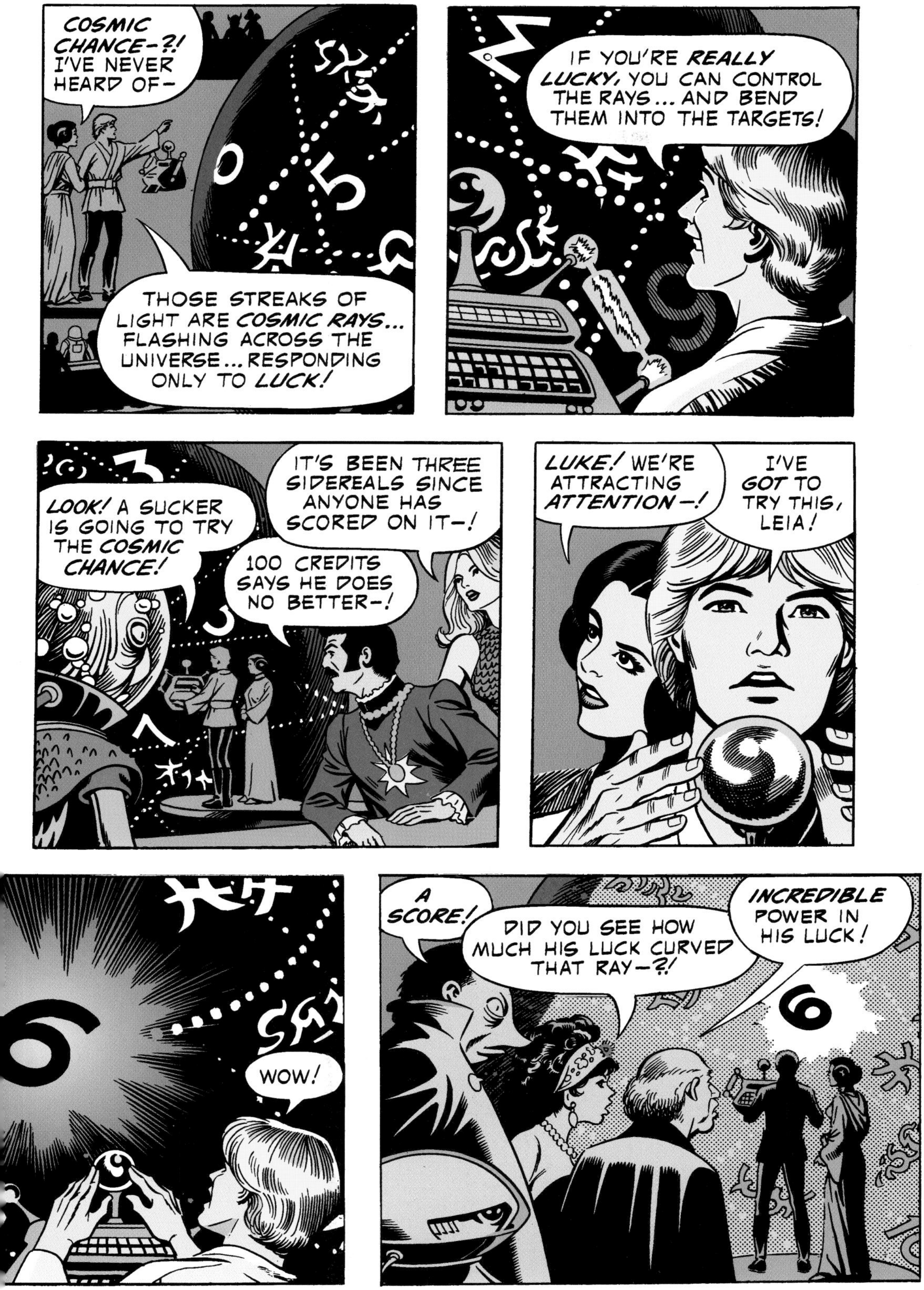
COSMIC CHANCE-?! I'VE NEVER HEARD OF-
THOSE STREAKS OF LIGHT ARE COSMIC RAYS... FLASHING ACROSS THE UNIVERSE... RESPONDING ONLY TO LUCK!
IF YOU'RE REALLY LUCKY, YOU CAN CONTROL THE RAYS... AND BEND THEM INTO THE TARGETS!
LOOK! A SUCKER IS GOING TO TRY THE COSMIC CHANCE!
IT'S BEEN THREE SIDEREALS SINCE ANYONE HAS SCORED ON IT-!
100 CREDITS SAYS HE DOES NO BETTER-!
LUKE! WE'RE ATTRACTING ATTENTION-!
I'VE GOT TO TRY THIS, LEIA!
WOW!
A SCORE!
DID YOU SEE HOW MUCH HIS LUCK CURVED THAT RAY-?!
INCREDIBLE POWER IN HIS LUCK!

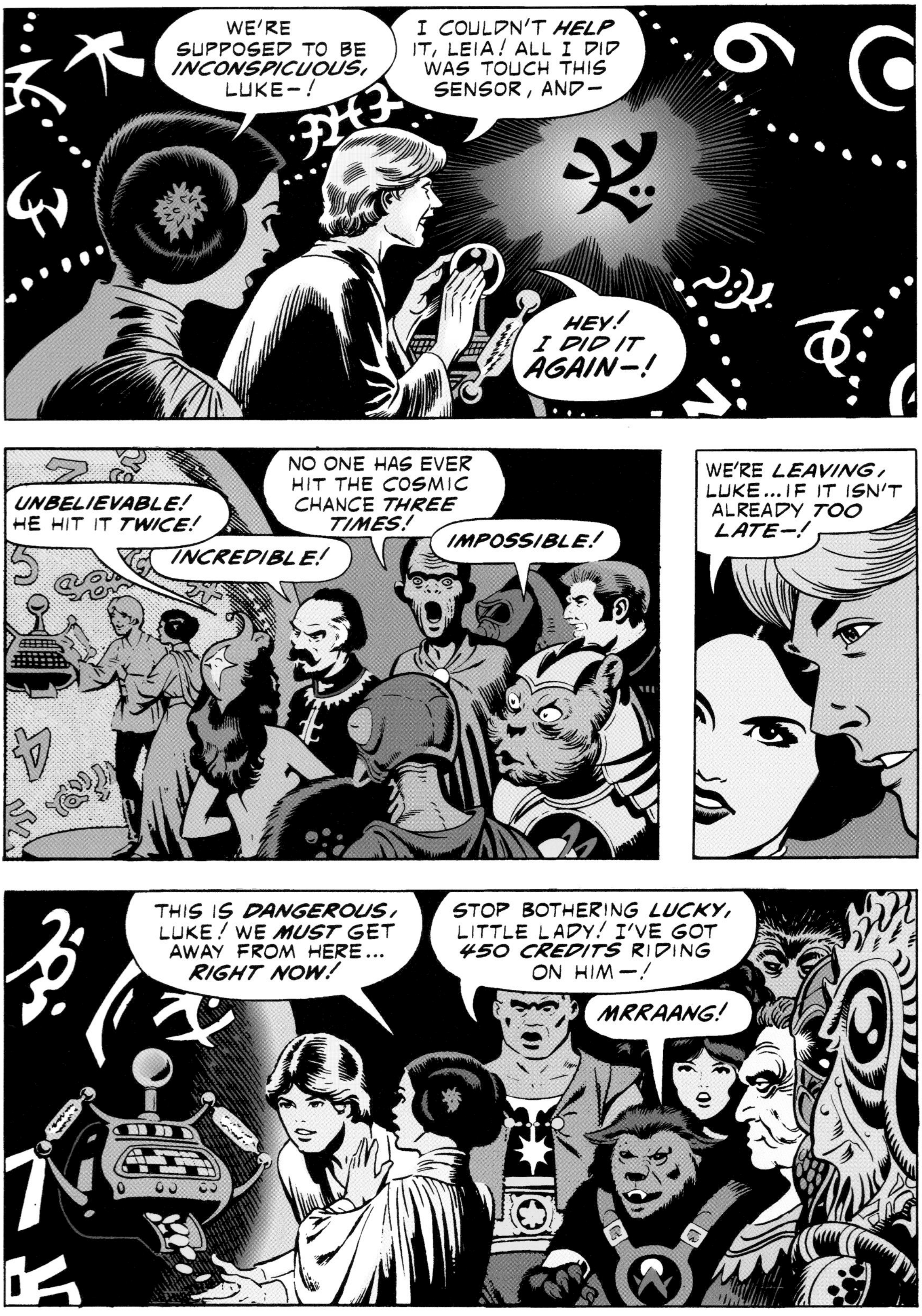
WE'RE SUPPOSED TO BE INCONSPICUOUS, LUKE—!
I COULDN'T HELP IT, LEIA! ALL I DID WAS TOUCH THIS SENSOR, AND—
HEY! I DID IT AGAIN—!
UNBELIEVABLE! HE HIT IT TWICE!
NO ONE HAS EVER HIT THE COSMIC CHANCE THREE TIMES!
INCREDIBLE!
IMPOSSIBLE!
WE'RE LEAVING, LUKE...IF IT ISN'T ALREADY TOO LATE—!
THIS IS DANGEROUS, LUKE! WE MUST GET AWAY FROM HERE... RIGHT NOW!
STOP BOTHERING LUCKY, LITTLE LADY! I'VE GOT 450 CREDITS RIDING ON HIM—!
MRRAANG!

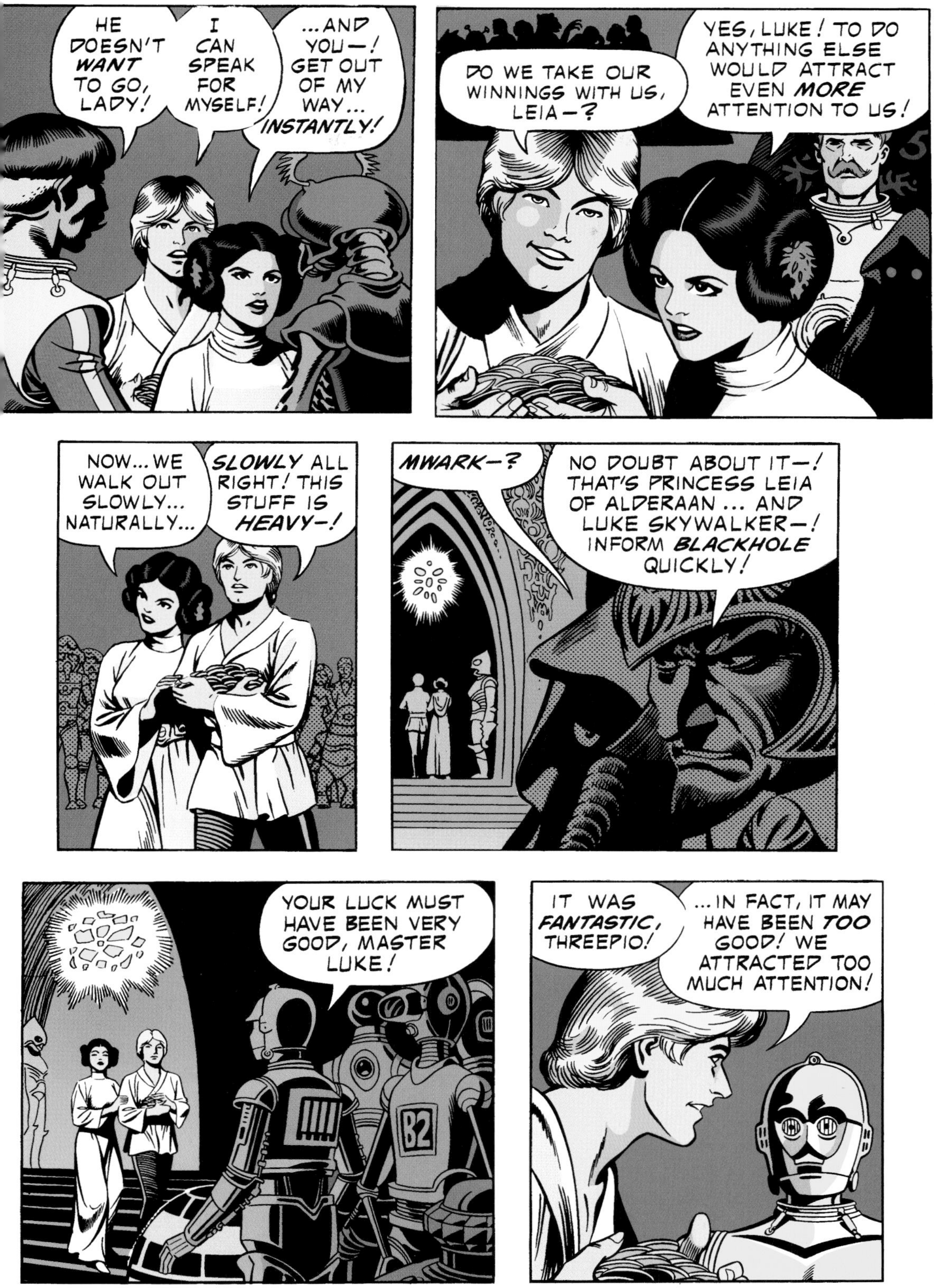
HE DOESN'T *WANT* TO GO, LADY!
I CAN SPEAK FOR MYSELF!
...AND YOU—! GET OUT OF MY WAY... *INSTANTLY!*
DO WE TAKE OUR WINNINGS WITH US, LEIA—?
YES, LUKE! TO DO ANYTHING ELSE WOULD ATTRACT EVEN *MORE* ATTENTION TO US!
NOW... WE WALK OUT SLOWLY... NATURALLY...
SLOWLY ALL RIGHT! THIS STUFF IS *HEAVY*—!
MWARK—?
NO DOUBT ABOUT IT—! THAT'S PRINCESS LEIA OF ALDERAAN ... AND LUKE SKYWALKER—! INFORM *BLACKHOLE* QUICKLY!
YOUR LUCK MUST HAVE BEEN VERY GOOD, MASTER LUKE!
IT WAS *FANTASTIC*, THREEPIO!
...IN FACT, IT MAY HAVE BEEN *TOO* GOOD! WE ATTRACTED TOO MUCH ATTENTION!

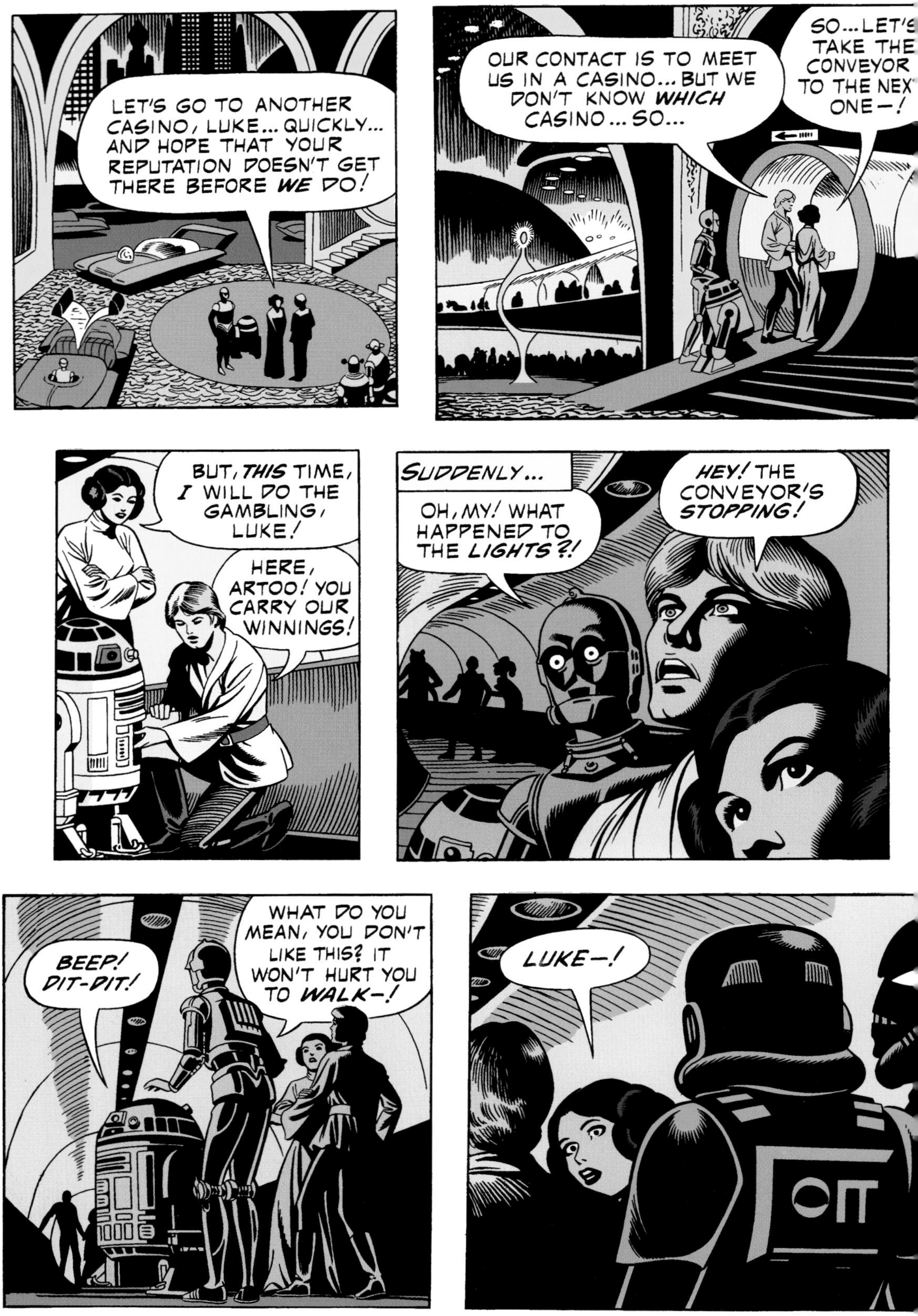
LET'S GO TO ANOTHER CASINO, LUKE... QUICKLY... AND HOPE THAT YOUR REPUTATION DOESN'T GET THERE BEFORE WE DO!
OUR CONTACT IS TO MEET US IN A CASINO... BUT WE DON'T KNOW WHICH CASINO... SO...
SO... LET'S TAKE THE CONVEYOR TO THE NEXT ONE—!
BUT, THIS TIME, I WILL DO THE GAMBLING, LUKE!
HERE, ARTOO! YOU CARRY OUR WINNINGS!
SUDDENLY...
OH, MY! WHAT HAPPENED TO THE LIGHTS?!
HEY! THE CONVEYOR'S STOPPING!
BEEP! DIT-DIT!
WHAT DO YOU MEAN, YOU DON'T LIKE THIS? IT WON'T HURT YOU TO WALK—!
LUKE—!

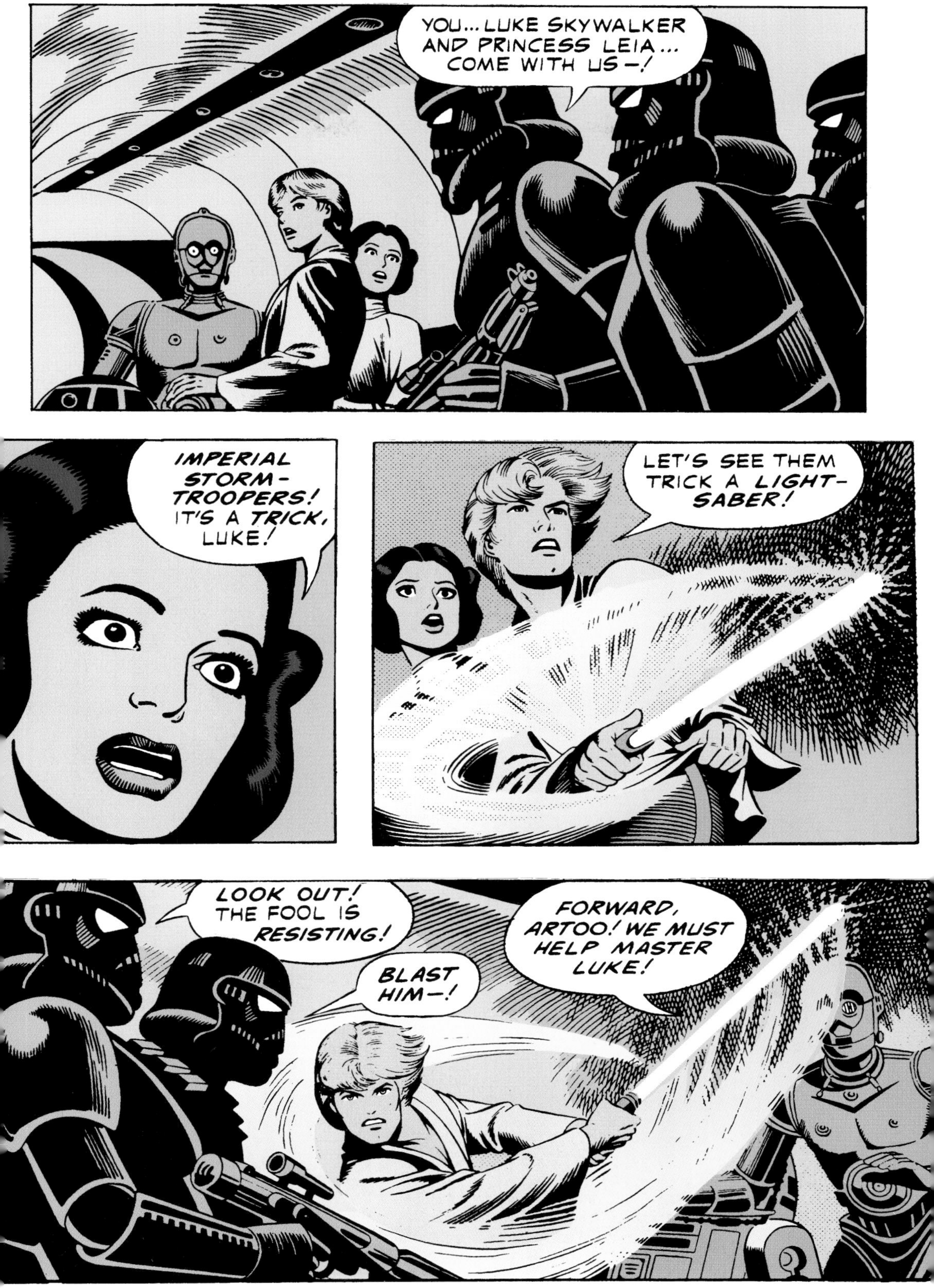
YOU... LUKE SKYWALKER AND PRINCESS LEIA... COME WITH US—!
IMPERIAL STORM-TROOPERS! IT'S A TRICK, LUKE!
LET'S SEE THEM TRICK A LIGHT-SABER!
LOOK OUT! THE FOOL IS RESISTING!
BLAST HIM—!
FORWARD, ARTOO! WE MUST HELP MASTER LUKE!

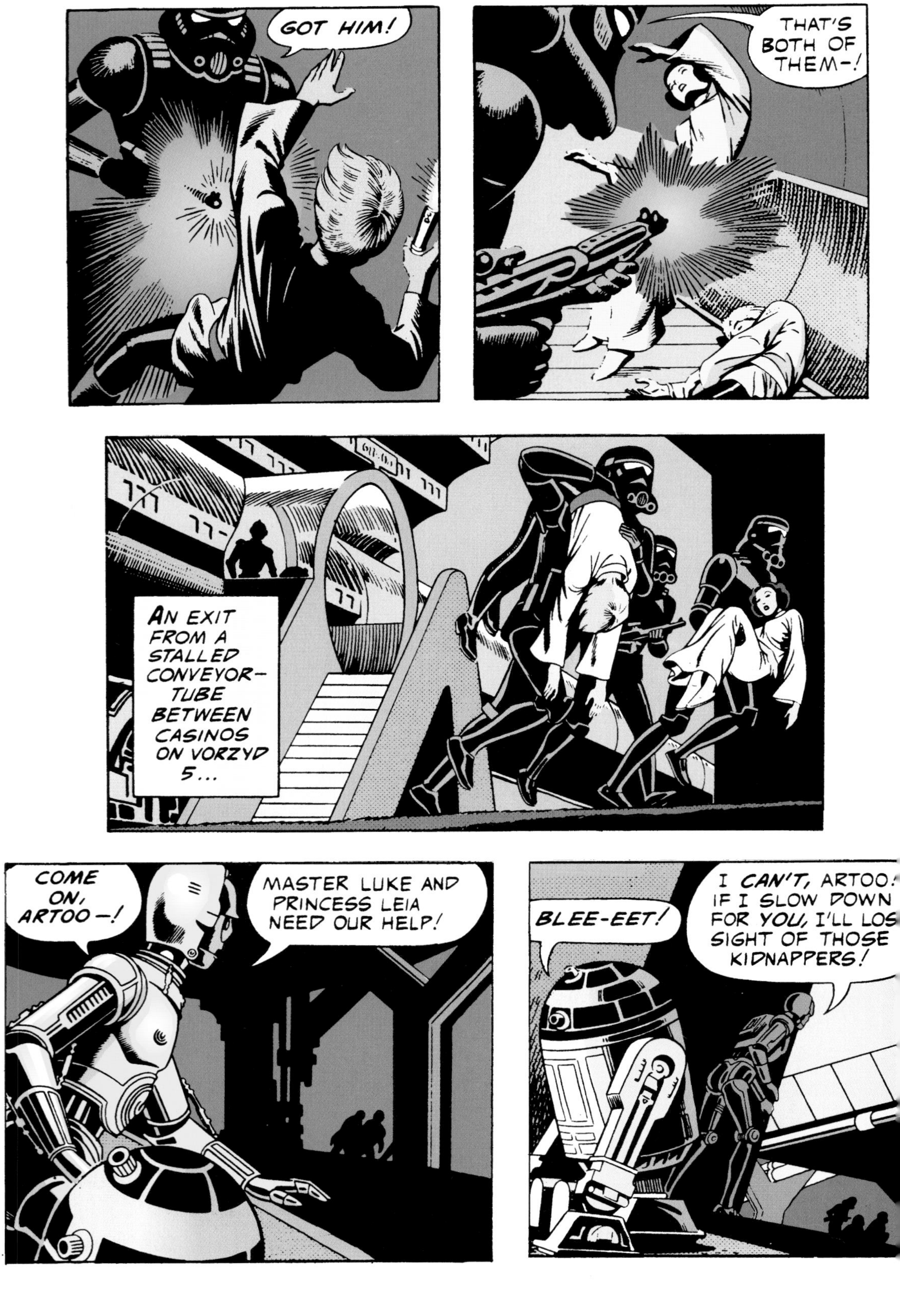
GOT HIM!
THAT'S BOTH OF THEM-!
AN EXIT FROM A STALLED CONVEYOR-TUBE BETWEEN CASINOS ON VORZYD 5...
COME ON, ARTOO-!
MASTER LUKE AND PRINCESS LEIA NEED OUR HELP!
BLEE-EET!
I CAN'T, ARTOO! IF I SLOW DOWN FOR YOU, I'LL LOS
SIGHT OF THOSE KIDNAPPERS!

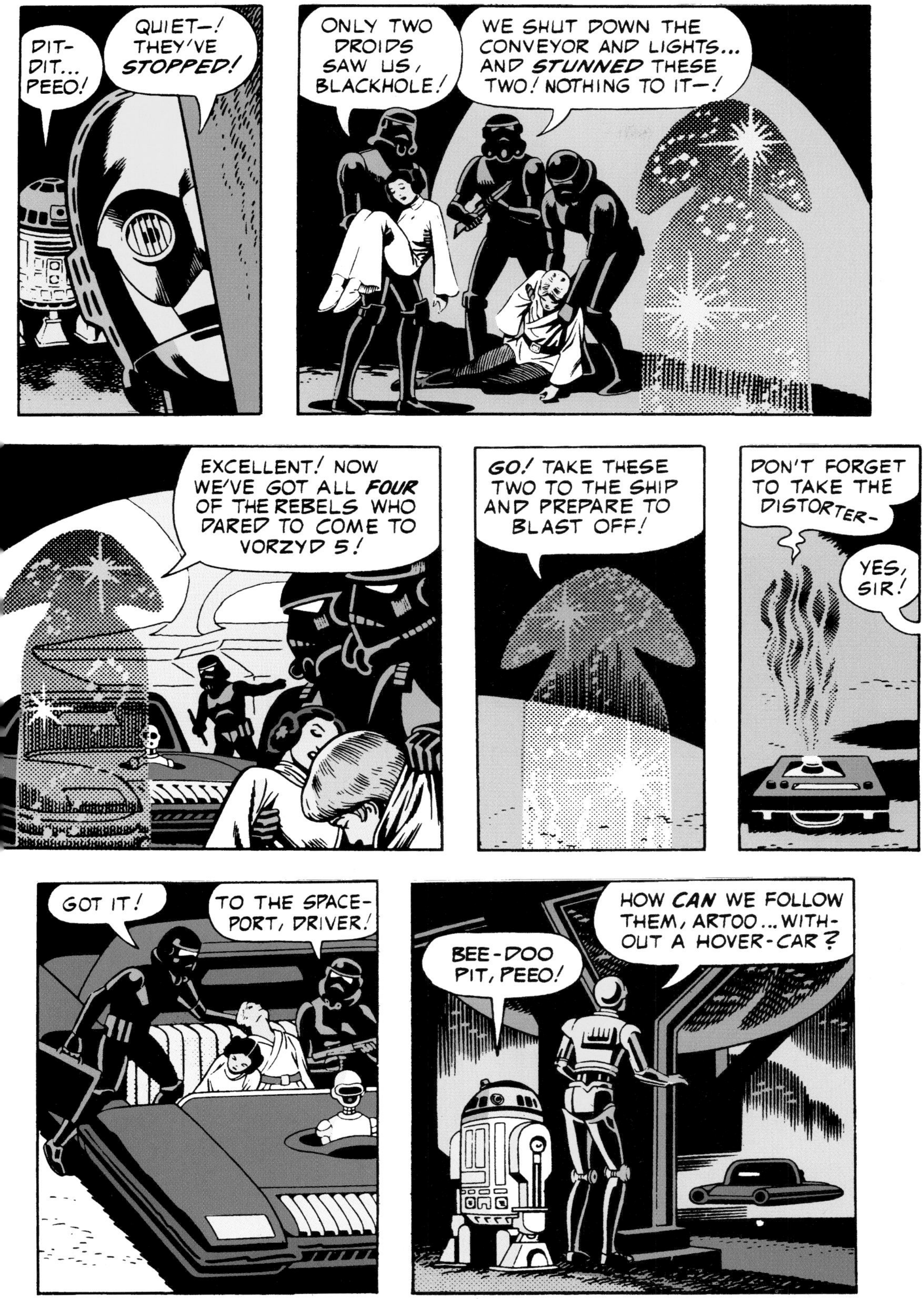
DIT-DIT... PEEO!
QUIET—! THEY'VE STOPPED!
ONLY TWO DROIDS SAW US, BLACKHOLE!
WE SHUT DOWN THE CONVEYOR AND LIGHTS... AND STUNNED THESE TWO! NOTHING TO IT—!
EXCELLENT! NOW WE'VE GOT ALL FOUR OF THE REBELS WHO DARED TO COME TO VORZYD 5!
GO! TAKE THESE TWO TO THE SHIP AND PREPARE TO BLAST OFF!
DON'T FORGET TO TAKE THE DISTORTER-
YES, SIR!
GOT IT!
TO THE SPACE-PORT, DRIVER!
HOW CAN WE FOLLOW THEM, ARTOO... WITH-OUT A HOVER-CAR?
BEE-DOO PIT, PEEO!

POOR MASTER LUKE... *KIDNAPPED!* WE NEED *HELP,* ARTOO! *HELP! POLICE-DROIDS! HELP!*

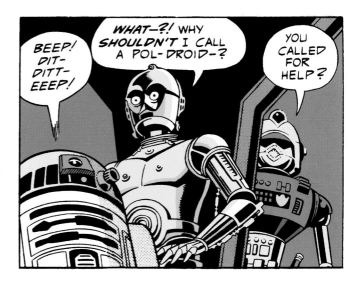

BEEP! DIT-DITT-EEEP!

WHAT—?! WHY *SHOULDN'T* I CALL A POL-DROID—?

YOU CALLED FOR HELP?

POLICE-DROID R-55 AT YOUR SERVICE—!

OUR OWNER NEEDS *HELP!* HE WAS TAKEN AWAY BY— *ULK!*

YES—? YOUR OWNER'S NAME AND IDENTIFICATION, PLEASE?

HIS NAME IS LU— *URP!*

BLEEP! PEEO DIT-DIT-BAP!

A *SLIGHT* MALFUNCTION! IT SOUNDS TO ME MORE AS IF YOUR FRIEND HAS BLOWN HIS *COMPUTER!* YOU MAY CONTINUE TO THE REPAIR CENTER WITH HIM!

LISTEN, YOU WALKING BLOB OF GREASE! WHY DID YOU *ZAP* ME... AND TELL THAT POLICE-DROID I HAVE A *SERIOUS MALFUNCTION?*

BLEEO. DEE-DIT *WHEEP!* VLOOEE.

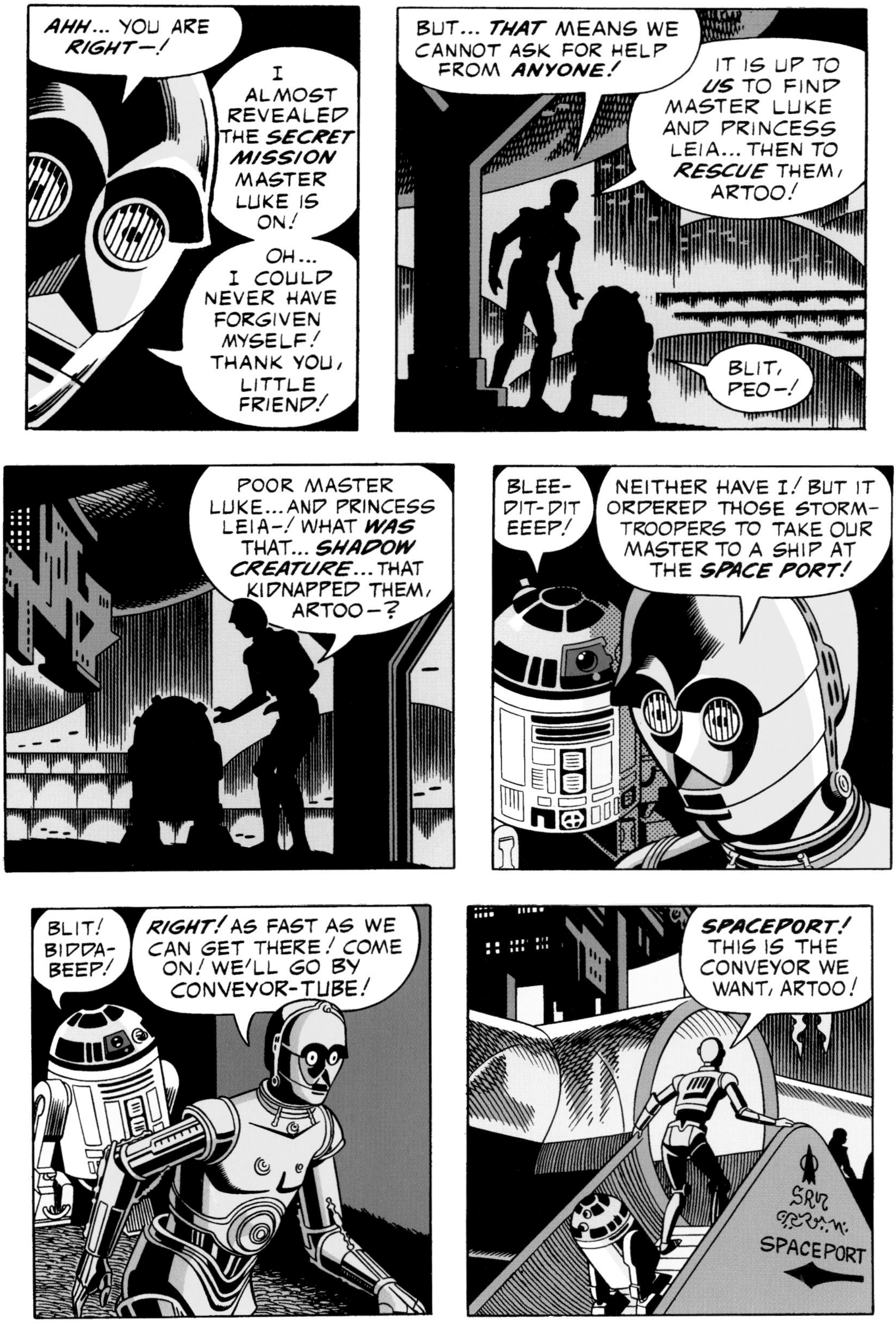
AHH... YOU ARE RIGHT—!
I ALMOST REVEALED THE SECRET MISSION MASTER LUKE IS ON!
OH... I COULD NEVER HAVE FORGIVEN MYSELF! THANK YOU, LITTLE FRIEND!
BUT... THAT MEANS WE CANNOT ASK FOR HELP FROM ANYONE!
IT IS UP TO US TO FIND MASTER LUKE AND PRINCESS LEIA... THEN TO RESCUE THEM, ARTOO!
BLIT, PEO—!
POOR MASTER LUKE... AND PRINCESS LEIA—! WHAT WAS THAT... SHADOW CREATURE... THAT KIDNAPPED THEM, ARTOO—?
BLEE-DIT-DIT EEEP!
NEITHER HAVE I! BUT IT ORDERED THOSE STORM-TROOPERS TO TAKE OUR MASTER TO A SHIP AT THE SPACE PORT!
BLIT! BIDDA-BEEP!
RIGHT! AS FAST AS WE CAN GET THERE! COME ON! WE'LL GO BY CONVEYOR-TUBE!
SPACEPORT! THIS IS THE CONVEYOR WE WANT, ARTOO!
SPACEPORT

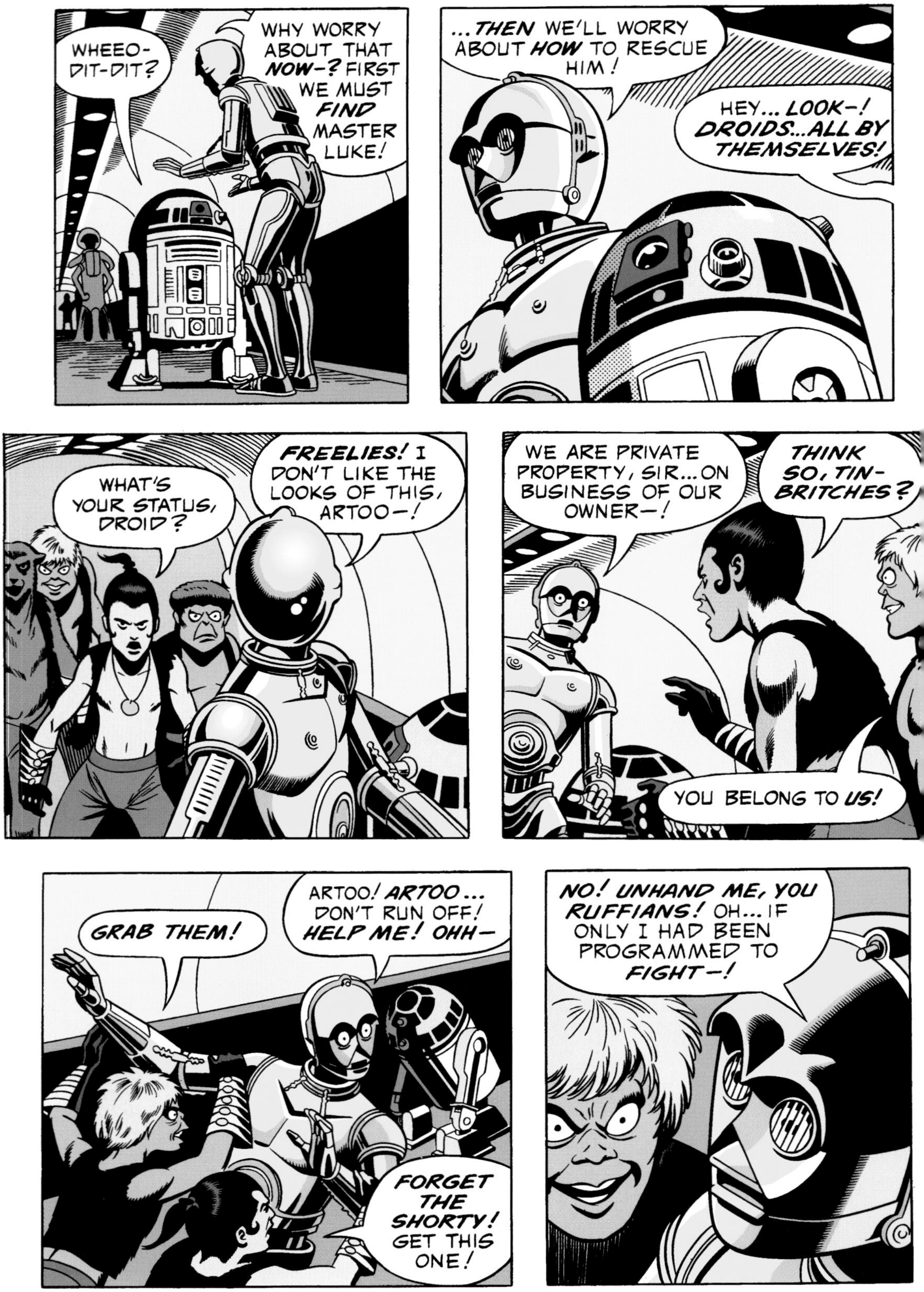
WHEEO-DIT-DIT?
WHY WORRY ABOUT THAT NOW-? FIRST WE MUST FIND MASTER LUKE!
...THEN WE'LL WORRY ABOUT HOW TO RESCUE HIM!
HEY... LOOK-! DROIDS...ALL BY THEMSELVES!
WHAT'S YOUR STATUS, DROID?
FREELIES! I DON'T LIKE THE LOOKS OF THIS, ARTOO-!
WE ARE PRIVATE PROPERTY, SIR...ON BUSINESS OF OUR OWNER-!
THINK SO, TIN-BRITCHES?
YOU BELONG TO US!
GRAB THEM!
ARTOO! ARTOO... DON'T RUN OFF! HELP ME! OHH-
FORGET THE SHORTY! GET THIS ONE!
NO! UNHAND ME, YOU RUFFIANS! OH... IF ONLY I HAD BEEN PROGRAMMED TO FIGHT-!

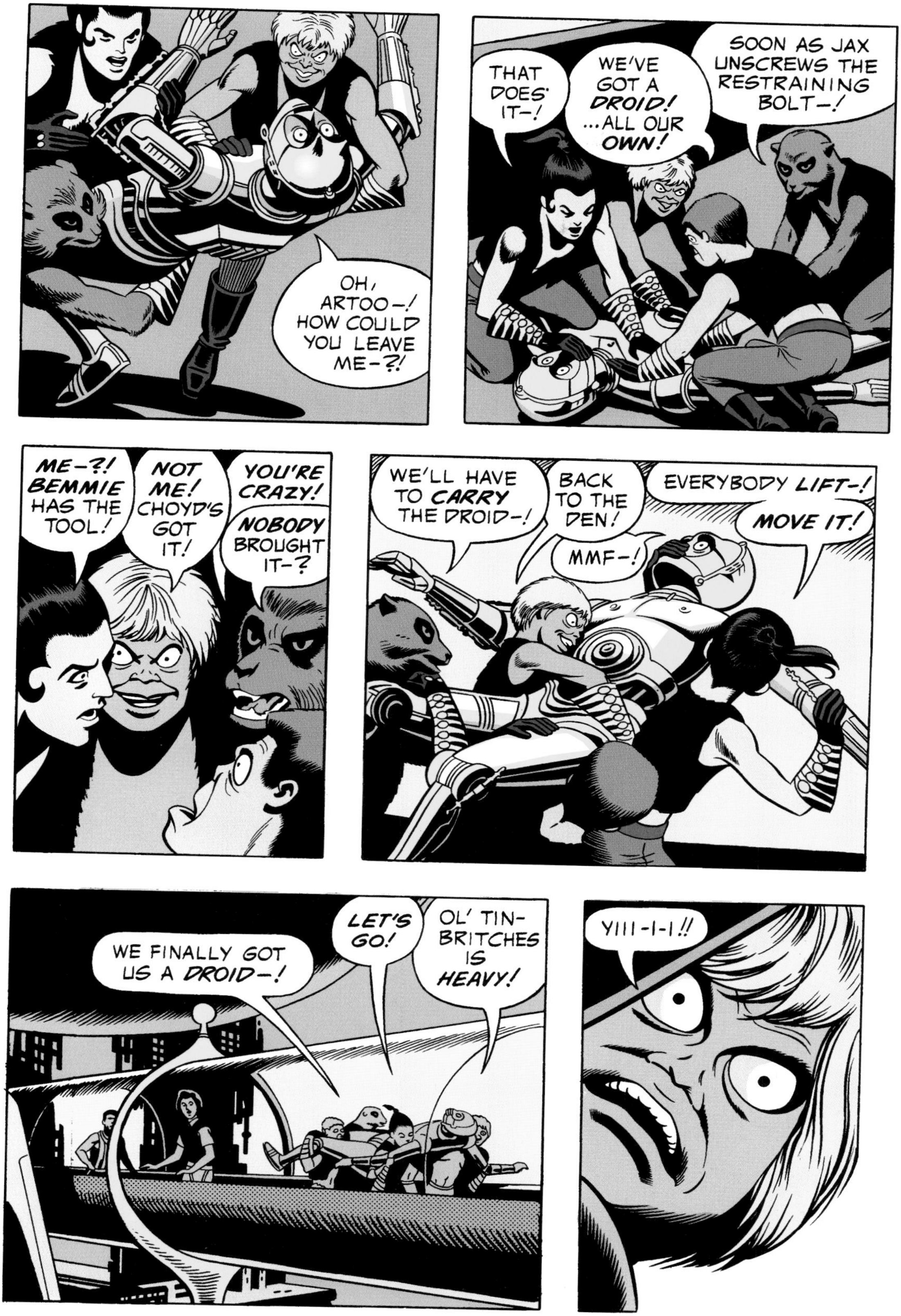

OH, ARTOO–! HOW COULD YOU LEAVE ME–?!
THAT DOES' IT–!
WE'VE GOT A DROID! ...ALL OUR OWN!
SOON AS JAX UNSCREWS THE RESTRAINING BOLT–!
ME–?! BEMMIE HAS THE TOOL!
NOT ME! CHOYD'S GOT IT!
YOU'RE CRAZY!
NOBODY BROUGHT IT–?
WE'LL HAVE TO CARRY THE DROID–!
BACK TO THE DEN!
MMF–!
EVERYBODY LIFT–!
MOVE IT!
WE FINALLY GOT US A DROID–!
LET'S GO!
OL' TIN-BRITCHES IS HEAVY!
YIII-I-I!!

POLICE-DROID!
STOP!
BLAST OUT'A HERE!
CRASH!
ARREST THEM, OFFICER--! THEY WERE STEALING ME--!
BLEE-DIT, PEEO?
ARTOO-DETOO! YOU DIDN'T RUN OFF AND LEAVE ME?! IT WAS YOU WHO BROUGHT THE POLICE-DROID!
OH, ARTOO... HOW CAN WE HOPE TO RESCUE MASTER LUKE...AND PRINCESS LEIA? I CAN'T EVEN PROTECT MYSELF!

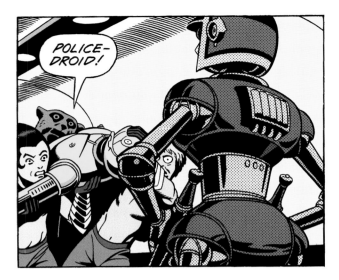

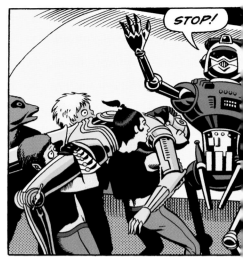

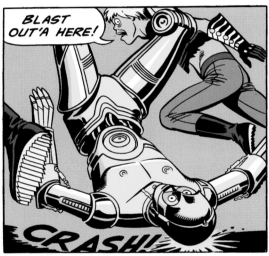

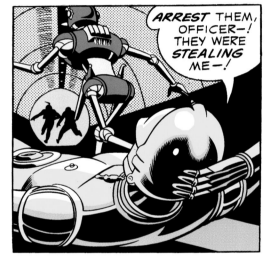

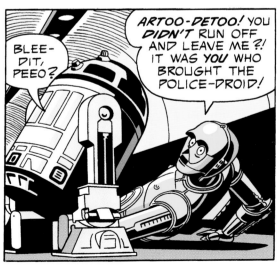

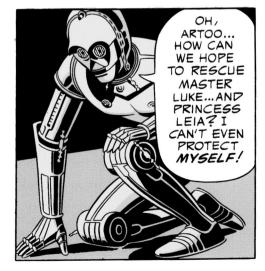

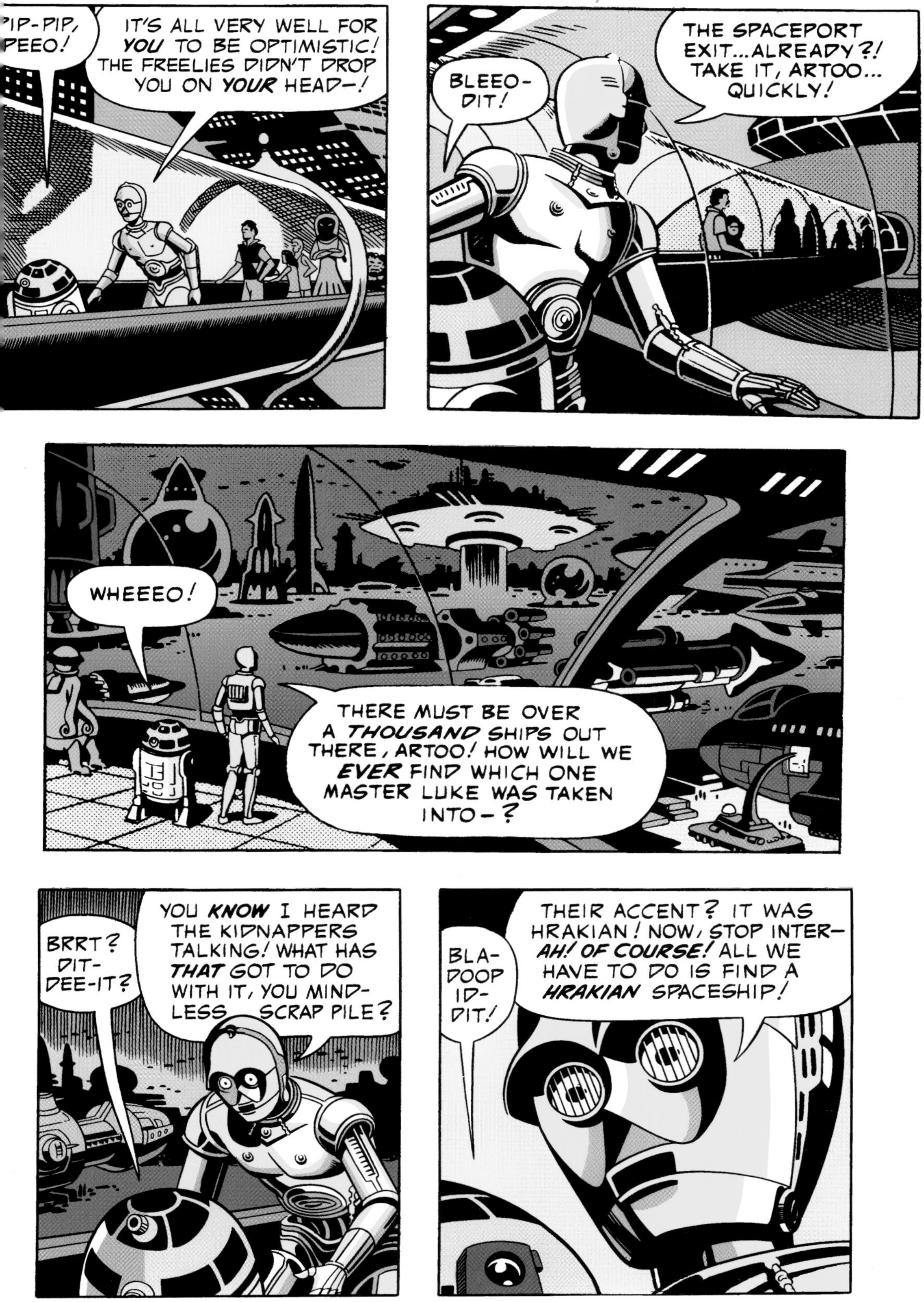
PIP-PIP, PEEO!
IT'S ALL VERY WELL FOR YOU TO BE OPTIMISTIC! THE FREELIES DIDN'T DROP YOU ON YOUR HEAD—!
BLEEO-DIT!
THE SPACEPORT EXIT...ALREADY?! TAKE IT, ARTOO... QUICKLY!
WHEEEO!
THERE MUST BE OVER A THOUSAND SHIPS OUT THERE, ARTOO! HOW WILL WE EVER FIND WHICH ONE MASTER LUKE WAS TAKEN INTO—?
BRRT? DIT-DEE-IT?
YOU KNOW I HEARD THE KIDNAPPERS TALKING! WHAT HAS THAT GOT TO DO WITH IT, YOU MINDLESS SCRAP PILE?
BLA-DOOP ID-DIT!
THEIR ACCENT? IT WAS HRAKIAN! NOW, STOP INTER— AH! OF COURSE! ALL WE HAVE TO DO IS FIND A HRAKIAN SPACESHIP!

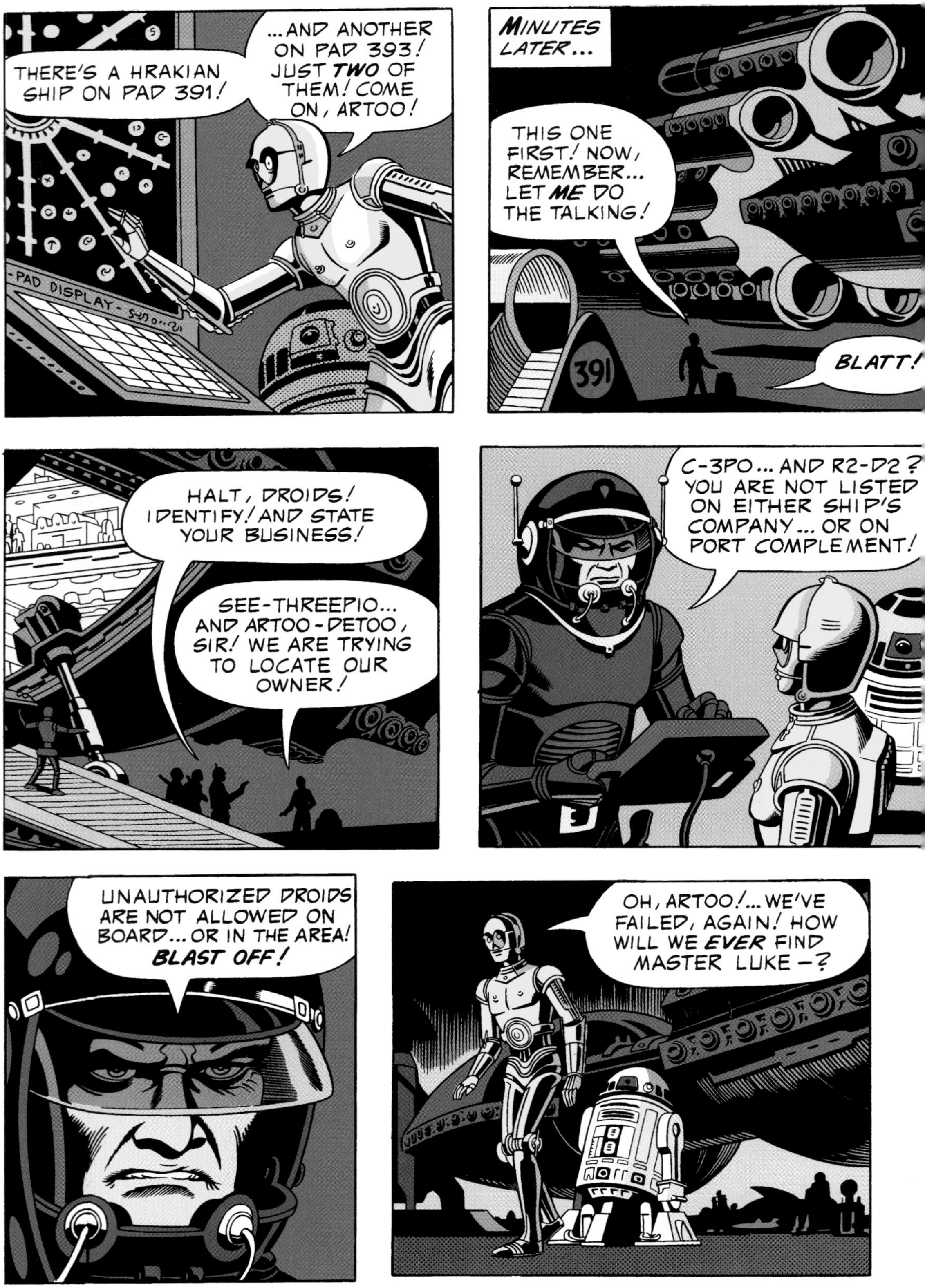
THERE'S A HRAKIAN SHIP ON PAD 391!
...AND ANOTHER ON PAD 393! JUST TWO OF THEM! COME ON, ARTOO!
-PAD DISPLAY-
MINUTES LATER...
THIS ONE FIRST! NOW, REMEMBER... LET ME DO THE TALKING!
391
BLATT!
HALT, DROIDS! IDENTIFY! AND STATE YOUR BUSINESS!
SEE-THREEPIO... AND ARTOO-DETOO, SIR! WE ARE TRYING TO LOCATE OUR OWNER!
C-3PO... AND R2-D2? YOU ARE NOT LISTED ON EITHER SHIP'S COMPANY... OR ON PORT COMPLEMENT!
UNAUTHORIZED DROIDS ARE NOT ALLOWED ON BOARD... OR IN THE AREA! BLAST OFF!
OH, ARTOO!... WE'VE FAILED, AGAIN! HOW WILL WE EVER FIND MASTER LUKE -?

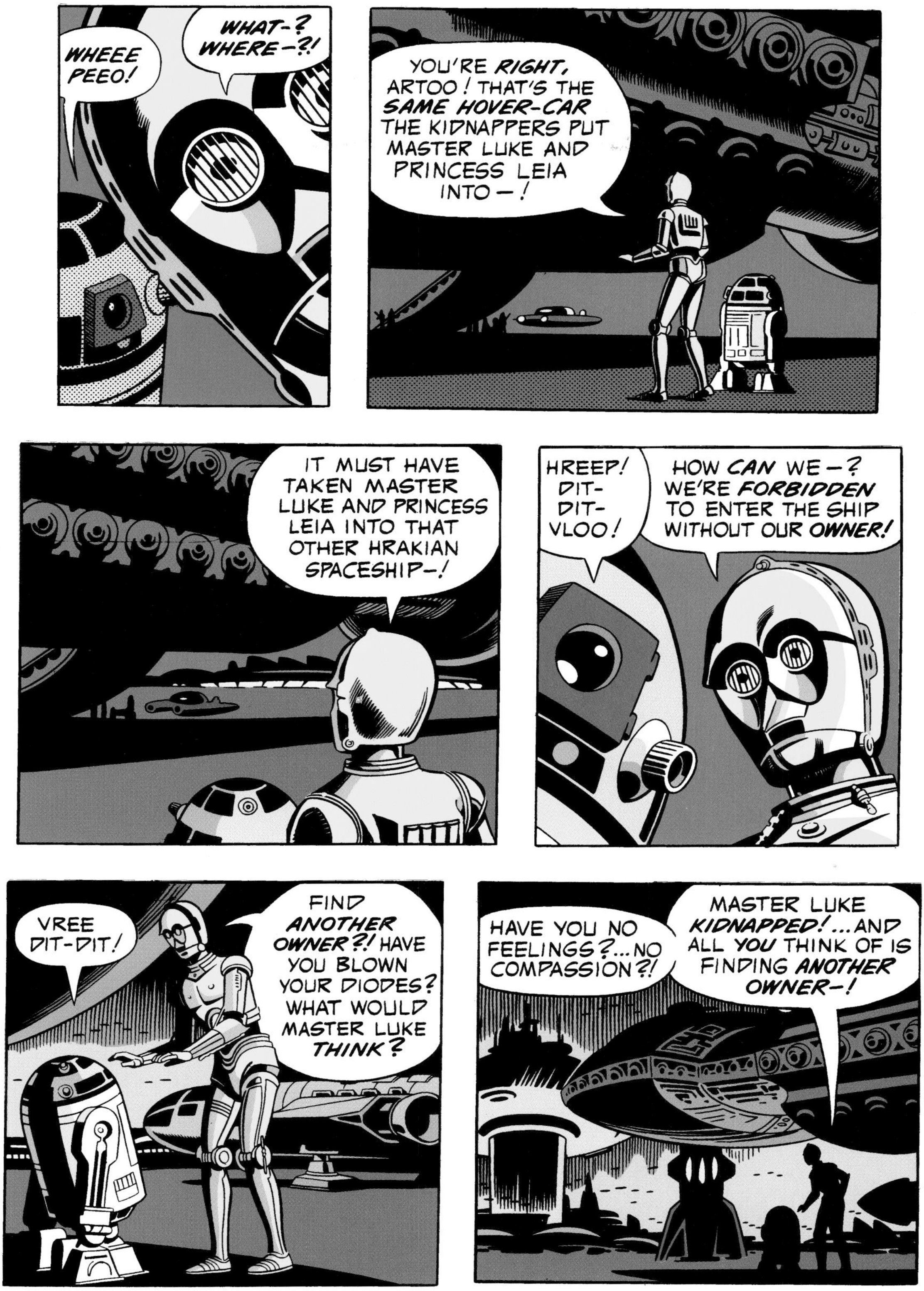
WHEEE PEEO!
WHAT-? WHERE-?!
YOU'RE RIGHT, ARTOO! THAT'S THE SAME HOVER-CAR THE KIDNAPPERS PUT MASTER LUKE AND PRINCESS LEIA INTO-!
IT MUST HAVE TAKEN MASTER LUKE AND PRINCESS LEIA INTO THAT OTHER HRAKIAN SPACESHIP-!
HREEP! DIT-DIT-VLOO!
HOW CAN WE-? WE'RE FORBIDDEN TO ENTER THE SHIP WITHOUT OUR OWNER!
VREE DIT-DIT!
FIND ANOTHER OWNER?! HAVE YOU BLOWN YOUR DIODES? WHAT WOULD MASTER LUKE THINK?
HAVE YOU NO FEELINGS?...NO COMPASSION?!
MASTER LUKE KIDNAPPED!...AND ALL YOU THINK OF IS FINDING ANOTHER OWNER-!

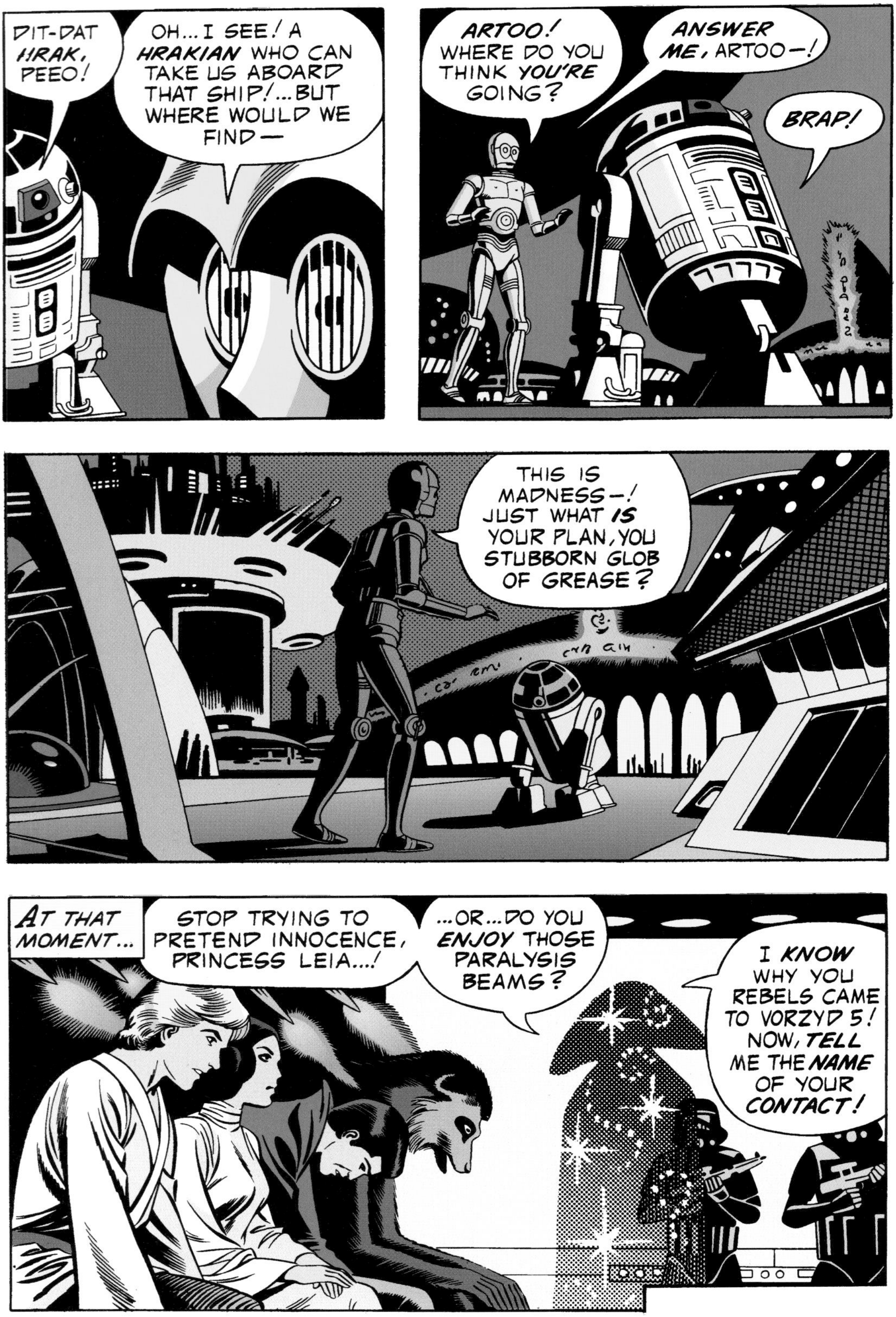
DIT-DAT HRAK, PEEO!
OH...I SEE! A HRAKIAN WHO CAN TAKE US ABOARD THAT SHIP!...BUT WHERE WOULD WE FIND—
ARTOO! WHERE DO YOU THINK YOU'RE GOING?
ANSWER ME, ARTOO—!
BRAP!
THIS IS MADNESS—! JUST WHAT IS YOUR PLAN, YOU STUBBORN GLOB OF GREASE?
AT THAT MOMENT...
STOP TRYING TO PRETEND INNOCENCE, PRINCESS LEIA...!
...OR...DO YOU ENJOY THOSE PARALYSIS BEAMS?
I KNOW WHY YOU REBELS CAME TO VORZYD 5! NOW, TELL ME THE NAME OF YOUR CONTACT!

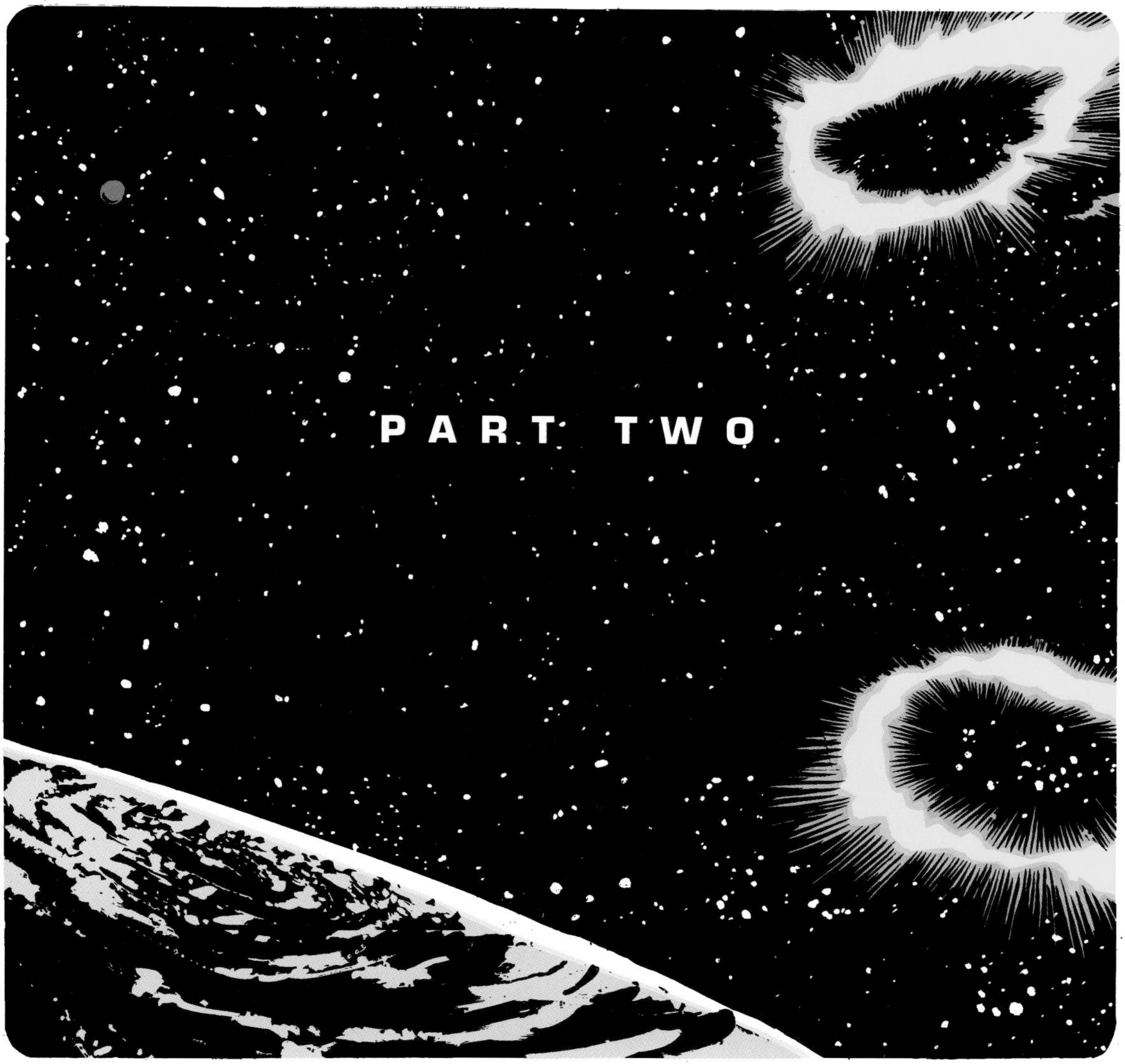
PART TWO

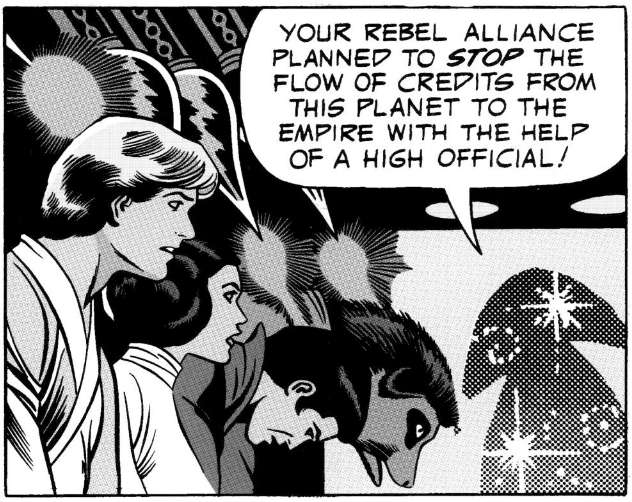
YOUR REBEL ALLIANCE PLANNED TO STOP THE FLOW OF CREDITS FROM THIS PLANET TO THE EMPIRE WITH THE HELP OF A HIGH OFFICIAL!

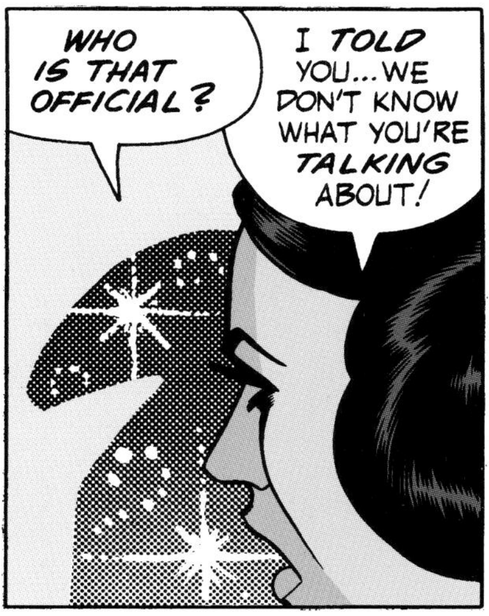
WHO IS THAT OFFICIAL?
I TOLD YOU...WE DON'T KNOW WHAT YOU'RE TALKING ABOUT!

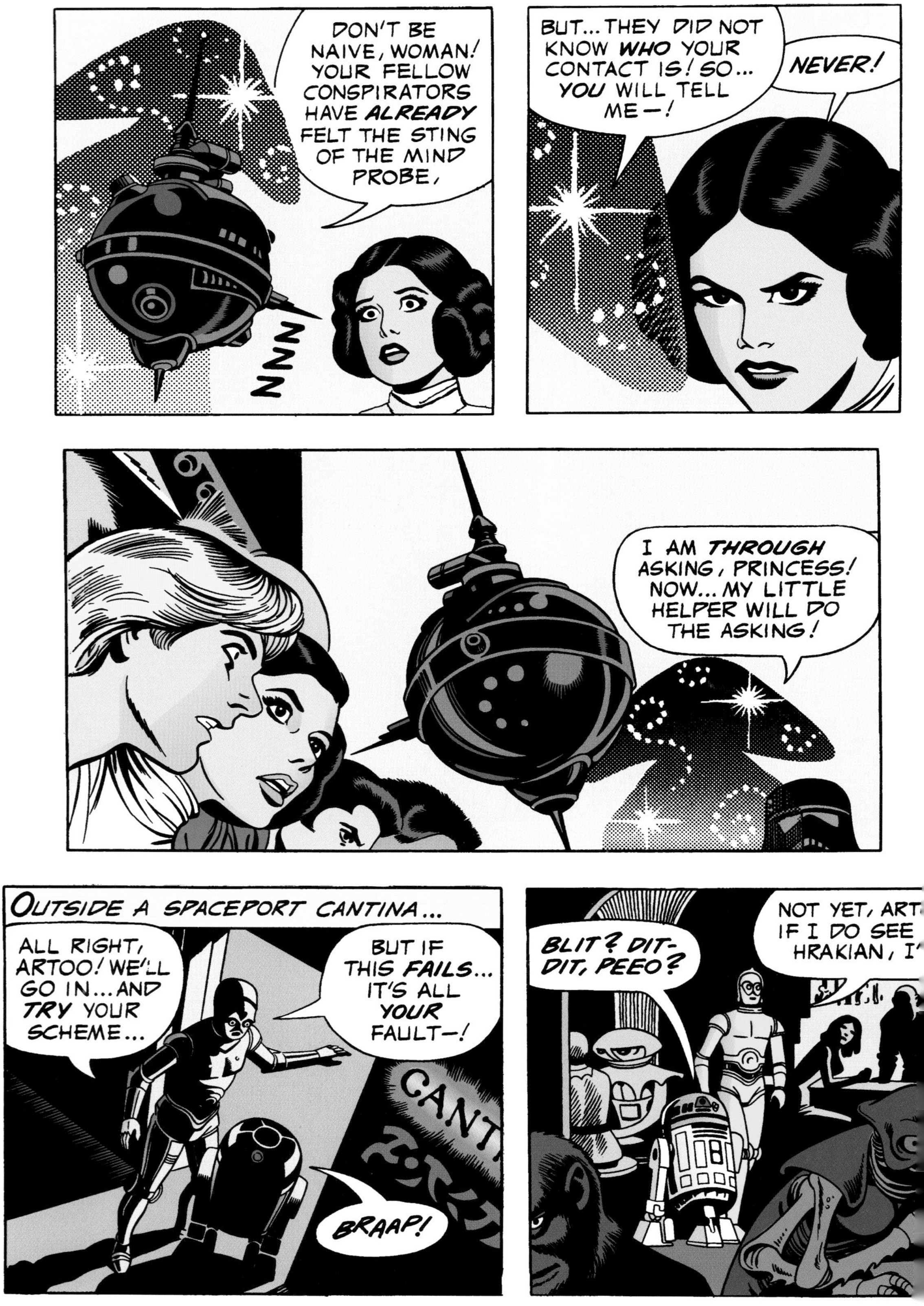
DON'T BE NAIVE, WOMAN! YOUR FELLOW CONSPIRATORS HAVE ALREADY FELT THE STING OF THE MIND PROBE,
NNN
BUT... THEY DID NOT KNOW WHO YOUR CONTACT IS! SO... YOU WILL TELL ME—!
NEVER!
I AM THROUGH ASKING, PRINCESS! NOW... MY LITTLE HELPER WILL DO THE ASKING!
OUTSIDE A SPACEPORT CANTINA...
ALL RIGHT, ARTOO! WE'LL GO IN... AND TRY YOUR SCHEME...
BUT IF THIS FAILS... IT'S ALL YOUR FAULT—!
BRAAP!
CANT
BLIT? DIT-DIT, PEEO?
NOT YET, ART
IF I DO SEE
HRAKIAN, I'

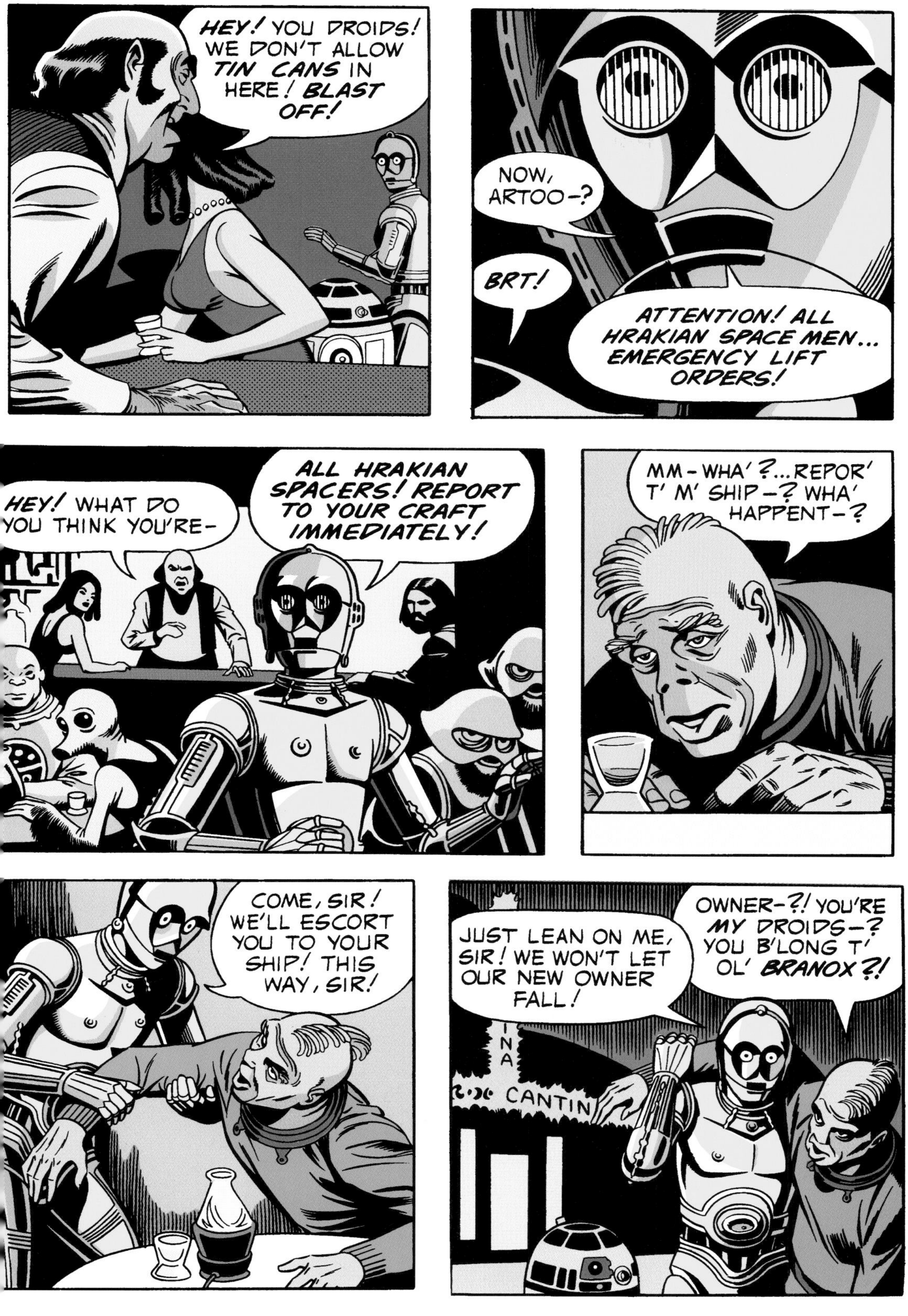
HEY! YOU DROIDS! WE DON'T ALLOW TIN CANS IN HERE! BLAST OFF!
NOW, ARTOO-?
BRT!
ATTENTION! ALL HRAKIAN SPACE MEN... EMERGENCY LIFT ORDERS!
HEY! WHAT DO YOU THINK YOU'RE-
ALL HRAKIAN SPACERS! REPORT TO YOUR CRAFT IMMEDIATELY!
MM-WHA'?...REPOR' T' M' SHIP-? WHA' HAPPENT-?
COME, SIR! WE'LL ESCORT YOU TO YOUR SHIP! THIS WAY, SIR!
JUST LEAN ON ME, SIR! WE WON'T LET OUR NEW OWNER FALL!
OWNER-?! YOU'RE MY DROIDS-? YOU B'LONG T' OL' BRANOX?!
CANTIN

IN A MANNER OF SPEAKING, SIR... WHILE WE HELP EACH OTHER GET ON BOARD YOUR SHIP!

THIS WAY, SIR!

BACK *EARLY* TONIGHT, EH, BRANOX?

'MERGENCY—

OUR OWNER'S NOT FEELING WELL, SIR! WE'LL SEE THAT HE GETS TO HIS QUARTERS!

INSIDE THE HRAKIAN SPACESHIP...

BRRT! VRUU PEEO!

ER... YOU GO AHEAD, SIR—! WE MUST...REGISTER WITH THE DROID STEWARD—!

HUH—?

WHAT MAKES YOU THINK WE CAN FIND MASTER LUKE BY GOING INTO SHIP'S DROID CONTROL!

BLAP!

THIS IS NO TIME TO GET FLIPPANT, YOU—*UH-OH!* SOMEONE'S *HERE*, ARTOO!

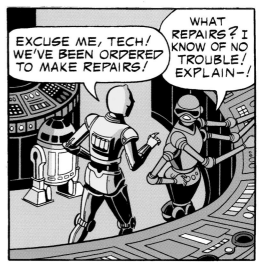

EXCUSE ME, TECH! WE'VE BEEN ORDERED TO MAKE REPAIRS!

WHAT REPAIRS? I KNOW OF NO TROUBLE! EXPLAIN—!

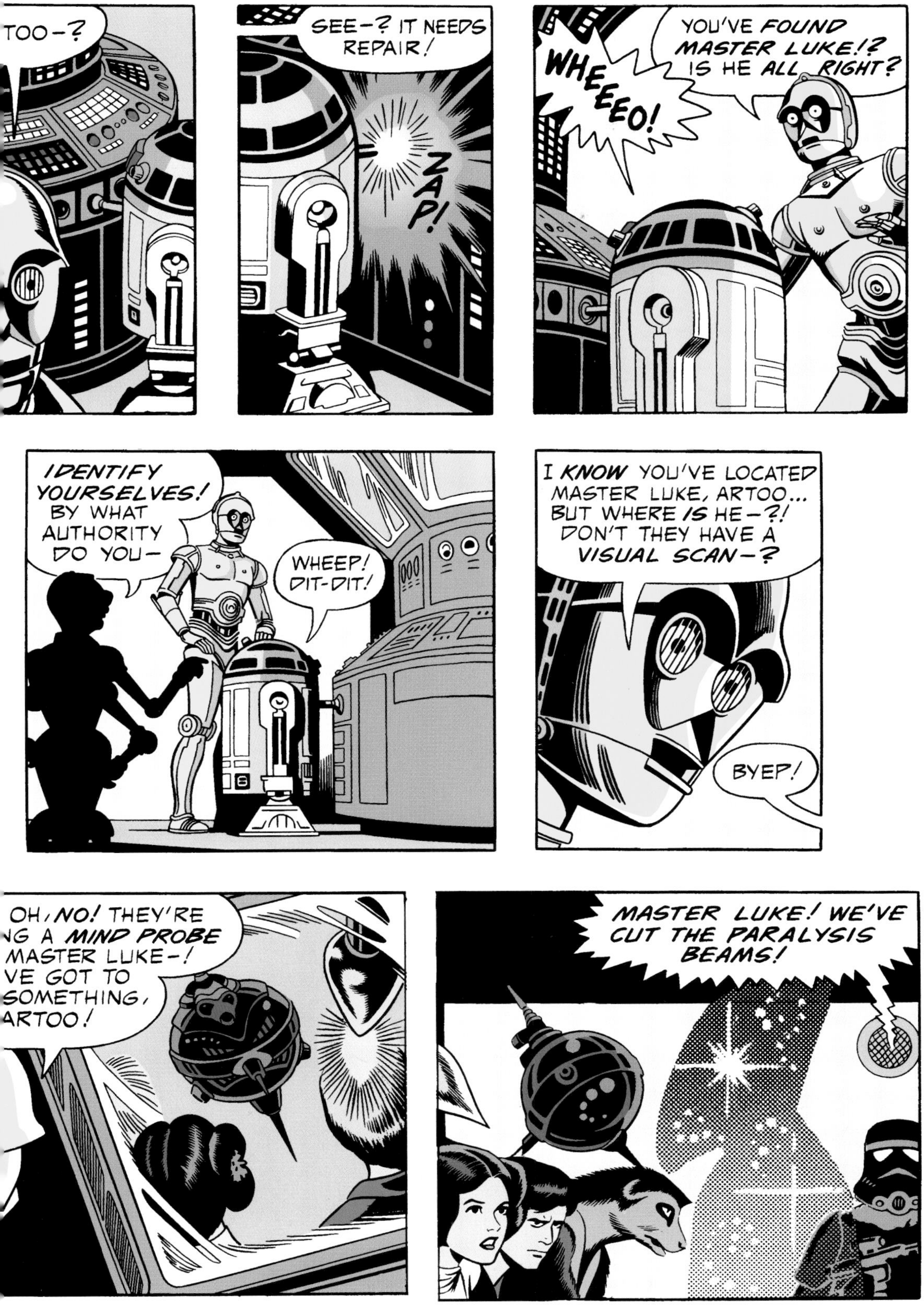
TOO—?
SEE—? IT NEEDS REPAIR!
ZAP!
WHEEEEO!
YOU'VE FOUND MASTER LUKE!? IS HE ALL RIGHT?
IDENTIFY YOURSELVES! BY WHAT AUTHORITY DO YOU—
WHEEP! DIT-DIT!
I KNOW YOU'VE LOCATED MASTER LUKE, ARTOO... BUT WHERE IS HE—?! DON'T THEY HAVE A VISUAL SCAN—?
BYEP!
OH, NO! THEY'RE NG A MIND PROBE MASTER LUKE—! VE GOT TO SOMETHING, ARTOO!
MASTER LUKE! WE'VE CUT THE PARALYSIS BEAMS!

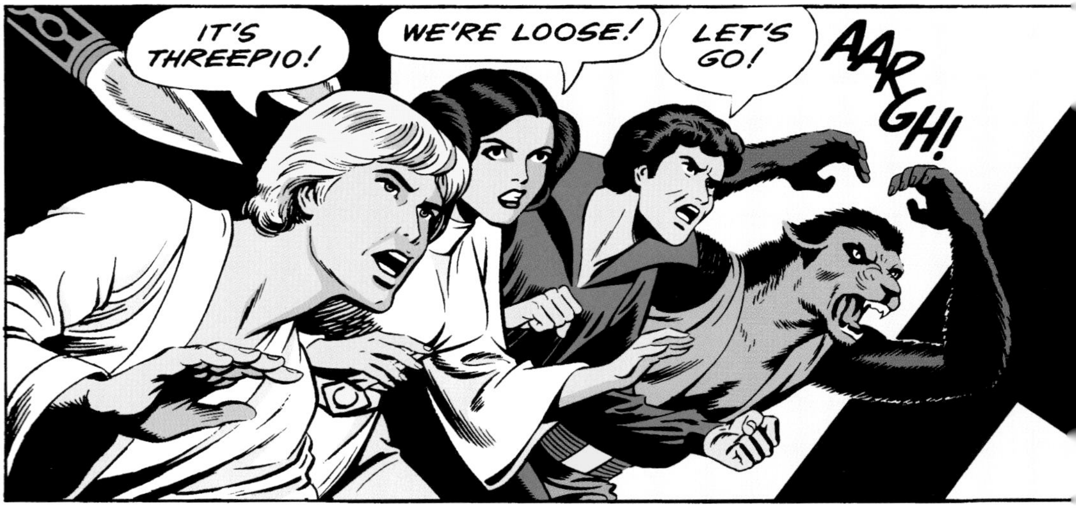
IT'S THREEPIO!
WE'RE LOOSE!
LET'S GO!
AARGH!

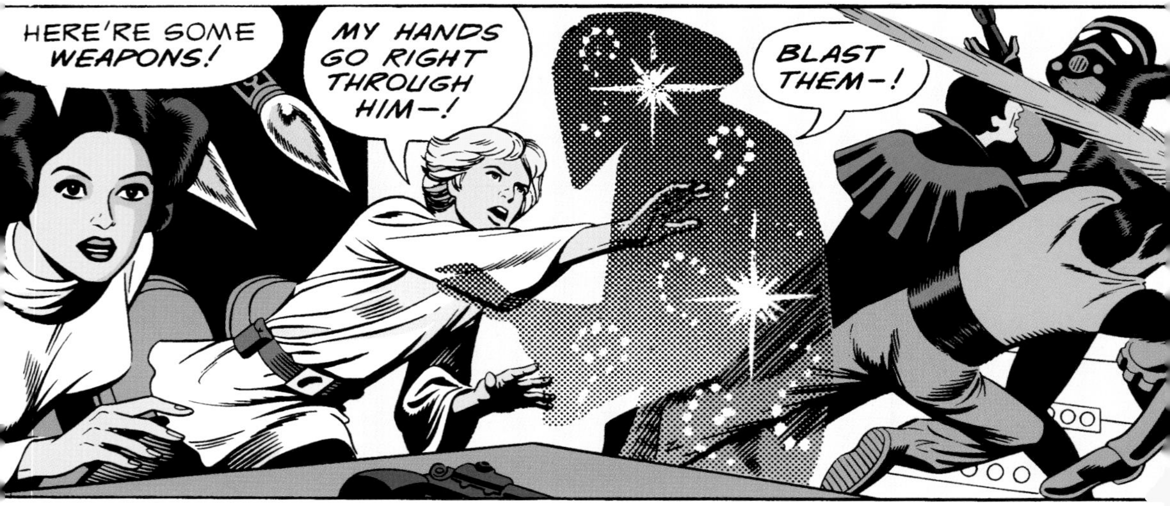
HERE'RE SOME WEAPONS!
MY HANDS GO RIGHT THROUGH HIM—!
BLAST THEM—!

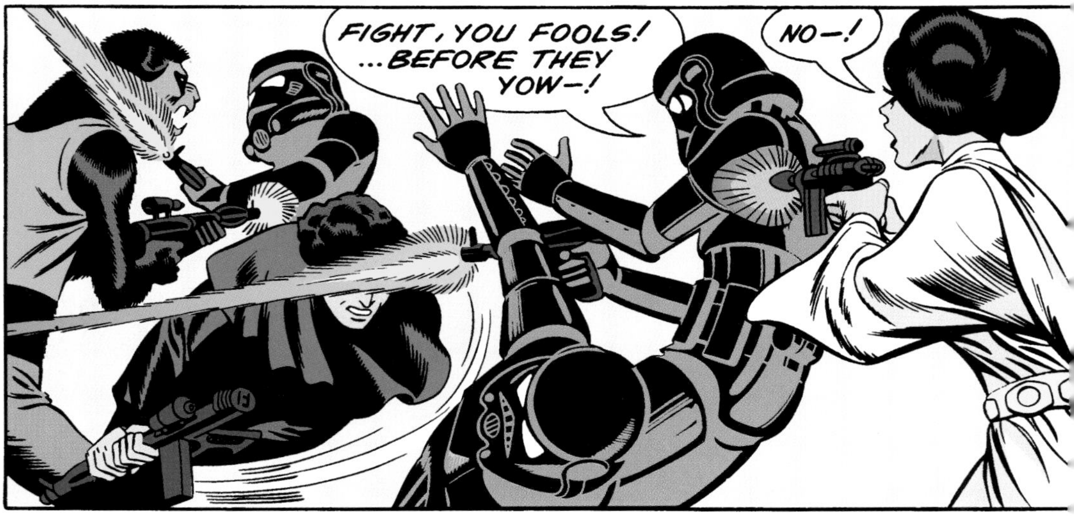
FIGHT, YOU FOOLS! ...BEFORE THEY YOW—!
NO—!

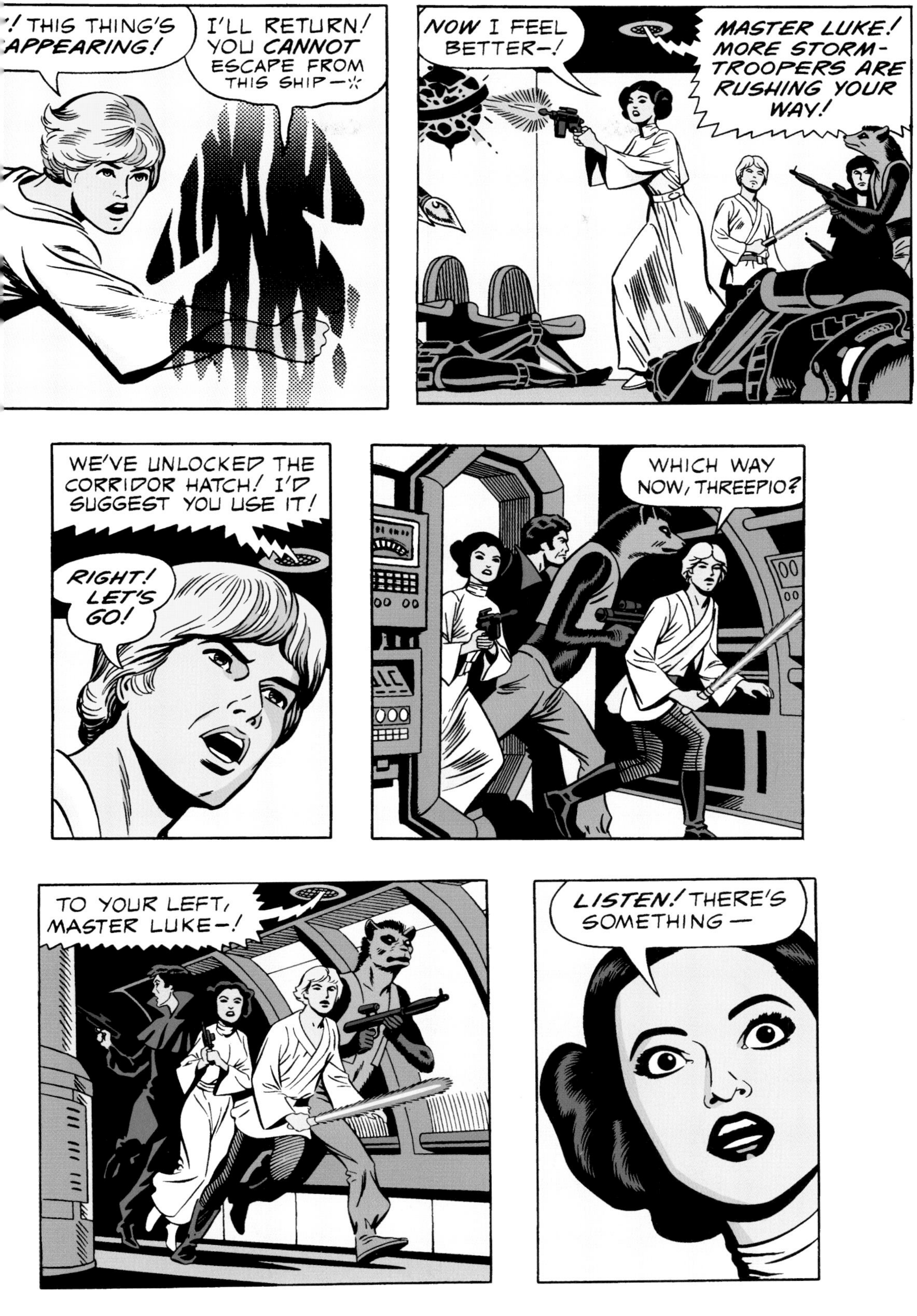
! THIS THING'S APPEARING!
I'LL RETURN! YOU CANNOT ESCAPE FROM THIS SHIP—
NOW I FEEL BETTER—!
MASTER LUKE! MORE STORM-TROOPERS ARE RUSHING YOUR WAY!
WE'VE UNLOCKED THE CORRIDOR HATCH! I'D SUGGEST YOU USE IT!
RIGHT! LET'S GO!
WHICH WAY NOW, THREEPIO?
TO YOUR LEFT, MASTER LUKE—!
LISTEN! THERE'S SOMETHING—

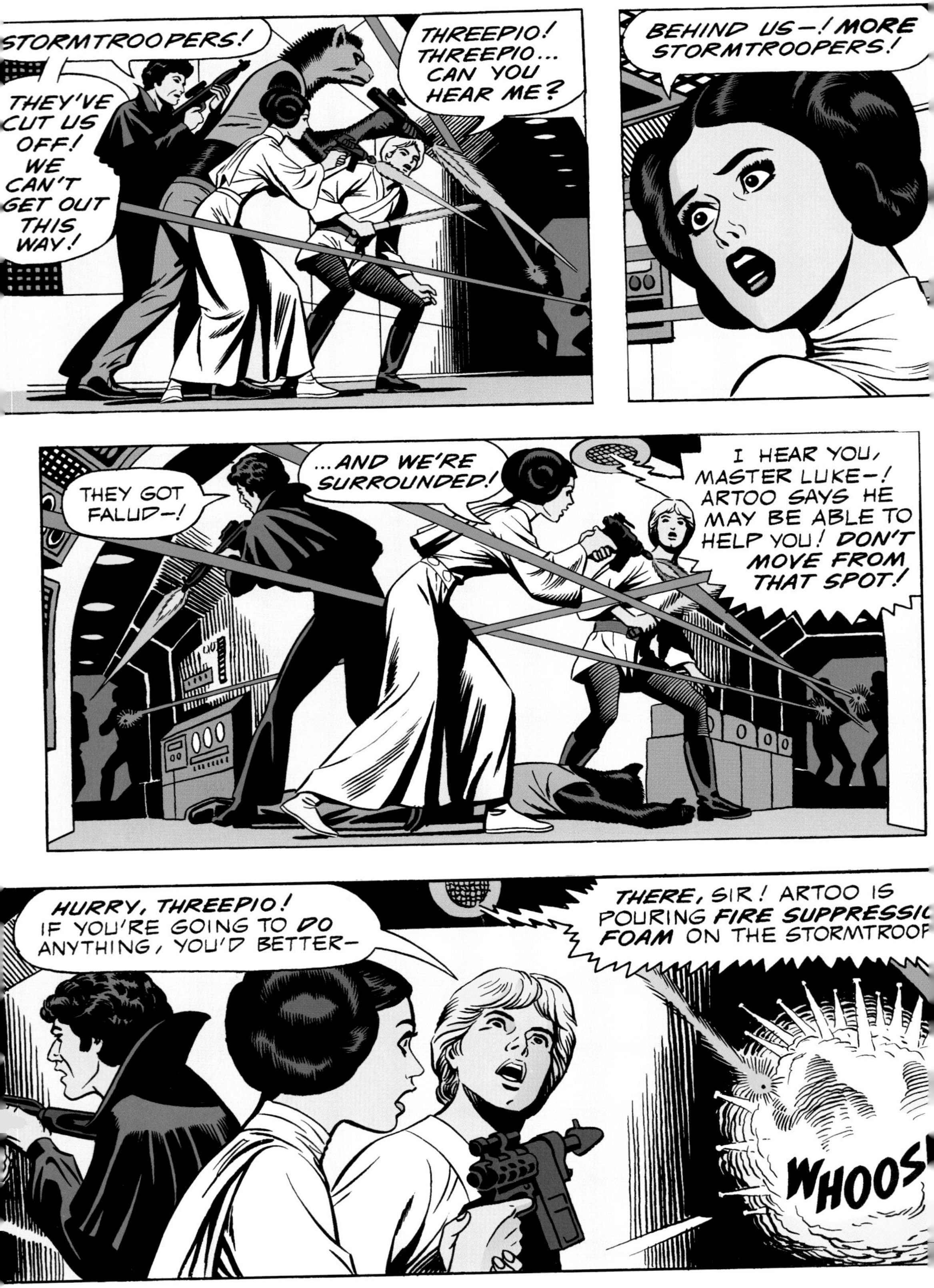
STORMTROOPERS!
THEY'VE CUT US OFF! WE CAN'T GET OUT THIS WAY!
THREEPIO! THREEPIO... CAN YOU HEAR ME?
BEHIND US—! MORE STORMTROOPERS!
THEY GOT FALUD—!
...AND WE'RE SURROUNDED!
I HEAR YOU, MASTER LUKE—! ARTOO SAYS HE MAY BE ABLE TO HELP YOU! DON'T MOVE FROM THAT SPOT!
HURRY, THREEPIO! IF YOU'RE GOING TO DO ANYTHING, YOU'D BETTER—
THERE, SIR! ARTOO IS POURING FIRE SUPPRESSI FOAM ON THE STORMTROOP
WHOOS

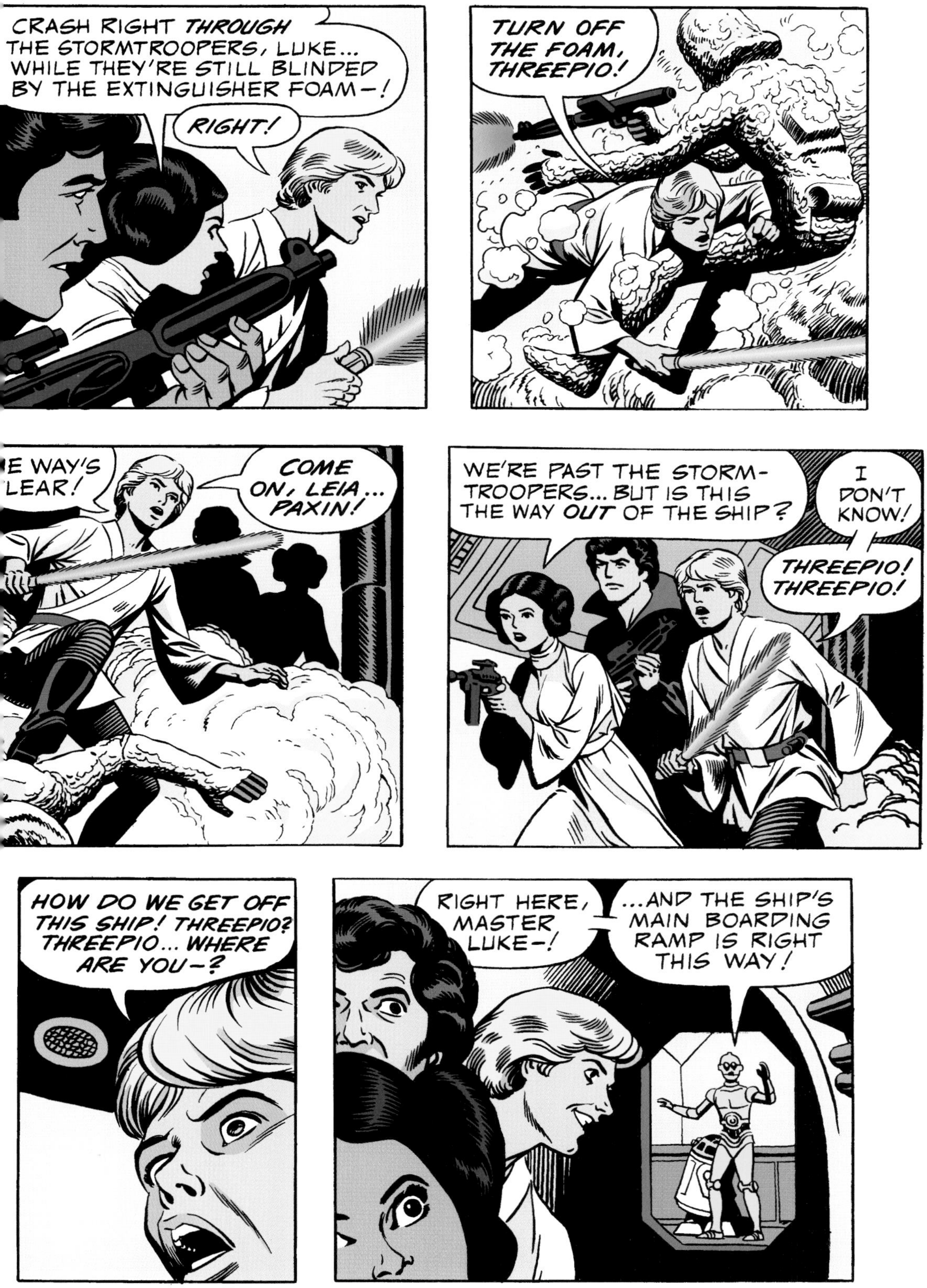
CRASH RIGHT THROUGH THE STORMTROOPERS, LUKE... WHILE THEY'RE STILL BLINDED BY THE EXTINGUISHER FOAM—!
RIGHT!
TURN OFF THE FOAM, THREEPIO!
E WAY'S LEAR!
COME ON, LEIA... PAXIN!
WE'RE PAST THE STORM-TROOPERS... BUT IS THIS THE WAY OUT OF THE SHIP?
I DON'T KNOW!
THREEPIO! THREEPIO!
HOW DO WE GET OFF THIS SHIP! THREEPIO? THREEPIO... WHERE ARE YOU—?
RIGHT HERE, MASTER LUKE—!
...AND THE SHIP'S MAIN BOARDING RAMP IS RIGHT THIS WAY!

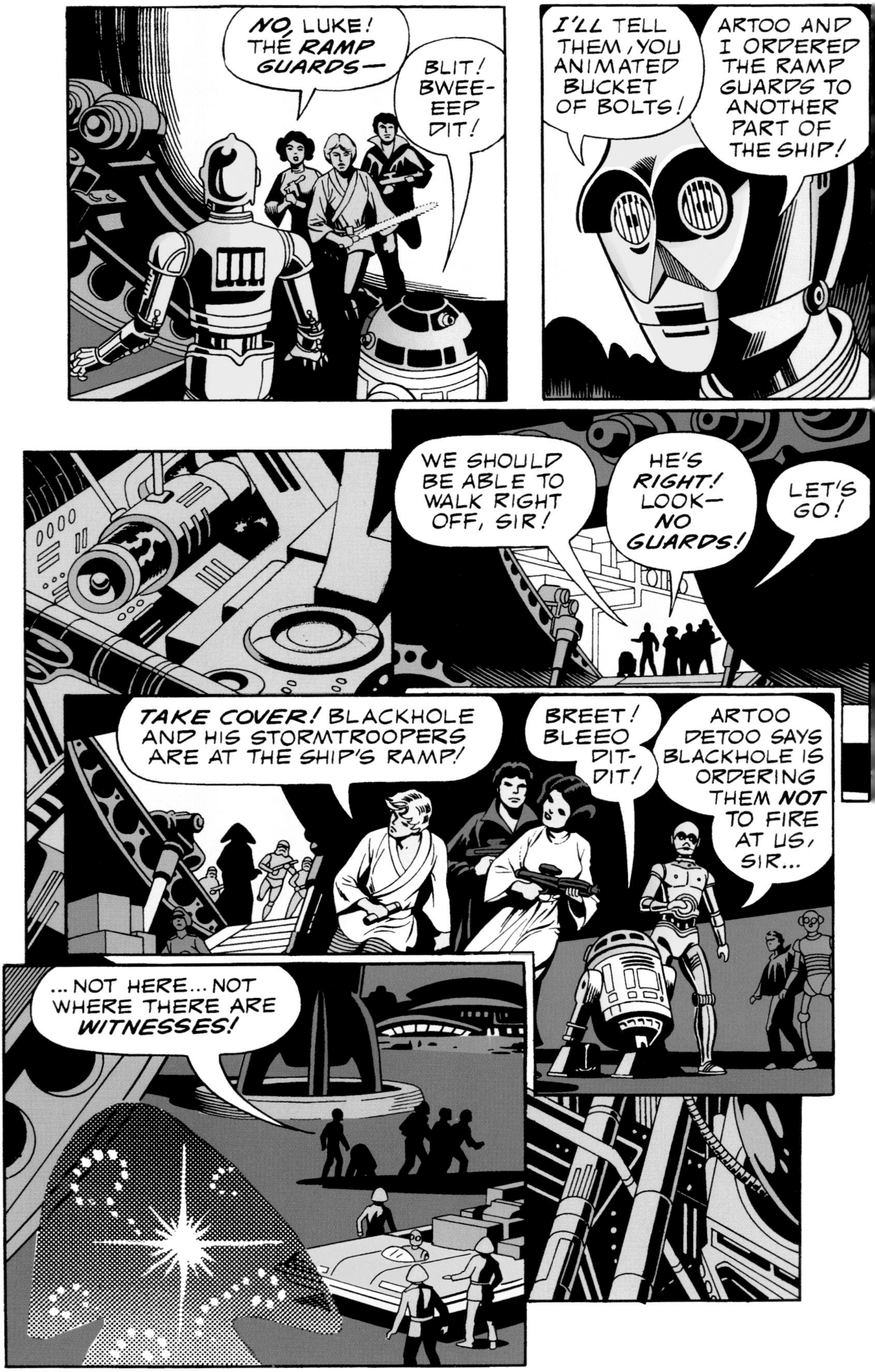
NO, LUKE! THE RAMP GUARDS—
BLIT! BWEE-EEP DIT!
I'LL TELL THEM, YOU ANIMATED BUCKET OF BOLTS!
ARTOO AND I ORDERED THE RAMP GUARDS TO ANOTHER PART OF THE SHIP!
WE SHOULD BE ABLE TO WALK RIGHT OFF, SIR!
HE'S RIGHT! LOOK— NO GUARDS!
LET'S GO!
TAKE COVER! BLACKHOLE AND HIS STORMTROOPERS ARE AT THE SHIP'S RAMP!
BREET! BLEEO DIT-DIT!
ARTOO DETOO SAYS BLACKHOLE IS ORDERING THEM NOT TO FIRE AT US, SIR...
...NOT HERE... NOT WHERE THERE ARE WITNESSES!

WE'RE *SAFE*... AT LEAST FOR THE MOMENT!

IF ONLY FALUD COULD HAVE MADE IT, TOO —!

HE DIDN'T DIE IN VAIN! THE REBELLION AGAINST THE EMPIRE WILL CONTINUE!

ER...IN ECRET ONGHOLD...

THEN FIRST TLE NST KHOLE ED IN RAW!

YOUR CONCLUSION IS CORRECT, MISTRESS MNEMOS!

I MUST KNOW MORE ABOUT *BLACKHOLE*, THREEPIO...BUT I CANNOT RELY SOLELY ON VOCAL COMMUNICATION!

SO ATTACH LEAD "B" TO YOUR RESTRAINING BOLT!

YES, MISTRESS MNEMOS!

NOW...GIVE ME THE SHARPEST MEMORY YOU HAVE...*AH!*

BLACKHOLE APPEARED TO BE SOME FORM OF *PROJECTION*, MISTRESS MNEMOS! MASTER LUKE'S BLOWS WENT RIGHT *THROUGH* IT!

IT SPOKE WITH A MALE HUMAN VOICE.

A VOICE I CAN ONLY DESCRIBE AS *SINISTER*... *THREATENING*... AND *EVIL*!

CONTROL YOURSELF, DEAR CHILD—! *EVIL* IS FOR *HUMANS* TO JUDGE!

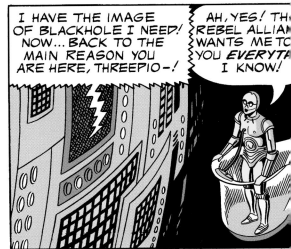

I HAVE THE IMAGE OF BLACKHOLE I NEED! NOW... BACK TO THE MAIN REASON YOU ARE HERE, THREEPIO—!

AH, YES! TH REBEL ALLIA WANTS ME T YOU *EVERYT* I KNOW!

MASTER MECHANIC FORBID! MY BANKS ARE OVERFLOWING WITH TRIVIA AS IT IS!

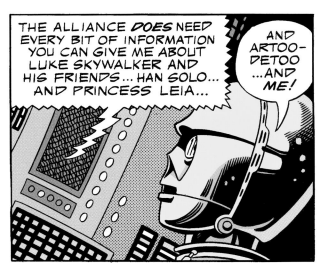

THE ALLIANCE *DOES* NEED EVERY BIT OF INFORMATION YOU CAN GIVE ME ABOUT LUKE SKYWALKER AND HIS FRIENDS... HAN SOLO... AND PRINCESS LEIA...

AND ARTOO-DETOO ...AND *ME*!

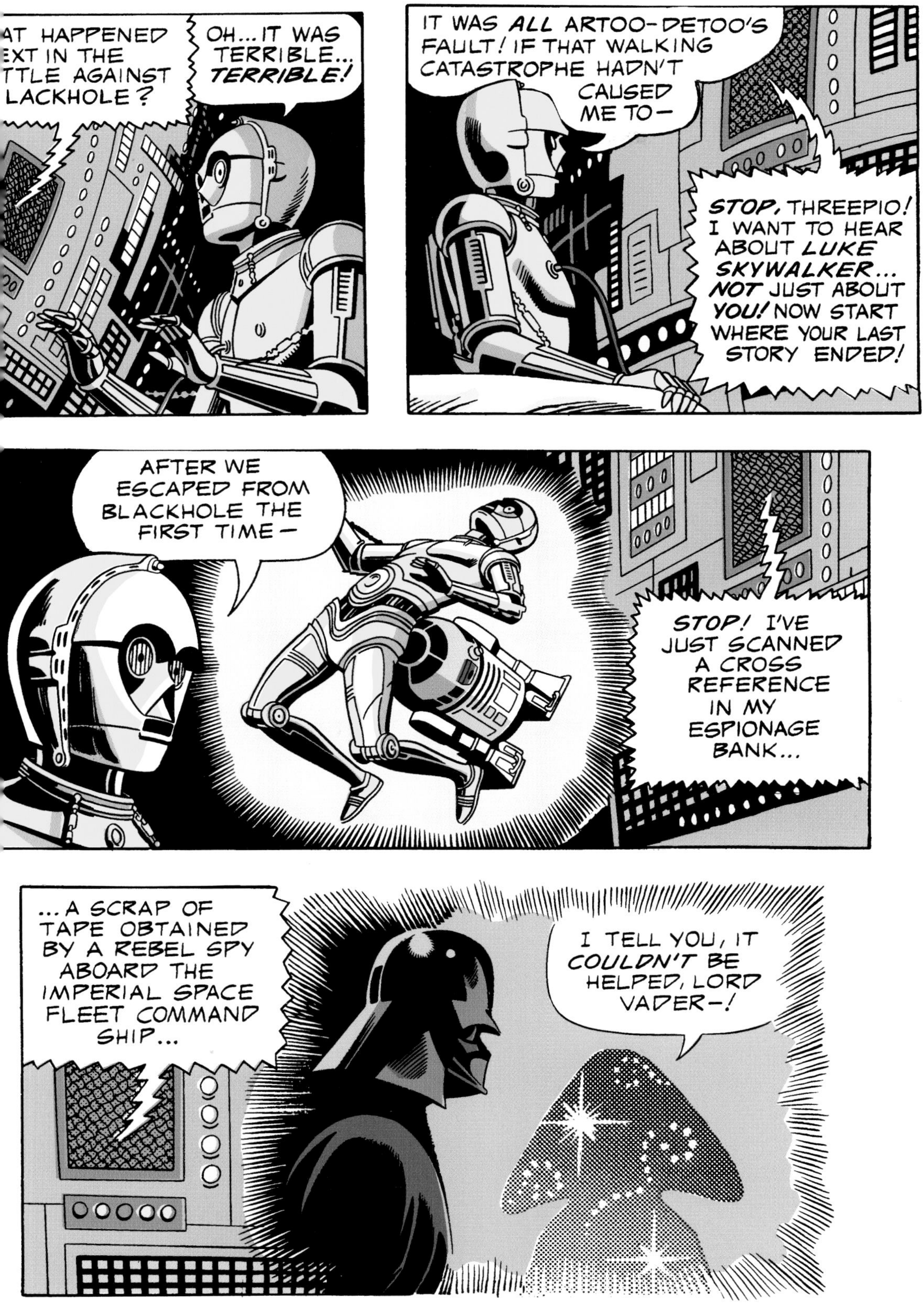
AT HAPPENED
EXT IN THE
TTLE AGAINST
LACKHOLE?
OH...IT WAS TERRIBLE... TERRIBLE!
IT WAS ALL ARTOO-DETOO'S FAULT! IF THAT WALKING CATASTROPHE HADN'T CAUSED ME TO—
STOP, THREEPIO! I WANT TO HEAR ABOUT LUKE SKYWALKER... NOT JUST ABOUT YOU! NOW START WHERE YOUR LAST STORY ENDED!
AFTER WE ESCAPED FROM BLACKHOLE THE FIRST TIME—
STOP! I'VE JUST SCANNED A CROSS REFERENCE IN MY ESPIONAGE BANK...
...A SCRAP OF TAPE OBTAINED BY A REBEL SPY ABOARD THE IMPERIAL SPACE FLEET COMMAND SHIP...
I TELL YOU, IT COULDN'T BE HELPED, LORD VADER—!

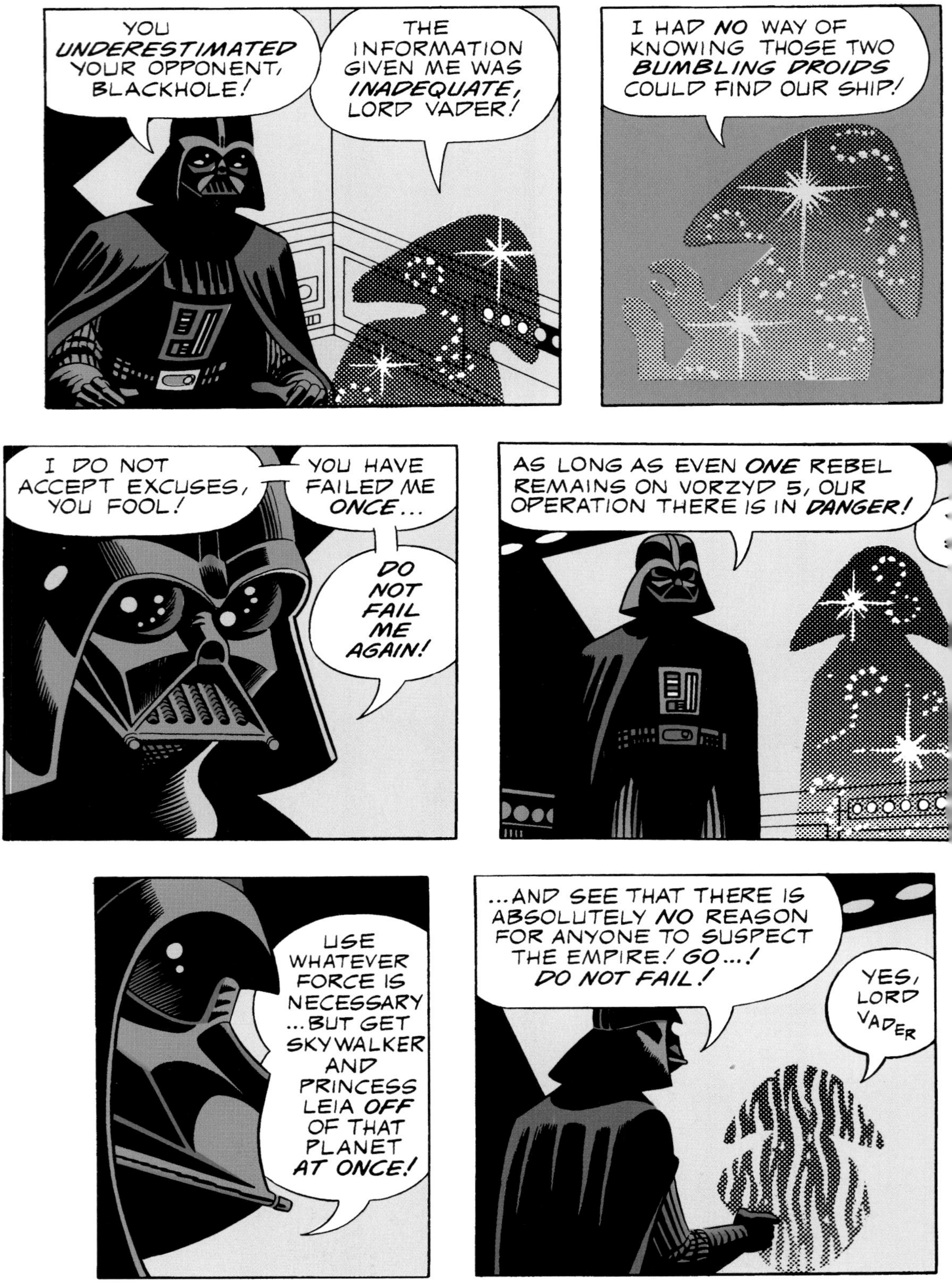
YOU UNDERESTIMATED YOUR OPPONENT, BLACKHOLE!
THE INFORMATION GIVEN ME WAS INADEQUATE, LORD VADER!
I HAD NO WAY OF KNOWING THOSE TWO BUMBLING DROIDS COULD FIND OUR SHIP!
I DO NOT ACCEPT EXCUSES, YOU FOOL!
YOU HAVE FAILED ME ONCE...
DO NOT FAIL ME AGAIN!
AS LONG AS EVEN ONE REBEL REMAINS ON VORZYD 5, OUR OPERATION THERE IS IN DANGER!
USE WHATEVER FORCE IS NECESSARY ...BUT GET SKYWALKER AND PRINCESS LEIA OFF OF THAT PLANET AT ONCE!
...AND SEE THAT THERE IS ABSOLUTELY NO REASON FOR ANYONE TO SUSPECT THE EMPIRE! GO...! DO NOT FAIL!
YES, LORD VADER

AH!...I THOUGHT I DETECTED *DARTH VADER'S* TOUCH IN BLACKHOLE'S OPERATIONS!

YOU MEAN ARTOO-DETOO WAS RIGHT ALL ALONG?!

"*WHEN* WE WERE ON VORZYD 5, ARTOO KEPT INSISTING THAT I WARN MASTER LUKE..."

FOR THE LAST TIME, ARTOO...I WILL *NOT* TELL MASTER LUKE ABOUT YOUR ABSURD SUSPICIONS-!

ARTOO-DETOO! COME *BACK* HERE! WE DON'T HAVE PERMISSION TO LEAVE THE SHIP-!

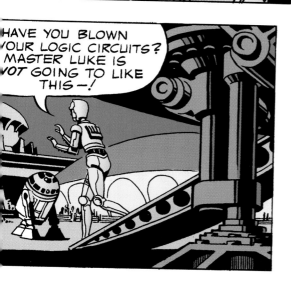

HAVE YOU BLOWN YOUR LOGIC CIRCUITS? MASTER LUKE IS *NOT* GOING TO LIKE THIS-!

THIS IS *DANGEROUS,* ARTOO-DETOO! DON'T YOU REMEMBER THE *LAST* TIME WE TOOK A CONVEYOR TUBE-?

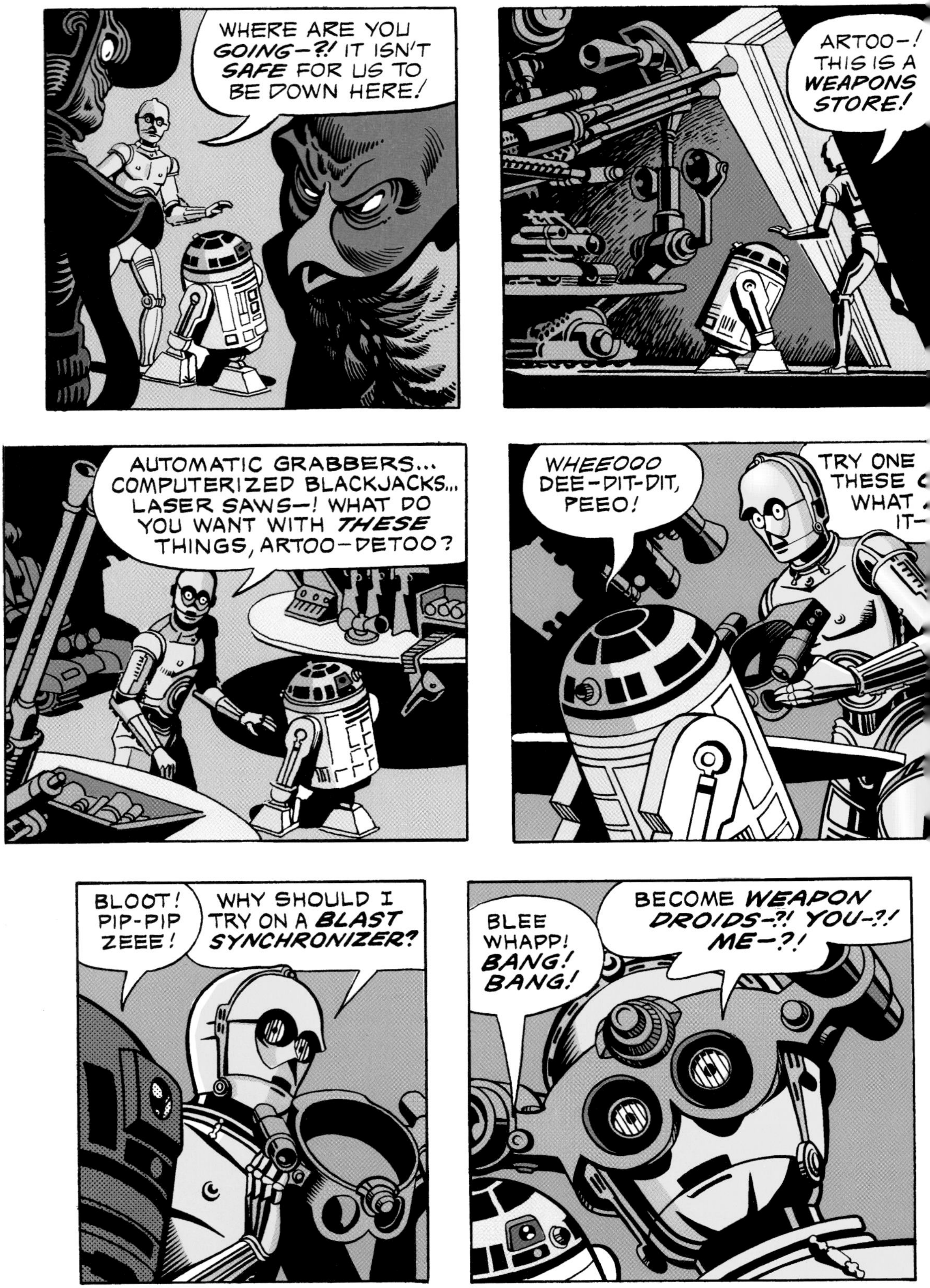
WHERE ARE YOU GOING—?! IT ISN'T SAFE FOR US TO BE DOWN HERE!
ARTOO—! THIS IS A WEAPONS STORE!
AUTOMATIC GRABBERS... COMPUTERIZED BLACKJACKS... LASER SAWS—! WHAT DO YOU WANT WITH THESE THINGS, ARTOO-DETOO?
WHEEOOO DEE-DIT-DIT, PEEO!
TRY ONE
THESE
WHAT
IT—
BLOOT! PIP-PIP ZEEE!
WHY SHOULD I TRY ON A BLAST SYNCHRONIZER?
BLEE WHAPP! BANG! BANG!
BECOME WEAPON DROIDS—?! YOU—?! ME—?!

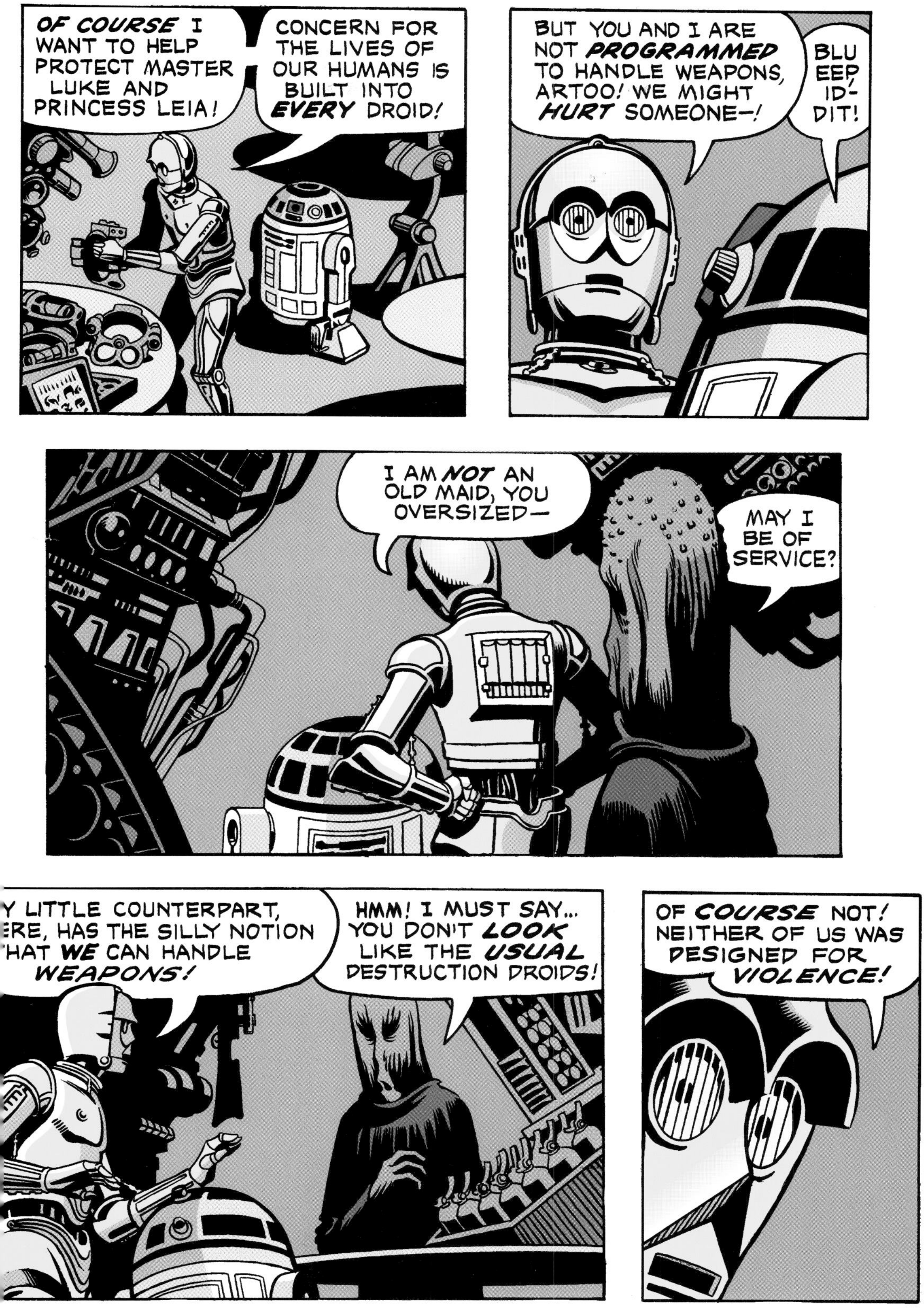

OF COURSE I WANT TO HELP PROTECT MASTER LUKE AND PRINCESS LEIA!
CONCERN FOR THE LIVES OF OUR HUMANS IS BUILT INTO EVERY DROID!
BUT YOU AND I ARE NOT PROGRAMMED TO HANDLE WEAPONS, ARTOO! WE MIGHT HURT SOMEONE--!
BLU EEP ID-DIT!
I AM NOT AN OLD MAID, YOU OVERSIZED--
MAY I BE OF SERVICE?
Y LITTLE COUNTERPART, ERE, HAS THE SILLY NOTION HAT WE CAN HANDLE WEAPONS!
HMM! I MUST SAY... YOU DON'T LOOK LIKE THE USUAL DESTRUCTION DROIDS!
OF COURSE NOT! NEITHER OF US WAS DESIGNED FOR VIOLENCE!

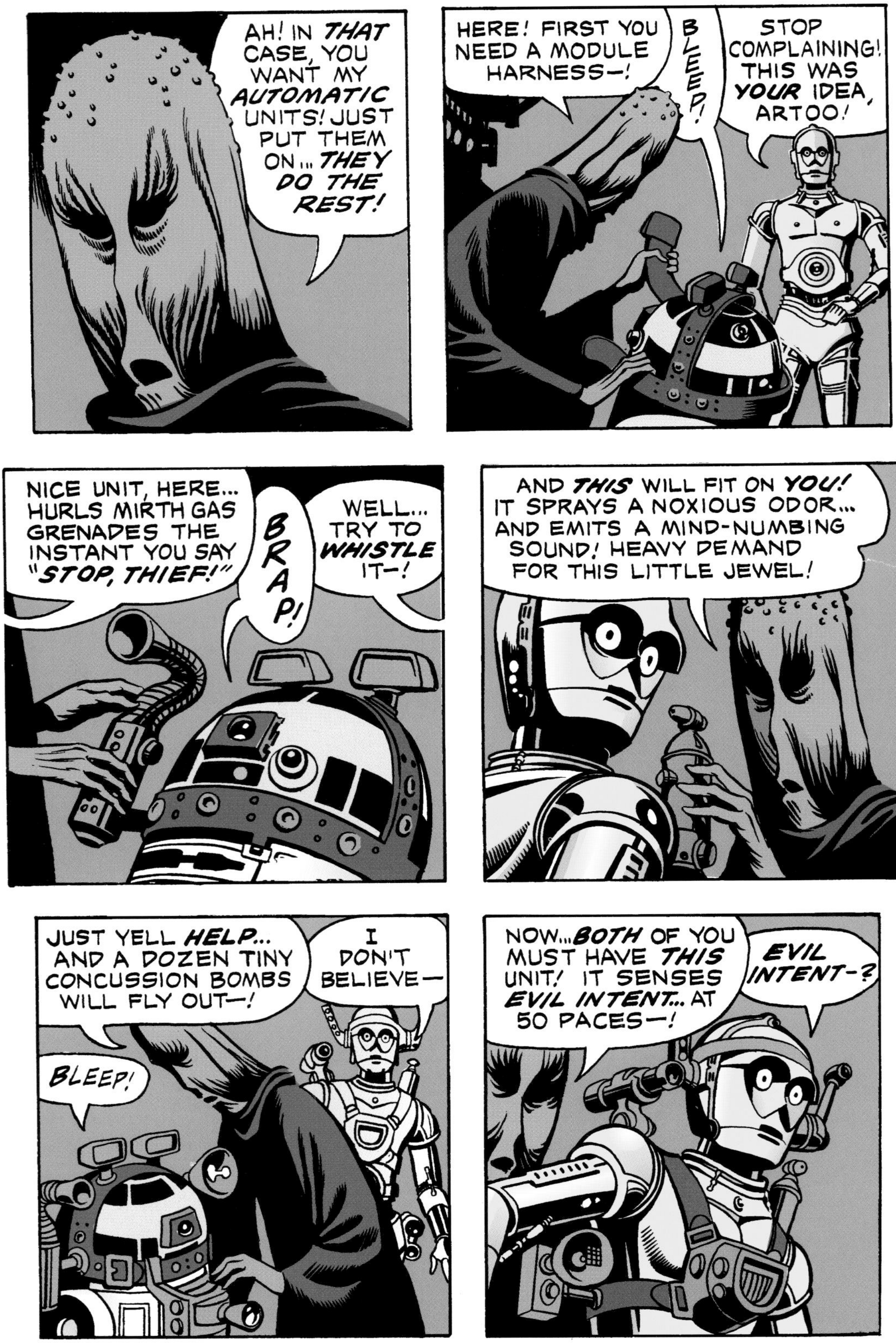
AH! IN THAT CASE, YOU WANT MY AUTOMATIC UNITS! JUST PUT THEM ON... THEY DO THE REST!
HERE! FIRST YOU NEED A MODULE HARNESS—!
BLEEP!
STOP COMPLAINING! THIS WAS YOUR IDEA, ARTOO!
NICE UNIT, HERE... HURLS MIRTH GAS GRENADES THE INSTANT YOU SAY "STOP, THIEF!"
BRAP!
WELL... TRY TO WHISTLE IT—!
AND THIS WILL FIT ON YOU! IT SPRAYS A NOXIOUS ODOR... AND EMITS A MIND-NUMBING SOUND! HEAVY DEMAND FOR THIS LITTLE JEWEL!
JUST YELL HELP... AND A DOZEN TINY CONCUSSION BOMBS WILL FLY OUT—!
I DON'T BELIEVE—
BLEEP!
NOW... BOTH OF YOU MUST HAVE THIS UNIT! IT SENSES EVIL INTENT... AT 50 PACES—!
EVIL INTENT—?

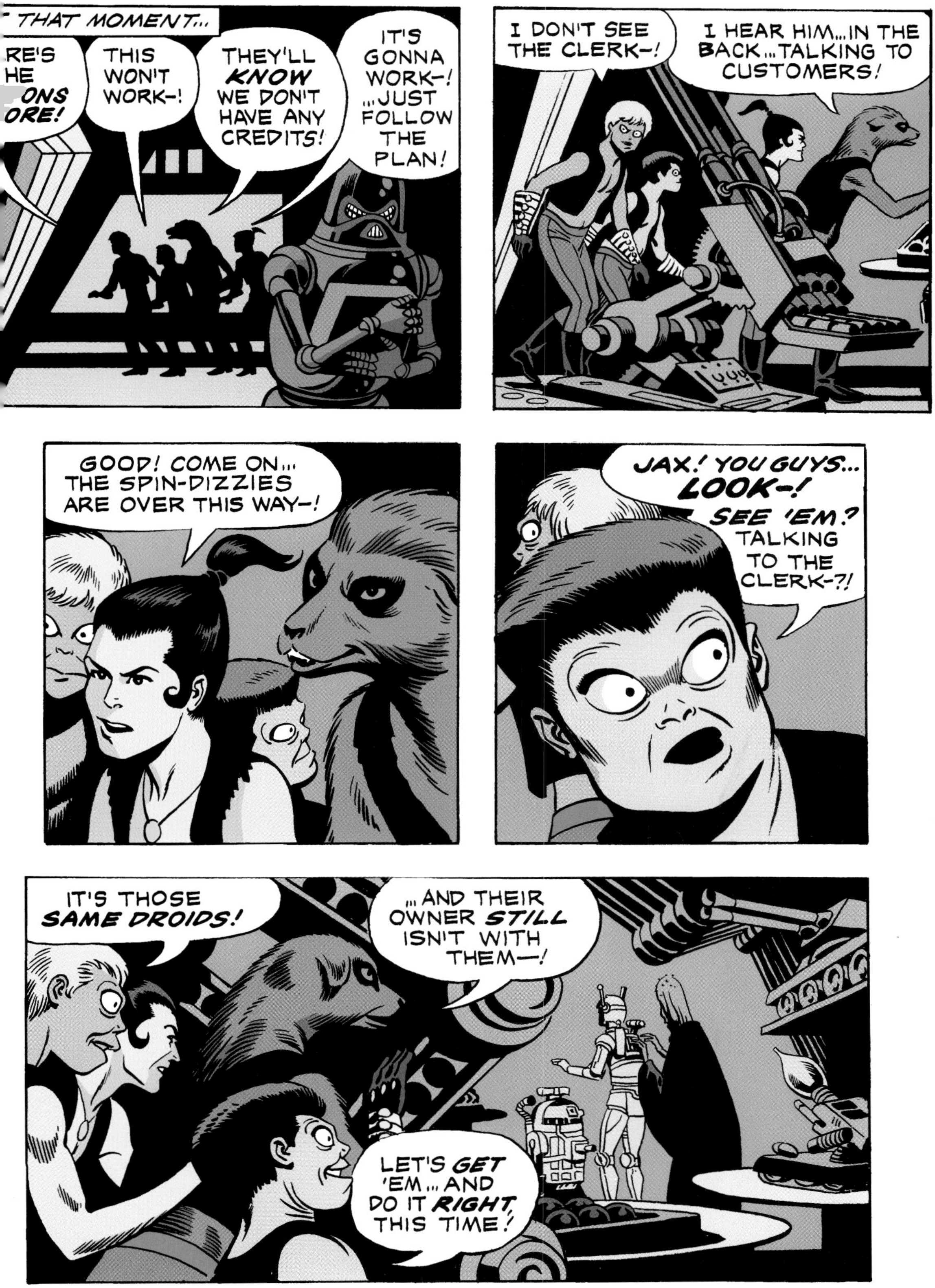

THAT MOMENT...
RE'S
HE
ONS
ORE!
THIS WON'T WORK-!
THEY'LL KNOW WE DON'T HAVE ANY CREDITS!
IT'S GONNA WORK-! ...JUST FOLLOW THE PLAN!
I DON'T SEE THE CLERK-!
I HEAR HIM... IN THE BACK... TALKING TO CUSTOMERS!
GOOD! COME ON... THE SPIN-DIZZIES ARE OVER THIS WAY-!
JAX! YOU GUYS... LOOK-! SEE 'EM? TALKING TO THE CLERK-?!
IT'S THOSE SAME DROIDS!
...AND THEIR OWNER STILL ISN'T WITH THEM—!
LET'S GET 'EM... AND DO IT RIGHT, THIS TIME!

WHAT'S ALL THAT STUFF THEY'RE BUYING--?
PROTECTIVE GEAR... AUTOMATIC DEFENSES...
ONCE THEY TURN IT ON, WE WON'T EVEN BE ABLE TO GET NEAR THEM!
RIGHT! SO... WE HIT THEM NOW!
THERE YOU ARE, SIRS... ARMED TO THE TEETH, SO TO SPEAK... ALL AT THE TOUCH OF YOUR MASTER SWITCH!
I FEEL LIKE A WALKING BOMB!
OUR TEST AREA IS OVER HERE... IF YOU WOULD CARE TO TRY OUT YOUR NEW CAPABILITIES!
PAAA-DOO-DIT! OOOO
DON'T COMPLAIN TO ME IF YOU CAN HARDLY MOVE! THIS IS ALL YOUR IDEA!
TALK ABOUT GAMBLER'S LUCK--!
THE SAME DROIDS.. JUST WAITING FOR US TO GRAB 'EM!
A DR
TWO DR
ALL O
OW

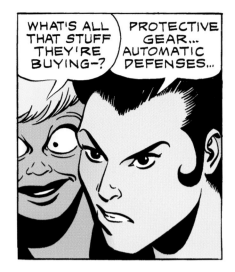

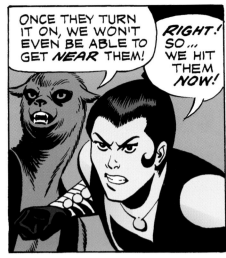

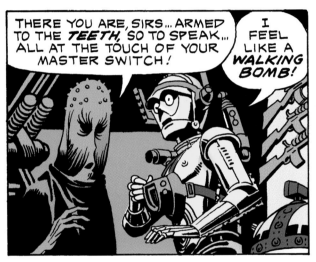

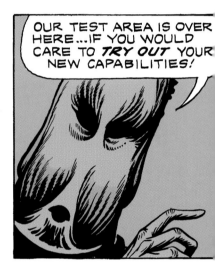

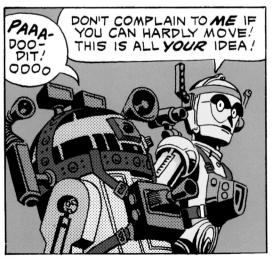

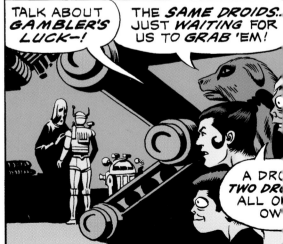

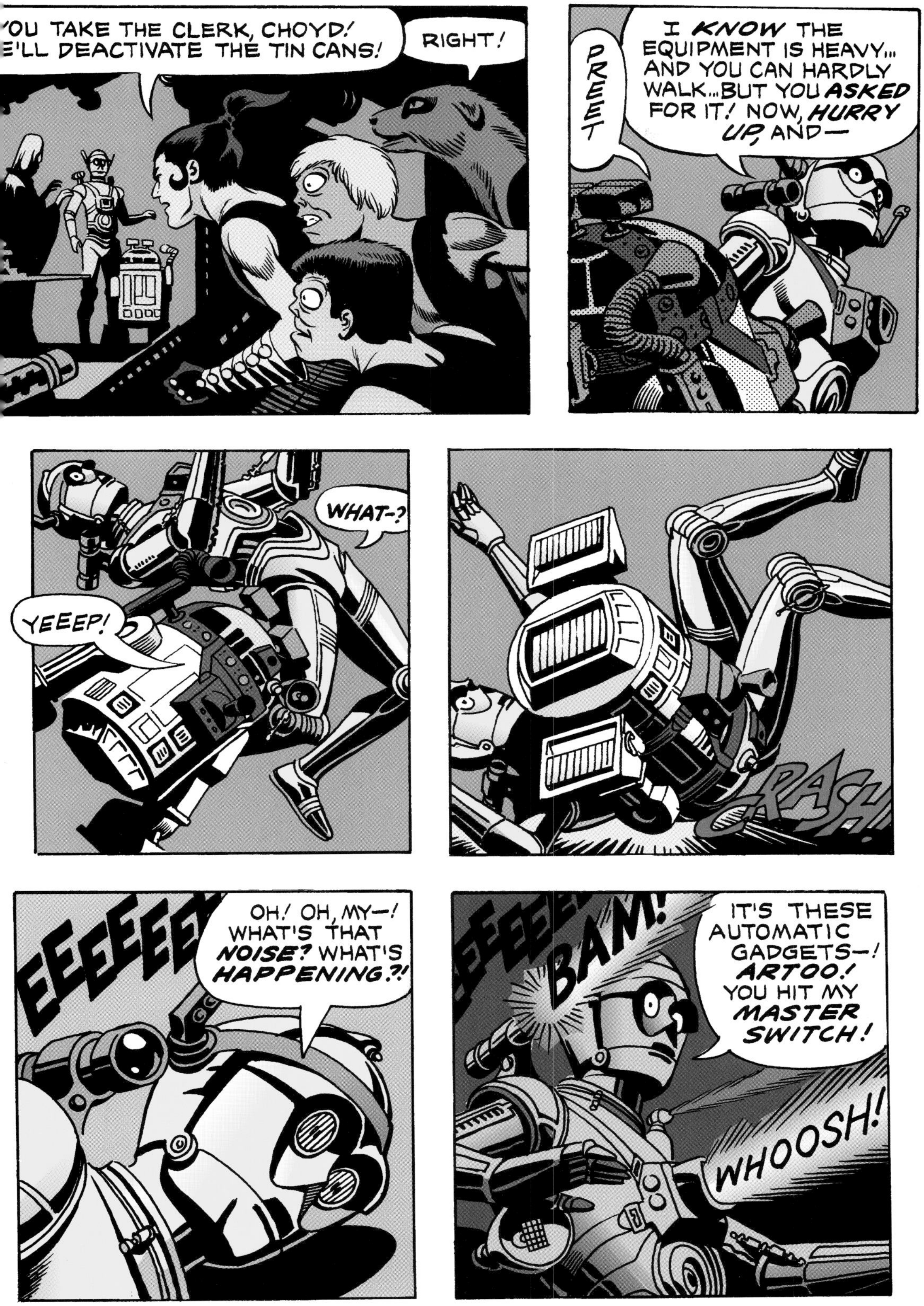
OU TAKE THE CLERK, CHOYD! E'LL DEACTIVATE THE TIN CANS!
RIGHT!
PREET
I KNOW THE EQUIPMENT IS HEAVY... AND YOU CAN HARDLY WALK...BUT YOU ASKED FOR IT! NOW, HURRY UP, AND—
WHAT-?
YEEEP!
CRASH!
EEEEEEE
OH! OH, MY—! WHAT'S THAT NOISE? WHAT'S HAPPENING?!
BAM!
IT'S THESE AUTOMATIC GADGETS—! ARTOO! YOU HIT MY MASTER SWITCH!
WHOOSH!

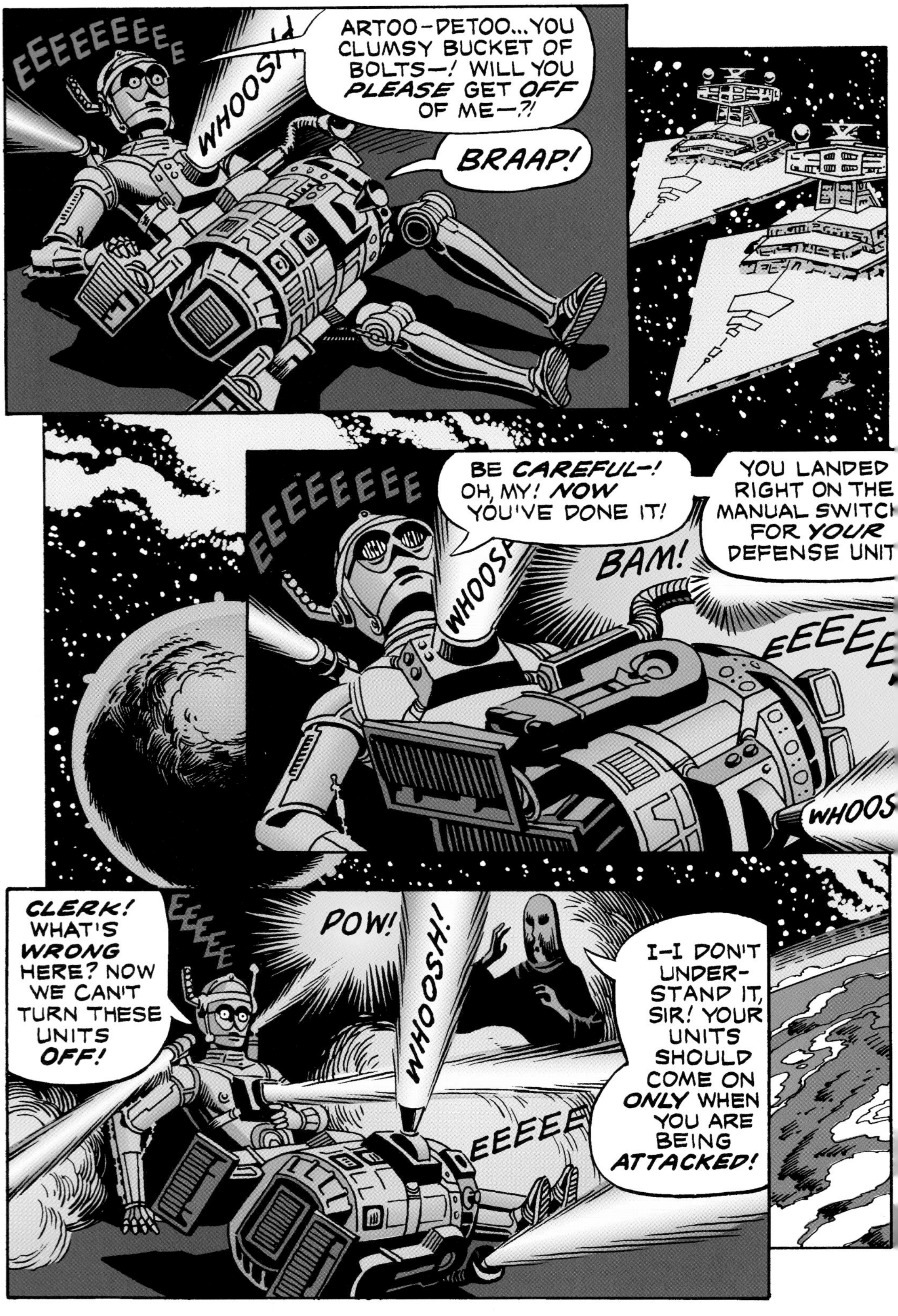
EEEEEEEEE
WHOOSH!
ARTOO-DETOO...YOU CLUMSY BUCKET OF BOLTS—! WILL YOU PLEASE GET OFF OF ME—?!
BRAAP!
EEEEEEEEE
BE CAREFUL—! OH, MY! NOW YOU'VE DONE IT!
YOU LANDED RIGHT ON THE MANUAL SWITCH FOR YOUR DEFENSE UNIT
WHOOSH
BAM!
EEEEE
WHOOS
CLERK! WHAT'S WRONG HERE? NOW WE CAN'T TURN THESE UNITS OFF!
EEEEEE
POW!
WHOOSH!
EEEEE
I-I DON'T UNDER-STAND IT, SIR! YOUR UNITS SHOULD COME ON ONLY WHEN YOU ARE BEING ATTACKED!

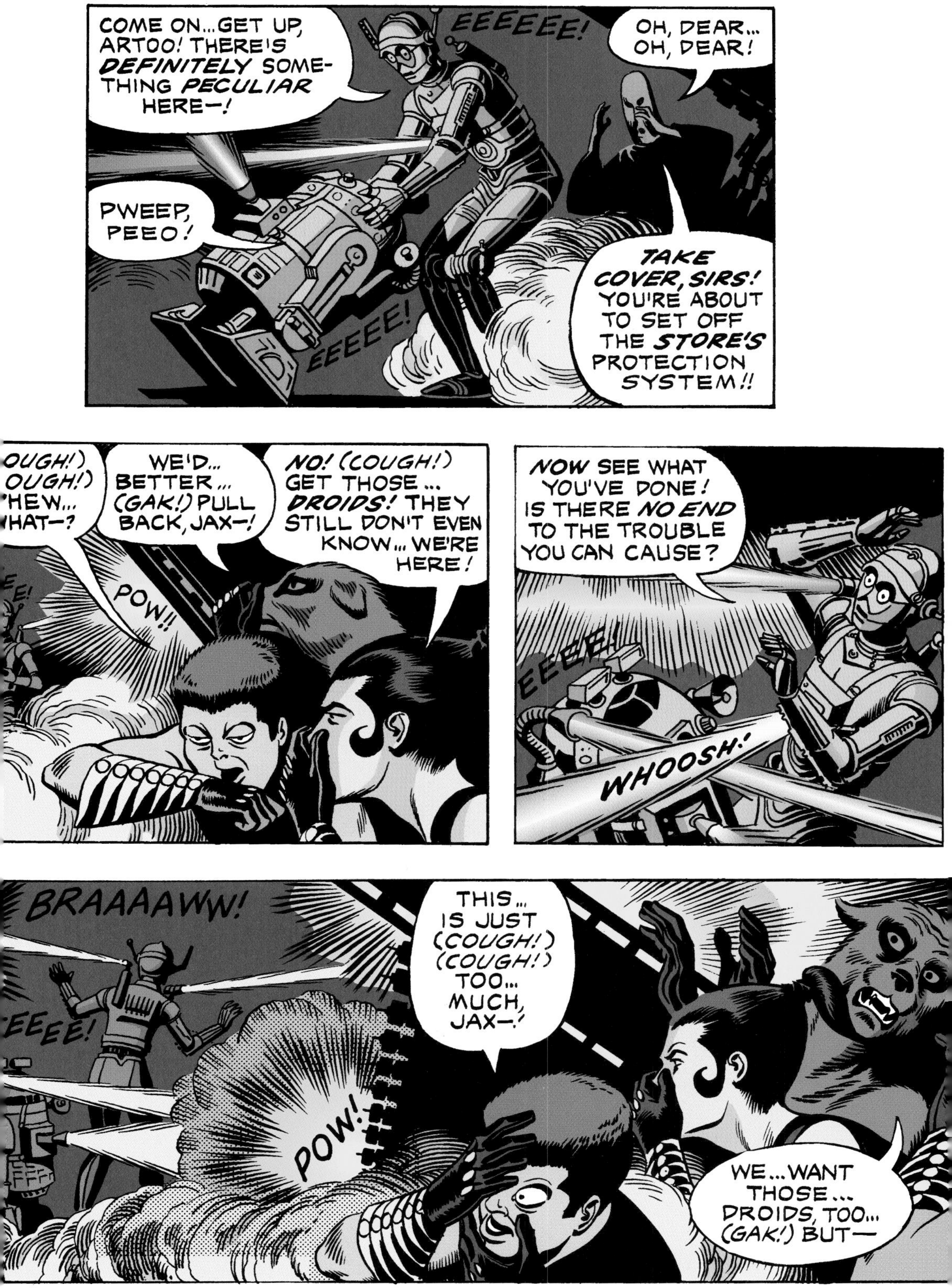
COME ON...GET UP, ARTOO! THERE'S DEFINITELY SOMETHING PECULIAR HERE—!
EEEEEE!
OH, DEAR... OH, DEAR!
PWEEP, PEEO!
EEEEE!
TAKE COVER, SIRS! YOU'RE ABOUT TO SET OFF THE STORE'S PROTECTION SYSTEM!!
WE'D... BETTER... (GAK!) PULL BACK, JAX—!
NO! (COUGH!) GET THOSE... DROIDS! THEY STILL DON'T EVEN KNOW... WE'RE HERE!
POW!!
NOW SEE WHAT YOU'VE DONE! IS THERE NO END TO THE TROUBLE YOU CAN CAUSE?
EEEE!
WHOOSH!
BRAAAAWW!
EEEEE!
THIS... IS JUST (COUGH!) (COUGH!) TOO... MUCH, JAX—!
POW!
WE...WANT THOSE... DROIDS, TOO... (GAK!) BUT—

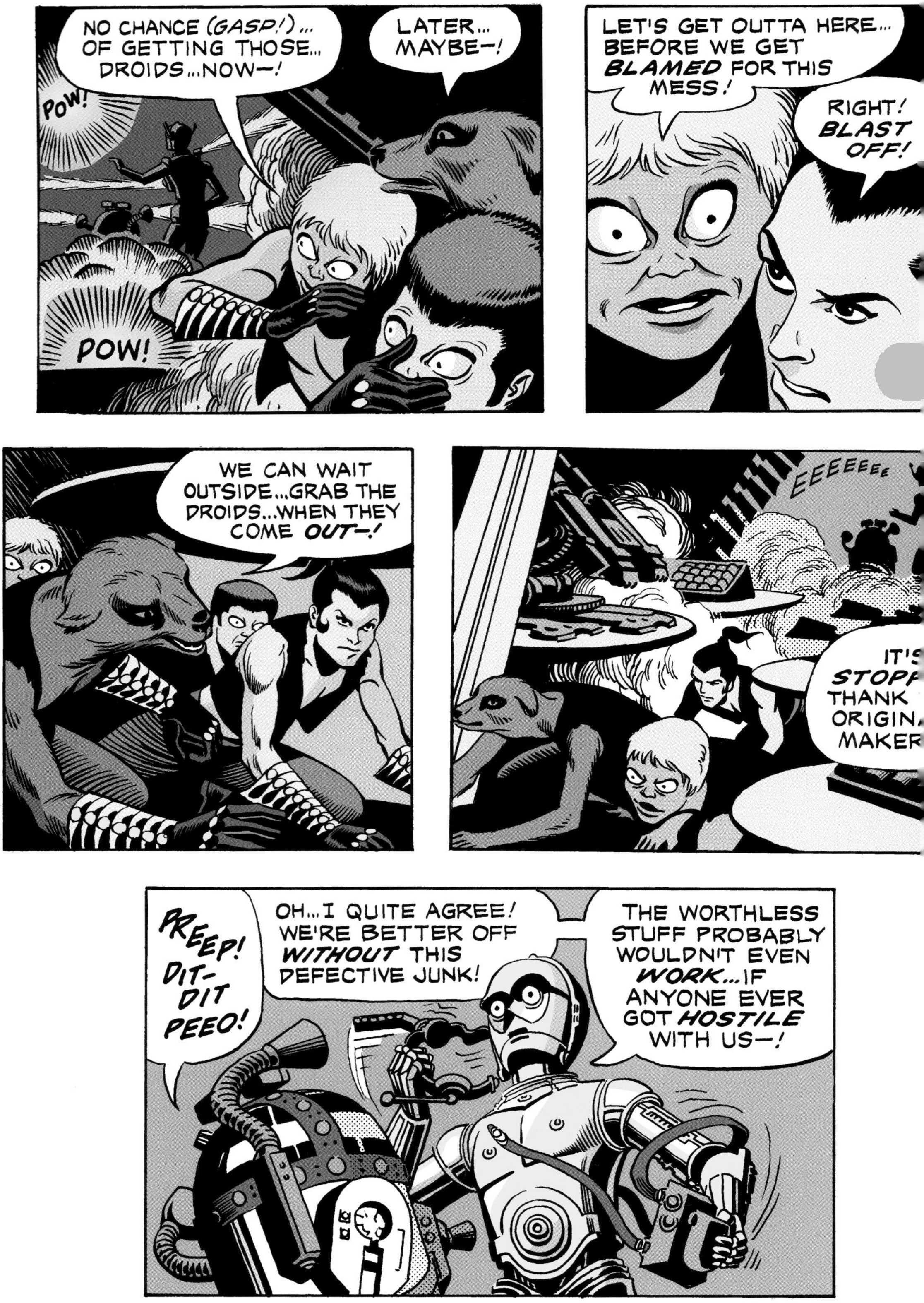

NO CHANCE (GASP!)... OF GETTING THOSE... DROIDS...NOW—!
LATER... MAYBE—!
POW!
POW!
LET'S GET OUTTA HERE... BEFORE WE GET BLAMED FOR THIS MESS!
RIGHT! BLAST OFF!
WE CAN WAIT OUTSIDE...GRAB THE DROIDS...WHEN THEY COME OUT—!
EEEEEEEe
IT'S STOPP THANK ORIGIN MAKER
PREEP! DIT-DIT PEEO!
OH...I QUITE AGREE! WE'RE BETTER OFF WITHOUT THIS DEFECTIVE JUNK!
THE WORTHLESS STUFF PROBABLY WOULDN'T EVEN WORK...IF ANYONE EVER GOT HOSTILE WITH US—!

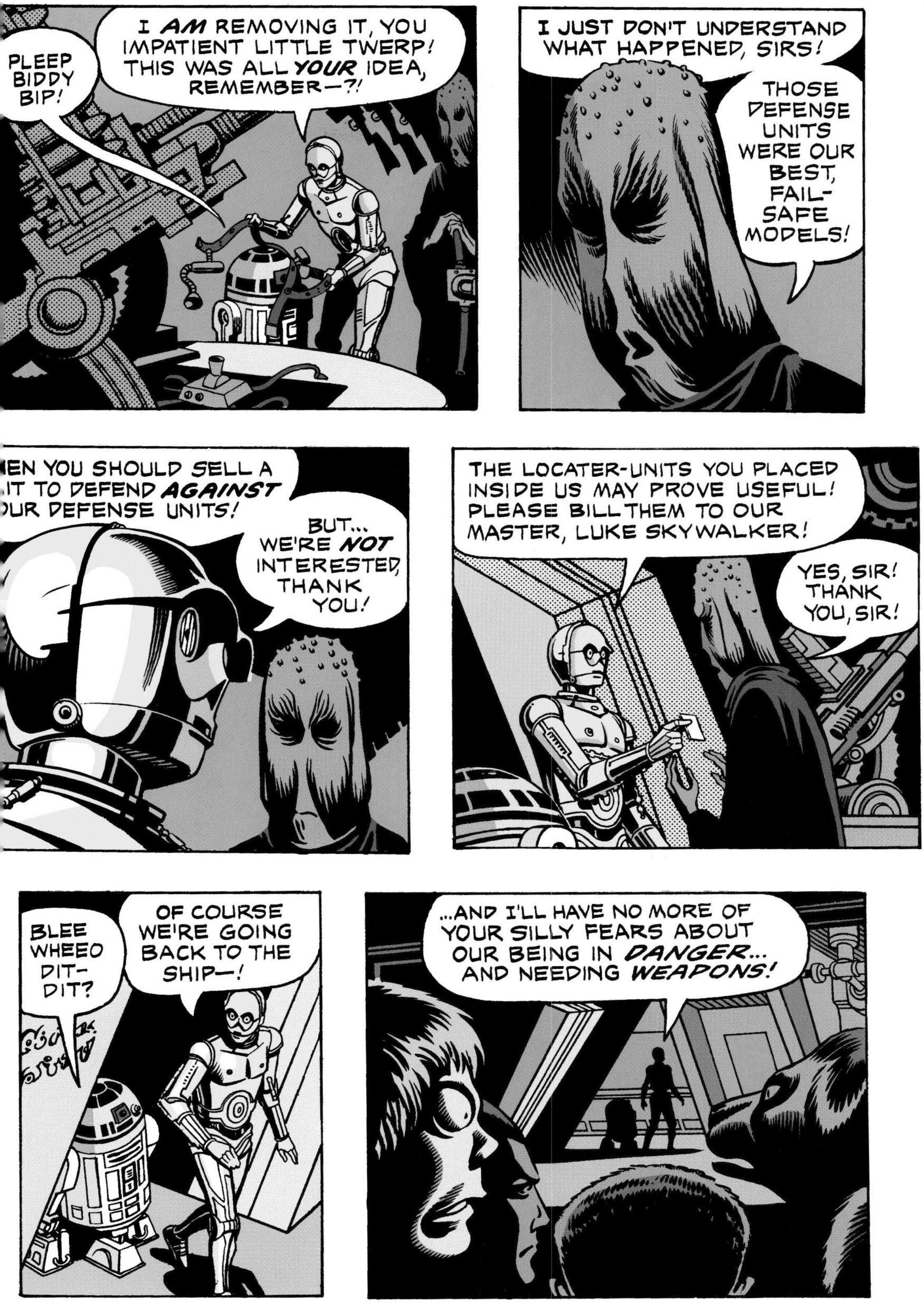
PLEEP BIDDY BIP!
I *AM* REMOVING IT, YOU IMPATIENT LITTLE TWERP! THIS WAS ALL *YOUR* IDEA, REMEMBER—?!
I JUST DON'T UNDERSTAND WHAT HAPPENED, SIRS!
THOSE DEFENSE UNITS WERE OUR BEST, FAIL-SAFE MODELS!
EN YOU SHOULD SELL A IT TO DEFEND *AGAINST* UR DEFENSE UNITS!
BUT... WE'RE *NOT* INTERESTED, THANK YOU!
THE LOCATER-UNITS YOU PLACED INSIDE US MAY PROVE USEFUL! PLEASE BILL THEM TO OUR MASTER, LUKE SKYWALKER!
YES, SIR! THANK YOU, SIR!
BLEE WHEEO DIT-DIT?
OF COURSE WE'RE GOING BACK TO THE SHIP—!
...AND I'LL HAVE NO MORE OF YOUR SILLY FEARS ABOUT OUR BEING IN *DANGER*... AND NEEDING *WEAPONS*!

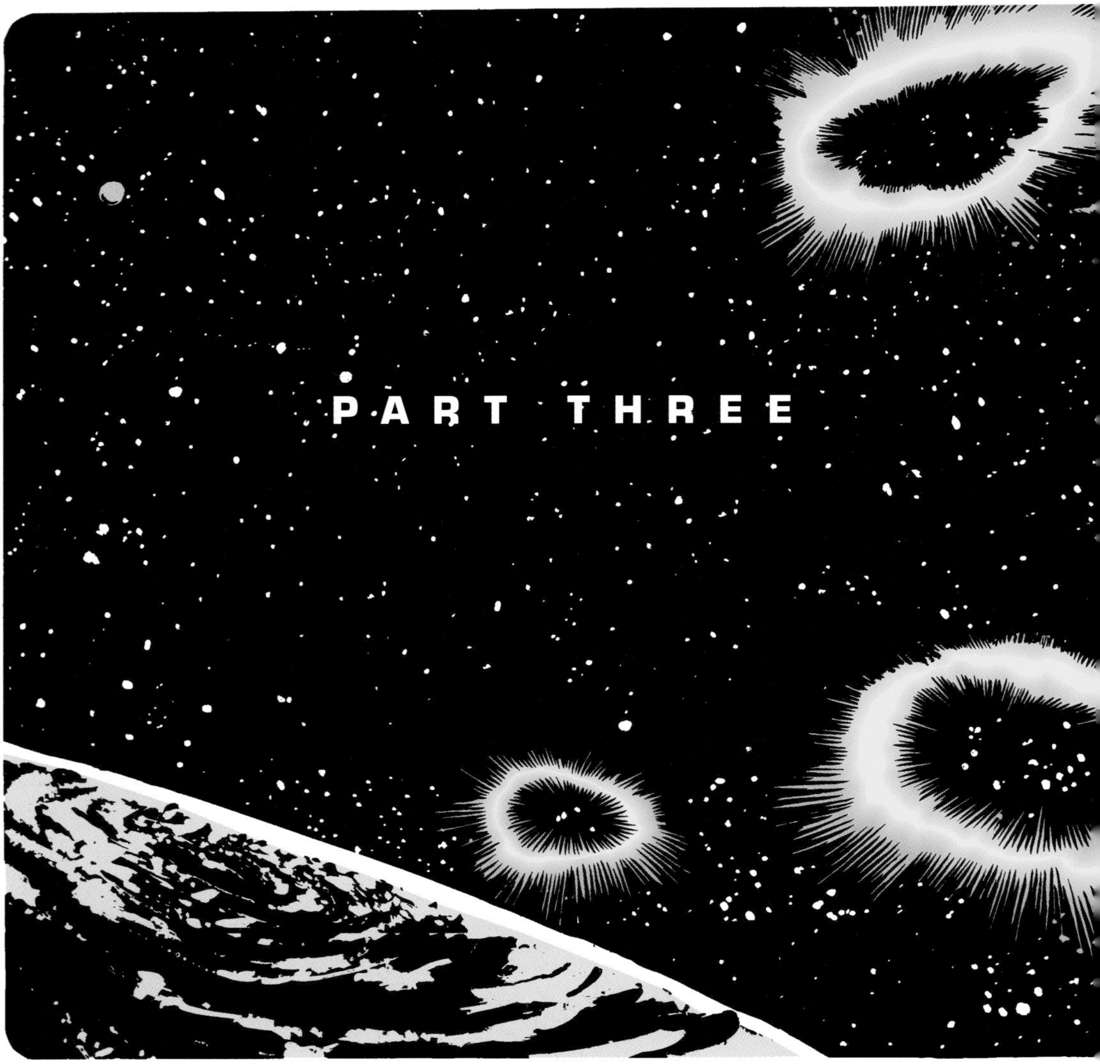
PART THREE

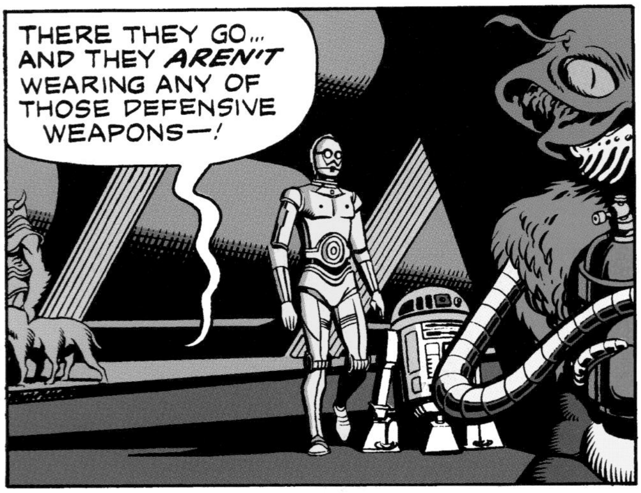
THERE THEY GO... AND THEY AREN'T WEARING ANY OF THOSE DEFENSIVE WEAPONS—!

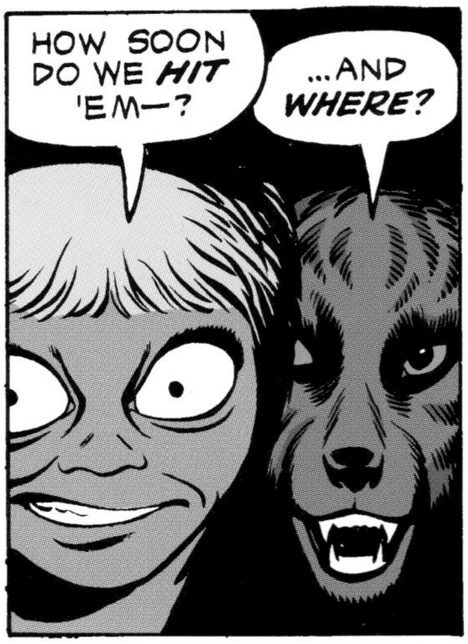
HOW SOON DO WE HIT 'EM—?
...AND WHERE?

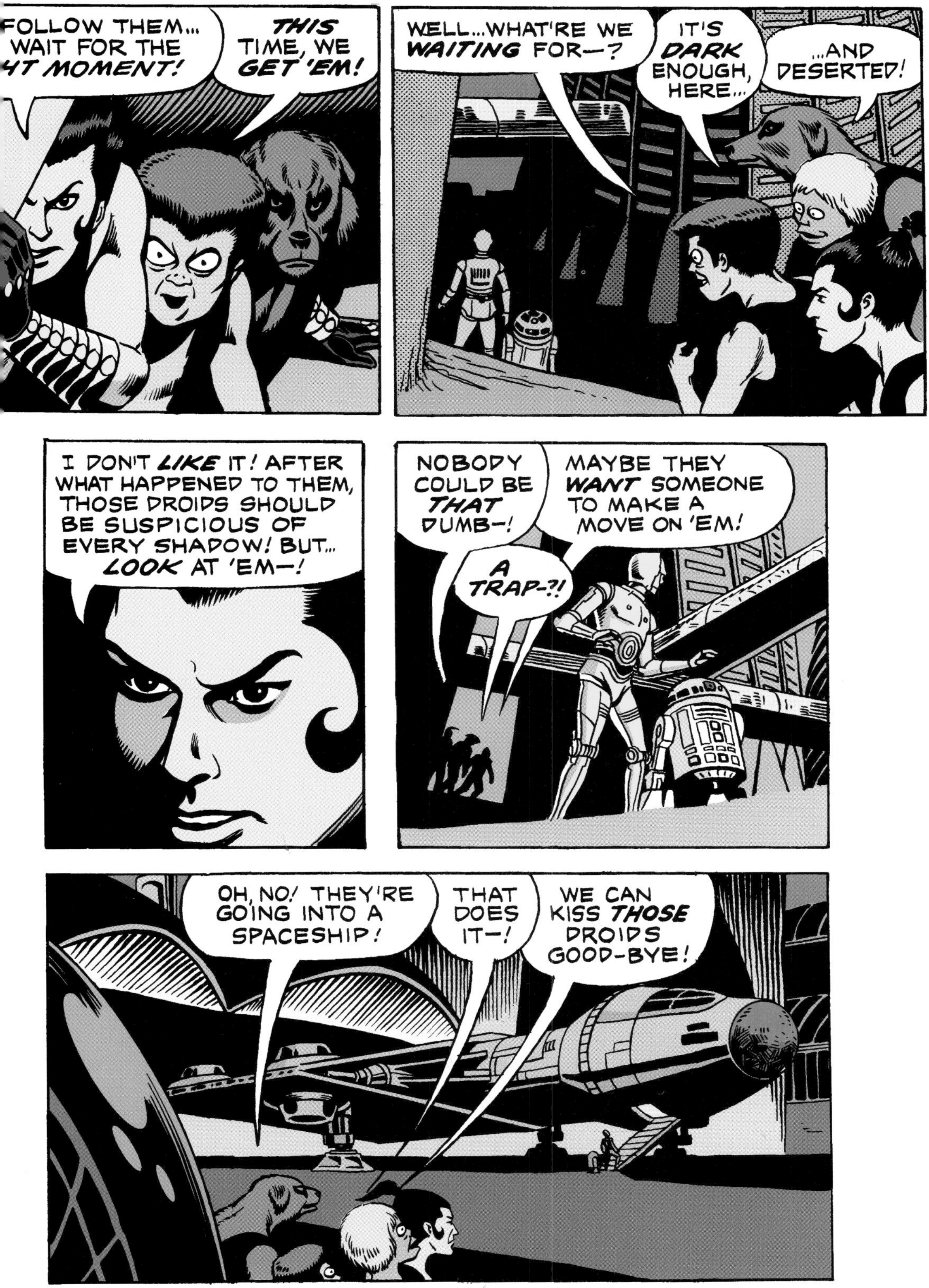
FOLLOW THEM... WAIT FOR THE
HT MOMENT!
THIS TIME, WE GET 'EM!
WELL...WHAT'RE WE WAITING FOR—?
IT'S DARK ENOUGH, HERE...
...AND DESERTED!
I DON'T LIKE IT! AFTER WHAT HAPPENED TO THEM, THOSE DROIDS SHOULD BE SUSPICIOUS OF EVERY SHADOW! BUT... LOOK AT 'EM—!
NOBODY COULD BE THAT DUMB—!
MAYBE THEY WANT SOMEONE TO MAKE A MOVE ON 'EM!
A TRAP-?!
OH, NO! THEY'RE GOING INTO A SPACESHIP!
THAT DOES IT—!
WE CAN KISS THOSE DROIDS GOOD-BYE!

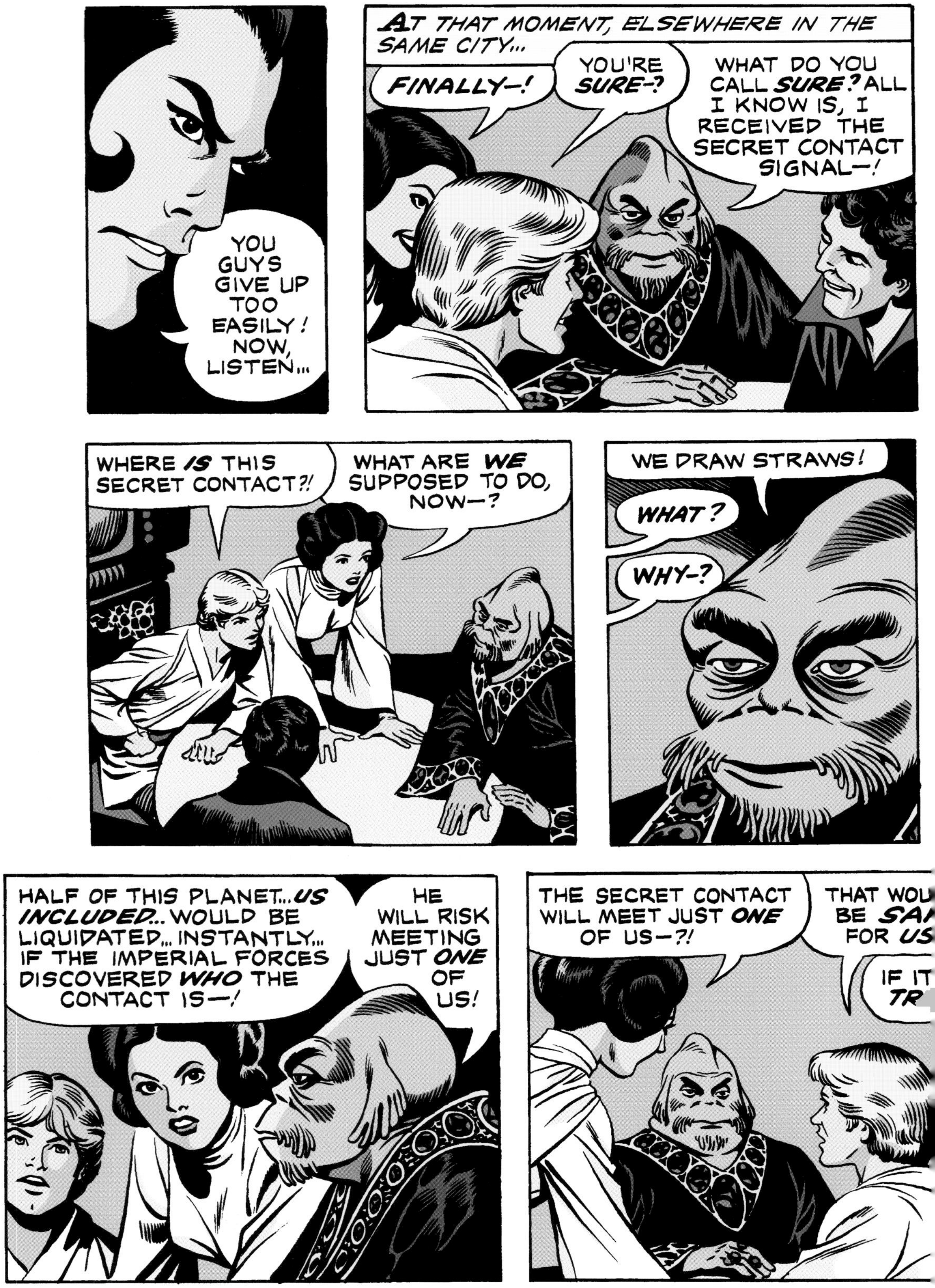
YOU GUYS GIVE UP TOO EASILY! NOW, LISTEN...
AT THAT MOMENT, ELSEWHERE IN THE SAME CITY...
FINALLY—!
YOU'RE SURE—?
WHAT DO YOU CALL SURE? ALL I KNOW IS, I RECEIVED THE SECRET CONTACT SIGNAL—!
WHERE IS THIS SECRET CONTACT?!
WHAT ARE WE SUPPOSED TO DO, NOW—?
WE DRAW STRAWS!
WHAT?
WHY—?
HALF OF THIS PLANET... US INCLUDED... WOULD BE LIQUIDATED... INSTANTLY... IF THE IMPERIAL FORCES DISCOVERED WHO THE CONTACT IS—!
HE WILL RISK MEETING JUST ONE OF US!
THE SECRET CONTACT WILL MEET JUST ONE OF US—?!
THAT WOU BE SA FOR US
IF IT TR

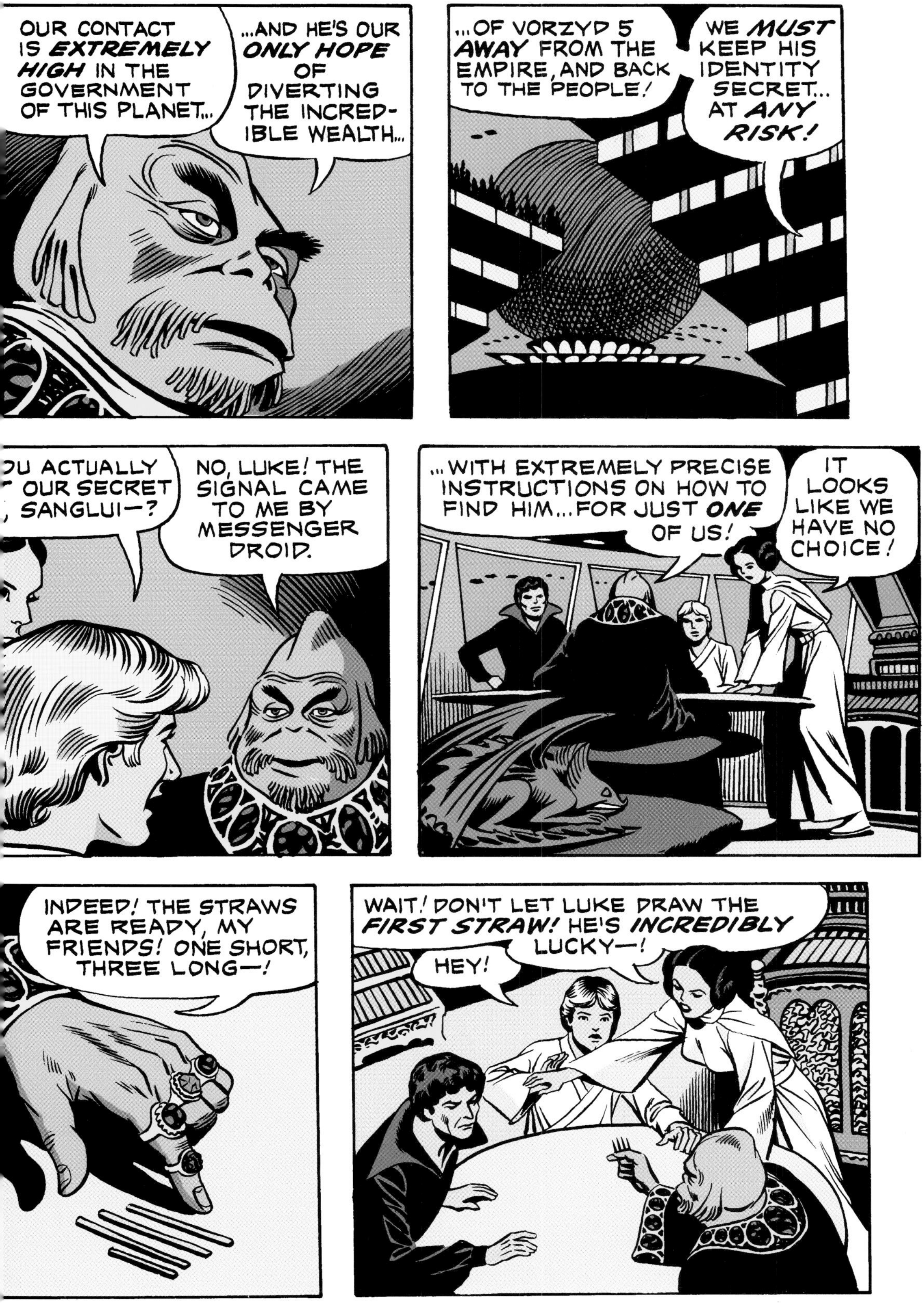

OUR CONTACT IS EXTREMELY HIGH IN THE GOVERNMENT OF THIS PLANET...
...AND HE'S OUR ONLY HOPE OF DIVERTING THE INCREDIBLE WEALTH...
...OF VORZYD 5 AWAY FROM THE EMPIRE, AND BACK TO THE PEOPLE!
WE MUST KEEP HIS IDENTITY SECRET... AT ANY RISK!
ACTUALLY OUR SECRET SANGLUI—?
NO, LUKE! THE SIGNAL CAME TO ME BY MESSENGER DROID.
...WITH EXTREMELY PRECISE INSTRUCTIONS ON HOW TO FIND HIM... FOR JUST ONE OF US!
IT LOOKS LIKE WE HAVE NO CHOICE!
INDEED! THE STRAWS ARE READY, MY FRIENDS! ONE SHORT, THREE LONG—!
WAIT! DON'T LET LUKE DRAW THE FIRST STRAW! HE'S INCREDIBLY LUCKY—!
HEY!

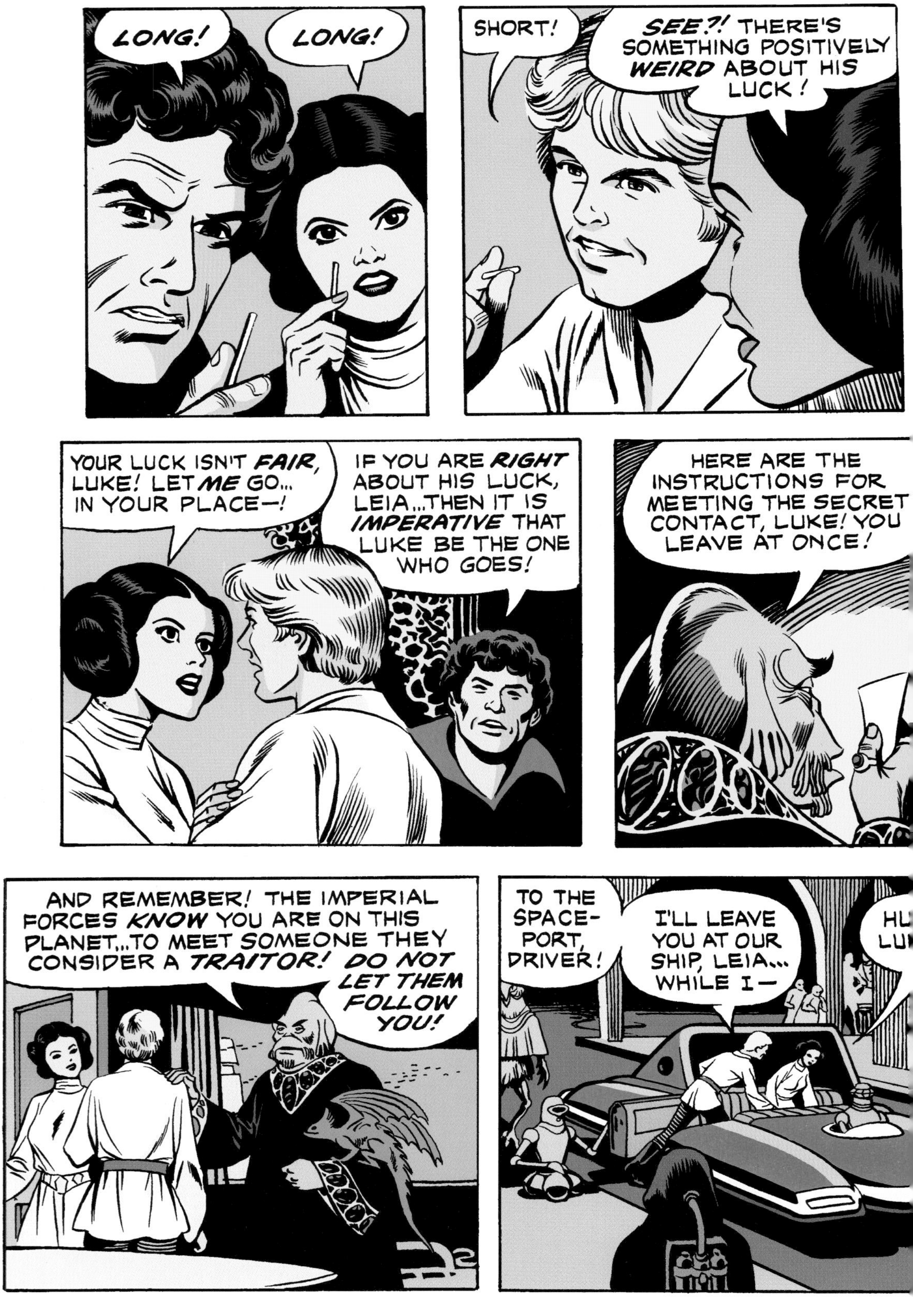
LONG!
LONG!
SHORT!
SEE?! THERE'S SOMETHING POSITIVELY WEIRD ABOUT HIS LUCK!
YOUR LUCK ISN'T FAIR, LUKE! LET ME GO... IN YOUR PLACE—!
IF YOU ARE RIGHT ABOUT HIS LUCK, LEIA...THEN IT IS IMPERATIVE THAT LUKE BE THE ONE WHO GOES!
HERE ARE THE INSTRUCTIONS FOR MEETING THE SECRET CONTACT, LUKE! YOU LEAVE AT ONCE!
AND REMEMBER! THE IMPERIAL FORCES KNOW YOU ARE ON THIS PLANET...TO MEET SOMEONE THEY CONSIDER A TRAITOR! DO NOT LET THEM FOLLOW YOU!
TO THE SPACE-PORT, DRIVER!
I'LL LEAVE YOU AT OUR SHIP, LEIA... WHILE I—

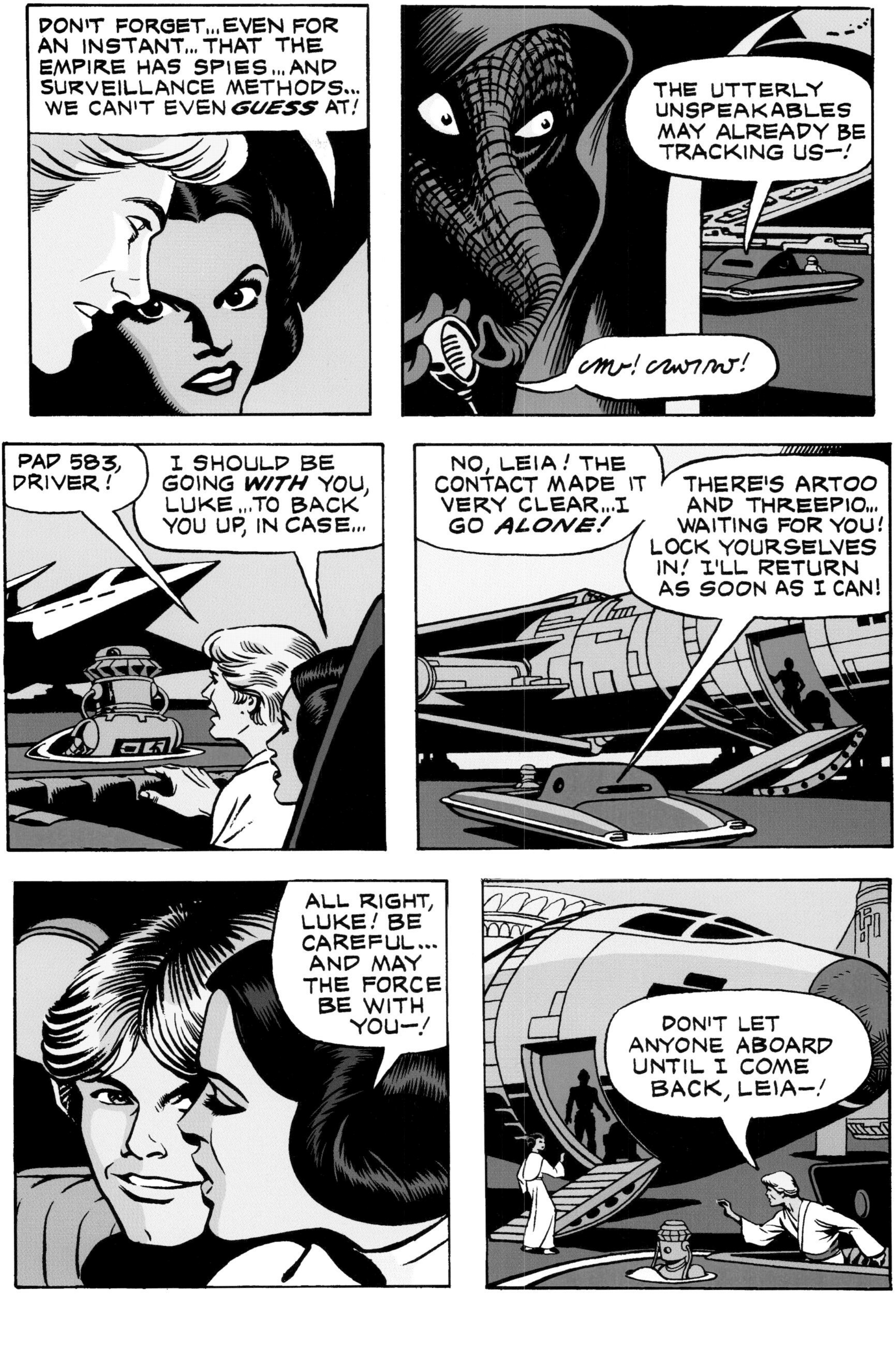
DON'T FORGET... EVEN FOR AN INSTANT... THAT THE EMPIRE HAS SPIES... AND SURVEILLANCE METHODS... WE CAN'T EVEN GUESS AT!
THE UTTERLY UNSPEAKABLES MAY ALREADY BE TRACKING US—!
PAD 583, DRIVER!
I SHOULD BE GOING WITH YOU, LUKE... TO BACK YOU UP, IN CASE...
NO, LEIA! THE CONTACT MADE IT VERY CLEAR... I GO ALONE!
THERE'S ARTOO AND THREEPIO... WAITING FOR YOU! LOCK YOURSELVES IN! I'LL RETURN AS SOON AS I CAN!
ALL RIGHT, LUKE! BE CAREFUL... AND MAY THE FORCE BE WITH YOU—!
DON'T LET ANYONE ABOARD UNTIL I COME BACK, LEIA—!

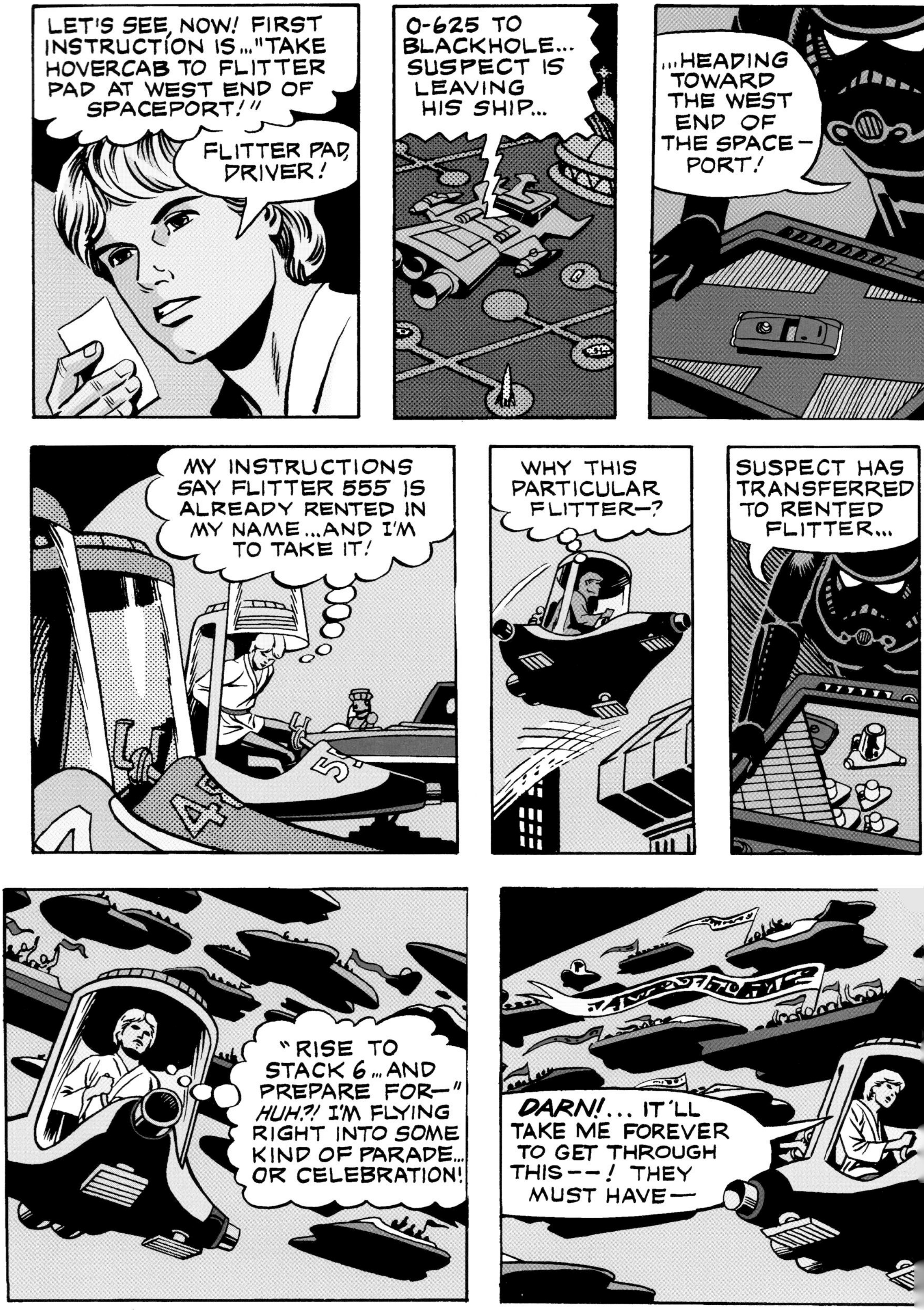
LET'S SEE, NOW! FIRST INSTRUCTION IS..."TAKE HOVERCAB TO FLITTER PAD AT WEST END OF SPACEPORT!"
FLITTER PAD, DRIVER!
0-625 TO BLACKHOLE... SUSPECT IS LEAVING HIS SHIP...
...HEADING TOWARD THE WEST END OF THE SPACE-PORT!
MY INSTRUCTIONS SAY FLITTER 555 IS ALREADY RENTED IN MY NAME...AND I'M TO TAKE IT!
WHY THIS PARTICULAR FLITTER—?
SUSPECT HAS TRANSFERRED TO RENTED FLITTER...
"RISE TO STACK 6...AND PREPARE FOR—" HUH?! I'M FLYING RIGHT INTO SOME KIND OF PARADE... OR CELEBRATION!
DARN!... IT'LL TAKE ME FOREVER TO GET THROUGH THIS--! THEY MUST HAVE—

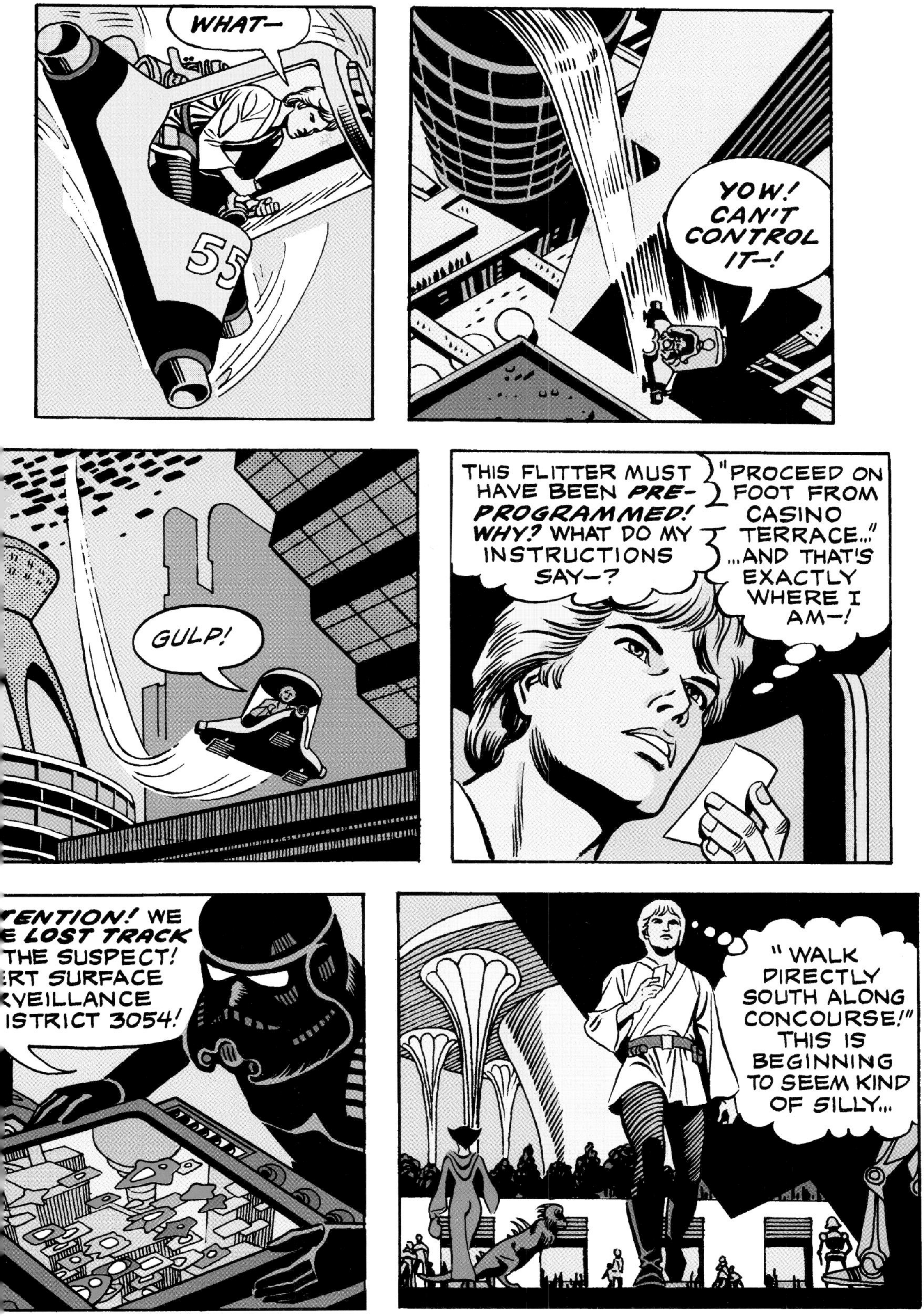
WHAT—
YOW! CAN'T CONTROL IT—!
GULP!
THIS FLITTER MUST HAVE BEEN PRE-PROGRAMMED! WHY? WHAT DO MY INSTRUCTIONS SAY—?
"PROCEED ON FOOT FROM CASINO TERRACE..." ...AND THAT'S EXACTLY WHERE I AM—!
TENTION! WE E LOST TRACK THE SUSPECT! ERT SURFACE VEILLANCE ISTRICT 3054!
"WALK DIRECTLY SOUTH ALONG CONCOURSE!" THIS IS BEGINNING TO SEEM KIND OF SILLY...

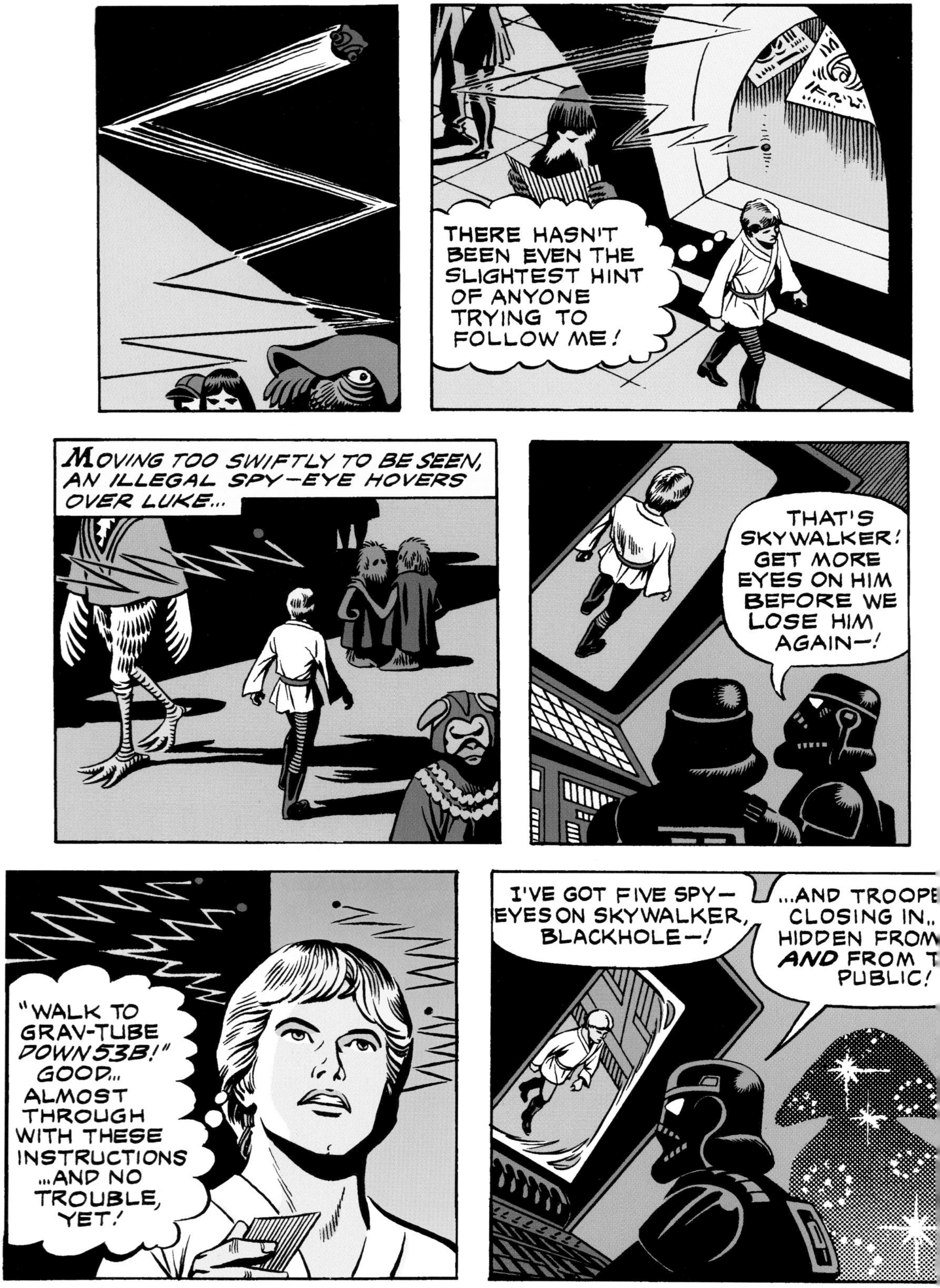
THERE HASN'T BEEN EVEN THE SLIGHTEST HINT OF ANYONE TRYING TO FOLLOW ME!
MOVING TOO SWIFTLY TO BE SEEN, AN ILLEGAL SPY-EYE HOVERS OVER LUKE...
THAT'S SKYWALKER! GET MORE EYES ON HIM BEFORE WE LOSE HIM AGAIN--!
"WALK TO GRAV-TUBE DOWN 53B!" GOOD... ALMOST THROUGH WITH THESE INSTRUCTIONS ...AND NO TROUBLE, YET!
I'VE GOT FIVE SPY-EYES ON SKYWALKER, BLACKHOLE--!
...AND TROOPE CLOSING IN.. HIDDEN FROM AND FROM T PUBLIC!

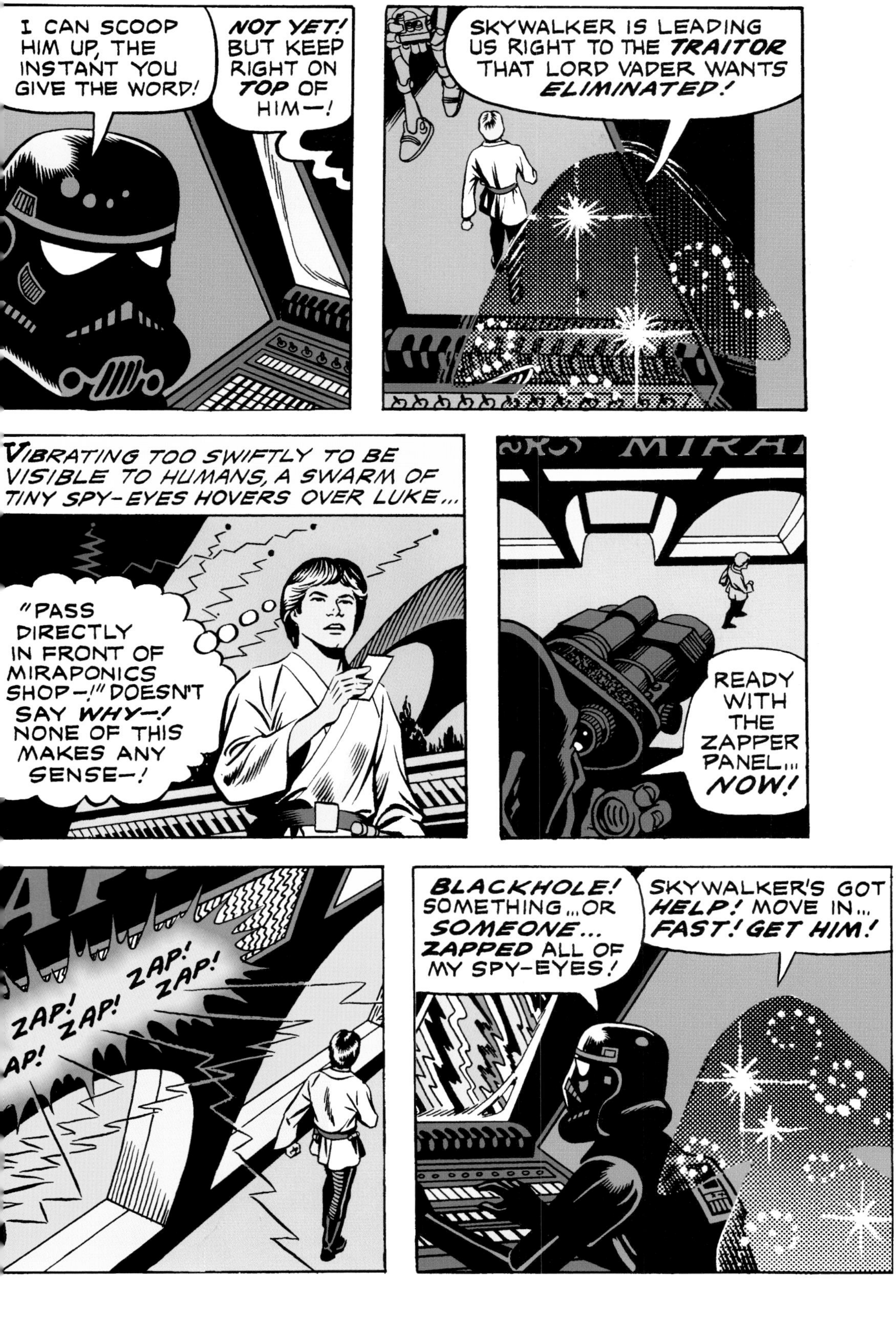
I CAN SCOOP HIM UP, THE INSTANT YOU GIVE THE WORD!
NOT YET! BUT KEEP RIGHT ON TOP OF HIM--!
SKYWALKER IS LEADING US RIGHT TO THE TRAITOR THAT LORD VADER WANTS ELIMINATED!
VIBRATING TOO SWIFTLY TO BE VISIBLE TO HUMANS, A SWARM OF TINY SPY-EYES HOVERS OVER LUKE...
"PASS DIRECTLY IN FRONT OF MIRAPONICS SHOP--!" DOESN'T SAY WHY--! NONE OF THIS MAKES ANY SENSE--!
READY WITH THE ZAPPER PANEL... NOW!
ZAP! ZAP! ZAP! ZAP! AP!
BLACKHOLE! SOMETHING...OR SOMEONE... ZAPPED ALL OF MY SPY-EYES!
SKYWALKER'S GOT HELP! MOVE IN... FAST! GET HIM!

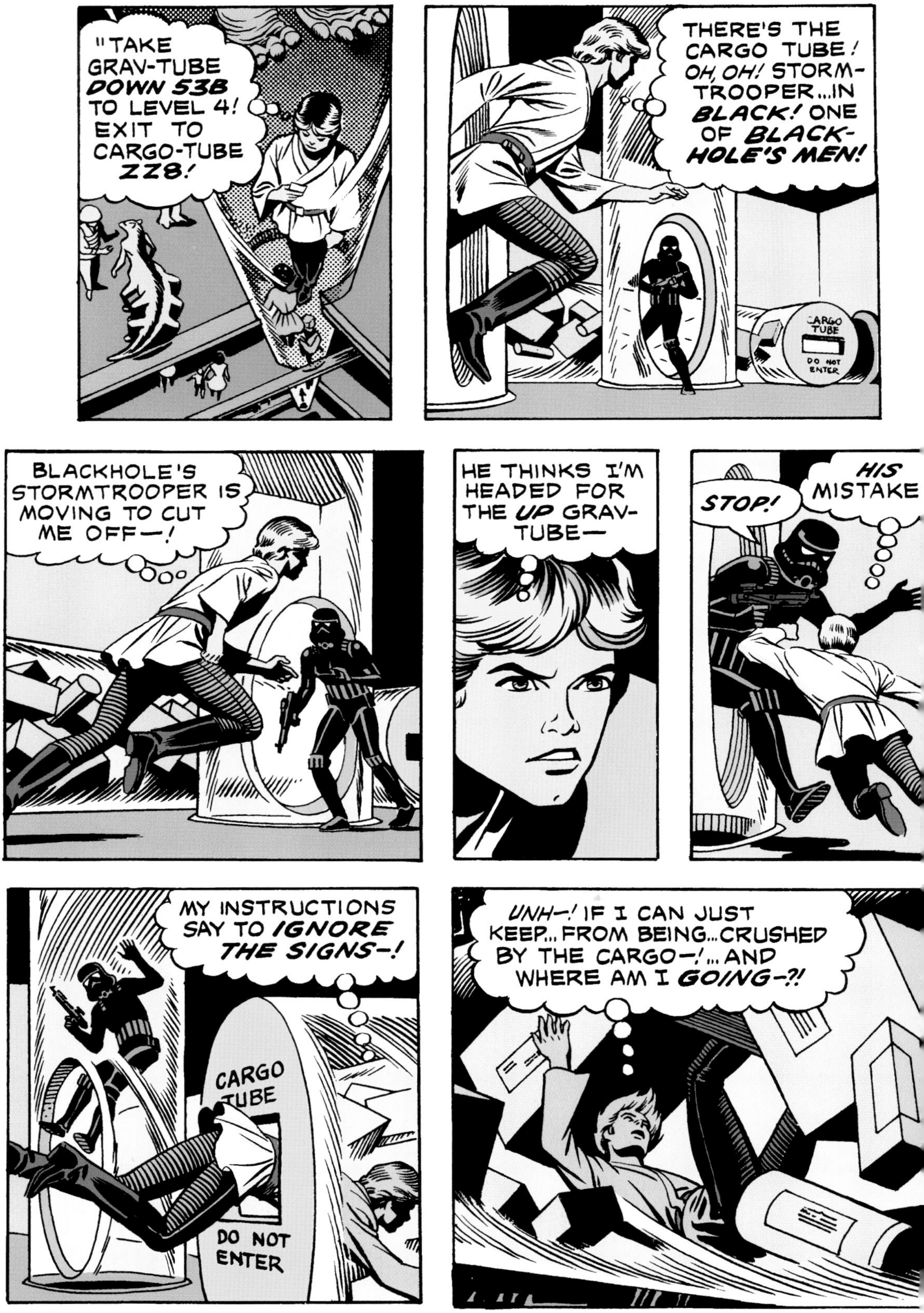
"TAKE GRAV-TUBE DOWN 53B TO LEVEL 4! EXIT TO CARGO-TUBE ZZ8!
THERE'S THE CARGO TUBE! OH, OH! STORM-TROOPER...IN BLACK! ONE OF BLACK-HOLE'S MEN!
CARGO TUBE
DO NOT ENTER
BLACKHOLE'S STORMTROOPER IS MOVING TO CUT ME OFF—!
HE THINKS I'M HEADED FOR THE UP GRAV-TUBE—
STOP!
HIS MISTAKE
MY INSTRUCTIONS SAY TO IGNORE THE SIGNS—!
CARGO TUBE
DO NOT ENTER
UNH—! IF I CAN JUST KEEP... FROM BEING...CRUSHED BY THE CARGO—!... AND WHERE AM I GOING—?!

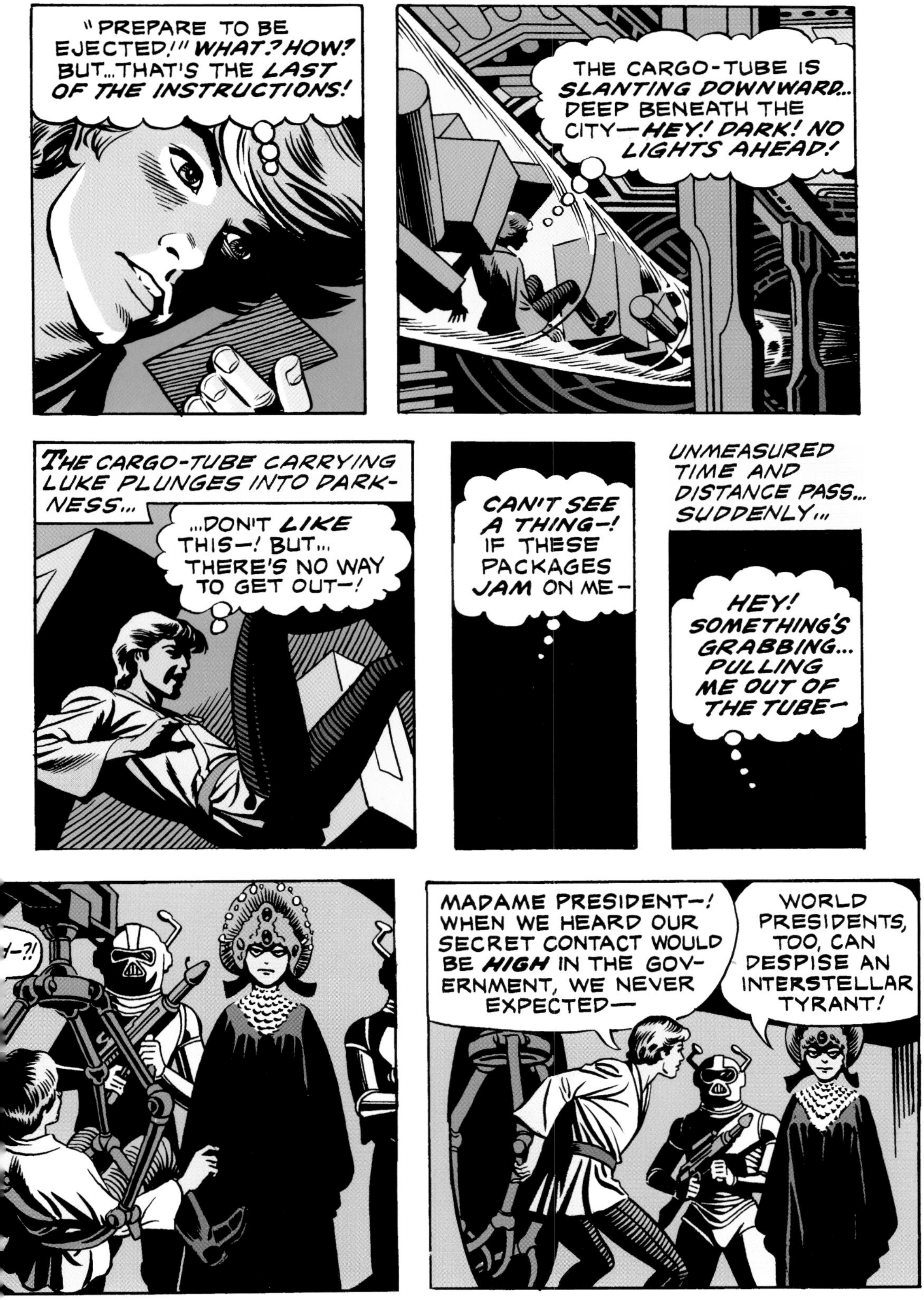
"PREPARE TO BE EJECTED!" WHAT? HOW? BUT...THAT'S THE LAST OF THE INSTRUCTIONS!
THE CARGO-TUBE IS SLANTING DOWNWARD... DEEP BENEATH THE CITY—HEY! DARK! NO LIGHTS AHEAD!
THE CARGO-TUBE CARRYING LUKE PLUNGES INTO DARKNESS...
...DON'T LIKE THIS—! BUT... THERE'S NO WAY TO GET OUT—!
CAN'T SEE A THING—! IF THESE PACKAGES JAM ON ME—
UNMEASURED TIME AND DISTANCE PASS... SUDDENLY...
HEY! SOMETHING'S GRABBING... PULLING ME OUT OF THE TUBE—
MADAME PRESIDENT—! WHEN WE HEARD OUR SECRET CONTACT WOULD BE HIGH IN THE GOVERNMENT, WE NEVER EXPECTED—
WORLD PRESIDENTS, TOO, CAN DESPISE AN INTERSTELLAR TYRANT!

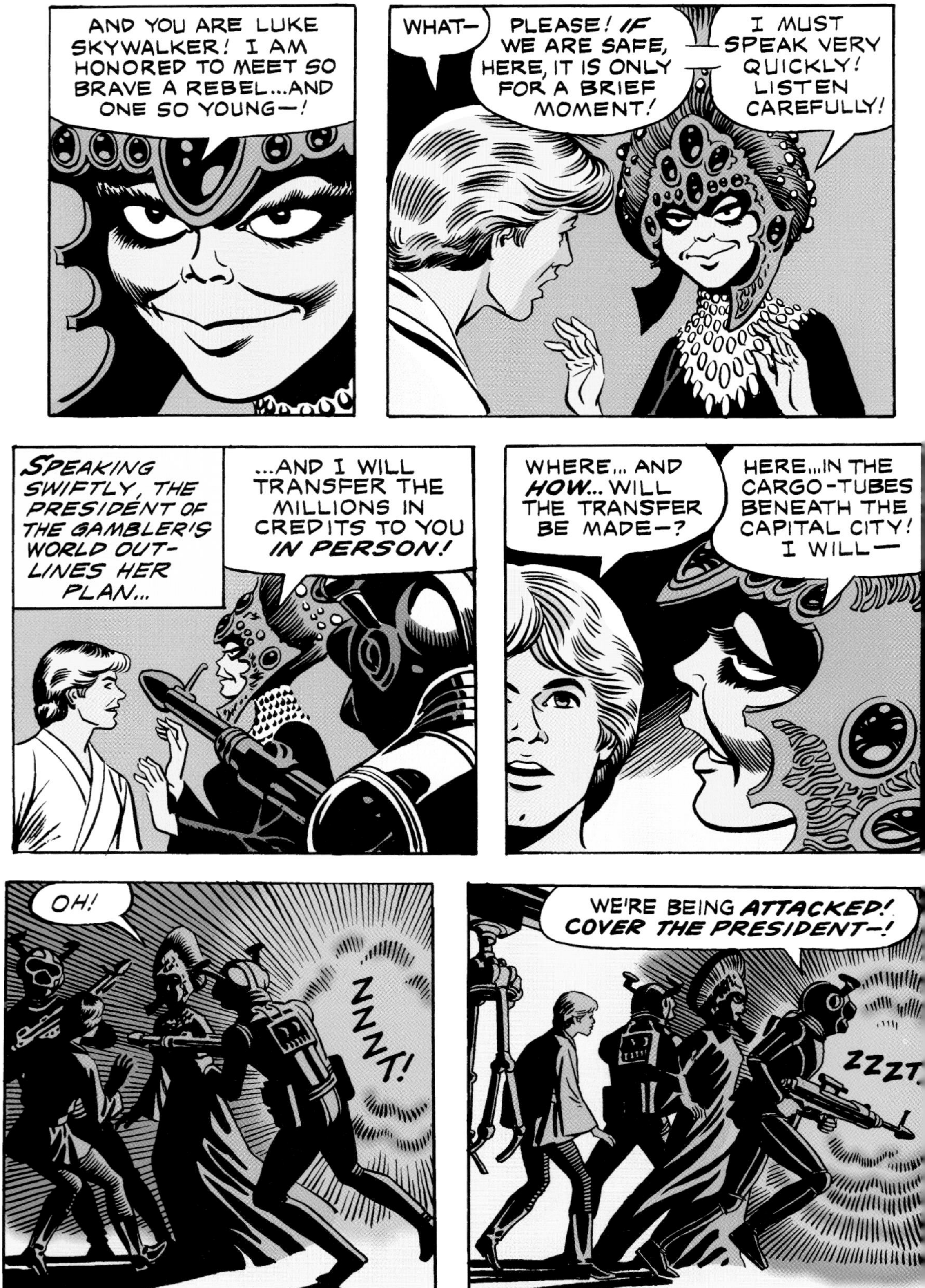
AND YOU ARE LUKE SKYWALKER! I AM HONORED TO MEET SO BRAVE A REBEL...AND ONE SO YOUNG—!
WHAT—
PLEASE! *IF* WE ARE SAFE, HERE, IT IS ONLY FOR A BRIEF MOMENT!
I MUST SPEAK VERY QUICKLY! LISTEN CAREFULLY!
SPEAKING SWIFTLY, THE PRESIDENT OF THE GAMBLER'S WORLD OUTLINES HER PLAN...
...AND I WILL TRANSFER THE MILLIONS IN CREDITS TO YOU *IN PERSON!*
WHERE... AND *HOW*... WILL THE TRANSFER BE MADE—?
HERE...IN THE CARGO-TUBES BENEATH THE CAPITAL CITY! I WILL—
OH!
NNNT!
WE'RE BEING *ATTACKED!* *COVER THE PRESIDENT—!*
ZZZT

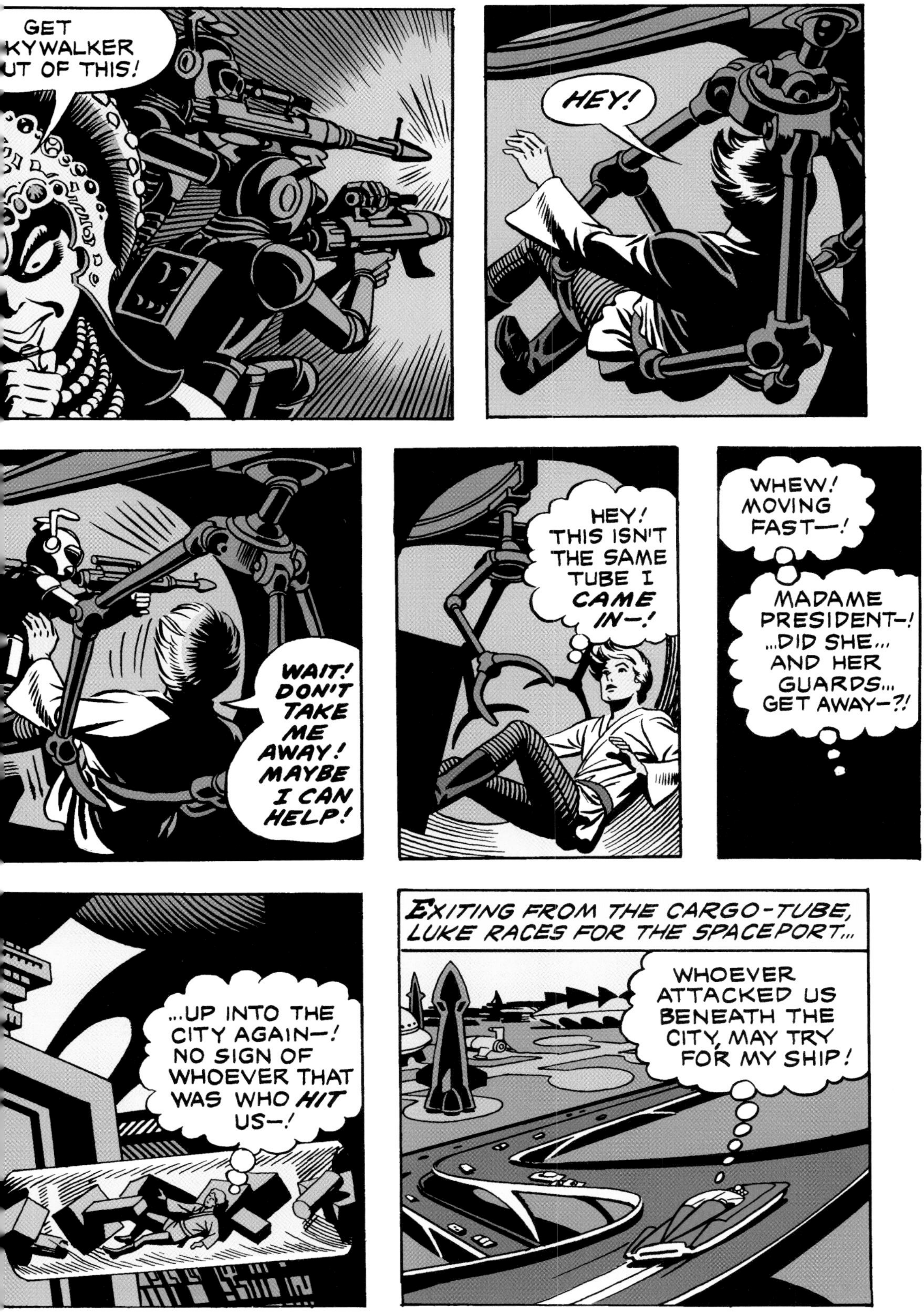
GET KYWALKER UT OF THIS!
HEY!
WAIT! DON'T TAKE ME AWAY! MAYBE I CAN HELP!
HEY! THIS ISN'T THE SAME TUBE I CAME IN—!
WHEW! MOVING FAST—!
MADAME PRESIDENT—! ...DID SHE... AND HER GUARDS... GET AWAY—?!
...UP INTO THE CITY AGAIN—! NO SIGN OF WHOEVER THAT WAS WHO HIT US—!
EXITING FROM THE CARGO-TUBE, LUKE RACES FOR THE SPACEPORT...
WHOEVER ATTACKED US BENEATH THE CITY, MAY TRY FOR MY SHIP!

LOOKS ALL RIGHT! ...AND THERE'S THREEPIO!

MASTER LUKE! THANK THE ORIGINAL MAKER! IT'S TERRIBLE... *TERRIBLE,* SIR—!

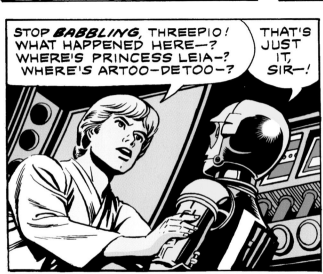

STOP *BABBLING,* THREEPIO! WHAT HAPPENED HERE—? WHERE'S PRINCESS LEIA—? WHERE'S ARTOO-DETOO—?

THAT'S JUST IT, SIR—!

THEY WERE *TAKEN*...BY A SWARM OF *FREELIES*... WHO *TRICKED* ME INTO LETTING THEM ABOARD!

FREELIES?! WHAT ARE—

JUVENILES, SIR ...OF VARIOUS SPECIES! THEY *KIDNAPPED* PRINCESS LEIA AND ARTOO-DETOO... AND LEFT ME HERE WITH A *MESSAGE* FOR YOU!

KIDNAPPED—!? WHY? WHY WOULD THOSE... *FREELIES*...TAKE LEIA AND ARTOO-DETOO—?

FOR *RANS* MASTE LUKE

RANSOM!? OW DID THEY KNOW—?

ONE OF THE FREELIES IS THE OFFSPRING OF *FALUD*... THE REBEL WHO WAS KILLED WHEN WE ESCAPED FROM BLACKHOLE'S SPACE-SHIP—!

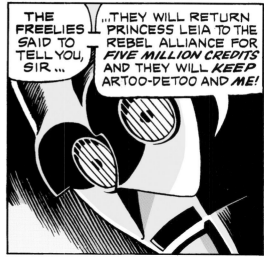

THE FREELIES SAID TO TELL YOU, SIR...

"...THEY WILL RETURN PRINCESS LEIA TO THE REBEL ALLIANCE FOR *FIVE MILLION CREDITS* AND THEY WILL *KEEP* ARTOO-DETOO AND *ME*!

FIVE MILLION CREDITS RANSOM FOR PRINCESS LEIA! THE REBEL ALLIANCE WOULD PAY IT, OF COURSE...

"...BUT HOW DO I KNOW SHE'S SAFE *NOW*?! ...OR THAT THE FREELIES WOULD *RELEASE* HER—?

IF ONLY I KNEW WHERE THEY HAVE *TAKEN* HER...

TRY R A SCUE!

I KNOW WHERE SHE IS, MASTER LUKE!...THAT IS... I CAN LEAD YOU TO WHERE THE FREELIES HAVE TAKEN *ARTOO-DETOO!*

ARTOO HAD THE SILLY NOTION THAT HE AND I COULD WEAR WEAPONS AND *PROTECT* YOU, MASTER LUKE!

IT WAS A *DISASTROUS FAILURE!*

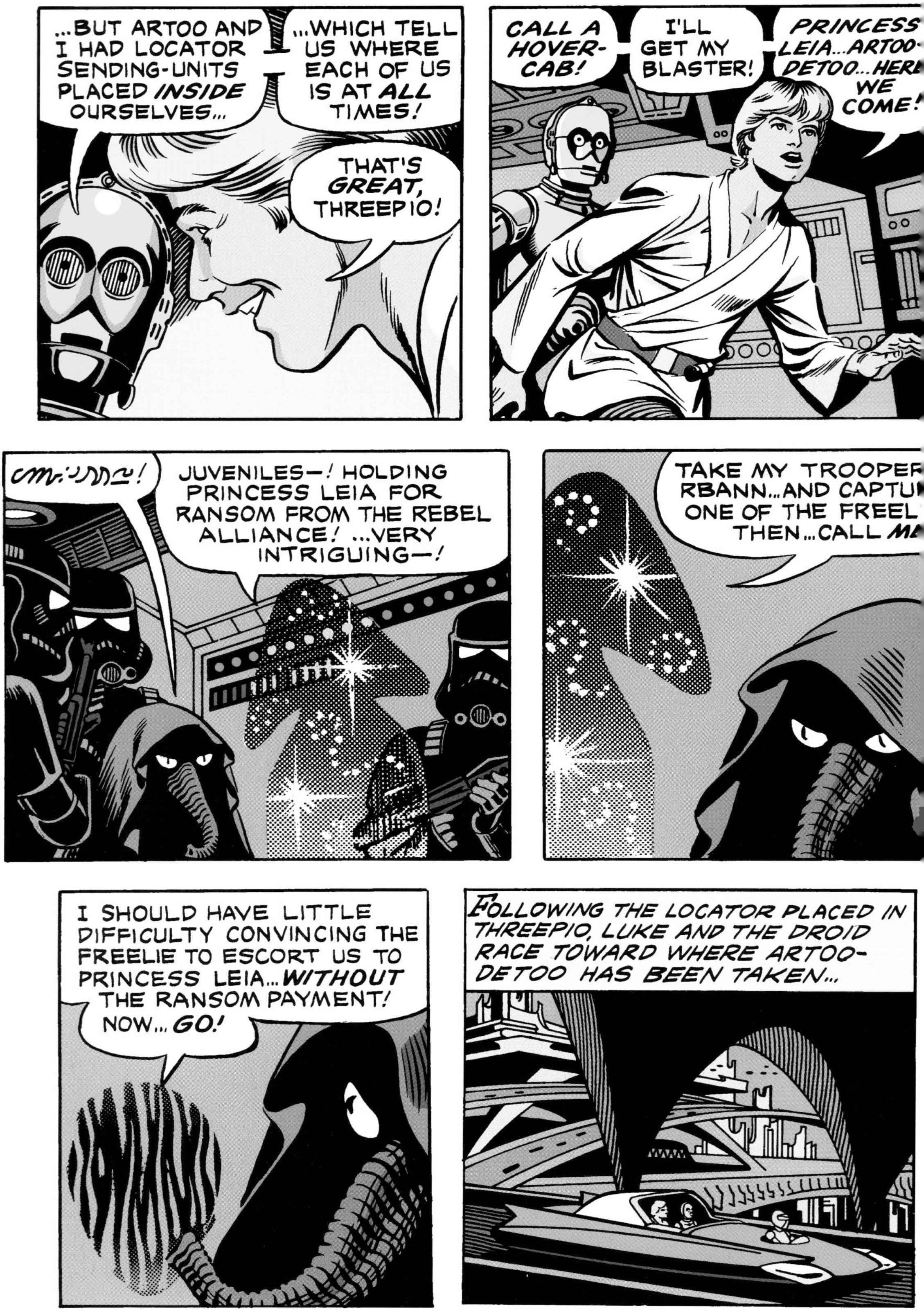
...BUT ARTOO AND I HAD LOCATOR SENDING-UNITS PLACED *INSIDE* OURSELVES...
...WHICH TELL US WHERE EACH OF US IS AT *ALL* TIMES!
THAT'S *GREAT,* THREEPIO!
CALL A HOVER-CAB!
I'LL GET MY BLASTER!
PRINCESS LEIA...ARTOO-DETOO...HER WE COME!
JUVENILES—! HOLDING PRINCESS LEIA FOR RANSOM FROM THE REBEL ALLIANCE! ...VERY INTRIGUING—!
TAKE MY TROOPER RBANN...AND CAPTU ONE OF THE FREEL THEN...CALL M
I SHOULD HAVE LITTLE DIFFICULTY CONVINCING THE FREELIE TO ESCORT US TO PRINCESS LEIA...*WITHOUT* THE RANSOM PAYMENT! NOW... *GO!*
FOLLOWING THE LOCATOR PLACED IN THREEPIO, LUKE AND THE DROID RACE TOWARD WHERE ARTOO-DETOO HAS BEEN TAKEN...

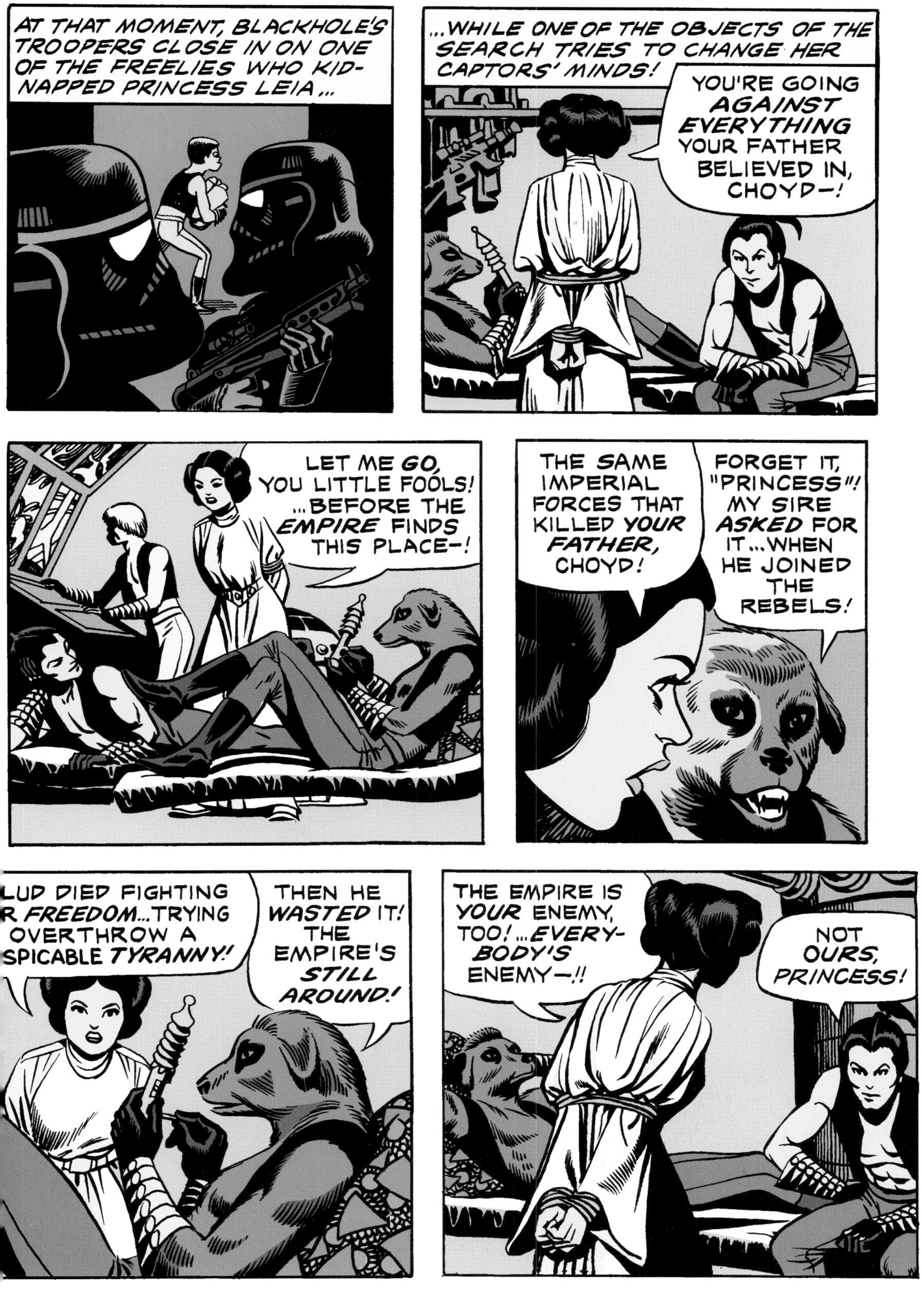
AT THAT MOMENT, BLACKHOLE'S TROOPERS CLOSE IN ON ONE OF THE FREELIES WHO KID-NAPPED PRINCESS LEIA...
...WHILE ONE OF THE OBJECTS OF THE SEARCH TRIES TO CHANGE HER CAPTORS' MINDS!
YOU'RE GOING *AGAINST EVERYTHING* YOUR FATHER BELIEVED IN, CHOYD-!
LET ME *GO*, YOU LITTLE FOOLS! ...BEFORE THE *EMPIRE* FINDS THIS PLACE-!
THE SAME IMPERIAL FORCES THAT KILLED *YOUR FATHER*, CHOYD!
FORGET IT, "PRINCESS"! MY SIRE *ASKED* FOR IT...WHEN HE JOINED THE REBELS!
LUD DIED FIGHTING R *FREEDOM*...TRYING OVERTHROW A SPICABLE *TYRANNY*!
THEN HE *WASTED* IT! THE EMPIRE'S *STILL AROUND*!
THE EMPIRE IS *YOUR* ENEMY, TOO! ...*EVERY-BODY'S* ENEMY-!!
NOT *OURS*, PRINCESS!

THE EMPIRE DOESN'T EVEN KNOW WE FREELIES EXIST! *NOBODY* DOES!

...AND THAT'S THE WAY WE *WANT* IT!

FREELIES LOOK OUT FOR OL' *NUMBER ONE*... EVERYONE *ELSE* BETTER *WATCH OUT* FOR FREELIES!

THAT'S THE WAY IT IS, THEN-?

...THE EMPIRE CAN STOMP ON THE REST OF THE GALAXY...

...AS LONG AS NO ONE BOTHERS YOU FREELIES?!

THAT'S IT!

YOU GO BETTE

ALL WE WANT FROM THE GALAXY IS *FIVE MILLION CREDITS* AND *TWO DROIDS*... IN RETURN FOR LETTING *YOU GO-!*

DEEP IN THE OLDEST, LITTLE-USED PORTION OF THE CAPITAL CITY...

ARTOO'S SIGNAL IS VERY STRONG, HERE, MASTER LUKE-!

THAT'S GOOD BECAUSE THIS AS FAR AS THE HOVER-CAB CAN GO! *COME ON-*

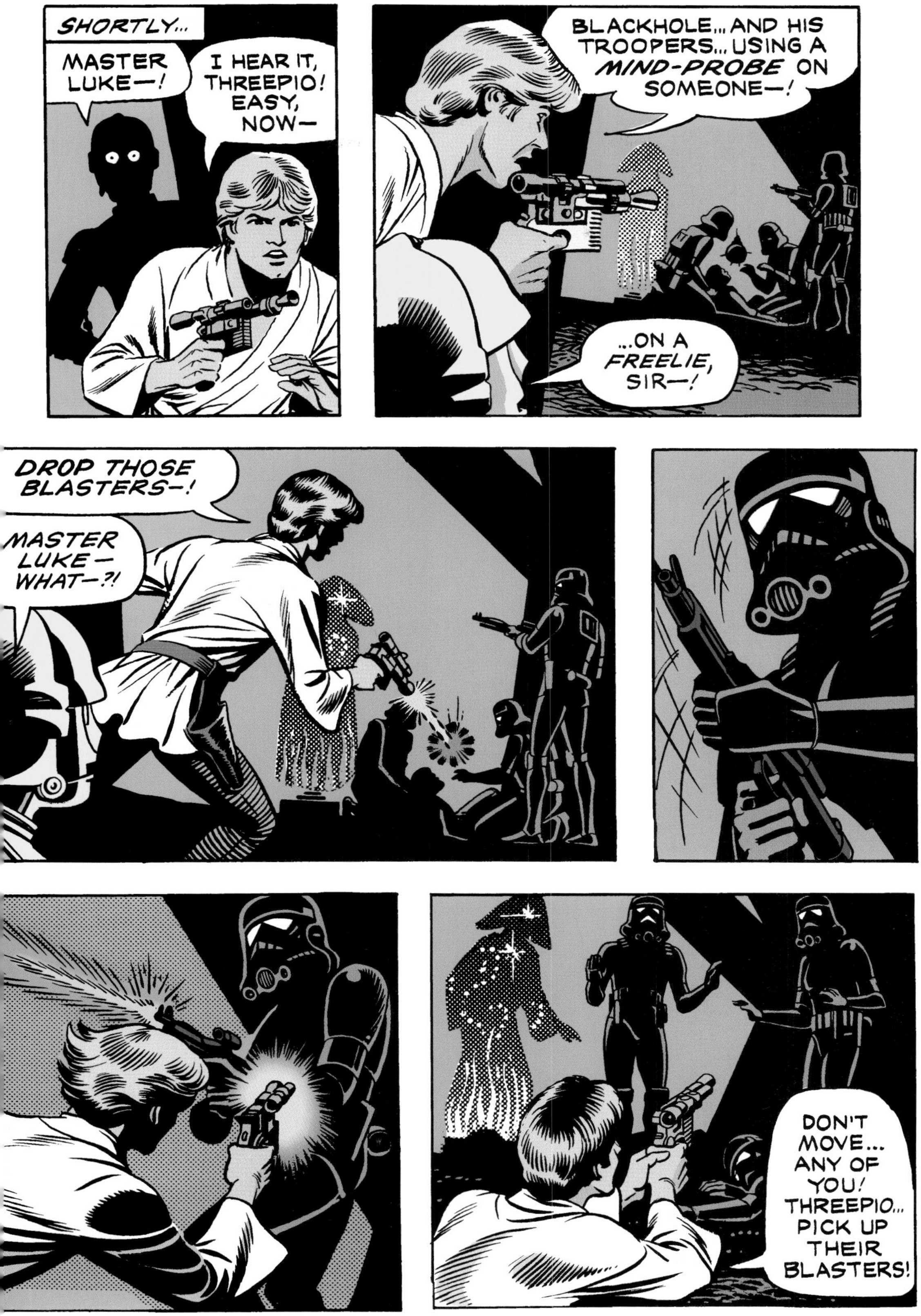
SHORTLY...
MASTER LUKE—!
I HEAR IT, THREEPIO! EASY, NOW—
BLACKHOLE... AND HIS TROOPERS... USING A *MIND-PROBE* ON SOMEONE—!
...ON A *FREELIE,* SIR—!
DROP THOSE BLASTERS—!
MASTER LUKE— WHAT—?!
DON'T MOVE... ANY OF YOU! THREEPIO... PICK UP THEIR BLASTERS!

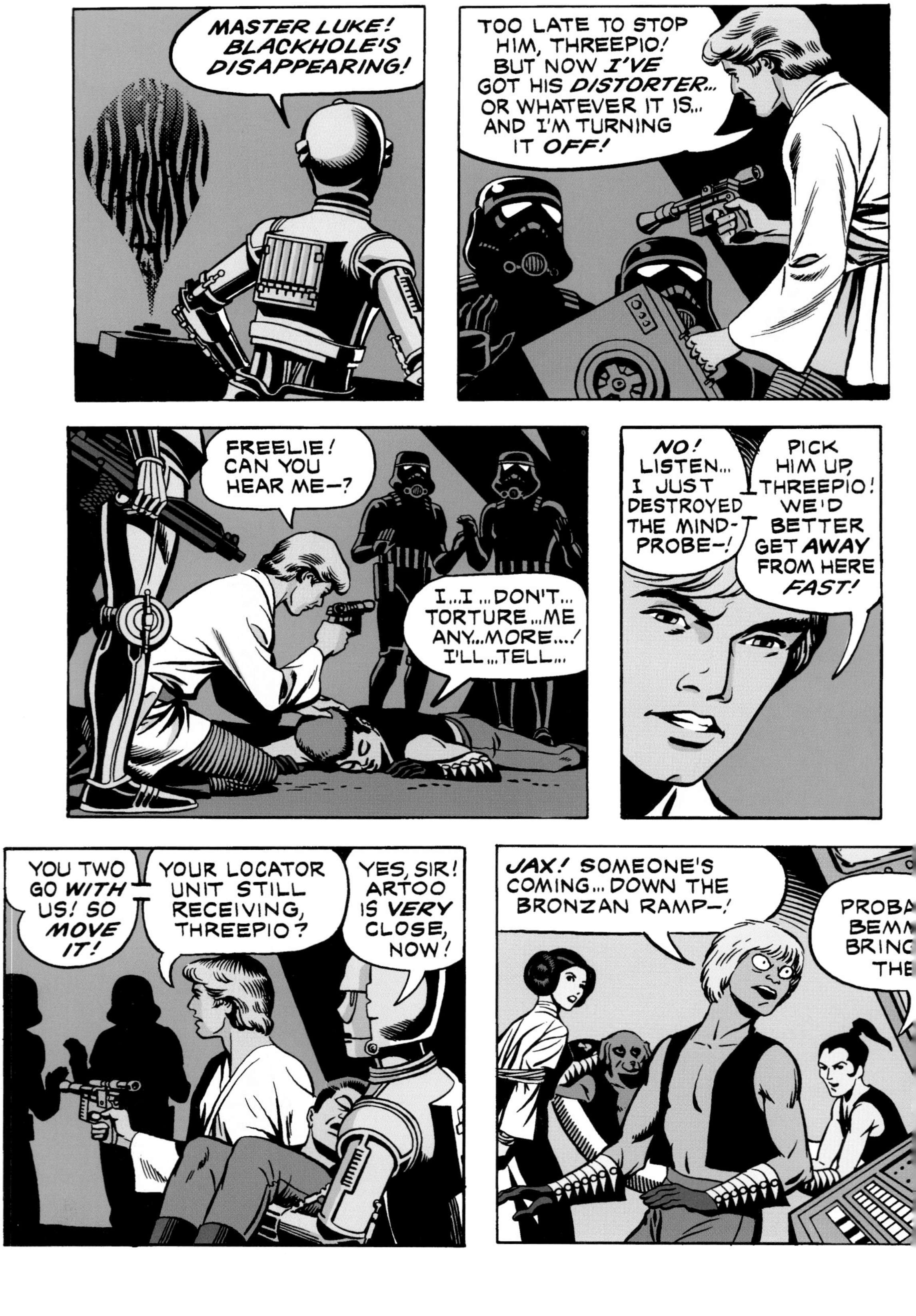
MASTER LUKE! BLACKHOLE'S DISAPPEARING!
TOO LATE TO STOP HIM, THREEPIO! BUT NOW I'VE GOT HIS DISTORTER... OR WHATEVER IT IS... AND I'M TURNING IT OFF!
FREELIE! CAN YOU HEAR ME--?
I...I ...DON'T... TORTURE...ME ANY...MORE....! I'LL...TELL...
NO! LISTEN... I JUST DESTROYED THE MIND-PROBE--!
PICK HIM UP, THREEPIO! WE'D BETTER GET AWAY FROM HERE FAST!
YOU TWO GO WITH US! SO MOVE IT!
YOUR LOCATOR UNIT STILL RECEIVING, THREEPIO?
YES, SIR! ARTOO IS VERY CLOSE, NOW!
JAX! SOMEONE'S COMING... DOWN THE BRONZAN RAMP--!

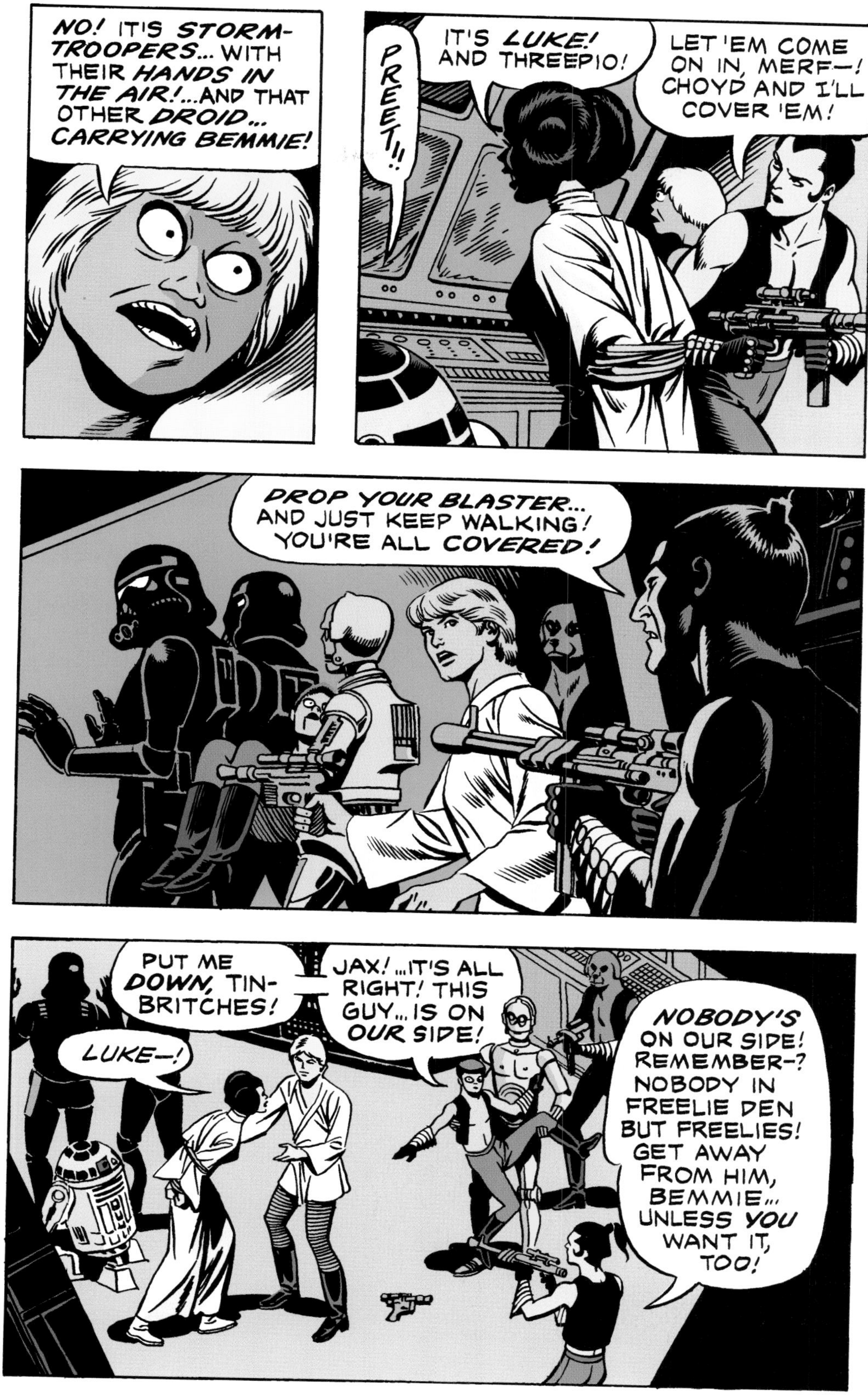
NO! IT'S STORM-TROOPERS... WITH THEIR HANDS IN THE AIR!...AND THAT OTHER DROID... CARRYING BEMMIE!
PREEET!!
IT'S LUKE! AND THREEPIO!
LET'EM COME ON IN, MERF—! CHOYD AND I'LL COVER 'EM!
DROP YOUR BLASTER... AND JUST KEEP WALKING! YOU'RE ALL COVERED!
PUT ME DOWN, TIN-BRITCHES!
JAX! ...IT'S ALL RIGHT! THIS GUY... IS ON OUR SIDE!
LUKE—!
NOBODY'S ON OUR SIDE! REMEMBER—? NOBODY IN FREELIE DEN BUT FREELIES! GET AWAY FROM HIM, BEMMIE... UNLESS YOU WANT IT, TOO!

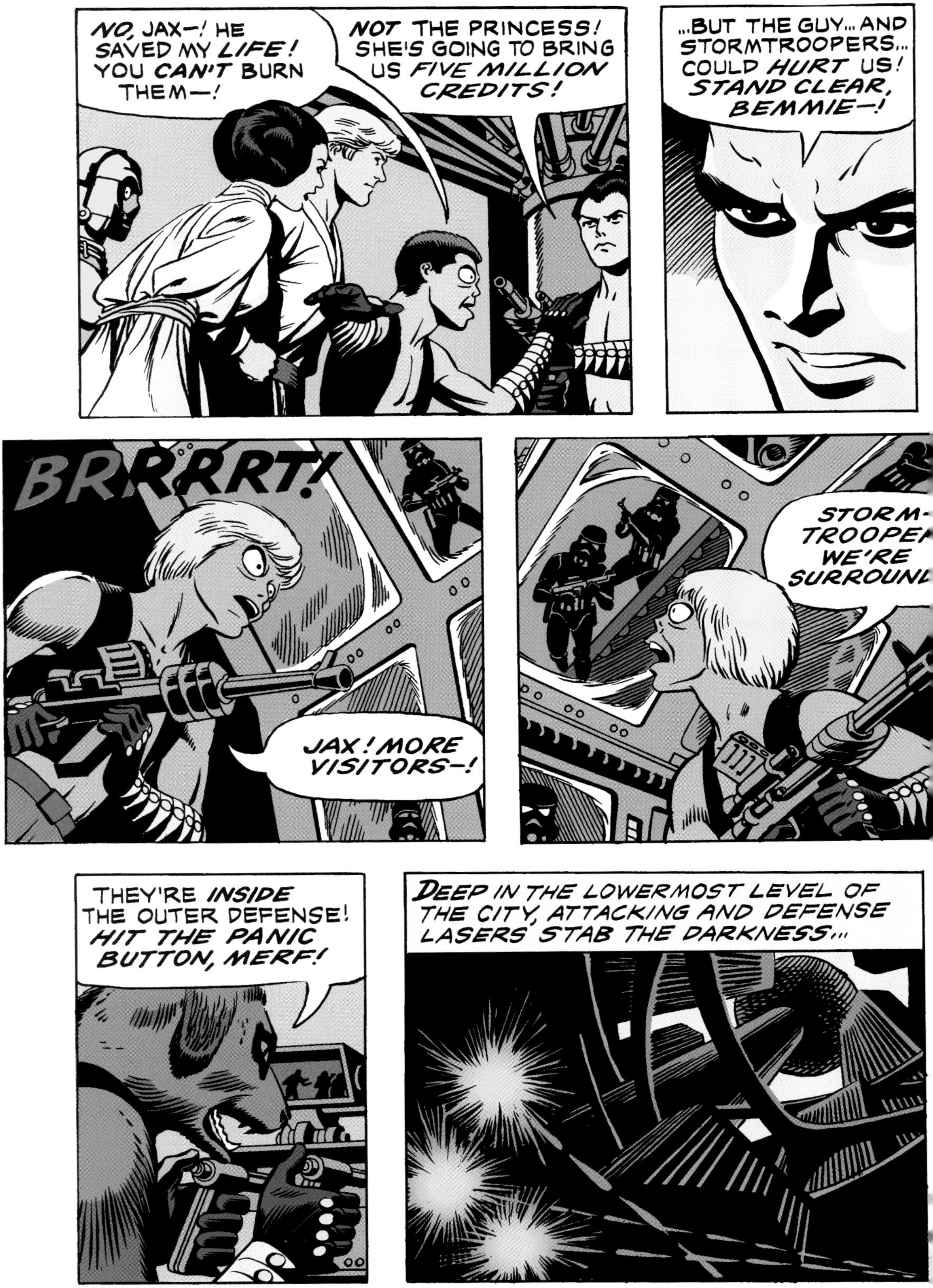
NO, JAX—! HE SAVED MY LIFE! YOU CAN'T BURN THEM—!
NOT THE PRINCESS! SHE'S GOING TO BRING US FIVE MILLION CREDITS!
...BUT THE GUY... AND STORMTROOPERS... COULD HURT US! STAND CLEAR, BEMMIE—!
BRRRRT!
JAX! MORE VISITORS—!
STORM- TROOPE WE'RE SURROUN
THEY'RE INSIDE THE OUTER DEFENSE! HIT THE PANIC BUTTON, MERF!
DEEP IN THE LOWERMOST LEVEL OF THE CITY, ATTACKING AND DEFENSE LASERS STAB THE DARKNESS...

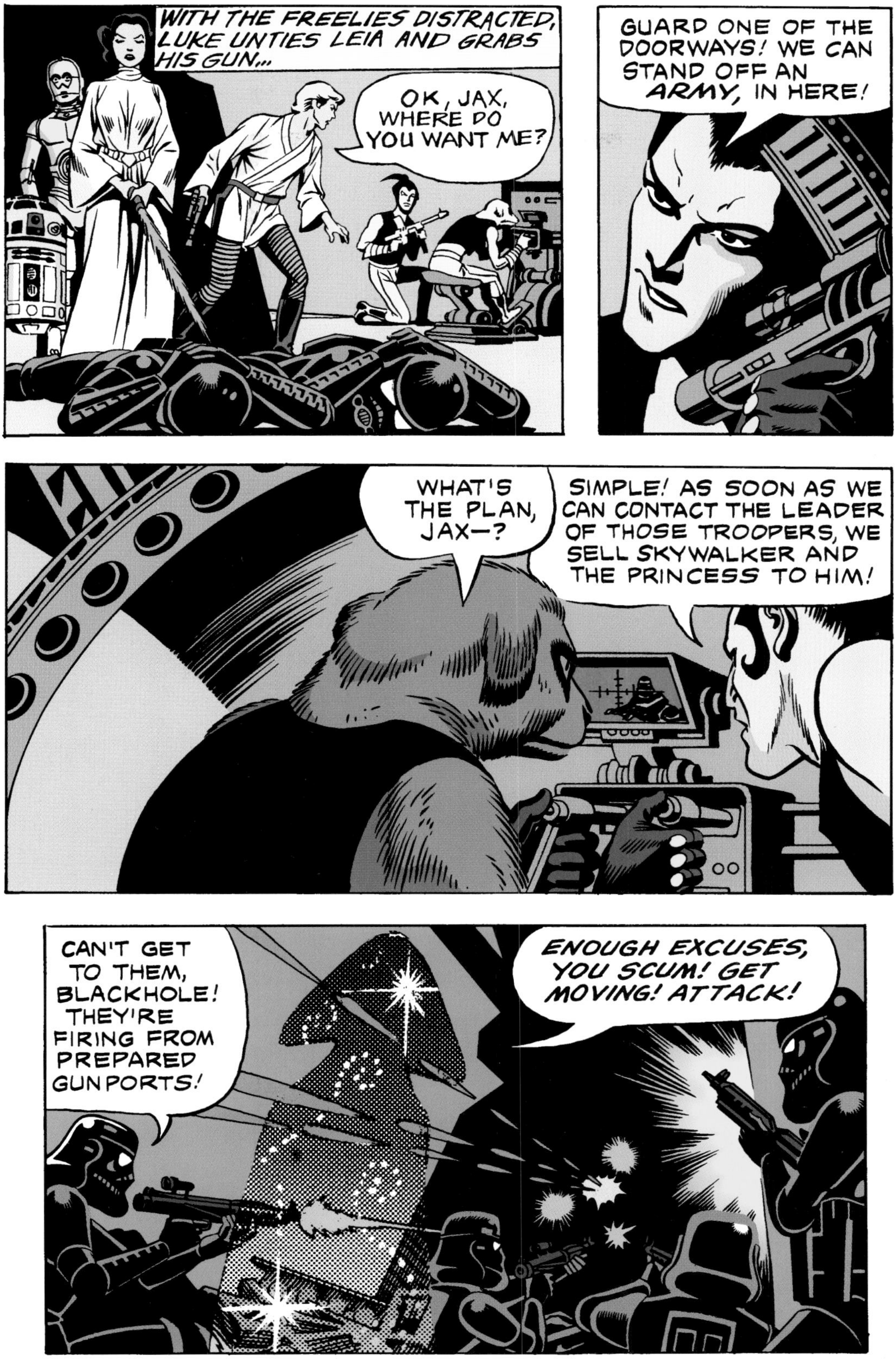
WITH THE FREELIES DISTRACTED, LUKE UNTIES LEIA AND GRABS HIS GUN...
OK, JAX, WHERE DO YOU WANT ME?
GUARD ONE OF THE DOORWAYS! WE CAN STAND OFF AN ARMY, IN HERE!
WHAT'S THE PLAN, JAX—?
SIMPLE! AS SOON AS WE CAN CONTACT THE LEADER OF THOSE TROOPERS, WE SELL SKYWALKER AND THE PRINCESS TO HIM!
CAN'T GET TO THEM, BLACKHOLE! THEY'RE FIRING FROM PREPARED GUNPORTS!
ENOUGH EXCUSES, YOU SCUM! GET MOVING! ATTACK!

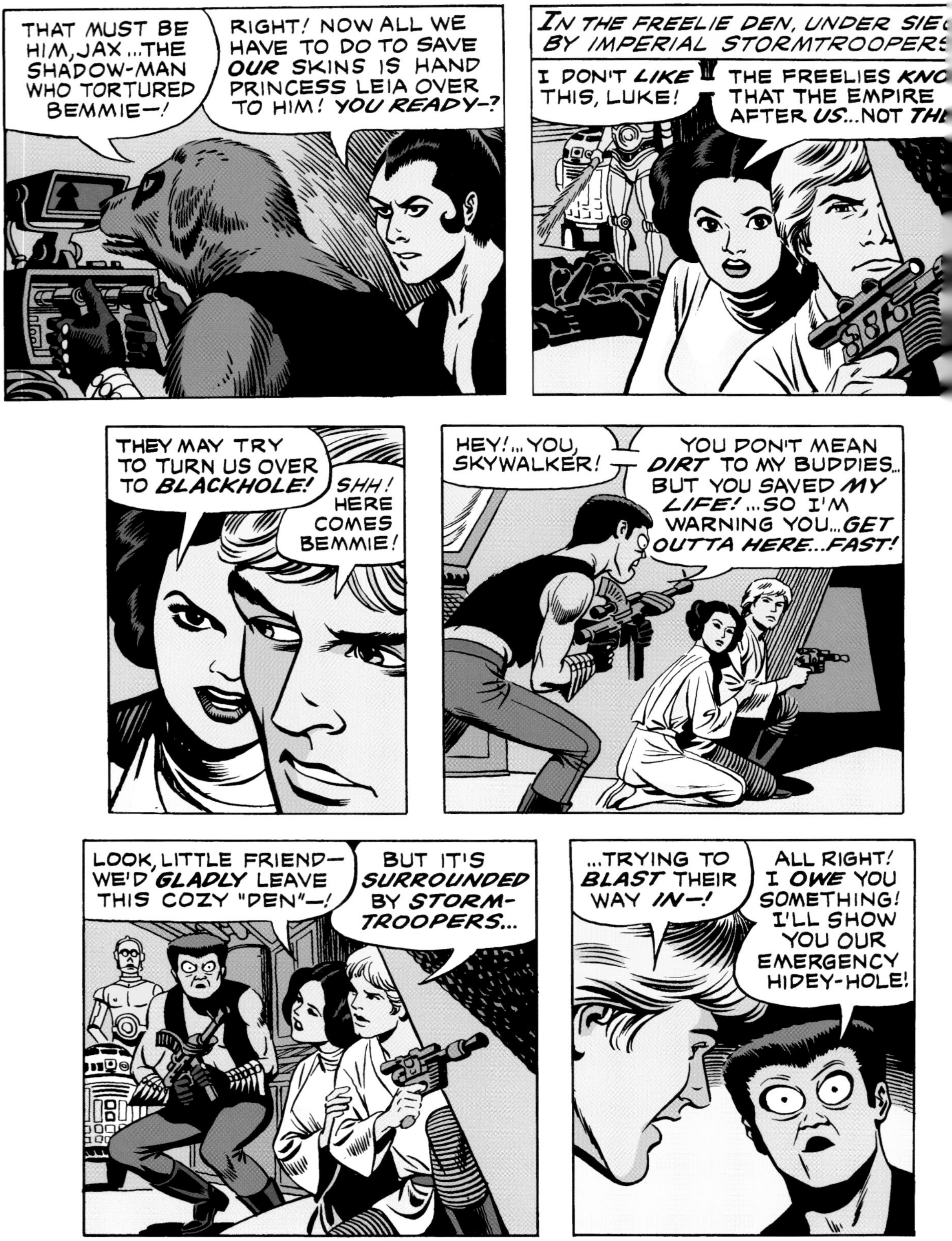
THAT MUST BE HIM, JAX...THE SHADOW-MAN WHO TORTURED BEMMIE—!
RIGHT! NOW ALL WE HAVE TO DO TO SAVE *OUR* SKINS IS HAND PRINCESS LEIA OVER TO HIM! *YOU READY—?*
IN THE FREELIE DEN, UNDER SIE BY IMPERIAL STORMTROOPERS
I DON'T *LIKE* THIS, LUKE!
THE FREELIES *KNO* THAT THE EMPIRE AFTER *US*...NOT *TH*
THEY MAY TRY TO TURN US OVER TO *BLACKHOLE!*
SHH! HERE COMES BEMMIE!
HEY!...YOU, SKYWALKER!
YOU DON'T MEAN *DIRT* TO MY BUDDIES... BUT YOU SAVED *MY LIFE!* ...SO I'M WARNING YOU...*GET OUTTA HERE...FAST!*
LOOK, LITTLE FRIEND— WE'D *GLADLY* LEAVE THIS COZY "DEN"—!
BUT IT'S *SURROUNDED* BY *STORM-TROOPERS...*
...TRYING TO *BLAST* THEIR WAY *IN—!*
ALL RIGHT! I *OWE* YOU SOMETHING! I'LL SHOW YOU OUR EMERGENCY HIDEY-HOLE!

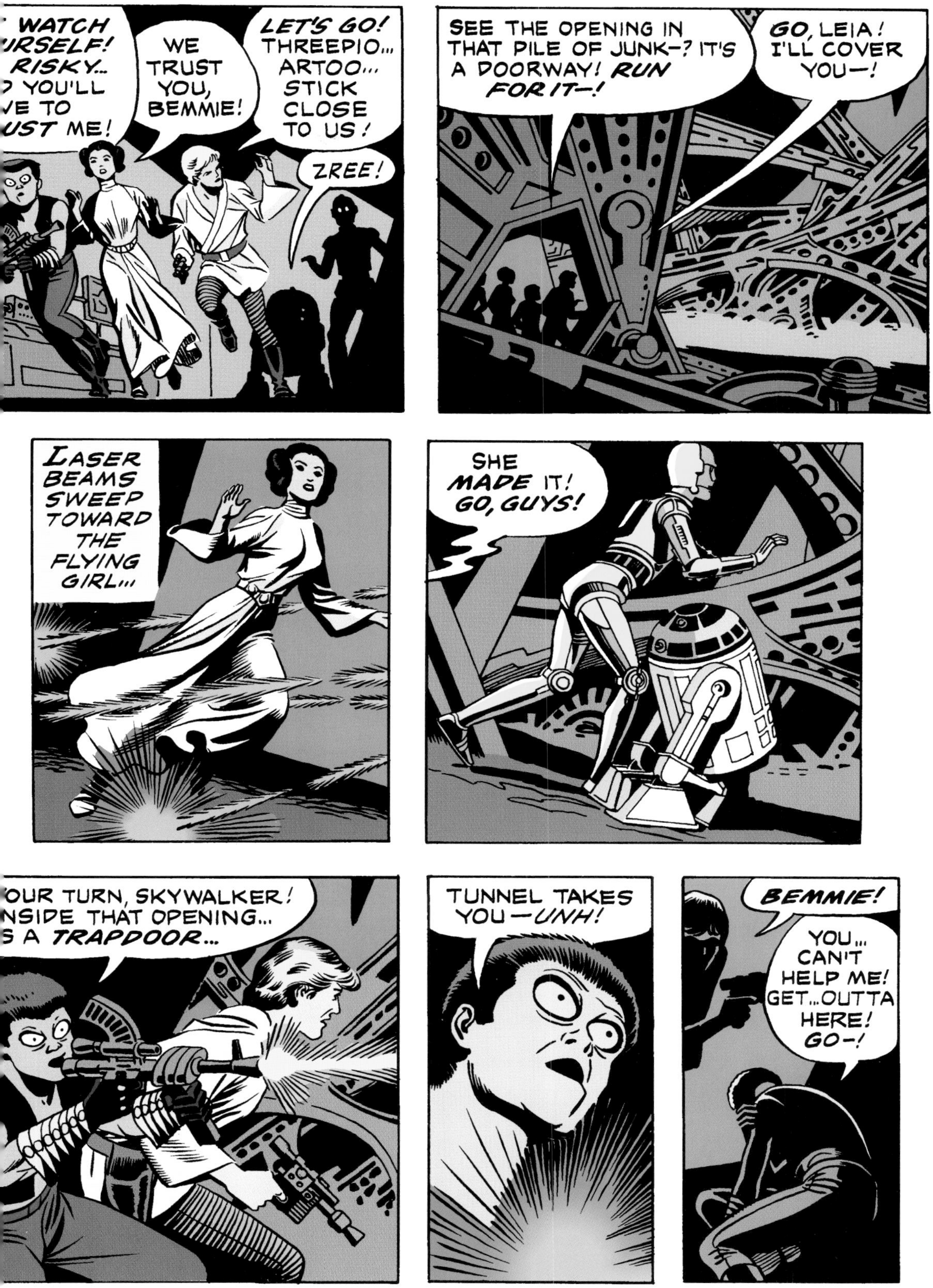
WATCH RSELF! RISKY... YOU'LL VE TO UST ME!
WE TRUST YOU, BEMMIE!
LET'S GO! THREEPIO... ARTOO... STICK CLOSE TO US!
ZREE!
SEE THE OPENING IN THAT PILE OF JUNK–? IT'S A DOORWAY! RUN FOR IT–!
GO, LEIA! I'LL COVER YOU–!
LASER BEAMS SWEEP TOWARD THE FLYING GIRL...
SHE MADE IT! GO, GUYS!
OUR TURN, SKYWALKER! NSIDE THAT OPENING... S A TRAPDOOR...
TUNNEL TAKES YOU–UNH!
BEMMIE!
YOU... CAN'T HELP ME! GET...OUTTA HERE! GO–!

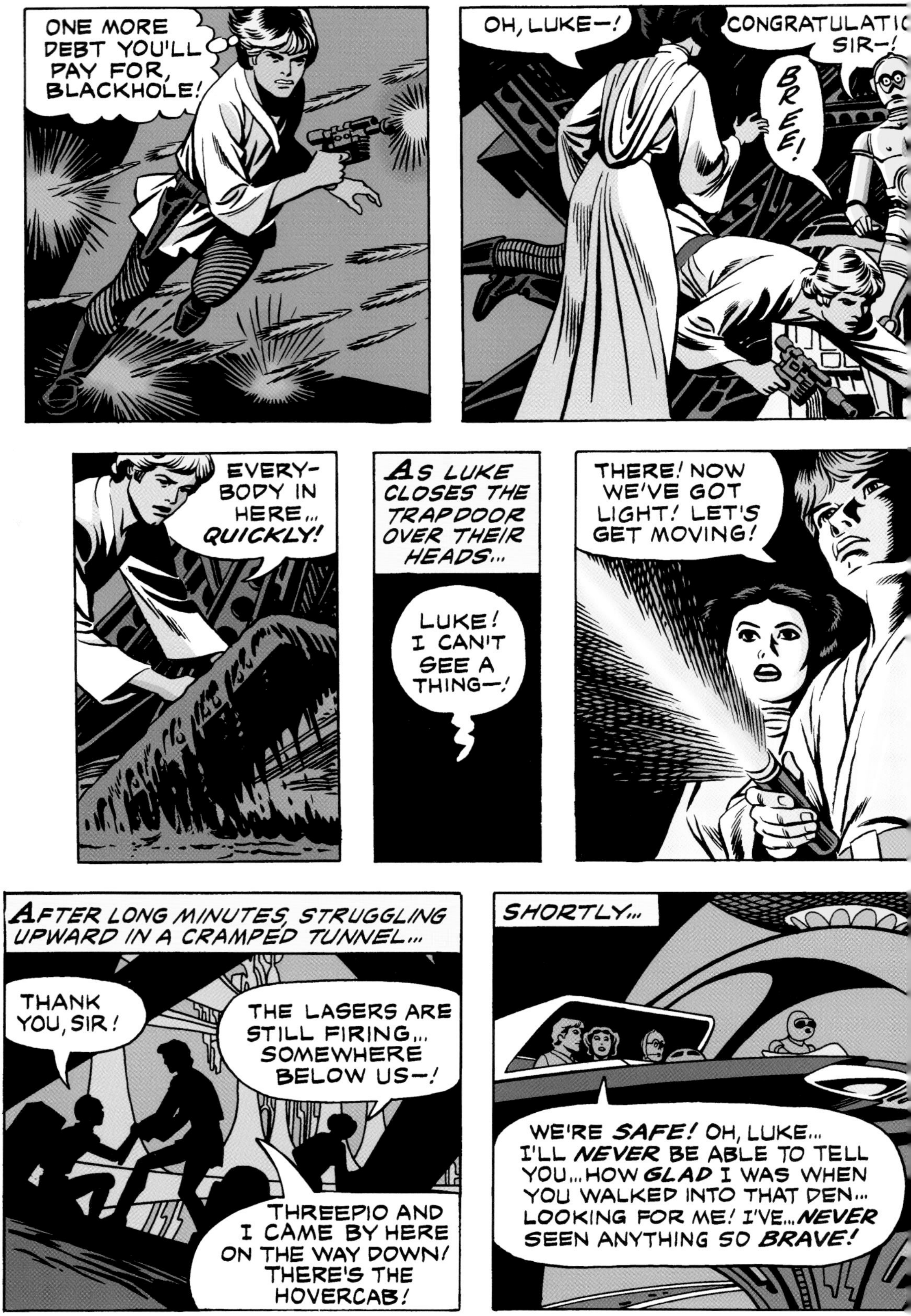
ONE MORE DEBT YOU'LL PAY FOR, BLACKHOLE!
OH, LUKE—!
CONGRATULATIO SIR—!
BREE!
EVERY-BODY IN HERE... QUICKLY!
AS LUKE CLOSES THE TRAPDOOR OVER THEIR HEADS...
LUKE! I CAN'T SEE A THING—!
THERE! NOW WE'VE GOT LIGHT! LET'S GET MOVING!
AFTER LONG MINUTES, STRUGGLING UPWARD IN A CRAMPED TUNNEL...
THANK YOU, SIR!
THE LASERS ARE STILL FIRING... SOMEWHERE BELOW US—!
THREEPIO AND I CAME BY HERE ON THE WAY DOWN! THERE'S THE HOVERCAB!
SHORTLY...
WE'RE SAFE! OH, LUKE... I'LL NEVER BE ABLE TO TELL YOU... HOW GLAD I WAS WHEN YOU WALKED INTO THAT DEN... LOOKING FOR ME! I'VE... NEVER SEEN ANYTHING SO BRAVE!

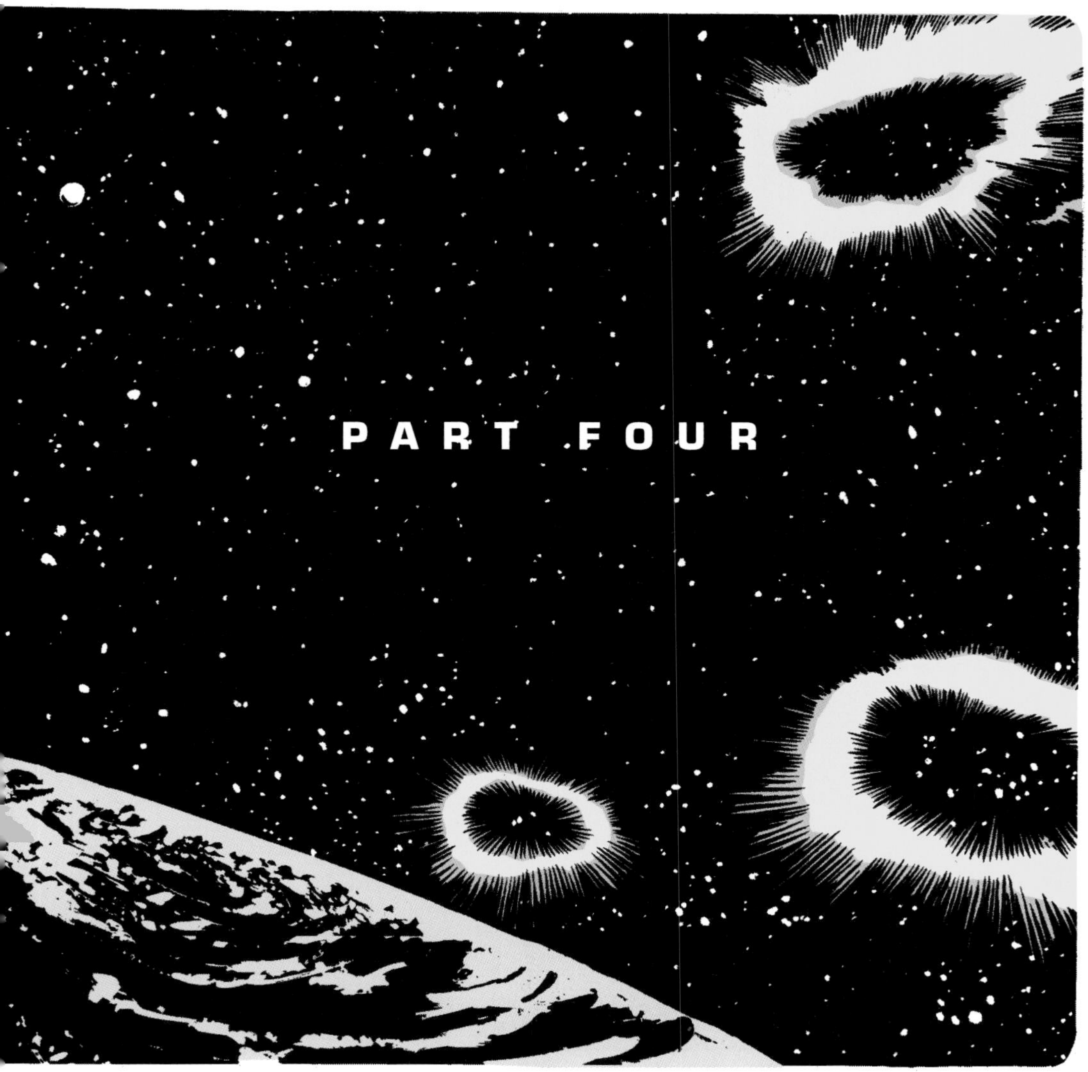
PART FOUR

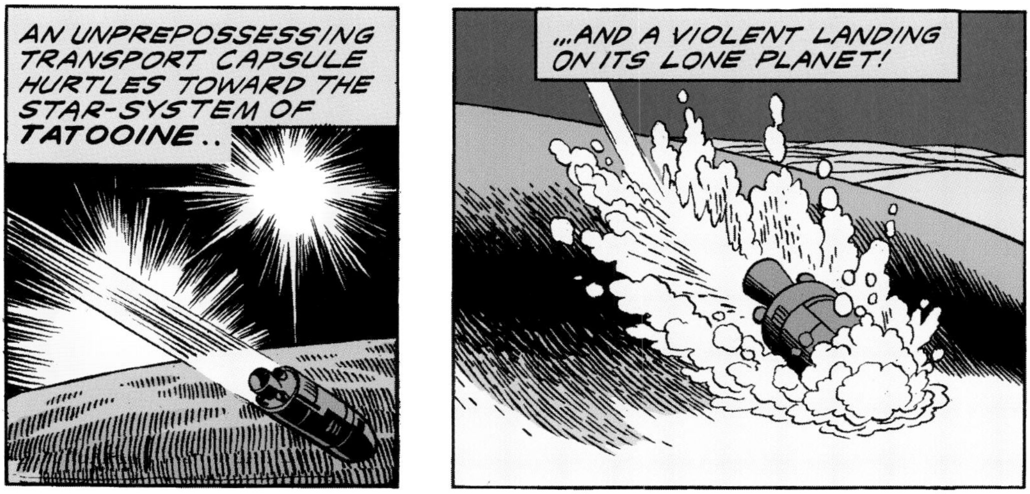
AN UNPREPOSSESSING TRANSPORT CAPSULE HURTLES TOWARD THE STAR-SYSTEM OF TATOOINE..
...AND A VIOLENT LANDING ON ITS LONE PLANET!

THE IMPACT RATTLES CERTAIN OF THE NATIVES AWAKE!

WARILY, THE METAL-SCAVENGING *JAWAS* APPROACH THE CRASH SITE...

...TESTING THE FALLEN TRANSPORT CAPSULE FO_ BOOBY TRAPS!

WHEN THEY ARE SATISFIED IT IS HARMLESS, THEY SIGNAL FOR *PICK-UP...*

IN RESPONSE, A MONSTROUS *SANDCRAWLER,* THEIR CUSTOMARY MODE OF TRANSPORTATION... COMES GRUMBLING OVER THE DUNES!

A SUCTION TUBE WHISKS THE CAPSULE INTO THE SANDCRAWLER'S METAL BELLY... THE JAWAS SCURRY ABOARD...

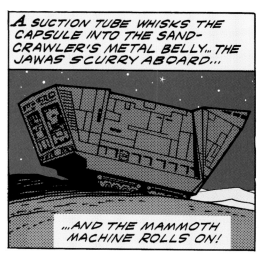

...AND THE MAMMOTH MACHINE ROLLS ON!

INSIDE, THE CREW CHIEF ORDERS THE CAPSULE *OPENED...*

URRGEPP... KRUTT *PUNNG!*

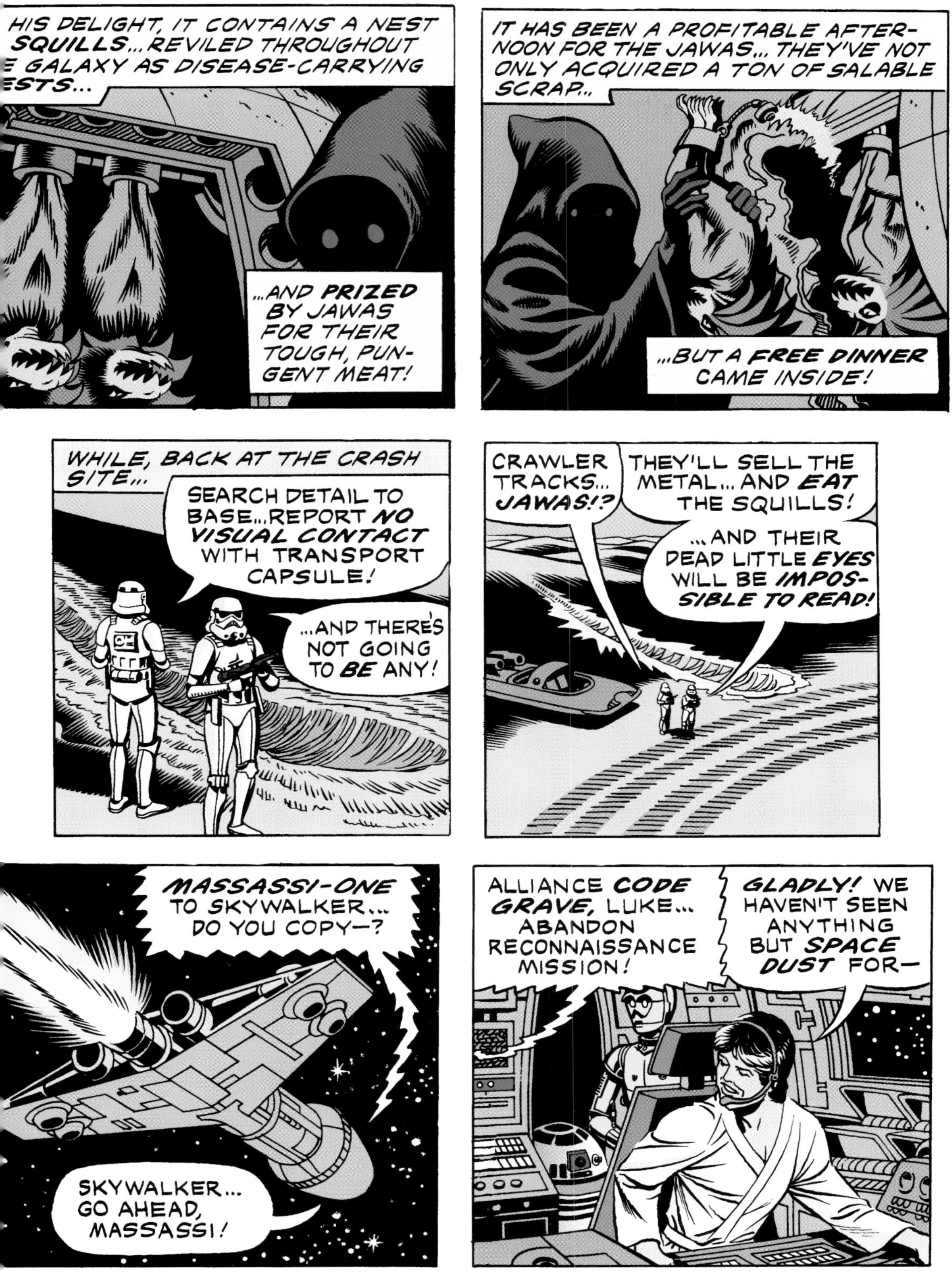
HIS DELIGHT, IT CONTAINS A NEST
SQUILLS... REVILED THROUGHOUT
E GALAXY AS DISEASE-CARRYING
ESTS...
...AND PRIZED BY JAWAS FOR THEIR TOUGH, PUNGENT MEAT!
IT HAS BEEN A PROFITABLE AFTERNOON FOR THE JAWAS... THEY'VE NOT ONLY ACQUIRED A TON OF SALABLE SCRAP...
...BUT A FREE DINNER CAME INSIDE!
WHILE, BACK AT THE CRASH SITE...
SEARCH DETAIL TO BASE...REPORT NO VISUAL CONTACT WITH TRANSPORT CAPSULE!
...AND THERE'S NOT GOING TO BE ANY!
CRAWLER TRACKS... JAWAS!?
THEY'LL SELL THE METAL... AND EAT THE SQUILLS!
...AND THEIR DEAD LITTLE EYES WILL BE IMPOSSIBLE TO READ!
MASSASSI-ONE TO SKYWALKER... DO YOU COPY--?
SKYWALKER... GO AHEAD, MASSASSI!
ALLIANCE CODE GRAVE, LUKE... ABANDON RECONNAISSANCE MISSION!
GLADLY! WE HAVEN'T SEEN ANYTHING BUT SPACE DUST FOR--

SET COURSE IMMEDIATELY FOR *TATOOINE!*

OBSERVERS ON *TATOOINE* REPORT THE LANDING OF AN UNSCHEDULED *TRANSPORT CAPSULE!* THE ALLIANCE IS *CONCERNED!*

SEND SOMEBODY ELSE!

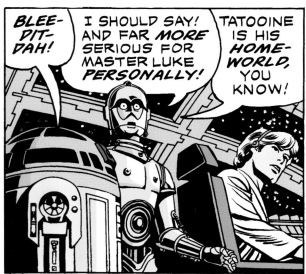

BLEE-DIT-DAH!

I SHOULD SAY! AND FAR *MORE* SERIOUS FOR MASTER LUKE *PERSONALLY!*

TATOOINE IS HIS *HOME-WORLD,* YOU KNOW!

YOUR *FAMILIARITY* WITH THE PLANET MAKES YOU IDEAL FOR—

I AM *NOT* GOING BACK THERE!

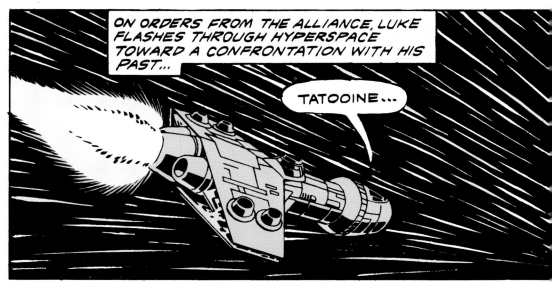

ON ORDERS FROM THE ALLIANCE, LUKE FLASHES THROUGH HYPERSPACE TOWARD A CONFRONTATION WITH HIS PAST...

TATOOINE...

JUST SAYING THE *NAME* MAKES ME *QUEASY*, THREEPIO! ...TOO MANY MEMORIES—!

I'M *ENTIRELY* SYMPATHETIC, MASTER LUKE!

MY OWN CIRCUITRY *BRISTLES* AT THE THOUGHT OF A CERTAIN *WELDER'S BENCH* ON *ALDERAAN!*

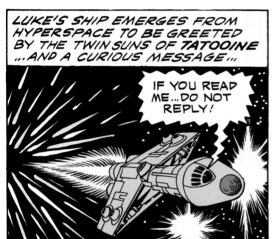

LUKE'S SHIP EMERGES FROM HYPERSPACE TO BE GREETED BY THE TWIN SUNS OF *TATOOINE* ...AND A CURIOUS MESSAGE...

IF YOU READ ME...DO NOT REPLY!

GO DIRECTLY TO MOS EISLEY CANTINA! ASK FOR *ANDUVIL* OF OGEM!

A FEMALE *ORGANIC* VOICE, WAS IT NOT?

A FEMININE VOICE...THAT HAD TO TALK *FAST*... OR *SEEM* LIKE IT!

I WONDER IF SHE'S WORKING WITH THE ALLIANCE... OR LAYING A *TRAP!*

MOS EISLEY SPACEPORT ON TATOOINE...

IT'S *CHANGED*, THREEPIO! IT'S *BIGGER*... BUSIER...

THERE'S MORE TRAFFIC HERE NOW THAN THIS WHOLE DUMP USED TO SEE IN A *YEAR—!*

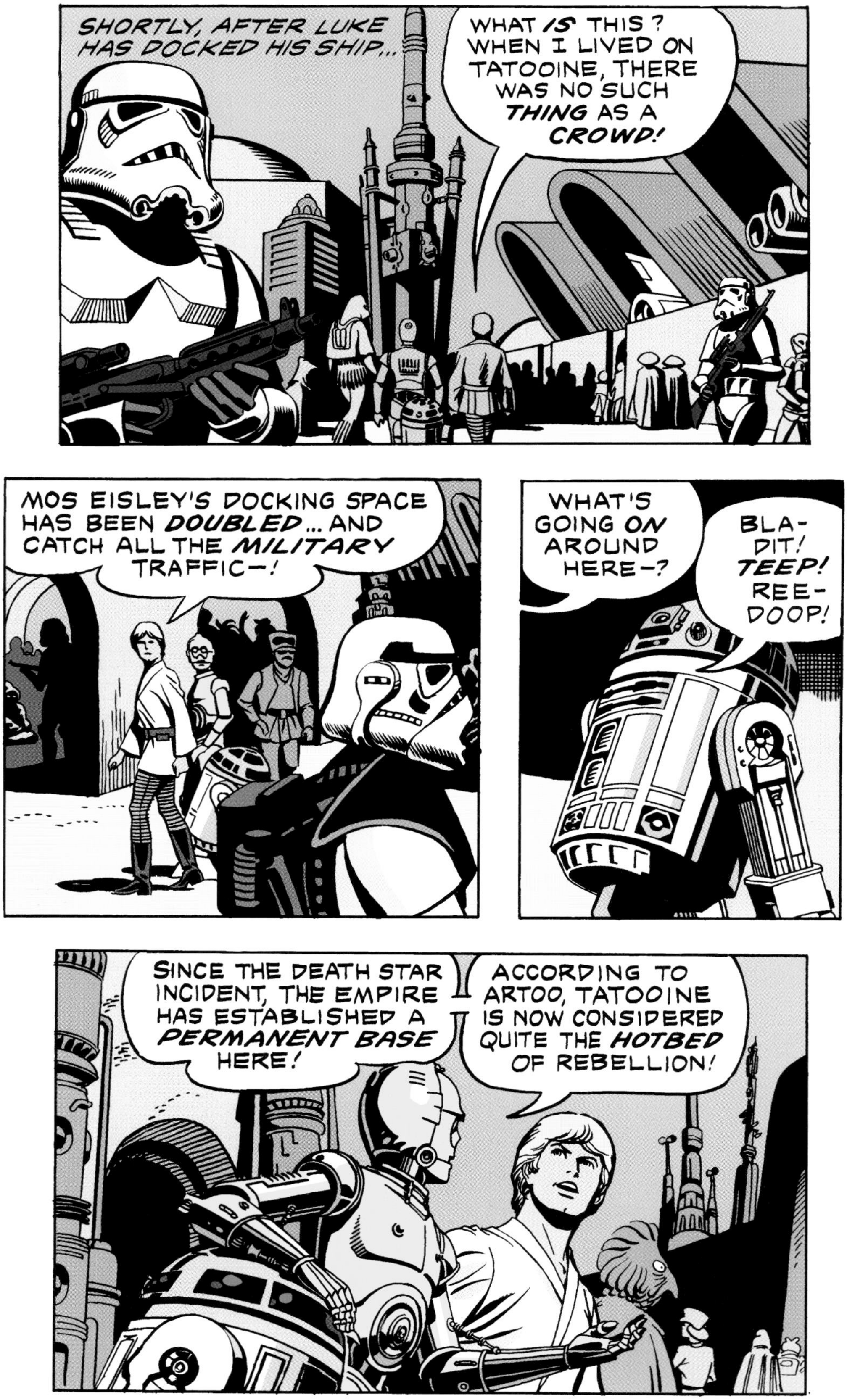
SHORTLY, AFTER LUKE HAS DOCKED HIS SHIP...
WHAT *IS* THIS? WHEN I LIVED ON TATOOINE, THERE WAS NO SUCH *THING* AS A *CROWD!*
MOS EISLEY'S DOCKING SPACE HAS BEEN *DOUBLED*... AND CATCH ALL THE *MILITARY* TRAFFIC—!
WHAT'S GOING *ON* AROUND HERE—?
BLA-DIT! *TEEP!* REE-DOOP!
SINCE THE DEATH STAR INCIDENT, THE EMPIRE HAS ESTABLISHED A *PERMANENT BASE* HERE!
ACCORDING TO ARTOO, TATOOINE IS NOW CONSIDERED QUITE THE *HOTBED* OF REBELLION!

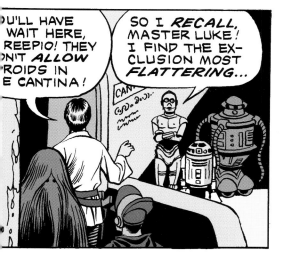

YOU'LL HAVE TO WAIT HERE, THREEPIO! THEY DON'T *ALLOW* DROIDS IN THE CANTINA!

SO I *RECALL*, MASTER LUKE! I FIND THE EXCLUSION MOST *FLATTERING*...

" ...THEY SEEM TO EXERCISE NO SELECTION *WHATEVER* IN THEIR *ORGANIC* PATRONS!"

LUKE FREEZES IN THE DOORWAY OF THE MOS EISLEY CANTINA, HIS VISION CLOUDED BY IMAGES OUT OF THE *PAST!*

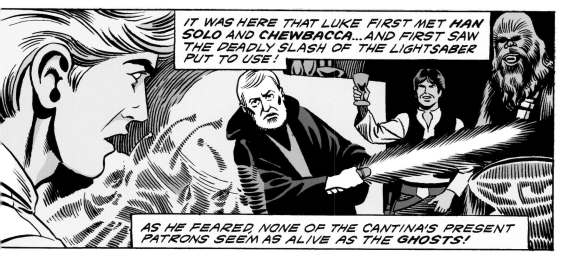

IT WAS HERE THAT LUKE FIRST MET *HAN SOLO* AND *CHEWBACCA*...AND FIRST SAW THE DEADLY SLASH OF THE LIGHTSABER PUT TO USE!

AS HE FEARED, NONE OF THE CANTINA'S PRESENT PATRONS SEEM AS ALIVE AS THE *GHOSTS!*

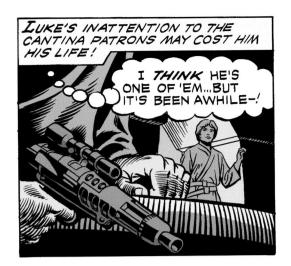

LUKE'S INATTENTION TO THE CANTINA PATRONS MAY COST HIM HIS LIFE!

I *THINK* HE'S ONE OF 'EM...BUT IT'S BEEN AWHILE—!

AW...WHAT THE GRIT! *JABBA THE HUTT* WILL LAY A COUPLE *THOUSAND* ON ME JUST FOR *THINKIN'* IT'S HIM—!

YAAGH—!

HE WAS GOING TO *VAPORIZE* YOU! YOU *KNOW* HIM—?

SORT OF—!

HE WORKED OFF-AND-ON FOR *JABBA THE HUTT!* THERE'S AN OLD *GRUDGE* INVOLVED!

SO I'VE *HEARD!*

YOU *HAVE?!*

I AM CALLED *ANDUYIL OF OGEM!*

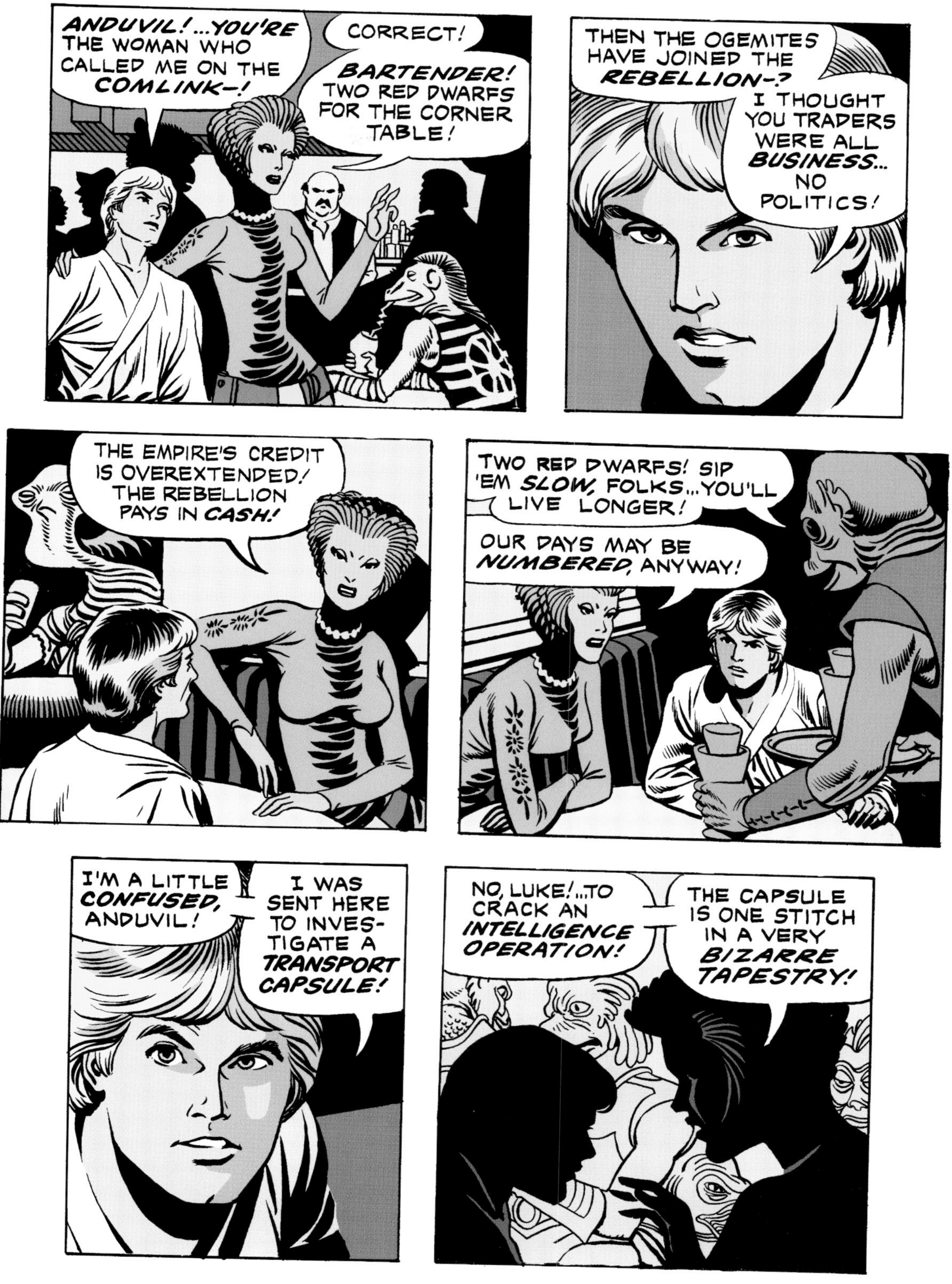

ANDUVIL!...YOU'RE THE WOMAN WHO CALLED ME ON THE COMLINK-!
CORRECT!
BARTENDER! TWO RED DWARFS FOR THE CORNER TABLE!
THEN THE OGEMITES HAVE JOINED THE REBELLION-?
I THOUGHT YOU TRADERS WERE ALL BUSINESS... NO POLITICS!
THE EMPIRE'S CREDIT IS OVEREXTENDED! THE REBELLION PAYS IN CASH!
TWO RED DWARFS! SIP 'EM SLOW, FOLKS...YOU'LL LIVE LONGER!
OUR DAYS MAY BE NUMBERED, ANYWAY!
I'M A LITTLE CONFUSED, ANDUVIL!
I WAS SENT HERE TO INVESTIGATE A TRANSPORT CAPSULE!
NO, LUKE!...TO CRACK AN INTELLIGENCE OPERATION!
THE CAPSULE IS ONE STITCH IN A VERY BIZARRE TAPESTRY!

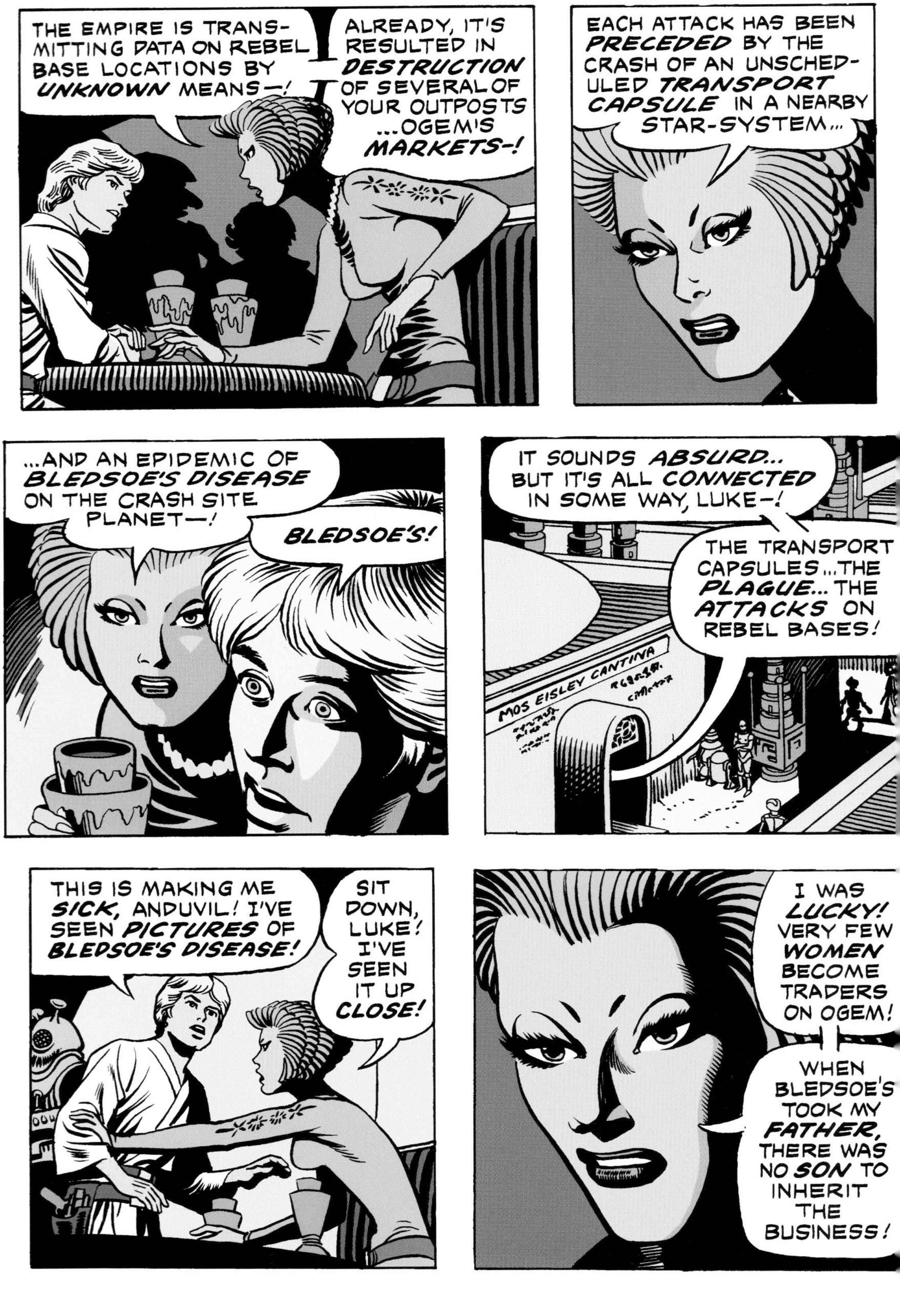
THE EMPIRE IS TRANSMITTING DATA ON REBEL BASE LOCATIONS BY UNKNOWN MEANS—!
ALREADY, IT'S RESULTED IN DESTRUCTION OF SEVERAL OF YOUR OUTPOSTS ...OGEM'S MARKETS—!
EACH ATTACK HAS BEEN PRECEDED BY THE CRASH OF AN UNSCHEDULED TRANSPORT CAPSULE IN A NEARBY STAR-SYSTEM...
...AND AN EPIDEMIC OF BLEDSOE'S DISEASE ON THE CRASH SITE PLANET—!
BLEDSOE'S!
IT SOUNDS ABSURD... BUT IT'S ALL CONNECTED IN SOME WAY, LUKE—!
THE TRANSPORT CAPSULES...THE PLAGUE... THE ATTACKS ON REBEL BASES!
MOS EISLEY CANTINA
THIS IS MAKING ME SICK, ANDUVIL! I'VE SEEN PICTURES OF BLEDSOE'S DISEASE!
SIT DOWN, LUKE! I'VE SEEN IT UP CLOSE!
I WAS LUCKY! VERY FEW WOMEN BECOME TRADERS ON OGEM!
WHEN BLEDSOE'S TOOK MY FATHER, THERE WAS NO SON TO INHERIT THE BUSINESS!

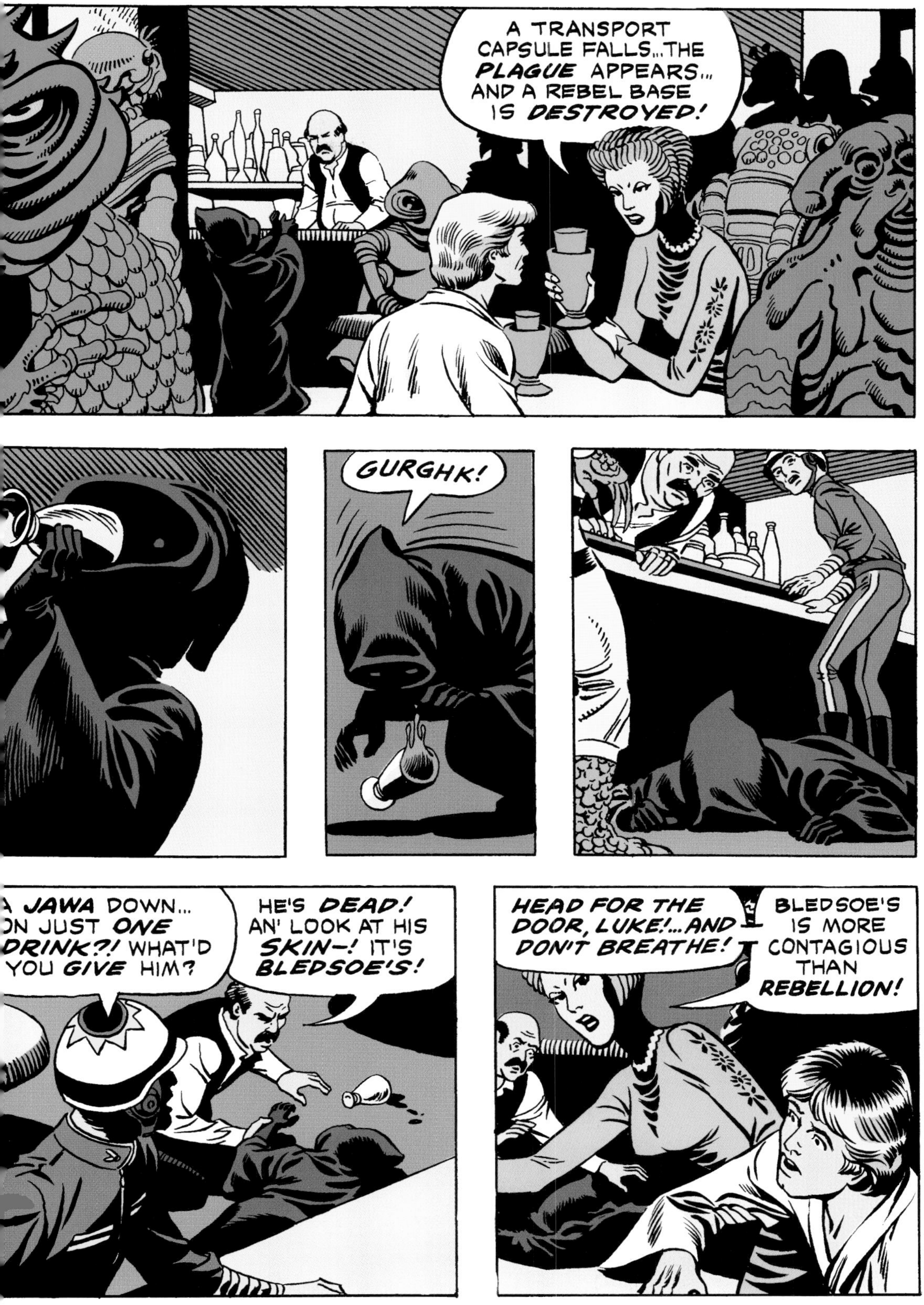
A TRANSPORT CAPSULE FALLS...THE PLAGUE APPEARS... AND A REBEL BASE IS DESTROYED!
GURGHK!
A JAWA DOWN... ON JUST ONE DRINK?! WHAT'D YOU GIVE HIM?
HE'S DEAD! AN' LOOK AT HIS SKIN--! IT'S BLEDSOE'S!
HEAD FOR THE DOOR, LUKE!...AND DON'T BREATHE!
BLEDSOE'S IS MORE CONTAGIOUS THAN REBELLION!

I'VE GOT A LANDSPEEDER... THIS WAY—!
EISLEY
WAIT, ANDUVIL—! THREEPIO... ARTOO! WHERE ARE THEY—?
THREEPIO! ARTOO—!
OVER HERE, MASTER LUKE! A RATHER SURLY SECURITY DROID CONSIGNED US TO THIS WAITING AREA!
MOVE IT, SKYWALKER! ...UNLESS YOU FIGURE YOU'RE IMMUNE TO BLEDSOE'S DISEASE!
MOMENTS LATER...
WE'LL BE SAFER AWAY FROM MOS EISLEY! TOO MUCH HEAVY BREATHING BACK THERE!
AN OUTBREAK OF BLEDSOE'S DISEASE IN MOS EISLEY SENDS LUKE AND ANDUVIL INTO THE TATOOINE DESERT...
WHERE CAN WE LAY LOW FOR AWHILE, LUKE—?
...WE'RE TUSKEN BAIT OUT HERE IN THE OPEN!
UH... HEAD FOR THE JUNDLAND WASTES! THERE'S A HOUSE—

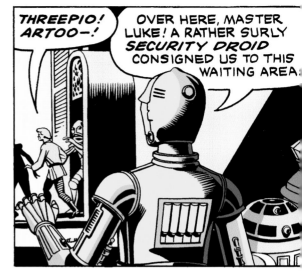

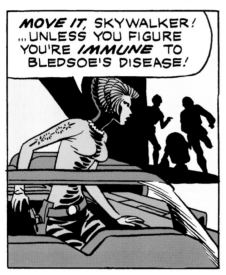

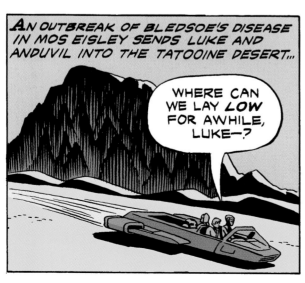

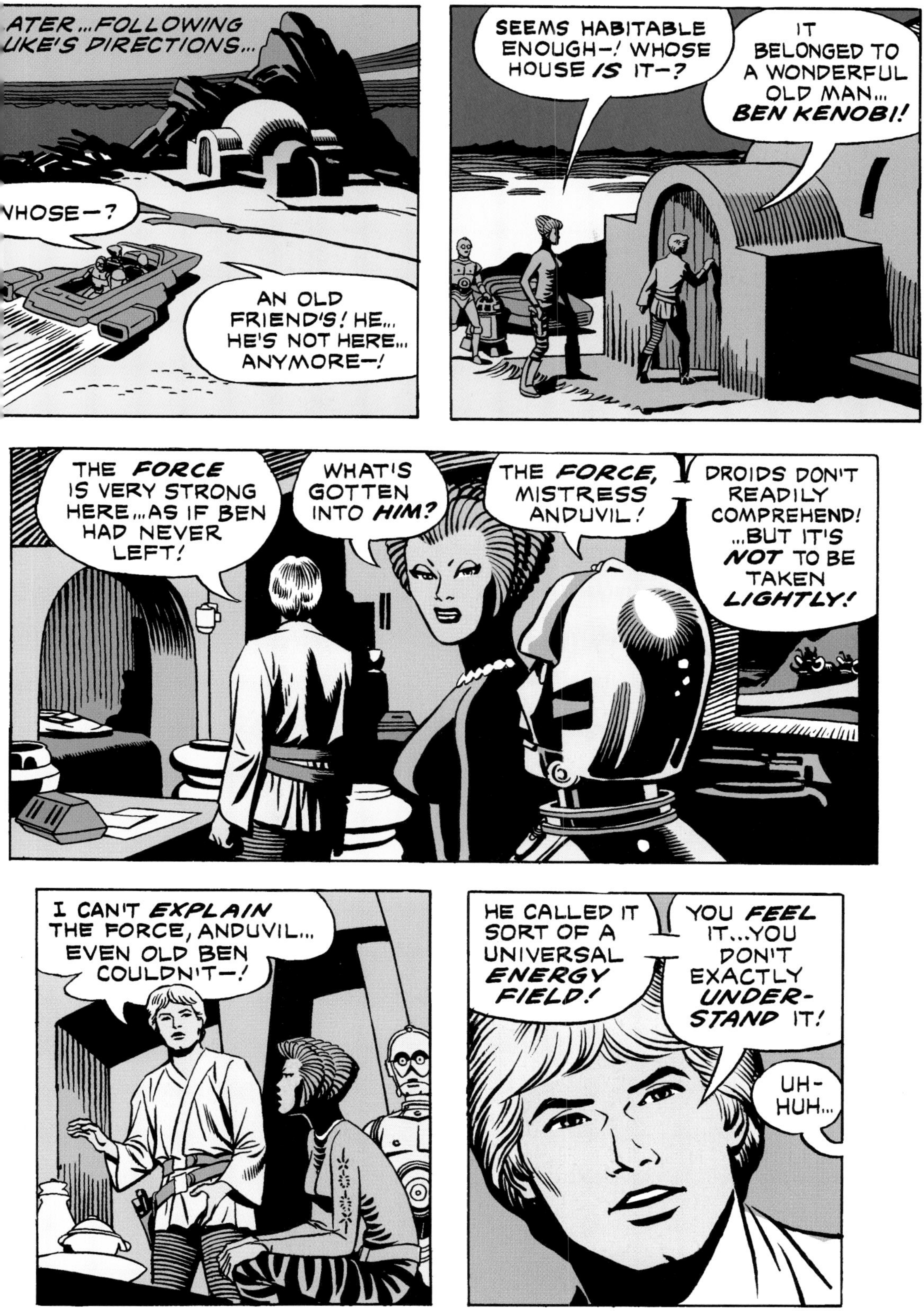
ATER...FOLLOWING UKE'S DIRECTIONS...
VHOSE—?
AN OLD FRIEND'S! HE... HE'S NOT HERE... ANYMORE—!
SEEMS HABITABLE ENOUGH—! WHOSE HOUSE IS IT—?
IT BELONGED TO A WONDERFUL OLD MAN... BEN KENOBI!
THE FORCE IS VERY STRONG HERE...AS IF BEN HAD NEVER LEFT!
WHAT'S GOTTEN INTO HIM?
THE FORCE, MISTRESS ANDUVIL!
DROIDS DON'T READILY COMPREHEND! ...BUT IT'S NOT TO BE TAKEN LIGHTLY!
I CAN'T EXPLAIN THE FORCE, ANDUVIL... EVEN OLD BEN COULDN'T—!
HE CALLED IT SORT OF A UNIVERSAL ENERGY FIELD!
YOU FEEL IT...YOU DON'T EXACTLY UNDER-STAND IT!
UH-HUH...

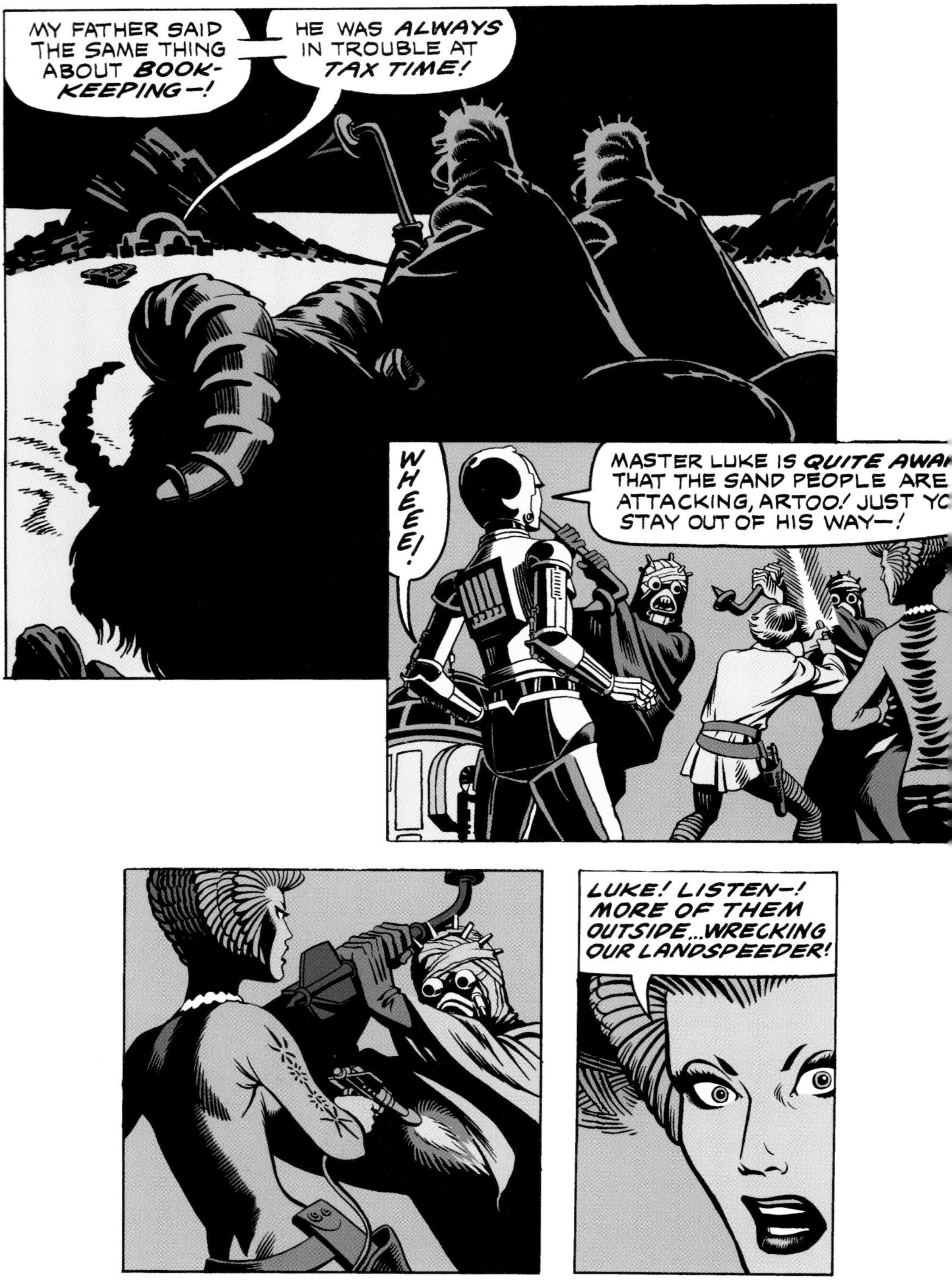
MY FATHER SAID THE SAME THING ABOUT BOOK-KEEPING—!
HE WAS ALWAYS IN TROUBLE AT TAX TIME!
WHEEEE!
MASTER LUKE IS QUITE AWA THAT THE SAND PEOPLE ARE ATTACKING, ARTOO! JUST YO STAY OUT OF HIS WAY—!
LUKE! LISTEN—! MORE OF THEM OUTSIDE...WRECKING OUR LANDSPEEDER!

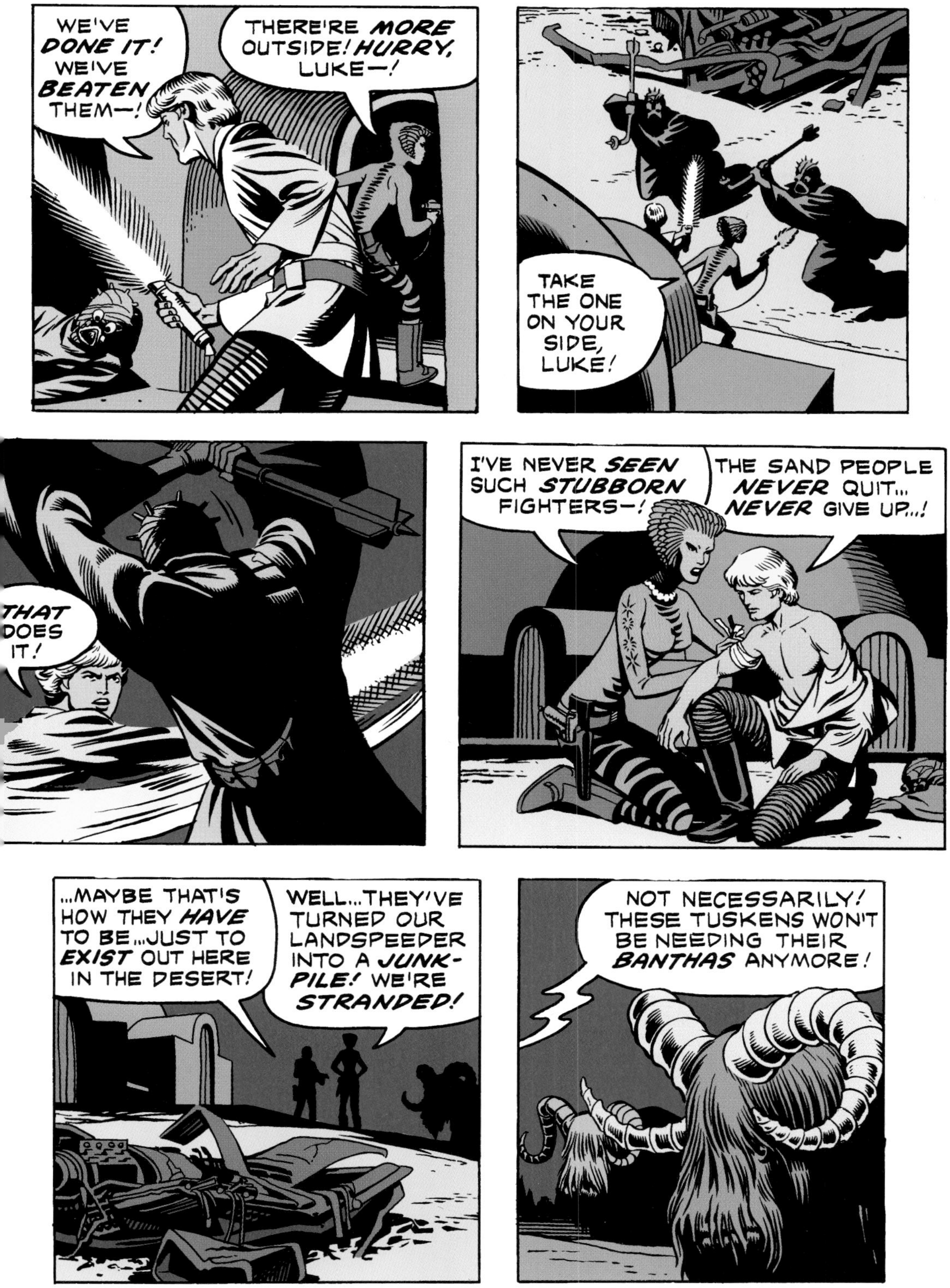
WE'VE DONE IT! WE'VE BEATEN THEM—!
THERE'RE MORE OUTSIDE! HURRY, LUKE—!
TAKE THE ONE ON YOUR SIDE, LUKE!
THAT DOES IT!
I'VE NEVER SEEN SUCH STUBBORN FIGHTERS—!
THE SAND PEOPLE NEVER QUIT... NEVER GIVE UP...!
...MAYBE THAT'S HOW THEY HAVE TO BE...JUST TO EXIST OUT HERE IN THE DESERT!
WELL...THEY'VE TURNED OUR LANDSPEEDER INTO A JUNK-PILE! WE'RE STRANDED!
NOT NECESSARILY! THESE TUSKENS WON'T BE NEEDING THEIR BANTHAS ANYMORE!

THEIR LANDSPEEDER DESTROYED BY TUSKEN RAIDERS, LUKE AND COMPANY RESUME THEIR JOURNEY ON *BANTHA-BACK*...

DON'T WORRY... WE'LL KNOW IT WHEN WE *SIGHT* IT!

ANY PARTICULAR *DESTINATION* IN MIND, ANDUVIL—?

I MUST SAY I PREFER MASTER LUKE'S *DIRECTNESS* TO THE OGEM FEMALE'S *EVASIVENESS*, ARTOO!

WE FLED THE *PLAGUE* IN MOS EISLEY...BUT *NOW* WHAT ARE WE GETTING INTO—?

PLOO DIT!

AS DAWN BANISHES THE COO... OF THE TATOOINE NIGHT...

ANDUVIL! *LOOK*—!

DIDN'T I SAY WE RECOGNIZE OU DESTINATION WHEN WE SAW

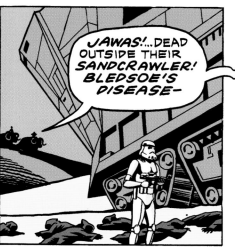

JAWAS!...DEAD OUTSIDE THEIR *SANDCRAWLER!* BLEDSOE'S *DISEASE*—

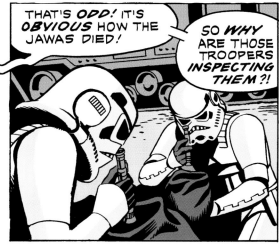

THAT'S *ODD!* IT'S *OBVIOUS* HOW THE JAWAS DIED!

SO *WHY* ARE THOSE TROOPERS *INSPECTING* THEM?!

THE TROOPERS RE CHECKING HE JAWAS' YES! WHY OULD HEY DO HAT?

BLEDSOE'S DISEASE CAN CAUSE A STRANGE *DISCOLORATION* OF THE PUPILS!

WHATEVER IT IS THEY'RE LOOKING FOR, THEY *HAVEN'T FOUND* IT!

SATISFIED THAT THE TROOPERS HAVE LEFT THE SANDCRAWLER, LUKE AND ANDUVIL INSPECT THE HUGE VEHICLE! *SUDDENLY...*

IT'S A SQUILL—!

IT'S OKAY! ...WOUND ISN'T DEEP! IT'LL HEAL—!

SQUILLS ARE *CARRIERS,* LUKE ... OF *BLEDSOE'S DISEASE!* YOU'RE ...IN FOR A *ROUGH TIME!*

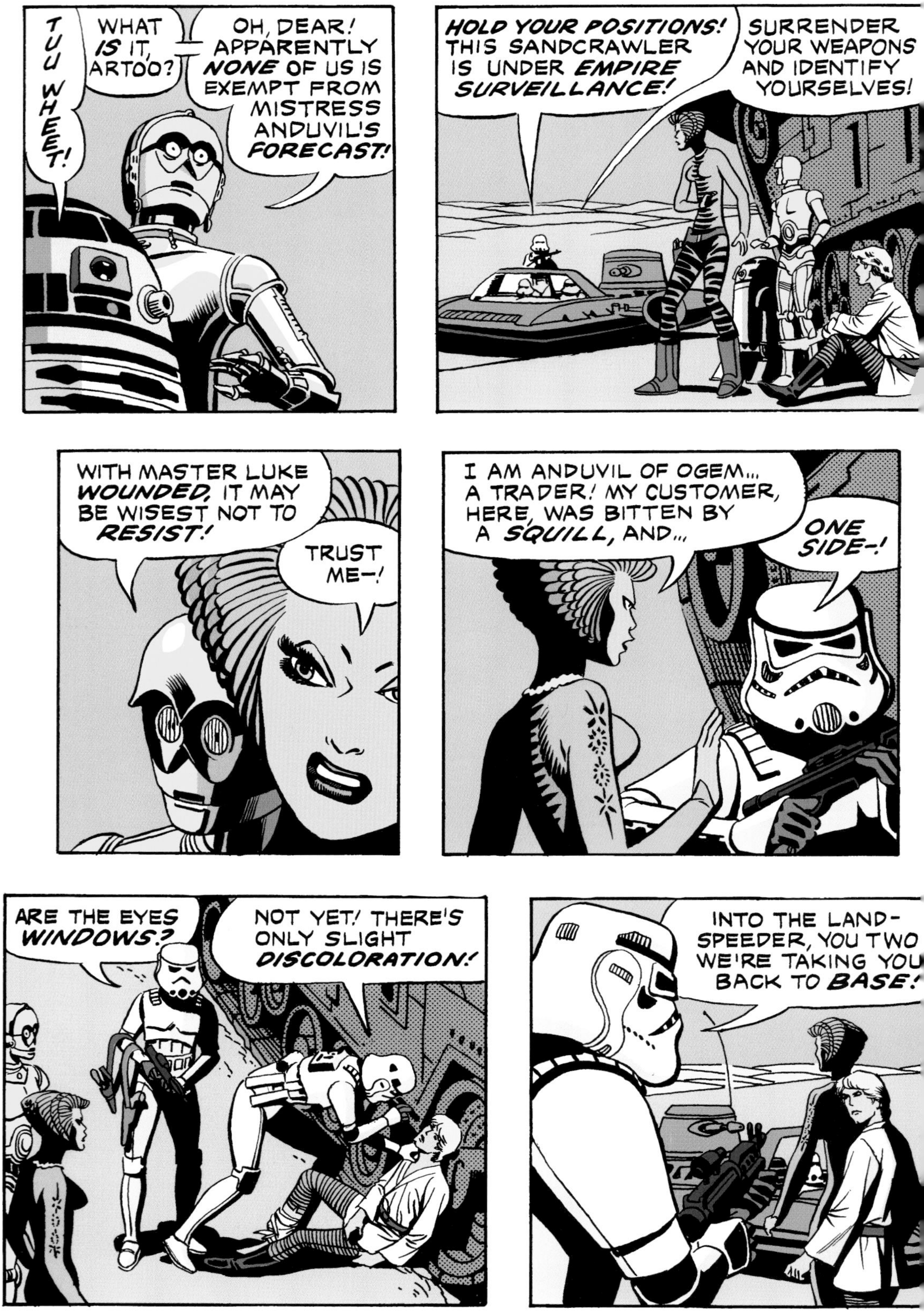
TUU WHEET!
WHAT IS IT, ARTOO?
OH, DEAR! APPARENTLY NONE OF US IS EXEMPT FROM MISTRESS ANDUVIL'S FORECAST!
HOLD YOUR POSITIONS! THIS SANDCRAWLER IS UNDER EMPIRE SURVEILLANCE!
SURRENDER YOUR WEAPONS AND IDENTIFY YOURSELVES!
WITH MASTER LUKE WOUNDED, IT MAY BE WISEST NOT TO RESIST!
TRUST ME--!
I AM ANDUVIL OF OGEM... A TRADER! MY CUSTOMER, HERE, WAS BITTEN BY A SQUILL, AND...
ONE SIDE--!
ARE THE EYES WINDOWS?
NOT YET! THERE'S ONLY SLIGHT DISCOLORATION!
INTO THE LAND-SPEEDER, YOU TWO WE'RE TAKING YOU BACK TO BASE!

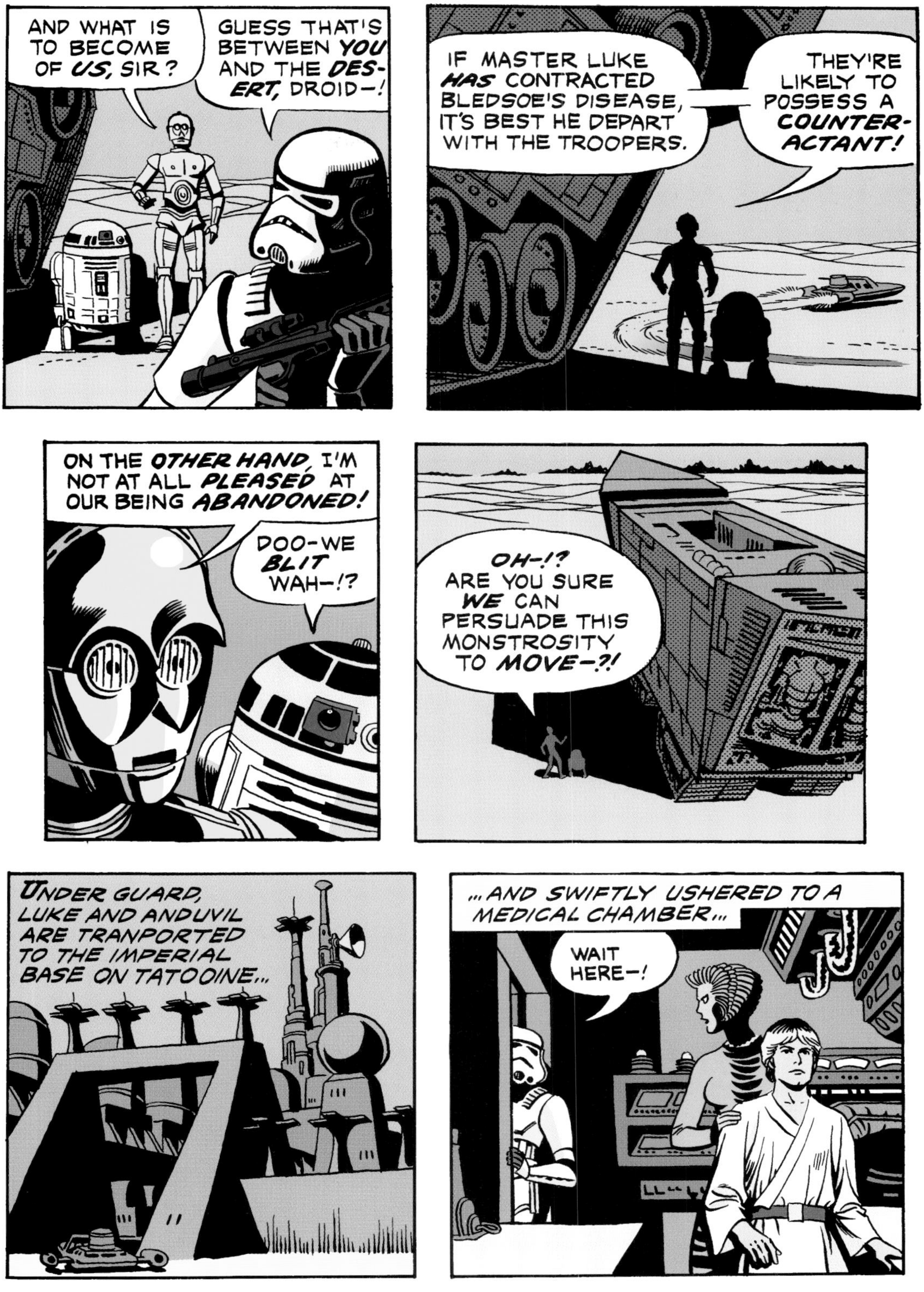
AND WHAT IS TO BECOME OF US, SIR?
GUESS THAT'S BETWEEN YOU AND THE DESERT, DROID—!
IF MASTER LUKE HAS CONTRACTED BLEDSOE'S DISEASE, IT'S BEST HE DEPART WITH THE TROOPERS.
THEY'RE LIKELY TO POSSESS A COUNTER-ACTANT!
ON THE OTHER HAND, I'M NOT AT ALL PLEASED AT OUR BEING ABANDONED!
DOO-WE BLIT WAH—!?
OH—!? ARE YOU SURE WE CAN PERSUADE THIS MONSTROSITY TO MOVE—?!
UNDER GUARD, LUKE AND ANDUVIL ARE TRANPORTED TO THE IMPERIAL BASE ON TATOOINE...
...AND SWIFTLY USHERED TO A MEDICAL CHAMBER...
WAIT HERE—!

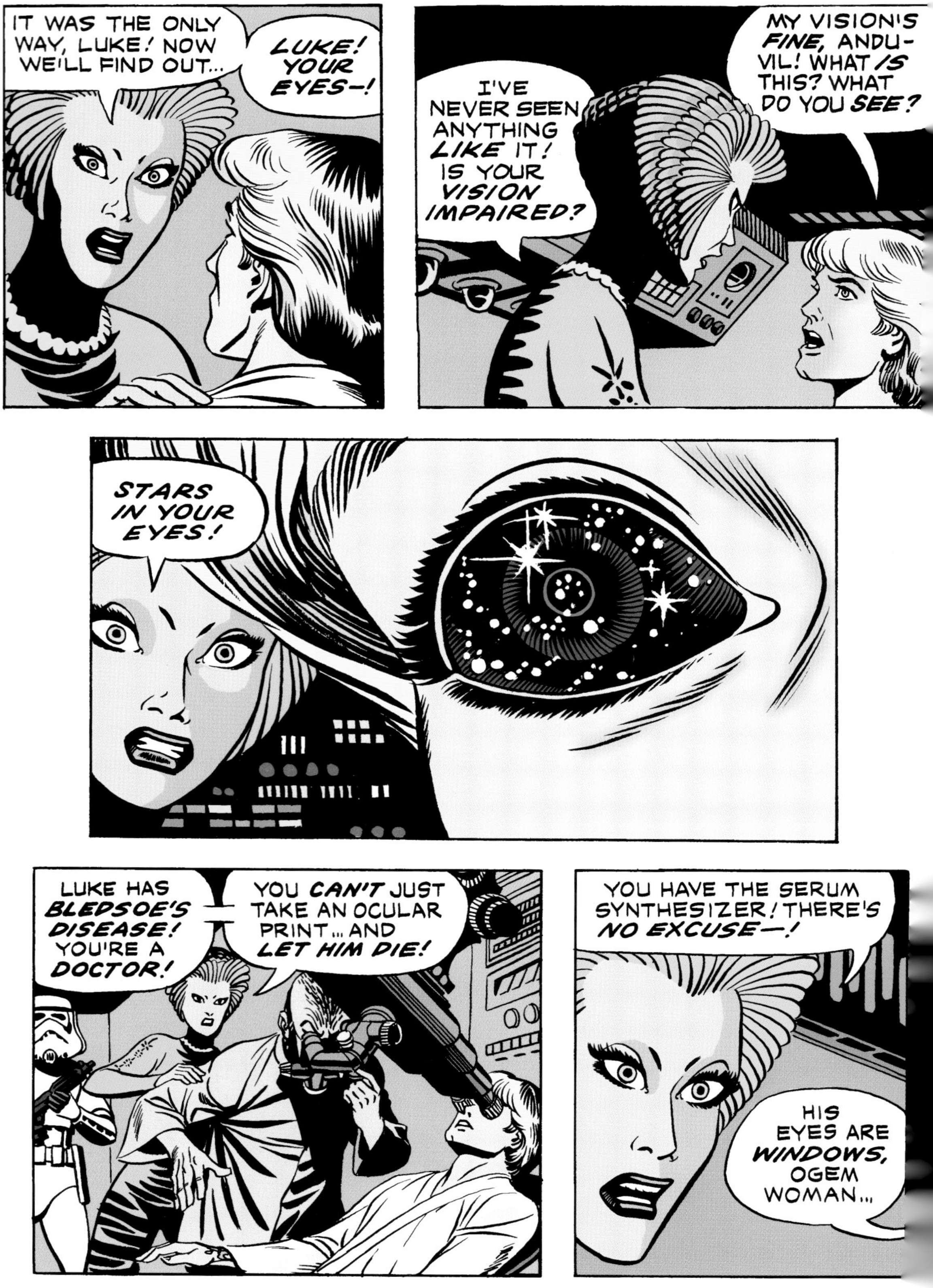

IT WAS THE ONLY WAY, LUKE! NOW WE'LL FIND OUT...
LUKE! YOUR EYES--!
I'VE NEVER SEEN ANYTHING LIKE IT! IS YOUR VISION IMPAIRED?
MY VISION'S FINE, ANDUVIL! WHAT IS THIS? WHAT DO YOU SEE?
STARS IN YOUR EYES!
LUKE HAS BLEDSOE'S DISEASE! YOU'RE A DOCTOR!
YOU CAN'T JUST TAKE AN OCULAR PRINT... AND LET HIM DIE!
YOU HAVE THE SERUM SYNTHESIZER! THERE'S NO EXCUSE--!
HIS EYES ARE WINDOWS, OGEM WOMAN...

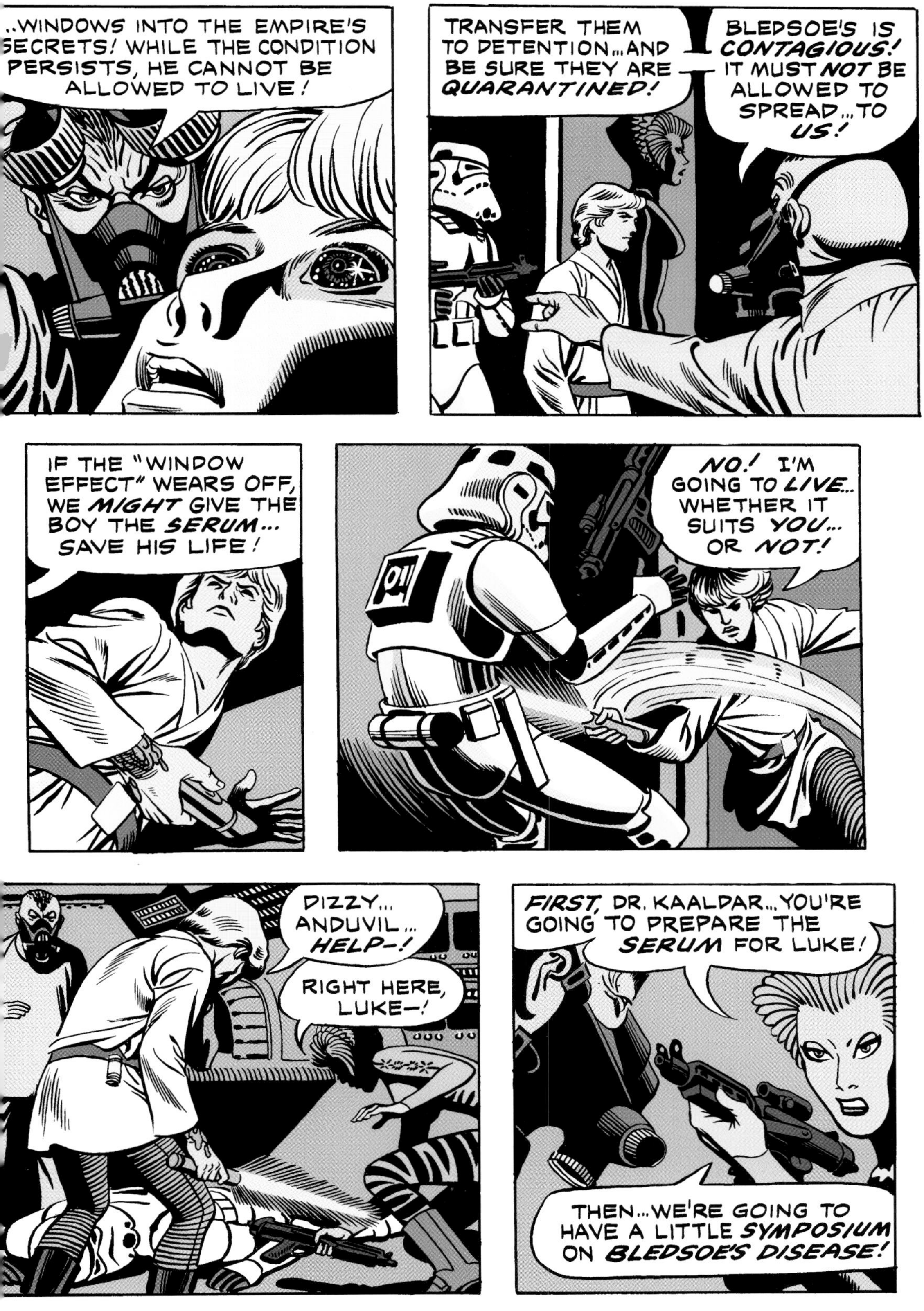
..WINDOWS INTO THE EMPIRE'S SECRETS! WHILE THE CONDITION PERSISTS, HE CANNOT BE ALLOWED TO LIVE!
TRANSFER THEM TO DETENTION...AND BE SURE THEY ARE QUARANTINED!
BLEDSOE'S IS CONTAGIOUS! IT MUST NOT BE ALLOWED TO SPREAD...TO US!
IF THE "WINDOW EFFECT" WEARS OFF, WE MIGHT GIVE THE BOY THE SERUM... SAVE HIS LIFE!
NO! I'M GOING TO LIVE... WHETHER IT SUITS YOU... OR NOT!
DIZZY... ANDUVIL... HELP-!
RIGHT HERE, LUKE-!
FIRST, DR. KAALDAR...YOU'RE GOING TO PREPARE THE SERUM FOR LUKE!
THEN...WE'RE GOING TO HAVE A LITTLE SYMPOSIUM ON BLEDSOE'S DISEASE!

A SHORT TIME LATER...

THERE... IT'S **DONE!** THE SERUM REQUIRES A BRIEF PERIOD TO TAKE EFFECT—!

GOOD! THAT GIVES **YOU** TIME TO SAVE **YOUR** LIFE!

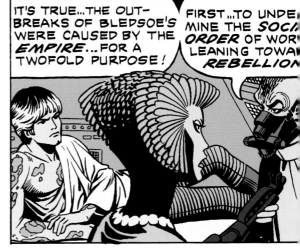

IT'S TRUE...THE OUT-BREAKS OF BLEDSOE'S WERE CAUSED BY THE **EMPIRE**...FOR A TWOFOLD PURPOSE!

FIRST...TO UNDER MINE THE **SOCIAL ORDER** OF WOR LEANING TOWA **REBELLION**

...AND ALSO TO TRANS-MIT THE **LOCATIONS** OF THE SECRET REBEL BASES!

I DON'T GET IT! **HOW?**

IN THE **EYES** OF THE VICTIMS! IT'S WHAT WE CALL THE **WINDOW EFFECT!**

THE EYES OF THE AFFLICTED SERVE AS **STAR MAPS!**

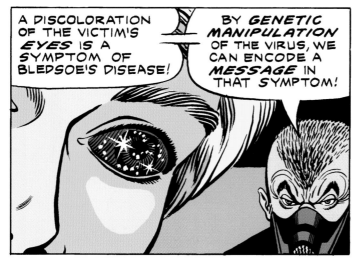

A DISCOLORATION OF THE VICTIM'S **EYES** IS A SYMPTOM OF BLEDSOE'S DISEASE!

BY **GENETIC MANIPULATION** OF THE VIRUS, WE CAN ENCODE A **MESSAGE** IN THAT SYMPTOM!

THE VIRUS BECOMES AN UNDETECTABLE COURIER OF **STAR CHARTS**...REVEAL-ING REBEL BASES FOR THE IMPERIAL SPACE FLEET TO **DESTROY!**

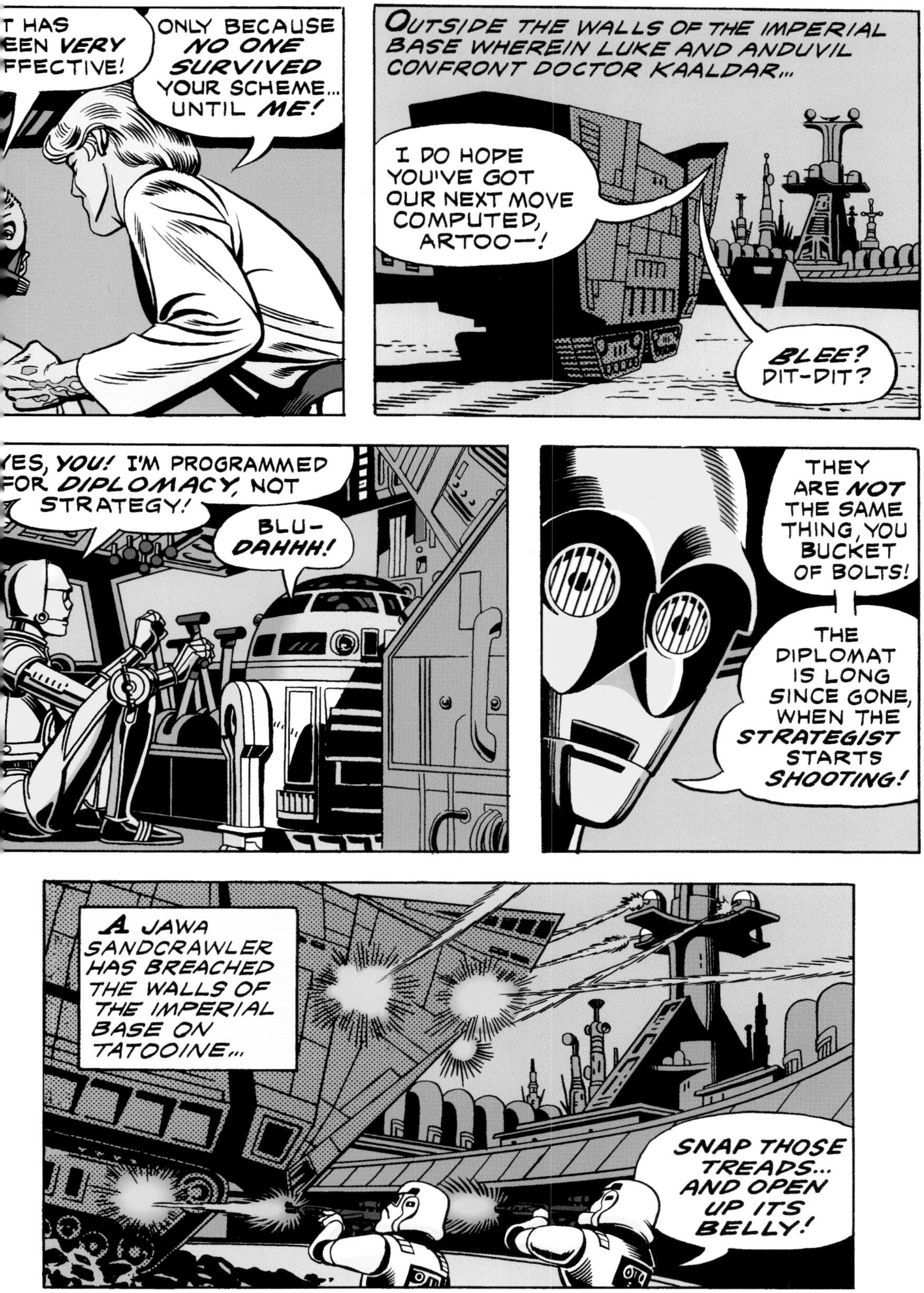
T HAS
EEN VERY
FFECTIVE!
ONLY BECAUSE NO ONE SURVIVED YOUR SCHEME... UNTIL ME!
OUTSIDE THE WALLS OF THE IMPERIAL BASE WHEREIN LUKE AND ANDUVIL CONFRONT DOCTOR KAALDAR...
I DO HOPE YOU'VE GOT OUR NEXT MOVE COMPUTED, ARTOO—!
BLEE? DIT-DIT?
YES, YOU! I'M PROGRAMMED FOR DIPLOMACY, NOT STRATEGY!
BLU-DAHHH!
THEY ARE NOT THE SAME THING, YOU BUCKET OF BOLTS!
THE DIPLOMAT IS LONG SINCE GONE, WHEN THE STRATEGIST STARTS SHOOTING!
A JAWA SANDCRAWLER HAS BREACHED THE WALLS OF THE IMPERIAL BASE ON TATOOINE...
SNAP THOSE TREADS... AND OPEN UP ITS BELLY!

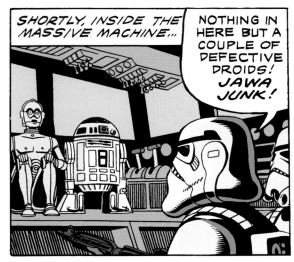

SHORTLY, INSIDE THE MASSIVE MACHINE...

NOTHING IN HERE BUT A COUPLE OF DEFECTIVE DROIDS! *JAWA JUNK!*

ONE 3PO, ONE R2 UNIT. COMMANDER! THERE'S NOTHING *ALIVE* IN THAT CRAWLER!

VERY WELL...DISPO OF THE DROIDS! AND TOW THAT HEA BACK OUT INTO THE DESERT!

IT'S *THREEPIO* AND *ARTOO!* I *CAN'T* LET THEM BE *SMELTED!*

YOU CAN'T LET *YOURSELF* BE *DISINTEGRATED*, EITHER—!

MAY THE *FORCE* BE WITH YOU, SKYWALKER!

UNLESS *I* FIND SOMETHING MORE *PRACTICAL*, YOU'RE GOING TO *NEED* IT!

ORDER YOUR MEN TO *RELEASE* THOSE DROIDS, COMMANDER... OR THIS COULD BECOME *VERY MESSY*—!

AAGH! WHAT *IS* THIS? WHO ARE *YOU*—?!

JUST A RUN OF THE MILL REBEL...WITH *BLEDSOE'S DISEASE!*

PUT A *RUSH* ON THAT ORDER, COMMANDER! I AM *STILL* CONTAGIOUS

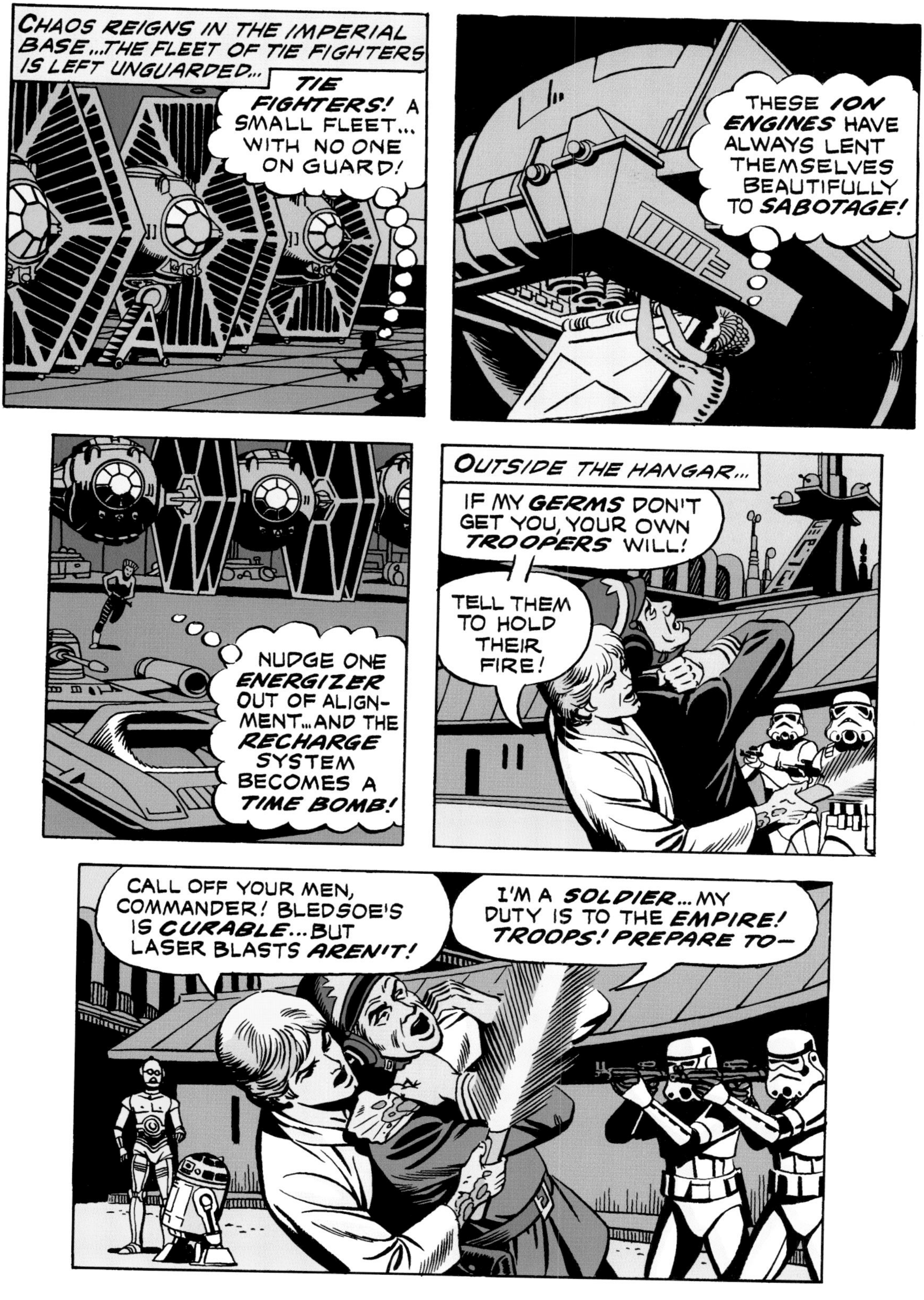
CHAOS REIGNS IN THE IMPERIAL BASE...THE FLEET OF TIE FIGHTERS IS LEFT UNGUARDED...
TIE FIGHTERS! A SMALL FLEET... WITH NO ONE ON GUARD!
THESE ION ENGINES HAVE ALWAYS LENT THEMSELVES BEAUTIFULLY TO SABOTAGE!
NUDGE ONE ENERGIZER OUT OF ALIGN-MENT...AND THE RECHARGE SYSTEM BECOMES A TIME BOMB!
OUTSIDE THE HANGAR...
IF MY GERMS DON'T GET YOU, YOUR OWN TROOPERS WILL!
TELL THEM TO HOLD THEIR FIRE!
CALL OFF YOUR MEN, COMMANDER! BLEDSOE'S IS CURABLE...BUT LASER BLASTS AREN'T!
I'M A SOLDIER...MY DUTY IS TO THE EMPIRE! TROOPS! PREPARE TO—

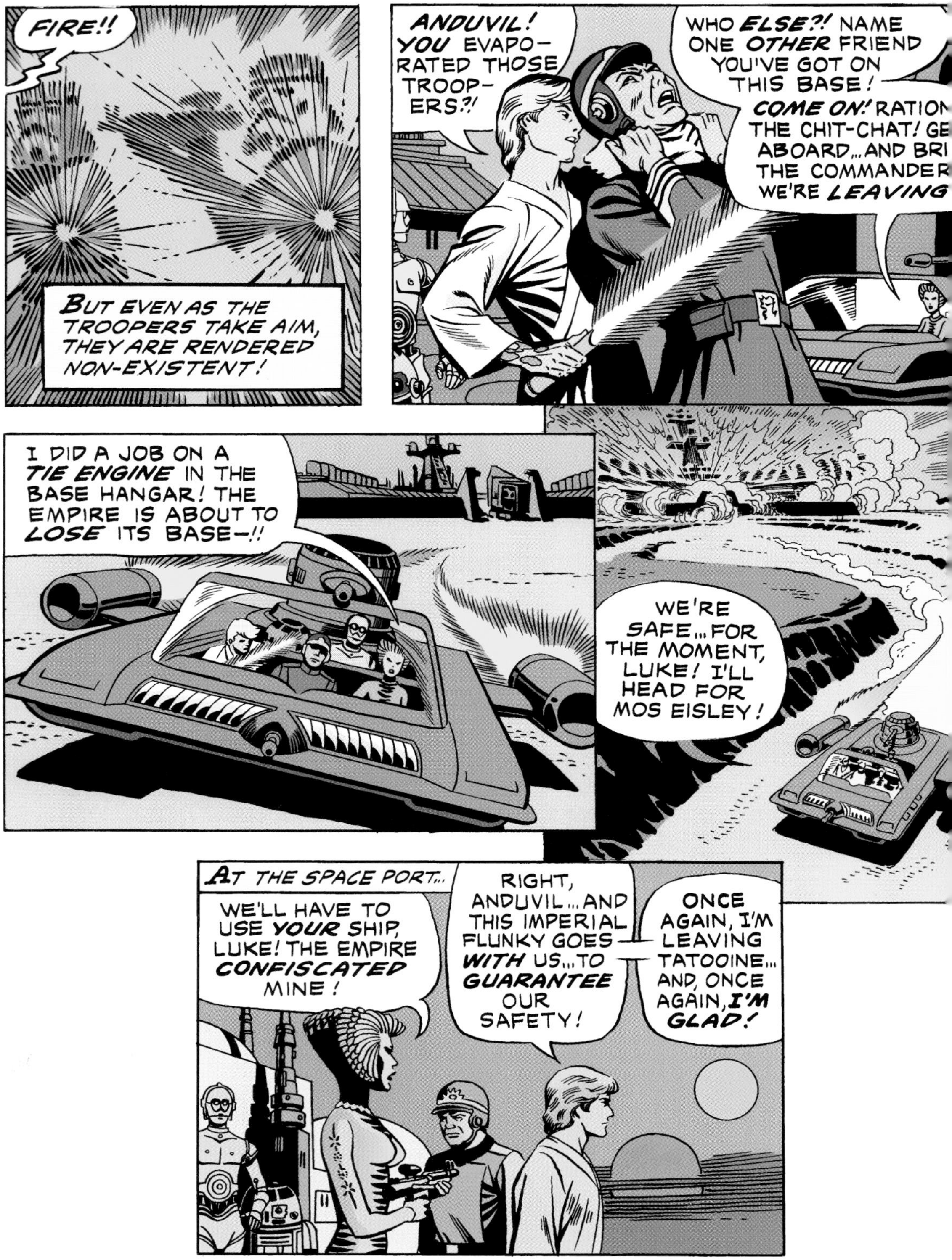
FIRE!!
BUT EVEN AS THE TROOPERS TAKE AIM, THEY ARE RENDERED NON-EXISTENT!
ANDUVIL! YOU EVAPO-RATED THOSE TROOP-ERS?!
WHO ELSE?! NAME ONE OTHER FRIEND YOU'VE GOT ON THIS BASE!
COME ON! RATION THE CHIT-CHAT! GE ABOARD... AND BRI THE COMMANDER WE'RE LEAVING
I DID A JOB ON A TIE ENGINE IN THE BASE HANGAR! THE EMPIRE IS ABOUT TO LOSE ITS BASE-!!
WE'RE SAFE... FOR THE MOMENT, LUKE! I'LL HEAD FOR MOS EISLEY!
AT THE SPACE PORT...
WE'LL HAVE TO USE YOUR SHIP, LUKE! THE EMPIRE CONFISCATED MINE!
RIGHT, ANDUVIL... AND THIS IMPERIAL FLUNKY GOES WITH US... TO GUARANTEE OUR SAFETY!
ONCE AGAIN, I'M LEAVING TATOOINE... AND, ONCE AGAIN, I'M GLAD!

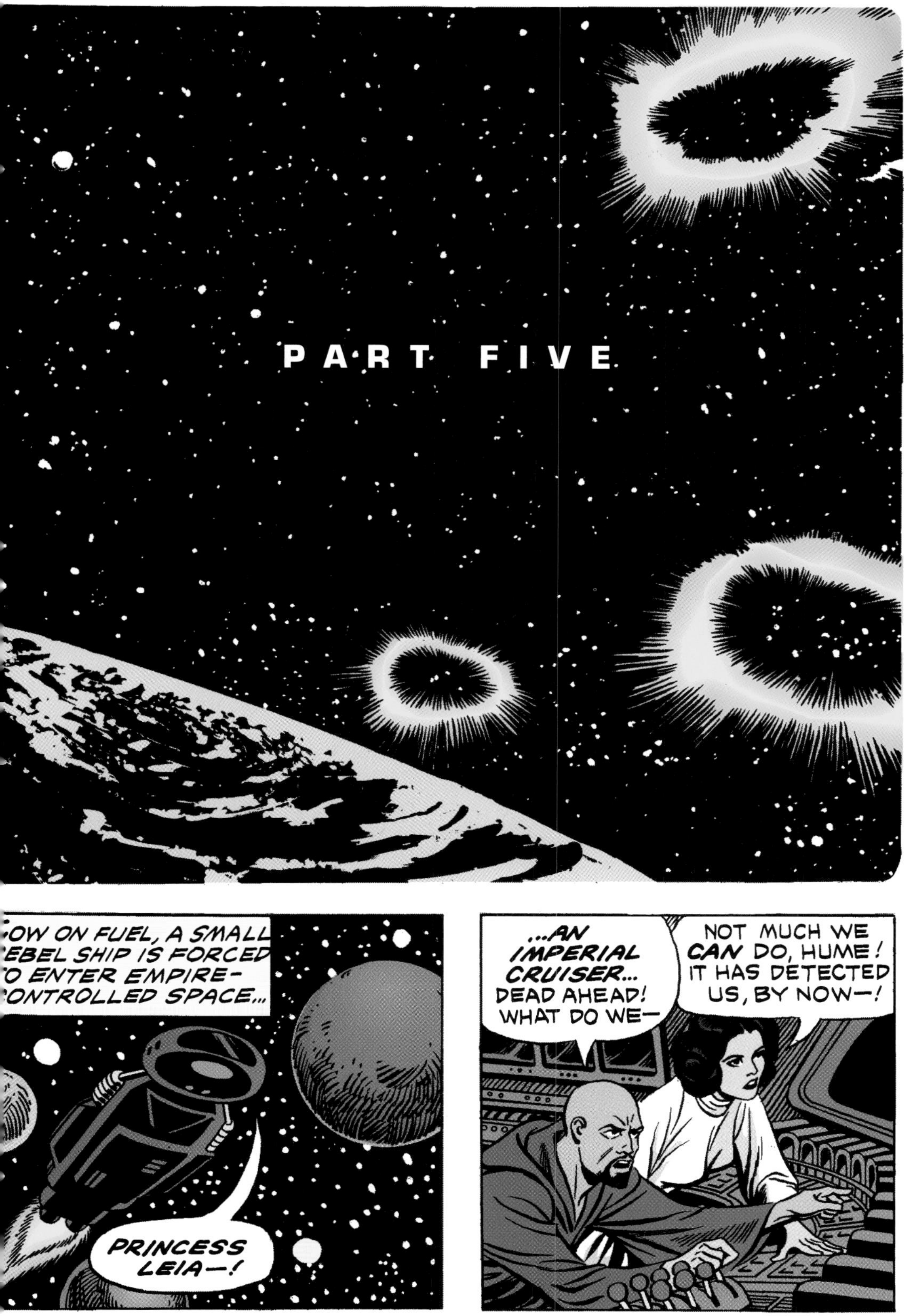
PART FIVE
OW ON FUEL, A SMALL EBEL SHIP IS FORCED O ENTER EMPIRE-ONTROLLED SPACE...
PRINCESS LEIA—!
...AN IMPERIAL CRUISER... DEAD AHEAD! WHAT DO WE—
NOT MUCH WE CAN DO, HUME! IT HAS DETECTED US, BY NOW—!

LORD VADER! UNIDENTIFIED CRAFT IN QUADRANT T²/5/ZERO!

NONE OF *OUR* SHIPS ARE IN THAT SECTOR, LORD VADER!

LAUNCH A *TIE FIGHTER* TO INVESTIGATE, *IMMEDIATELY!*

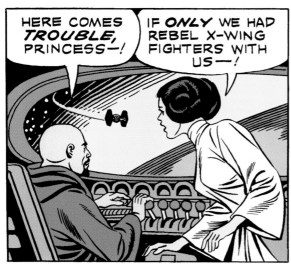

HERE COMES *TROUBLE,* PRINCESS—!

IF *ONLY* WE HAD REBEL X-WING FIGHTERS WITH US—!

WE HAVE *ONE* CHANCE, YOUR HIGHNESS! YOU CAN ESCAPE TO PHELARION IN THE GOSSAMER GLIDER!

NO, HUME! REFUSE TO LE, YOU TO THOS IMPERIAL *CU THROATS*

TIE FIGHTER ZG-35 TO COMMANDER! IDENTIFICATION OF INTRUDER CONFIRMED...CRAFT IS A REBEL *SHUTTLE!*

DISABLE THE SHUTT ZG-35! I WANT THOSE REBEL TAKEN *ALIVE*

HERE IT COMES, PRINCESS LEIA—! ...NO WAY FOR US TO ESCAPE...ON THE FUEL I HAVE LEFT—!
IT'S ON OUR TAIL! TURN LEFT, HUME!
I'M TRYING, PRINCESS! ...BUT THIS CRATE WASN'T MADE FOR FAST MANEUVERS!
WE'RE HIT! ...LOSING POWER—
THEN WE GO OUT FIGHTING, HUME! TRY TO—
FORGIVE ME, HIGHNESS!
THUD!
GUISING THE UNCONSCIOUS LEIA
IS OWN ROBE, HUME CARRIES HER
O AN AIR-LOCK AND PLACES HER
A GOSSAMER GLIDER...
GOOD LUCK, HIGHNESS!
THEN HE EJECTS HER!
YOU'LL NEED LUCK... ...THAT PLANET BELOW IS AN IMPERIAL LABOR COLONY!

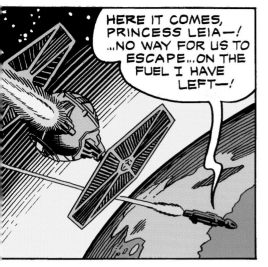

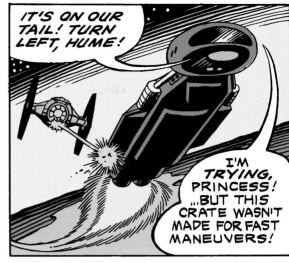

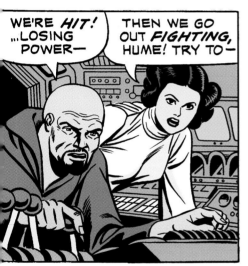

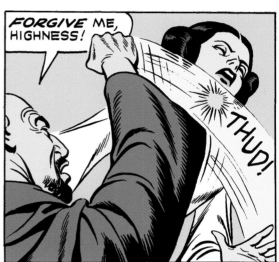

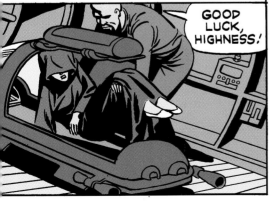

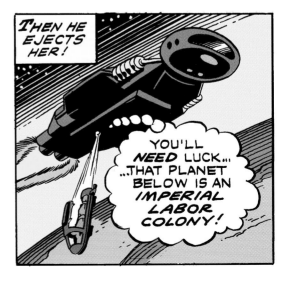

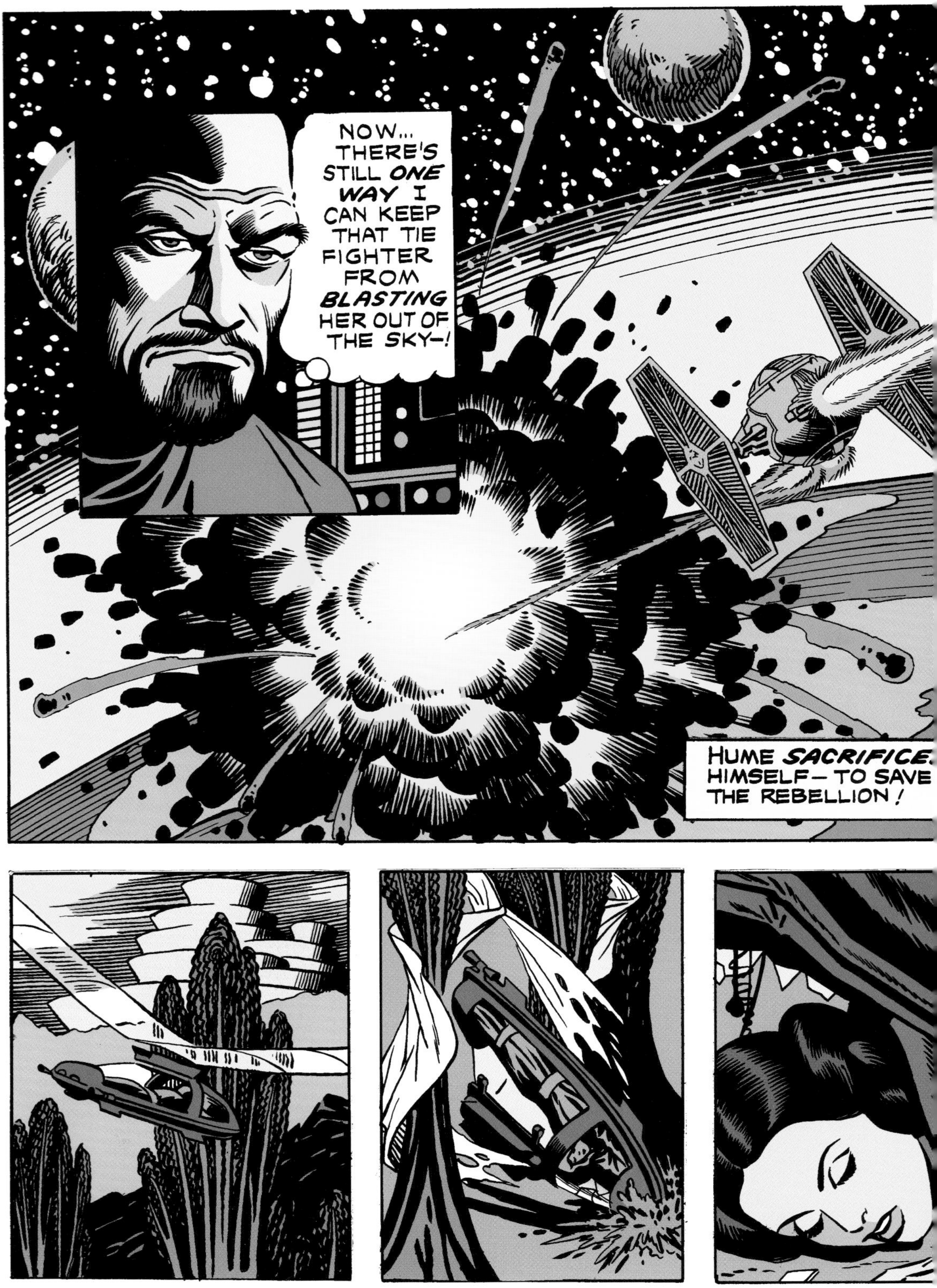
NOW... THERE'S STILL ONE WAY I CAN KEEP THAT TIE FIGHTER FROM BLASTING HER OUT OF THE SKY--!
HUME SACRIFICE HIMSELF-- TO SAVE THE REBELLION!

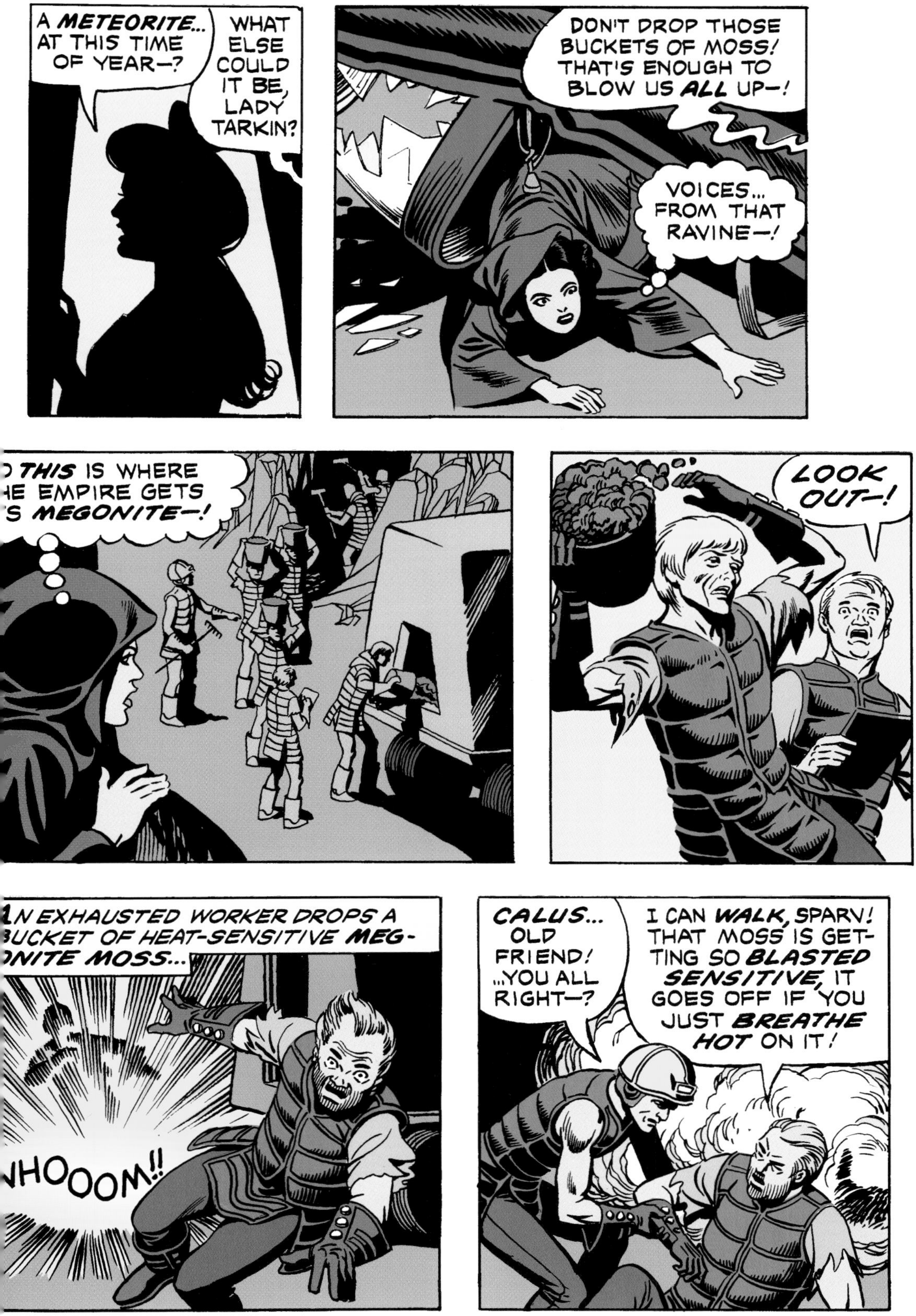
A METEORITE... AT THIS TIME OF YEAR—?
WHAT ELSE COULD IT BE, LADY TARKIN?
DON'T DROP THOSE BUCKETS OF MOSS! THAT'S ENOUGH TO BLOW US ALL UP—!
VOICES... FROM THAT RAVINE—!
THIS IS WHERE HE EMPIRE GETS 'S MEGONITE—!
LOOK OUT—!
N EXHAUSTED WORKER DROPS A BUCKET OF HEAT-SENSITIVE MEG-ONITE MOSS...
HOOOM!!
CALUS... OLD FRIEND! ...YOU ALL RIGHT—?
I CAN WALK, SPARV! THAT MOSS IS GETTING SO BLASTED SENSITIVE, IT GOES OFF IF YOU JUST BREATHE HOT ON IT!

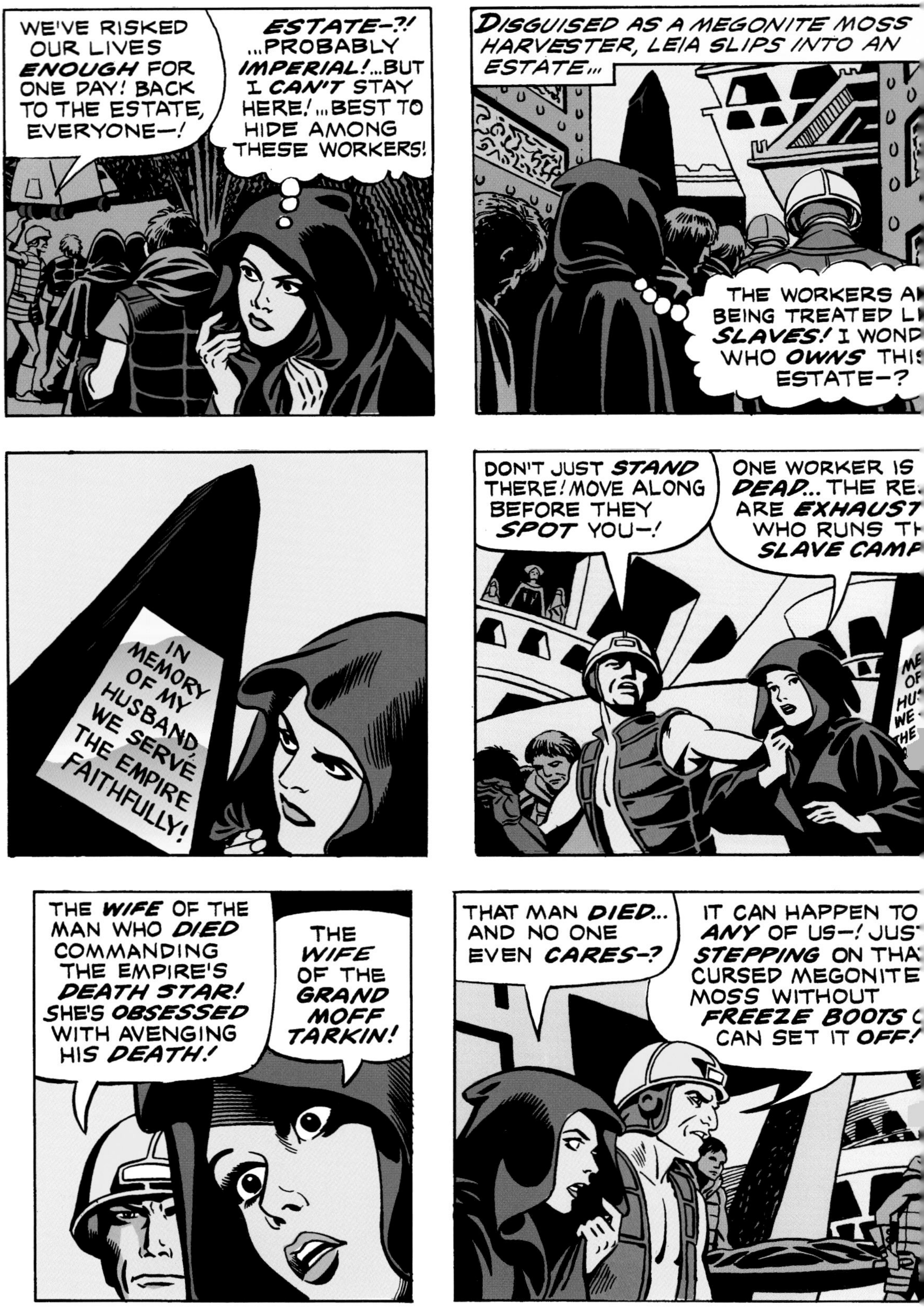
WE'VE RISKED OUR LIVES ENOUGH FOR ONE DAY! BACK TO THE ESTATE, EVERYONE—!
ESTATE—?! ...PROBABLY IMPERIAL!...BUT I CAN'T STAY HERE! ...BEST TO HIDE AMONG THESE WORKERS!
DISGUISED AS A MEGONITE MOSS HARVESTER, LEIA SLIPS INTO AN ESTATE...
THE WORKERS A BEING TREATED L SLAVES! I WOND WHO OWNS THIS ESTATE—?
IN MEMORY OF MY HUSBAND, WE SERVE THE EMPIRE FAITHFULLY!
DON'T JUST STAND THERE! MOVE ALONG BEFORE THEY SPOT YOU—!
ONE WORKER IS DEAD... THE RE ARE EXHAUST WHO RUNS TH SLAVE CAMP
THE WIFE OF THE MAN WHO DIED COMMANDING THE EMPIRE'S DEATH STAR! SHE'S OBSESSED WITH AVENGING HIS DEATH!
THE WIFE OF THE GRAND MOFF TARKIN!
THAT MAN DIED... AND NO ONE EVEN CARES—?
IT CAN HAPPEN TO ANY OF US—! JUS STEPPING ON THA CURSED MEGONITE MOSS WITHOUT FREEZE BOOTS CAN SET IT OFF!

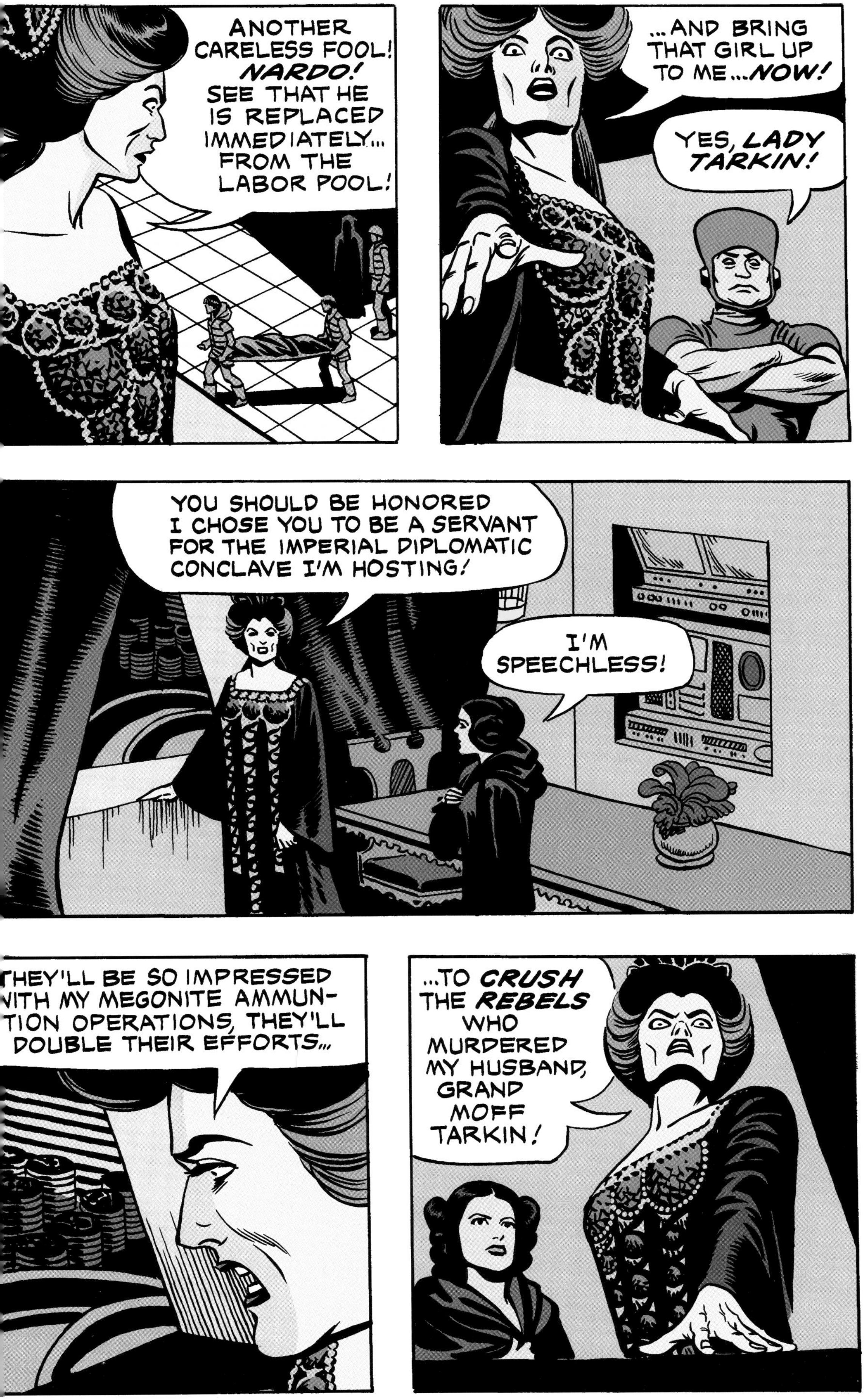
ANOTHER CARELESS FOOL! NARDO! SEE THAT HE IS REPLACED IMMEDIATELY... FROM THE LABOR POOL!
...AND BRING THAT GIRL UP TO ME...NOW!
YES, LADY TARKIN!
YOU SHOULD BE HONORED I CHOSE YOU TO BE A SERVANT FOR THE IMPERIAL DIPLOMATIC CONCLAVE I'M HOSTING!
I'M SPEECHLESS!
THEY'LL BE SO IMPRESSED WITH MY MEGONITE AMMUNITION OPERATIONS, THEY'LL DOUBLE THEIR EFFORTS...
...TO CRUSH THE REBELS WHO MURDERED MY HUSBAND, GRAND MOFF TARKIN!

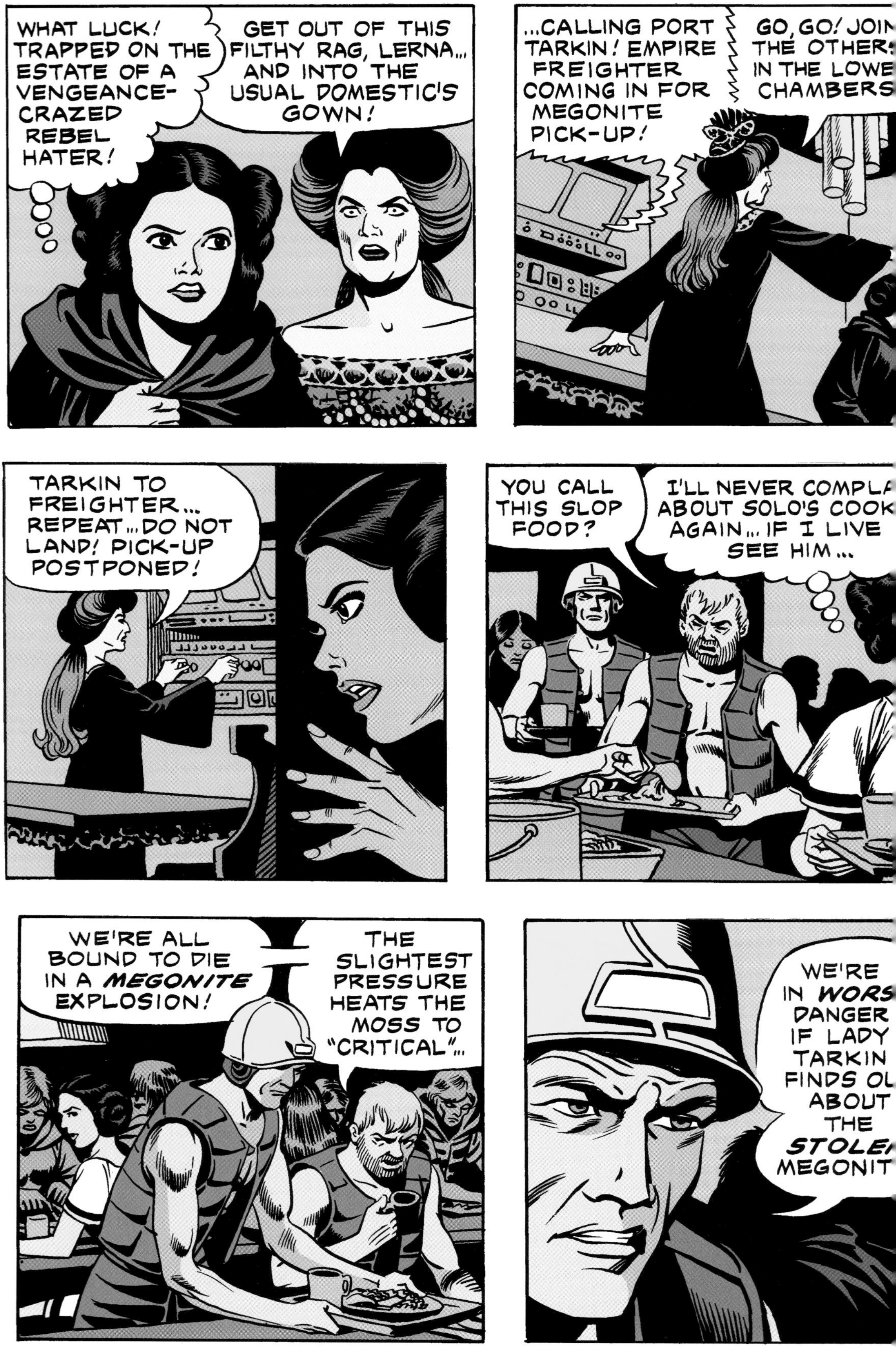
WHAT LUCK! TRAPPED ON THE ESTATE OF A VENGEANCE-CRAZED REBEL HATER!
GET OUT OF THIS FILTHY RAG, LERNA... AND INTO THE USUAL DOMESTIC'S GOWN!
...CALLING PORT TARKIN! EMPIRE FREIGHTER COMING IN FOR MEGONITE PICK-UP!
GO, GO! JOIN THE OTHER IN THE LOWE CHAMBERS
TARKIN TO FREIGHTER... REPEAT... DO NOT LAND! PICK-UP POSTPONED!
YOU CALL THIS SLOP FOOD?
I'LL NEVER COMPL ABOUT SOLO'S COOK AGAIN... IF I LIVE SEE HIM...
WE'RE ALL BOUND TO DIE IN A *MEGONITE* EXPLOSION!
THE SLIGHTEST PRESSURE HEATS THE MOSS TO "CRITICAL"...
WE'RE IN *WORS* DANGER IF LADY TARKIN FINDS OU ABOUT THE *STOLE* MEGONIT

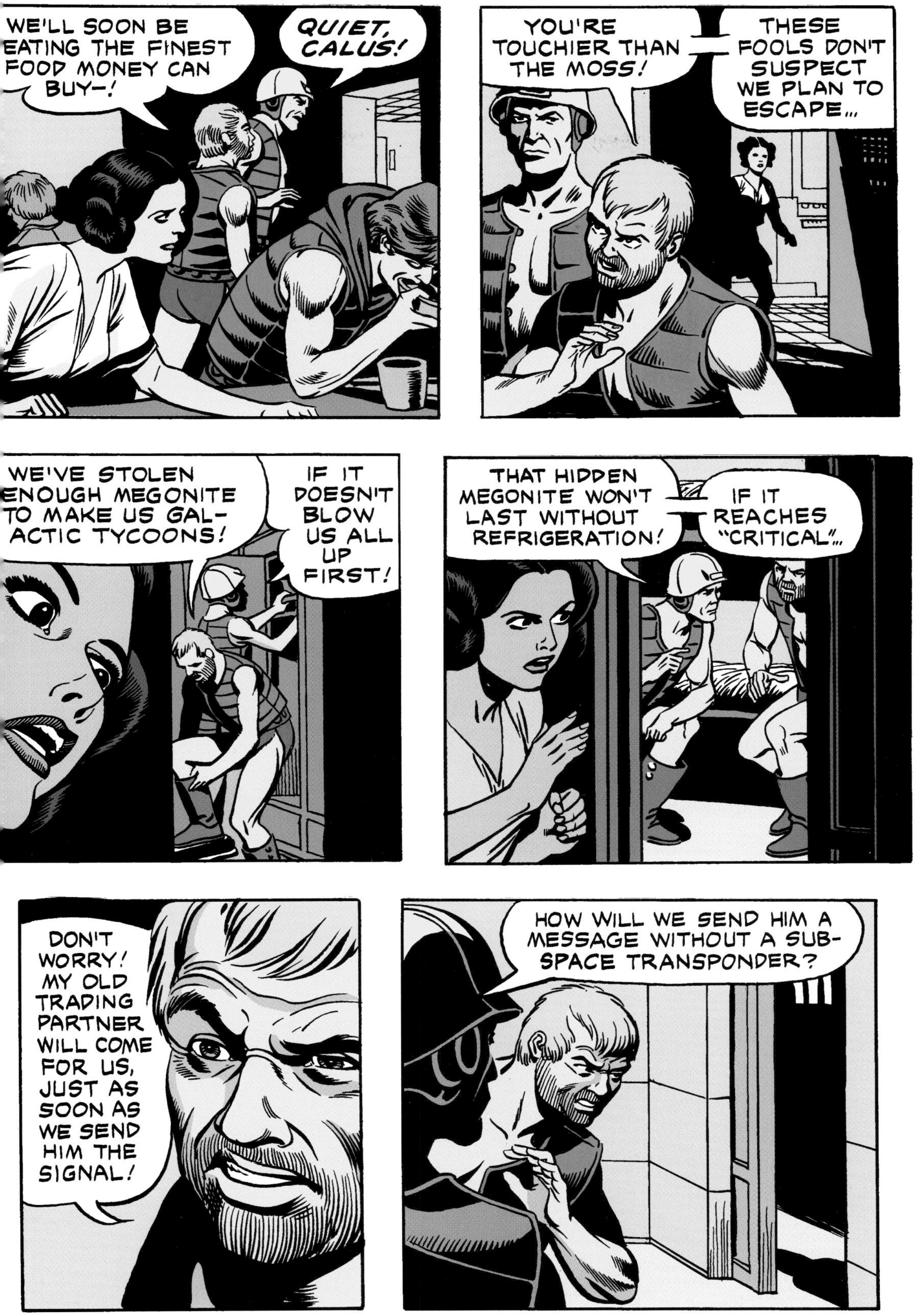
WE'LL SOON BE EATING THE FINEST FOOD MONEY CAN BUY-!
QUIET, CALUS!
YOU'RE TOUCHIER THAN THE MOSS!
THESE FOOLS DON'T SUSPECT WE PLAN TO ESCAPE...
WE'VE STOLEN ENOUGH MEGONITE TO MAKE US GAL-ACTIC TYCOONS!
IF IT DOESN'T BLOW US ALL UP FIRST!
THAT HIDDEN MEGONITE WON'T LAST WITHOUT REFRIGERATION!
IF IT REACHES "CRITICAL"...
DON'T WORRY! MY OLD TRADING PARTNER WILL COME FOR US, JUST AS SOON AS WE SEND HIM THE SIGNAL!
HOW WILL WE SEND HIM A MESSAGE WITHOUT A SUB-SPACE TRANSPONDER?

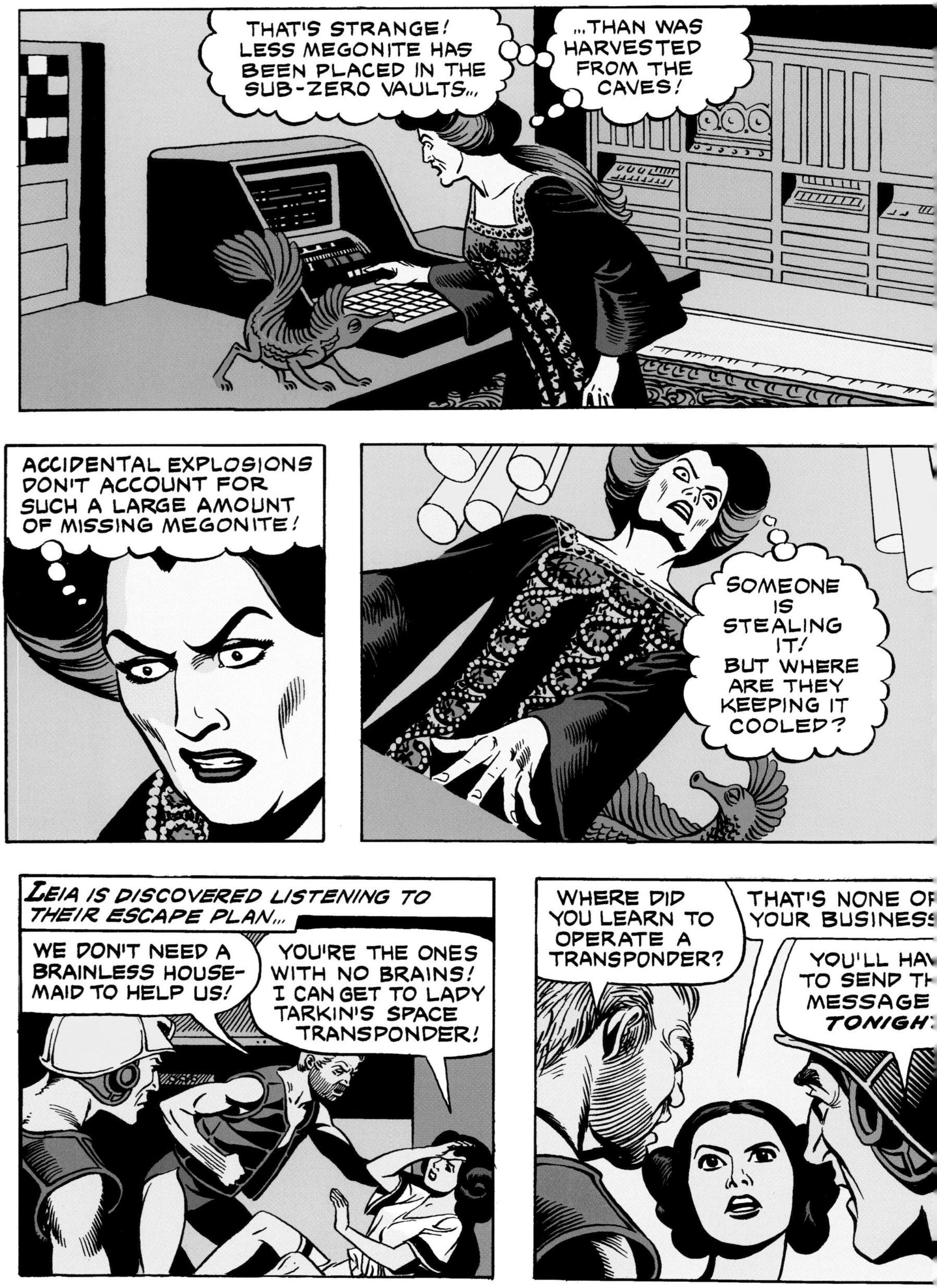
THAT'S STRANGE! LESS MEGONITE HAS BEEN PLACED IN THE SUB-ZERO VAULTS...
...THAN WAS HARVESTED FROM THE CAVES!
ACCIDENTAL EXPLOSIONS DON'T ACCOUNT FOR SUCH A LARGE AMOUNT OF MISSING MEGONITE!
SOMEONE IS STEALING IT! BUT WHERE ARE THEY KEEPING IT COOLED?
LEIA IS DISCOVERED LISTENING TO THEIR ESCAPE PLAN...
WE DON'T NEED A BRAINLESS HOUSE-MAID TO HELP US!
YOU'RE THE ONES WITH NO BRAINS! I CAN GET TO LADY TARKIN'S SPACE TRANSPONDER!
WHERE DID YOU LEARN TO OPERATE A TRANSPONDER?

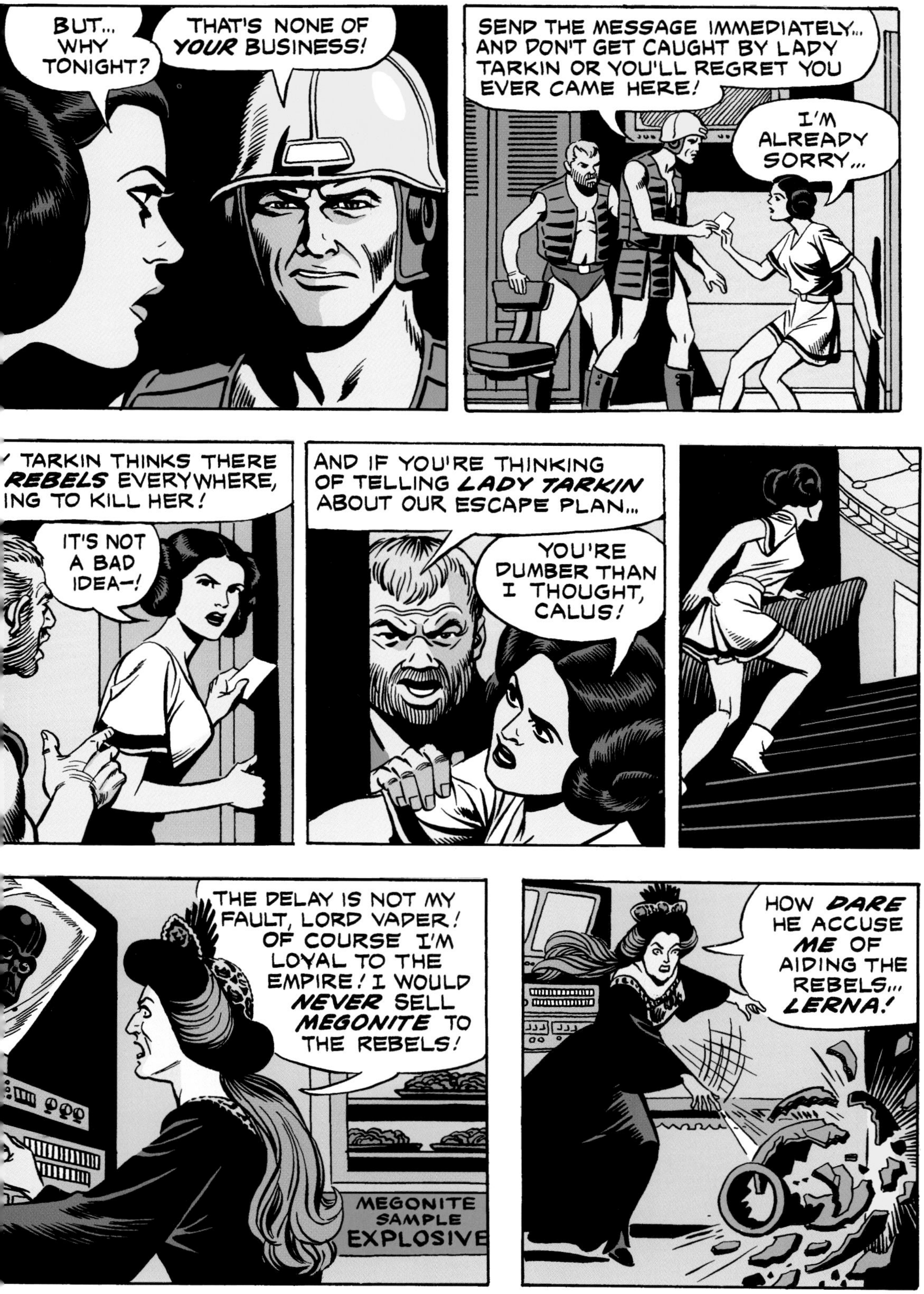
BUT... WHY TONIGHT?
THAT'S NONE OF YOUR BUSINESS!
SEND THE MESSAGE IMMEDIATELY... AND DON'T GET CAUGHT BY LADY TARKIN OR YOU'LL REGRET YOU EVER CAME HERE!
I'M ALREADY SORRY...
TARKIN THINKS THERE REBELS EVERYWHERE, ING TO KILL HER!
IT'S NOT A BAD IDEA--!
AND IF YOU'RE THINKING OF TELLING LADY TARKIN ABOUT OUR ESCAPE PLAN...
YOU'RE DUMBER THAN I THOUGHT, CALUS!
THE DELAY IS NOT MY FAULT, LORD VADER! OF COURSE I'M LOYAL TO THE EMPIRE! I WOULD NEVER SELL MEGONITE TO THE REBELS!
MEGONITE SAMPLE EXPLOSIVE
HOW DARE HE ACCUSE ME OF AIDING THE REBELS... LERNA!

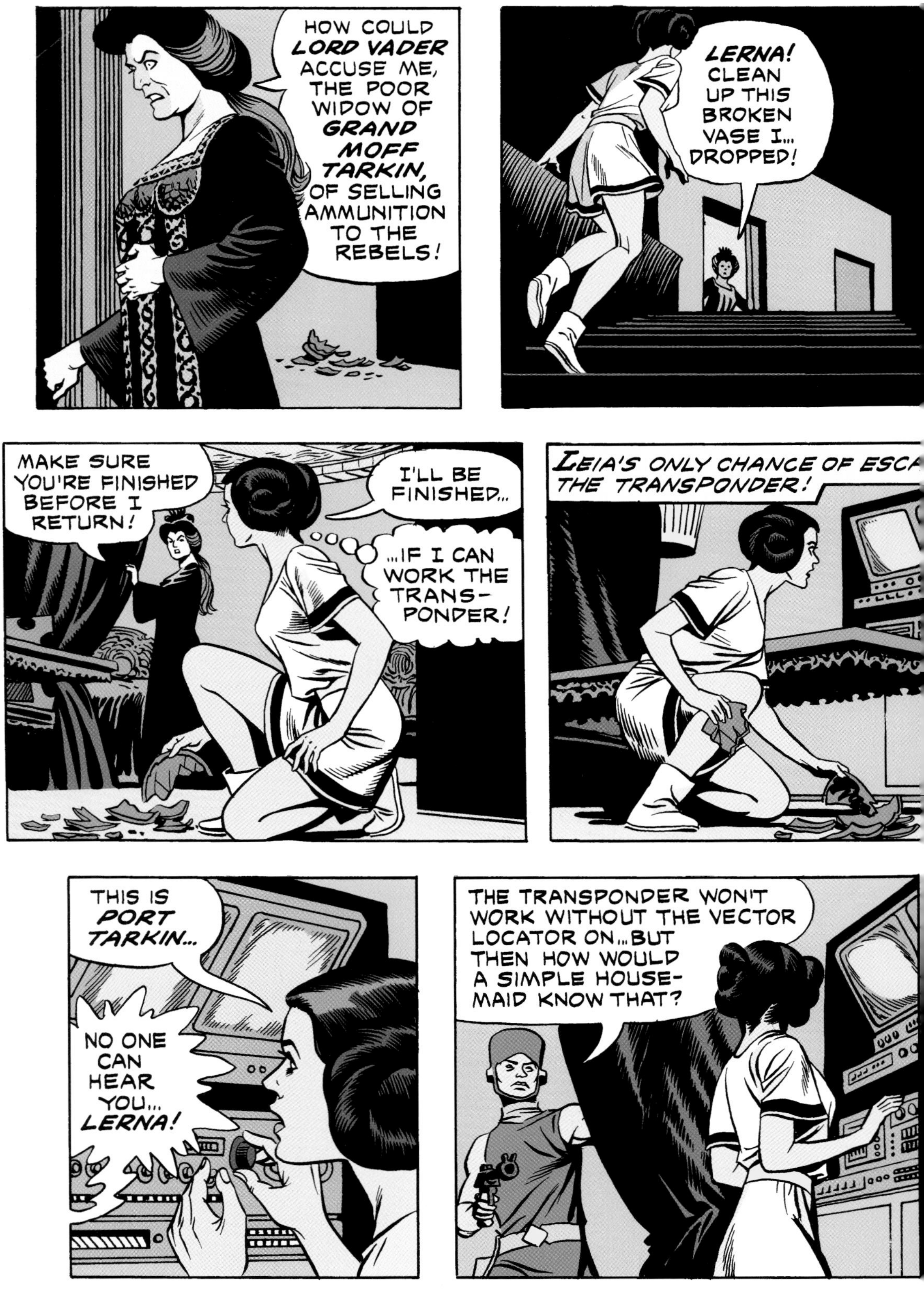
HOW COULD LORD VADER ACCUSE ME, THE POOR WIDOW OF GRAND MOFF TARKIN, OF SELLING AMMUNITION TO THE REBELS!
LERNA! CLEAN UP THIS BROKEN VASE I... DROPPED!
MAKE SURE YOU'RE FINISHED BEFORE I RETURN!
I'LL BE FINISHED...
...IF I CAN WORK THE TRANS- PONDER!
LEIA'S ONLY CHANCE OF ESCA
THE TRANSPONDER!
THIS IS PORT TARKIN...
NO ONE CAN HEAR YOU... LERNA!
THE TRANSPONDER WON'T WORK WITHOUT THE VECTOR LOCATOR ON... BUT THEN HOW WOULD A SIMPLE HOUSE- MAID KNOW THAT?

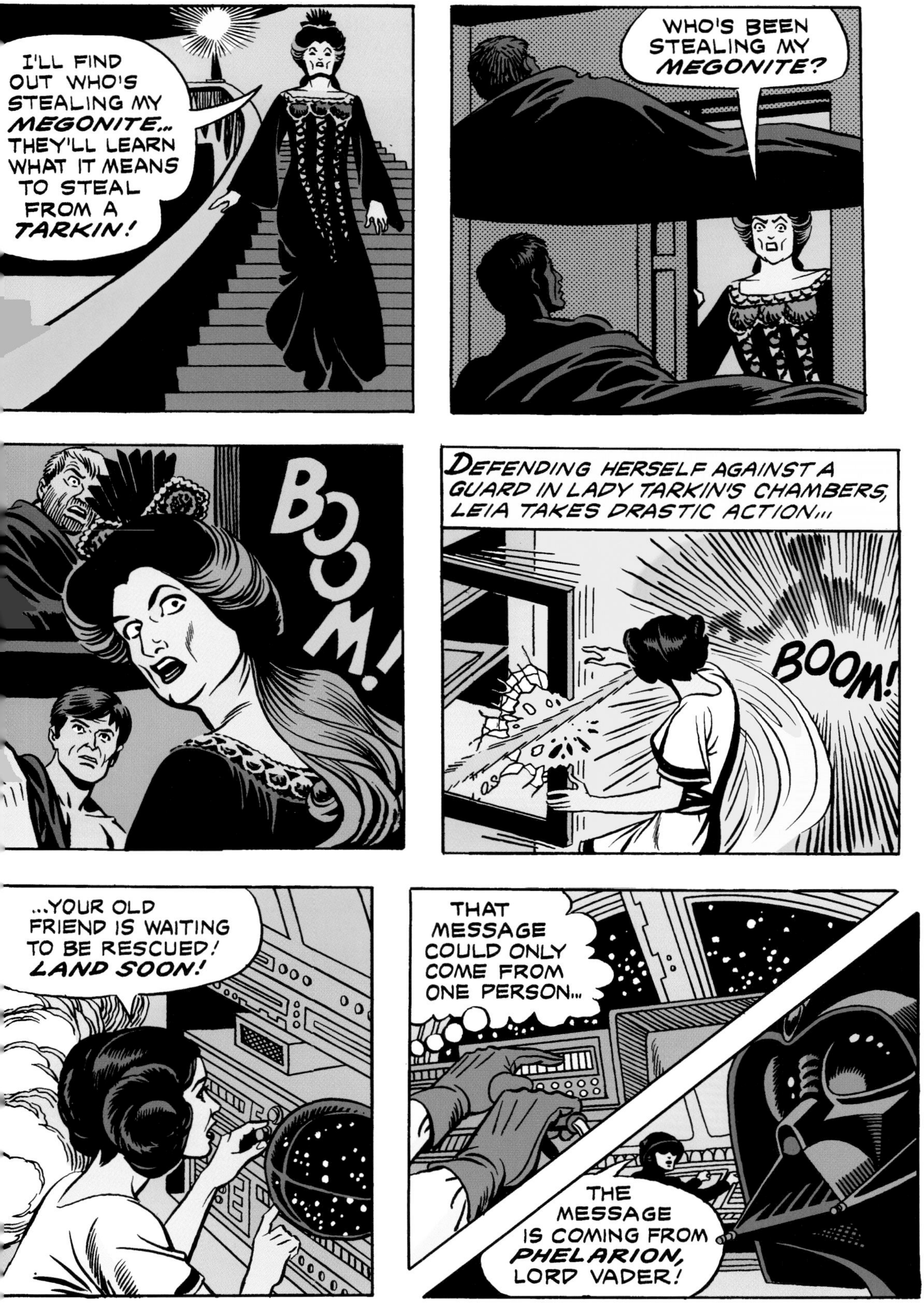
I'LL FIND OUT WHO'S STEALING MY MEGONITE... THEY'LL LEARN WHAT IT MEANS TO STEAL FROM A TARKIN!
WHO'S BEEN STEALING MY MEGONITE?
BOOM!
DEFENDING HERSELF AGAINST A GUARD IN LADY TARKIN'S CHAMBERS, LEIA TAKES DRASTIC ACTION...
BOOM!
...YOUR OLD FRIEND IS WAITING TO BE RESCUED! LAND SOON!
THAT MESSAGE COULD ONLY COME FROM ONE PERSON...
THE MESSAGE IS COMING FROM PHELARION, LORD VADER!

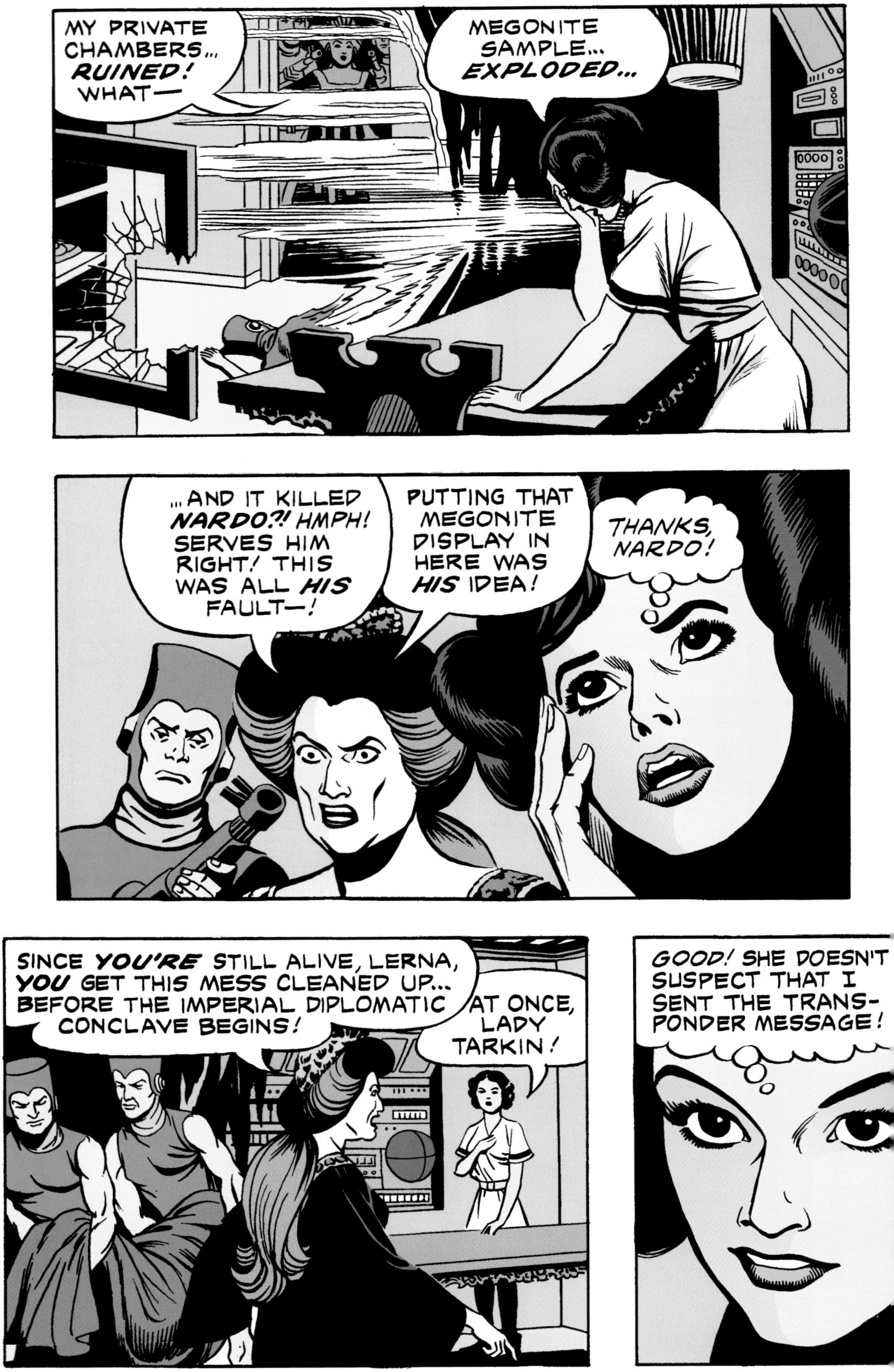
MY PRIVATE CHAMBERS... RUINED! WHAT—
MEGONITE SAMPLE... EXPLODED...
...AND IT KILLED NARDO?! HMPH! SERVES HIM RIGHT! THIS WAS ALL HIS FAULT—!
PUTTING THAT MEGONITE DISPLAY IN HERE WAS HIS IDEA!
THANKS, NARDO!
SINCE YOU'RE STILL ALIVE, LERNA, YOU GET THIS MESS CLEANED UP... BEFORE THE IMPERIAL DIPLOMATIC CONCLAVE BEGINS!
AT ONCE, LADY TARKIN!
GOOD! SHE DOESN'T SUSPECT THAT I SENT THE TRANS-PONDER MESSAGE!

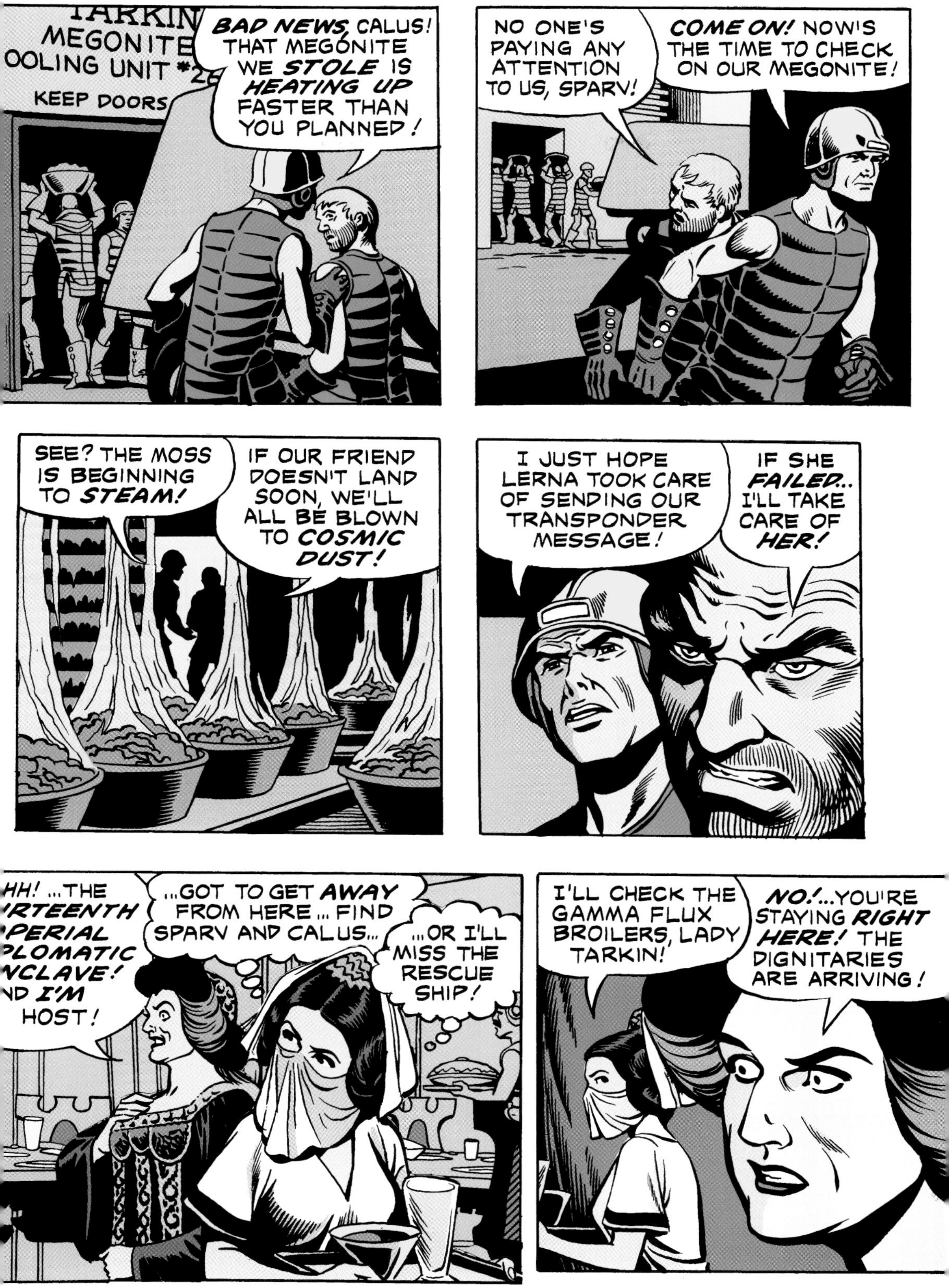

TARKIN
MEGONITE
OOLING UNIT #2
KEEP DOORS
BAD NEWS, CALUS! THAT MEGONITE WE STOLE IS HEATING UP FASTER THAN YOU PLANNED!
NO ONE'S PAYING ANY ATTENTION TO US, SPARV!
COME ON! NOW'S THE TIME TO CHECK ON OUR MEGONITE!
SEE? THE MOSS IS BEGINNING TO STEAM!
IF OUR FRIEND DOESN'T LAND SOON, WE'LL ALL BE BLOWN TO COSMIC DUST!
I JUST HOPE LERNA TOOK CARE OF SENDING OUR TRANSPONDER MESSAGE!
IF SHE FAILED.. I'LL TAKE CARE OF HER!
HH! ...THE IRTEENTH PERIAL PLOMATIC NCLAVE! ND I'M HOST!
...GOT TO GET AWAY FROM HERE... FIND SPARV AND CALUS...
...OR I'LL MISS THE RESCUE SHIP!
I'LL CHECK THE GAMMA FLUX BROILERS, LADY TARKIN!
NO!...YOU'RE STAYING RIGHT HERE! THE DIGNITARIES ARE ARRIVING!

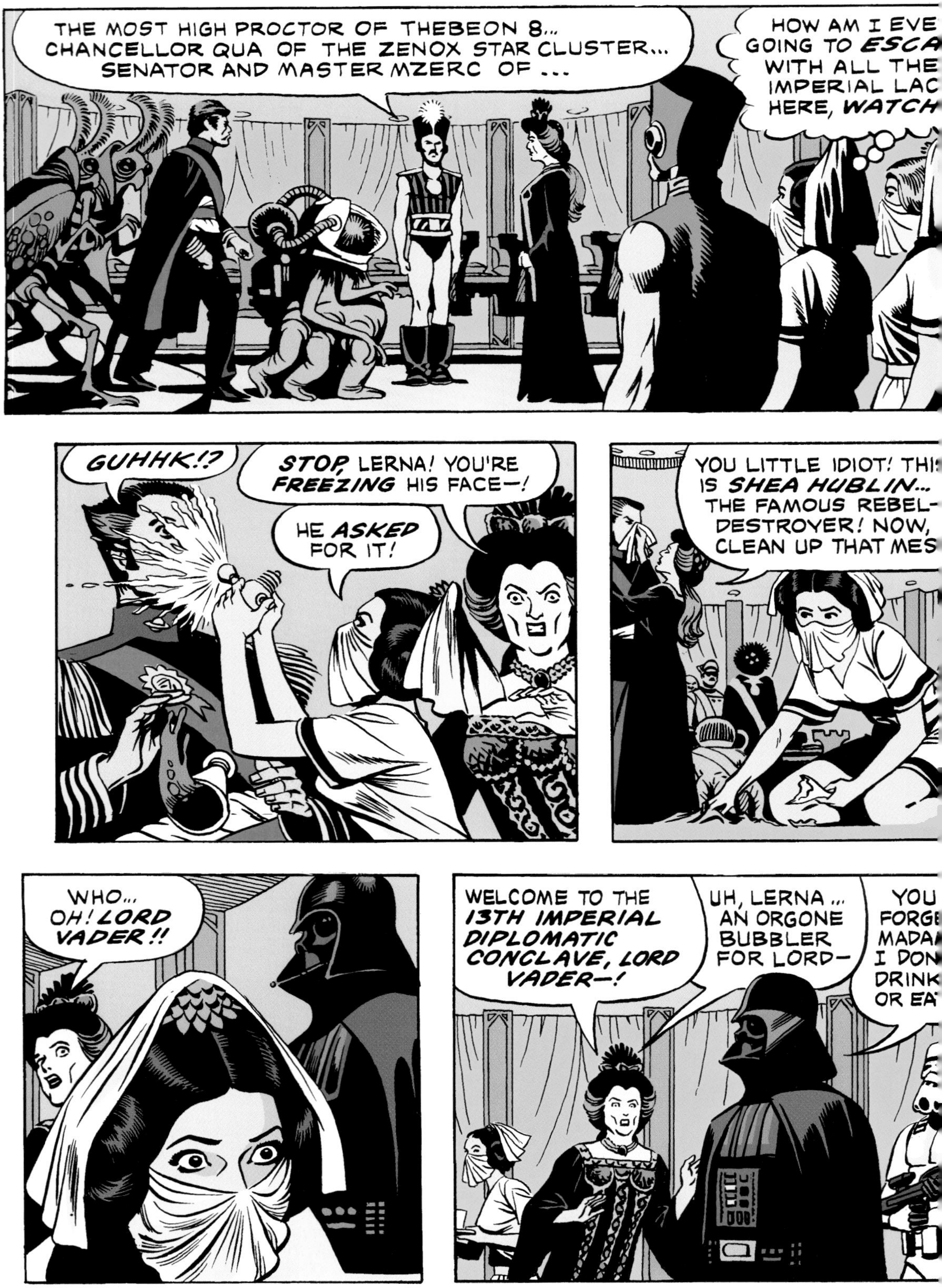
THE MOST HIGH PROCTOR OF THEBEON 8... CHANCELLOR QUA OF THE ZENOX STAR CLUSTER... SENATOR AND MASTER MZERC OF ...
HOW AM I EVE GOING TO ESCA WITH ALL THE IMPERIAL LAC HERE, WATCH
GUHHK!?
STOP, LERNA! YOU'RE FREEZING HIS FACE—!
HE ASKED FOR IT!
YOU LITTLE IDIOT! THI IS SHEA HUBLIN... THE FAMOUS REBEL-DESTROYER! NOW, CLEAN UP THAT MES
WHO... OH! LORD VADER!!
WELCOME TO THE 13TH IMPERIAL DIPLOMATIC CONCLAVE, LORD VADER—!
UH, LERNA... AN ORGONE BUBBLER FOR LORD—
YOU FORGE MADA I DON DRINK OR EA

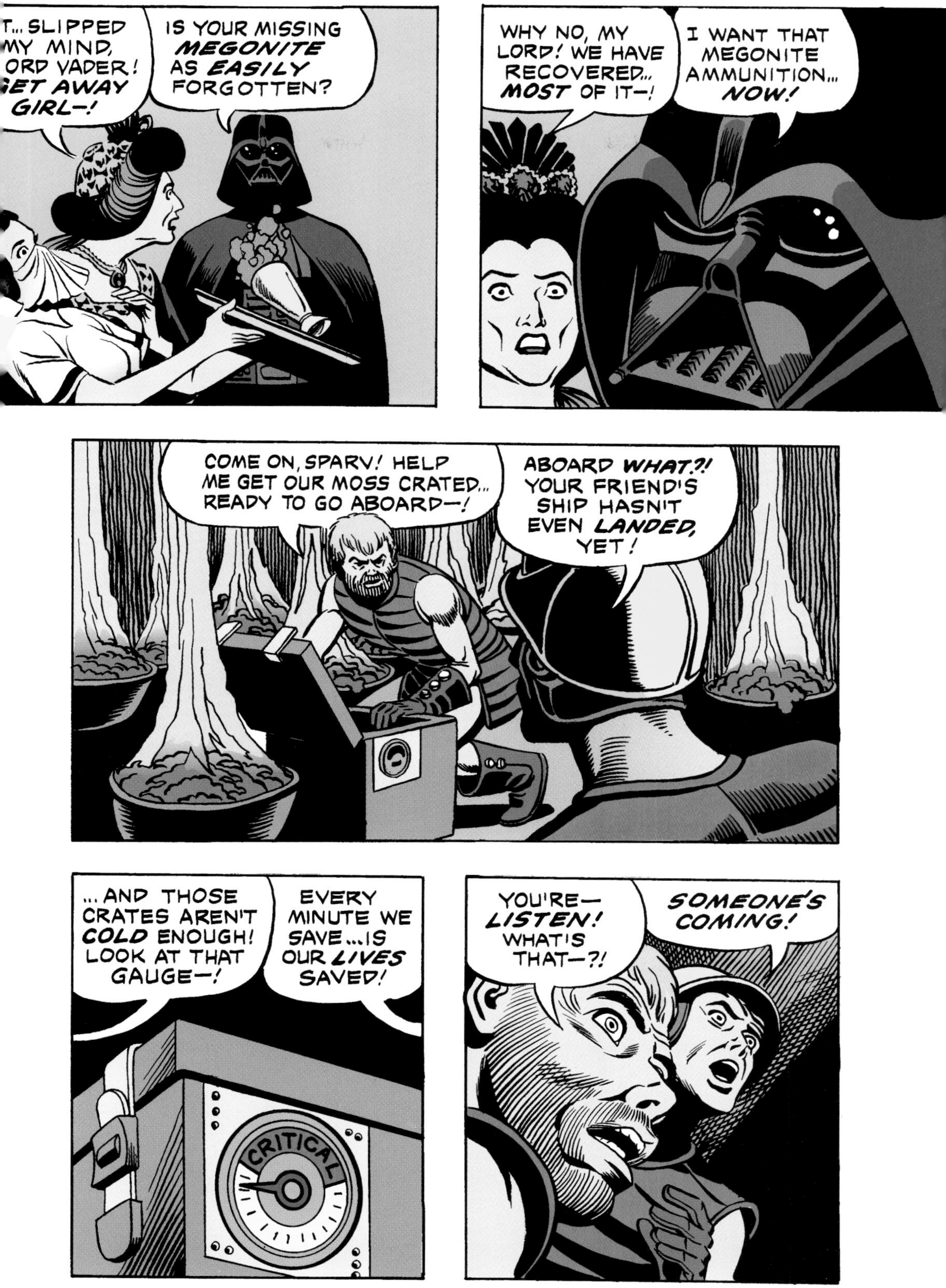
T... SLIPPED MY MIND, ORD VADER! ET AWAY GIRL—!
IS YOUR MISSING MEGONITE AS EASILY FORGOTTEN?
WHY NO, MY LORD! WE HAVE RECOVERED... MOST OF IT—!
I WANT THAT MEGONITE AMMUNITION... NOW!
COME ON, SPARV! HELP ME GET OUR MOSS CRATED... READY TO GO ABOARD—!
ABOARD WHAT?! YOUR FRIEND'S SHIP HASN'T EVEN LANDED, YET!
...AND THOSE CRATES AREN'T COLD ENOUGH! LOOK AT THAT GAUGE—!
EVERY MINUTE WE SAVE...IS OUR LIVES SAVED!
CRITICAL
YOU'RE— LISTEN! WHAT'S THAT—?!
SOMEONE'S COMING!

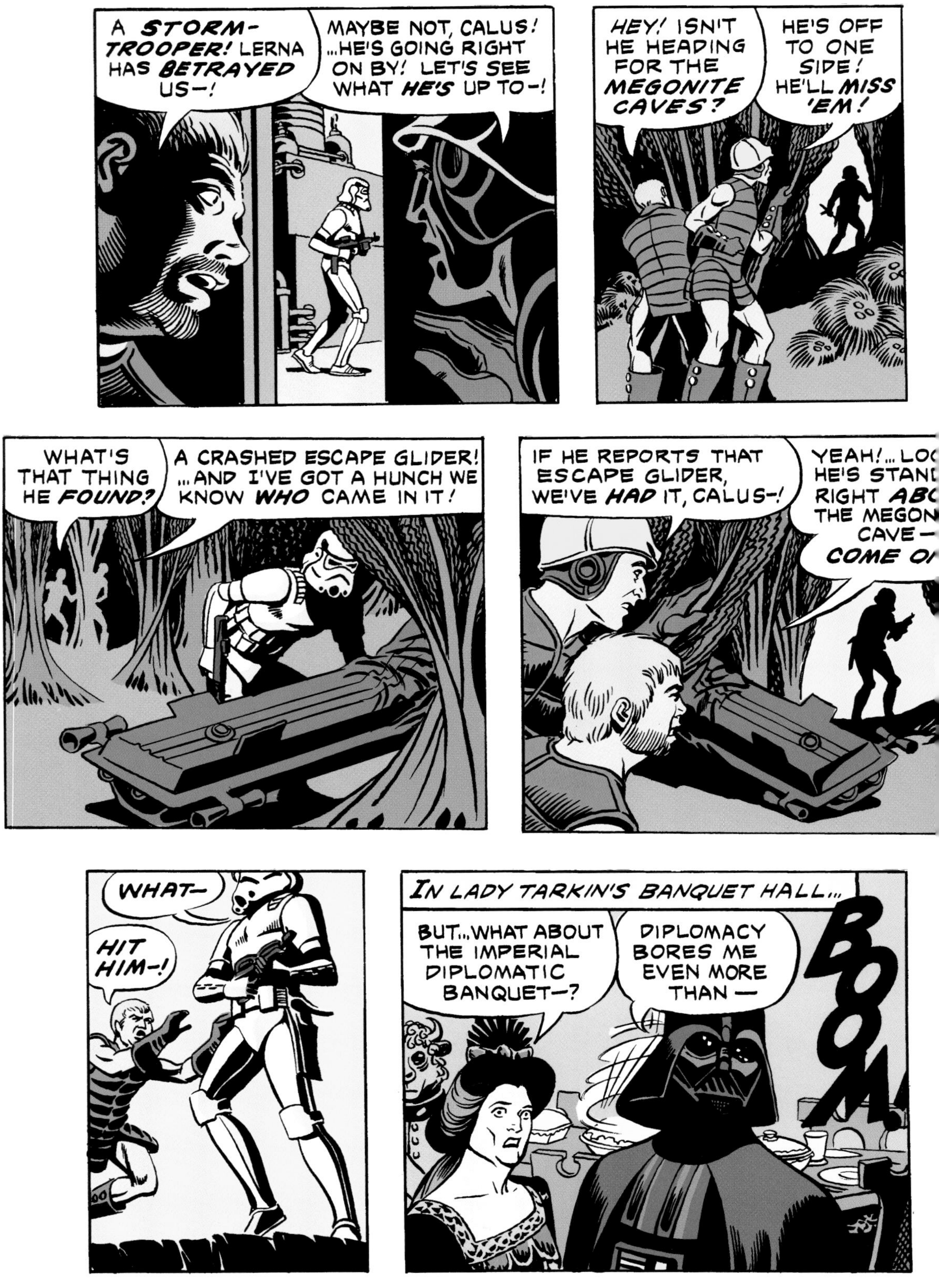
A STORM-TROOPER! LERNA HAS BETRAYED US—!
MAYBE NOT, CALUS! ...HE'S GOING RIGHT ON BY! LET'S SEE WHAT HE'S UP TO—!
HEY! ISN'T HE HEADING FOR THE MEGONITE CAVES?
HE'S OFF TO ONE SIDE! HE'LL MISS 'EM!
WHAT'S THAT THING HE FOUND?
A CRASHED ESCAPE GLIDER! ...AND I'VE GOT A HUNCH WE KNOW WHO CAME IN IT!
IF HE REPORTS THAT ESCAPE GLIDER, WE'VE HAD IT, CALUS—!
YEAH!... LO
HE'S STAN
RIGHT AB
THE MEGON
CAVE—
COME O
WHAT—
HIT HIM—!
IN LADY TARKIN'S BANQUET HALL...
BUT... WHAT ABOUT THE IMPERIAL DIPLOMATIC BANQUET—?
DIPLOMACY BORES ME EVEN MORE THAN —
BOOM

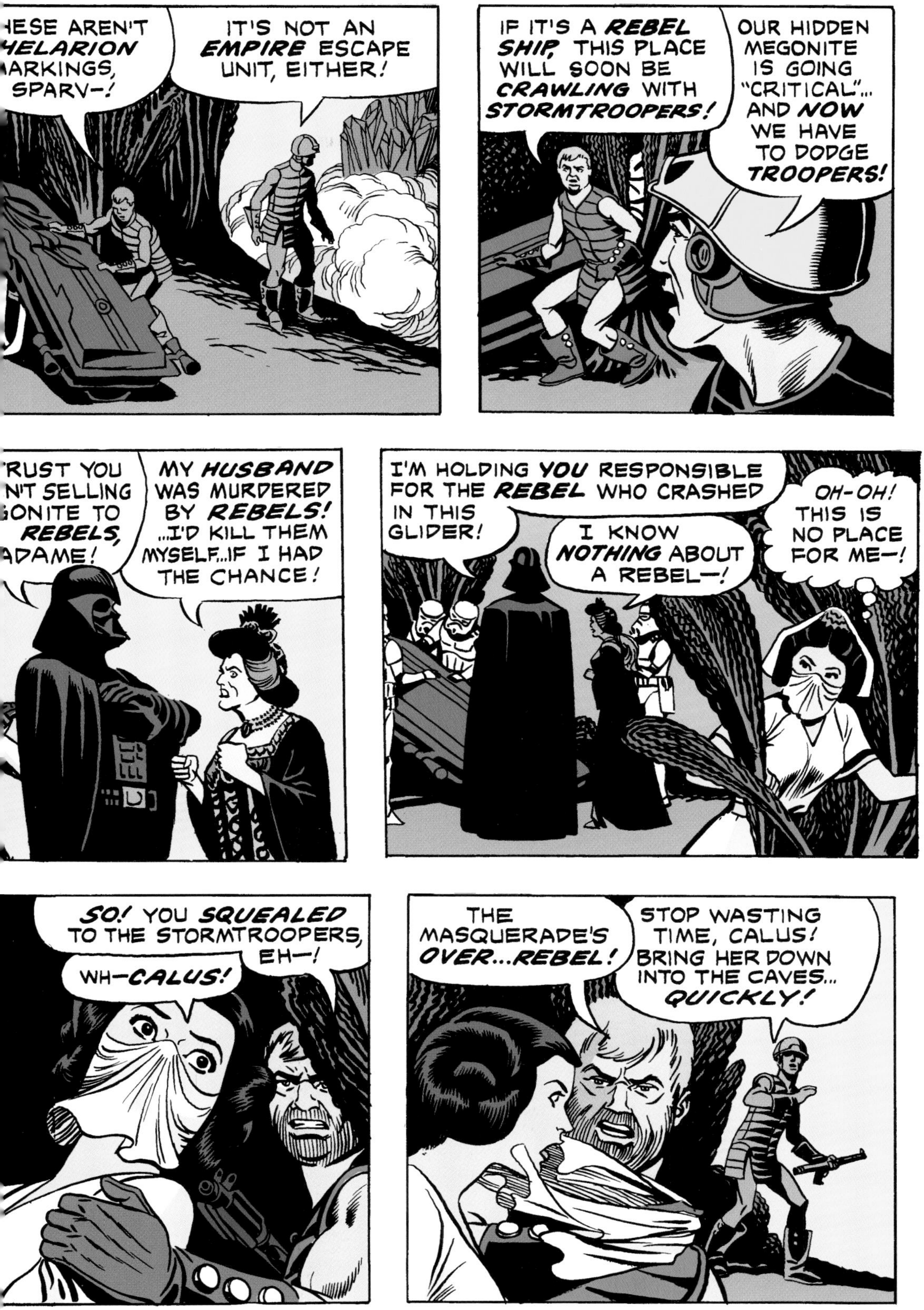

ESE AREN'T HELARION ARKINGS, SPARV—!
IT'S NOT AN EMPIRE ESCAPE UNIT, EITHER!
IF IT'S A REBEL SHIP, THIS PLACE WILL SOON BE CRAWLING WITH STORMTROOPERS!
OUR HIDDEN MEGONITE IS GOING "CRITICAL"... AND NOW WE HAVE TO DODGE TROOPERS!
RUST YOU N'T SELLING GONITE TO REBELS, ADAME!
MY HUSBAND WAS MURDERED BY REBELS! ...I'D KILL THEM MYSELF...IF I HAD THE CHANCE!
I'M HOLDING YOU RESPONSIBLE FOR THE REBEL WHO CRASHED IN THIS GLIDER!
I KNOW NOTHING ABOUT A REBEL—!
OH-OH! THIS IS NO PLACE FOR ME—!
SO! YOU SQUEALED TO THE STORMTROOPERS, EH—!
WH—CALUS!
THE MASQUERADE'S OVER...REBEL!
STOP WASTING TIME, CALUS! BRING HER DOWN INTO THE CAVES... QUICKLY!

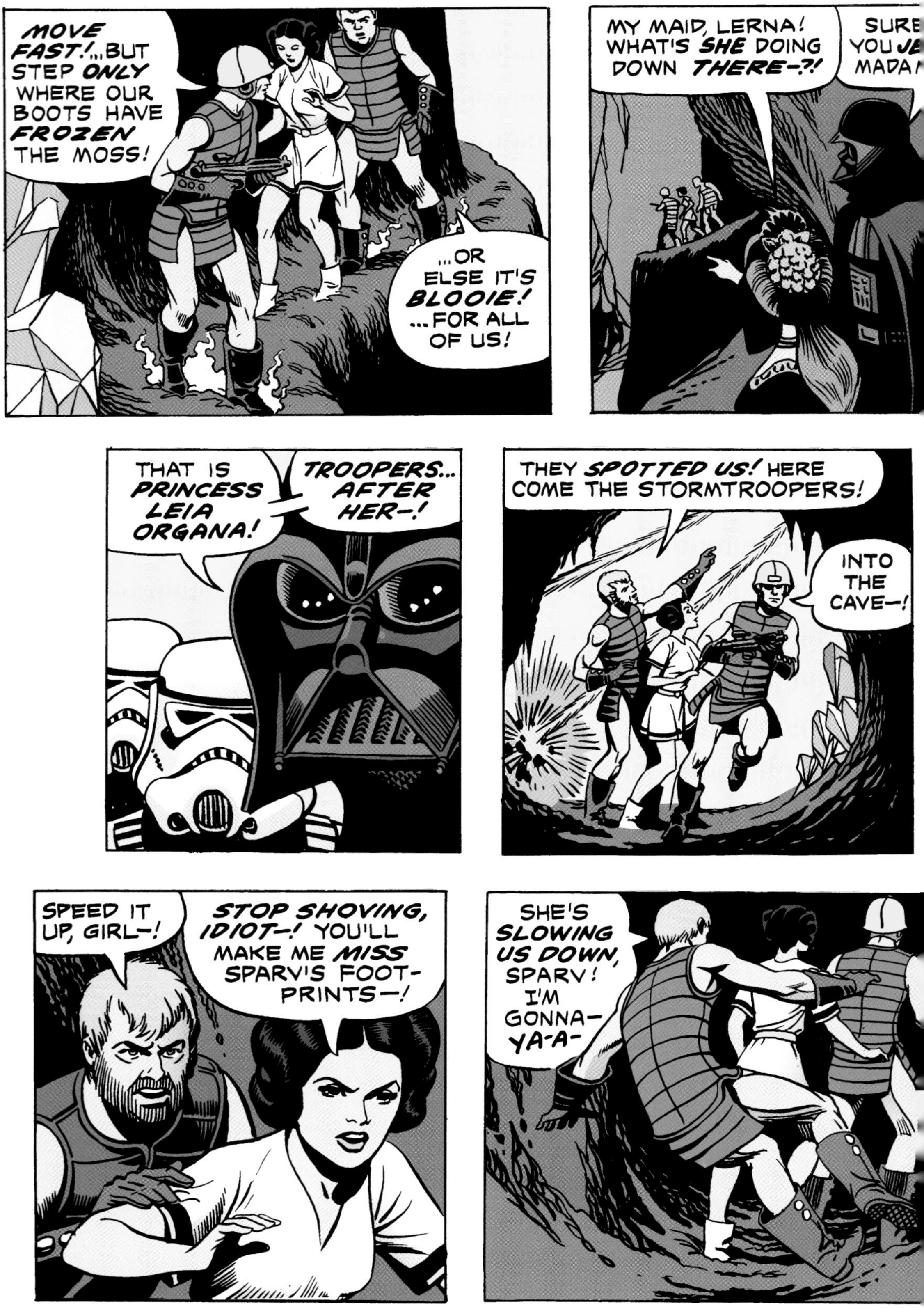
MOVE FAST!... BUT STEP ONLY WHERE OUR BOOTS HAVE FROZEN THE MOSS!
...OR ELSE IT'S BLOOIE! ...FOR ALL OF US!
MY MAID, LERNA! WHAT'S SHE DOING DOWN THERE--?!
SURE YOU
THAT IS PRINCESS LEIA ORGANA!
TROOPERS... AFTER HER--!
THEY SPOTTED US! HERE COME THE STORMTROOPERS!
INTO THE CAVE--!
SPEED IT UP, GIRL--!
STOP SHOVING, IDIOT--! YOU'LL MAKE ME MISS SPARV'S FOOT-PRINTS--!
SHE'S SLOWING US DOWN, SPARV! I'M GONNA-- YA-A-

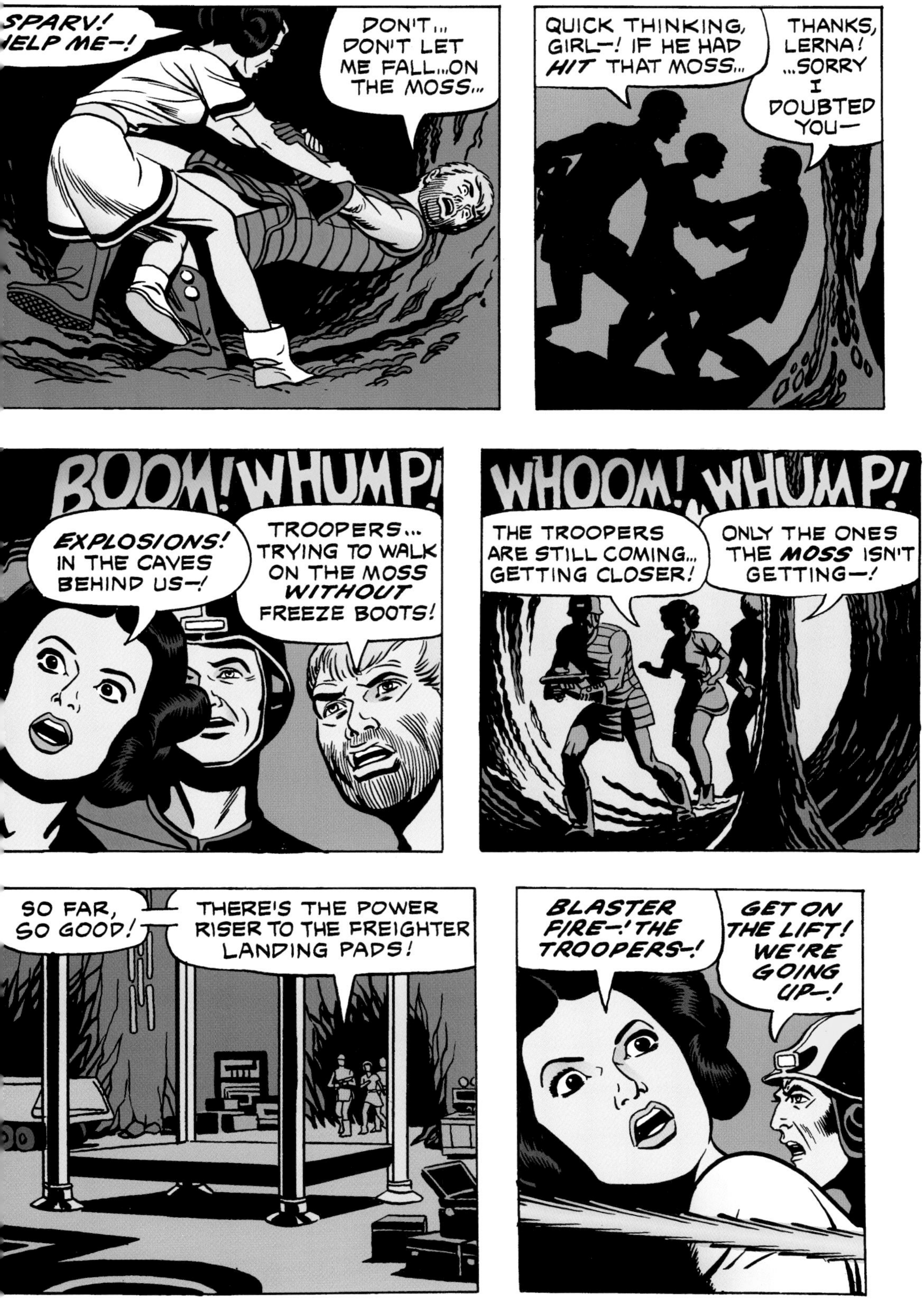
SPARV! HELP ME—!
DON'T... DON'T LET ME FALL...ON THE MOSS...
QUICK THINKING, GIRL—! IF HE HAD HIT THAT MOSS...
THANKS, LERNA! ...SORRY I DOUBTED YOU—
BOOM! WHUMP!
EXPLOSIONS! IN THE CAVES BEHIND US—!
TROOPERS... TRYING TO WALK ON THE MOSS WITHOUT FREEZE BOOTS!
WHOOM! WHUMP!
THE TROOPERS ARE STILL COMING... GETTING CLOSER!
ONLY THE ONES THE MOSS ISN'T GETTING—!
SO FAR, SO GOOD!
THERE'S THE POWER RISER TO THE FREIGHTER LANDING PADS!
BLASTER FIRE—! THE TROOPERS—!
GET ON THE LIFT! WE'RE GOING UP—!

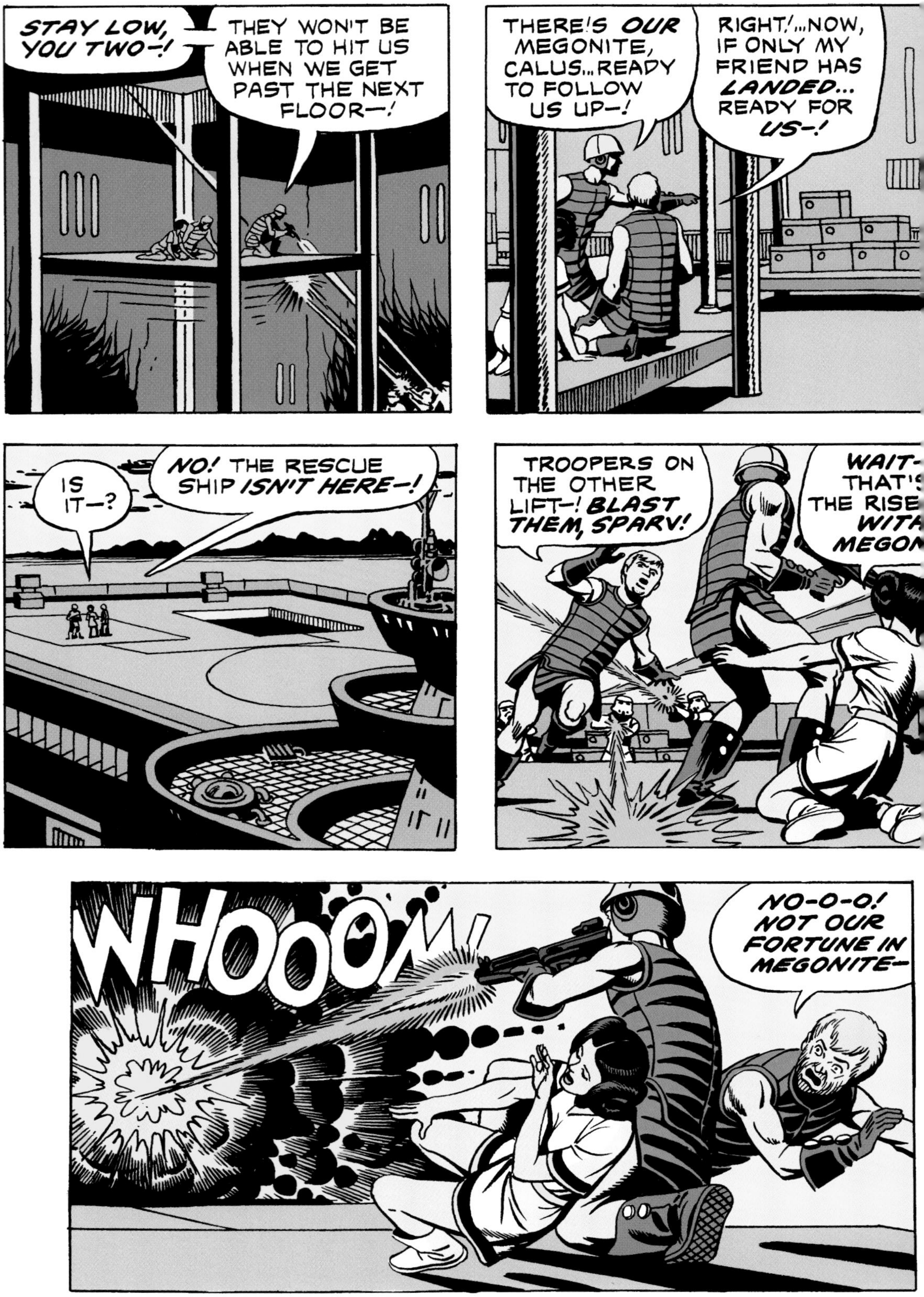
STAY LOW, YOU TWO—!
THEY WON'T BE ABLE TO HIT US WHEN WE GET PAST THE NEXT FLOOR—!
THERE'S OUR MEGONITE, CALUS...READY TO FOLLOW US UP—!
RIGHT!...NOW, IF ONLY MY FRIEND HAS LANDED... READY FOR US—!
IS IT—?
NO! THE RESCUE SHIP ISN'T HERE—!
TROOPERS ON THE OTHER LIFT—! BLAST THEM, SPARV!
WAIT— THAT'S THE RISE WITA MEGON
WHOOOM!
NO-O-O! NOT OUR FORTUNE IN MEGONITE—

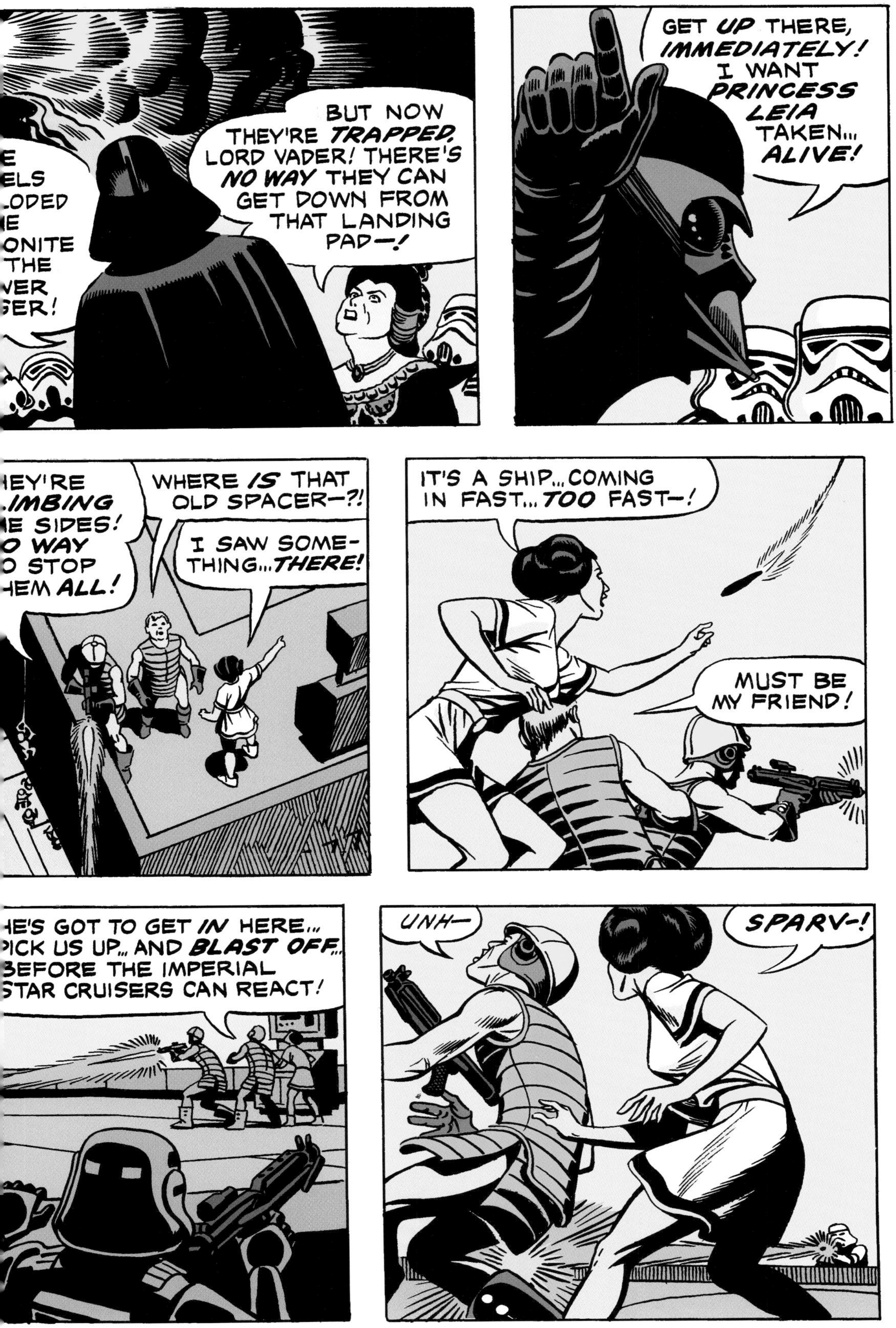

BUT NOW THEY'RE TRAPPED, LORD VADER! THERE'S NO WAY THEY CAN GET DOWN FROM THAT LANDING PAD—!
GET UP THERE, IMMEDIATELY! I WANT PRINCESS LEIA TAKEN... ALIVE!
WHERE IS THAT OLD SPACER—?!
I SAW SOMETHING... THERE!
IT'S A SHIP... COMING IN FAST... TOO FAST—!
MUST BE MY FRIEND!
STAR CRUISERS CAN REACT!
UNH—
SPARV—!

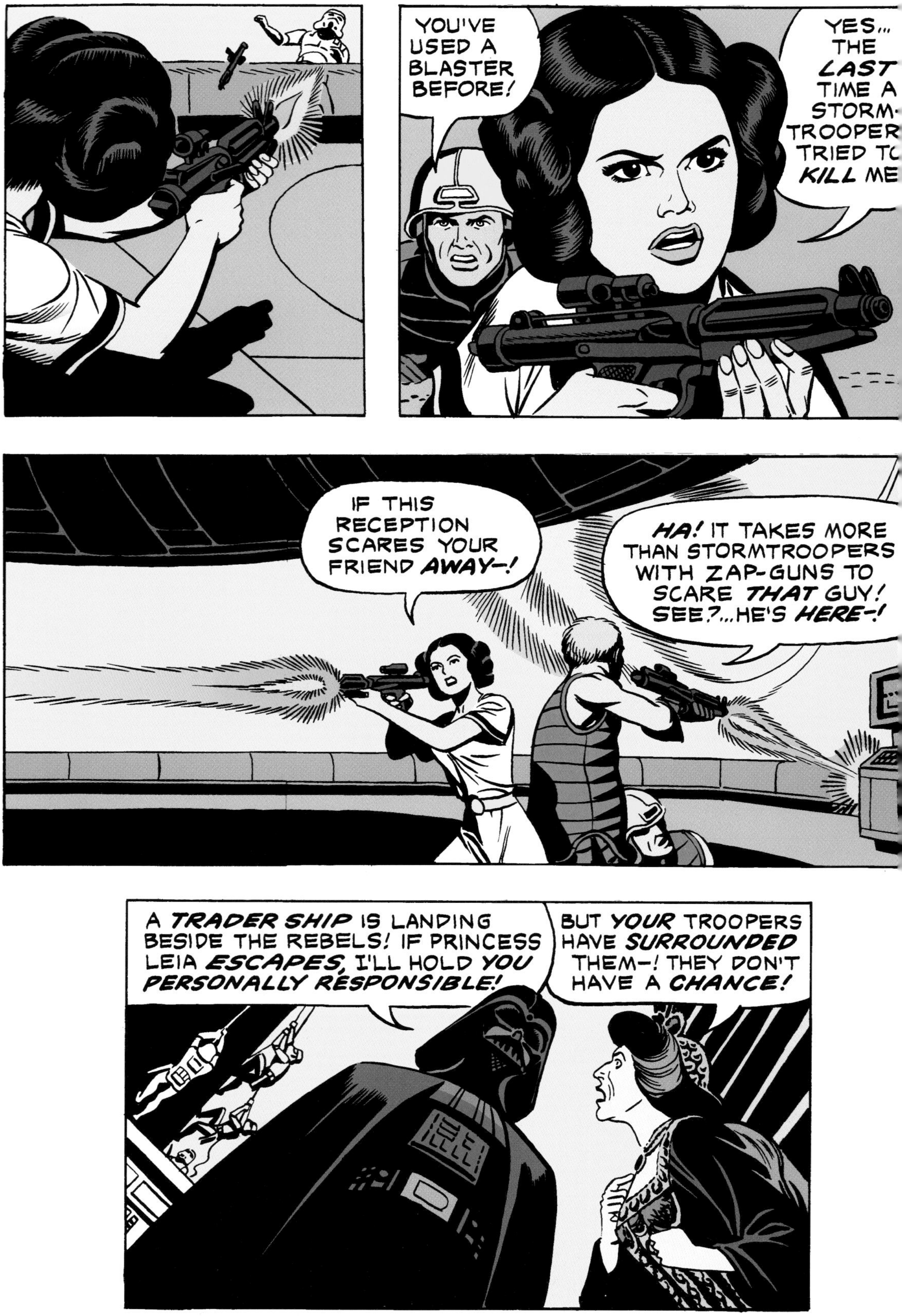

YOU'VE USED A BLASTER BEFORE!
YES... THE LAST TIME A STORM-TROOPER TRIED TO KILL ME
IF THIS RECEPTION SCARES YOUR FRIEND AWAY-!
HA! IT TAKES MORE THAN STORMTROOPERS WITH ZAP-GUNS TO SCARE THAT GUY! SEE?...HE'S HERE-!
A TRADER SHIP IS LANDING BESIDE THE REBELS! IF PRINCESS LEIA ESCAPES, I'LL HOLD YOU PERSONALLY RESPONSIBLE!
BUT YOUR TROOPERS HAVE SURROUNDED THEM-! THEY DON'T HAVE A CHANCE!

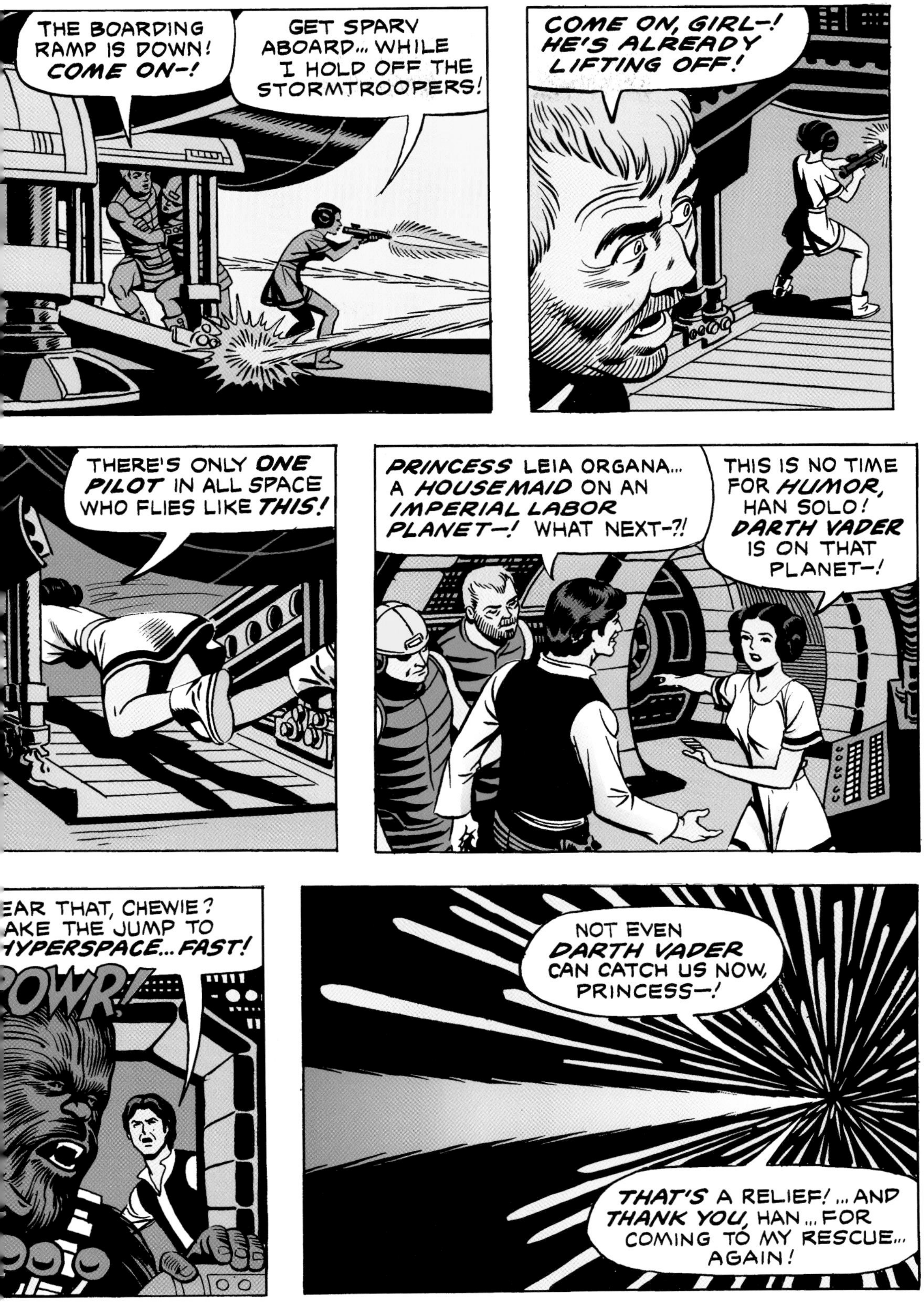
THE BOARDING RAMP IS DOWN! COME ON-!
GET SPARV ABOARD... WHILE I HOLD OFF THE STORMTROOPERS!
COME ON, GIRL-! HE'S ALREADY LIFTING OFF!
THERE'S ONLY ONE PILOT IN ALL SPACE WHO FLIES LIKE THIS!
PRINCESS LEIA ORGANA... A HOUSEMAID ON AN IMPERIAL LABOR PLANET-! WHAT NEXT-?!
THIS IS NO TIME FOR HUMOR, HAN SOLO! DARTH VADER IS ON THAT PLANET-!
EAR THAT, CHEWIE? AKE THE JUMP TO HYPERSPACE... FAST!
POWR!
NOT EVEN DARTH VADER CAN CATCH US NOW, PRINCESS-!
THAT'S A RELIEF! ...AND THANK YOU, HAN... FOR COMING TO MY RESCUE... AGAIN!

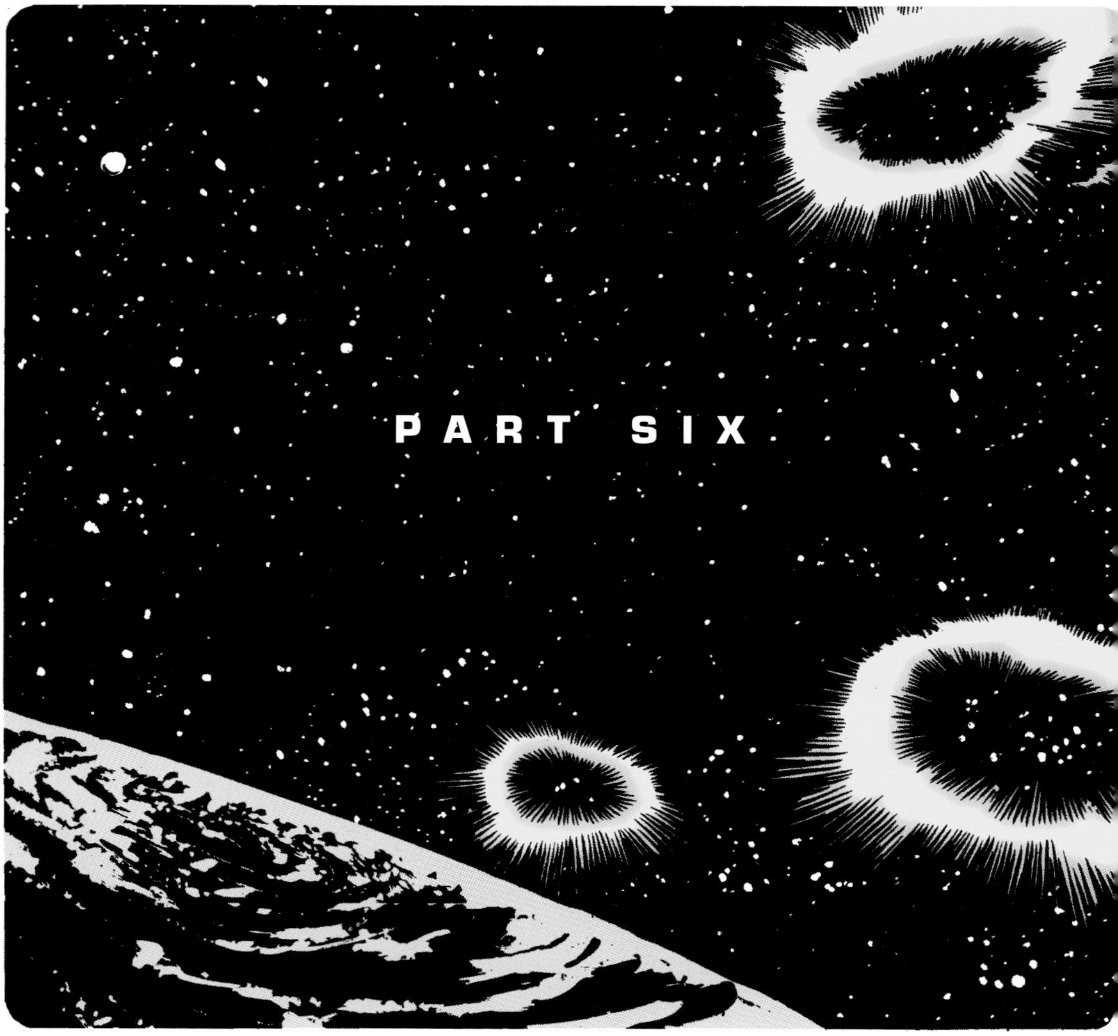
PART SIX

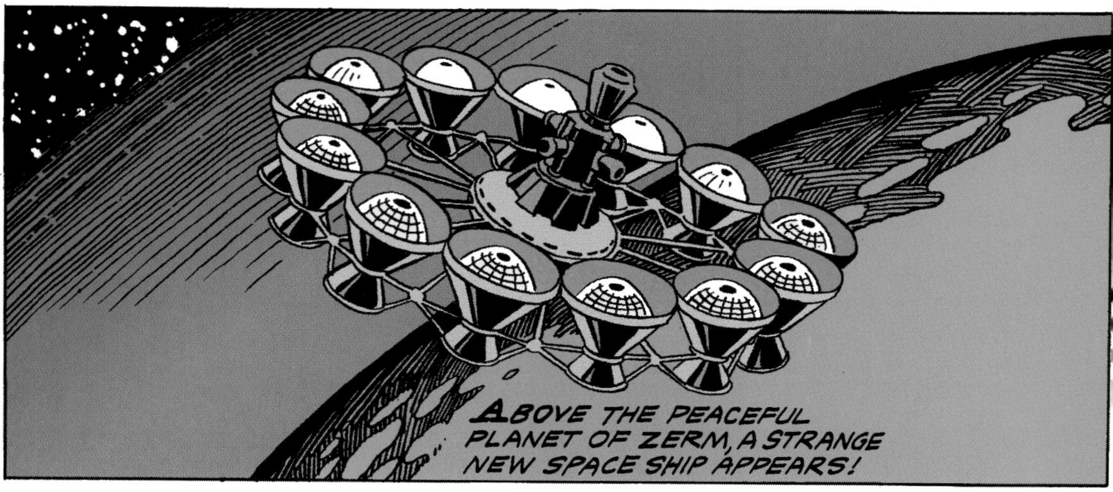
ABOVE THE PEACEFUL
PLANET OF ZERM, A STRANGE
NEW SPACE SHIP APPEARS!

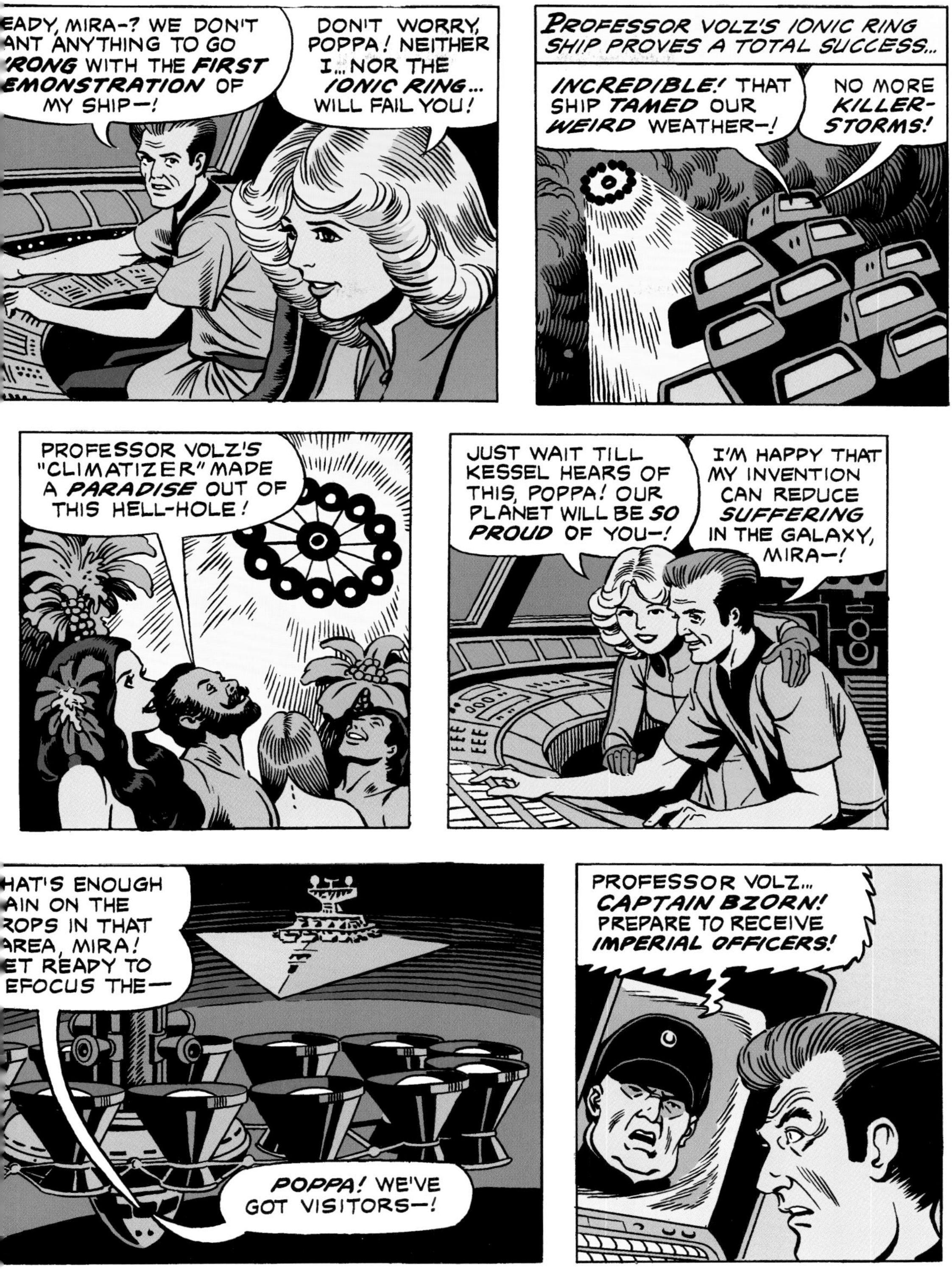
EADY, MIRA-? WE DON'T ANT ANYTHING TO GO 'RONG WITH THE FIRST EMONSTRATION OF MY SHIP—!
DON'T WORRY, POPPA! NEITHER I... NOR THE IONIC RING... WILL FAIL YOU!
PROFESSOR VOLZ'S IONIC RING SHIP PROVES A TOTAL SUCCESS...
INCREDIBLE! THAT SHIP TAMED OUR WEIRD WEATHER—!
NO MORE KILLER-STORMS!
PROFESSOR VOLZ'S "CLIMATIZER" MADE A PARADISE OUT OF THIS HELL-HOLE!
JUST WAIT TILL KESSEL HEARS OF THIS, POPPA! OUR PLANET WILL BE SO PROUD OF YOU—!
I'M HAPPY THAT MY INVENTION CAN REDUCE SUFFERING IN THE GALAXY, MIRA—!
HAT'S ENOUGH AIN ON THE ROPS IN THAT AREA, MIRA! ET READY TO EFOCUS THE—
POPPA! WE'VE GOT VISITORS—!
PROFESSOR VOLZ... CAPTAIN BZORN! PREPARE TO RECEIVE IMPERIAL OFFICERS!

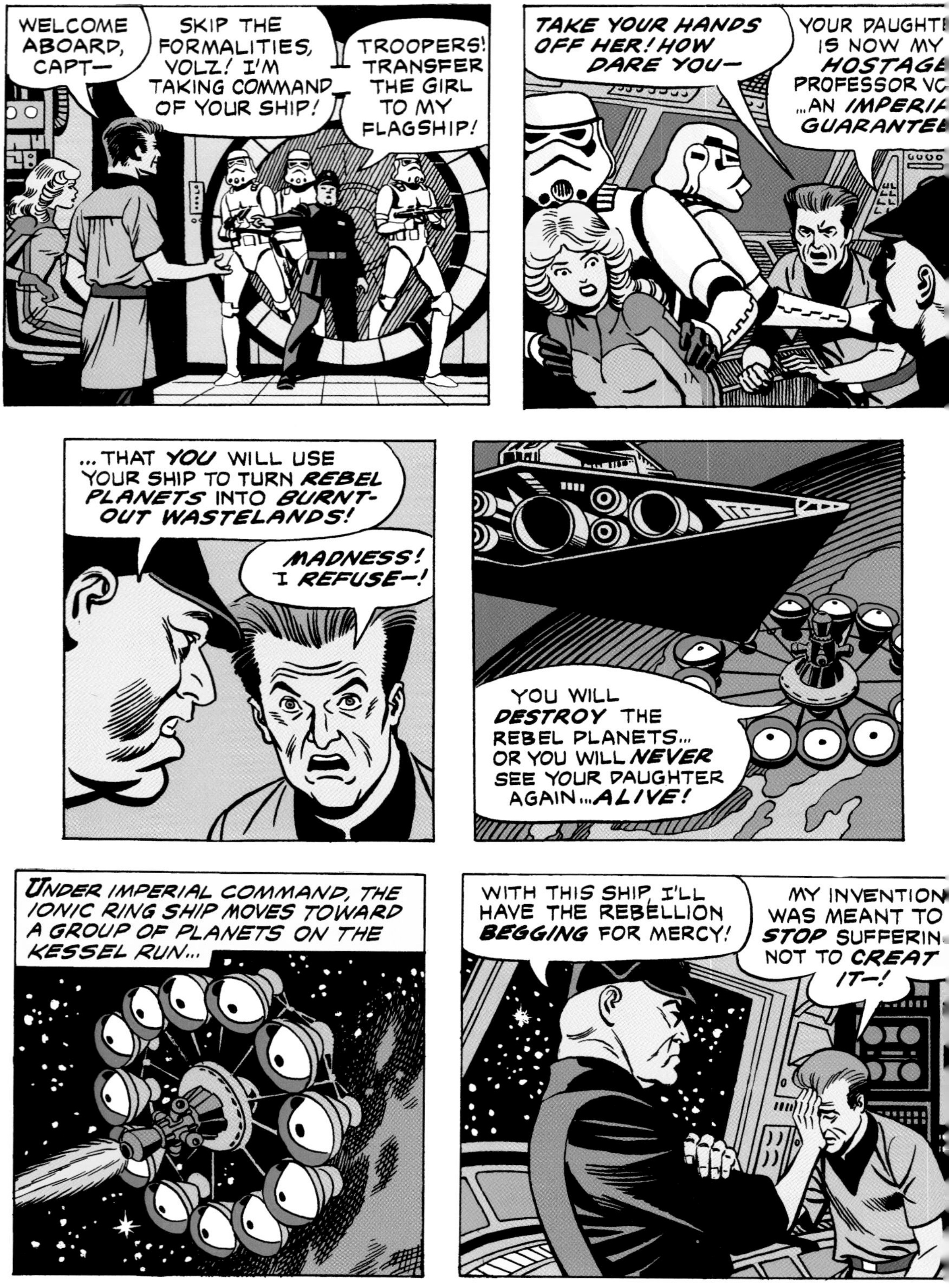

WELCOME ABOARD, CAPT—
SKIP THE FORMALITIES, VOLZ! I'M TAKING COMMAND OF YOUR SHIP!
TROOPERS! TRANSFER THE GIRL TO MY FLAGSHIP!
TAKE YOUR HANDS OFF HER! HOW DARE YOU—
YOUR DAUGHTE IS NOW MY HOSTAGE PROFESSOR VO ...AN IMPERIA GUARANTEE
...THAT YOU WILL USE YOUR SHIP TO TURN REBEL PLANETS INTO BURNT-OUT WASTELANDS!
MADNESS! I REFUSE—!
YOU WILL DESTROY THE REBEL PLANETS... OR YOU WILL NEVER SEE YOUR DAUGHTER AGAIN...ALIVE!
UNDER IMPERIAL COMMAND, THE IONIC RING SHIP MOVES TOWARD A GROUP OF PLANETS ON THE KESSEL RUN...
WITH THIS SHIP, I'LL HAVE THE REBELLION BEGGING FOR MERCY!
MY INVENTION WAS MEANT TO STOP SUFFERIN NOT TO CREAT IT—!

YOU'LL PREVENT YOUR *DAUGHTER'S* SUFFERING, VOLZ...AS LONG AS YOU OBEY *ME!*

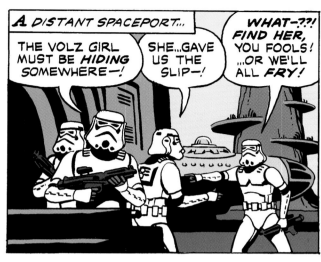

A *DISTANT SPACEPORT...*

THE VOLZ GIRL MUST BE *HIDING* SOMEWHERE—!

SHE...GAVE US THE SLIP—!

WHAT—??! FIND HER, YOU FOOLS! ...OR WE'LL ALL *FRY!*

ARE THE TROOPERS SEARCHING FOR OUR SPICE, MALO—?

OF COURSE NOT! OUR SPICE IS ON THE WAY TO *KESSEL* ABOARD *HAN SOLO'S* SHIP!

STOP *WORRYING,* CHEWIE—! WE'LL GET TO KESSEL ON TIME—!

...*AFTER* WE CHECK ON SKYWALKER!

SMALL *SECRET REBEL BASE* N THE PLANET *RANDA...*

GOOD TO SEE YOU, HAN—! LOOKS LIKE THE *FALCON'S* REALLY *LOADED!* WHAT—?

SPICE...ON ITS WAY TO *KESSEL*...JABBA PLANS TO *PROFIT* FROM AN IMPENDING FAMINE ...

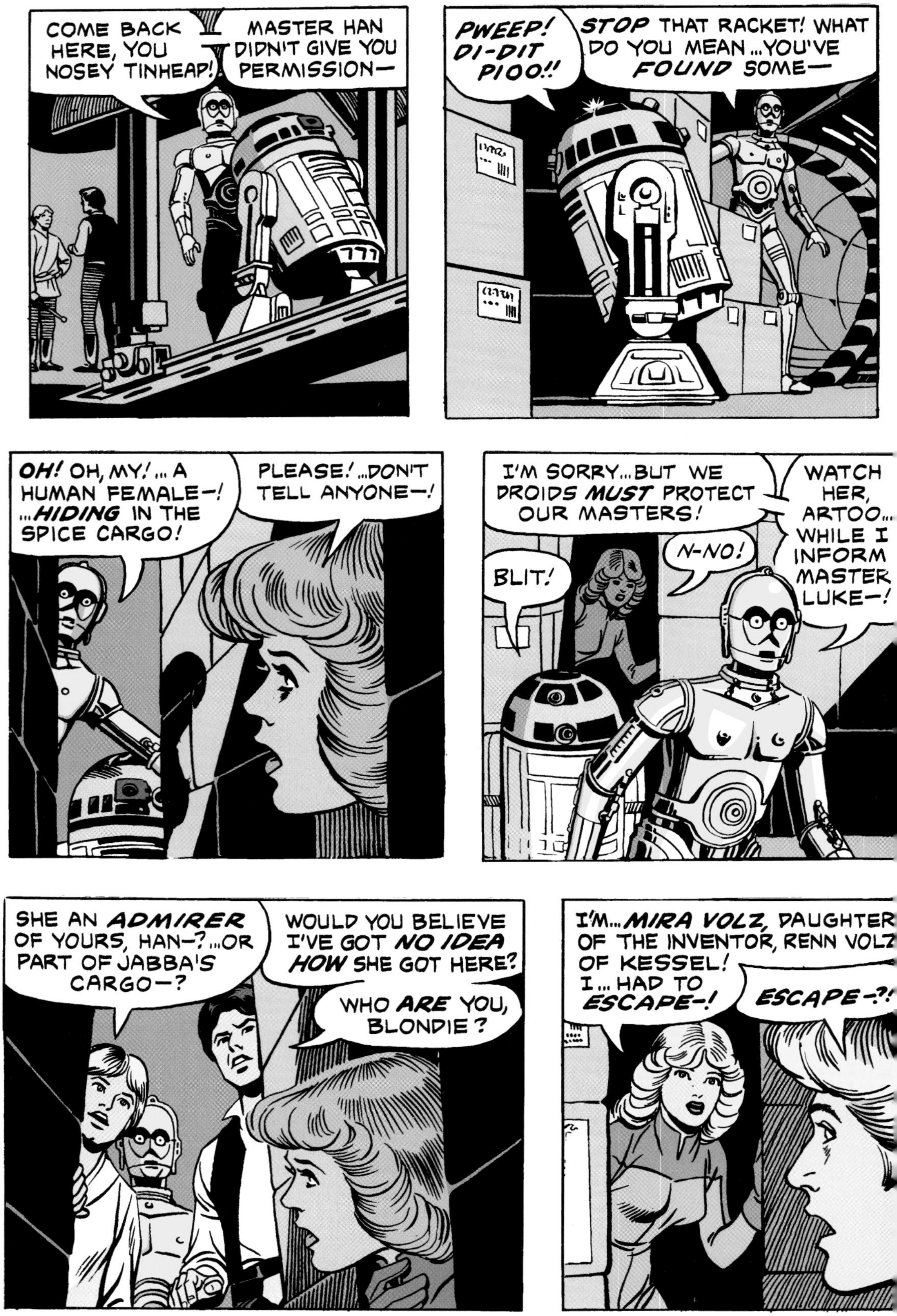
COME BACK HERE, YOU NOSEY TINHEAP!
MASTER HAN DIDN'T GIVE YOU PERMISSION—
PWEEP! DI-DIT PIOO!!
STOP THAT RACKET! WHAT DO YOU MEAN ...YOU'VE FOUND SOME—
OH! OH, MY! ... A HUMAN FEMALE—! ...HIDING IN THE SPICE CARGO!
PLEASE! ...DON'T TELL ANYONE—!
I'M SORRY...BUT WE DROIDS MUST PROTECT OUR MASTERS!
WATCH HER, ARTOO... WHILE I INFORM MASTER LUKE—!
N-NO!
BLIT!
SHE AN ADMIRER OF YOURS, HAN—? ...OR PART OF JABBA'S CARGO—?
WOULD YOU BELIEVE I'VE GOT NO IDEA HOW SHE GOT HERE?
WHO ARE YOU, BLONDIE?
I'M... MIRA VOLZ, DAUGHTER OF THE INVENTOR, RENN VOLZ OF KESSEL! I... HAD TO ESCAPE—!
ESCAPE—?!

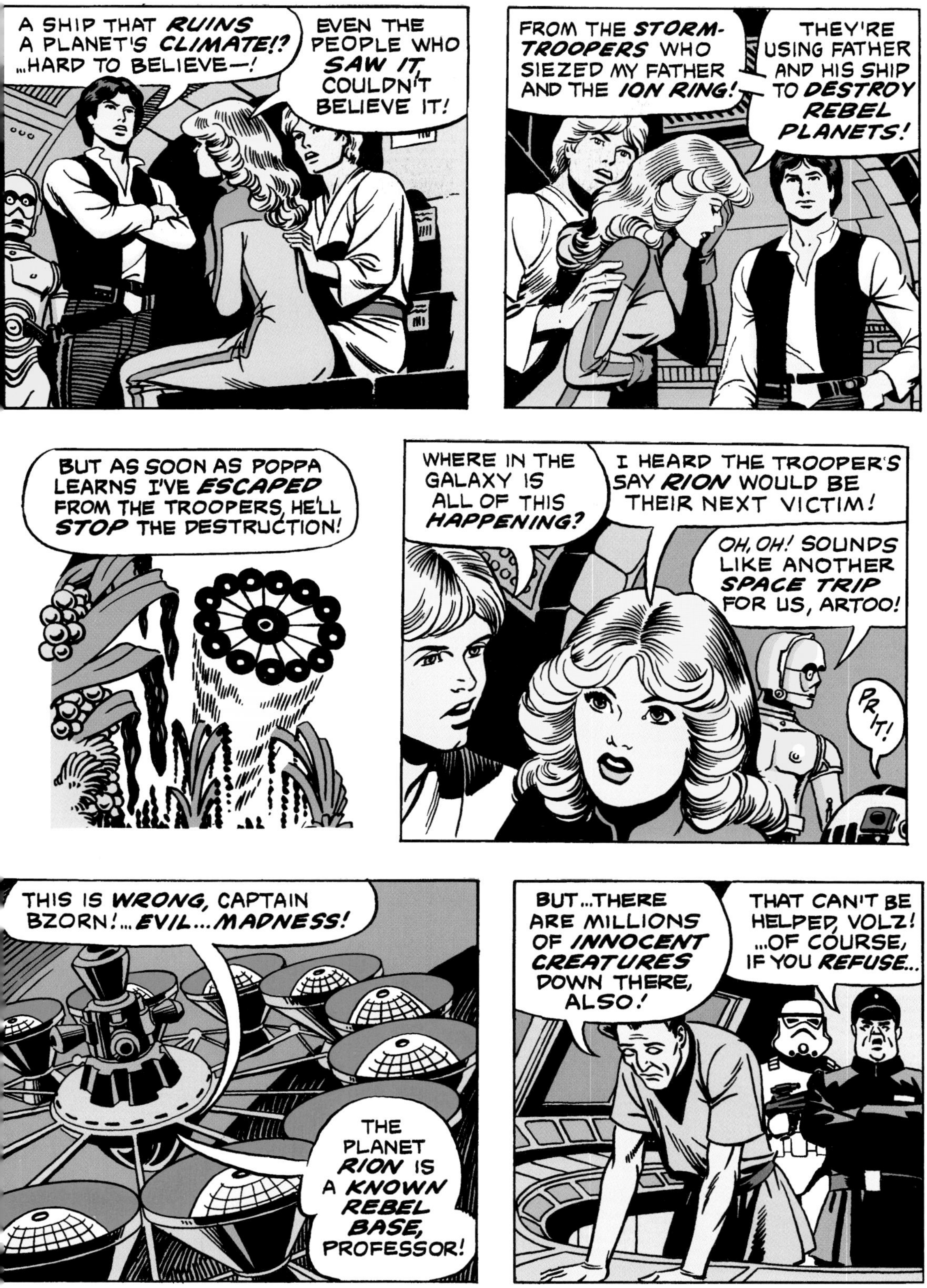
A SHIP THAT RUINS A PLANET'S CLIMATE!? ...HARD TO BELIEVE—!
EVEN THE PEOPLE WHO SAW IT, COULDN'T BELIEVE IT!
FROM THE STORM-TROOPERS WHO SIEZED MY FATHER AND THE ION RING!
THEY'RE USING FATHER AND HIS SHIP TO DESTROY REBEL PLANETS!
BUT AS SOON AS POPPA LEARNS I'VE ESCAPED FROM THE TROOPERS, HE'LL STOP THE DESTRUCTION!
WHERE IN THE GALAXY IS ALL OF THIS HAPPENING?
I HEARD THE TROOPER'S SAY RION WOULD BE THEIR NEXT VICTIM!
OH, OH! SOUNDS LIKE ANOTHER SPACE TRIP FOR US, ARTOO!
PRIT!
THIS IS WRONG, CAPTAIN BZORN!... EVIL... MADNESS!
THE PLANET RION IS A KNOWN REBEL BASE, PROFESSOR!
BUT... THERE ARE MILLIONS OF INNOCENT CREATURES DOWN THERE, ALSO!
THAT CAN'T BE HELPED, VOLZ! ...OF COURSE, IF YOU REFUSE...

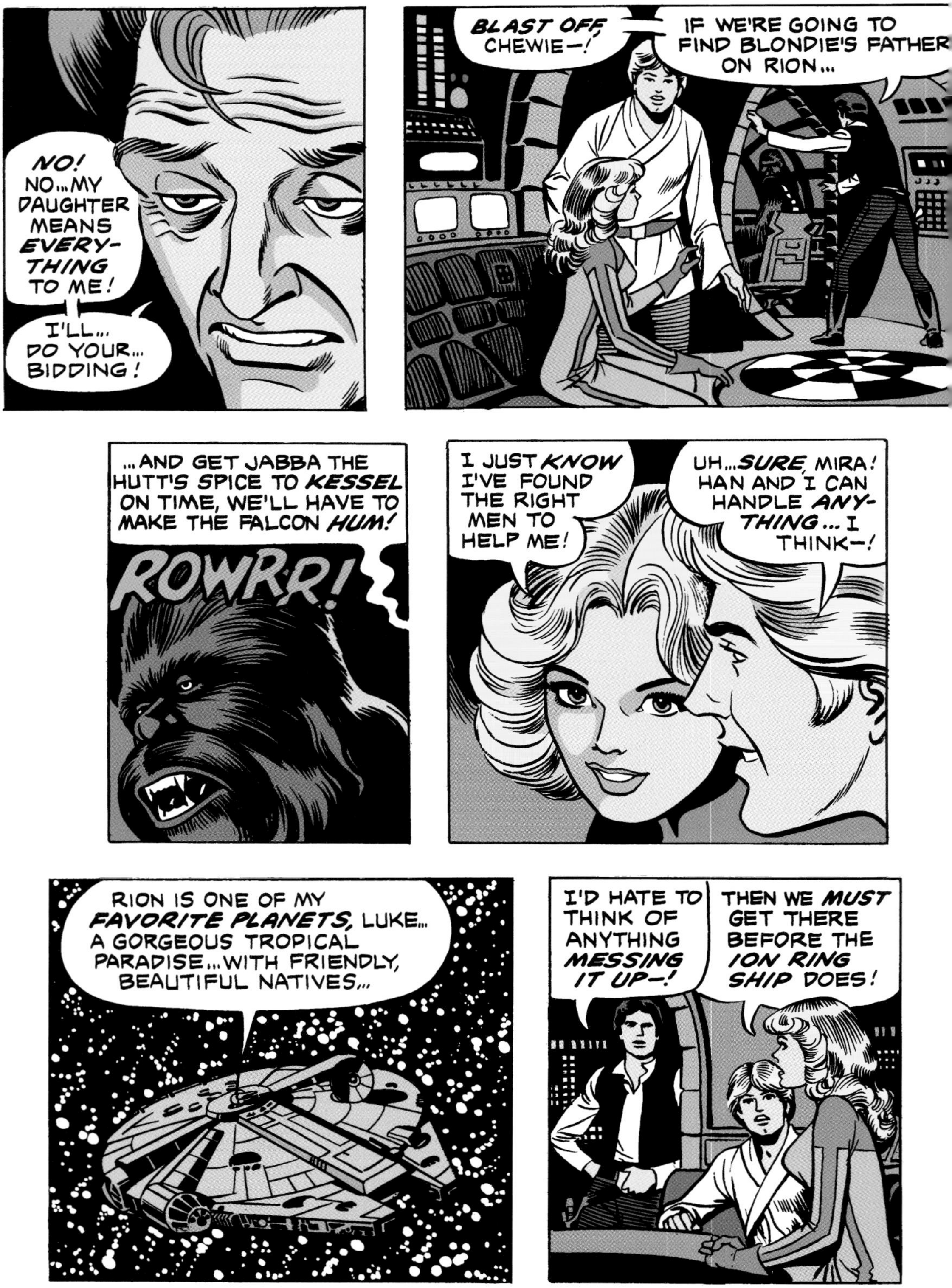
NO! NO... MY DAUGHTER MEANS EVERY-THING TO ME!
I'LL... DO YOUR... BIDDING!
BLAST OFF, CHEWIE—!
IF WE'RE GOING TO FIND BLONDIE'S FATHER ON RION...
...AND GET JABBA THE HUTT'S SPICE TO KESSEL ON TIME, WE'LL HAVE TO MAKE THE FALCON HUM!
ROWRR!
I JUST KNOW I'VE FOUND THE RIGHT MEN TO HELP ME!
UH... SURE, MIRA! HAN AND I CAN HANDLE ANY-THING... I THINK—!
RION IS ONE OF MY FAVORITE PLANETS, LUKE... A GORGEOUS TROPICAL PARADISE... WITH FRIENDLY, BEAUTIFUL NATIVES,...
I'D HATE TO THINK OF ANYTHING MESSING IT UP—!
THEN WE MUST GET THERE BEFORE THE ION RING SHIP DOES!

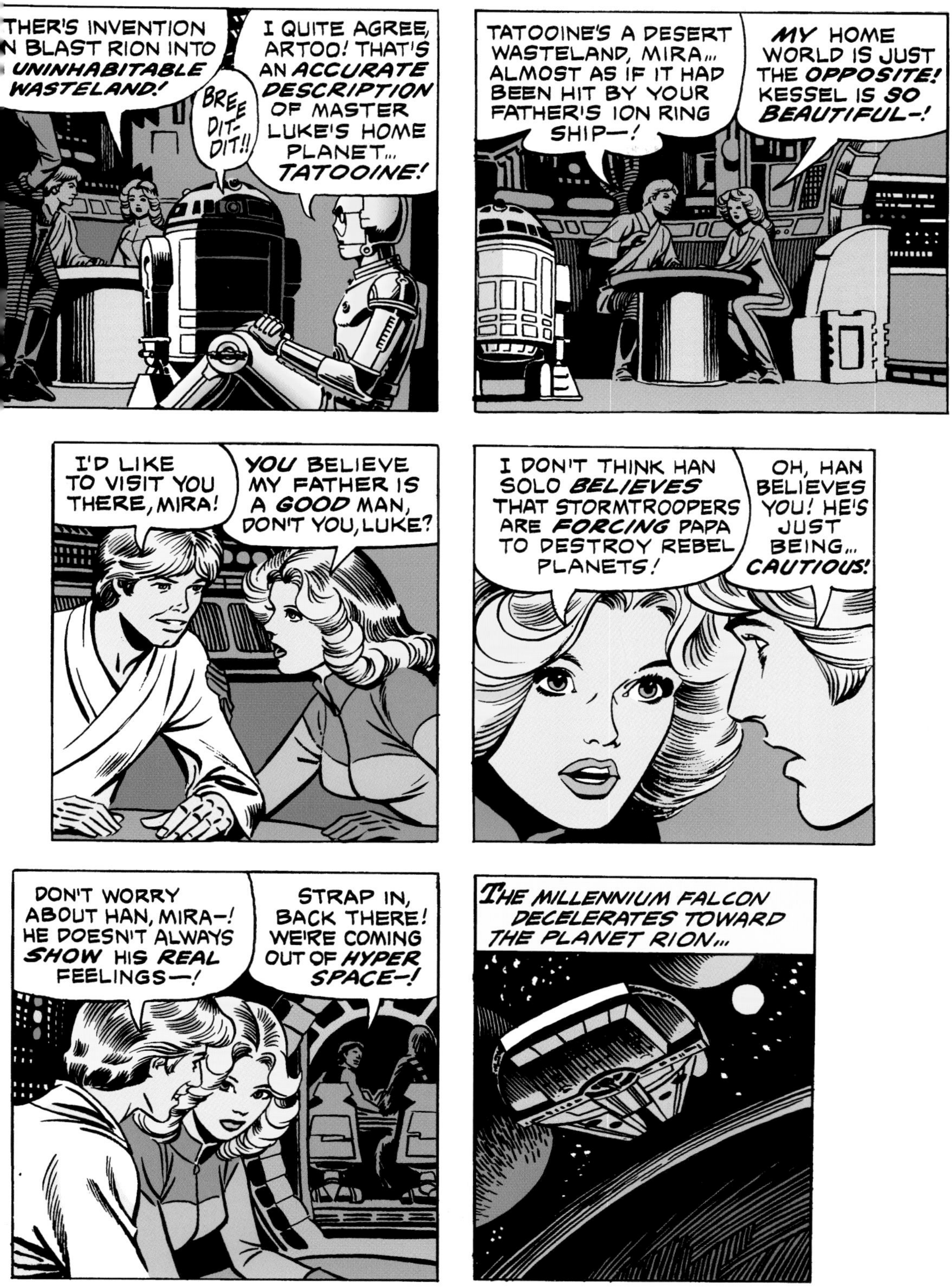
THER'S INVENTION N BLAST RION INTO UNINHABITABLE WASTELAND!
BREE DIT-DIT!!
I QUITE AGREE, ARTOO! THAT'S AN ACCURATE DESCRIPTION OF MASTER LUKE'S HOME PLANET... TATOOINE!
TATOOINE'S A DESERT WASTELAND, MIRA... ALMOST AS IF IT HAD BEEN HIT BY YOUR FATHER'S ION RING SHIP—!
MY HOME WORLD IS JUST THE OPPOSITE! KESSEL IS SO BEAUTIFUL—!
I'D LIKE TO VISIT YOU THERE, MIRA!
YOU BELIEVE MY FATHER IS A GOOD MAN, DON'T YOU, LUKE?
I DON'T THINK HAN SOLO BELIEVES THAT STORMTROOPERS ARE FORCING PAPA TO DESTROY REBEL PLANETS!
OH, HAN BELIEVES YOU! HE'S JUST BEING... CAUTIOUS!
DON'T WORRY ABOUT HAN, MIRA—! HE DOESN'T ALWAYS SHOW HIS REAL FEELINGS—!
STRAP IN, BACK THERE! WE'RE COMING OUT OF HYPER SPACE—!
THE MILLENNIUM FALCON DECELERATES TOWARD THE PLANET RION...

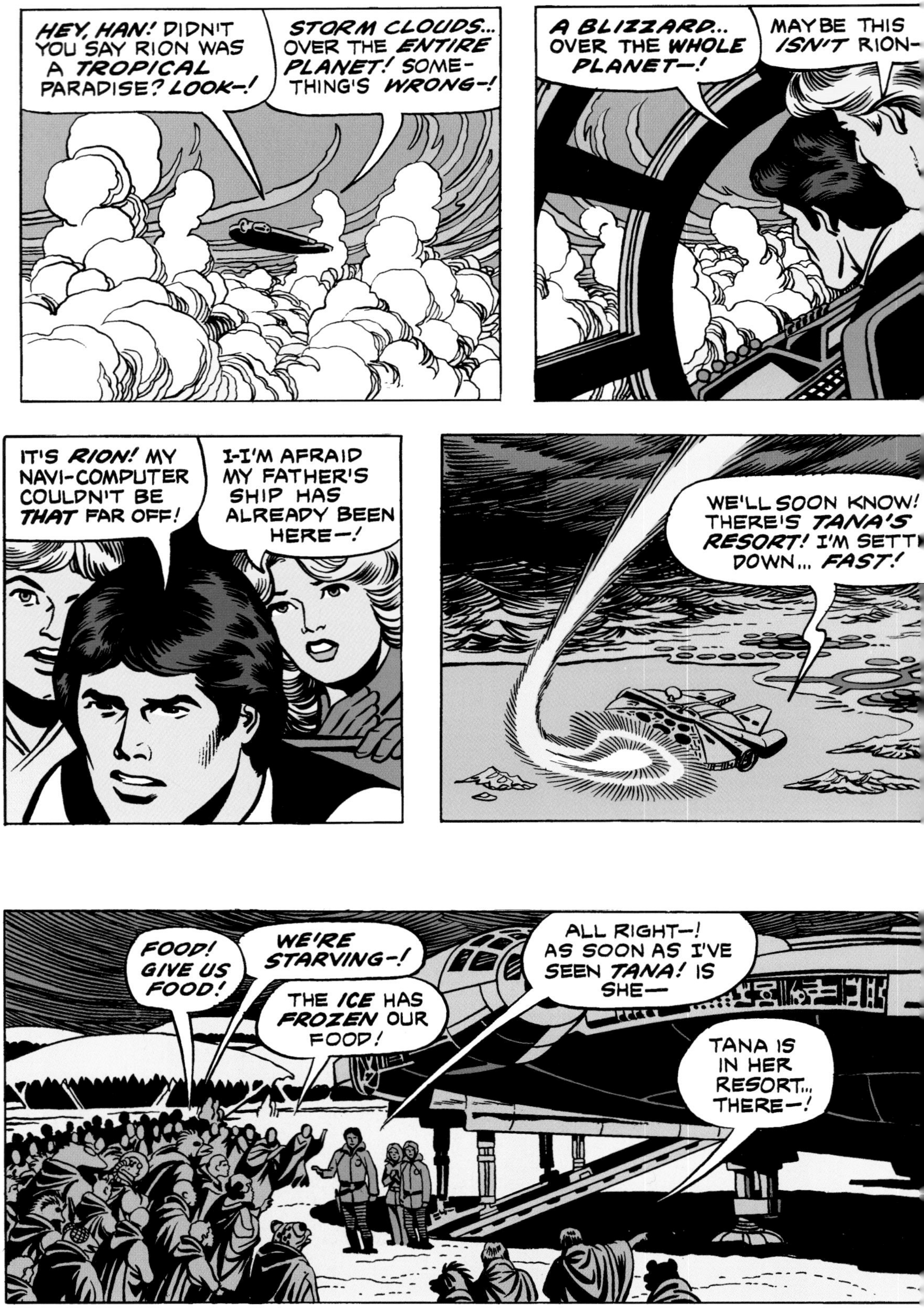
HEY, HAN! DIDN'T YOU SAY RION WAS A TROPICAL PARADISE? LOOK-!
STORM CLOUDS... OVER THE ENTIRE PLANET! SOME-THING'S WRONG-!
A BLIZZARD... OVER THE WHOLE PLANET-!
MAYBE THIS ISN'T RION-
IT'S RION! MY NAVI-COMPUTER COULDN'T BE THAT FAR OFF!
I-I'M AFRAID MY FATHER'S SHIP HAS ALREADY BEEN HERE-!
WE'LL SOON KNOW! THERE'S TANA'S RESORT! I'M SETT DOWN... FAST!
FOOD! GIVE US FOOD!
WE'RE STARVING-!
THE ICE HAS FROZEN OUR FOOD!
ALL RIGHT-! AS SOON AS I'VE SEEN TANA! IS SHE—
TANA IS IN HER RESORT... THERE-!

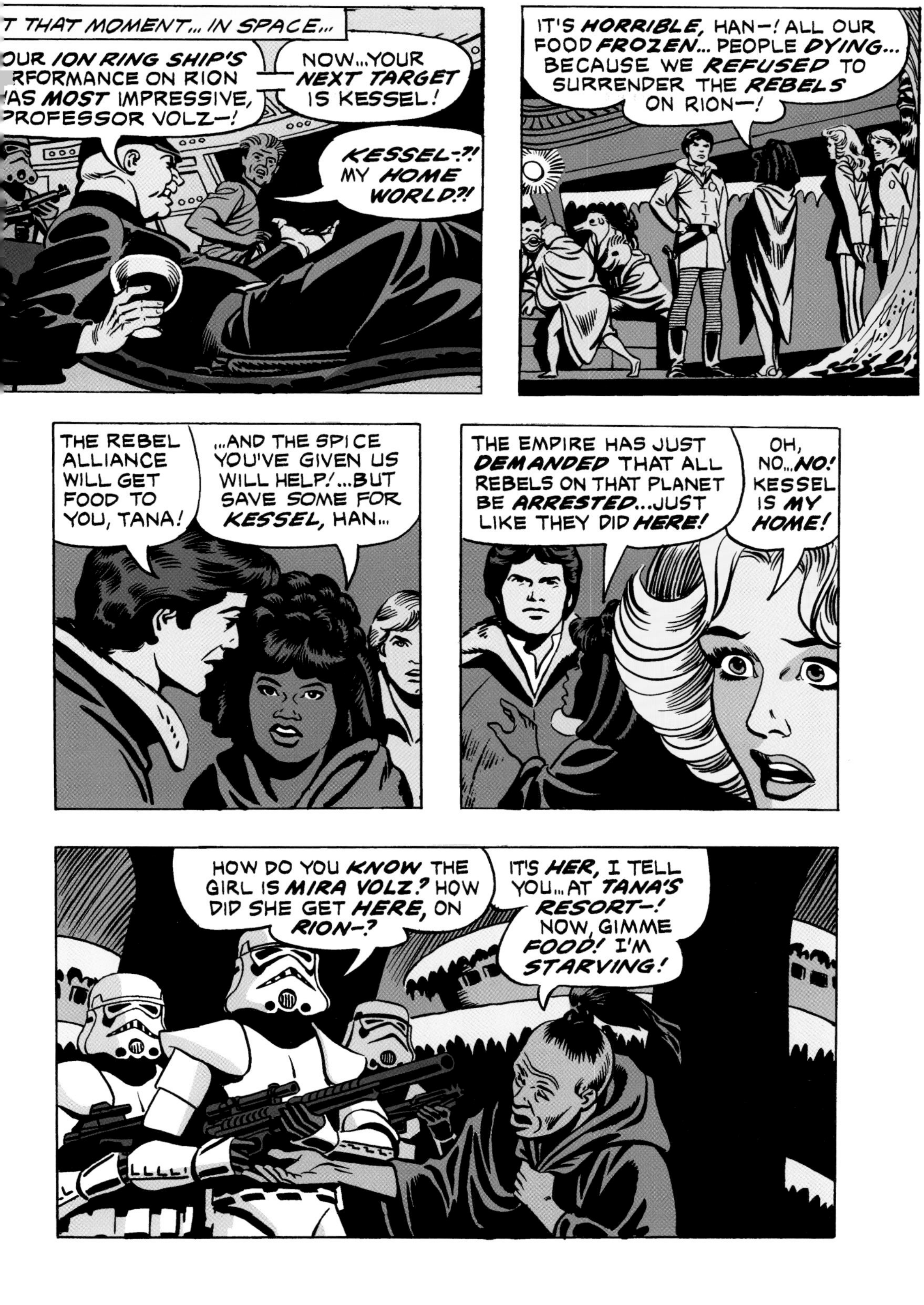
T THAT MOMENT... IN SPACE...
OUR ION RING SHIP'S RFORMANCE ON RION AS MOST IMPRESSIVE, PROFESSOR VOLZ—!
NOW... YOUR NEXT TARGET IS KESSEL!
KESSEL-?! MY HOME WORLD?!
IT'S HORRIBLE, HAN—! ALL OUR FOOD FROZEN... PEOPLE DYING... BECAUSE WE REFUSED TO SURRENDER THE REBELS ON RION—!
THE REBEL ALLIANCE WILL GET FOOD TO YOU, TANA!
...AND THE SPICE YOU'VE GIVEN US WILL HELP! ...BUT SAVE SOME FOR KESSEL, HAN...
THE EMPIRE HAS JUST DEMANDED THAT ALL REBELS ON THAT PLANET BE ARRESTED...JUST LIKE THEY DID HERE!
OH, NO...NO! KESSEL IS MY HOME!
HOW DO YOU KNOW THE GIRL IS MIRA VOLZ? HOW DID SHE GET HERE, ON RION—?
IT'S HER, I TELL YOU... AT TANA'S RESORT—! NOW, GIMME FOOD! I'M STARVING!

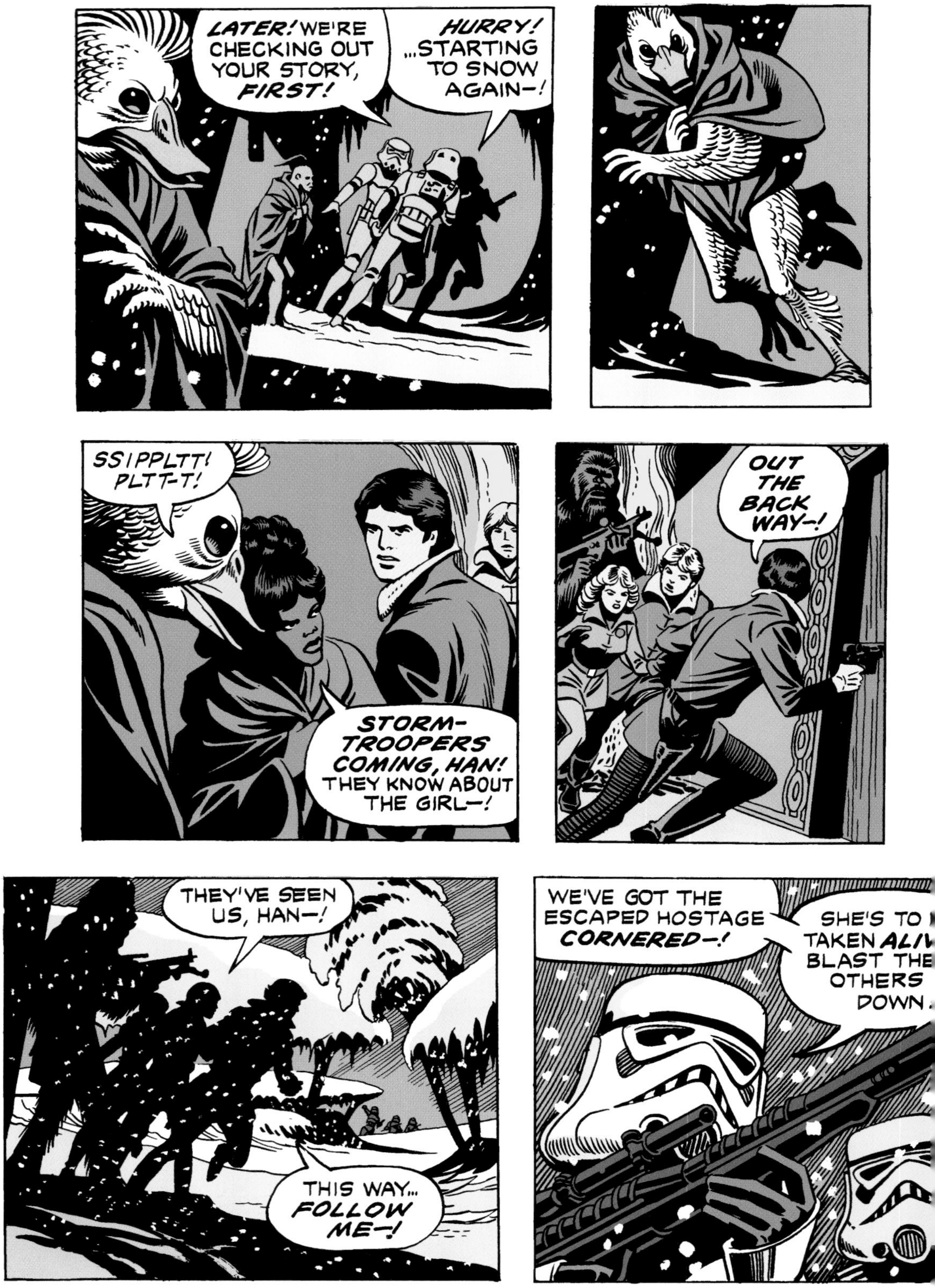

LATER! WE'RE CHECKING OUT YOUR STORY, FIRST!
HURRY! ...STARTING TO SNOW AGAIN-!
SSIPPLTT! PLTT-T!
STORM-TROOPERS COMING, HAN! THEY KNOW ABOUT THE GIRL-!
OUT THE BACK WAY-!
THEY'VE SEEN US, HAN-!
THIS WAY... FOLLOW ME-!
WE'VE GOT THE ESCAPED HOSTAGE CORNERED-!
SHE'S TO
TAKEN ALIV
BLAST THE
OTHERS
DOWN

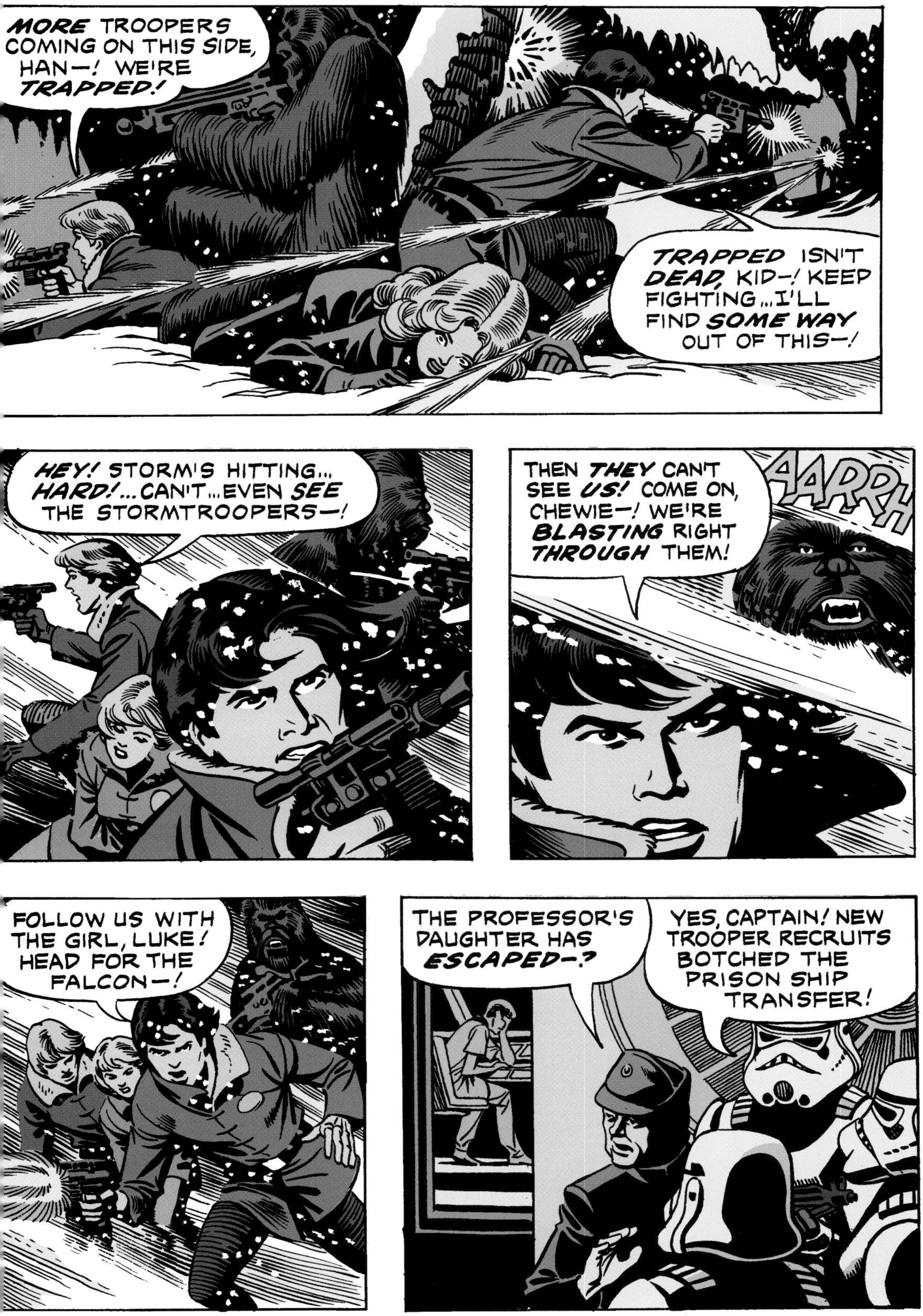
MORE TROOPERS COMING ON THIS SIDE, HAN—! WE'RE TRAPPED!
TRAPPED ISN'T DEAD, KID—! KEEP FIGHTING...I'LL FIND SOME WAY OUT OF THIS—!
HEY! STORM'S HITTING... HARD!...CAN'T...EVEN SEE THE STORMTROOPERS—!
THEN THEY CAN'T SEE US! COME ON, CHEWIE—! WE'RE BLASTING RIGHT THROUGH THEM!
AARRH
FOLLOW US WITH THE GIRL, LUKE! HEAD FOR THE FALCON—!
THE PROFESSOR'S DAUGHTER HAS ESCAPED—?
YES, CAPTAIN! NEW TROOPER RECRUITS BOTCHED THE PRISON SHIP TRANSFER!

VOLZ MUST *NOT* LEARN THAT WE NO LONGER HOLD HER *HOSTAGE!*

NO ONE IS TO SPEAK TO HIM BUT *ME!* THAT *IS AN ORDER!*

PLEASE... HOW IS *MIRA—?*

YOUR DAUGHTER IS PERFECTLY SAFE, VOL AS LONG AS YOU DO *EXACTLY AS I SAY*

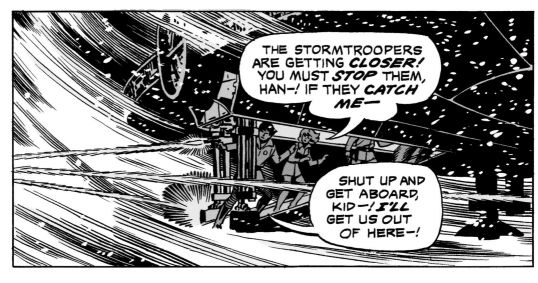

THE STORMTROOPERS ARE GETTING *CLOSER!* YOU MUST *STOP* THEM, HAN—! IF THEY *CATCH ME—*

SHUT UP AND GET ABOARD, KID—! *I'LL* GET US OUT OF HERE—!

BLAST OFF, CHEWIE—!

DON'T MIND HAN, MIRA! HE'LL BE IN A BETTER MOOD ONCE WE GET TO *KESSEL!*

I... I KNOW, LUKE! SO WILL I—!

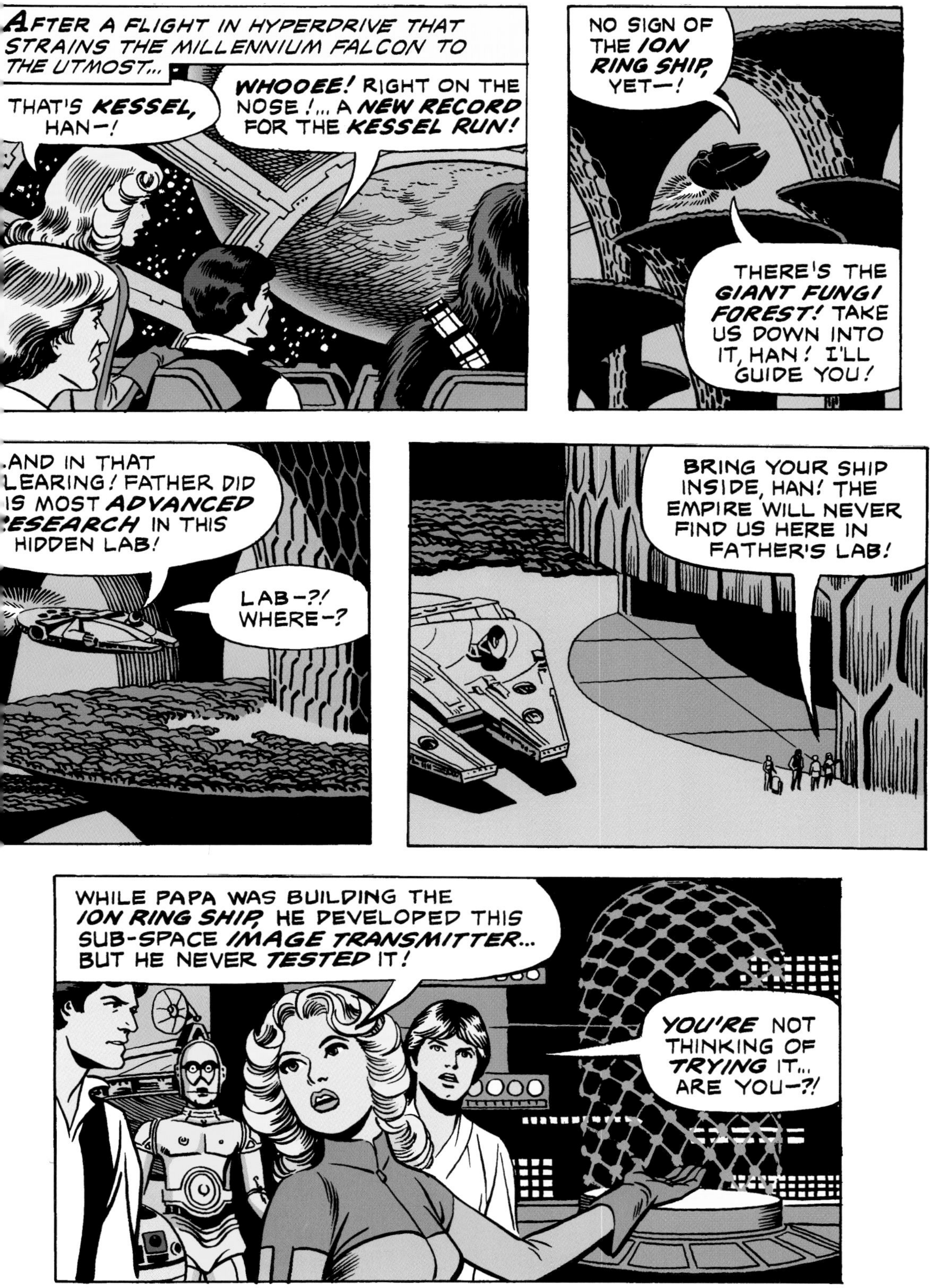
AFTER A FLIGHT IN HYPERDRIVE THAT STRAINS THE MILLENNIUM FALCON TO THE UTMOST...
THAT'S KESSEL, HAN—!
WHOOEE! RIGHT ON THE NOSE!... A NEW RECORD FOR THE KESSEL RUN!
NO SIGN OF THE ION RING SHIP, YET—!
THERE'S THE GIANT FUNGI FOREST! TAKE US DOWN INTO IT, HAN! I'LL GUIDE YOU!
.AND IN THAT LEARING! FATHER DID IS MOST ADVANCED ESEARCH IN THIS HIDDEN LAB!
LAB—?! WHERE—?
BRING YOUR SHIP INSIDE, HAN! THE EMPIRE WILL NEVER FIND US HERE IN FATHER'S LAB!
WHILE PAPA WAS BUILDING THE ION RING SHIP, HE DEVELOPED THIS SUB-SPACE IMAGE TRANSMITTER... BUT HE NEVER TESTED IT!
YOU'RE NOT THINKING OF TRYING IT... ARE YOU—?!

THE STORMTROOPERS ON THE *ION RING SHIP* CAN *JAM* ANY NORMAL MESSAGE I TRY TO SEND TO FATHER—!

...BUT *NOT* THIS SUB-SPACE IMAGE TRANSMISSION, EH? WORTH TRYING!

I'M JUST AFRAID THE TRANSMITTER MIGHT *HURT* YOU, MIRA—!

THANK YOU FC CARING LUKE

...BUT I MUST *TAKE* THAT CHANCE!

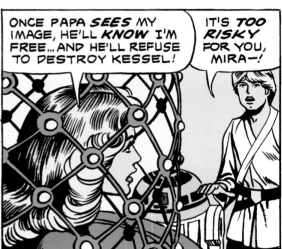

ONCE PAPA *SEES* MY IMAGE, HE'LL *KNOW* I'M FREE...AND HE'LL REFUSE TO DESTROY KESSEL!

IT'S *TOO RISKY* FOR YOU, MIRA—!

WE DON'T KNOW *ANYTHING* ABOUT HOW THIS TRANSMITTER *WORKS!*

R E E P! DIT-DIT!

MASTER LUKE! ARTOO HAS LOCATED THE *DATA STORAGE!*

...HE CAN OPERATE THE IMAGE TRANSMITTER!

THEN *HURRY—!* PLEASE START TRANSMITTING!

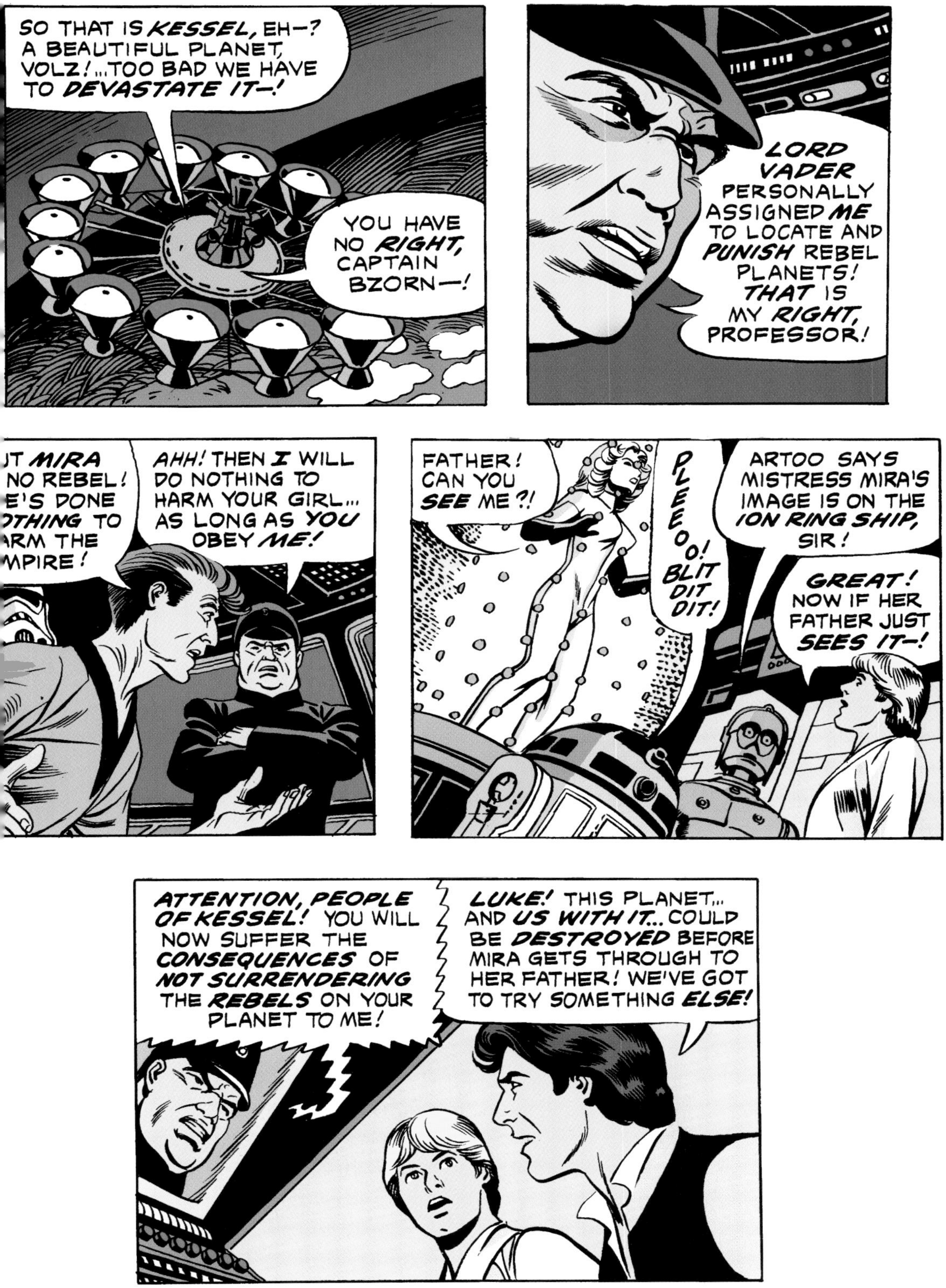

SO THAT IS KESSEL, EH—? A BEAUTIFUL PLANET, VOLZ!...TOO BAD WE HAVE TO DEVASTATE IT—!
YOU HAVE NO RIGHT, CAPTAIN BZORN—!
LORD VADER PERSONALLY ASSIGNED ME TO LOCATE AND PUNISH REBEL PLANETS! THAT IS MY RIGHT, PROFESSOR!
JT MIRA NO REBEL! E'S DONE OTHING TO ARM THE MPIRE!
AHH! THEN I WILL DO NOTHING TO HARM YOUR GIRL... AS LONG AS YOU OBEY ME!
FATHER! CAN YOU SEE ME?!
PLEEEOO! BLIT DIT DIT!
ARTOO SAYS MISTRESS MIRA'S IMAGE IS ON THE ION RING SHIP, SIR!
GREAT! NOW IF HER FATHER JUST SEES IT—!
ATTENTION, PEOPLE OF KESSEL! YOU WILL NOW SUFFER THE CONSEQUENCES OF NOT SURRENDERING THE REBELS ON YOUR PLANET TO ME!
LUKE! THIS PLANET... AND US WITH IT... COULD BE DESTROYED BEFORE MIRA GETS THROUGH TO HER FATHER! WE'VE GOT TO TRY SOMETHING ELSE!

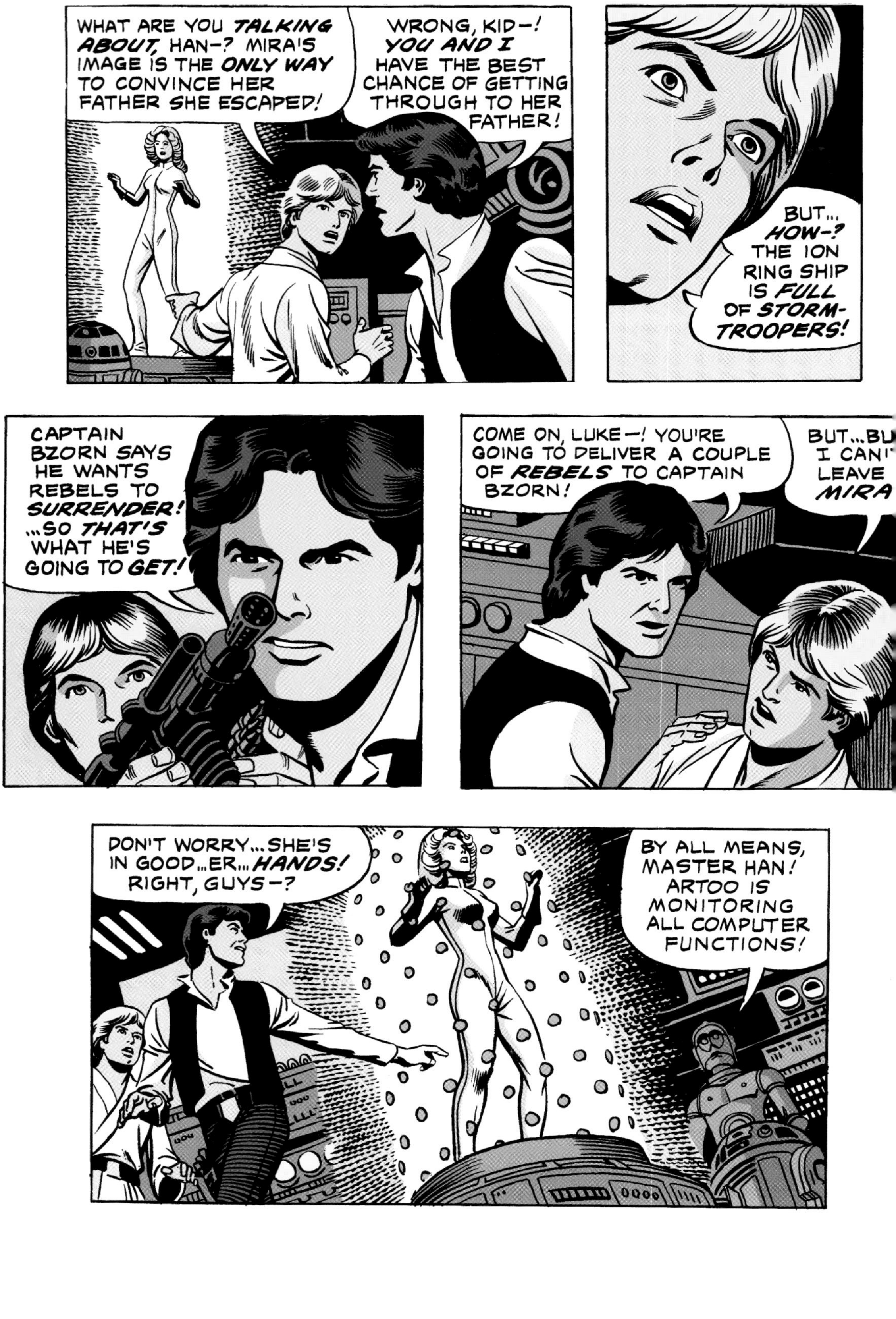
WHAT ARE YOU TALKING ABOUT, HAN-? MIRA'S IMAGE IS THE ONLY WAY TO CONVINCE HER FATHER SHE ESCAPED!
WRONG, KID-! YOU AND I HAVE THE BEST CHANCE OF GETTING THROUGH TO HER FATHER!
BUT... HOW-? THE ION RING SHIP IS FULL OF STORM-TROOPERS!
CAPTAIN BZORN SAYS HE WANTS REBELS TO SURRENDER! ...SO THAT'S WHAT HE'S GOING TO GET!
COME ON, LUKE-! YOU'RE GOING TO DELIVER A COUPLE OF REBELS TO CAPTAIN BZORN!
DON'T WORRY... SHE'S IN GOOD... ER... HANDS! RIGHT, GUYS-?
BY ALL MEANS, MASTER HAN! ARTOO IS MONITORING ALL COMPUTER FUNCTIONS!

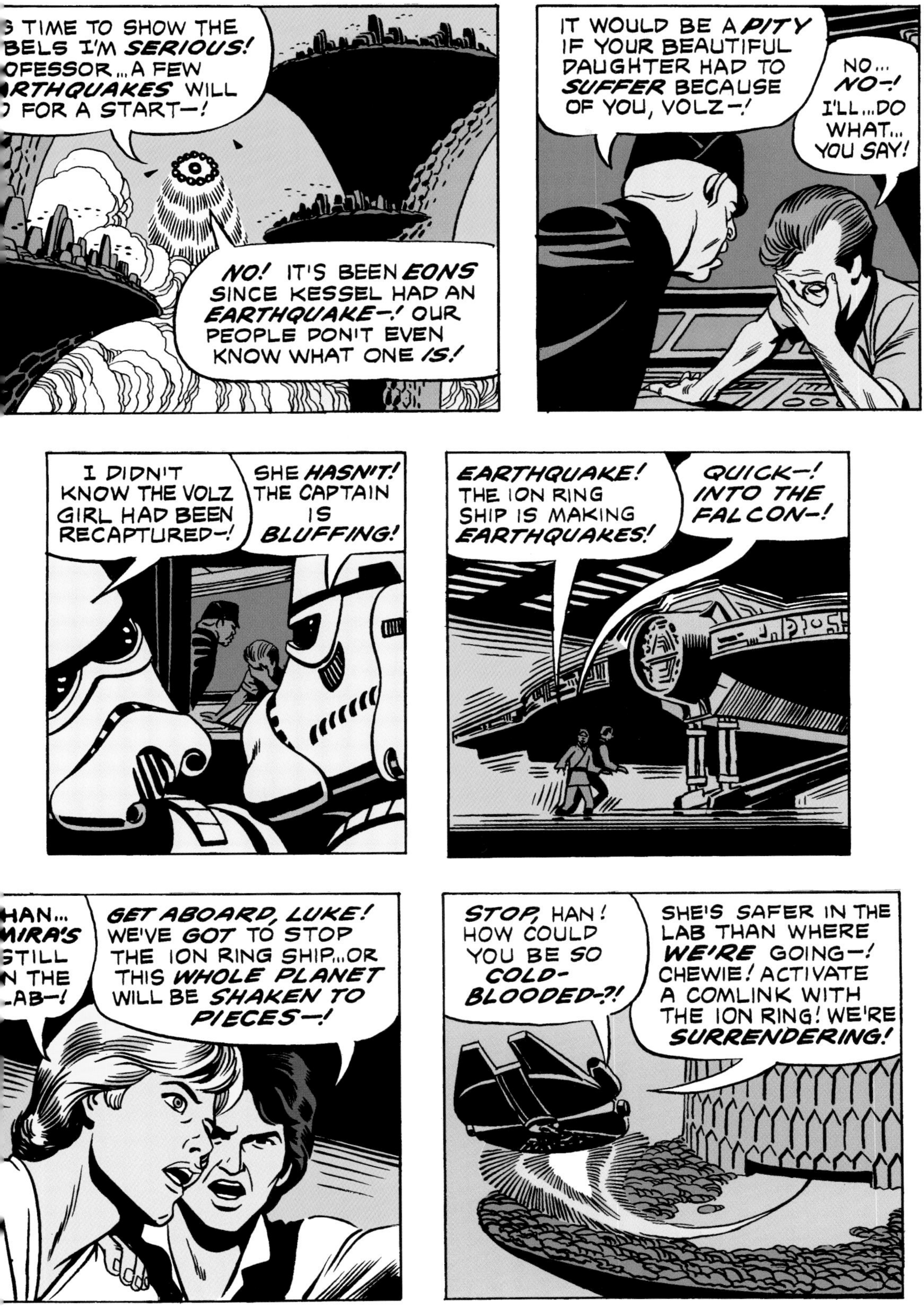

S TIME TO SHOW THE BELS I'M *SERIOUS!* OFESSOR... A FEW RTHQUAKES WILL FOR A START—!
NO! IT'S BEEN *EONS* SINCE KESSEL HAD AN *EARTHQUAKE*—! OUR PEOPLE DON'T EVEN KNOW WHAT ONE *IS!*
IT WOULD BE A *PITY* IF YOUR BEAUTIFUL DAUGHTER HAD TO *SUFFER* BECAUSE OF YOU, VOLZ—!
NO... *NO*—! I'LL...DO WHAT... YOU *SAY!*
I DIDN'T KNOW THE VOLZ GIRL HAD BEEN RECAPTURED—!
SHE *HASN'T!* THE CAPTAIN IS *BLUFFING!*
EARTHQUAKE! THE ION RING SHIP IS MAKING *EARTHQUAKES!*
QUICK—! INTO THE FALCON—!
HAN... MIRA'S STILL N THE AB—!
GET ABOARD, LUKE! WE'VE *GOT* TO STOP THE ION RING SHIP...OR THIS *WHOLE PLANET* WILL BE *SHAKEN TO PIECES*—!
STOP, HAN! HOW COULD YOU BE *SO COLD-BLOODED*—?!
SHE'S SAFER IN THE LAB THAN WHERE *WE'RE* GOING—! CHEWIE! ACTIVATE A COMLINK WITH THE ION RING! WE'RE *SURRENDERING!*

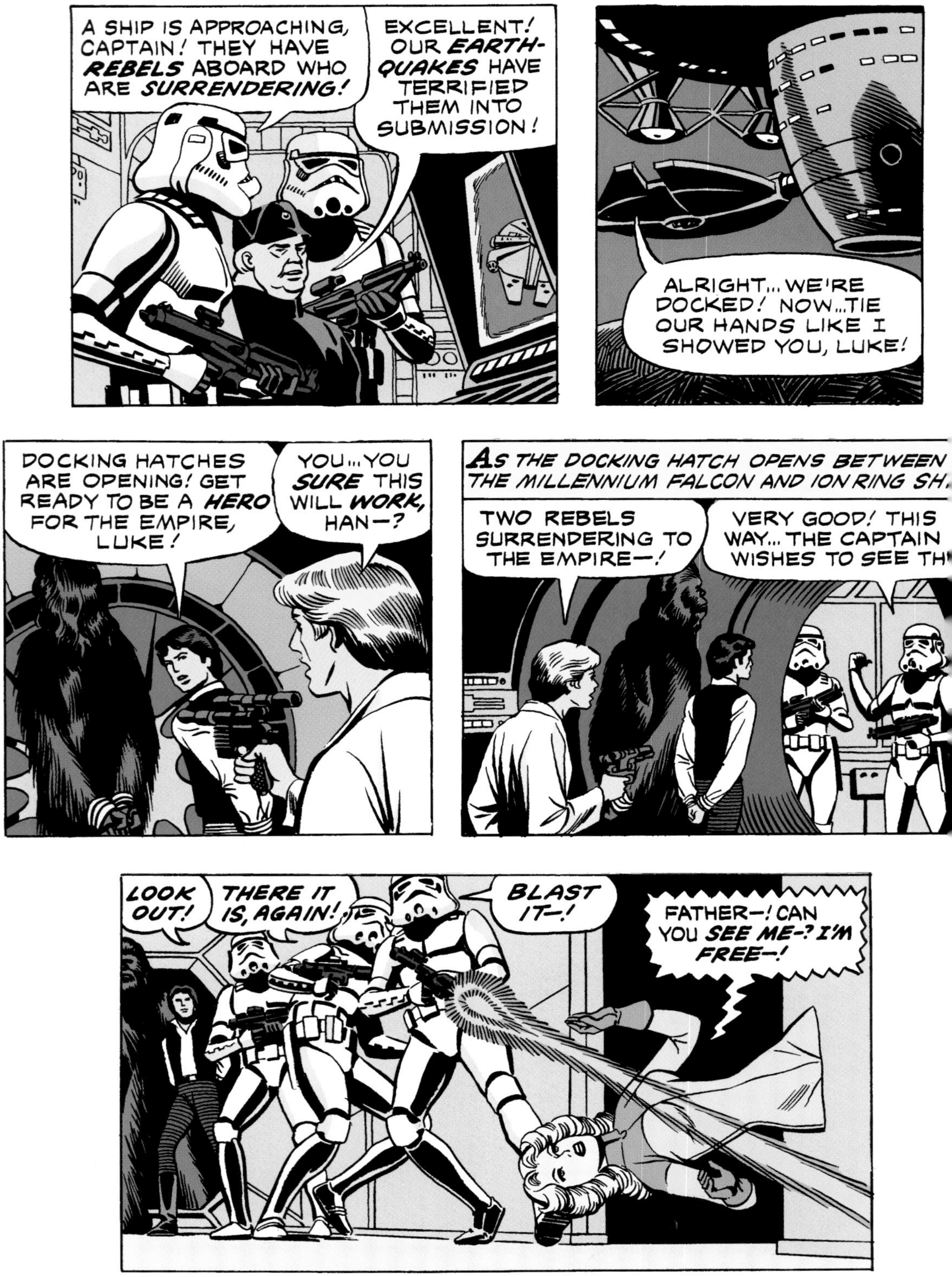
A SHIP IS APPROACHING, CAPTAIN! THEY HAVE REBELS ABOARD WHO ARE SURRENDERING!
EXCELLENT! OUR EARTH-QUAKES HAVE TERRIFIED THEM INTO SUBMISSION!
ALRIGHT... WE'RE DOCKED! NOW...TIE OUR HANDS LIKE I SHOWED YOU, LUKE!
DOCKING HATCHES ARE OPENING! GET READY TO BE A HERO FOR THE EMPIRE, LUKE!
YOU... YOU SURE THIS WILL WORK, HAN—?
AS THE DOCKING HATCH OPENS BETWEEN THE MILLENNIUM FALCON AND ION RING SH
TWO REBELS SURRENDERING TO THE EMPIRE—!
VERY GOOD! THIS WAY... THE CAPTAIN WISHES TO SEE TH
LOOK OUT!
THERE IT IS, AGAIN!
BLAST IT—!
FATHER—! CAN YOU SEE ME—? I'M FREE—!

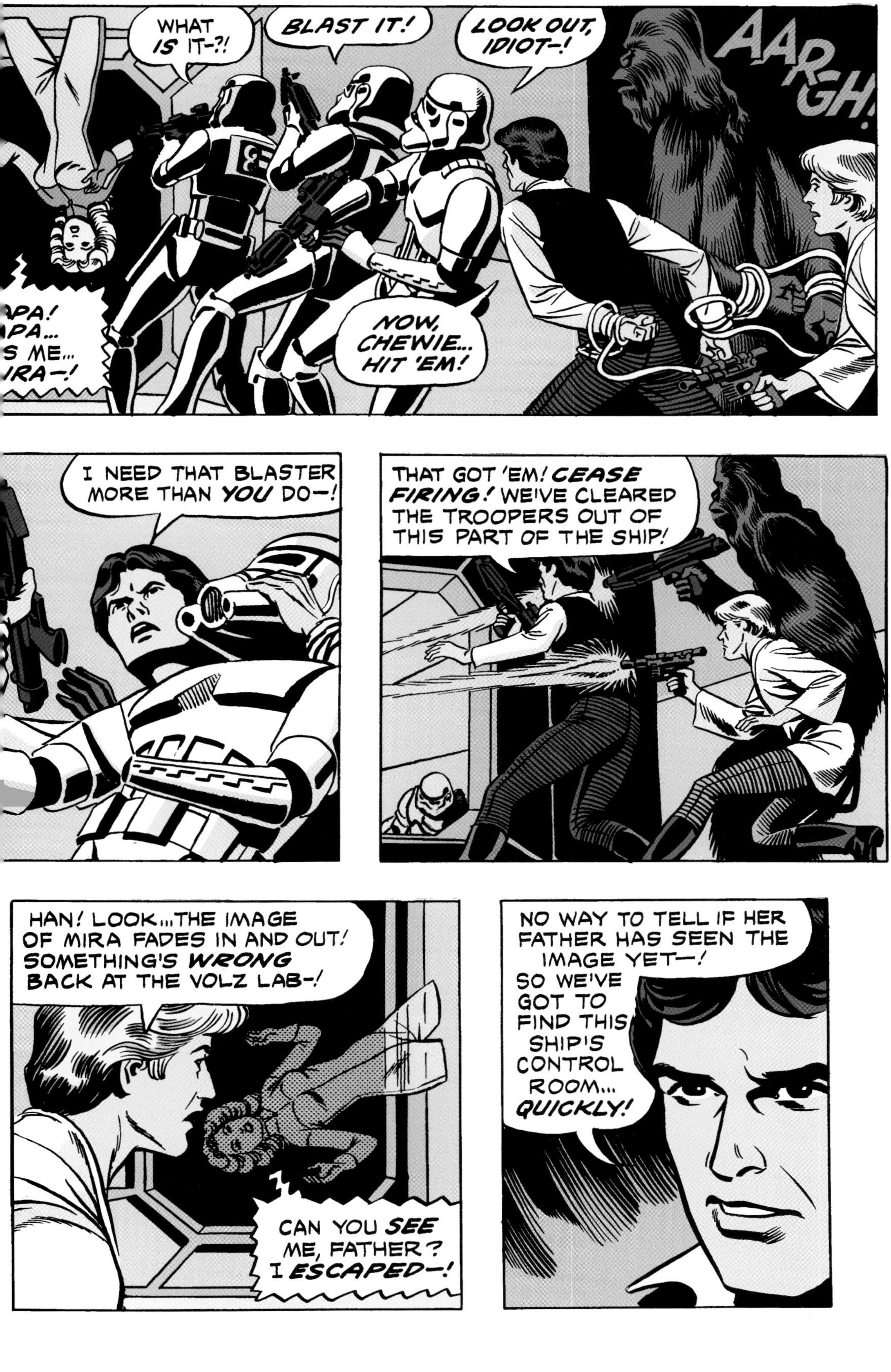
WHAT IS IT-?!
BLAST IT!
LOOK OUT, IDIOT—!
AARGH!
NOW, CHEWIE... HIT 'EM!
I NEED THAT BLASTER MORE THAN YOU DO—!
THAT GOT 'EM! CEASE FIRING! WE'VE CLEARED THE TROOPERS OUT OF THIS PART OF THE SHIP!
HAN! LOOK... THE IMAGE OF MIRA FADES IN AND OUT! SOMETHING'S WRONG BACK AT THE VOLZ LAB-!
CAN YOU SEE ME, FATHER? I ESCAPED—!
NO WAY TO TELL IF HER FATHER HAS SEEN THE IMAGE YET—!
SO WE'VE GOT TO FIND THIS SHIP'S CONTROL ROOM... QUICKLY!

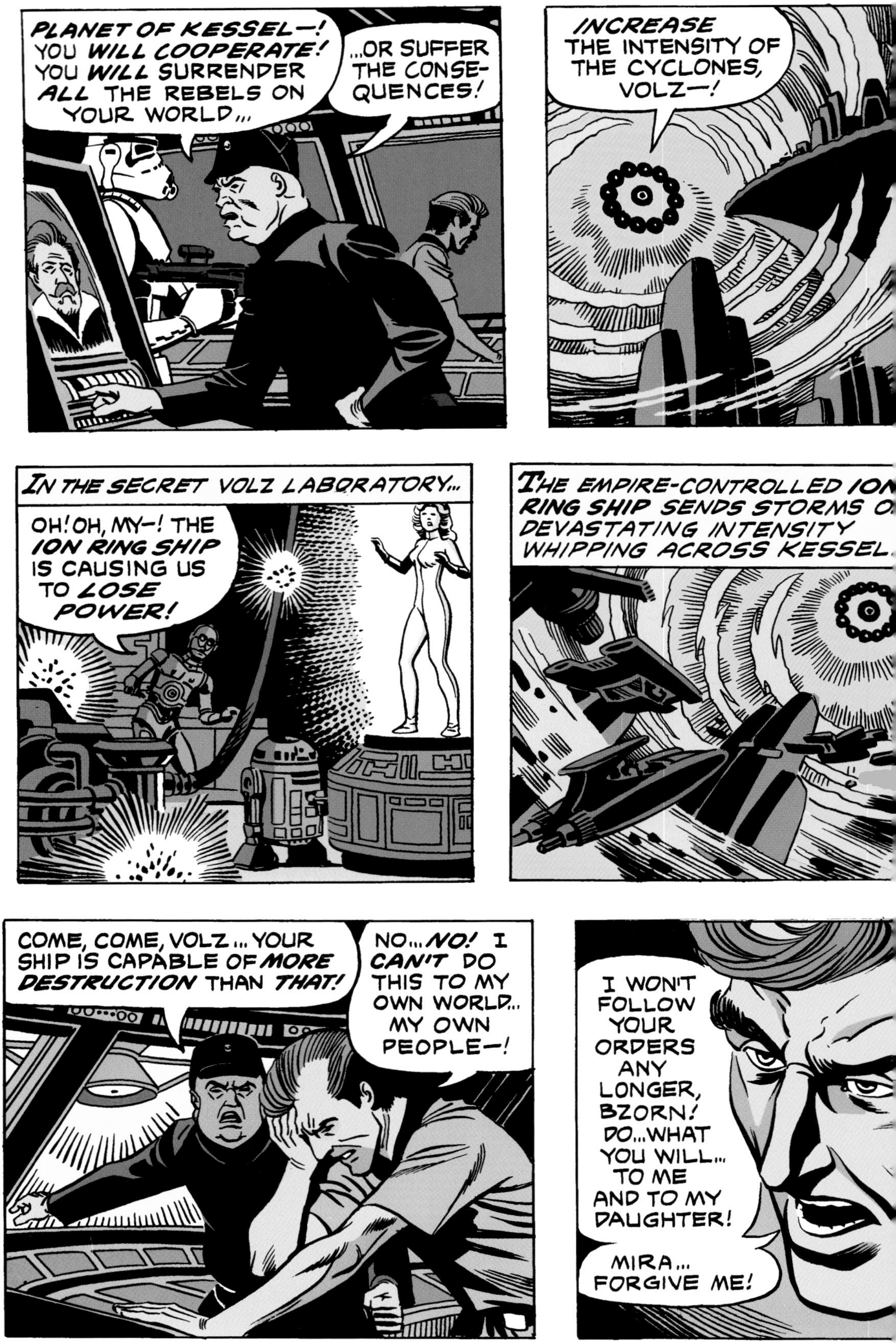
PLANET OF KESSEL—! YOU WILL COOPERATE! YOU WILL SURRENDER ALL THE REBELS ON YOUR WORLD...
...OR SUFFER THE CONSEQUENCES!
INCREASE THE INTENSITY OF THE CYCLONES, VOLZ—!
IN THE SECRET VOLZ LABORATORY...
OH! OH, MY—! THE ION RING SHIP IS CAUSING US TO LOSE POWER!
THE EMPIRE-CONTROLLED ION RING SHIP SENDS STORMS OF DEVASTATING INTENSITY WHIPPING ACROSS KESSEL.
COME, COME, VOLZ... YOUR SHIP IS CAPABLE OF MORE DESTRUCTION THAN THAT!
NO... NO! I CAN'T DO THIS TO MY OWN WORLD... MY OWN PEOPLE—!
I WON'T FOLLOW YOUR ORDERS ANY LONGER, BZORN! DO... WHAT YOU WILL... TO ME AND TO MY DAUGHTER!
MIRA... FORGIVE ME!

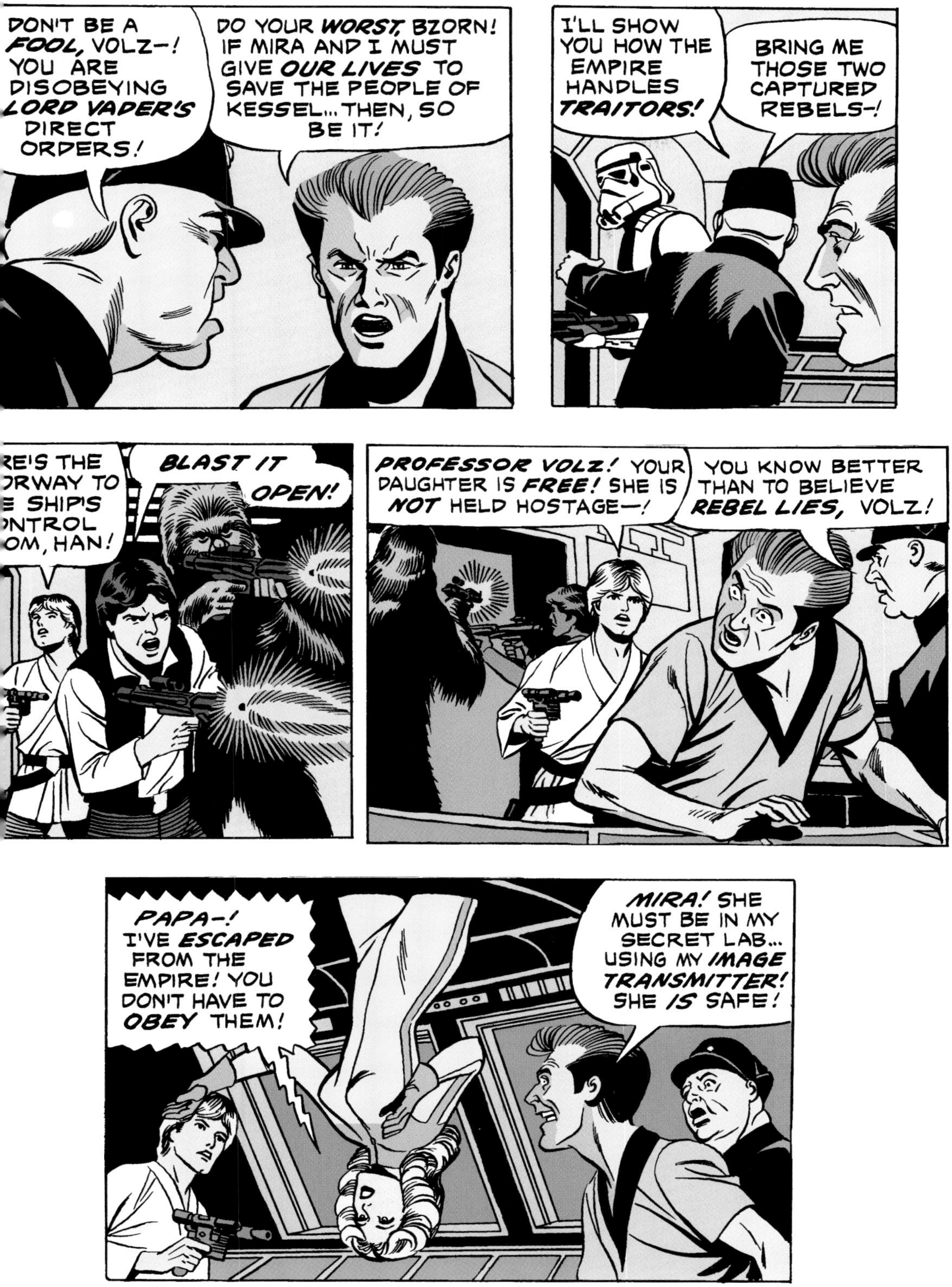
DON'T BE A FOOL, VOLZ--! YOU ARE DISOBEYING LORD VADER'S DIRECT ORDERS!
DO YOUR WORST, BZORN! IF MIRA AND I MUST GIVE OUR LIVES TO SAVE THE PEOPLE OF KESSEL... THEN, SO BE IT!
I'LL SHOW YOU HOW THE EMPIRE HANDLES TRAITORS!
BRING ME THOSE TWO CAPTURED REBELS--!
RE'S THE RWAY TO E SHIP'S NTROL OM, HAN!
BLAST IT OPEN!
PROFESSOR VOLZ! YOUR DAUGHTER IS FREE! SHE IS NOT HELD HOSTAGE--!
YOU KNOW BETTER THAN TO BELIEVE REBEL LIES, VOLZ!
PAPA--! I'VE ESCAPED FROM THE EMPIRE! YOU DON'T HAVE TO OBEY THEM!
MIRA! SHE MUST BE IN MY SECRET LAB... USING MY IMAGE TRANSMITTER! SHE IS SAFE!

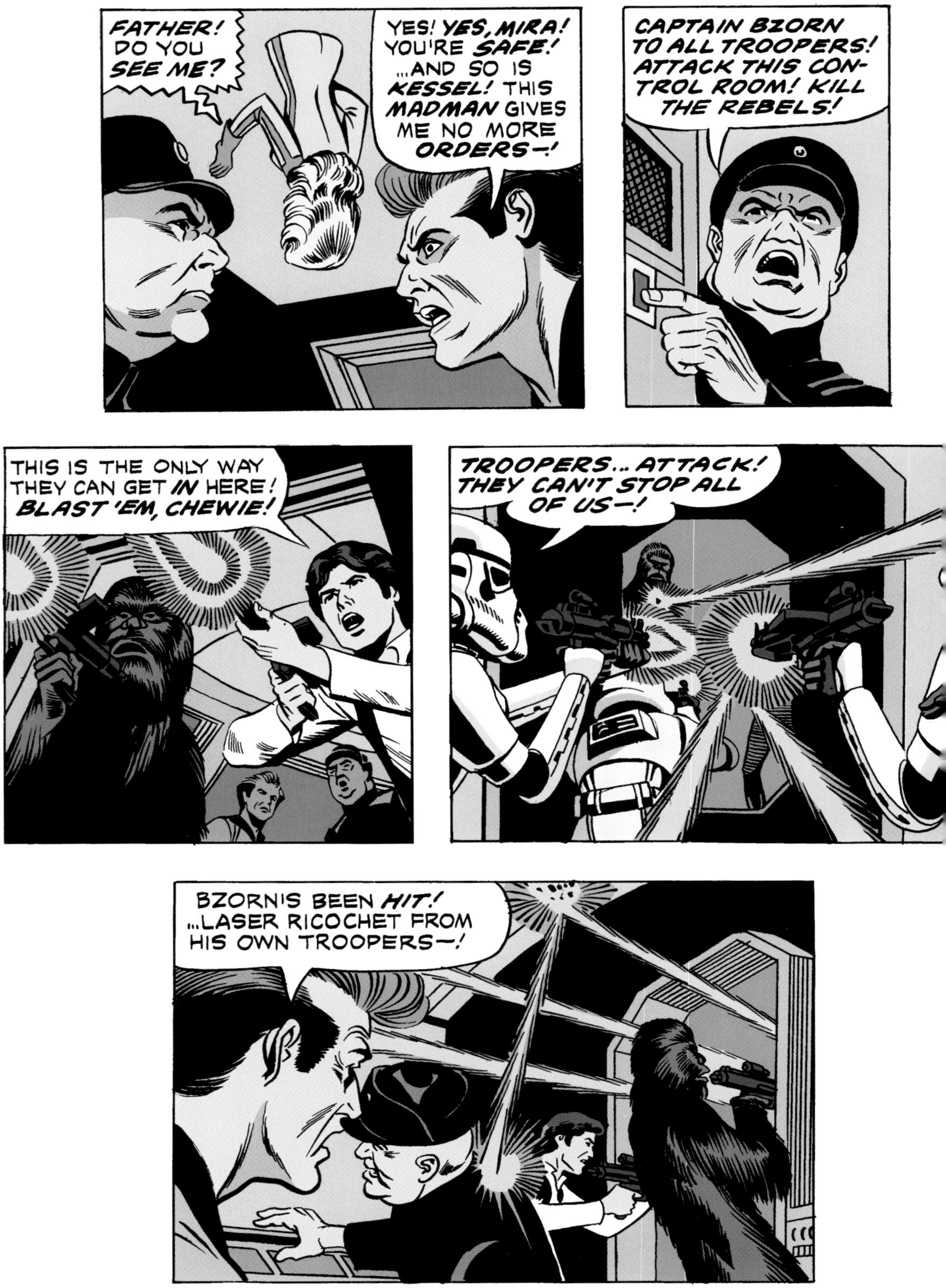
FATHER! DO YOU SEE ME?
YES! YES, MIRA! YOU'RE SAFE! ...AND SO IS KESSEL! THIS MADMAN GIVES ME NO MORE ORDERS--!
CAPTAIN BZORN TO ALL TROOPERS! ATTACK THIS CONTROL ROOM! KILL THE REBELS!
THIS IS THE ONLY WAY THEY CAN GET IN HERE! BLAST 'EM, CHEWIE!
TROOPERS... ATTACK! THEY CAN'T STOP ALL OF US--!
BZORN'S BEEN HIT! ...LASER RICOCHET FROM HIS OWN TROOPERS--!

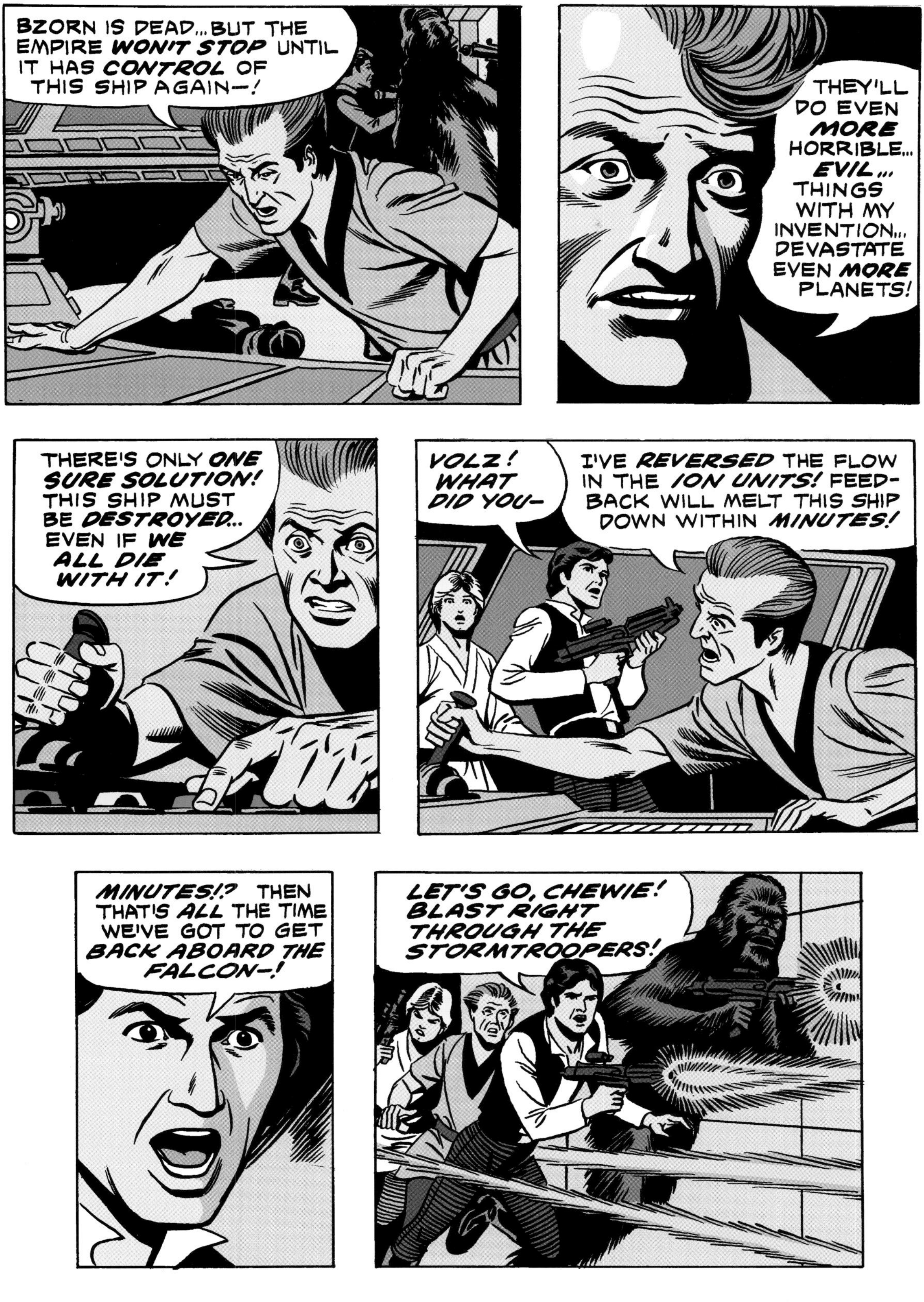
BZORN IS DEAD... BUT THE EMPIRE WON'T STOP UNTIL IT HAS CONTROL OF THIS SHIP AGAIN—!
THEY'LL DO EVEN MORE HORRIBLE... EVIL... THINGS WITH MY INVENTION... DEVASTATE EVEN MORE PLANETS!
THERE'S ONLY ONE SURE SOLUTION! THIS SHIP MUST BE DESTROYED... EVEN IF WE ALL DIE WITH IT!
VOLZ! WHAT DID YOU—
I'VE REVERSED THE FLOW IN THE ION UNITS! FEED-BACK WILL MELT THIS SHIP DOWN WITHIN MINUTES!
MINUTES!? THEN THAT'S ALL THE TIME WE'VE GOT TO GET BACK ABOARD THE FALCON—!
LET'S GO, CHEWIE! BLAST RIGHT THROUGH THE STORMTROOPERS!

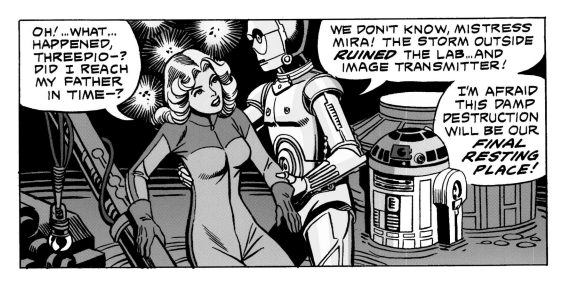

OH! ...WHAT... HAPPENED, THREEPIO—? DID I REACH MY FATHER IN TIME—?

WE DON'T KNOW, MISTRESS MIRA! THE STORM OUTSIDE *RUINED* THE LAB...AND IMAGE TRANSMITTER!

I'M AFRAID THIS DAMP DESTRUCTION WILL BE OUR *FINAL RESTING PLACE!*

THE ION RING SHIP SELF-DESTRUCTS IN THE AIR OVER THE PLANET KESSEL...

OH NO, *NO—!* PAPA—!

LOOK, MISTRESS MIRA! MASTER HAN'S SHIP IS LANDING—! MAYBE...

OH, LUKE—! EVERYONE IS *SAFE!* IT... SEEMS LIKE A *MIRACLE—!*

NOTHING TO IT, MIRA—! HAN WILL DO ALMOST *ANYTHI* TO SET A *NEW RECOR* FOR *THE KESSEL RU*

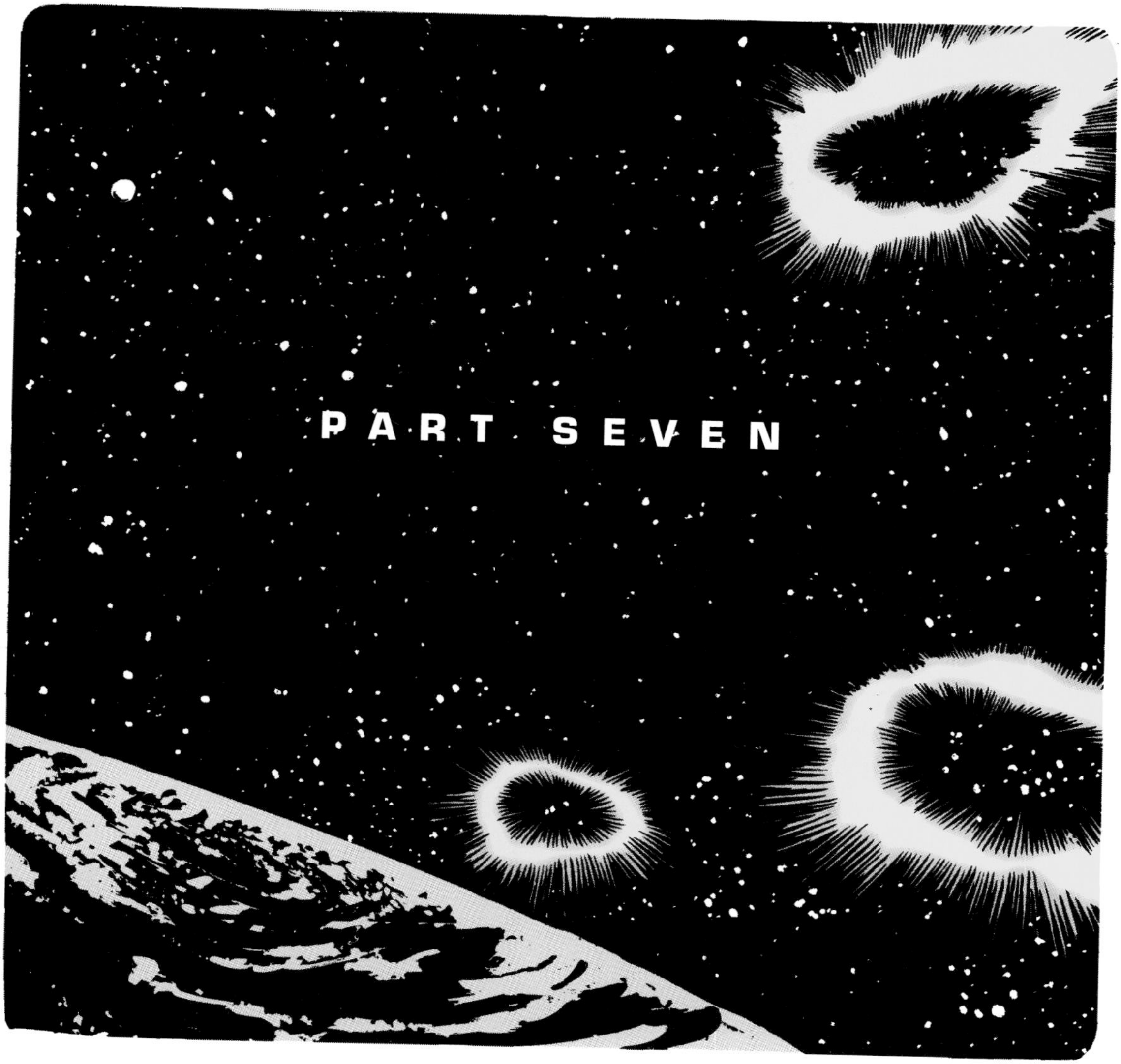
PART SEVEN

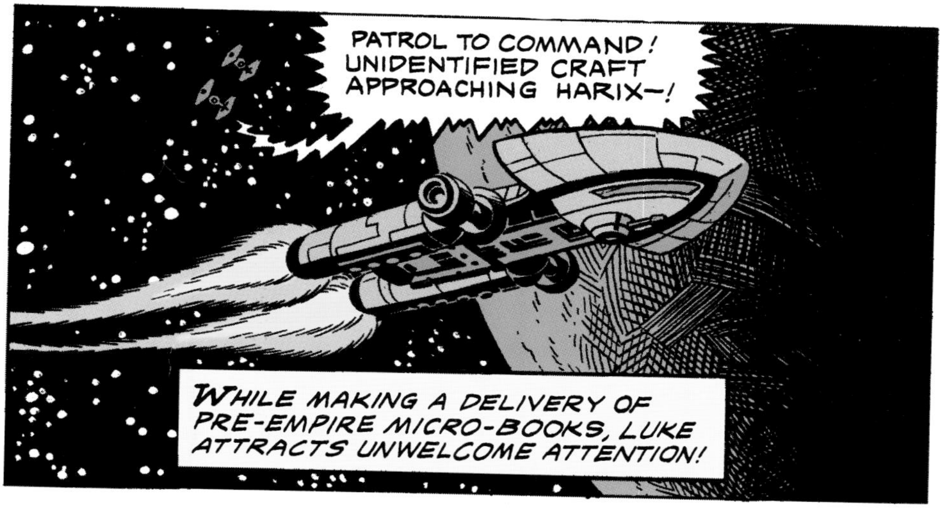
PATROL TO COMMAND! UNIDENTIFIED CRAFT APPROACHING HARIX--!
WHILE MAKING A DELIVERY OF PRE-EMPIRE MICRO-BOOKS, LUKE ATTRACTS UNWELCOME ATTENTION!

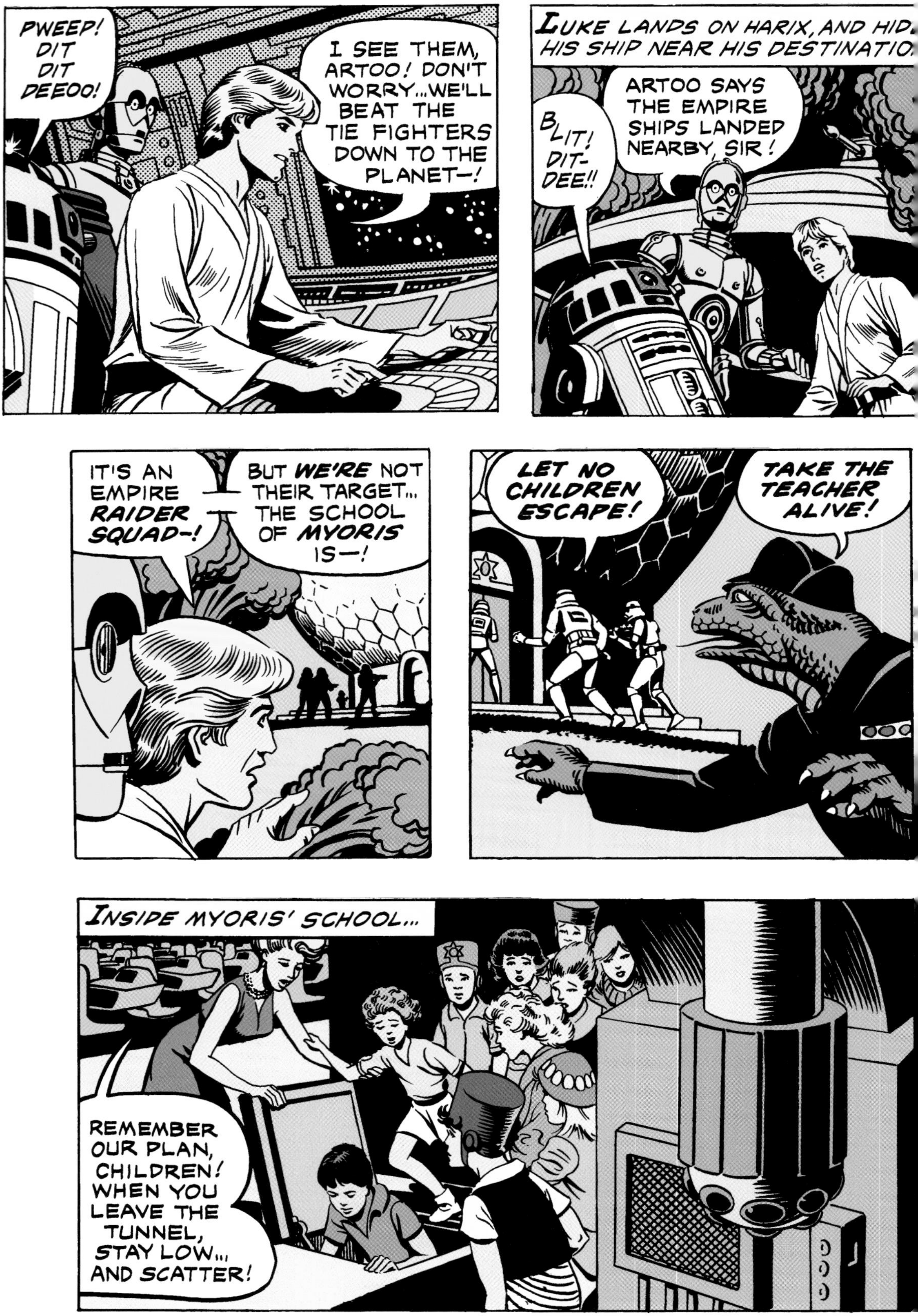
PWEEP! DIT DIT DEEOO!
I SEE THEM, ARTOO! DON'T WORRY...WE'LL BEAT THE TIE FIGHTERS DOWN TO THE PLANET—!
LUKE LANDS ON HARIX, AND HID
HIS SHIP NEAR HIS DESTINATIO
BLIT! DIT-DEE!!
ARTOO SAYS THE EMPIRE SHIPS LANDED NEARBY, SIR!
IT'S AN EMPIRE RAIDER SQUAD—!
BUT WE'RE NOT THEIR TARGET... THE SCHOOL OF MYORIS IS—!
LET NO CHILDREN ESCAPE!
TAKE THE TEACHER ALIVE!
INSIDE MYORIS' SCHOOL...
REMEMBER OUR PLAN, CHILDREN! WHEN YOU LEAVE THE TUNNEL, STAY LOW... AND SCATTER!

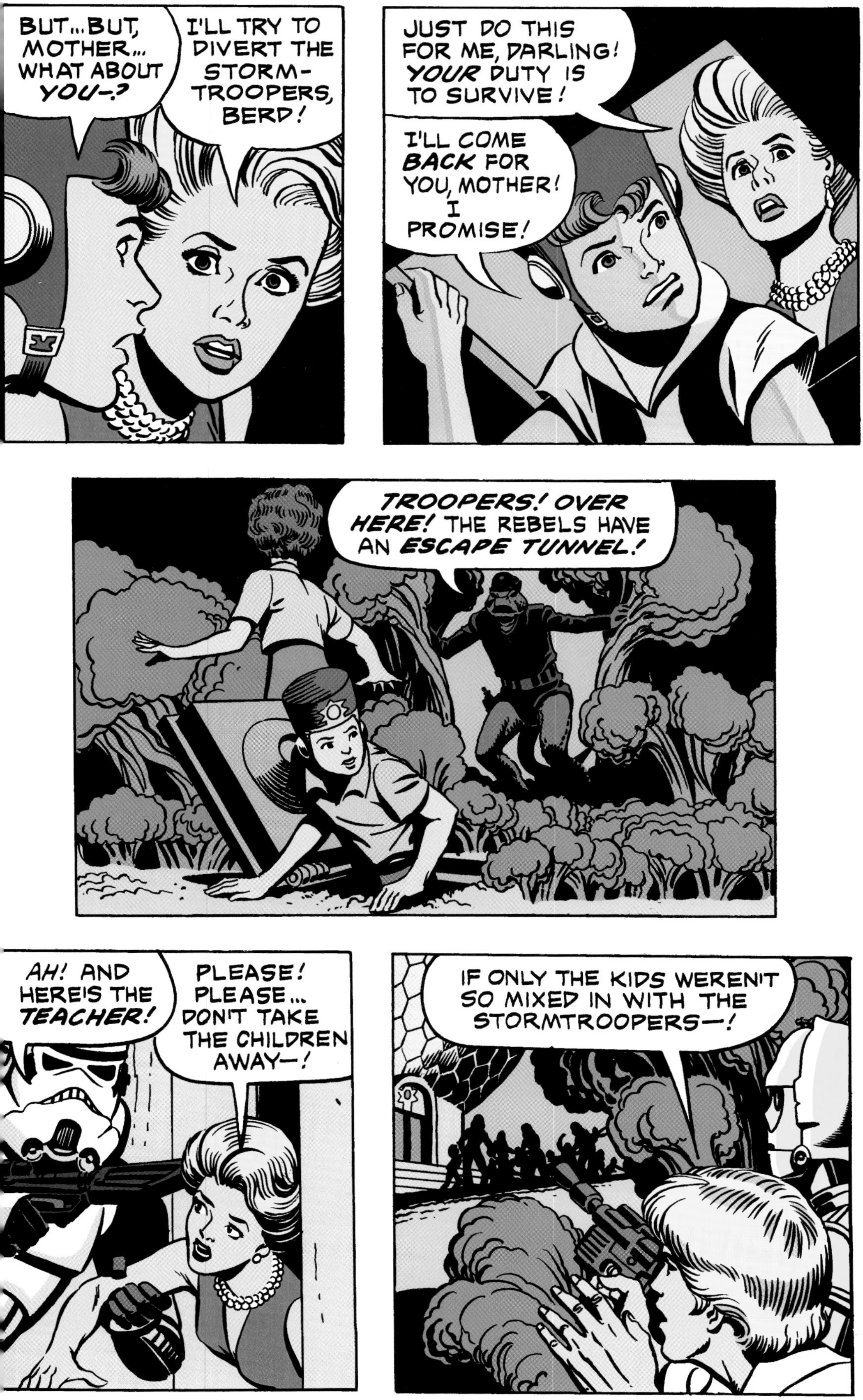
BUT... BUT, MOTHER... WHAT ABOUT YOU-?
I'LL TRY TO DIVERT THE STORM-TROOPERS, BERD!
JUST DO THIS FOR ME, DARLING! YOUR DUTY IS TO SURVIVE!
I'LL COME BACK FOR YOU, MOTHER! I PROMISE!
TROOPERS! OVER HERE! THE REBELS HAVE AN ESCAPE TUNNEL!
AH! AND HERE'S THE TEACHER!
PLEASE! PLEASE... DON'T TAKE THE CHILDREN AWAY-!
IF ONLY THE KIDS WEREN'T SO MIXED IN WITH THE STORMTROOPERS-!

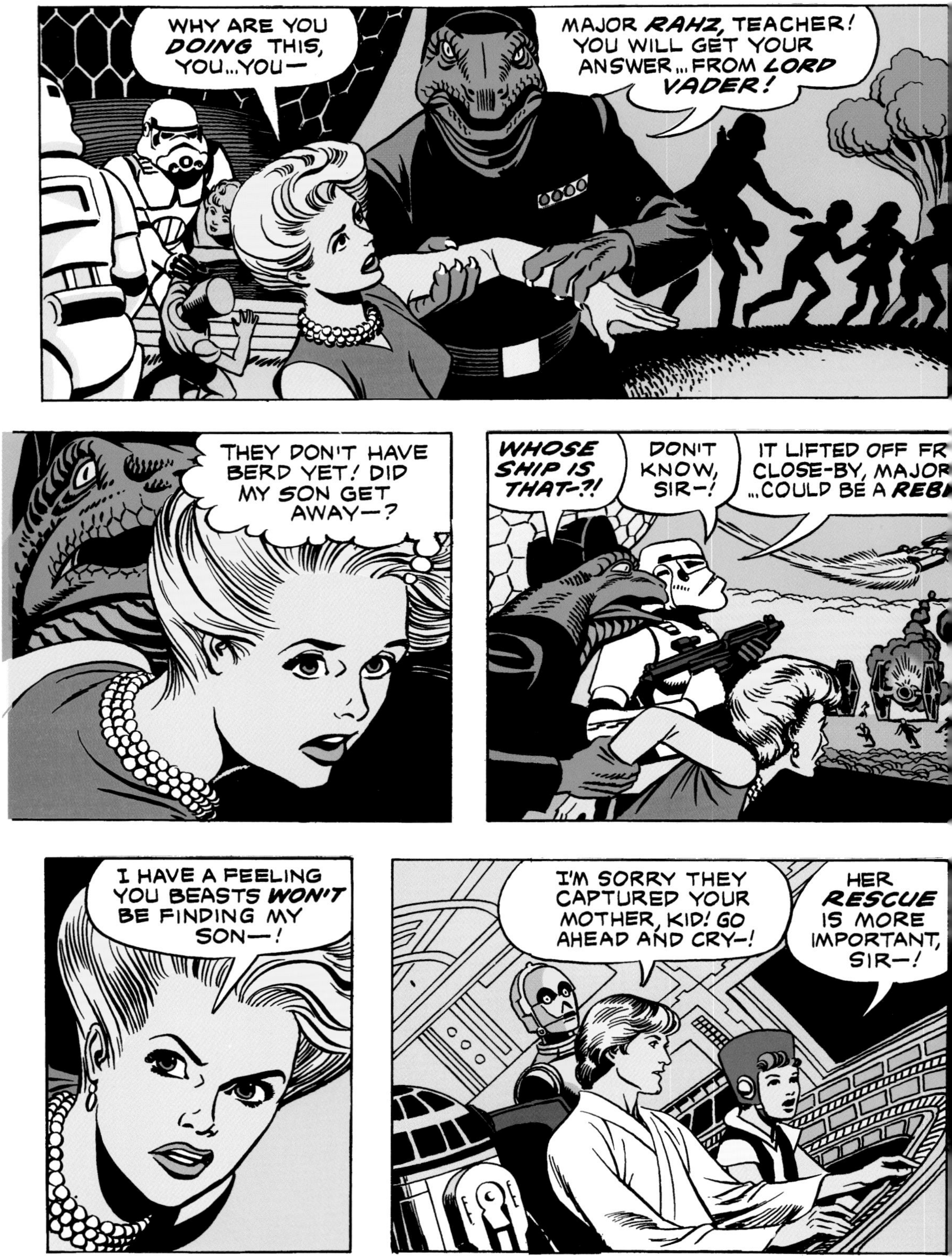
WHY ARE YOU DOING THIS, YOU...YOU—
MAJOR RAHZ, TEACHER! YOU WILL GET YOUR ANSWER... FROM LORD VADER!
THEY DON'T HAVE BERD YET! DID MY SON GET AWAY—?
WHOSE SHIP IS THAT–?!
DON'T KNOW, SIR–!
IT LIFTED OFF FR CLOSE-BY, MAJOR ...COULD BE A REB
I HAVE A FEELING YOU BEASTS WON'T BE FINDING MY SON—!
I'M SORRY THEY CAPTURED YOUR MOTHER, KID! GO AHEAD AND CRY–!
HER RESCUE IS MORE IMPORTANT, SIR–!

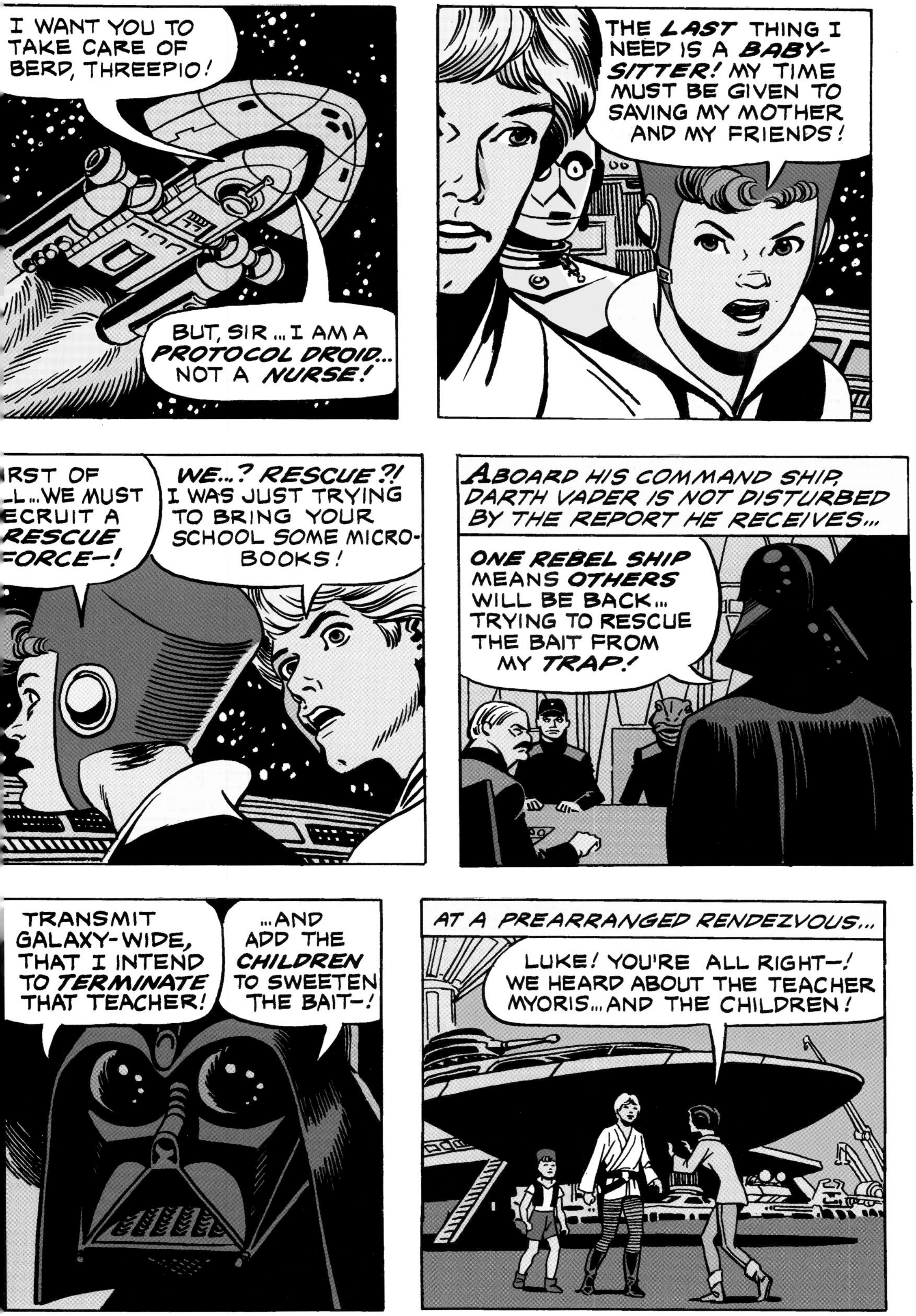
I WANT YOU TO TAKE CARE OF BERD, THREEPIO!
BUT, SIR ... I AM A PROTOCOL DROID... NOT A NURSE!
THE LAST THING I NEED IS A BABY-SITTER! MY TIME MUST BE GIVEN TO SAVING MY MOTHER AND MY FRIENDS!
RST OF L...WE MUST ECRUIT A RESCUE ORCE-!
WE...? RESCUE?! I WAS JUST TRYING TO BRING YOUR SCHOOL SOME MICRO-BOOKS!
ABOARD HIS COMMAND SHIP, DARTH VADER IS NOT DISTURBED BY THE REPORT HE RECEIVES...
ONE REBEL SHIP MEANS OTHERS WILL BE BACK... TRYING TO RESCUE THE BAIT FROM MY TRAP!
TRANSMIT GALAXY-WIDE, THAT I INTEND TO TERMINATE THAT TEACHER!
...AND ADD THE CHILDREN TO SWEETEN THE BAIT-!
AT A PREARRANGED RENDEZVOUS...
LUKE! YOU'RE ALL RIGHT-! WE HEARD ABOUT THE TEACHER MYORIS... AND THE CHILDREN!

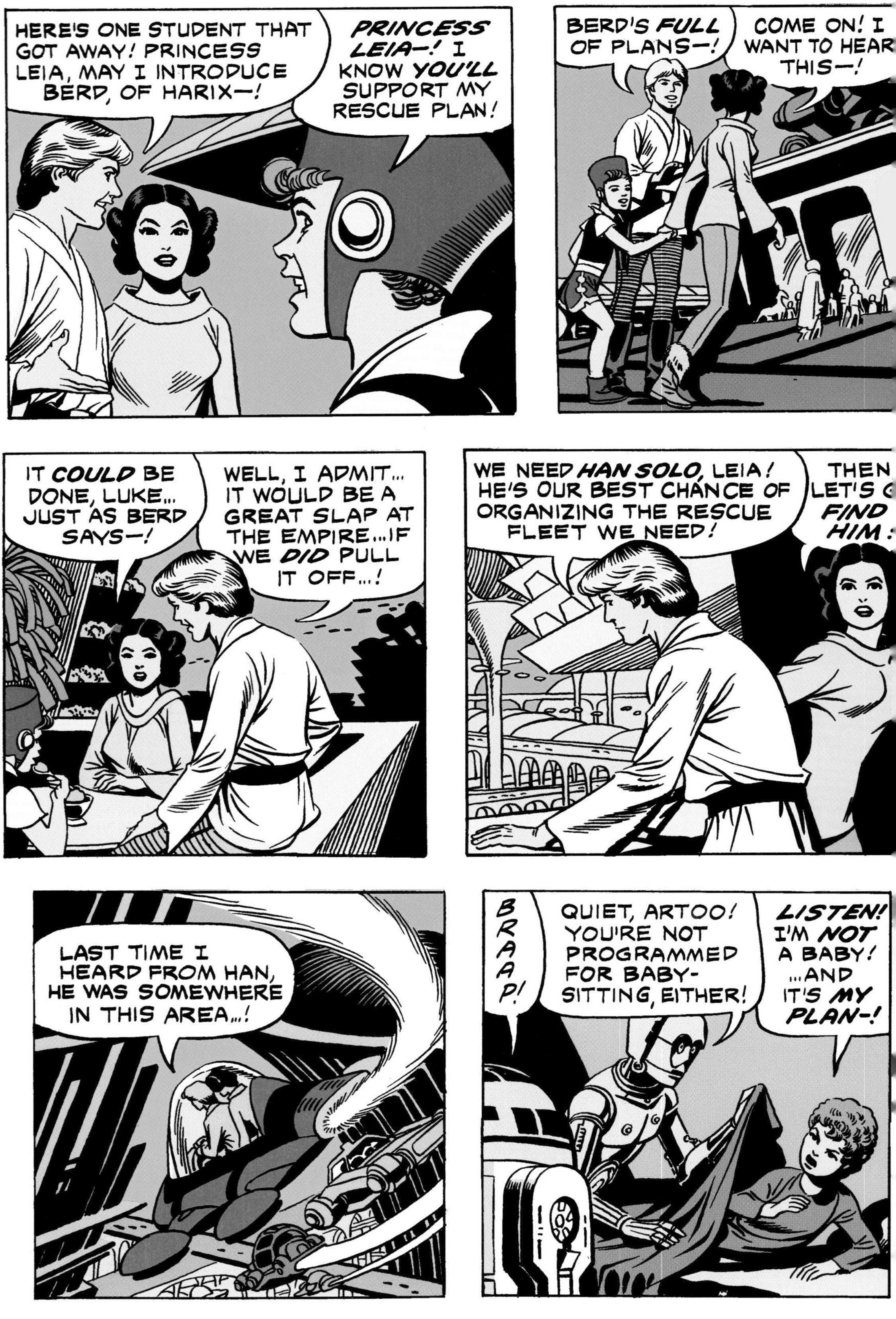
HERE'S ONE STUDENT THAT GOT AWAY! PRINCESS LEIA, MAY I INTRODUCE BERD, OF HARIX—!
PRINCESS LEIA—! I KNOW YOU'LL SUPPORT MY RESCUE PLAN!
BERD'S FULL OF PLANS—!
COME ON! I WANT TO HEAR THIS—!
IT COULD BE DONE, LUKE... JUST AS BERD SAYS—!
WELL, I ADMIT... IT WOULD BE A GREAT SLAP AT THE EMPIRE...IF WE DID PULL IT OFF...!
WE NEED HAN SOLO, LEIA! HE'S OUR BEST CHANCE OF ORGANIZING THE RESCUE FLEET WE NEED!
THEN LET'S FIND HIM
LAST TIME I HEARD FROM HAN, HE WAS SOMEWHERE IN THIS AREA...!
BRAAAP!
QUIET, ARTOO! YOU'RE NOT PROGRAMMED FOR BABY-SITTING, EITHER!
LISTEN! I'M NOT A BABY! ...AND IT'S MY PLAN—!

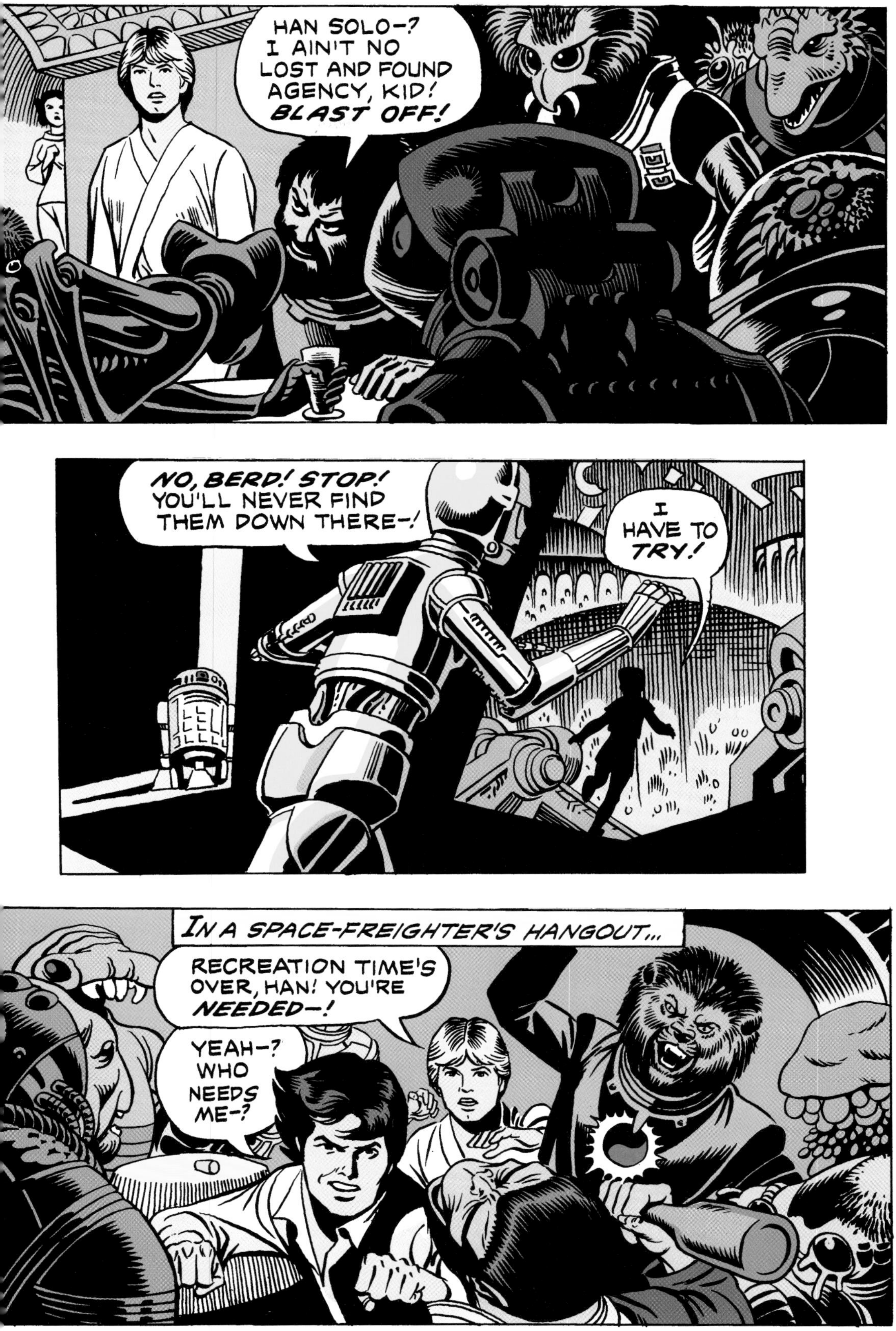
HAN SOLO-? I AIN'T NO LOST AND FOUND AGENCY, KID! BLAST OFF!
NO, BERD! STOP! YOU'LL NEVER FIND THEM DOWN THERE-!
I HAVE TO TRY!
IN A SPACE-FREIGHTER'S HANGOUT...
RECREATION TIME'S OVER, HAN! YOU'RE NEEDED-!
YEAH-? WHO NEEDS ME-?

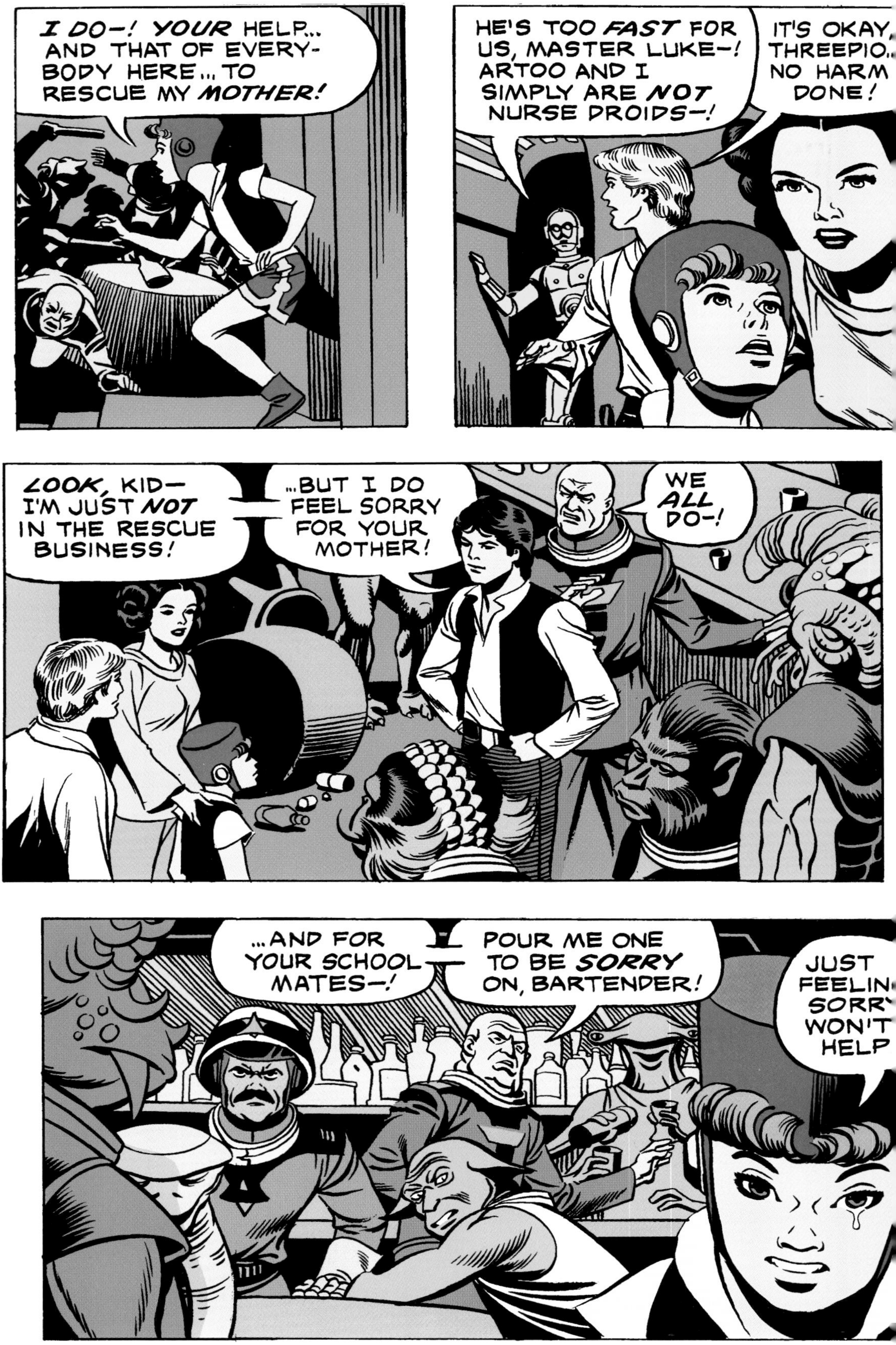
I DO-! YOUR HELP... AND THAT OF EVERY-BODY HERE... TO RESCUE MY MOTHER!
HE'S TOO FAST FOR US, MASTER LUKE-! ARTOO AND I SIMPLY ARE NOT NURSE DROIDS-!
IT'S OKAY, THREEPIO. NO HARM DONE!
LOOK, KID- I'M JUST NOT IN THE RESCUE BUSINESS!
...BUT I DO FEEL SORRY FOR YOUR MOTHER!
WE ALL DO-!
...AND FOR YOUR SCHOOL MATES-!
POUR ME ONE TO BE SORRY ON, BARTENDER!
JUST FEELIN SORR WON'T HELP

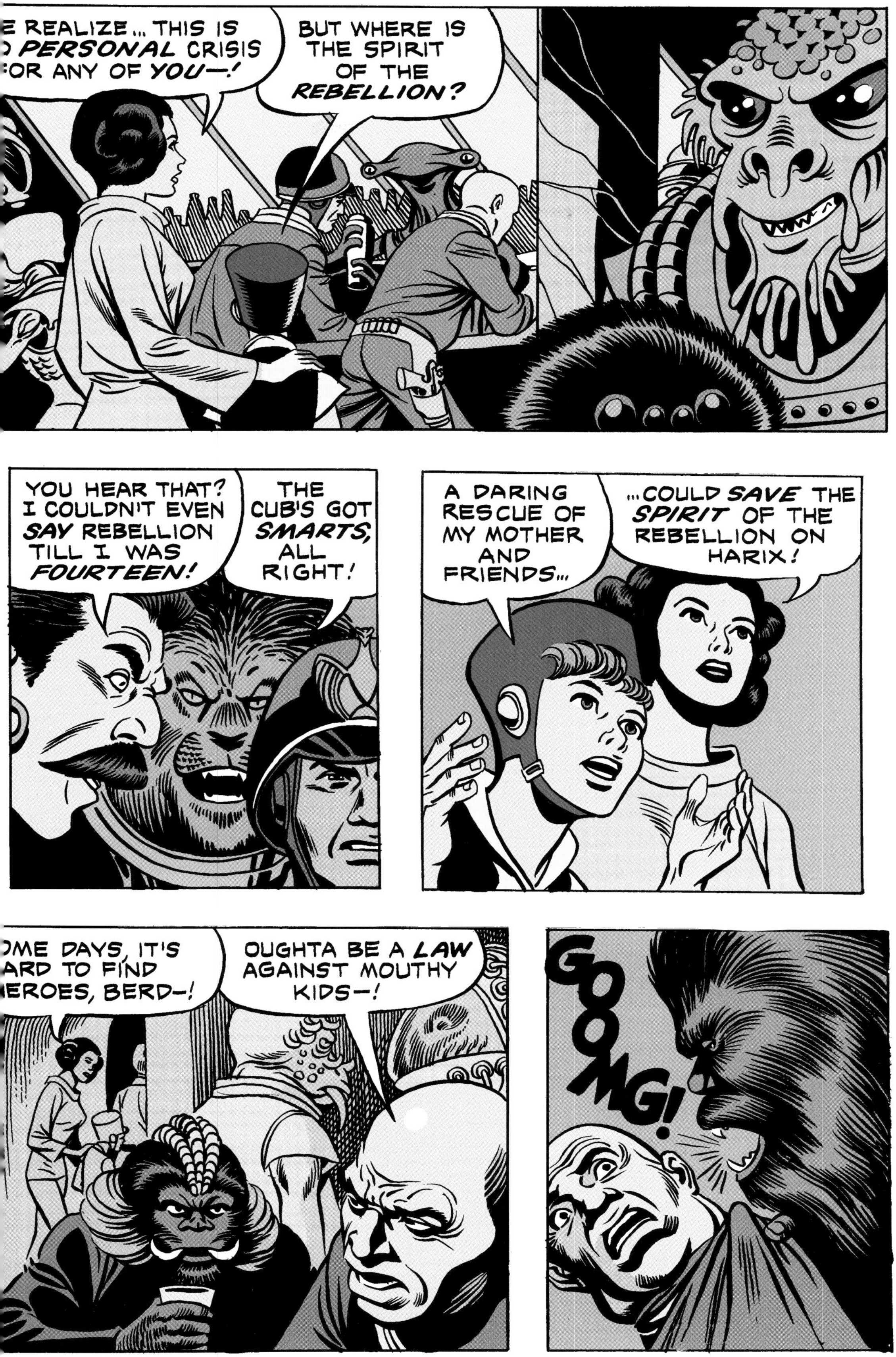
E REALIZE... THIS IS
PERSONAL CRISIS
OR ANY OF YOU—!
BUT WHERE IS THE SPIRIT OF THE REBELLION?
YOU HEAR THAT? I COULDN'T EVEN SAY REBELLION TILL I WAS FOURTEEN!
THE CUB'S GOT SMARTS, ALL RIGHT!
A DARING RESCUE OF MY MOTHER AND FRIENDS...
...COULD SAVE THE SPIRIT OF THE REBELLION ON HARIX!
OME DAYS, IT'S
ARD TO FIND
EROES, BERD—!
OUGHTA BE A LAW AGAINST MOUTHY KIDS—!
GOOMG!

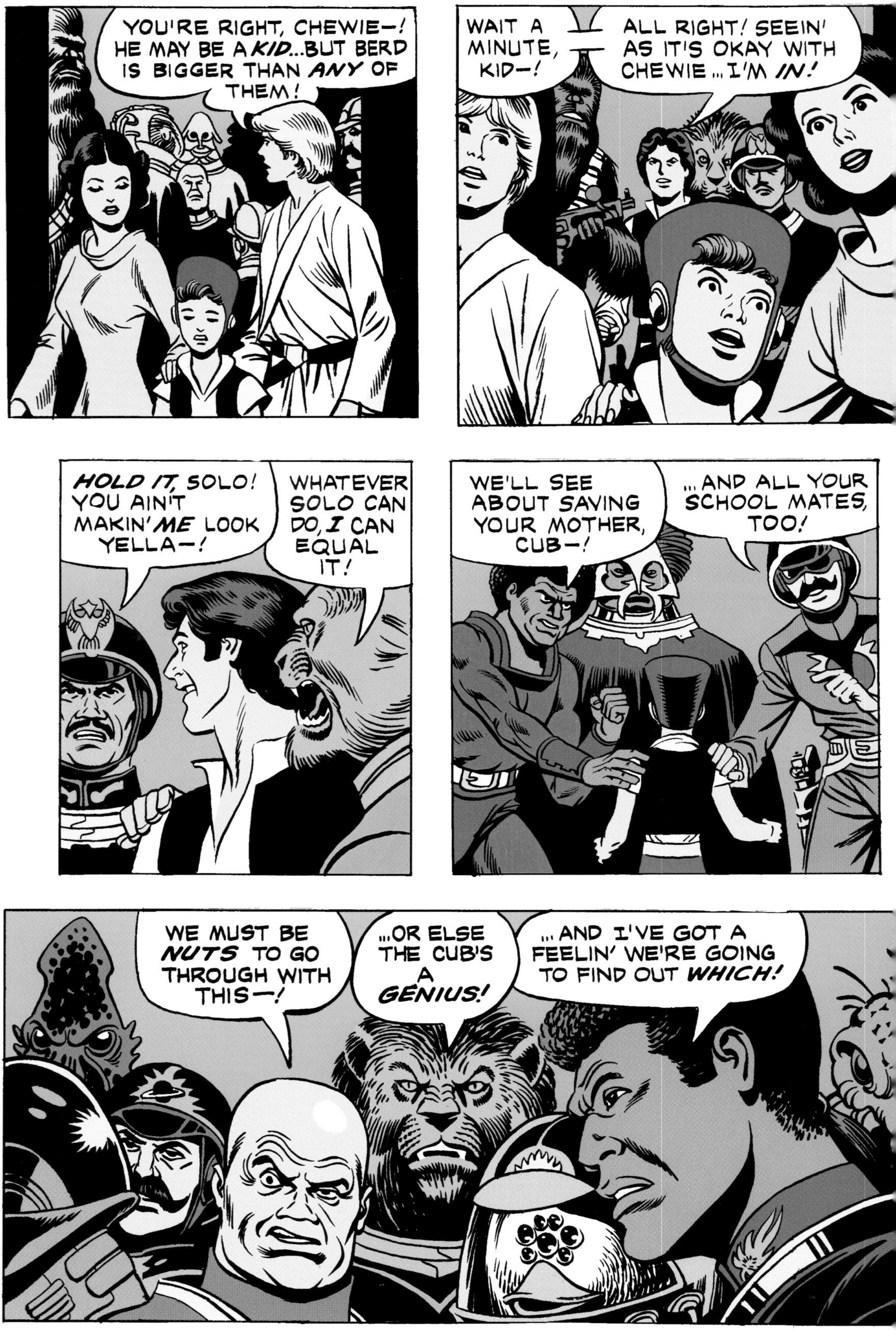
YOU'RE RIGHT, CHEWIE—! HE MAY BE A KID...BUT BERD IS BIGGER THAN ANY OF THEM!
WAIT A MINUTE, KID—!
ALL RIGHT! SEEIN' AS IT'S OKAY WITH CHEWIE ... I'M IN!
HOLD IT, SOLO! YOU AIN'T MAKIN' ME LOOK YELLA—!
WHATEVER SOLO CAN DO, I CAN EQUAL IT!
WE'LL SEE ABOUT SAVING YOUR MOTHER, CUB—!
...AND ALL YOUR SCHOOL MATES, TOO!
WE MUST BE NUTS TO GO THROUGH WITH THIS—!
...OR ELSE THE CUB'S A GENIUS!
... AND I'VE GOT A FEELIN' WE'RE GOING TO FIND OUT WHICH!

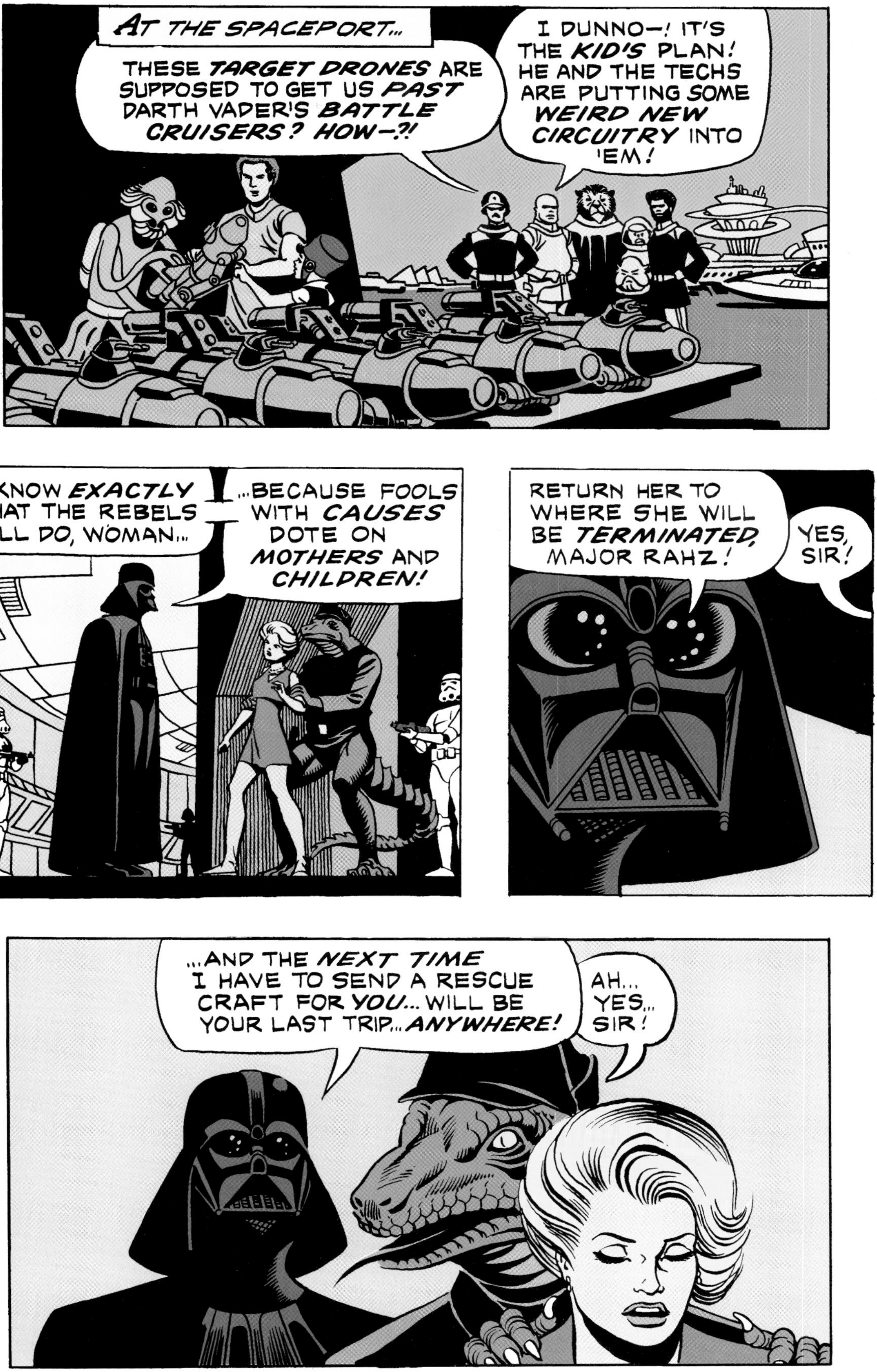
AT THE SPACEPORT...
THESE TARGET DRONES ARE SUPPOSED TO GET US PAST DARTH VADER'S BATTLE CRUISERS? HOW–?!
I DUNNO–! IT'S THE KID'S PLAN! HE AND THE TECHS ARE PUTTING SOME WEIRD NEW CIRCUITRY INTO 'EM!
KNOW EXACTLY HAT THE REBELS ILL DO, WOMAN...
...BECAUSE FOOLS WITH CAUSES DOTE ON MOTHERS AND CHILDREN!
RETURN HER TO WHERE SHE WILL BE TERMINATED, MAJOR RAHZ!
YES, SIR!
...AND THE NEXT TIME I HAVE TO SEND A RESCUE CRAFT FOR YOU... WILL BE YOUR LAST TRIP... ANYWHERE!
AH... YES... SIR!

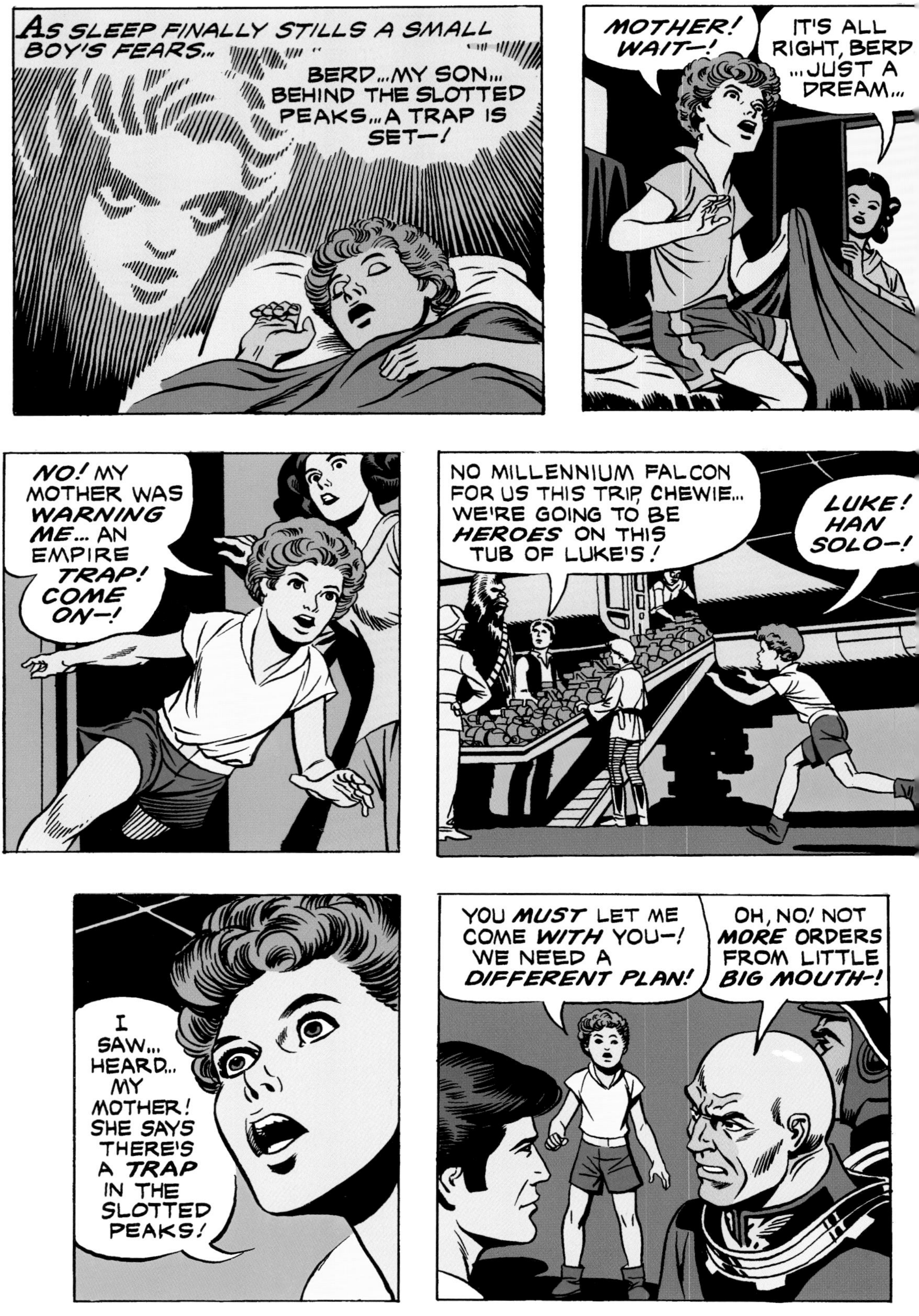
AS SLEEP FINALLY STILLS A SMALL BOY'S FEARS...
BERD...MY SON... BEHIND THE SLOTTED PEAKS...A TRAP IS SET--!
MOTHER! WAIT--!
IT'S ALL RIGHT, BERD ...JUST A DREAM...
NO! MY MOTHER WAS WARNING ME... AN EMPIRE TRAP! COME ON--!
NO MILLENNIUM FALCON FOR US THIS TRIP, CHEWIE... WE'RE GOING TO BE HEROES ON THIS TUB OF LUKE'S!
LUKE! HAN SOLO--!
I SAW... HEARD... MY MOTHER! SHE SAYS THERE'S A TRAP IN THE SLOTTED PEAKS!
YOU MUST LET ME COME WITH YOU--! WE NEED A DIFFERENT PLAN!
OH, NO! NOT MORE ORDERS FROM LITTLE BIG MOUTH--!

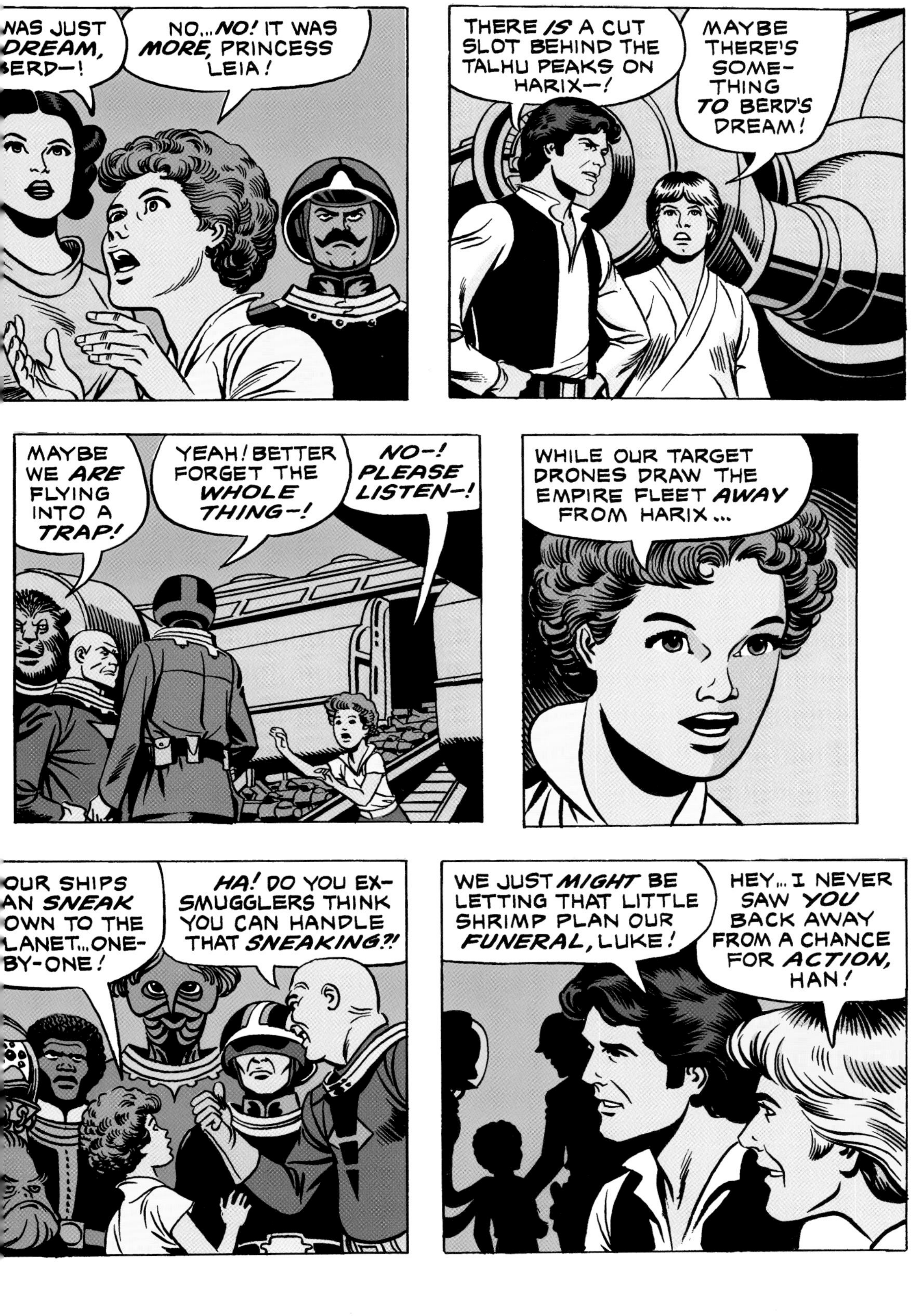

NAS JUST DREAM, ERD—!
NO...NO! IT WAS MORE, PRINCESS LEIA!
THERE IS A CUT SLOT BEHIND THE TALHU PEAKS ON HARIX—!
MAYBE THERE'S SOME-THING TO BERD'S DREAM!
MAYBE WE ARE FLYING INTO A TRAP!
YEAH! BETTER FORGET THE WHOLE THING—!
NO—! PLEASE LISTEN—!
WHILE OUR TARGET DRONES DRAW THE EMPIRE FLEET AWAY FROM HARIX...
OUR SHIPS AN SNEAK OWN TO THE LANET...ONE-BY-ONE!
HA! DO YOU EX-SMUGGLERS THINK YOU CAN HANDLE THAT SNEAKING?!
WE JUST MIGHT BE LETTING THAT LITTLE SHRIMP PLAN OUR FUNERAL, LUKE!
HEY... I NEVER SAW YOU BACK AWAY FROM A CHANCE FOR ACTION, HAN!

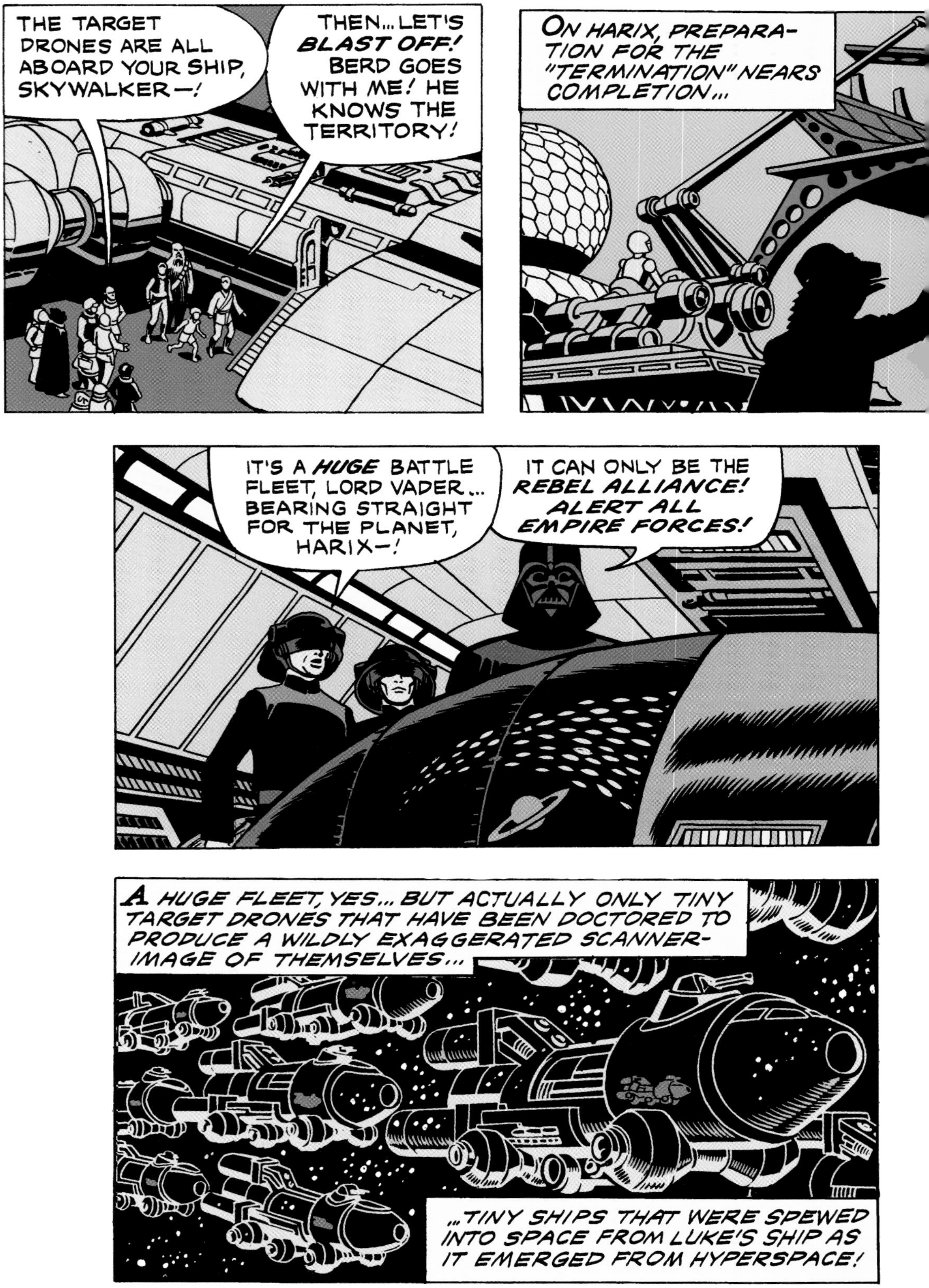
THE TARGET DRONES ARE ALL ABOARD YOUR SHIP, SKYWALKER—!
THEN... LET'S *BLAST OFF!* BERD GOES WITH ME! HE KNOWS THE TERRITORY!
ON HARIX, PREPARATION FOR THE "TERMINATION" NEARS COMPLETION...
IT'S A *HUGE* BATTLE FLEET, LORD VADER... BEARING STRAIGHT FOR THE PLANET, HARIX—!
IT CAN ONLY BE THE *REBEL ALLIANCE! ALERT ALL EMPIRE FORCES!*
A HUGE FLEET, YES... BUT ACTUALLY ONLY TINY TARGET DRONES THAT HAVE BEEN DOCTORED TO PRODUCE A WILDLY EXAGGERATED SCANNER-IMAGE OF THEMSELVES...
...TINY SHIPS THAT WERE SPEWED INTO SPACE FROM LUKE'S SHIP AS IT EMERGED FROM HYPERSPACE!

LANDING ON HARIX, LUKE, HAN AND CHEWIE DISCOVER THAT BERD'S DREAM OF AN EMPIRE TRAP IS REALITY!

WHEW! THERE'S *NO WAY* OUR FLEET OF FREIGHTERS COULD HANDLE *THOSE* BABIES—!

WE'RE *DEAD* IF DARTH VADER GETS AN ATTACK SIGNAL TO THEM!

UNLESS...WE CAN [P]UT THOSE TIE [FI]GHTERS OUT OF [C]OMMISSION...ALL [A]T *ONE WHACK!*

ARGH?

HUH-?! *HOW?!*

IF WE COULD JUST MAKE IT ACROSS...AND UP THAT SHAELO CLIFF...

THEY'D SHOOT US BEFORE WE MADE *TWENTY FEET—!*

NOT IF *CHEWIE* KEEPS THEM WATCHING *HIM*... ON *THIS* SIDE—!

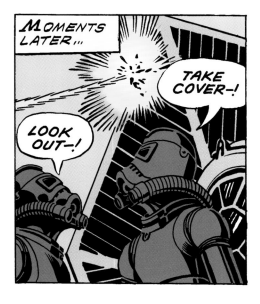

MOMENTS LATER...

TAKE COVER–!

LOOK OUT–!

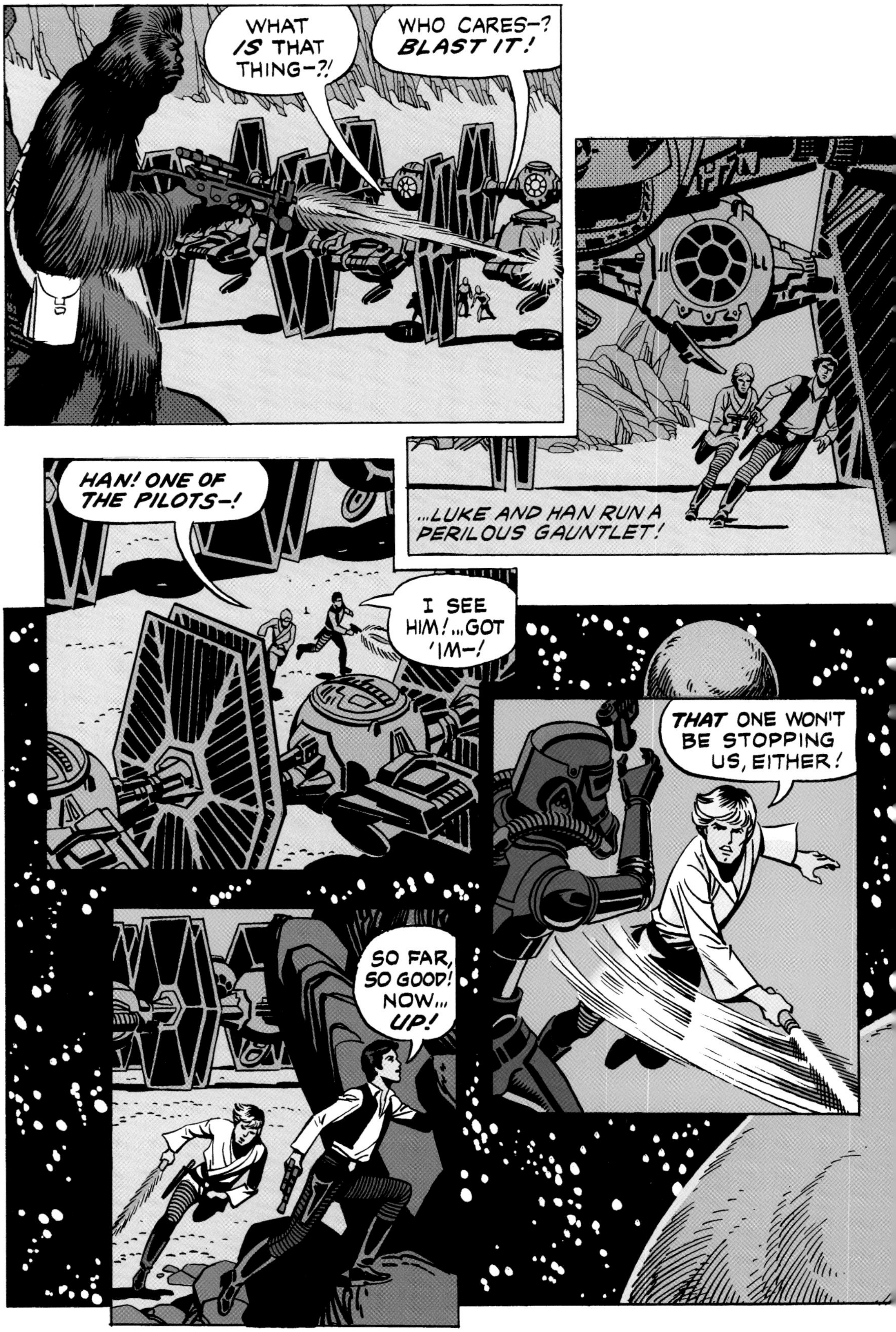
WHAT *IS* THAT THING–?!
WHO CARES–? *BLAST IT!*
...LUKE AND HAN RUN A PERILOUS GAUNTLET!
HAN! ONE OF THE PILOTS–!
I SEE HIM!...GOT 'IM–!
THAT ONE WON'T BE STOPPING US, EITHER!
SO FAR, SO GOOD! NOW... *UP!*

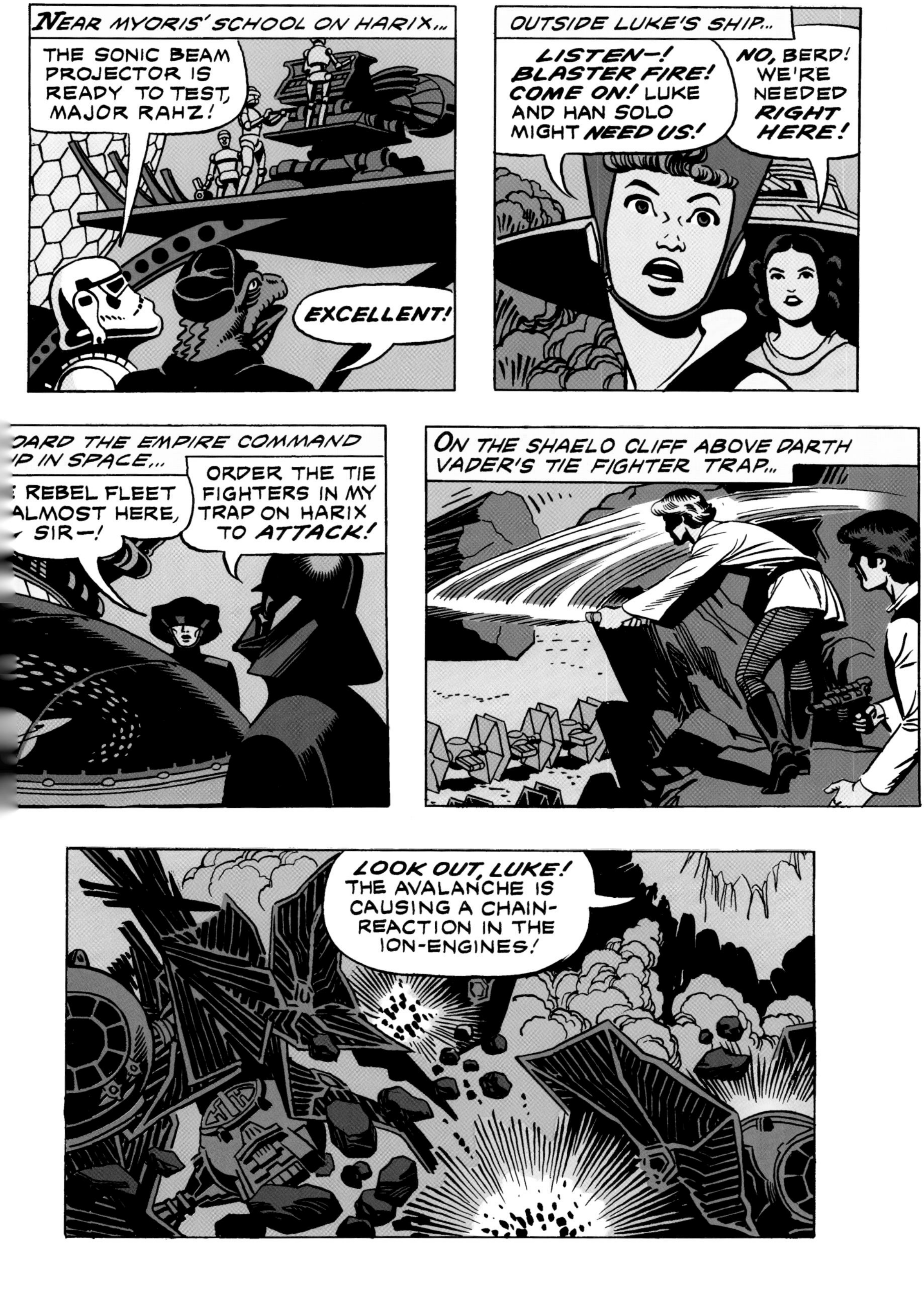
NEAR MYORIS' SCHOOL ON HARIX...
THE SONIC BEAM PROJECTOR IS READY TO TEST, MAJOR RAHZ!
EXCELLENT!
OUTSIDE LUKE'S SHIP...
LISTEN—! BLASTER FIRE! COME ON! LUKE AND HAN SOLO MIGHT NEED US!
NO, BERD! WE'RE NEEDED RIGHT HERE!
OARD THE EMPIRE COMMAND
P IN SPACE,...
REBEL FLEET
ALMOST HERE,
SIR—!
ORDER THE TIE FIGHTERS IN MY TRAP ON HARIX TO ATTACK!
ON THE SHAELO CLIFF ABOVE DARTH VADER'S TIE FIGHTER TRAP...
LOOK OUT, LUKE! THE AVALANCHE IS CAUSING A CHAIN-REACTION IN THE ION-ENGINES!

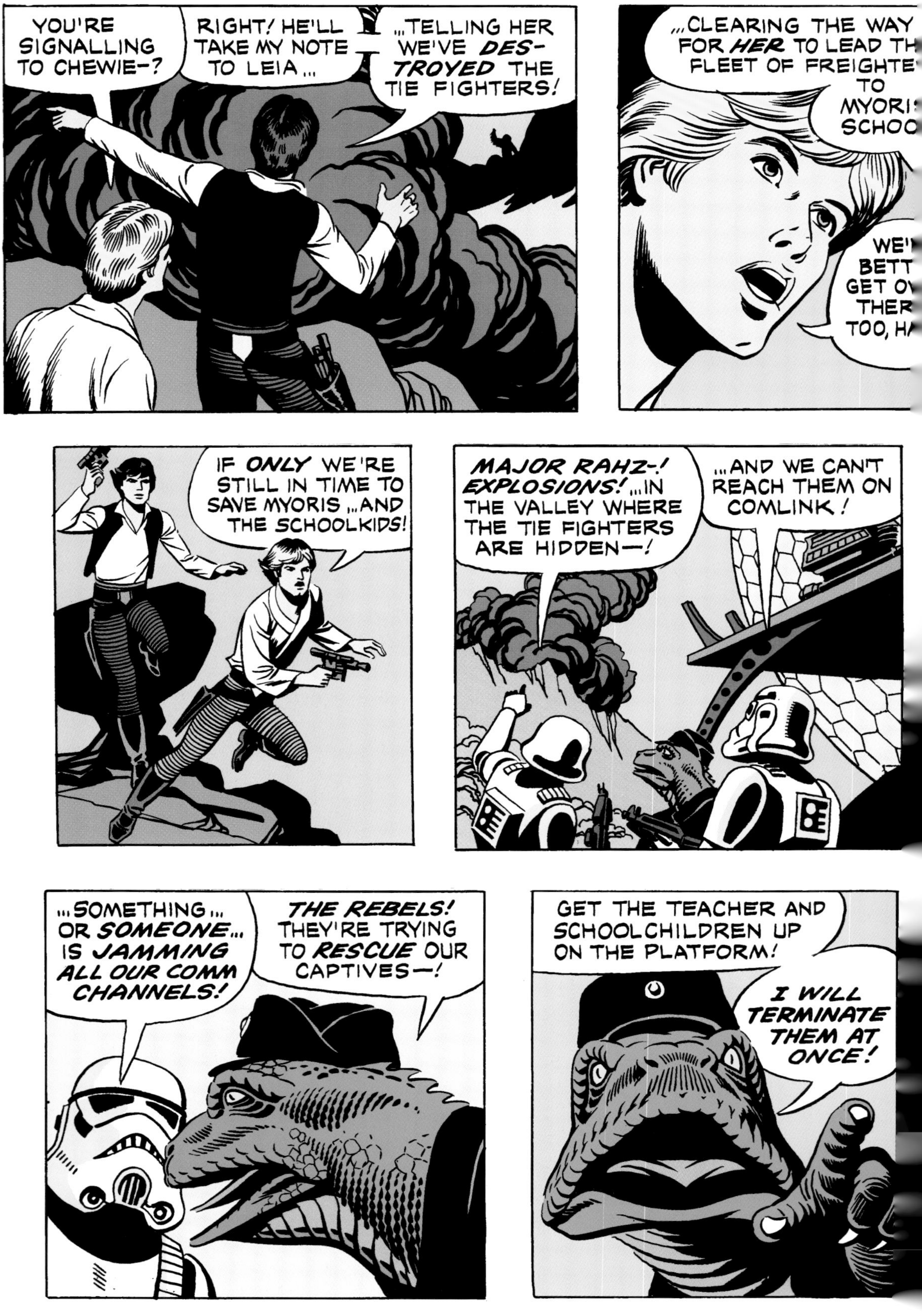
YOU'RE SIGNALLING TO CHEWIE-?
RIGHT! HE'LL TAKE MY NOTE TO LEIA...
...TELLING HER WE'VE DESTROYED THE TIE FIGHTERS!
...CLEARING THE WAY FOR HER TO LEAD TH
FLEET OF FREIGHTE
TO MYORI
SCHOO
WE'
BETT
GET O
THER
TOO, H
IF ONLY WE'RE STILL IN TIME TO SAVE MYORIS ...AND THE SCHOOLKIDS!
MAJOR RAHZ-! EXPLOSIONS! ...IN THE VALLEY WHERE THE TIE FIGHTERS ARE HIDDEN—!
...AND WE CAN'T REACH THEM ON COMLINK!
...SOMETHING... OR SOMEONE... IS JAMMING ALL OUR COMM CHANNELS!
THE REBELS! THEY'RE TRYING TO RESCUE OUR CAPTIVES—!
GET THE TEACHER AND SCHOOLCHILDREN UP ON THE PLATFORM!
I WILL TERMINATE THEM AT ONCE!

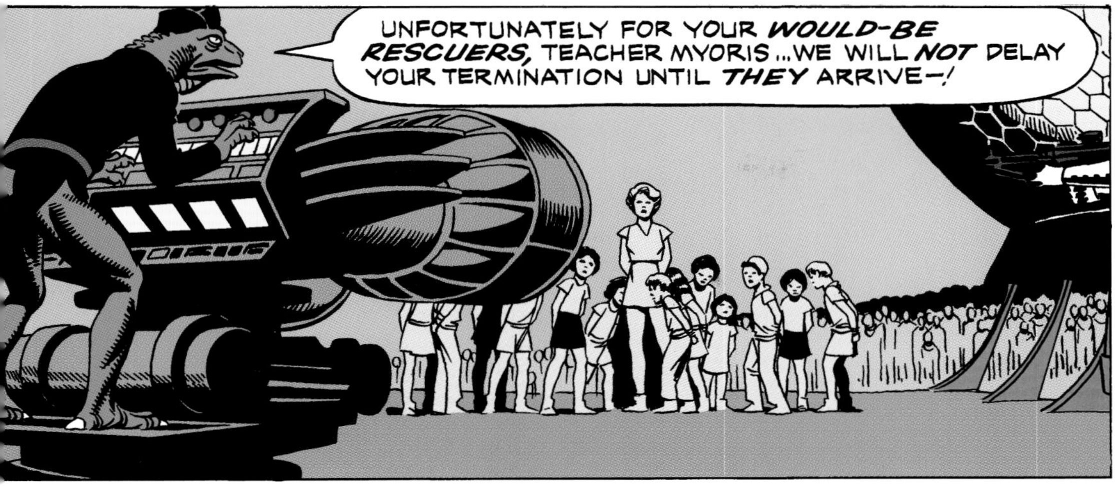
UNFORTUNATELY FOR YOUR *WOULD-BE RESCUERS,* TEACHER MYORIS ... WE WILL *NOT* DELAY YOUR TERMINATION UNTIL *THEY* ARRIVE—!

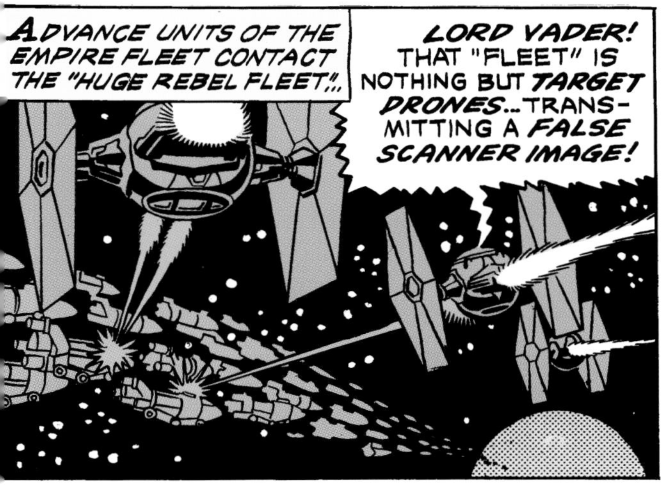
ADVANCE UNITS OF THE EMPIRE FLEET CONTACT THE "HUGE REBEL FLEET"...
LORD VADER! THAT "FLEET" IS NOTHING BUT *TARGET DRONES*... TRANS-MITTING A *FALSE SCANNER IMAGE!*

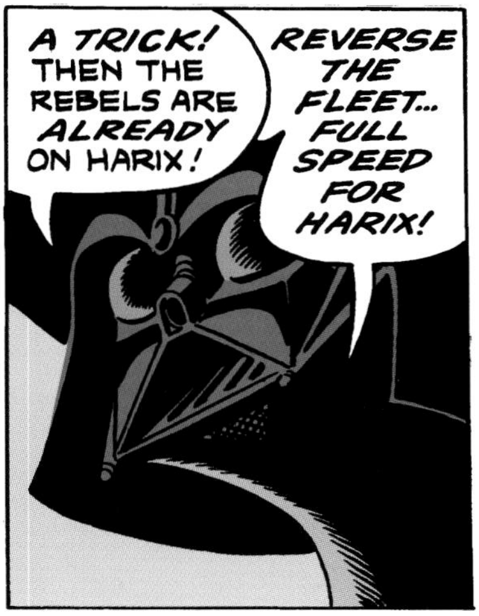
A TRICK! THEN THE REBELS ARE *ALREADY* ON HARIX!
REVERSE THE FLEET... FULL SPEED FOR HARIX!

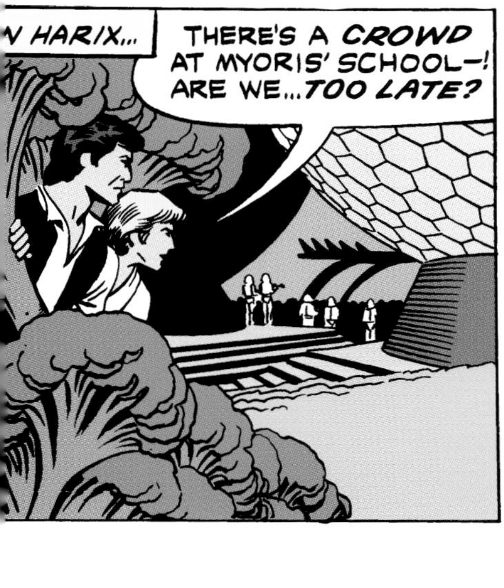
N HARIX...
THERE'S A *CROWD* AT MYORIS' SCHOOL—! ARE WE... *TOO LATE?*

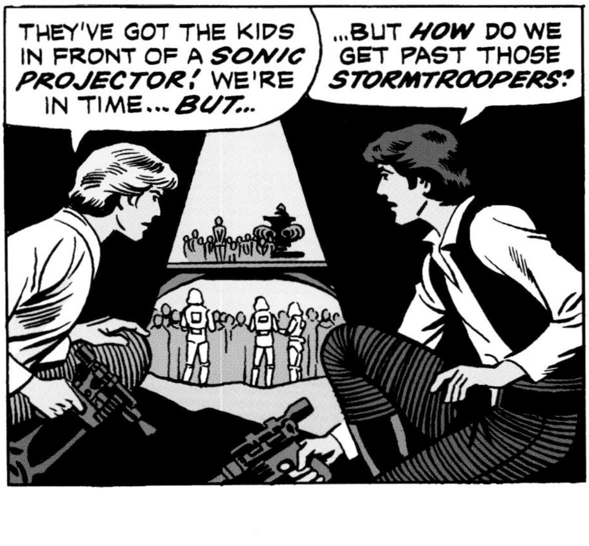
THEY'VE GOT THE KIDS IN FRONT OF A *SONIC PROJECTOR!* WE'RE IN TIME... *BUT...*
...BUT *HOW* DO WE GET PAST THOSE *STORMTROOPERS?*

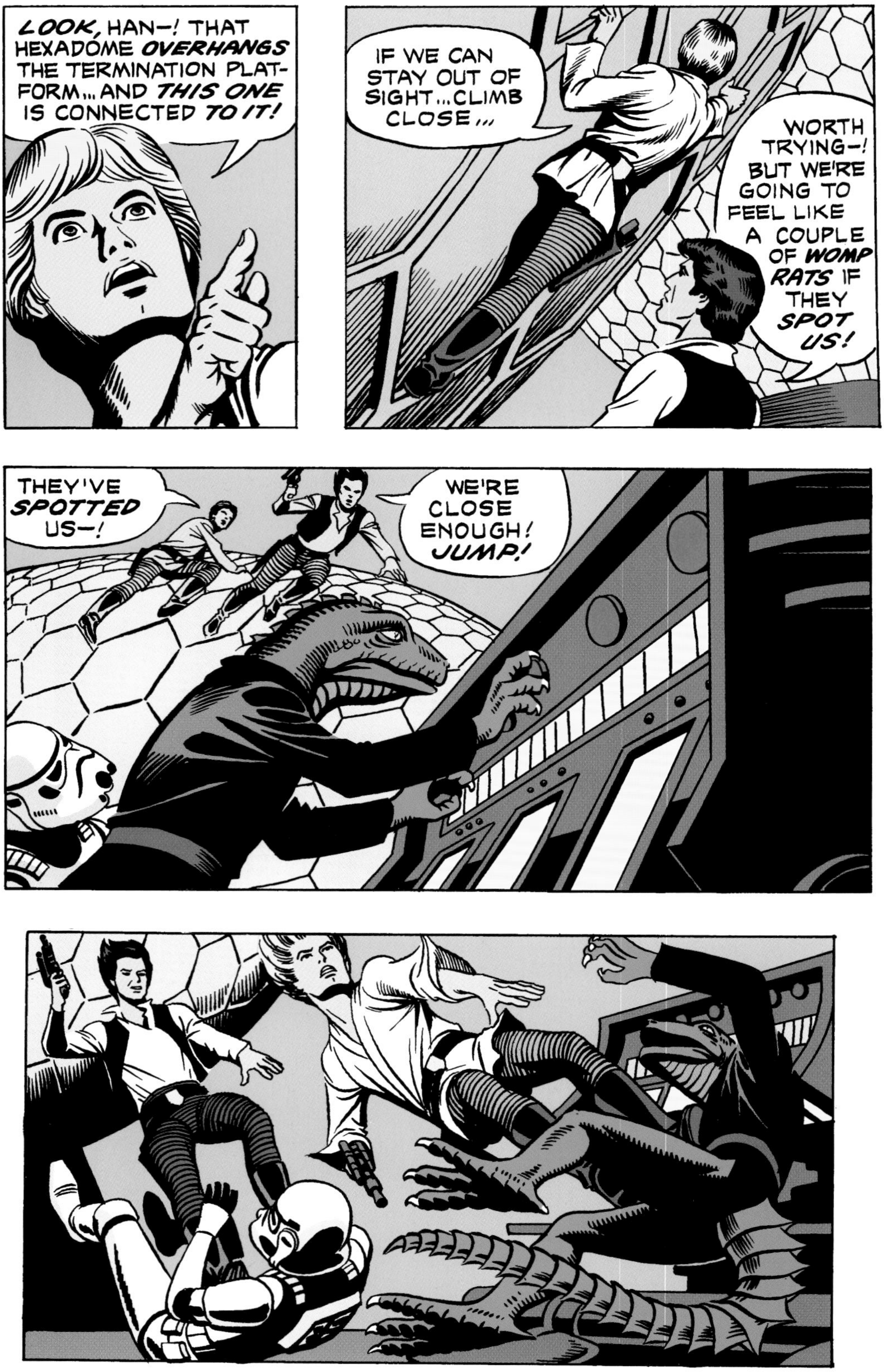
LOOK, HAN—! THAT HEXADOME OVERHANGS THE TERMINATION PLATFORM... AND THIS ONE IS CONNECTED TO IT!
IF WE CAN STAY OUT OF SIGHT... CLIMB CLOSE...
WORTH TRYING—! BUT WE'RE GOING TO FEEL LIKE A COUPLE OF WOMP RATS IF THEY SPOT US!
THEY'VE SPOTTED US—!
WE'RE CLOSE ENOUGH! JUMP!

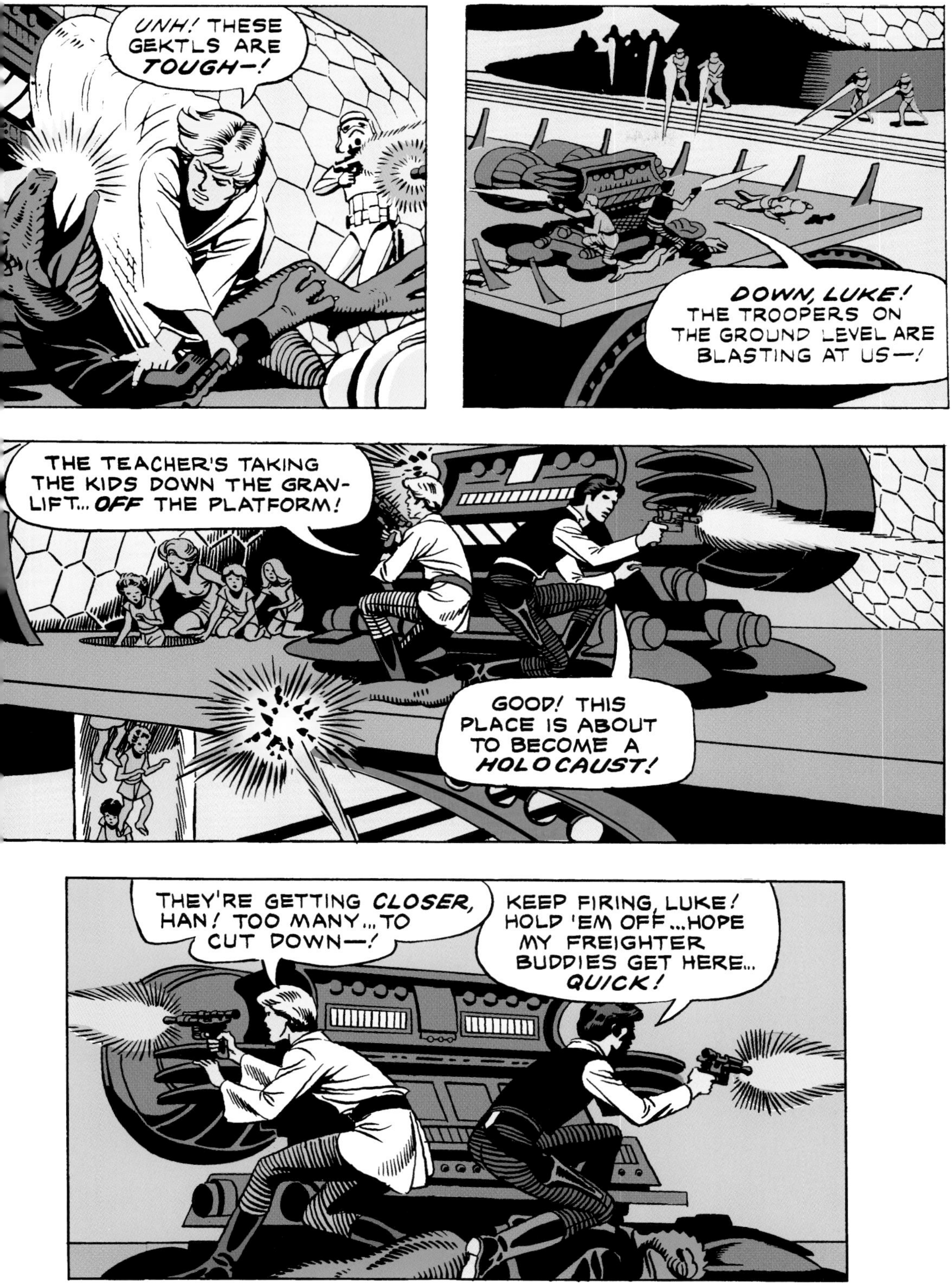
UNH! THESE GEKTLS ARE TOUGH—!
DOWN, LUKE! THE TROOPERS ON THE GROUND LEVEL ARE BLASTING AT US—!
THE TEACHER'S TAKING THE KIDS DOWN THE GRAV-LIFT... OFF THE PLATFORM!
GOOD! THIS PLACE IS ABOUT TO BECOME A HOLOCAUST!
THEY'RE GETTING CLOSER, HAN! TOO MANY... TO CUT DOWN—!
KEEP FIRING, LUKE! HOLD 'EM OFF...HOPE MY FREIGHTER BUDDIES GET HERE... QUICK!

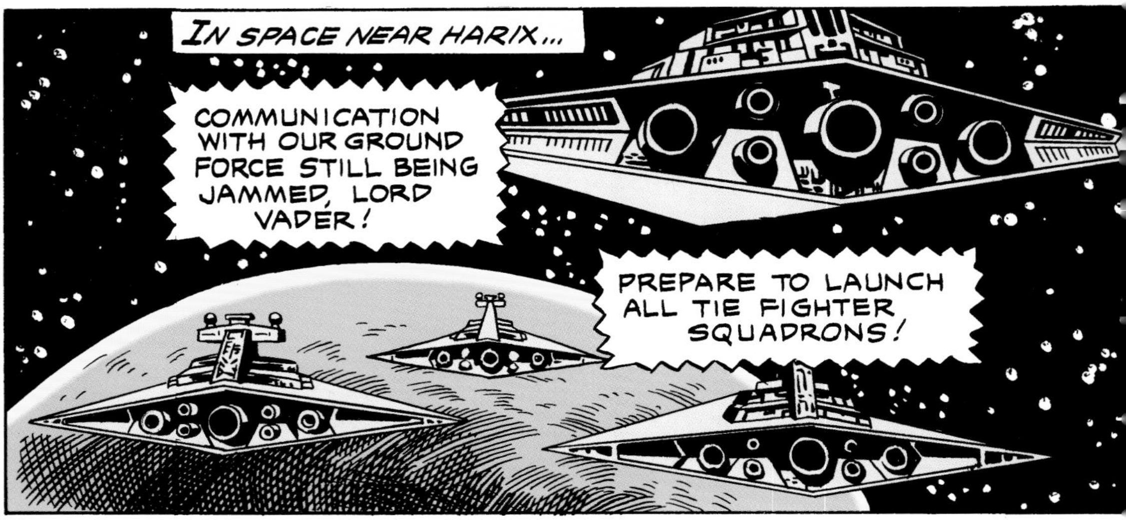
IN SPACE NEAR HARIX...
COMMUNICATION WITH OUR GROUND FORCE STILL BEING JAMMED, LORD VADER!
PREPARE TO LAUNCH ALL TIE FIGHTER SQUADRONS!

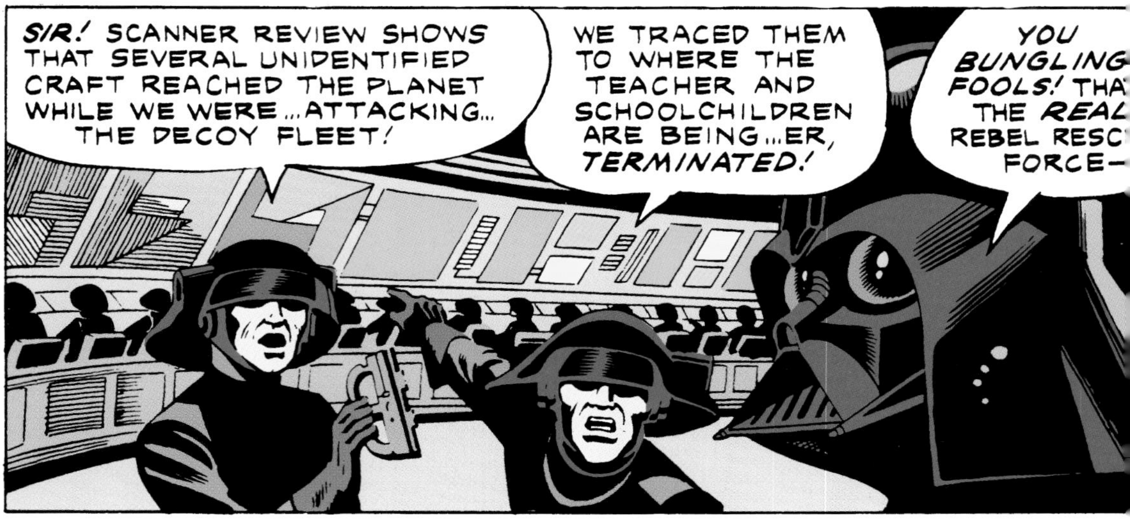
SIR! SCANNER REVIEW SHOWS THAT SEVERAL UNIDENTIFIED CRAFT REACHED THE PLANET WHILE WE WERE...ATTACKING... THE DECOY FLEET!
WE TRACED THEM TO WHERE THE TEACHER AND SCHOOLCHILDREN ARE BEING...ER, TERMINATED!
YOU BUNGLING FOOLS! THA THE REAL REBEL RESC FORCE—

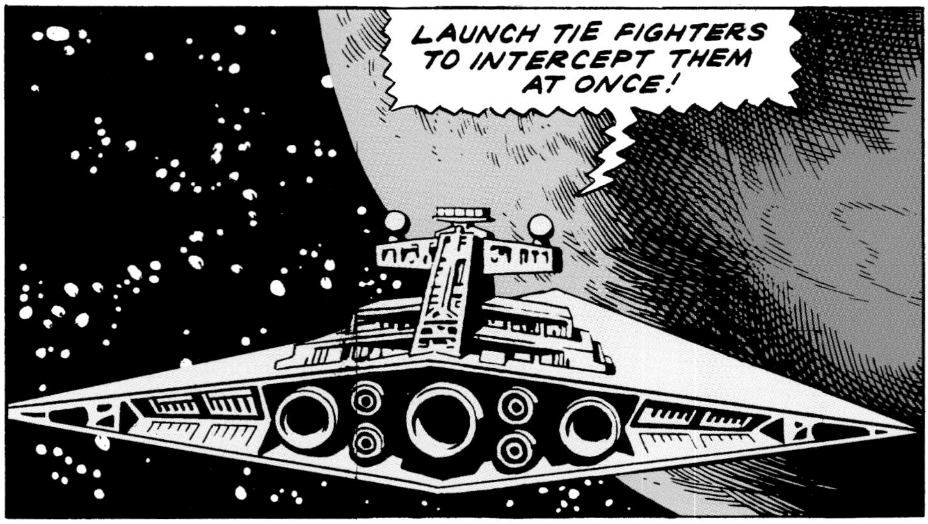
LAUNCH TIE FIGHTERS TO INTERCEPT THEM AT ONCE!

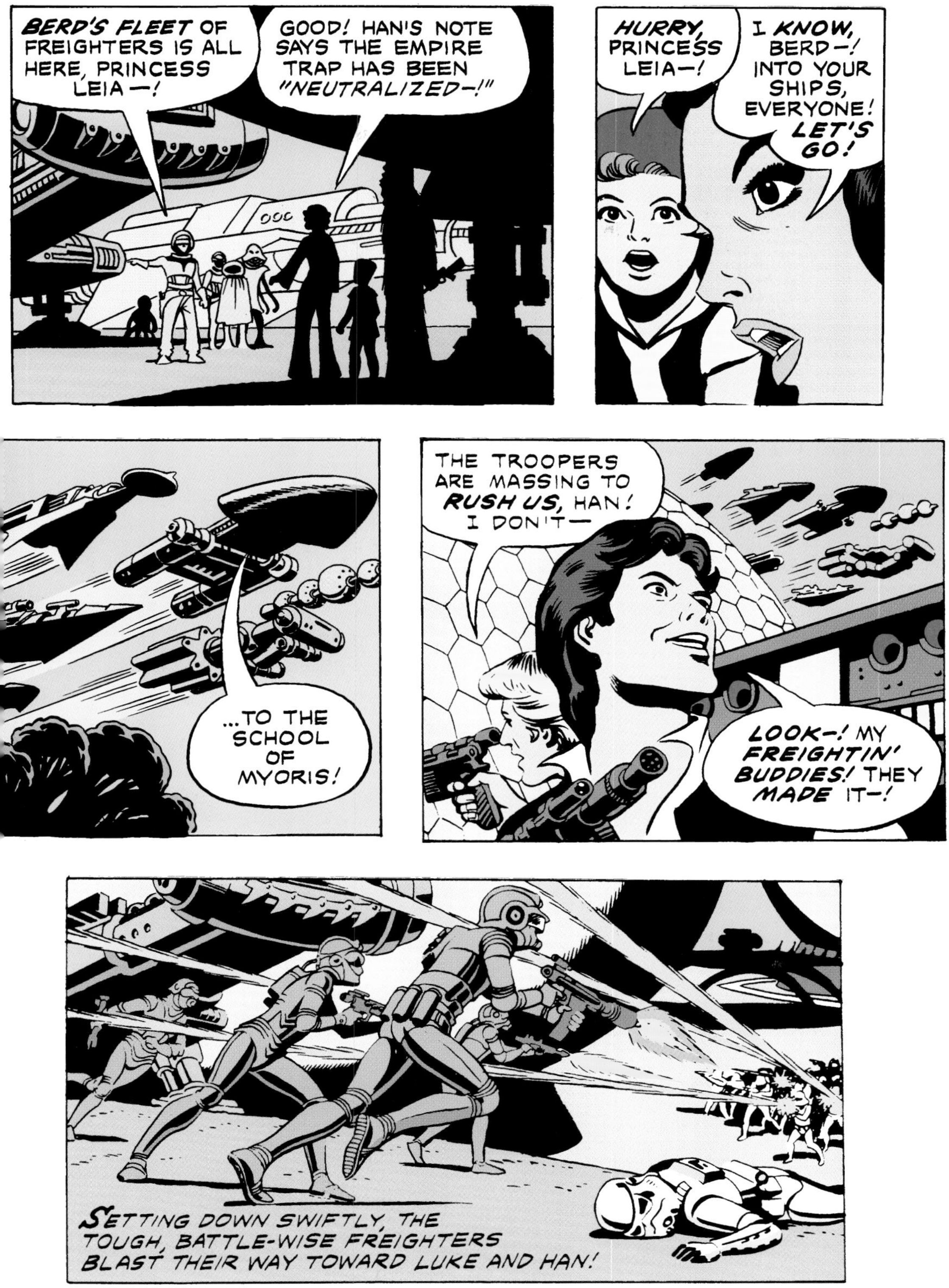
BERD'S FLEET OF FREIGHTERS IS ALL HERE, PRINCESS LEIA—!
GOOD! HAN'S NOTE SAYS THE EMPIRE TRAP HAS BEEN "NEUTRALIZED—!"
HURRY, PRINCESS LEIA—!
I KNOW, BERD—! INTO YOUR SHIPS, EVERYONE! LET'S GO!
...TO THE SCHOOL OF MYORIS!
THE TROOPERS ARE MASSING TO RUSH US, HAN! I DON'T—
LOOK—! MY FREIGHTIN' BUDDIES! THEY MADE IT—!
SETTING DOWN SWIFTLY, THE TOUGH, BATTLE-WISE FREIGHTERS BLAST THEIR WAY TOWARD LUKE AND HAN!

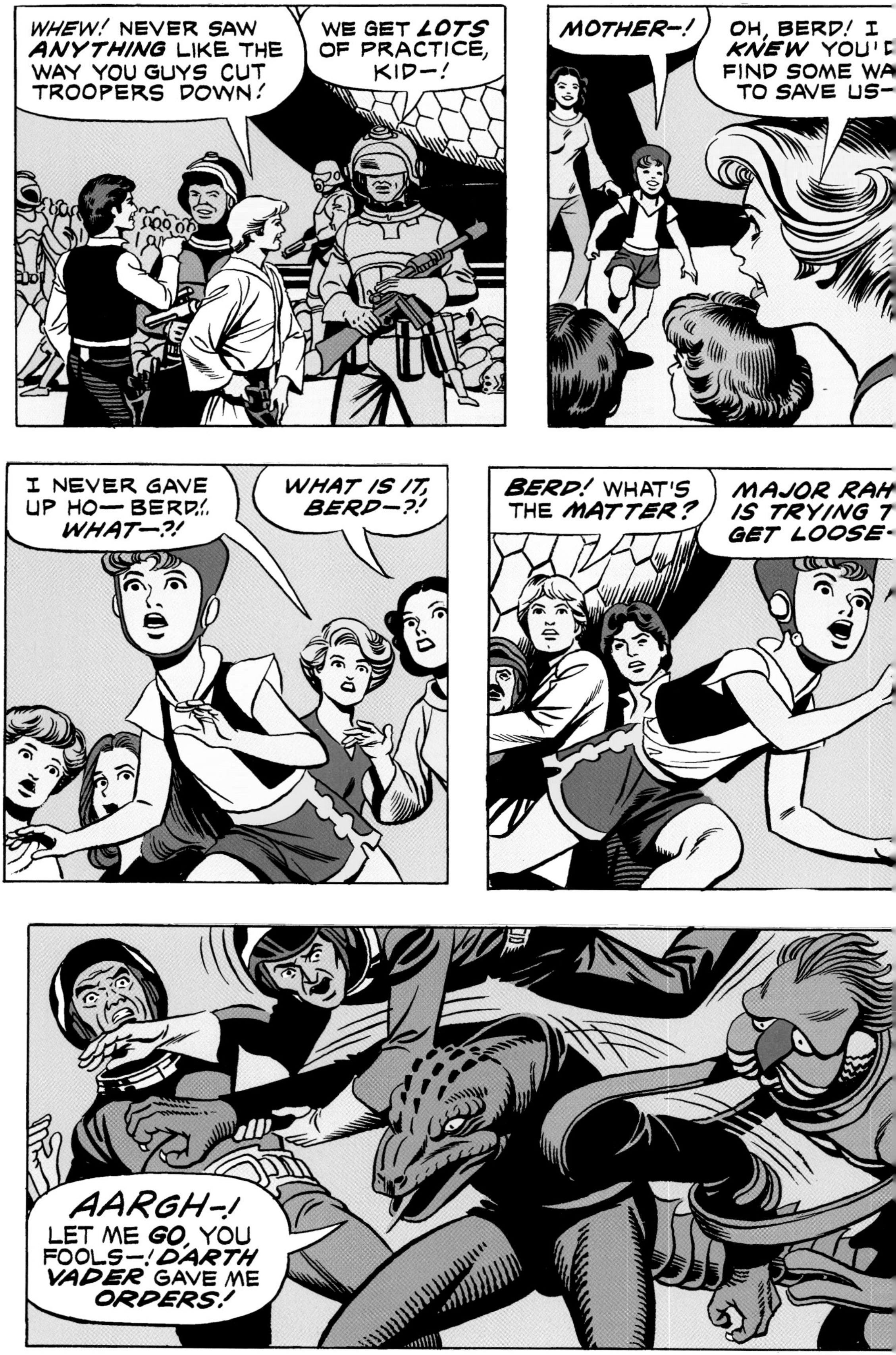
WHEW! NEVER SAW ANYTHING LIKE THE WAY YOU GUYS CUT TROOPERS DOWN!
WE GET LOTS OF PRACTICE, KID–!
MOTHER–!
OH, BERD! I KNEW YOU'D FIND SOME WA TO SAVE US–
I NEVER GAVE UP HO— BERD!. WHAT–?!
WHAT IS IT, BERD–?!
BERD! WHAT'S THE MATTER?
MAJOR RAH IS TRYING T GET LOOSE–
AARGH–! LET ME GO, YOU FOOLS–! DARTH VADER GAVE ME ORDERS!

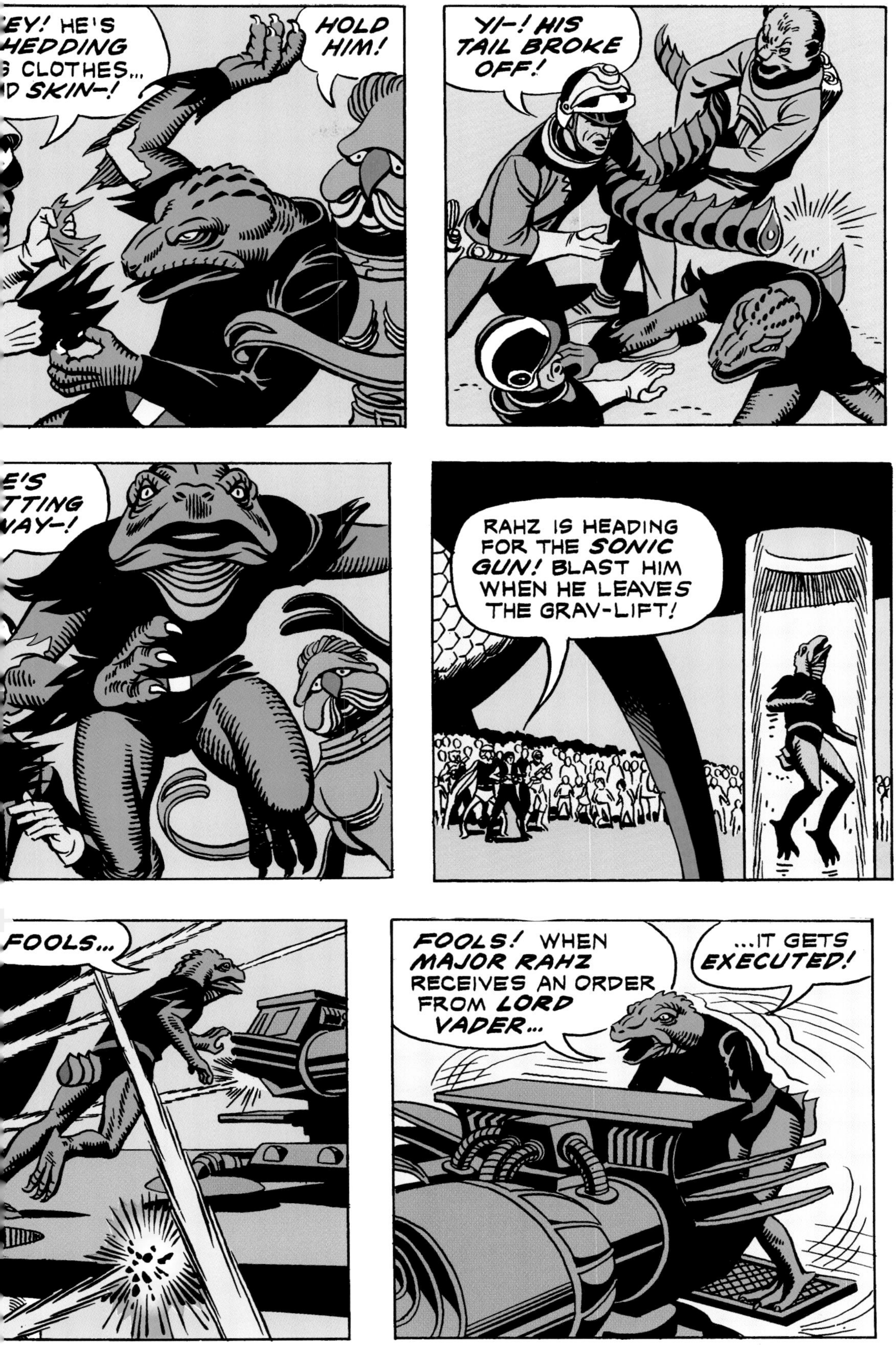
EY! HE'S
HEDDING
S CLOTHES...
D SKIN-!
HOLD HIM!
YI-! HIS TAIL BROKE OFF!
E'S
TTING
WAY-!
RAHZ IS HEADING FOR THE SONIC GUN! BLAST HIM WHEN HE LEAVES THE GRAV-LIFT!
FOOLS...
FOOLS! WHEN MAJOR RAHZ RECEIVES AN ORDER FROM LORD VADER...
...IT GETS EXECUTED!

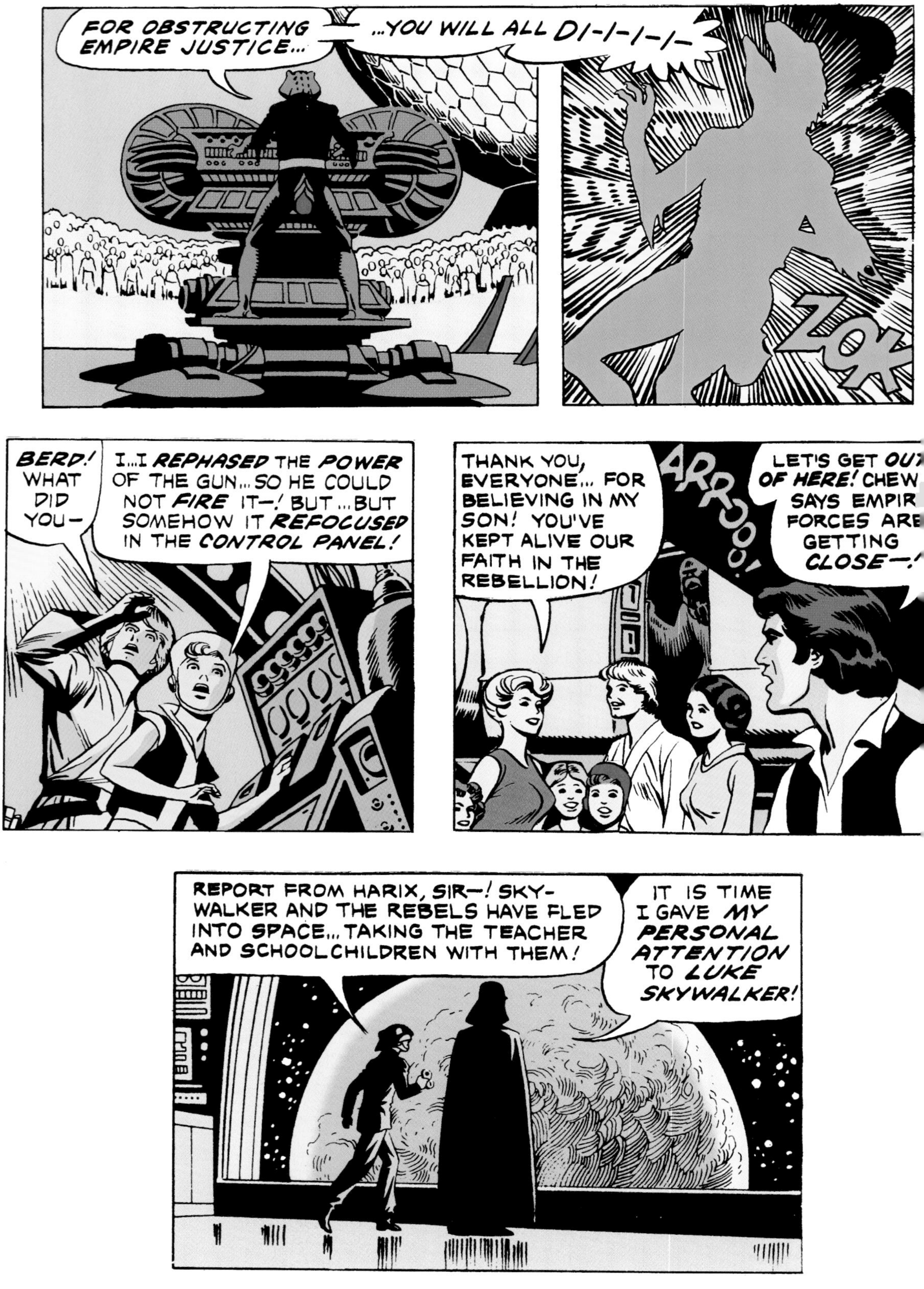
FOR OBSTRUCTING EMPIRE JUSTICE...
...YOU WILL ALL DI-I-I-I-I-
ZOK
BERD! WHAT DID YOU—
I...I REPHASED THE POWER OF THE GUN... SO HE COULD NOT FIRE IT—! BUT... BUT SOMEHOW IT REFOCUSED IN THE CONTROL PANEL!
THANK YOU, EVERYONE... FOR BELIEVING IN MY SON! YOU'VE KEPT ALIVE OUR FAITH IN THE REBELLION!
ARROOO!
LET'S GET OU OF HERE! CHEW SAYS EMPIR FORCES ARE GETTING CLOSE—!
REPORT FROM HARIX, SIR—! SKY-WALKER AND THE REBELS HAVE FLED INTO SPACE... TAKING THE TEACHER AND SCHOOLCHILDREN WITH THEM!
IT IS TIME I GAVE MY PERSONAL ATTENTION TO LUKE SKYWALKER!

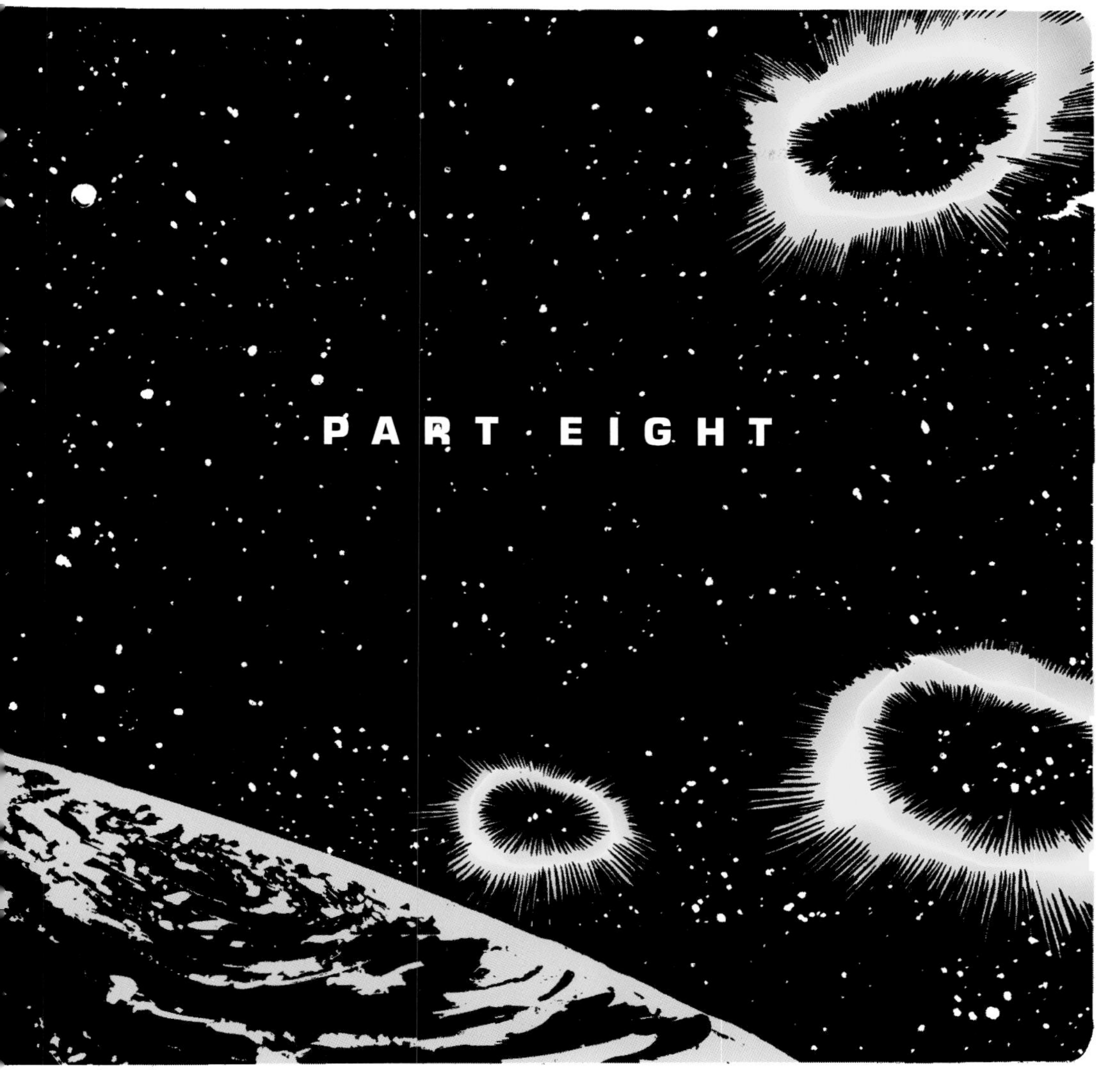
PART EIGHT

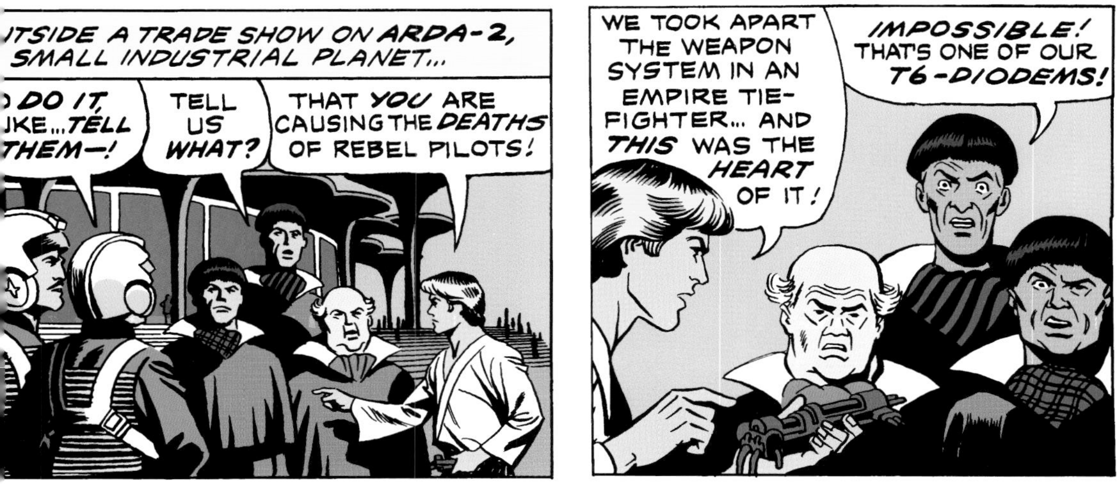
TSIDE A TRADE SHOW ON ARDA-2, SMALL INDUSTRIAL PLANET...
DO IT, IKE...TELL THEM—!
TELL US WHAT?
THAT YOU ARE CAUSING THE DEATHS OF REBEL PILOTS!
WE TOOK APART THE WEAPON SYSTEM IN AN EMPIRE TIE-FIGHTER... AND THIS WAS THE HEART OF IT!
IMPOSSIBLE! THAT'S ONE OF OUR T6-DIODEMS!

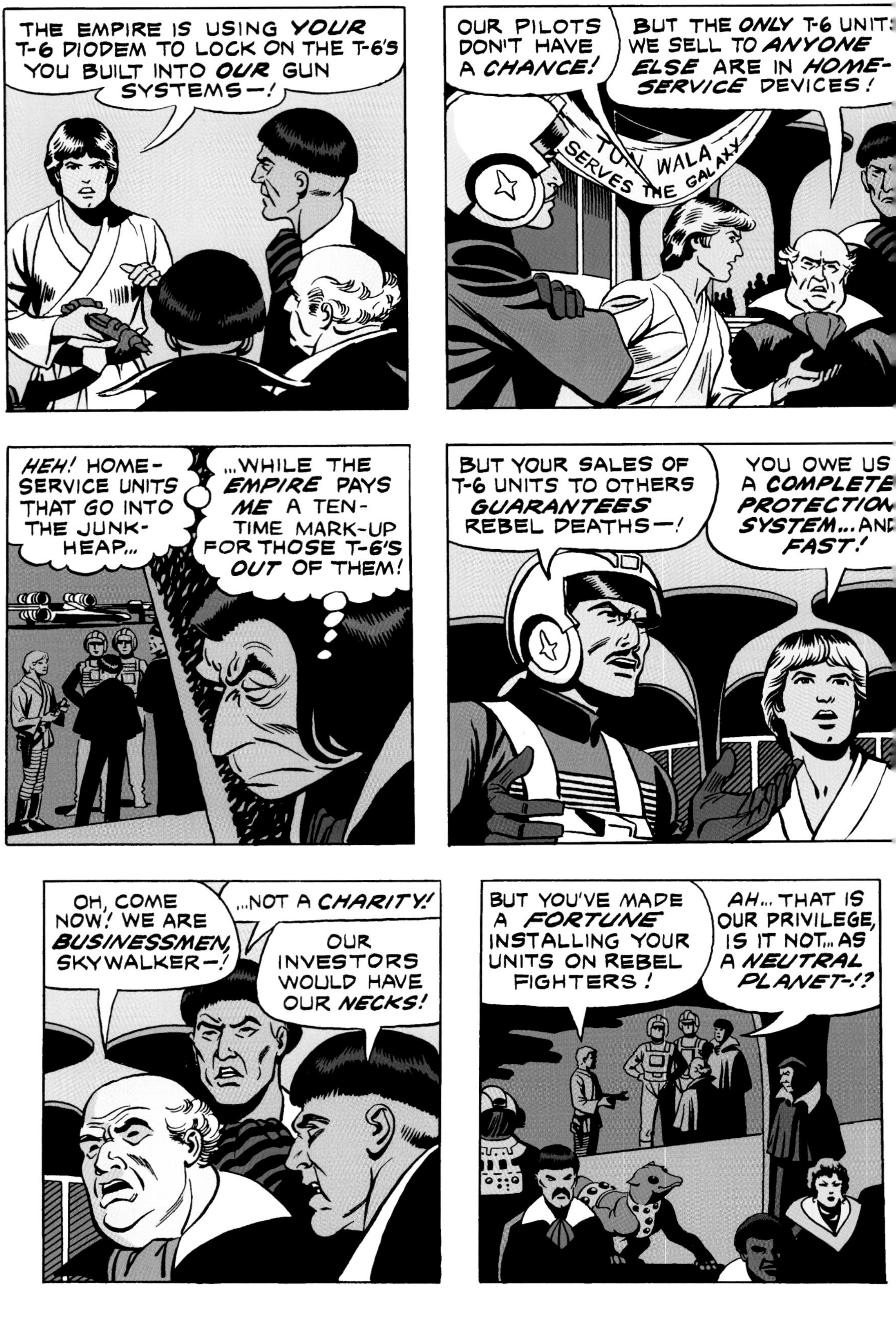
THE EMPIRE IS USING *YOUR* T-6 DIODEM TO LOCK ON THE T-6'S YOU BUILT INTO *OUR* GUN SYSTEMS—!
OUR PILOTS DON'T HAVE A *CHANCE!*
BUT THE *ONLY* T-6 UNIT WE SELL TO *ANYONE ELSE* ARE IN *HOME-SERVICE* DEVICES!
WALA
SERVES THE GALAXY
HEH! HOME-SERVICE UNITS THAT GO INTO THE JUNK-HEAP...
...WHILE THE *EMPIRE* PAYS *ME* A TEN-TIME MARK-UP FOR THOSE T-6'S *OUT* OF THEM!
BUT YOUR SALES OF T-6 UNITS TO OTHERS *GUARANTEES* REBEL DEATHS—!
YOU OWE US A *COMPLETE PROTECTION SYSTEM*... AN *FAST!*
OH, COME NOW! WE ARE *BUSINESSMEN,* SKYWALKER—!
...NOT A *CHARITY!*
OUR INVESTORS WOULD HAVE OUR *NECKS!*
BUT YOU'VE MADE A *FORTUNE* INSTALLING YOUR UNITS ON REBEL FIGHTERS!
AH... THAT IS OUR PRIVILEGE, IS IT NOT... AS A *NEUTRAL PLANET*-!?

HERE, MY GOOD FELLOW...ARE THE *REWARDS* OF NEUTRALITY!

I SEE *TROUBLE*... AND *SOMEBODY* PUTTING YOU INTO *DARTH VADER'S* POCKET!

TUN WALA SERVES THE GALAXY

NONSENSE! NEUTRAL PLANETS ARE *VALUABLE* TO BOTH SIDES... IN *EVERY* WAR!

SURELY THE REBEL ALLIANCE WILL BE ABLE TO PAY FOR WHAT IT NEEDS—!

...S TIME YOU HEARD ...ROM SOMEONE WHO ...NOWS ABOUT ...USTING THE ...PIRE...*PRINCESS LEIA*—!

PRINCESS LEIA...OF ALDERAAN? NO!

THE PRINCESS IS HERE FOR YOUR TRADE SHOW... BUT SHE'S STILL OUT AT THE QUALO'S PLACE!

FINE... BRING HER IN—!

NO! NOT TO PULL HEART STRINGS... AND CRIMP MY TRADE LINES TO THE *EMPIRE!*

...GOT THAT, KIROS? GET THERE FIRST... AND KEEP PRINCESS LEIA *AWAY* FROM THE TRADE SHOW!

NO—! IT'S NOT *RIGHT!*

MAG DOUM *KNOWS* THAT, SON!

WE'VE GOT NO CHOICE! COME ON! WE'LL HAVE TO MOVE... *FAST!*

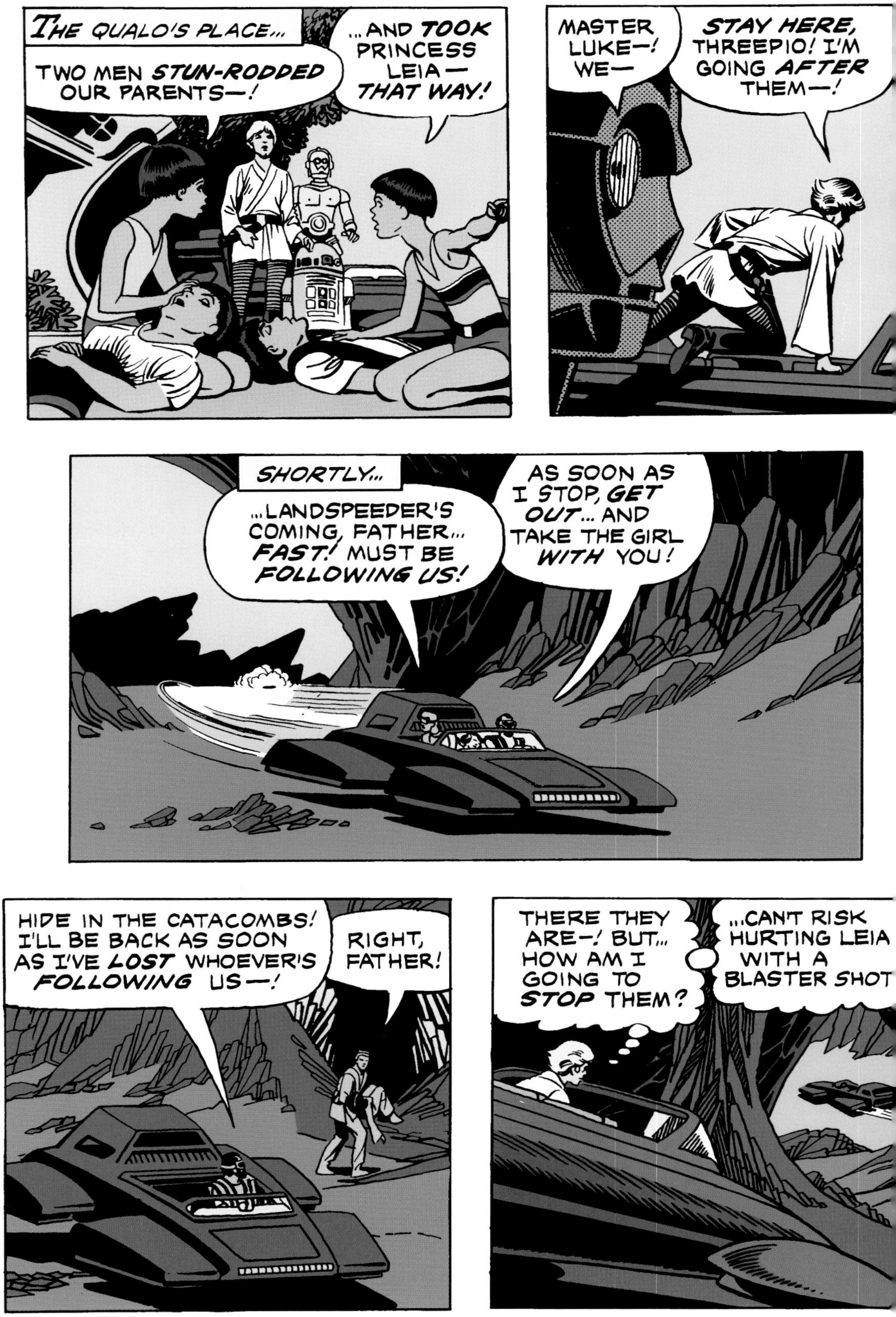
THE QUALO'S PLACE...
TWO MEN STUN-RODDED OUR PARENTS—!
...AND TOOK PRINCESS LEIA— THAT WAY!
MASTER LUKE—! WE—
STAY HERE, THREEPIO! I'M GOING AFTER THEM—!
SHORTLY...
...LANDSPEEDER'S COMING, FATHER... FAST! MUST BE FOLLOWING US!
AS SOON AS I STOP, GET OUT... AND TAKE THE GIRL WITH YOU!
HIDE IN THE CATACOMBS! I'LL BE BACK AS SOON AS I'VE LOST WHOEVER'S FOLLOWING US—!
RIGHT, FATHER!
THERE THEY ARE—! BUT... HOW AM I GOING TO STOP THEM?
...CAN'T RISK HURTING LEIA WITH A BLASTER SHOT

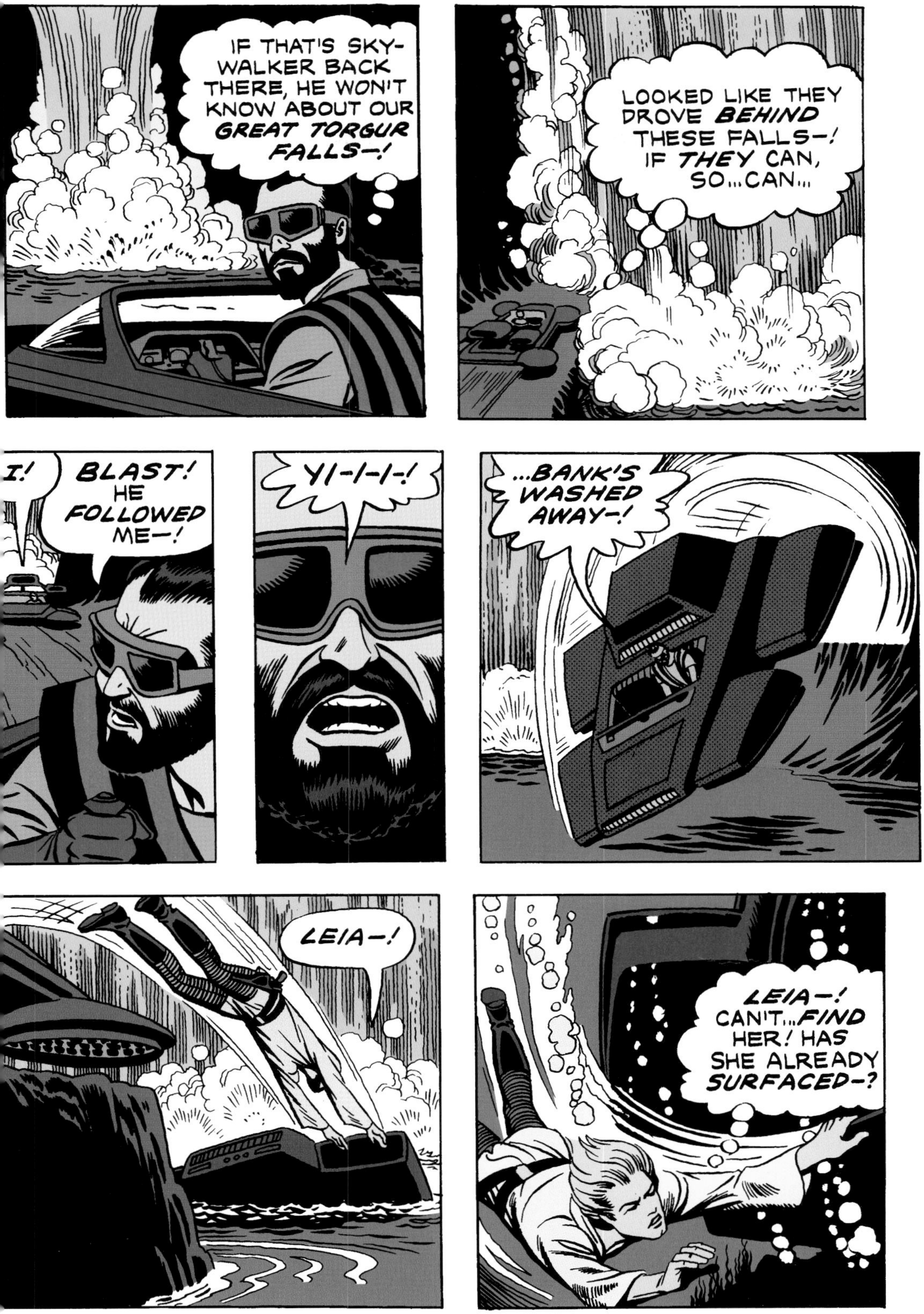
IF THAT'S SKY-WALKER BACK THERE, HE WON'T KNOW ABOUT OUR GREAT TORGUR FALLS—!
LOOKED LIKE THEY DROVE BEHIND THESE FALLS—! IF THEY CAN, SO...CAN...
I!
BLAST! HE FOLLOWED ME—!
YI-I-I-!
...BANK'S WASHED AWAY—!
LEIA—!
LEIA—! CAN'T...FIND HER! HAS SHE ALREADY SURFACED—?

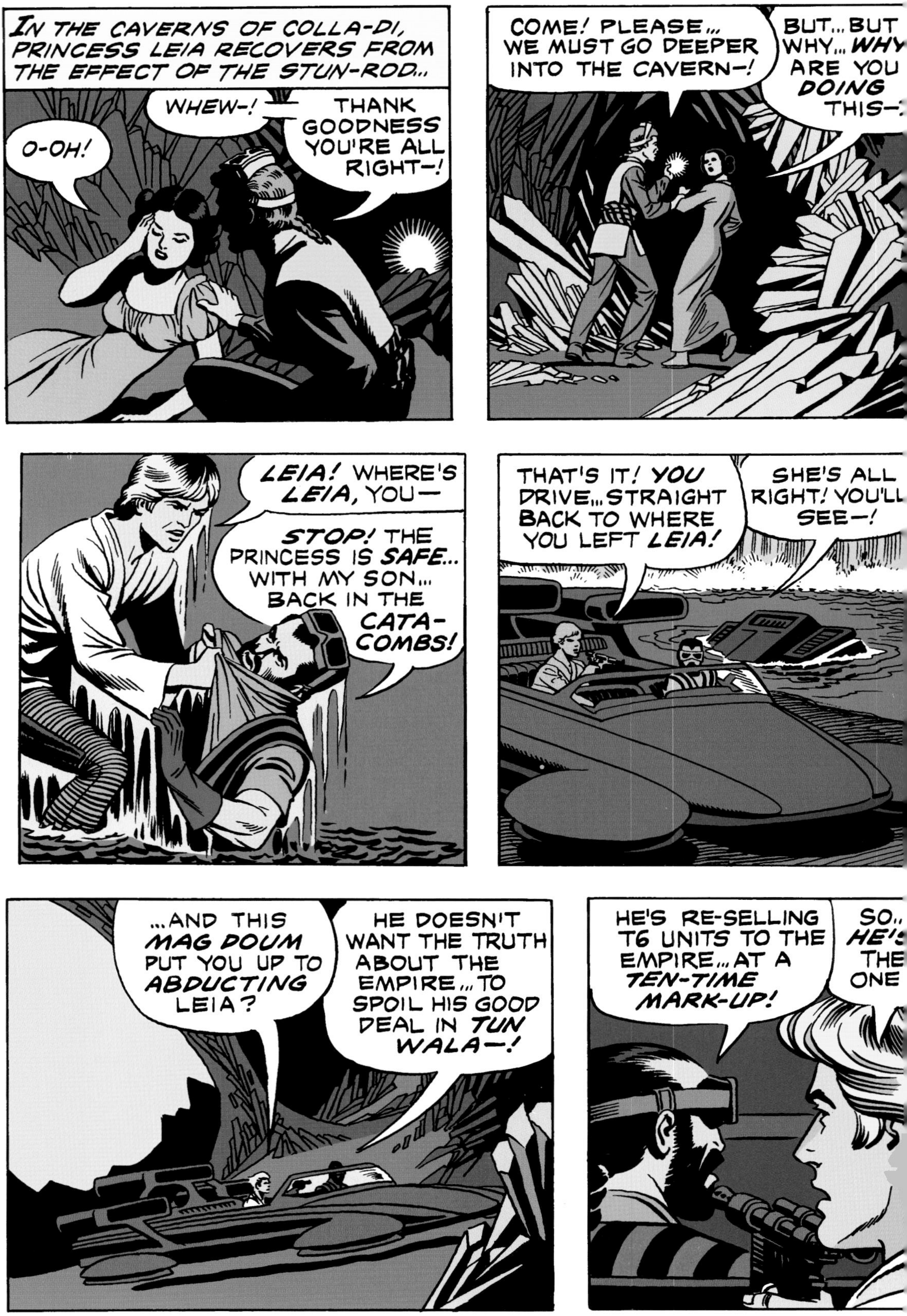
IN THE CAVERNS OF COLLA-DI, PRINCESS LEIA RECOVERS FROM THE EFFECT OF THE STUN-ROD...
O-OH!
WHEW-!
THANK GOODNESS YOU'RE ALL RIGHT-!
COME! PLEASE... WE MUST GO DEEPER INTO THE CAVERN-!
BUT... BUT WHY... WHY ARE YOU DOING THIS-
LEIA! WHERE'S LEIA, YOU—
STOP! THE PRINCESS IS SAFE... WITH MY SON... BACK IN THE CATA-COMBS!
THAT'S IT! YOU DRIVE... STRAIGHT BACK TO WHERE YOU LEFT LEIA!
SHE'S ALL RIGHT! YOU'LL SEE-!
...AND THIS MAG DOUM PUT YOU UP TO ABDUCTING LEIA?
HE DOESN'T WANT THE TRUTH ABOUT THE EMPIRE... TO SPOIL HIS GOOD DEAL IN TUN WALA-!
HE'S RE-SELLING T6 UNITS TO THE EMPIRE... AT A TEN-TIME MARK-UP!
SO.. HE'S THE ONE

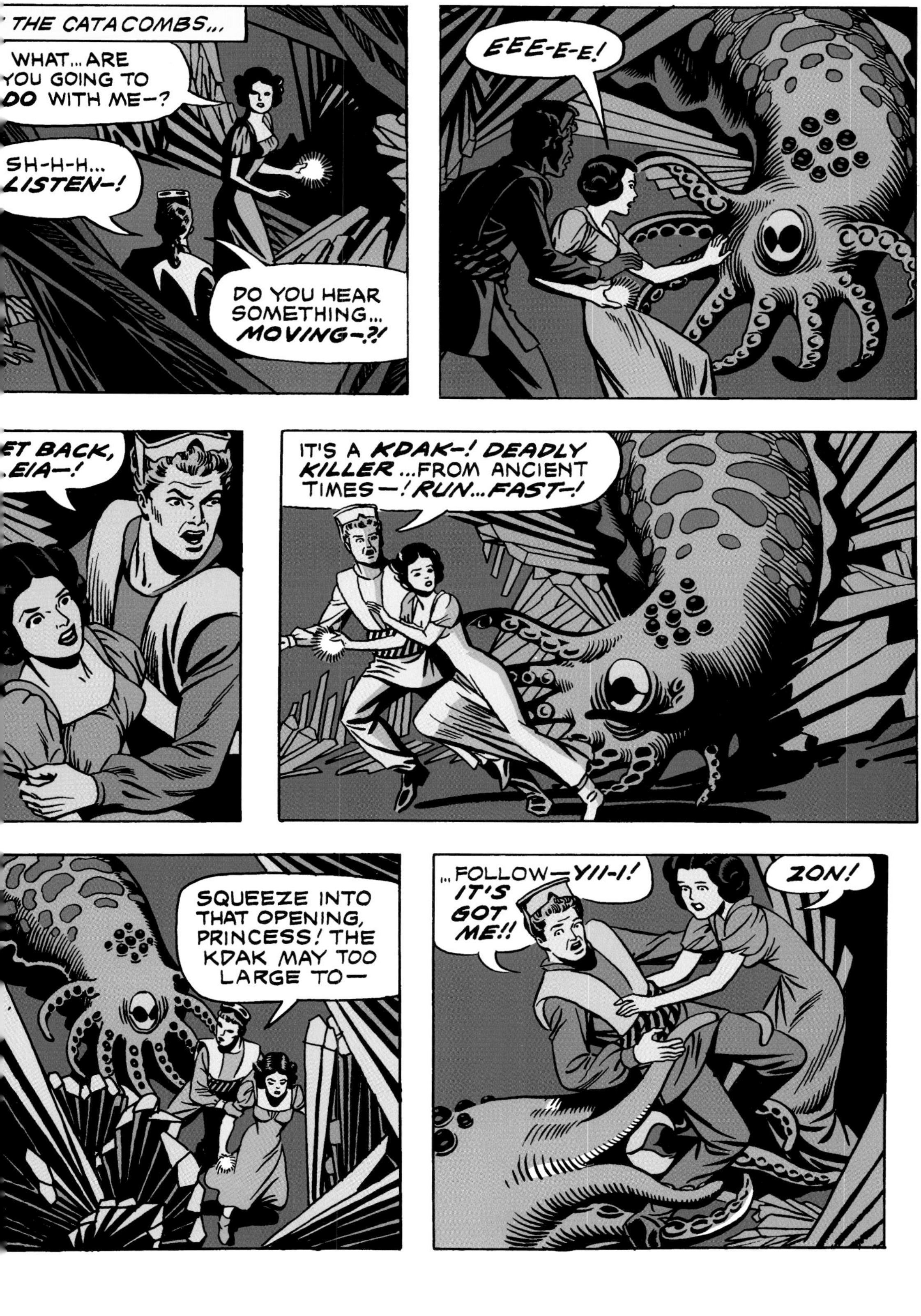
THE CATACOMBS...
WHAT... ARE YOU GOING TO DO WITH ME--?
SH-H-H... LISTEN--!
DO YOU HEAR SOMETHING... MOVING--?!
EEE-E-E!
ET BACK, EIA--!
IT'S A KDAK--! DEADLY KILLER ...FROM ANCIENT TIMES--! RUN... FAST--!
SQUEEZE INTO THAT OPENING, PRINCESS! THE KDAK MAY TOO LARGE TO--
...FOLLOW--YII-I! IT'S GOT ME!!
ZON!

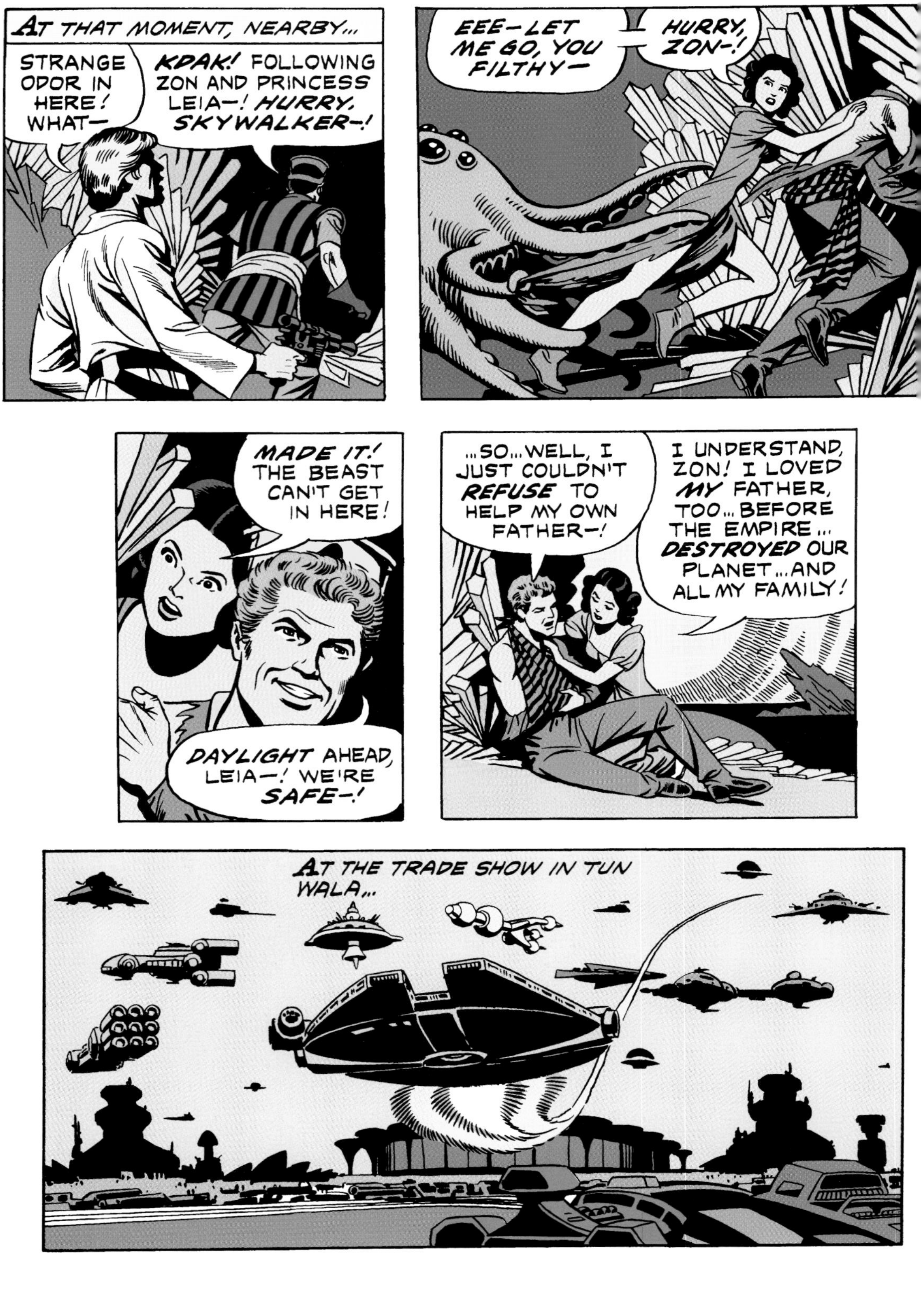
AT THAT MOMENT, NEARBY...
STRANGE ODOR IN HERE! WHAT—
KDAK! FOLLOWING ZON AND PRINCESS LEIA—! HURRY, SKYWALKER—!
EEE—LET ME GO, YOU FILTHY—
HURRY, ZON—!
MADE IT! THE BEAST CAN'T GET IN HERE!
DAYLIGHT AHEAD, LEIA—! WE'RE SAFE—!
...SO...WELL, I JUST COULDN'T REFUSE TO HELP MY OWN FATHER—!
I UNDERSTAND, ZON! I LOVED MY FATHER, TOO...BEFORE THE EMPIRE... DESTROYED OUR PLANET...AND ALL MY FAMILY!
AT THE TRADE SHOW IN TUN WALA...

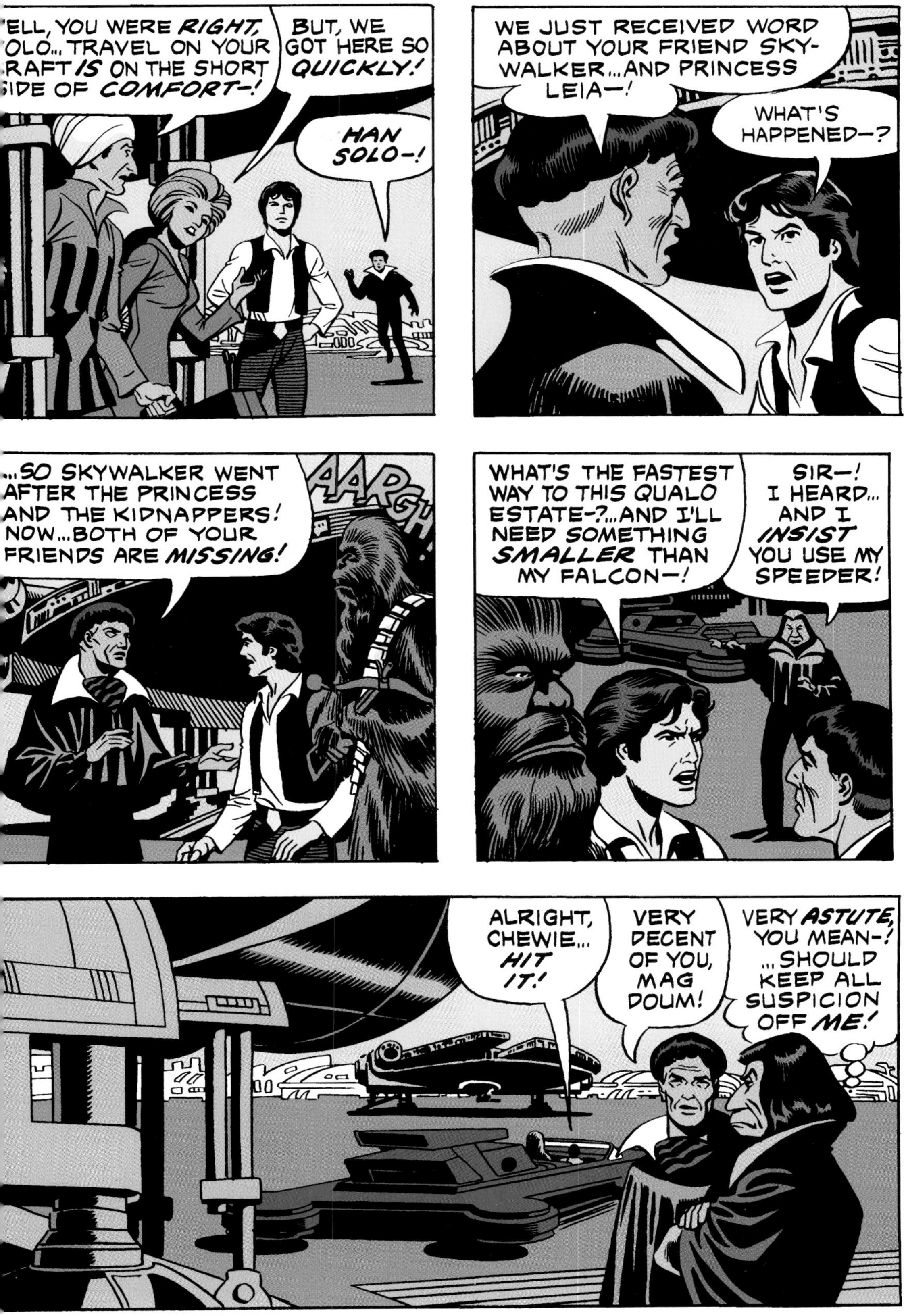
ELL, YOU WERE RIGHT, OLO... TRAVEL ON YOUR RAFT IS ON THE SHORT IDE OF COMFORT-!
BUT, WE GOT HERE SO QUICKLY!
HAN SOLO-!
WE JUST RECEIVED WORD ABOUT YOUR FRIEND SKY-WALKER...AND PRINCESS LEIA-!
WHAT'S HAPPENED-?
...SO SKYWALKER WENT AFTER THE PRINCESS AND THE KIDNAPPERS! NOW...BOTH OF YOUR FRIENDS ARE MISSING!
AARGH
WHAT'S THE FASTEST WAY TO THIS QUALO ESTATE-?...AND I'LL NEED SOMETHING SMALLER THAN MY FALCON-!
SIR-! I HEARD... AND I INSIST YOU USE MY SPEEDER!
ALRIGHT, CHEWIE... HIT IT!
VERY DECENT OF YOU, MAG DOUM!
VERY ASTUTE, YOU MEAN-! ...SHOULD KEEP ALL SUSPICION OFF ME!

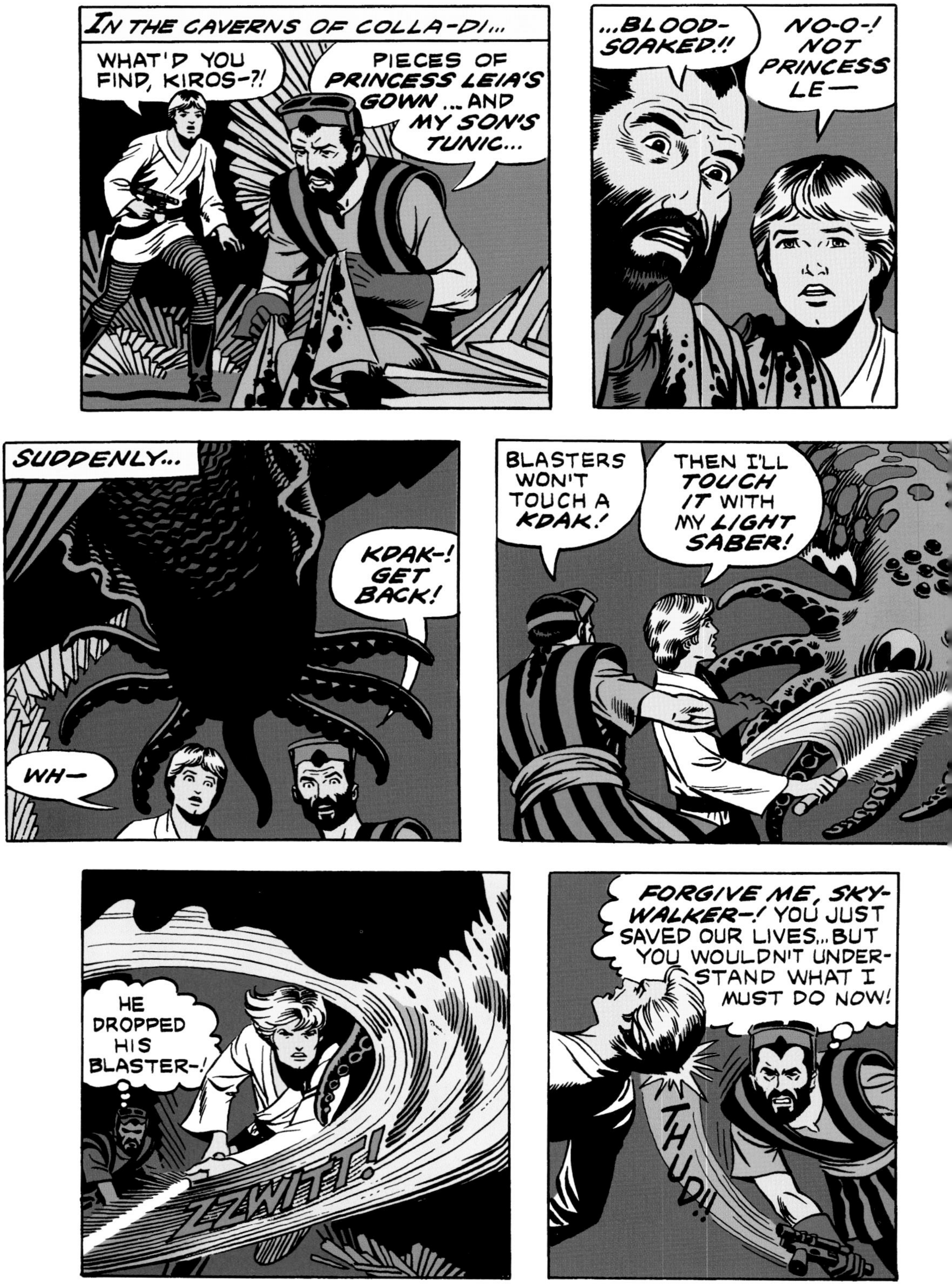
IN THE CAVERNS OF COLLA-DI...
WHAT'D YOU FIND, KIROS-?!
PIECES OF PRINCESS LEIA'S GOWN ... AND MY SON'S TUNIC...
...BLOOD-SOAKED!!
NO-O-! NOT PRINCESS LE—
SUDDENLY...
KDAK-! GET BACK!
WH—
BLASTERS WON'T TOUCH A KDAK!
THEN I'LL TOUCH IT WITH MY LIGHT SABER!
HE DROPPED HIS BLASTER-!
ZZWITT!
FORGIVE ME, SKY-WALKER-! YOU JUST SAVED OUR LIVES... BUT YOU WOULDN'T UNDER-STAND WHAT I MUST DO NOW!
THUD!!

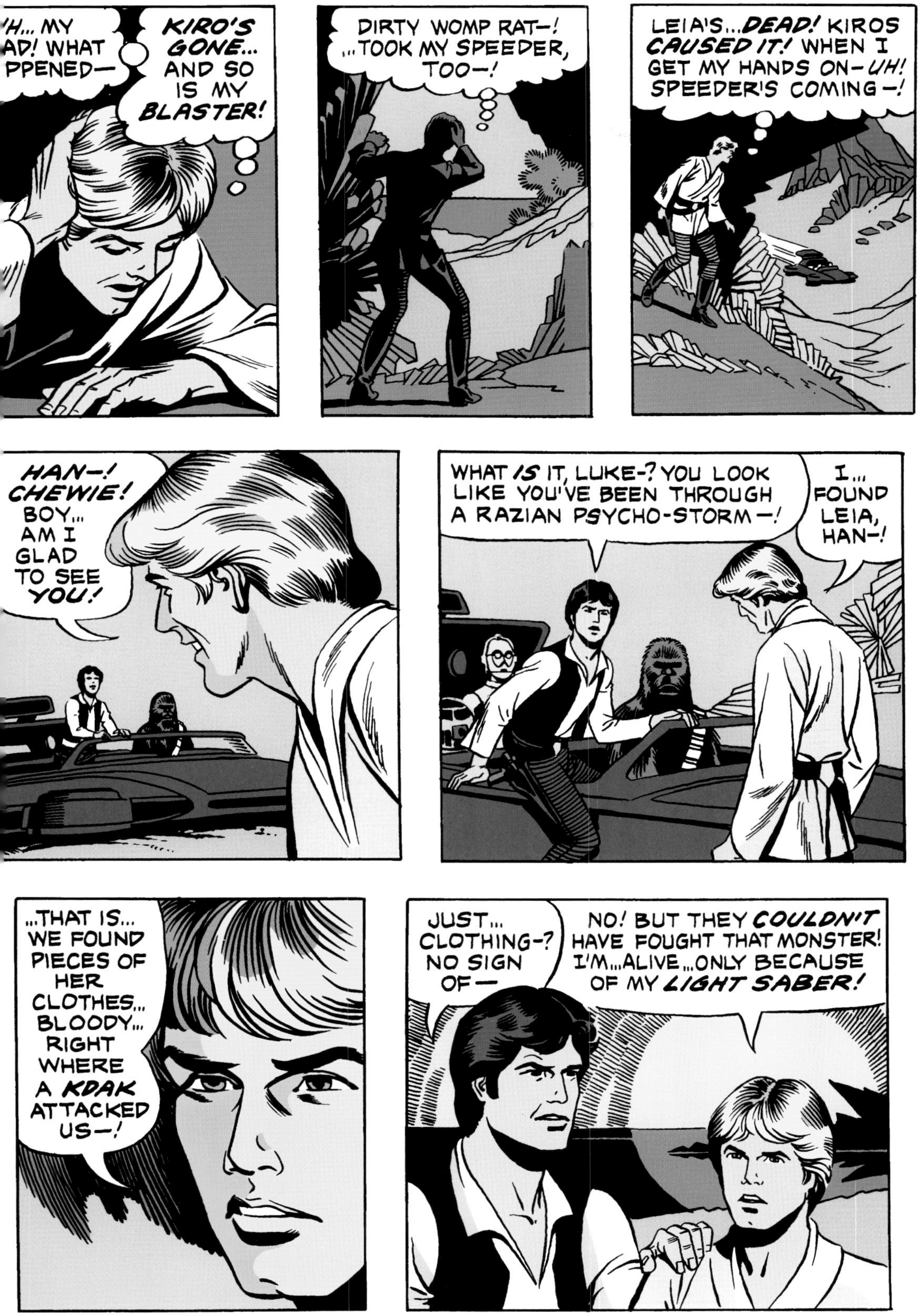

'H... MY
AD! WHAT
PPENED—
KIRO'S GONE... AND SO IS MY BLASTER!
DIRTY WOMP RAT—! ...TOOK MY SPEEDER, TOO—!
LEIA'S...DEAD! KIROS CAUSED IT! WHEN I GET MY HANDS ON—UH! SPEEDER'S COMING—!
HAN—! CHEWIE! BOY... AM I GLAD TO SEE YOU!
WHAT IS IT, LUKE—? YOU LOOK LIKE YOU'VE BEEN THROUGH A RAZIAN PSYCHO-STORM—!
I... FOUND LEIA, HAN—!
...THAT IS... WE FOUND PIECES OF HER CLOTHES... BLOODY... RIGHT WHERE A KDAK ATTACKED US—!
JUST... CLOTHING—? NO SIGN OF—
NO! BUT THEY COULDN'T HAVE FOUGHT THAT MONSTER! I'M...ALIVE...ONLY BECAUSE OF MY LIGHT SABER!

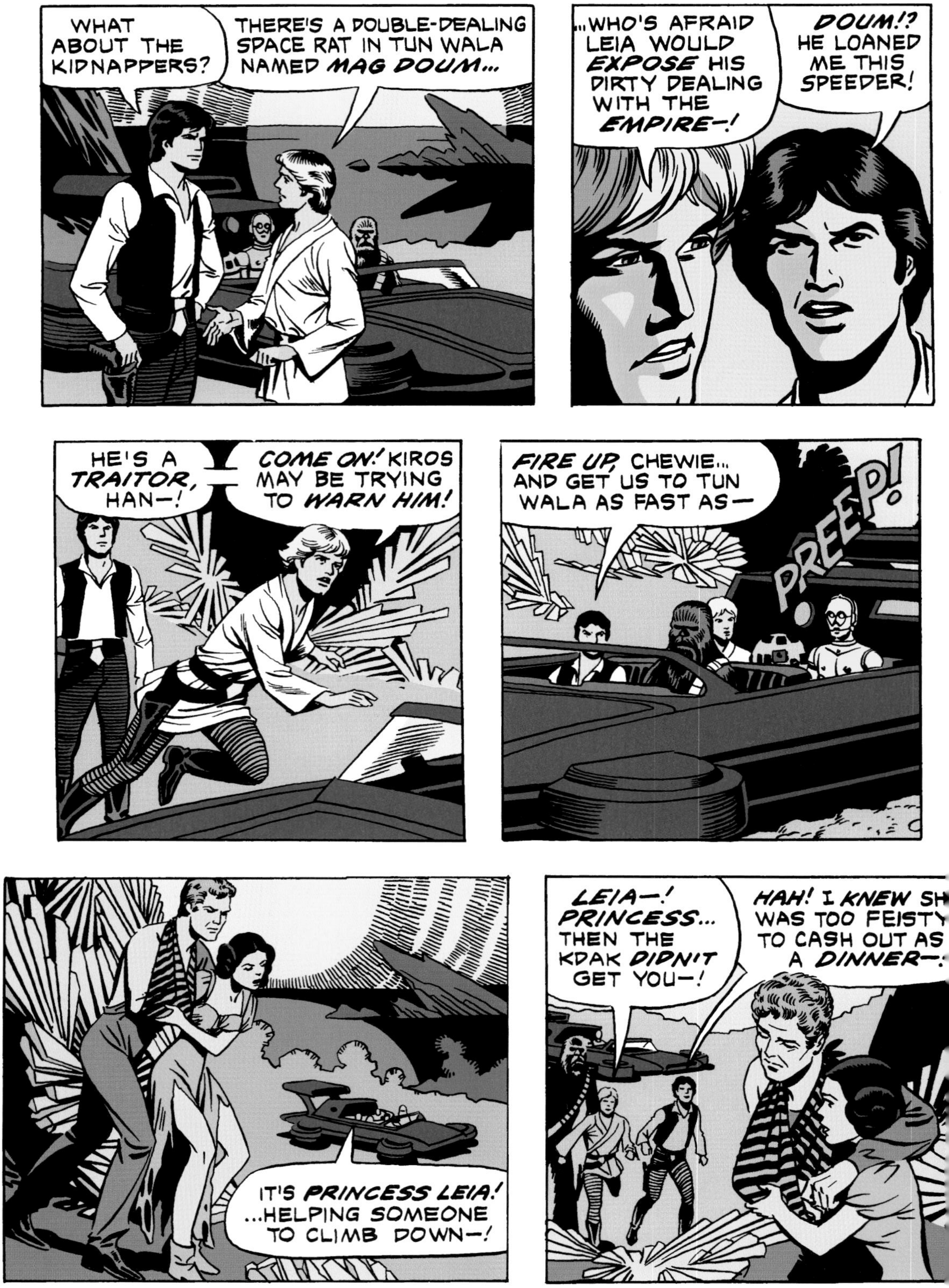

WHAT ABOUT THE KIDNAPPERS?
THERE'S A DOUBLE-DEALING SPACE RAT IN TUN WALA NAMED *MAG DOUM*...
...WHO'S AFRAID LEIA WOULD *EXPOSE* HIS DIRTY DEALING WITH THE *EMPIRE*—!
DOUM!? HE LOANED ME THIS SPEEDER!
HE'S A *TRAITOR,* HAN—!
COME ON! KIROS MAY BE TRYING TO *WARN HIM!*
FIRE UP, CHEWIE... AND GET US TO TUN WALA AS FAST AS—
PREEP!
IT'S *PRINCESS LEIA!* ...HELPING SOMEONE TO CLIMB DOWN—!
LEIA—! PRINCESS... THEN THE KDAK *DIDN'T* GET YOU—!
HAH! I *KNEW* SH WAS TOO FEISTY TO CASH OUT AS A *DINNER*—!

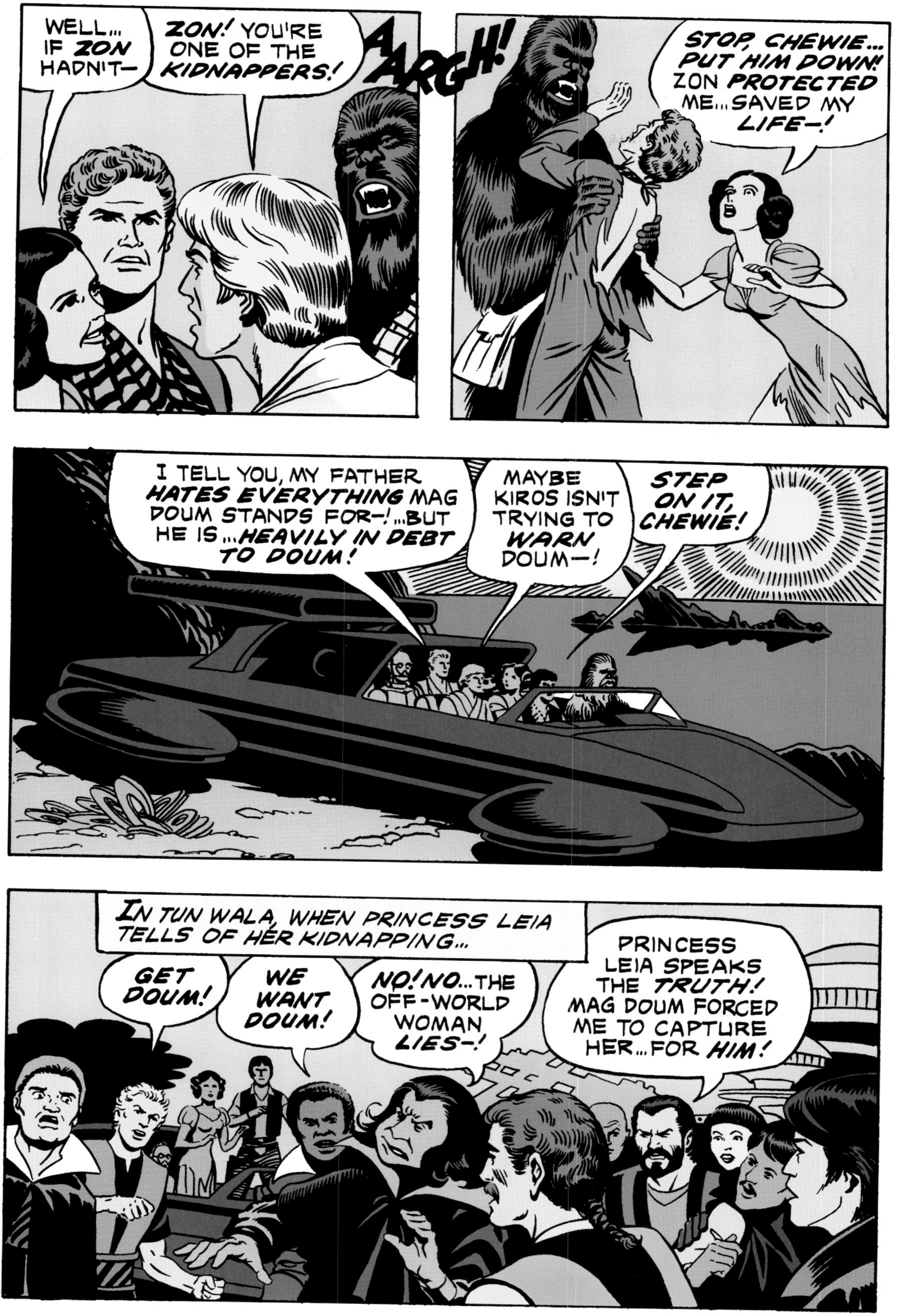
WELL... IF ZON HADN'T—
ZON! YOU'RE ONE OF THE KIDNAPPERS!
AARGH!
STOP, CHEWIE... PUT HIM DOWN! ZON PROTECTED ME... SAVED MY LIFE—!
I TELL YOU, MY FATHER HATES EVERYTHING MAG DOUM STANDS FOR—!...BUT HE IS... HEAVILY IN DEBT TO DOUM!
MAYBE KIROS ISN'T TRYING TO WARN DOUM—!
STEP ON IT, CHEWIE!
IN TUN WALA, WHEN PRINCESS LEIA TELLS OF HER KIDNAPPING...
GET DOUM!
WE WANT DOUM!
NO! NO... THE OFF-WORLD WOMAN LIES—!
PRINCESS LEIA SPEAKS THE TRUTH! MAG DOUM FORCED ME TO CAPTURE HER... FOR HIM!

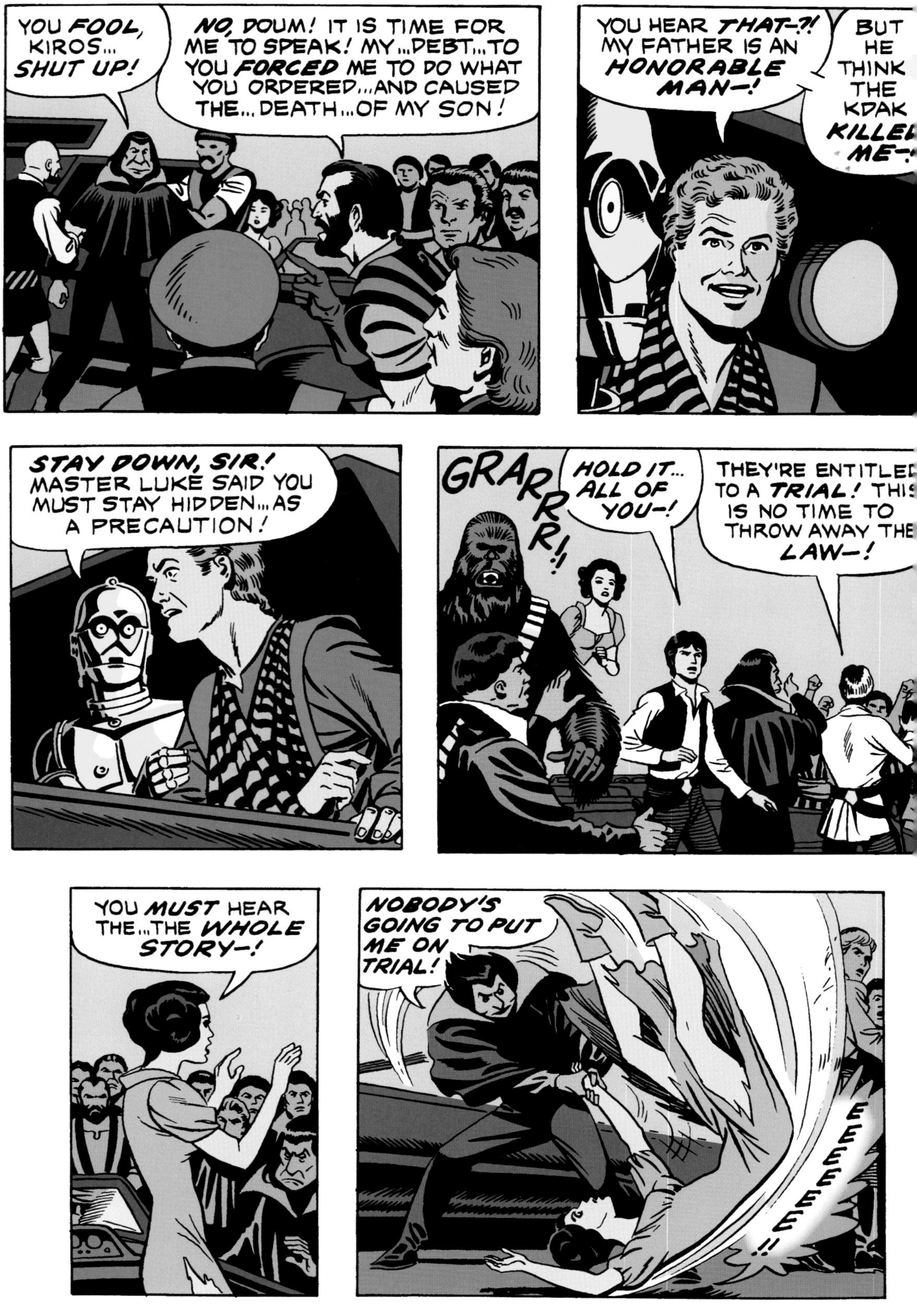

YOU FOOL, KIROS... SHUT UP!
NO, DOUM! IT IS TIME FOR ME TO SPEAK! MY...DEBT...TO YOU FORCED ME TO DO WHAT YOU ORDERED...AND CAUSED THE... DEATH...OF MY SON!
YOU HEAR THAT—?! MY FATHER IS AN HONORABLE MAN—!
BUT HE THINK THE KDAK KILLE ME—
STAY DOWN, SIR! MASTER LUKE SAID YOU MUST STAY HIDDEN...AS A PRECAUTION!
GRARRR!!
HOLD IT... ALL OF YOU—!
THEY'RE ENTITLE TO A TRIAL! THI IS NO TIME TO THROW AWAY THE LAW—!
YOU MUST HEAR THE...THE WHOLE STORY—!
NOBODY'S GOING TO PUT ME ON TRIAL!
EEEEEEE!!

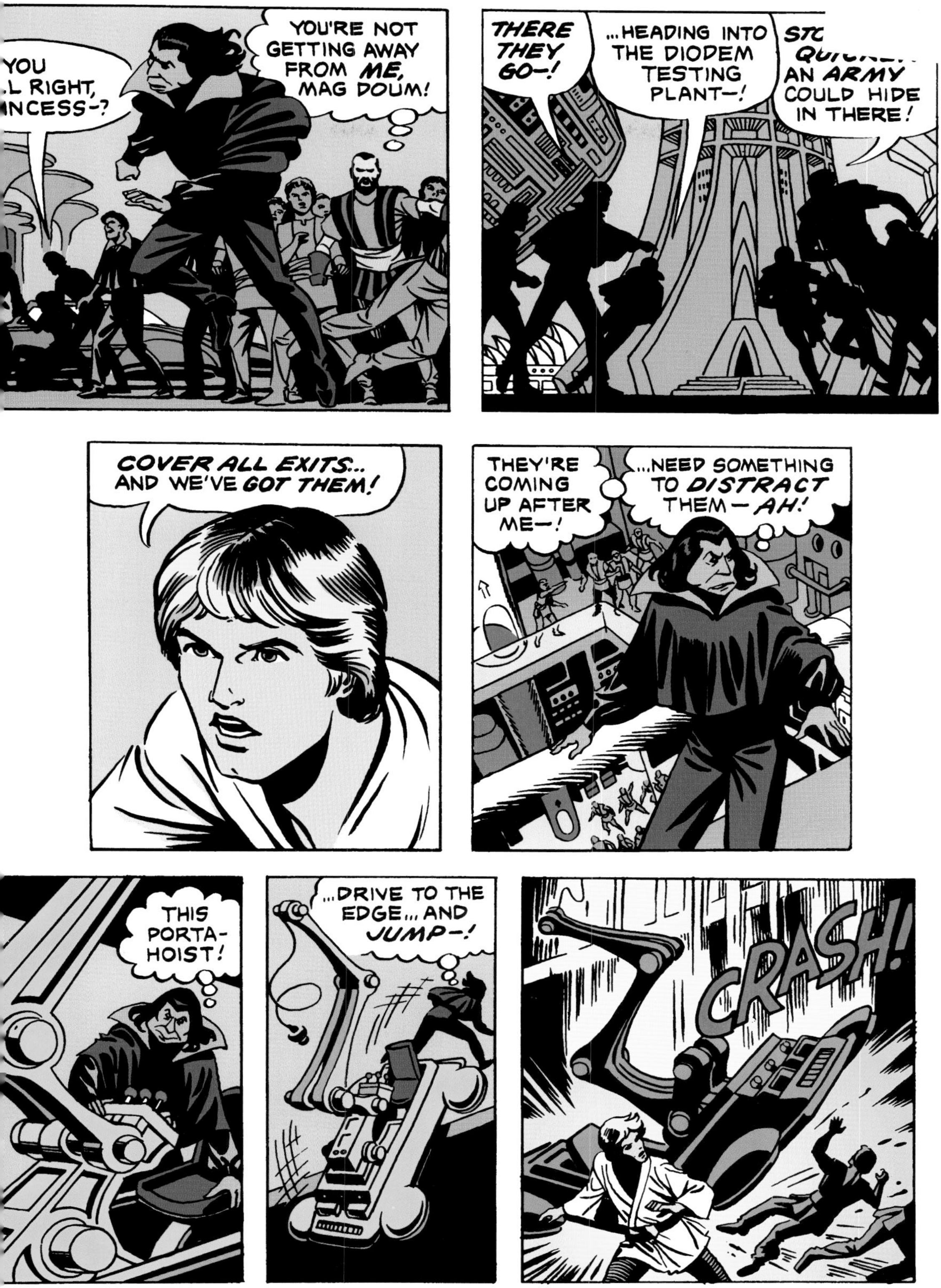

YOU'RE NOT GETTING AWAY FROM ME, MAG DOUM!
THERE THEY GO--!
...HEADING INTO THE DIODEM TESTING PLANT--!
AN ARMY COULD HIDE IN THERE!
COVER ALL EXITS... AND WE'VE GOT THEM!
THEY'RE COMING UP AFTER ME--!
...NEED SOMETHING TO DISTRACT THEM -- AH!
THIS PORTA-HOIST!
...DRIVE TO THE EDGE... AND JUMP--!
CRASH!

THAT CAME DOWN FROM THE FIFTH LEVEL—! MUST BE WHERE DOUM IS!
YOU'RE PUTTING ON TOO MUCH OF A SHOW, MAG DOUM—!
I THINK I KNOW WHAT YOU'RE UP TO—!
IF I CAN DRAW ENOUGH OF THEM UP HERE, THEY WON STAND BETWEE ME AND MY SHIP
HE GOT AWAY!
DESPITE THE CROWD HUNTING HIM, MAG DOUM MANAGES TO REACH HIS SPACE SHIP, AND BLAST OFF!
QUICKLY! ONE OF YOUR X-WINGS CAN SHOOT HIM DOWN—!
WHY SHOULD WE—? TO QUOTE YOU, TEMORA... "WE'RE NOT A CHARITY!"

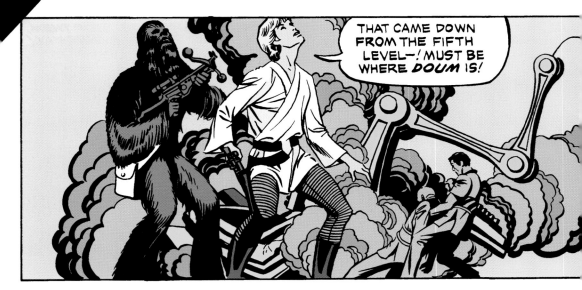

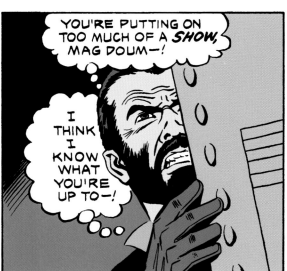

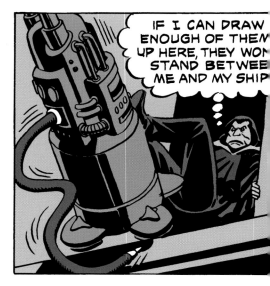

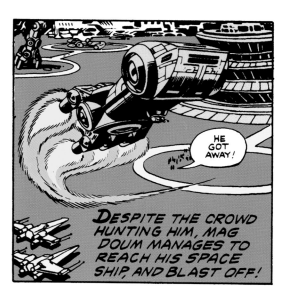

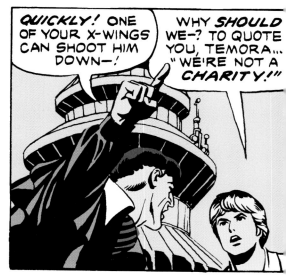

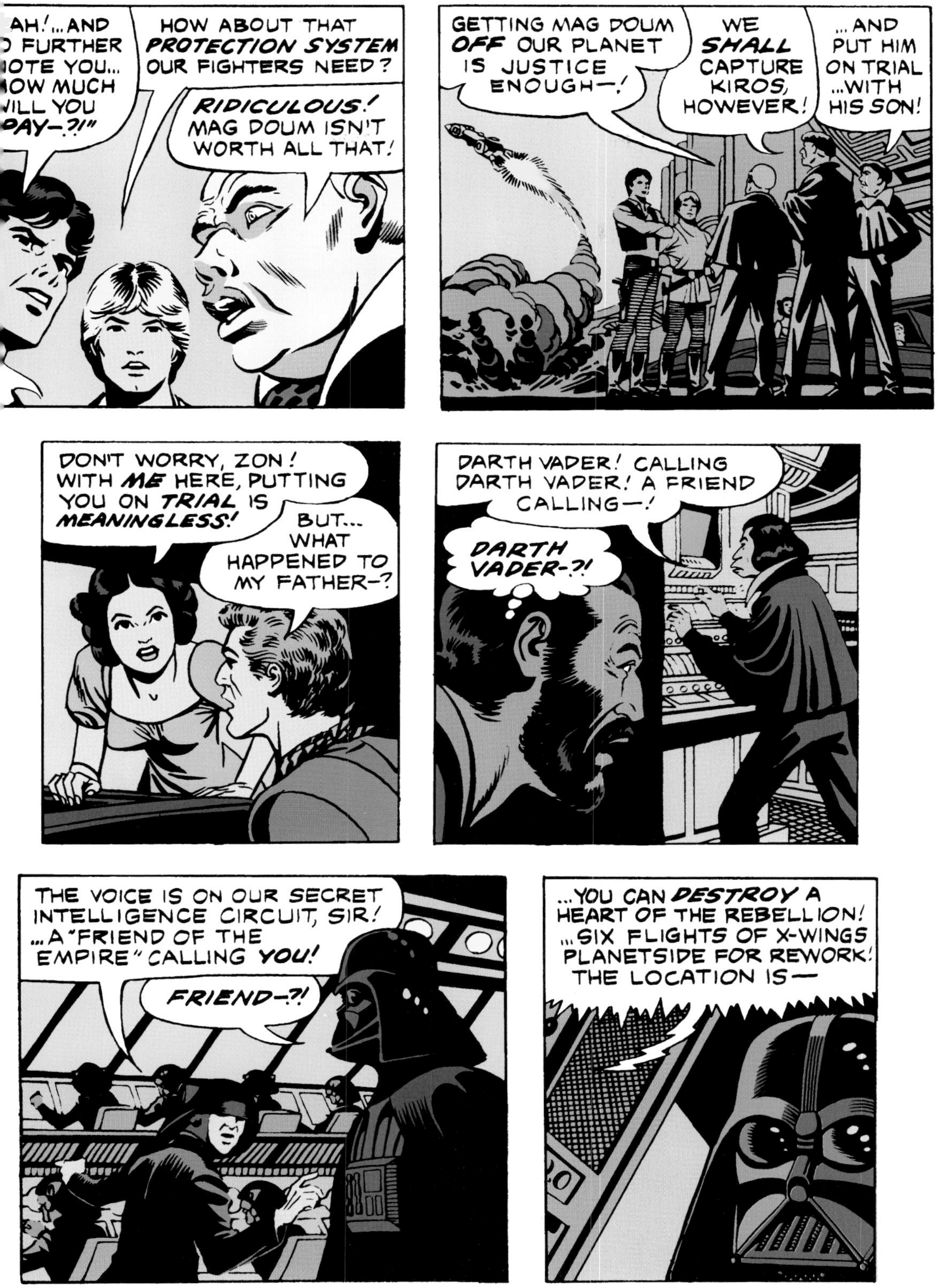
AH!...AND
FURTHER
OTE YOU...
OW MUCH
ILL YOU
AY-?!"
HOW ABOUT THAT PROTECTION SYSTEM OUR FIGHTERS NEED?
RIDICULOUS! MAG DOUM ISN'T WORTH ALL THAT!
GETTING MAG DOUM OFF OUR PLANET IS JUSTICE ENOUGH—!
WE SHALL CAPTURE KIROS, HOWEVER!
...AND PUT HIM ON TRIAL ...WITH HIS SON!
DON'T WORRY, ZON! WITH ME HERE, PUTTING YOU ON TRIAL IS MEANINGLESS!
BUT... WHAT HAPPENED TO MY FATHER—?
DARTH VADER! CALLING DARTH VADER! A FRIEND CALLING—!
DARTH VADER-?!
THE VOICE IS ON OUR SECRET INTELLIGENCE CIRCUIT, SIR! ...A "FRIEND OF THE EMPIRE" CALLING YOU!
FRIEND-?!
...YOU CAN DESTROY A HEART OF THE REBELLION! ...SIX FLIGHTS OF X-WINGS PLANETSIDE FOR REWORK! THE LOCATION IS—

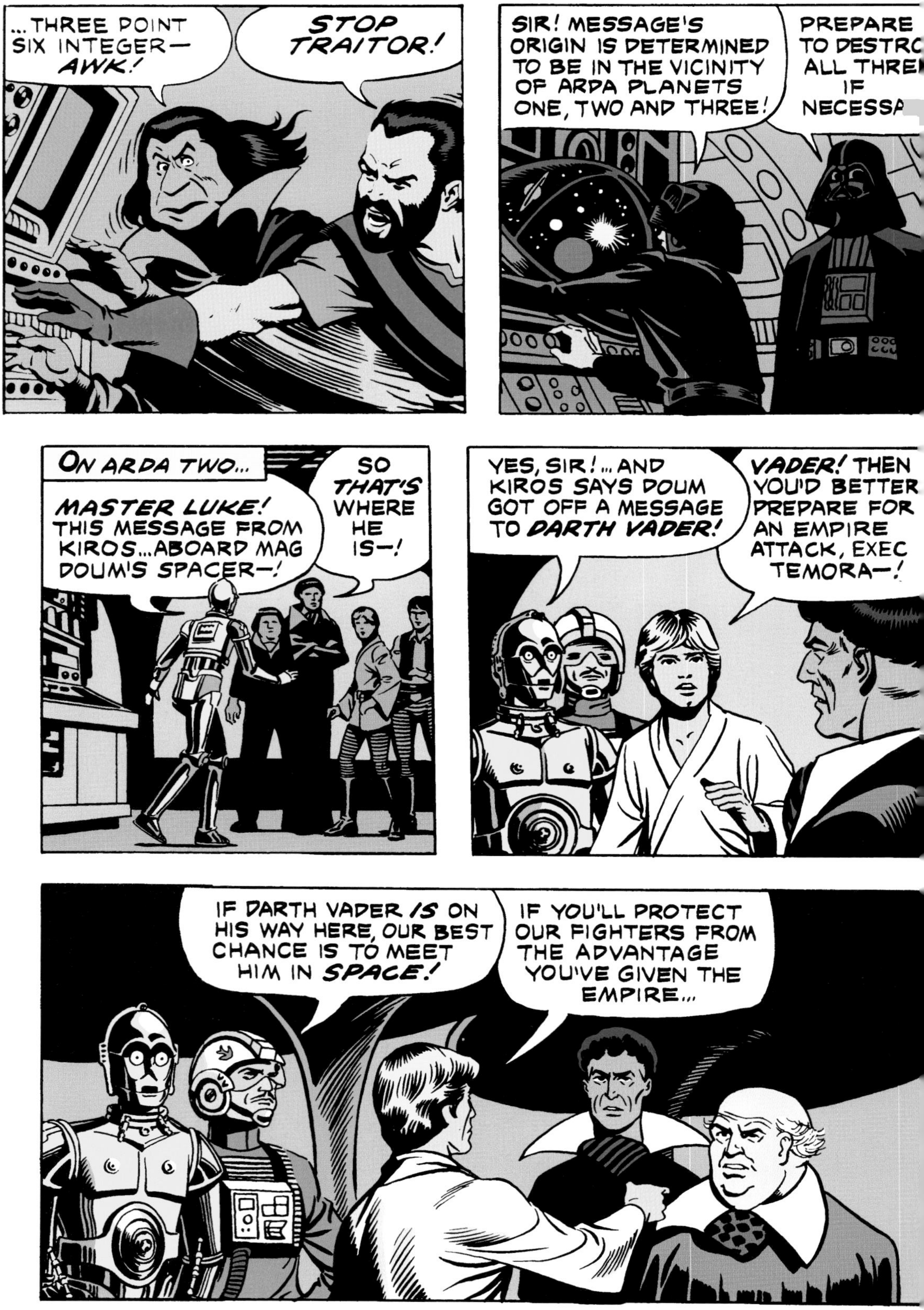
...THREE POINT SIX INTEGER— AWK!
STOP TRAITOR!
SIR! MESSAGE'S ORIGIN IS DETERMINED TO BE IN THE VICINITY OF ARDA PLANETS ONE, TWO AND THREE!
PREPARE TO DESTRO ALL THRE IF NECESSA
ON ARDA TWO...
MASTER LUKE! THIS MESSAGE FROM KIROS...ABOARD MAG DOUM'S SPACER—!
SO THAT'S WHERE HE IS—!
YES, SIR!...AND KIROS SAYS DOUM GOT OFF A MESSAGE TO DARTH VADER!
VADER! THEN YOU'D BETTER PREPARE FOR AN EMPIRE ATTACK, EXEC TEMORA—!
IF DARTH VADER IS ON HIS WAY HERE, OUR BEST CHANCE IS TO MEET HIM IN SPACE!
IF YOU'LL PROTECT OUR FIGHTERS FROM THE ADVANTAGE YOU'VE GIVEN THE EMPIRE...

...IN PAYMENT, WE'LL ATTACK VADER'S FLEET...TRY TO KEEP THEM *OFF* OF YOUR PLANET—!

THE CHOICE IS *YOURS*, EXEC TEMORA!

WE ...WILL NOT BE PANICKED BY A *RUMOR!* WHY...DARTH VADER MAY BE USING *YOU*...TO TEST *OUR NEUTRALITY—!*

N A TUN WALA DETENTION BLOCK...

AN *EMPIRE FLEET*... COMING TO *ATTACK US*–.?!

I'VE GOT TO GET *OUT* OF HERE!

I CAN FLY AN X-WING! THEY'LL NEED EVERY FIGHTER PILOT ON ARDA! *MAKE THEM RELEASE ME, PRINCESS!*

I'M AFRAID THERE'S NOT A *THING* I CAN DO, ZON!

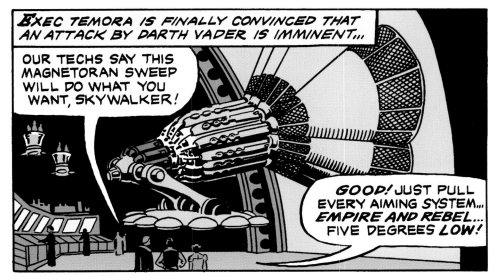

EXEC TEMORA IS FINALLY CONVINCED THAT AN ATTACK BY DARTH VADER IS IMMINENT...

OUR TECHS SAY THIS MAGNETORAN SWEEP WILL DO WHAT YOU WANT, SKYWALKER!

GOOD! JUST PULL EVERY AIMING SYSTEM... *EMPIRE AND REBEL...* FIVE DEGREES *LOW!*

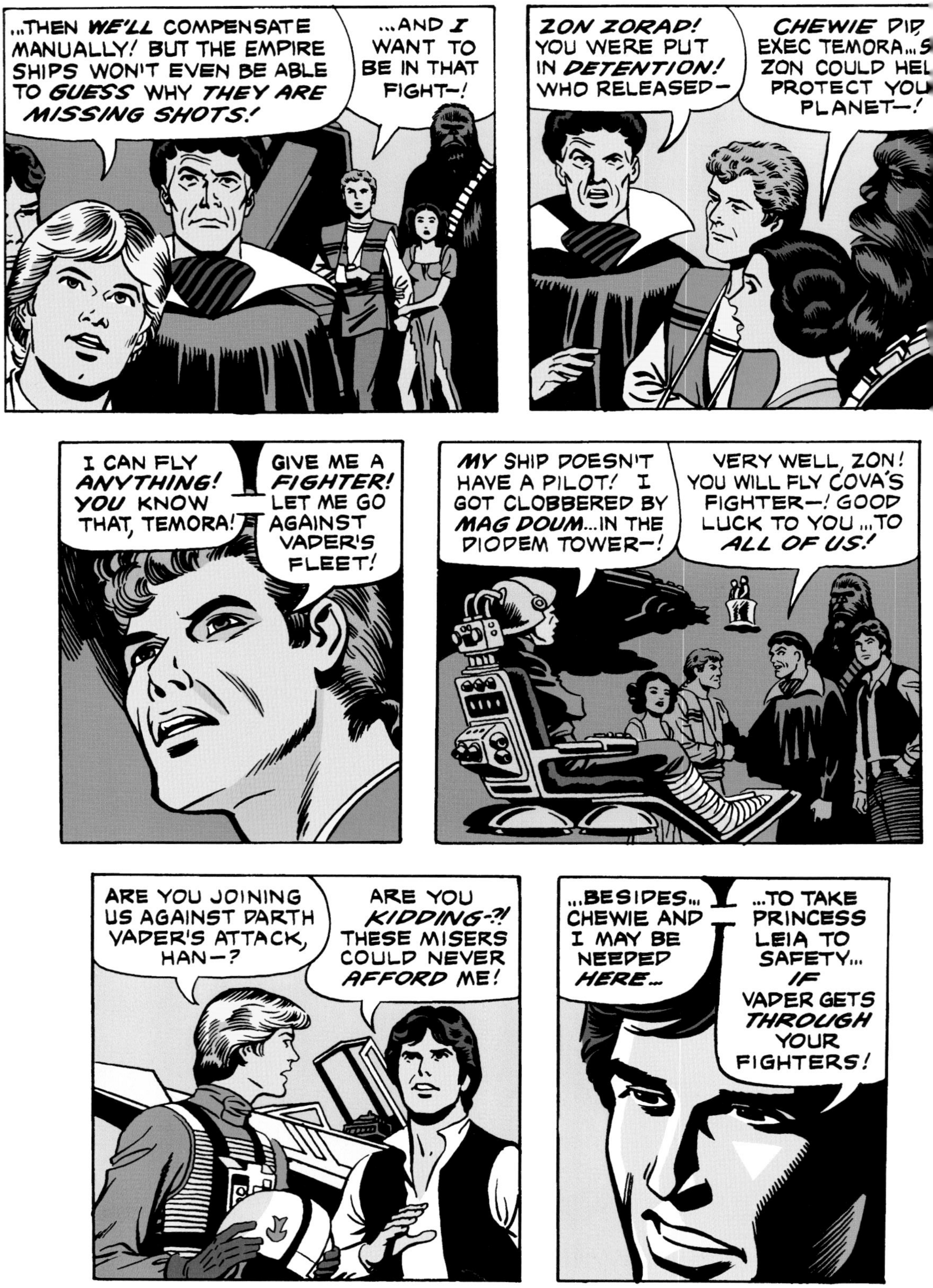

...THEN *WE'LL* COMPENSATE MANUALLY! BUT THE EMPIRE SHIPS WON'T EVEN BE ABLE TO *GUESS* WHY *THEY ARE MISSING SHOTS!*
...AND *I* WANT TO BE IN THAT FIGHT—!
ZON ZORAD! YOU WERE PUT IN *DETENTION!* WHO RELEASED—
CHEWIE DID EXEC TEMORA...S ZON COULD HEL PROTECT YOU PLANET—!
I CAN FLY *ANYTHING!* *YOU* KNOW THAT, TEMORA!
GIVE ME A *FIGHTER!* LET ME GO AGAINST VADER'S FLEET!
MY SHIP DOESN'T HAVE A PILOT! I GOT CLOBBERED BY *MAG DOUM*...IN THE DIODEM TOWER—!
VERY WELL, ZON! YOU WILL FLY COVA'S FIGHTER—! GOOD LUCK TO YOU ...TO *ALL OF US!*
ARE YOU JOINING US AGAINST DARTH VADER'S ATTACK, HAN—?
ARE YOU *KIDDING*-?! THESE MISERS COULD NEVER *AFFORD* ME!
...BESIDES... CHEWIE AND I MAY BE NEEDED *HERE*...
...TO TAKE PRINCESS LEIA TO SAFETY... *IF* VADER GETS *THROUGH* YOUR FIGHTERS!

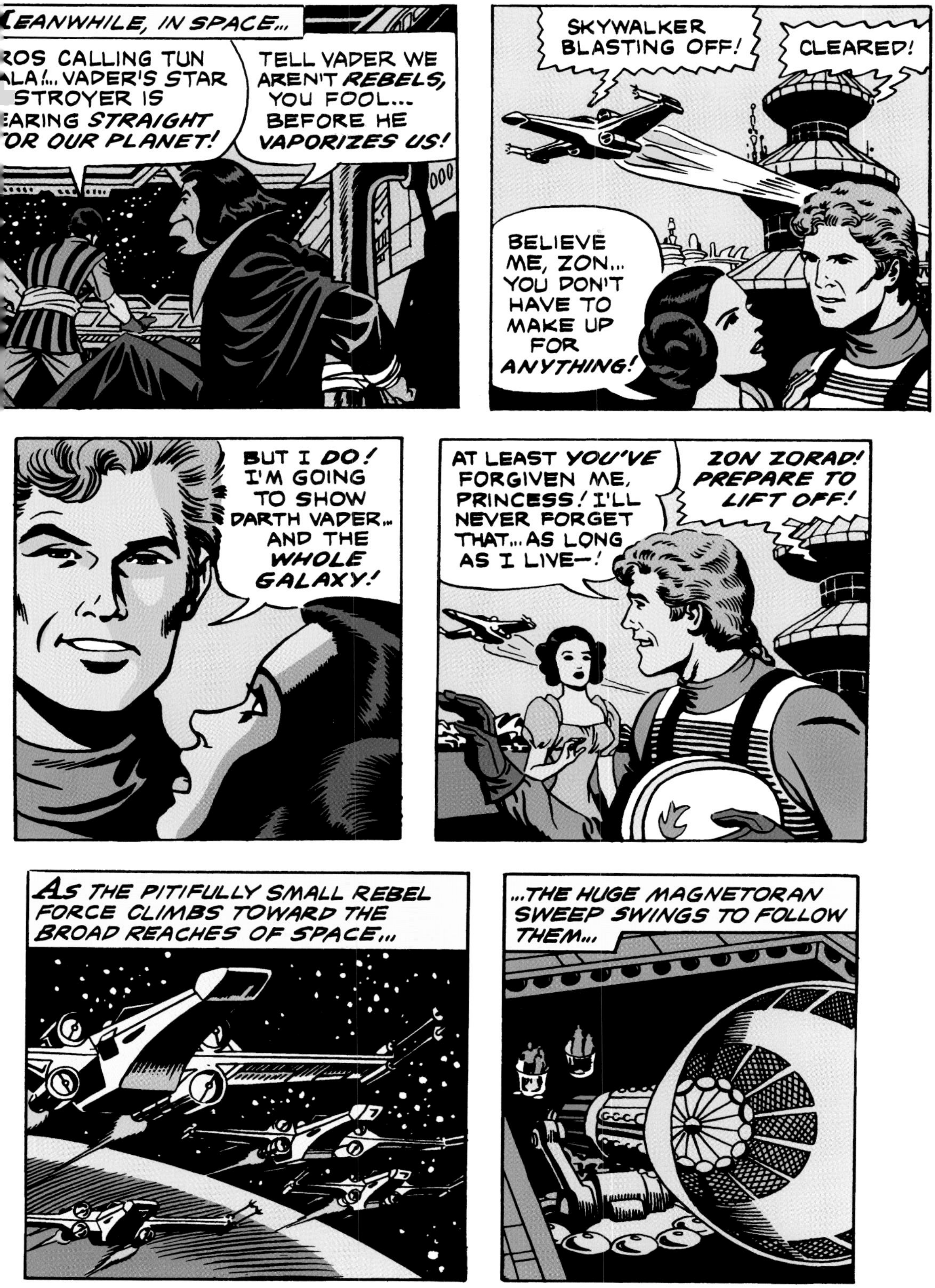

MEANWHILE, IN SPACE...
ROS CALLING TUN ALA!... VADER'S STAR STROYER IS EARING STRAIGHT FOR OUR PLANET!
TELL VADER WE AREN'T REBELS, YOU FOOL... BEFORE HE VAPORIZES US!
SKYWALKER BLASTING OFF!
CLEARED!
BELIEVE ME, ZON... YOU DON'T HAVE TO MAKE UP FOR ANYTHING!
BUT I DO! I'M GOING TO SHOW DARTH VADER... AND THE WHOLE GALAXY!
AT LEAST YOU'VE FORGIVEN ME, PRINCESS! I'LL NEVER FORGET THAT... AS LONG AS I LIVE--!
ZON ZORAD! PREPARE TO LIFT OFF!
AS THE PITIFULLY SMALL REBEL FORCE CLIMBS TOWARD THE BROAD REACHES OF SPACE...
...THE HUGE MAGNETORAN SWEEP SWINGS TO FOLLOW THEM...

SKYWALKER! I *MUST* LET MY FATHER KNOW I'M ALIVE—!

I UNDERSTAND, ZON! WE'RE ALMOST IN COMLINK RANGE, NOW!

LORD VADER! A FREIGHTER... HEADING DIRECTLY TOWARD US!

...WITH X-WING FIGHTERS FOLLOWIN IT—!

JUST *SIX* REBEL SHIPS?!

LAUNCH THREE FLIGHTS OF TIE-FIGHTERS!

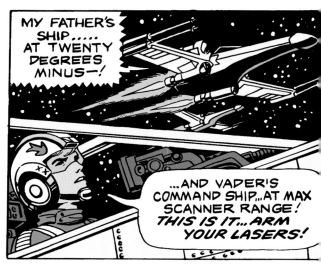

MY FATHER'S SHIP..... AT TWENTY DEGREES MINUS—!

...AND VADER'S COMMAND SHIP...AT MAX SCANNER RANGE! THIS IS IT...ARM YOUR LASERS!

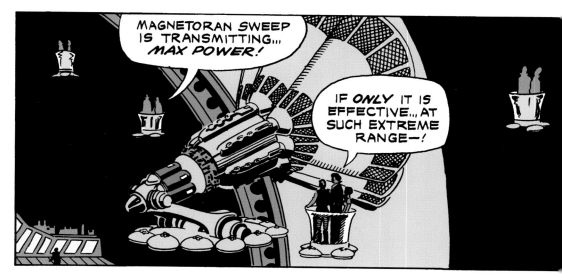

MAGNETORAN SWEEP IS TRANSMITTING... *MAX POWER!*

IF *ONLY* IT IS EFFECTIVE... AT SUCH EXTREME RANGE—!

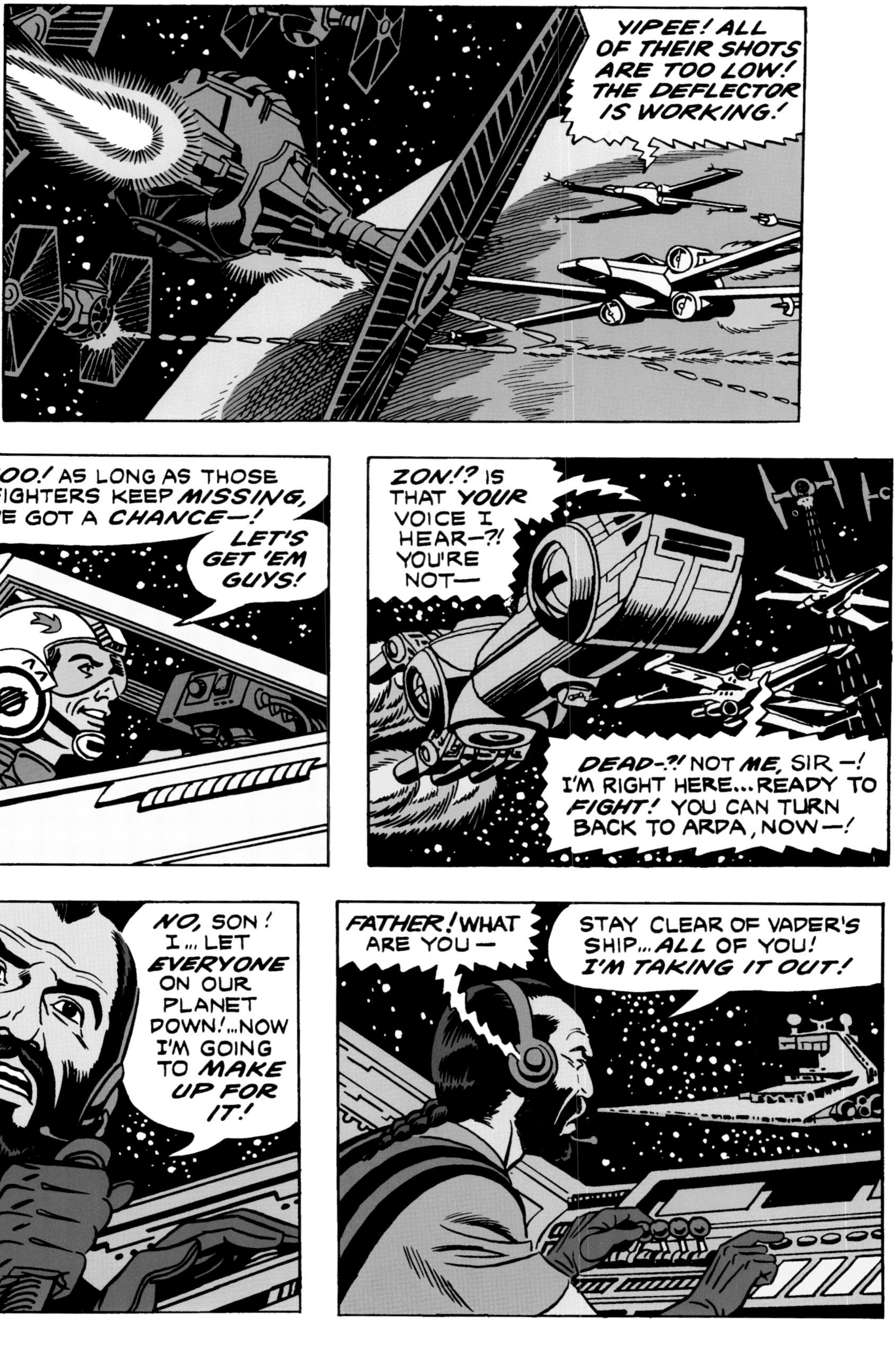
YIPEE! ALL OF THEIR SHOTS ARE TOO LOW! THE DEFLECTOR IS WORKING!
AHOO! AS LONG AS THOSE IE-FIGHTERS KEEP MISSING, E'VE GOT A CHANCE—!
LET'S GET 'EM GUYS!
ZON!? IS THAT YOUR VOICE I HEAR—?! YOU'RE NOT—
DEAD-?! NOT ME, SIR—! I'M RIGHT HERE...READY TO FIGHT! YOU CAN TURN BACK TO ARDA, NOW—!
NO, SON! I... LET EVERYONE ON OUR PLANET DOWN!...NOW I'M GOING TO MAKE UP FOR IT!
FATHER! WHAT ARE YOU—
STAY CLEAR OF VADER'S SHIP...ALL OF YOU! I'M TAKING IT OUT!

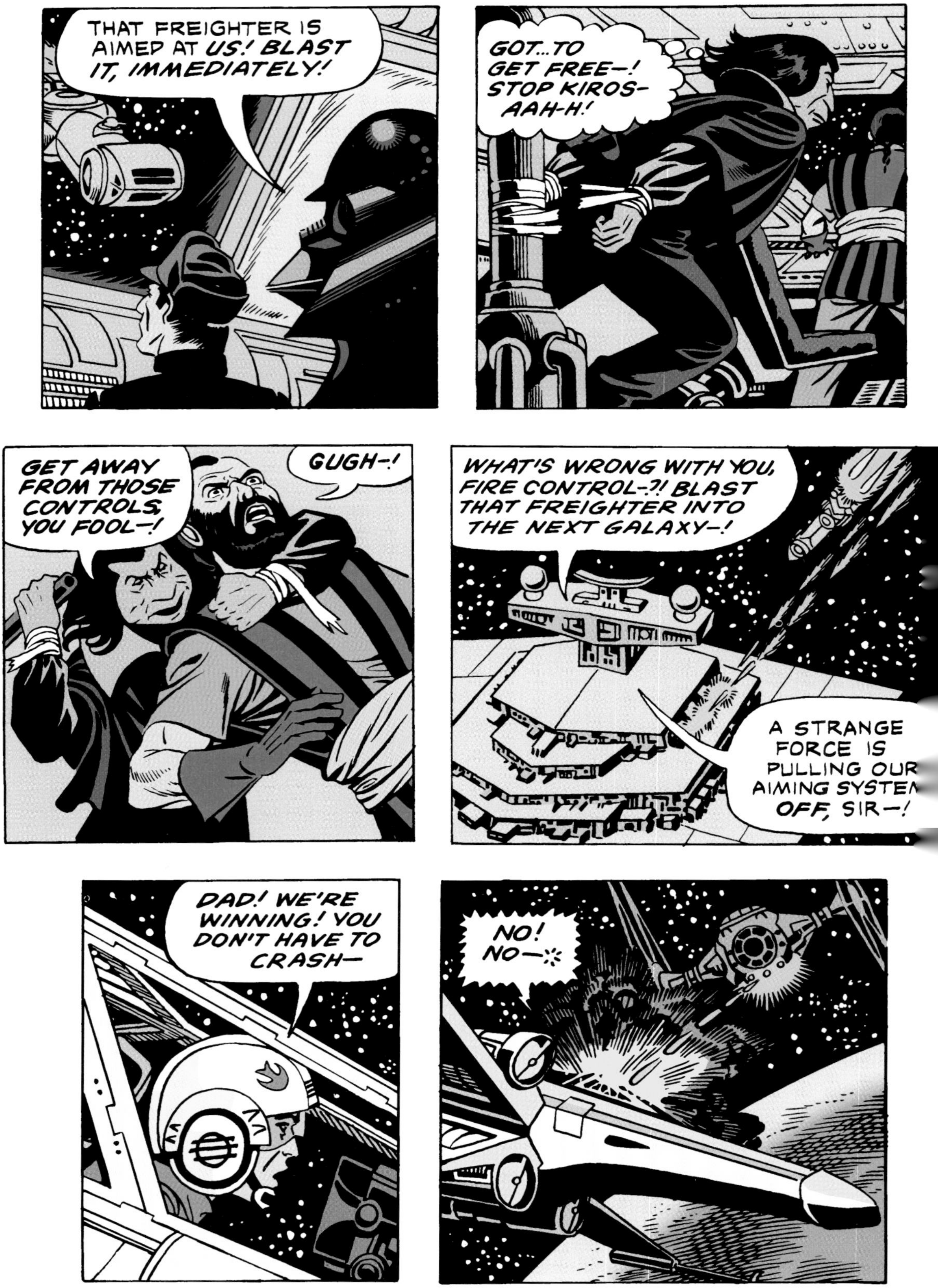
THAT FREIGHTER IS AIMED AT US! BLAST IT, IMMEDIATELY!
GOT...TO GET FREE--! STOP KIROS-- AAH-H!
GET AWAY FROM THOSE CONTROLS, YOU FOOL--!
GUGH--!
WHAT'S WRONG WITH YOU, FIRE CONTROL--?! BLAST THAT FREIGHTER INTO THE NEXT GALAXY--!
A STRANGE FORCE IS PULLING OUR AIMING SYSTEM OFF, SIR--!
DAD! WE'RE WINNING! YOU DON'T HAVE TO CRASH--
NO! NO--

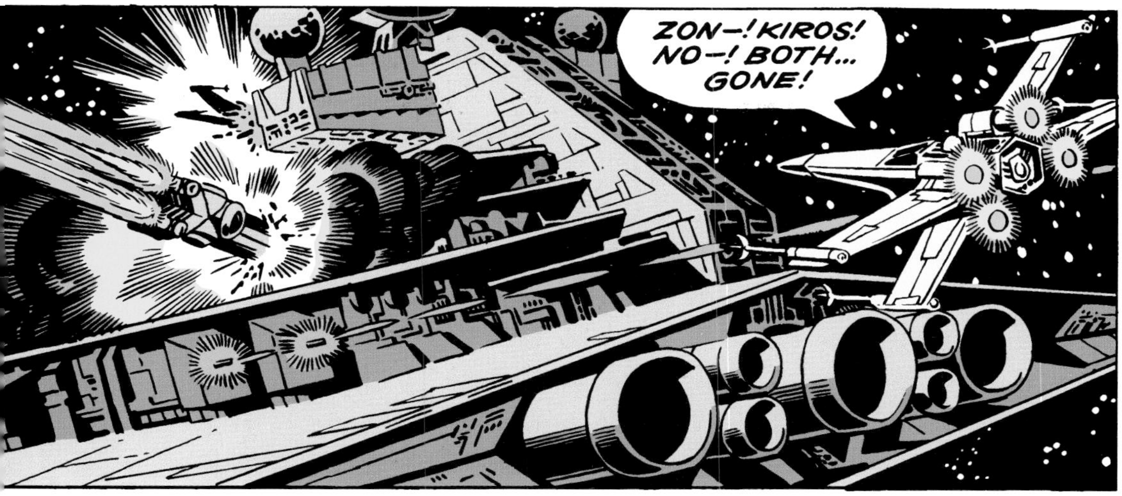
ZON—! KIROS! NO—! BOTH... GONE!

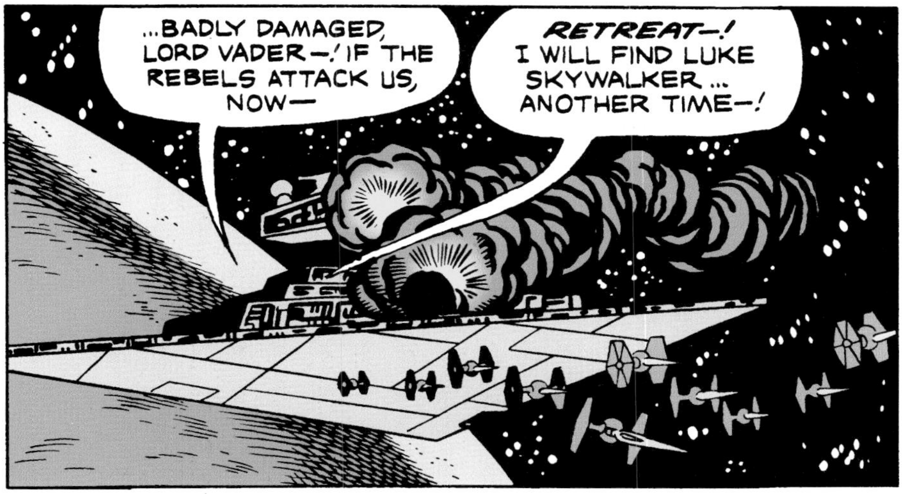
...BADLY DAMAGED, LORD VADER—! IF THE REBELS ATTACK US, NOW—
RETREAT—! I WILL FIND LUKE SKYWALKER ... ANOTHER TIME—!

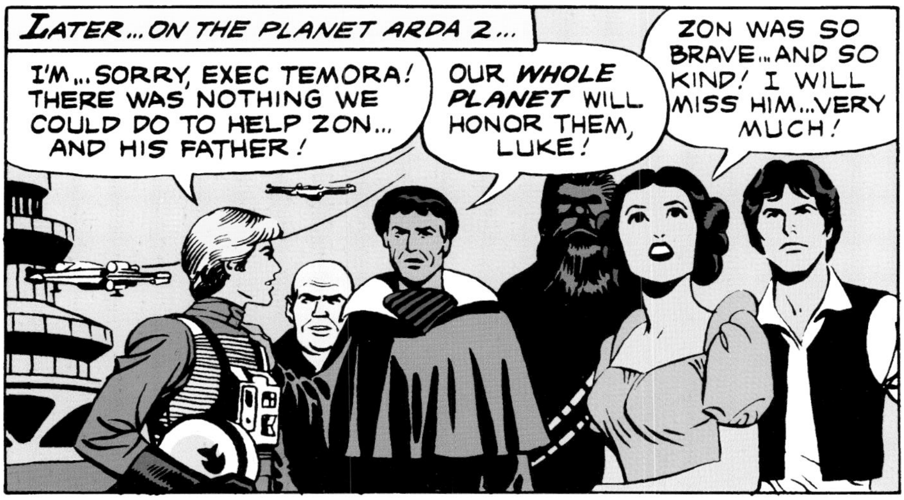
LATER... ON THE PLANET ARDA 2...
I'M... SORRY, EXEC TEMORA! THERE WAS NOTHING WE COULD DO TO HELP ZON... AND HIS FATHER!
OUR WHOLE PLANET WILL HONOR THEM, LUKE!
ZON WAS SO BRAVE... AND SO KIND! I WILL MISS HIM... VERY MUCH!

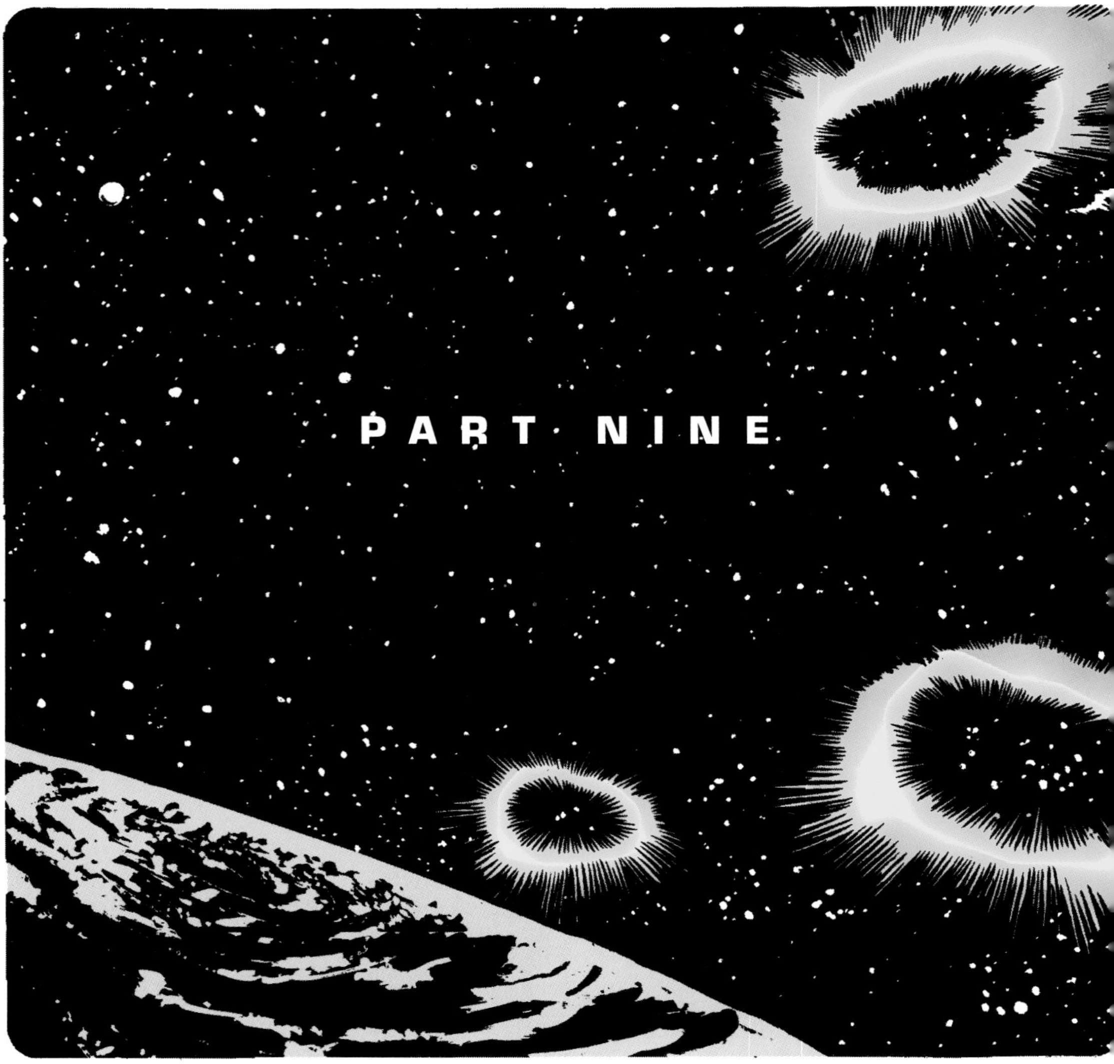
PART NINE

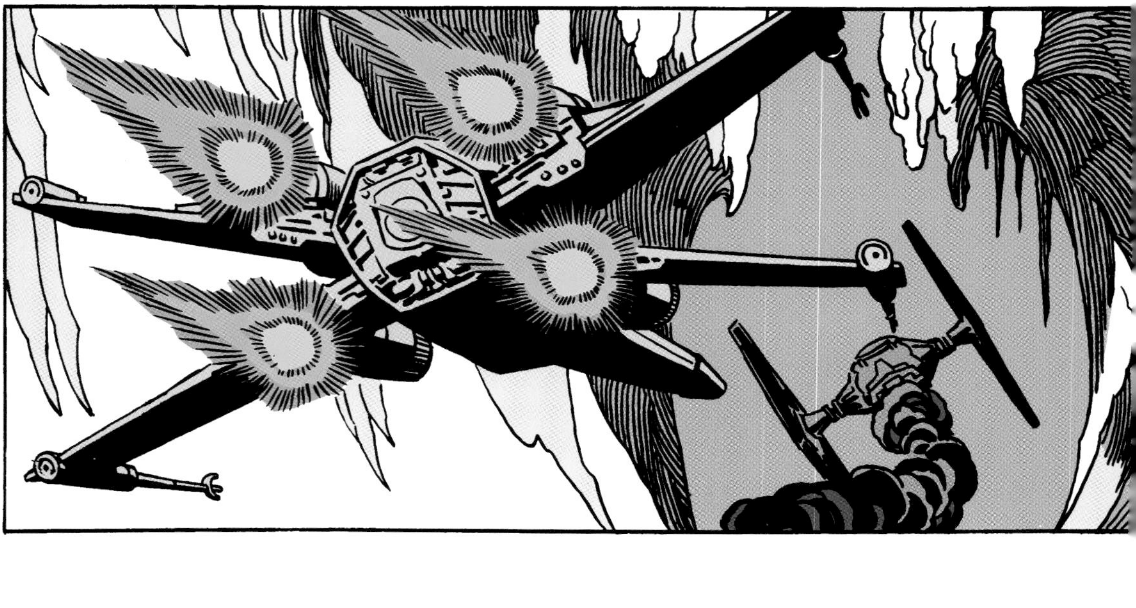

THE DISABLED EMPIRE FIGHTER TRIES TO LOSE LUKE IN THE ICE CANYONS OF OTA...

LAND THAT THING, YOU IDIOT... BEFORE YOU BRING THESE ICE CLIFFS *DOWN* ON US—!

...TOO LATE—!

TONS OF FALLING ICE AND SNOW FORCE BOTH CRAFT TO CRASH-LAND...

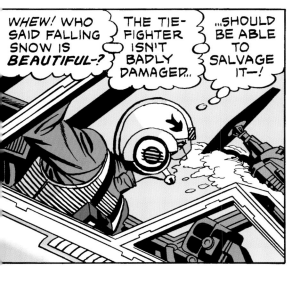

WHEW! WHO SAID FALLING SNOW IS *BEAUTIFUL*—?

THE TIE-FIGHTER ISN'T BADLY DAMAGED...

...SHOULD BE ABLE TO SALVAGE IT—!

NOW... WHAT ABOUT THE PILOT—?

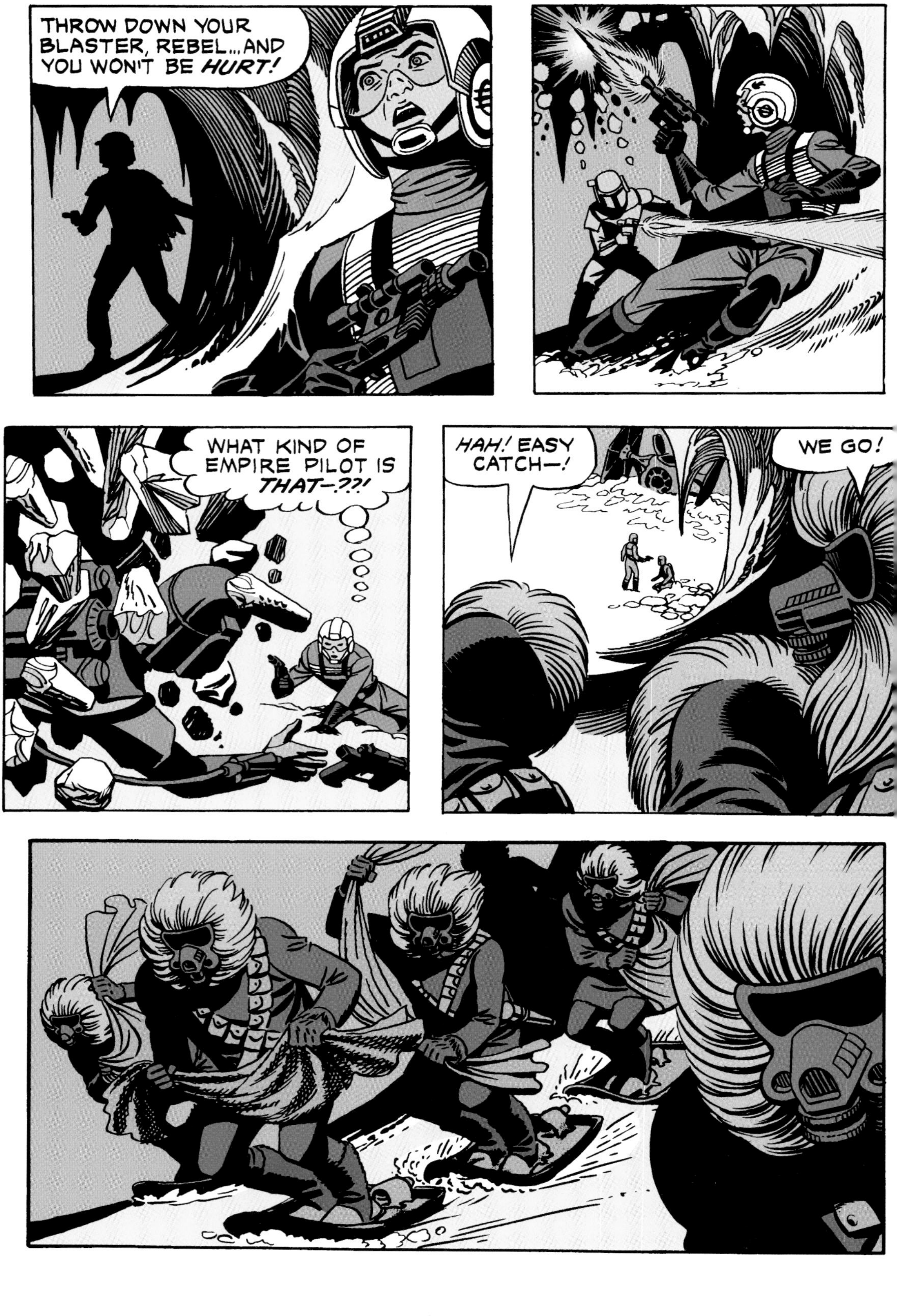
THROW DOWN YOUR BLASTER, REBEL...AND YOU WON'T BE *HURT!*
WHAT KIND OF EMPIRE PILOT IS *THAT-??!*
HAH! EASY CATCH-!
WE GO!

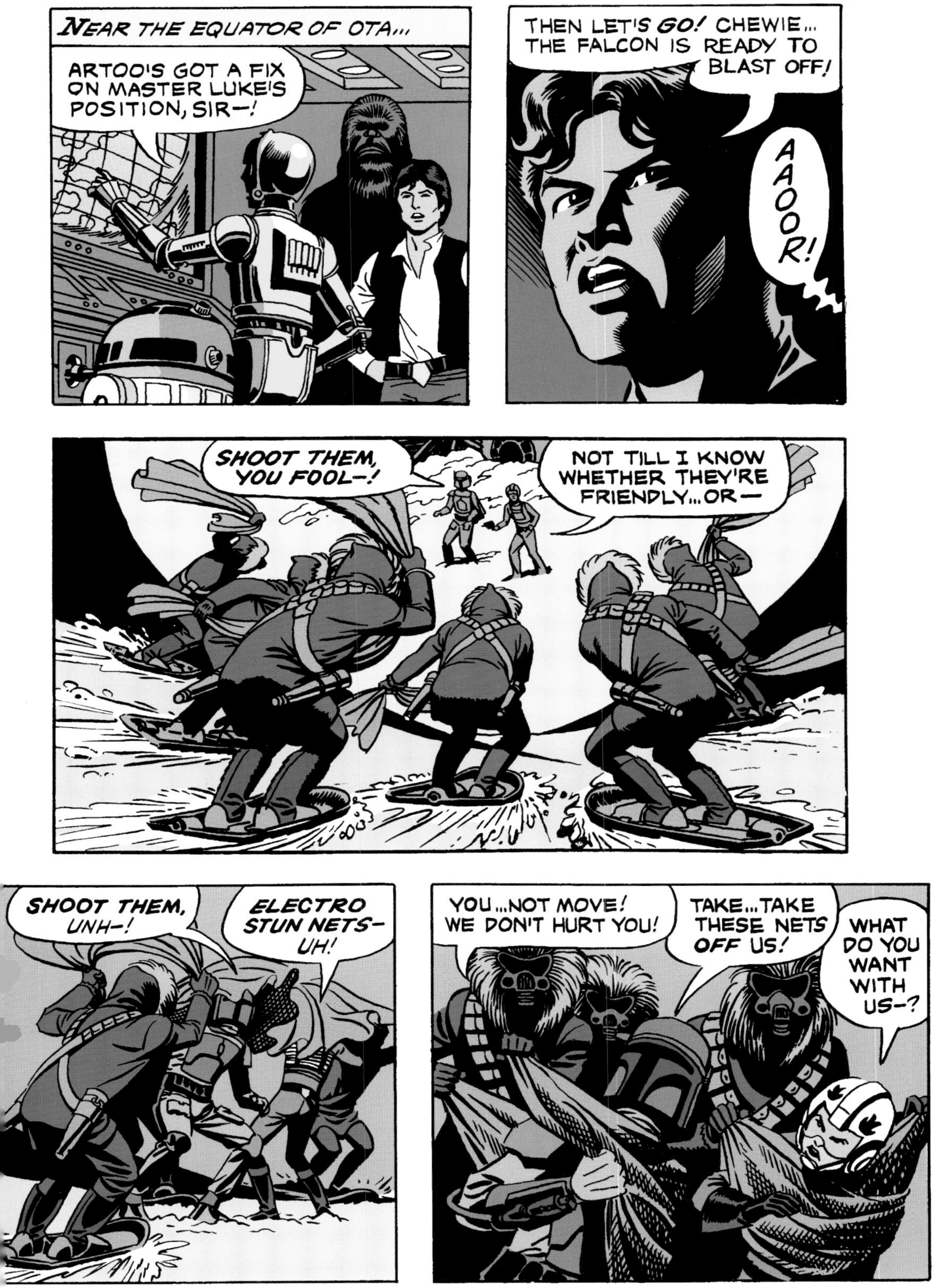
NEAR THE EQUATOR OF OTA...
ARTOO'S GOT A FIX ON MASTER LUKE'S POSITION, SIR—!
THEN LET'S GO! CHEWIE... THE FALCON IS READY TO BLAST OFF!
AAOOR!
SHOOT THEM, YOU FOOL—!
NOT TILL I KNOW WHETHER THEY'RE FRIENDLY...OR—
SHOOT THEM, UNH—!
ELECTRO STUN NETS— UH!
YOU...NOT MOVE! WE DON'T HURT YOU!
TAKE...TAKE THESE NETS OFF US!
WHAT DO YOU WANT WITH US—?

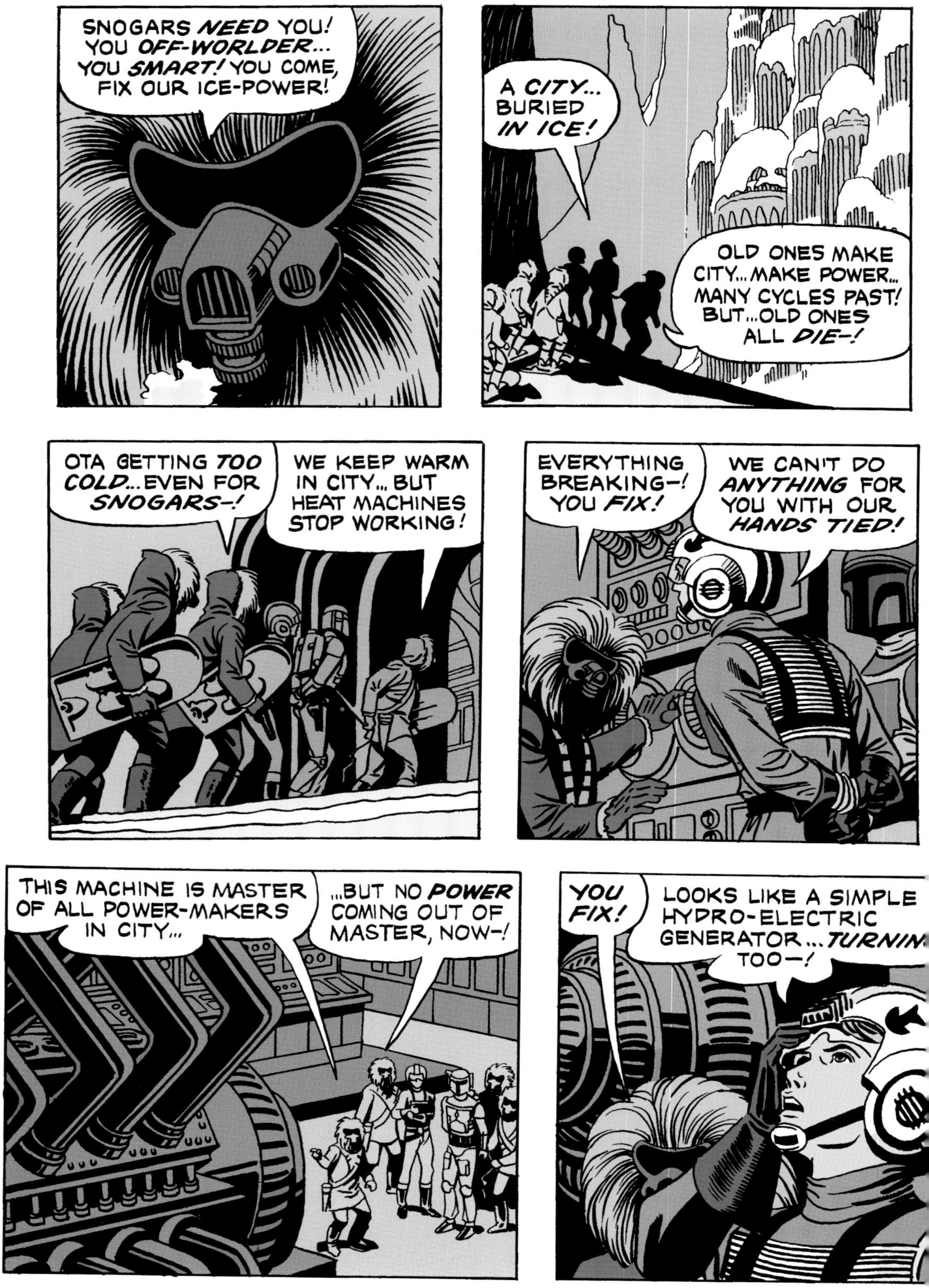

SNOGARS NEED YOU! YOU OFF-WORLDER... YOU SMART! YOU COME, FIX OUR ICE-POWER!
A CITY... BURIED IN ICE!
OLD ONES MAKE CITY... MAKE POWER... MANY CYCLES PAST! BUT...OLD ONES ALL DIE-!
OTA GETTING TOO COLD... EVEN FOR SNOGARS-!
WE KEEP WARM IN CITY... BUT HEAT MACHINES STOP WORKING!
EVERYTHING BREAKING-! YOU FIX!
WE CAN'T DO ANYTHING FOR YOU WITH OUR HANDS TIED!
THIS MACHINE IS MASTER OF ALL POWER-MAKERS IN CITY...
...BUT NO POWER COMING OUT OF MASTER, NOW-!
YOU FIX!
LOOKS LIKE A SIMPLE HYDRO-ELECTRIC GENERATOR... TURNIN TOO-!

GET READY TO BREAK FREE, REBEL! I SEE THE PROBLEM...AND IT'S GOING TO HELP *US*–!

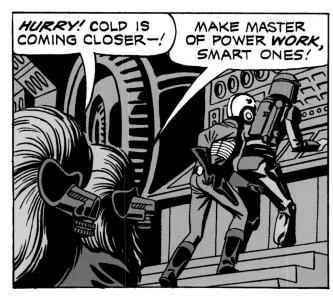

HURRY! COLD IS COMING CLOSER–!

MAKE MASTER OF POWER *WORK*, SMART ONES!

THE OVERLOAD BREAKER HAS TURNED THE GENER-ATOR *OFF!* SOMETHING'S WRONG INSIDE IT–!

EEEEEEEEEEEEEE!

UNLESS YOU WANT TO STAY HERE AND *FREEZE*, REBEL—

...GET READY TO RUN–!

EEEEEEEE

RUN!...FOR THE CITY ENTRANCE–!

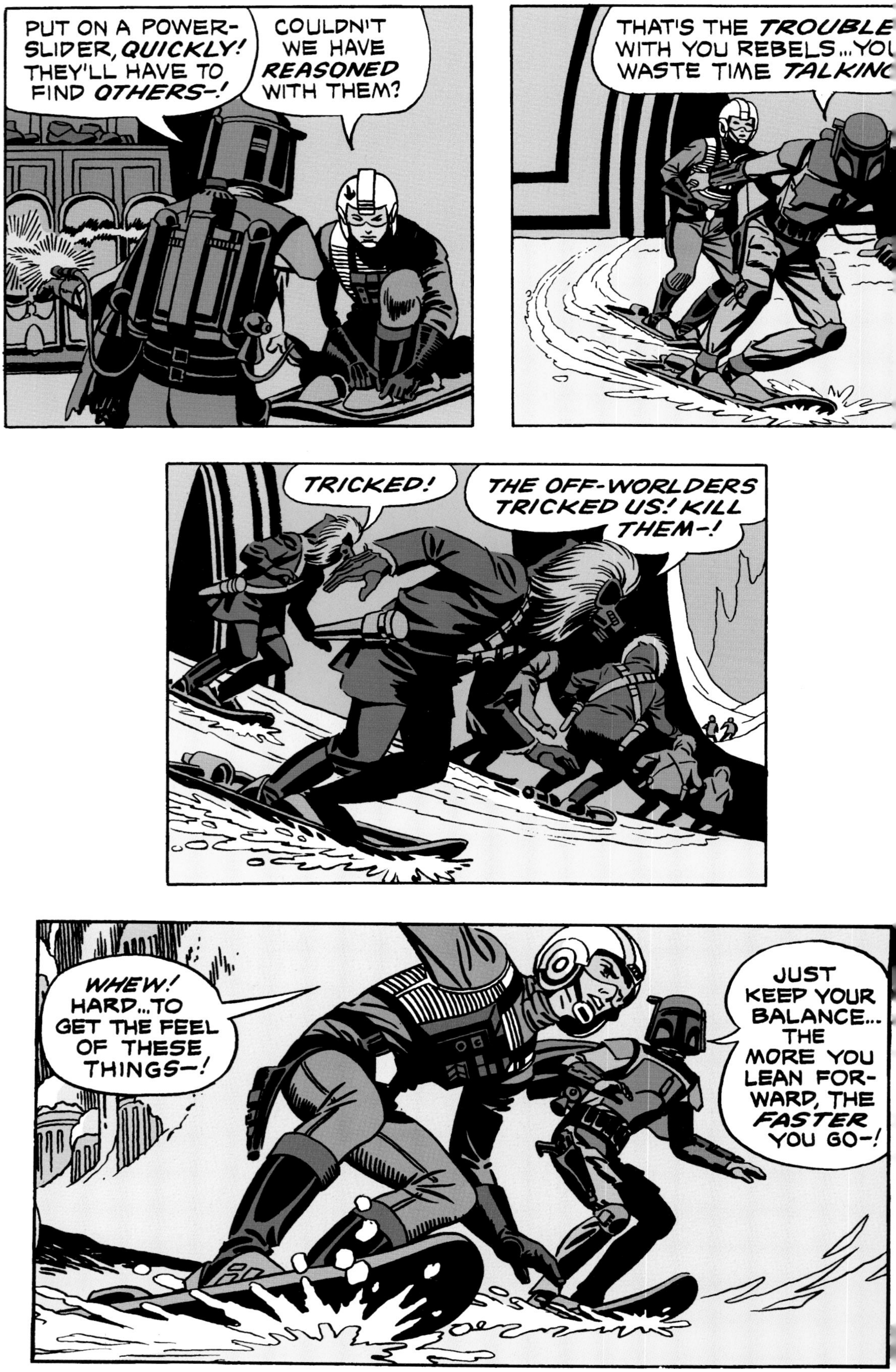
PUT ON A POWER-SLIDER, QUICKLY! THEY'LL HAVE TO FIND OTHERS--!
COULDN'T WE HAVE REASONED WITH THEM?
THAT'S THE TROUBLE WITH YOU REBELS...YOU WASTE TIME TALKIN
TRICKED!
THE OFF-WORLDERS TRICKED US! KILL THEM--!
WHEW! HARD...TO GET THE FEEL OF THESE THINGS--!
JUST KEEP YOUR BALANCE... THE MORE YOU LEAN FORWARD, THE FASTER YOU GO--!

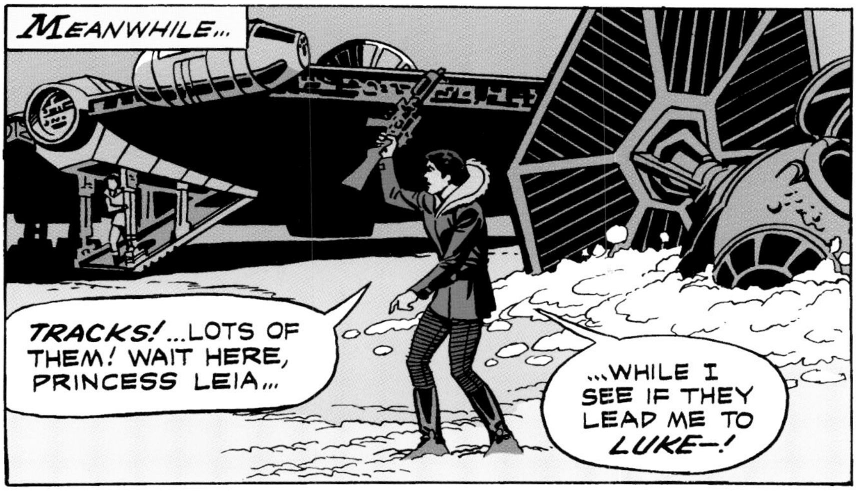
MEANWHILE...
TRACKS! ...LOTS OF THEM! WAIT HERE, PRINCESS LEIA...
...WHILE I SEE IF THEY LEAD ME TO LUKE—!

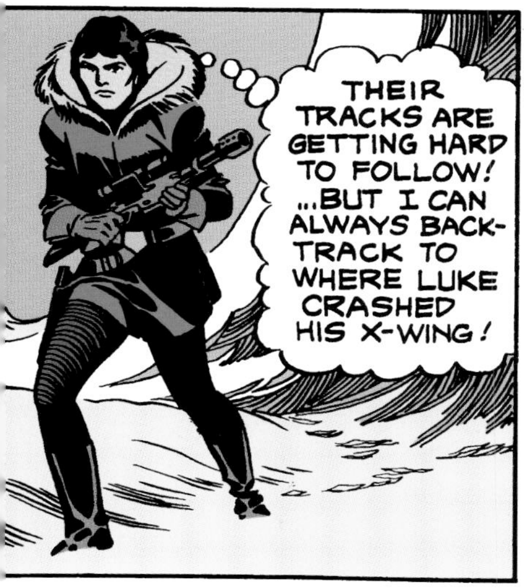
THEIR TRACKS ARE GETTING HARD TO FOLLOW! ...BUT I CAN ALWAYS BACK-TRACK TO WHERE LUKE CRASHED HIS X-WING!

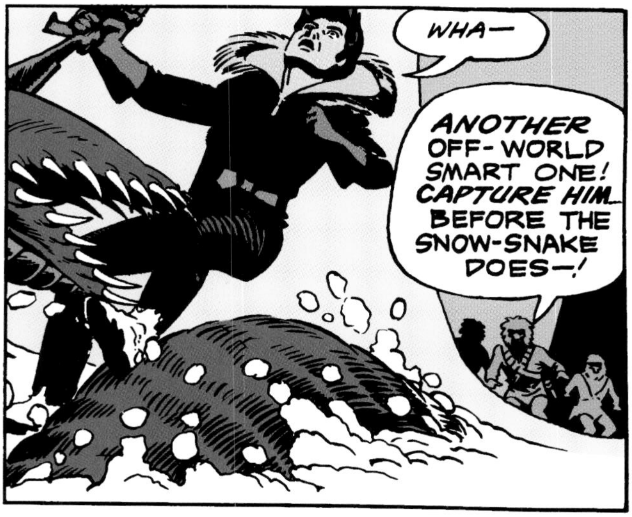
WHA—
ANOTHER OFF-WORLD SMART ONE! CAPTURE HIM BEFORE THE SNOW-SNAKE DOES—!

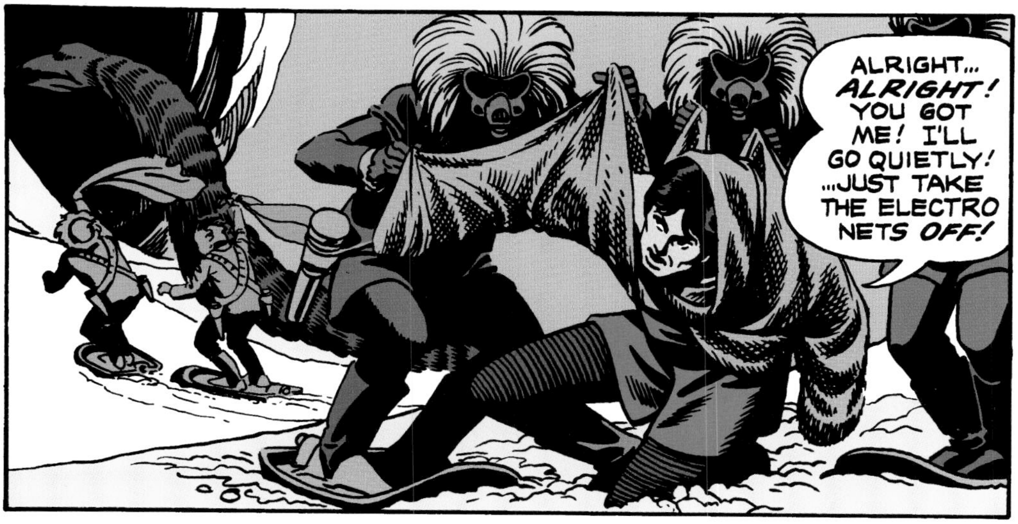
ALRIGHT... ALRIGHT! YOU GOT ME! I'LL GO QUIETLY! ...JUST TAKE THE ELECTRO NETS OFF!

SOMETHING'S WRONG, CHEWIE! HAN SHOULD HAVE FOUND LUKE BY NOW! *GO FIND HAN, CHEWIE...*

...AND PLEASE...BRING HIM...AND LUKE... BACK—!

HEY! THAT'S *HAN SOLO*—! HE MUST'VE BEEN SEARCHING FOR *ME!* C'MON... WE'VE GOT TO *HELP HIM*—!

HAN SOLO! WHAT INCREDIBLE GOOD LUCK—!

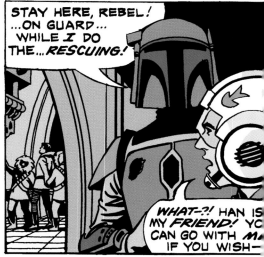

STAY HERE, REBEL! ...ON GUARD... WHILE *I* DO THE...*RESCUING!*

WHAT—?! HAN IS MY *FRIEND!* YO CAN GO WITH M IF YOU WISH—

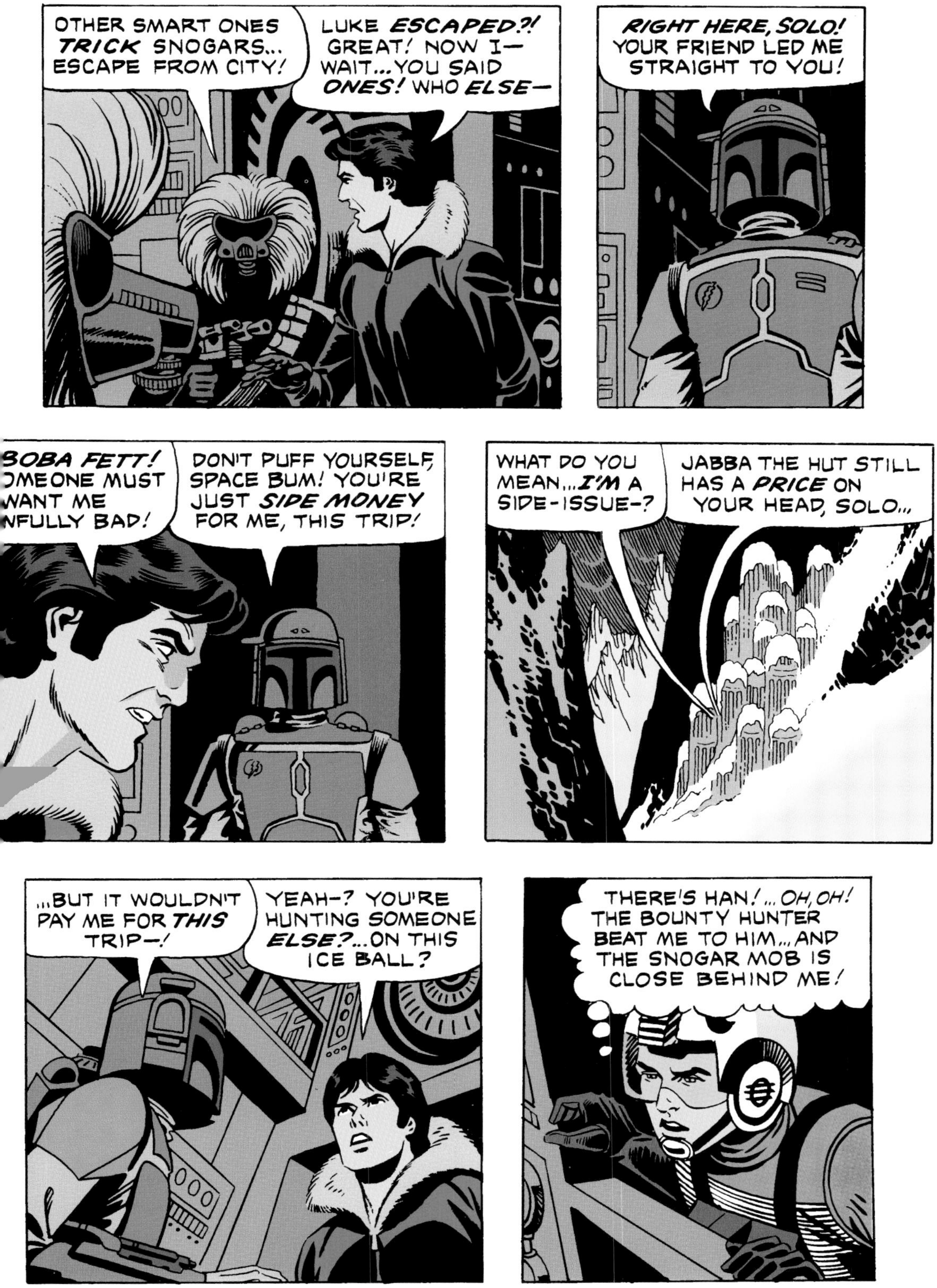
OTHER SMART ONES TRICK SNOGARS... ESCAPE FROM CITY!
LUKE ESCAPED?! GREAT! NOW I— WAIT...YOU SAID ONES! WHO ELSE—
RIGHT HERE, SOLO! YOUR FRIEND LED ME STRAIGHT TO YOU!
BOBA FETT! OMEONE MUST WANT ME NFULLY BAD!
DON'T PUFF YOURSELF, SPACE BUM! YOU'RE JUST SIDE MONEY FOR ME, THIS TRIP!
WHAT DO YOU MEAN...I'M A SIDE-ISSUE-?
JABBA THE HUT STILL HAS A PRICE ON YOUR HEAD, SOLO...
...BUT IT WOULDN'T PAY ME FOR THIS TRIP—!
YEAH-? YOU'RE HUNTING SOMEONE ELSE?...ON THIS ICE BALL?
THERE'S HAN!... OH, OH! THE BOUNTY HUNTER BEAT ME TO HIM...AND THE SNOGAR MOB IS CLOSE BEHIND ME!

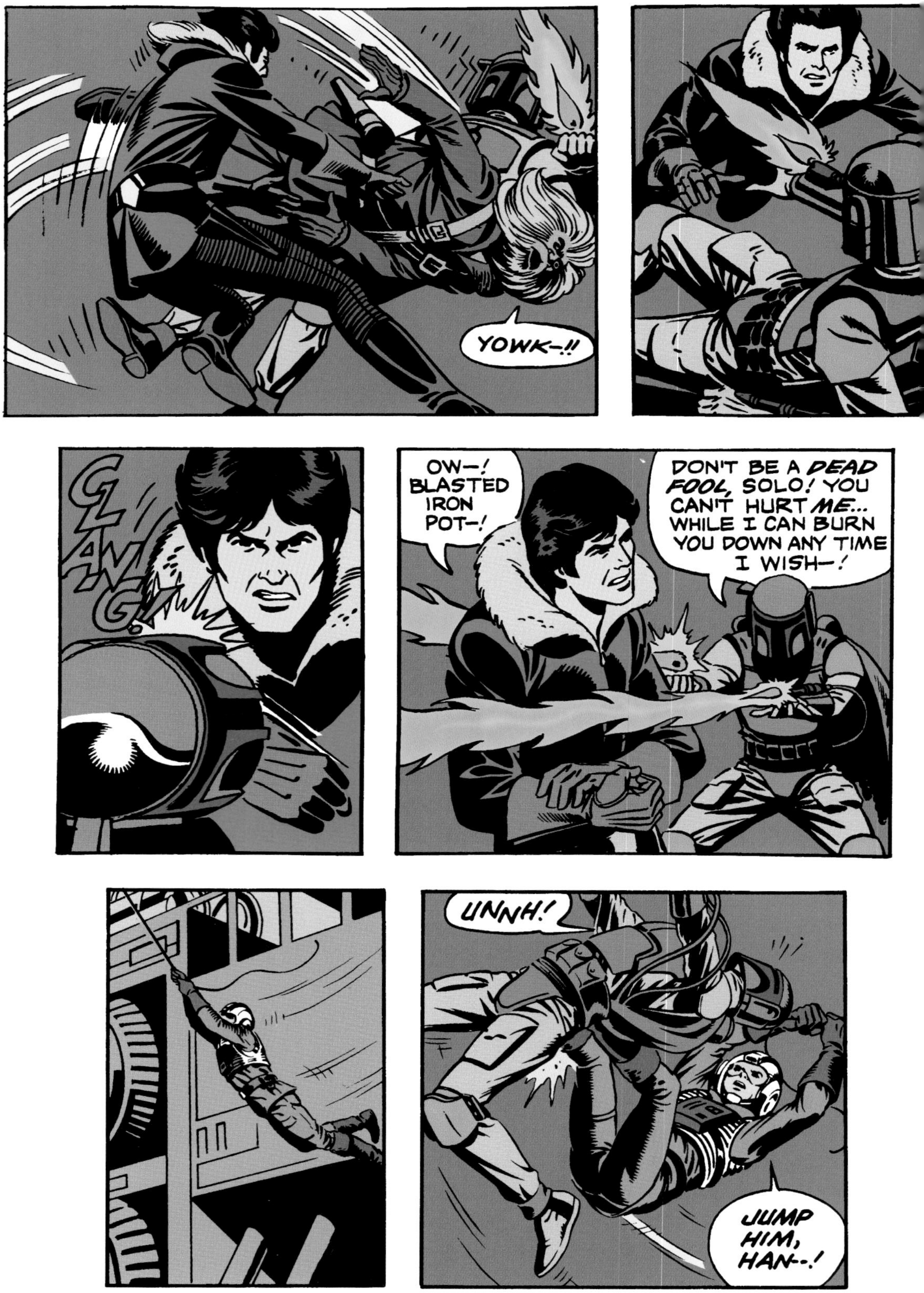
YOWK-!!
CLANG!
OW-! BLASTED IRON POT-!
DON'T BE A DEAD FOOL, SOLO! YOU CAN'T HURT ME... WHILE I CAN BURN YOU DOWN ANY TIME I WISH-!
UNNH!
JUMP HIM, HAN-!

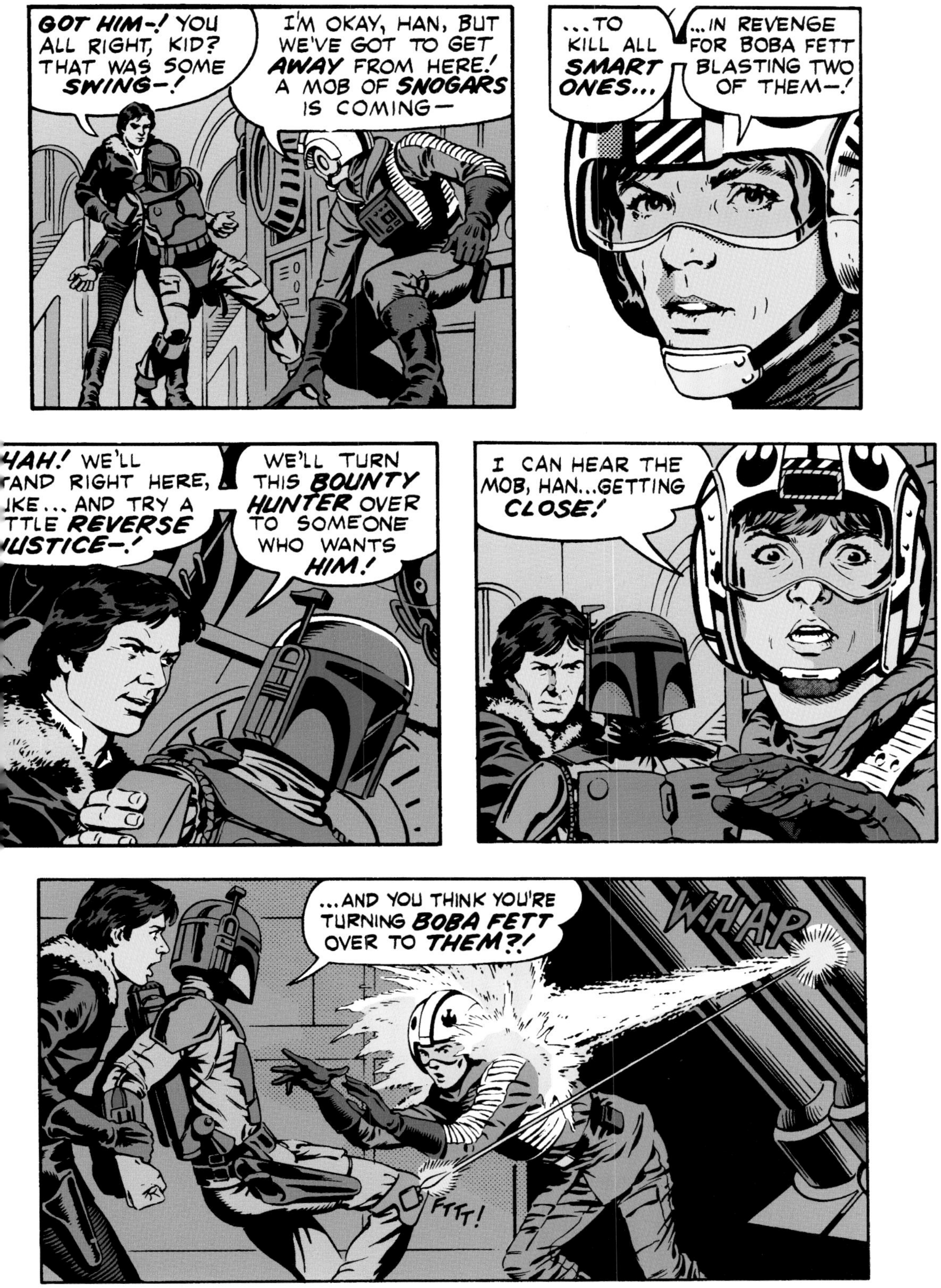
GOT HIM–! YOU ALL RIGHT, KID? THAT WAS SOME SWING–!
I'M OKAY, HAN, BUT WE'VE GOT TO GET AWAY FROM HERE! A MOB OF SNOGARS IS COMING—
...TO KILL ALL SMART ONES...
...IN REVENGE FOR BOBA FETT BLASTING TWO OF THEM–!
AH! WE'LL TAND RIGHT HERE, IKE... AND TRY A TTLE REVERSE USTICE–!
WE'LL TURN THIS BOUNTY HUNTER OVER TO SOMEONE WHO WANTS HIM!
I CAN HEAR THE MOB, HAN...GETTING CLOSE!
...AND YOU THINK YOU'RE TURNING BOBA FETT OVER TO THEM?!
WHAP
FTTT!

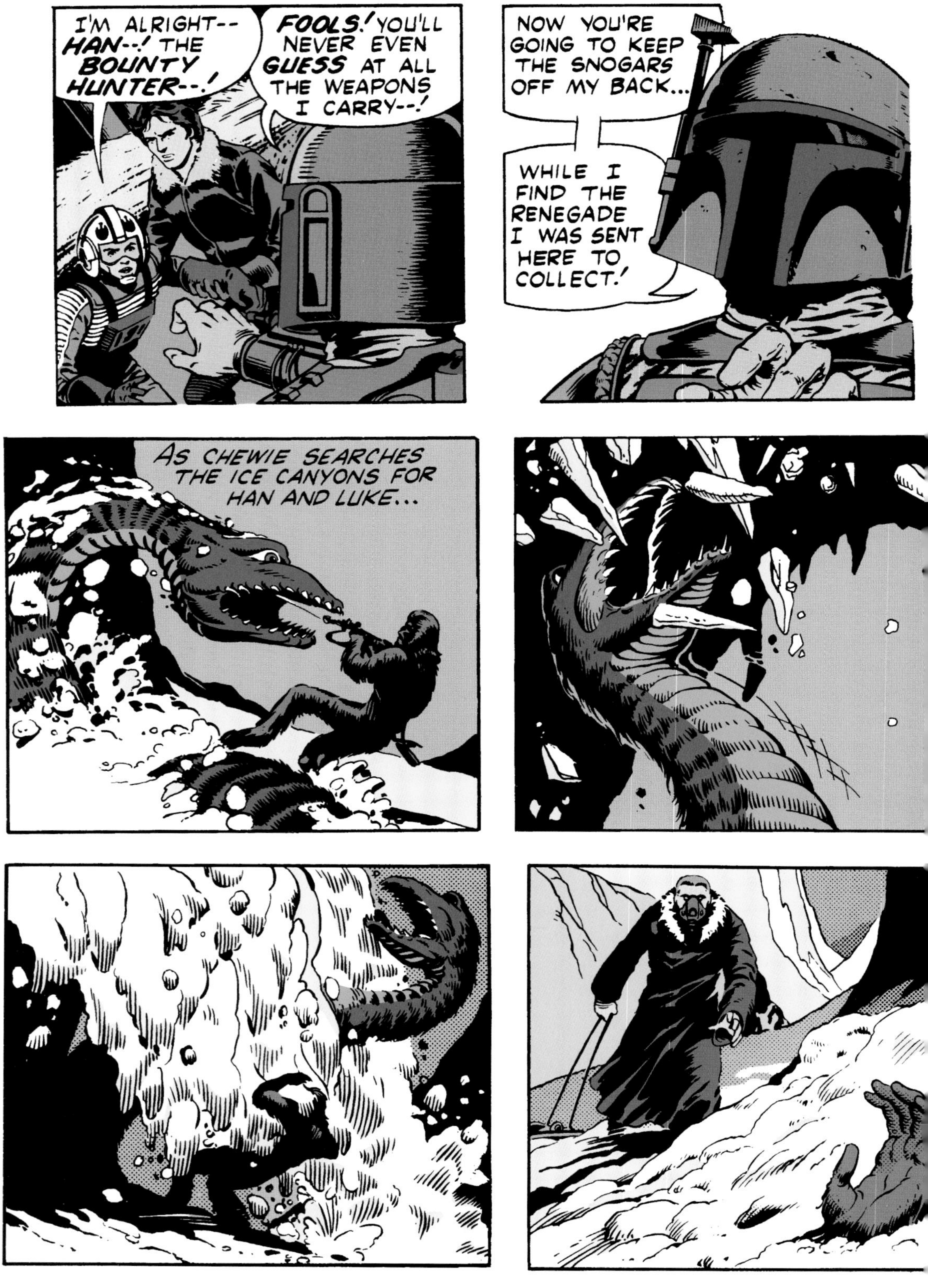
I'M ALRIGHT-- HAN--! THE BOUNTY HUNTER--!
FOOLS! YOU'LL NEVER EVEN GUESS AT ALL THE WEAPONS I CARRY--!
NOW YOU'RE GOING TO KEEP THE SNOGARS OFF MY BACK...
WHILE I FIND THE RENEGADE I WAS SENT HERE TO COLLECT!
AS CHEWIE SEARCHES THE ICE CANYONS FOR HAN AND LUKE...

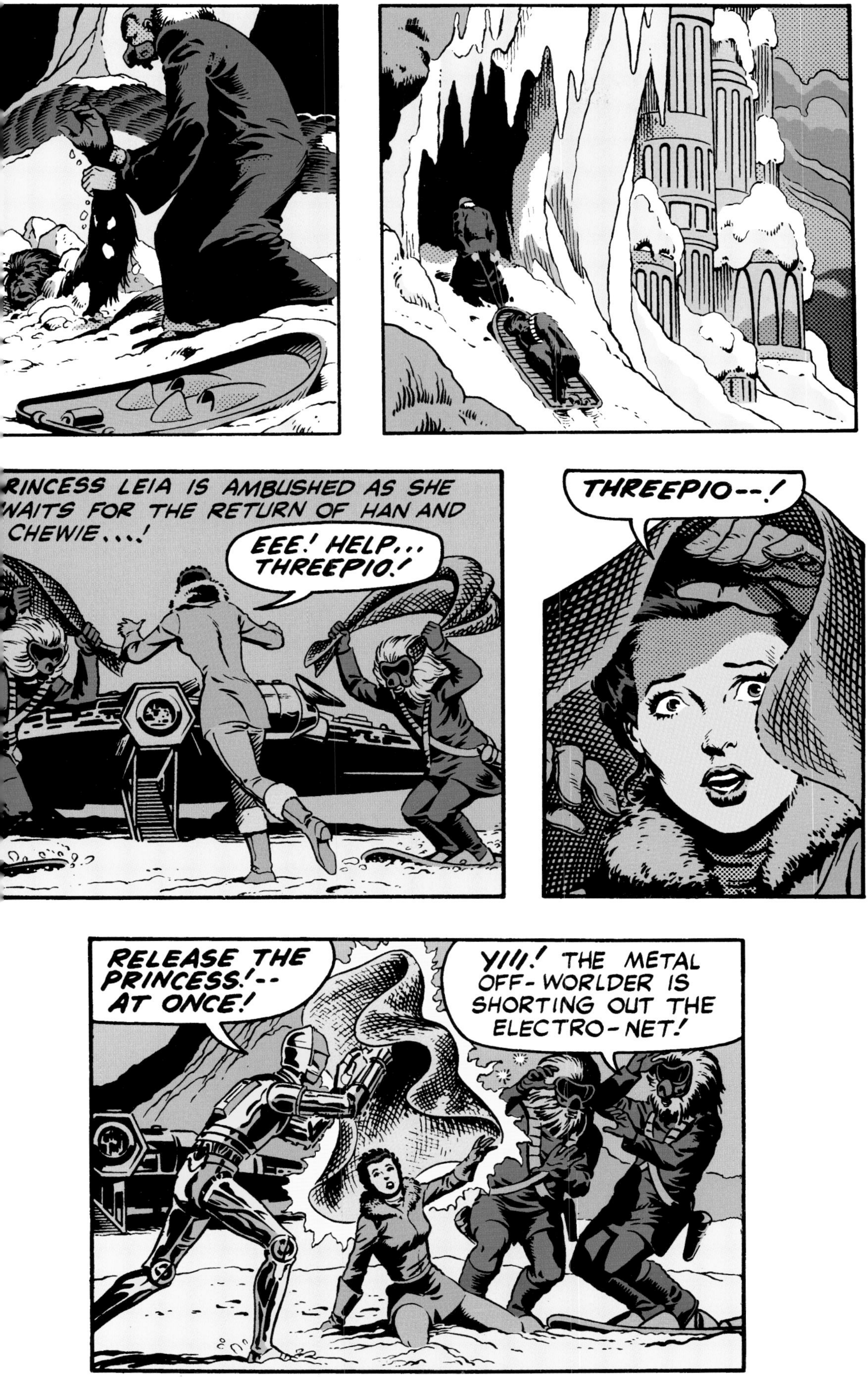
RINCESS LEIA IS AMBUSHED AS SHE WAITS FOR THE RETURN OF HAN AND CHEWIE....!
EEE! HELP... THREEPIO!
THREEPIO--!
RELEASE THE PRINCESS!-- AT ONCE!
YIII! THE METAL OFF-WORLDER IS SHORTING OUT THE ELECTRO-NET!

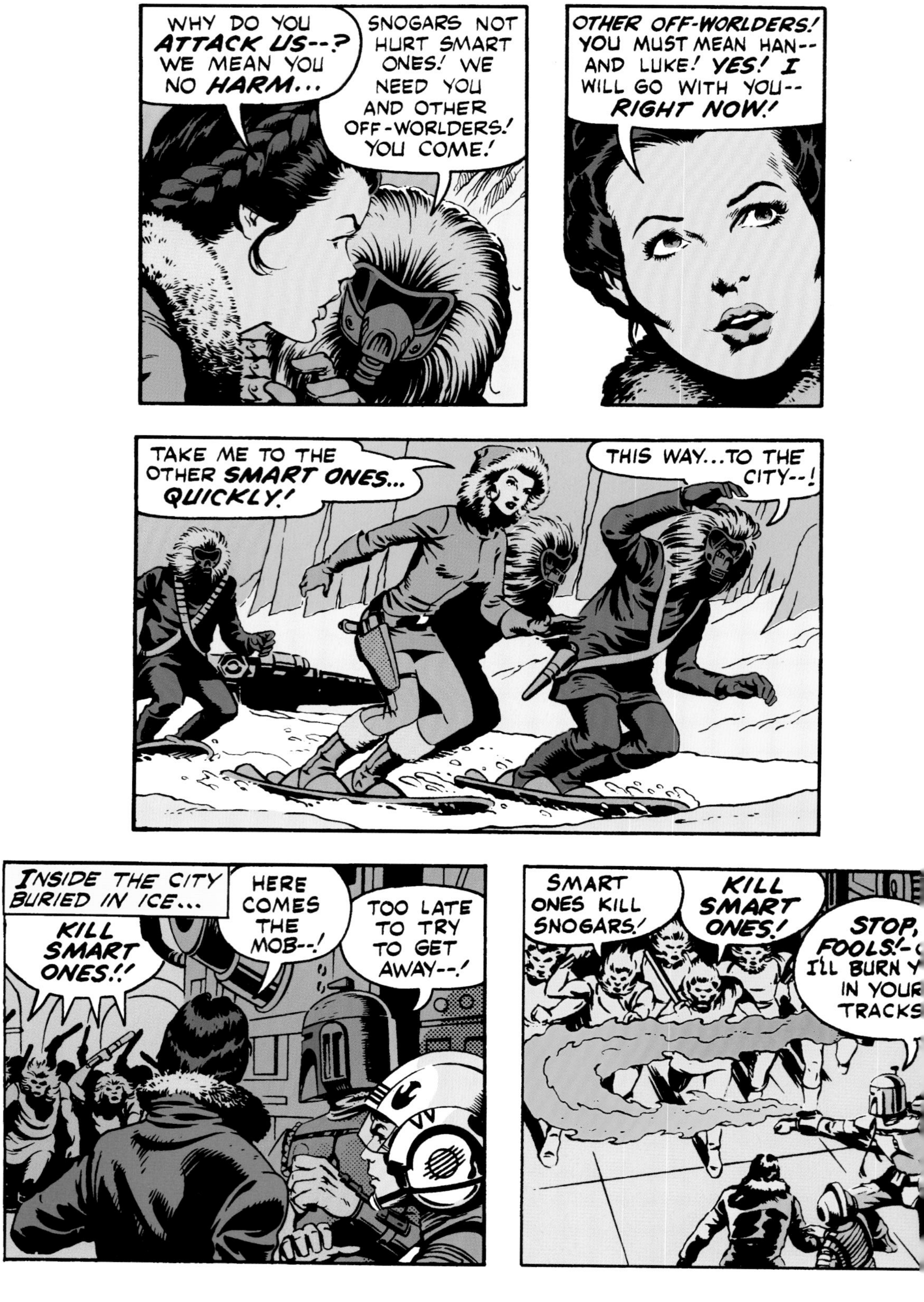
WHY DO YOU ATTACK US--? WE MEAN YOU NO HARM...
SNOGARS NOT HURT SMART ONES! WE NEED YOU AND OTHER OFF-WORLDERS! YOU COME!
OTHER OFF-WORLDERS! YOU MUST MEAN HAN--AND LUKE! YES! I WILL GO WITH YOU--RIGHT NOW!
TAKE ME TO THE OTHER SMART ONES... QUICKLY!
THIS WAY...TO THE CITY--!
INSIDE THE CITY BURIED IN ICE...
KILL SMART ONES!!
HERE COMES THE MOB--!
TOO LATE TO TRY TO GET AWAY--!
SMART ONES KILL SNOGARS!
KILL SMART ONES!
STOP, FOOLS!-- I'LL BURN Y IN YOUR TRACKS

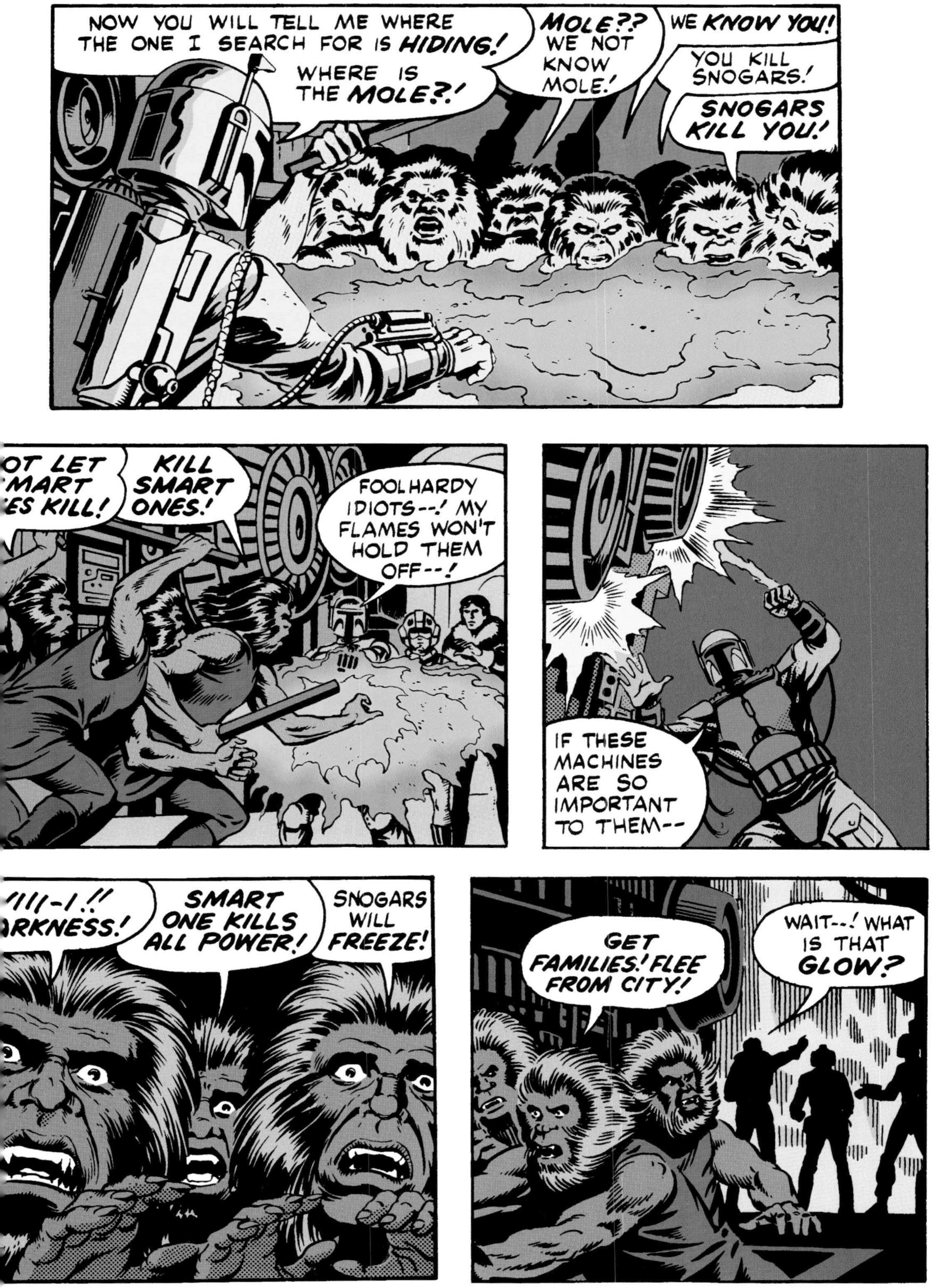

NOW YOU WILL TELL ME WHERE THE ONE I SEARCH FOR IS HIDING!
WHERE IS THE MOLE?!
MOLE?? WE NOT KNOW MOLE!
WE KNOW YOU!
YOU KILL SNOGARS!
SNOGARS KILL YOU!
OT LET MART ES KILL!
KILL SMART ONES!
FOOLHARDY IDIOTS--! MY FLAMES WON'T HOLD THEM OFF--!
IF THESE MACHINES ARE SO IMPORTANT TO THEM--
ARKNESS!
SMART ONE KILLS ALL POWER!
SNOGARS WILL FREEZE!
GET FAMILIES! FLEE FROM CITY!
WAIT--! WHAT IS THAT GLOW?

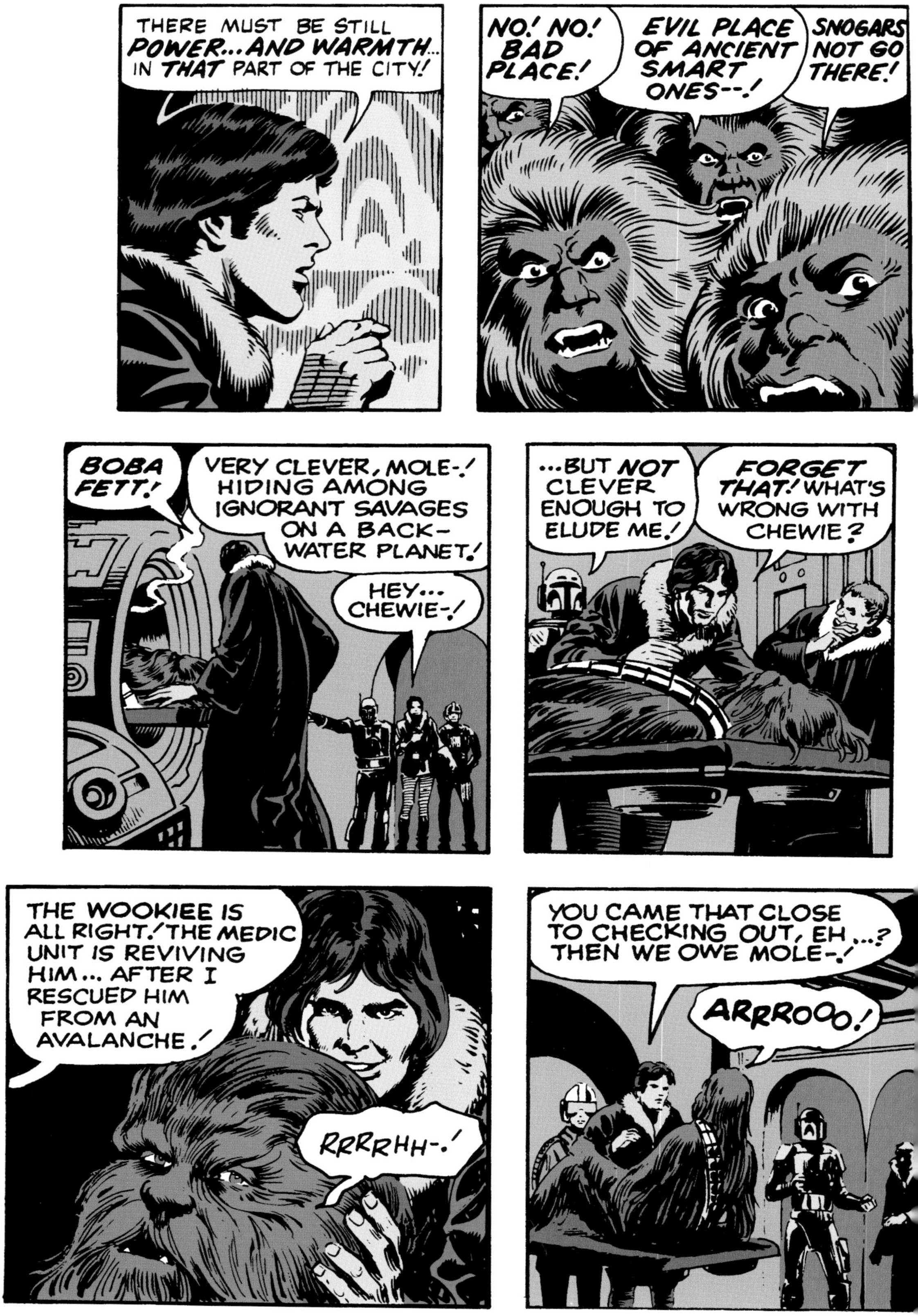

THERE MUST BE STILL POWER... AND WARMTH... IN THAT PART OF THE CITY!
NO! NO! BAD PLACE!
EVIL PLACE OF ANCIENT SMART ONES--!
SNOGARS NOT GO THERE!
BOBA FETT!
VERY CLEVER, MOLE-! HIDING AMONG IGNORANT SAVAGES ON A BACK-WATER PLANET!
HEY... CHEWIE-!
...BUT NOT CLEVER ENOUGH TO ELUDE ME!
FORGET THAT! WHAT'S WRONG WITH CHEWIE?
THE WOOKIEE IS ALL RIGHT! THE MEDIC UNIT IS REVIVING HIM... AFTER I RESCUED HIM FROM AN AVALANCHE!
RRRRHH-!
YOU CAME THAT CLOSE TO CHECKING OUT, EH...? THEN WE OWE MOLE-!
ARRROOO!

YOU RAN OUT ON *LORD VADER* FOR *THIS?* HIDING IN RUINS... NURSING WOOKIEES.'

I'LL NEVER SPY FOR *DARTH VADER* AGAIN... NOR FOR ANYONE ELSE! YOU'RE WASTING YOUR TIME, FETT! I'LL NEVER RETURN TO SERVE THE EMPIRE!

I KNEW I COULDN'T HIDE FROM VADER *FOREVER* BUT NOBODY WILL EVER TAKE ME BACK TO HIS *SWEET MERCY!*

YOU ARE A *TRAITOR* MOLE... AND YOU KNOW THE PENALTY FOR TRAITORS! LORD VADER WANTS YOU... ALIVE!... JUST AS I INTEND TO DELIVER YOU!

AND WE'RE LEAVING NOW! YOU'RE COMING TOO, SOLO! JABBA THE HUTT WILL PAY ME A COUPLE CREDITS FOR YOUR HIDE!

YOU KNOW THIS CITY, MOLE! GUIDE US STRAIGHT TO A QUICK EXIT... AND NOTHING *CUTE.* UNDERSTAND?

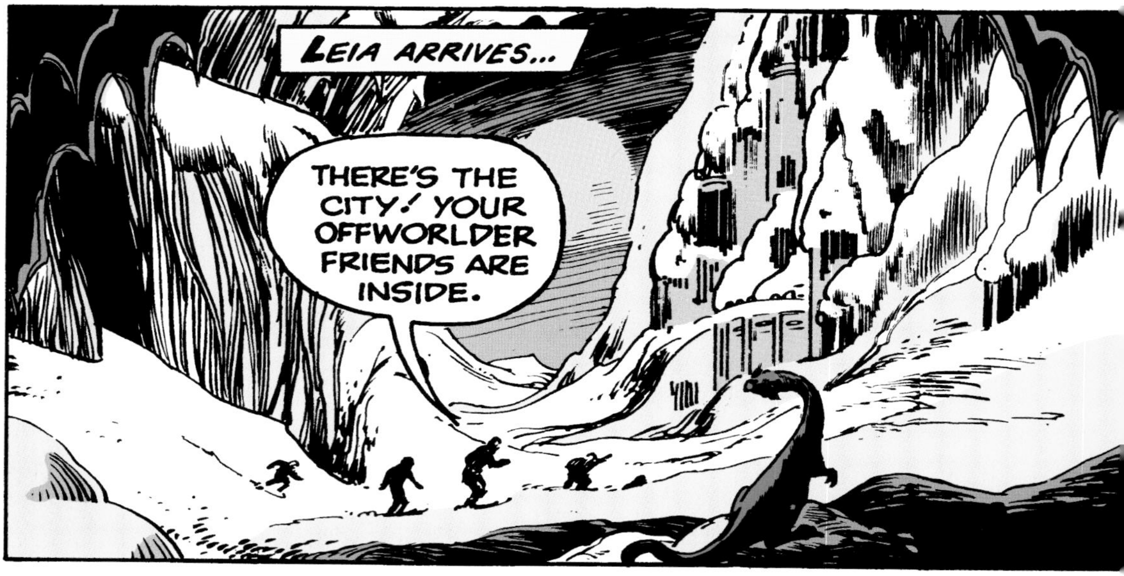
LEIA ARRIVES...
THERE'S THE CITY! YOUR OFFWORLDER FRIENDS ARE INSIDE.

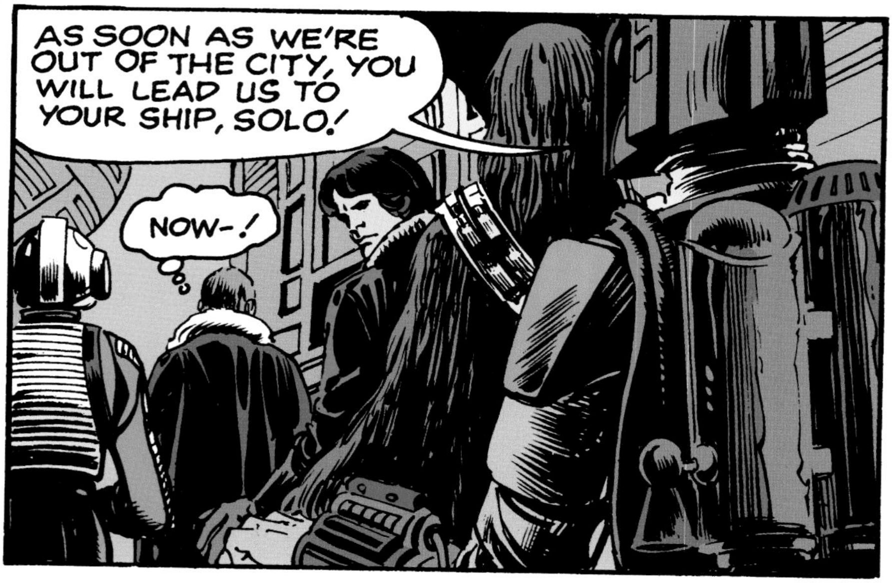
AS SOON AS WE'RE OUT OF THE CITY, YOU WILL LEAD US TO YOUR SHIP, SOLO!
NOW-!

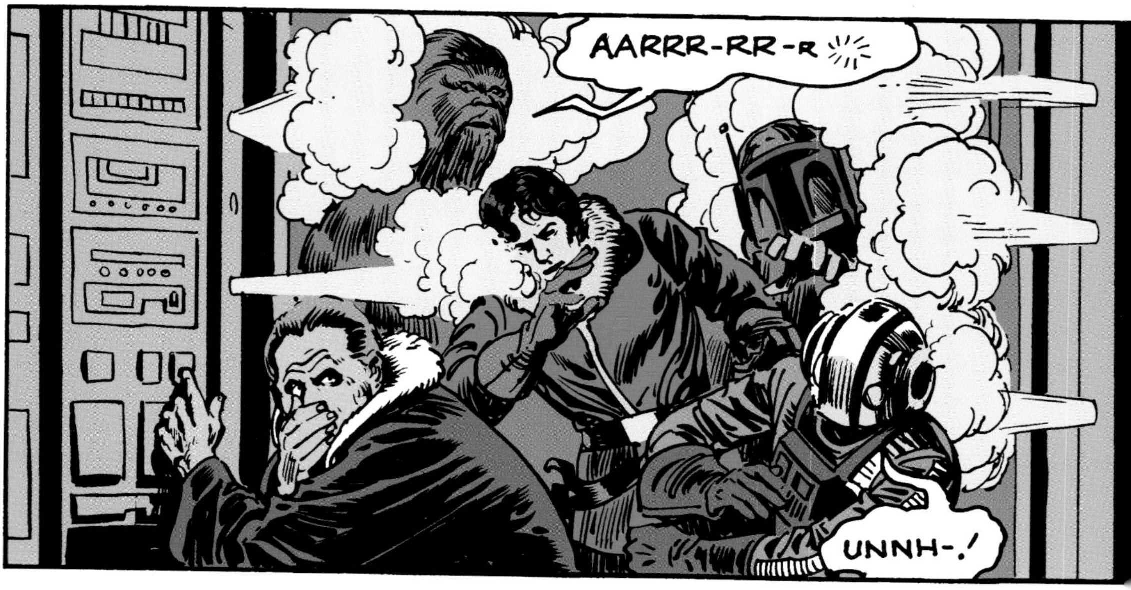
AARRR-RR-R
UNNH-!

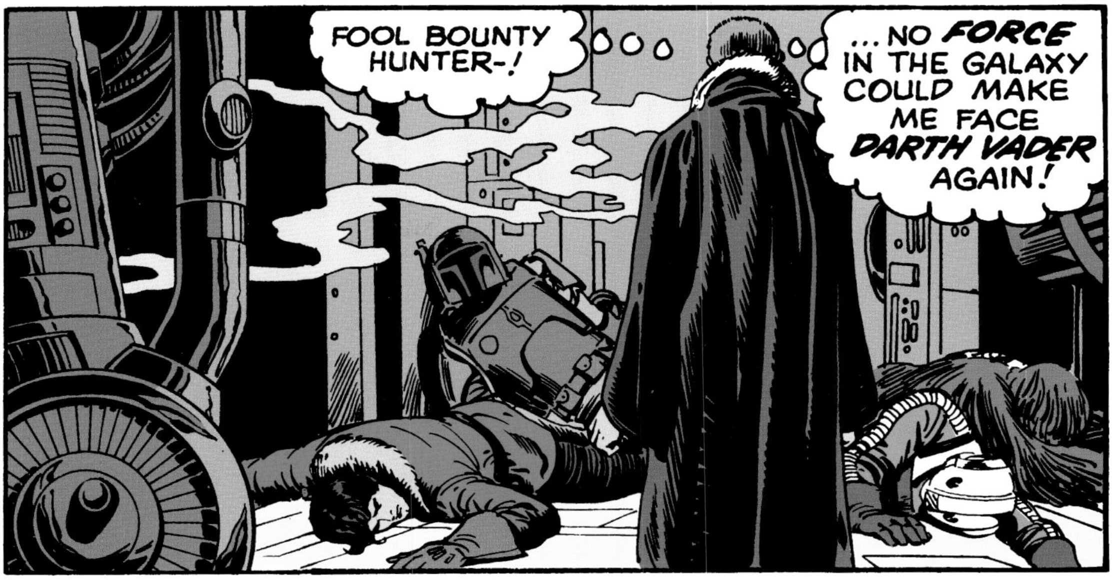
FOOL BOUNTY HUNTER-!
...NO FORCE IN THE GALAXY COULD MAKE ME FACE DARTH VADER AGAIN!

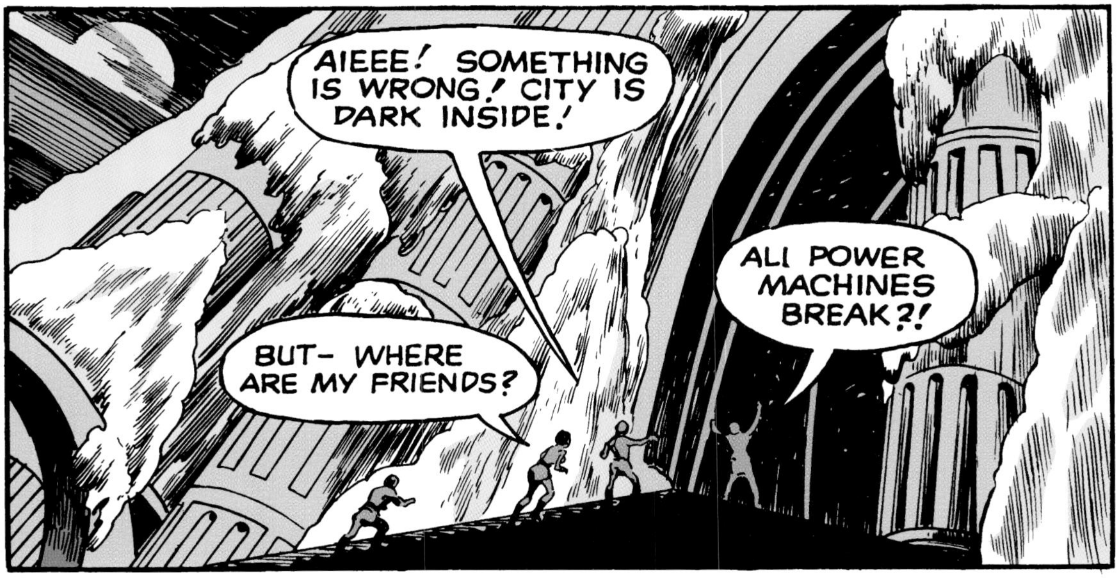
AIEEE! SOMETHING IS WRONG! CITY IS DARK INSIDE!
ALI POWER MACHINES BREAK?!
BUT- WHERE ARE MY FRIENDS?

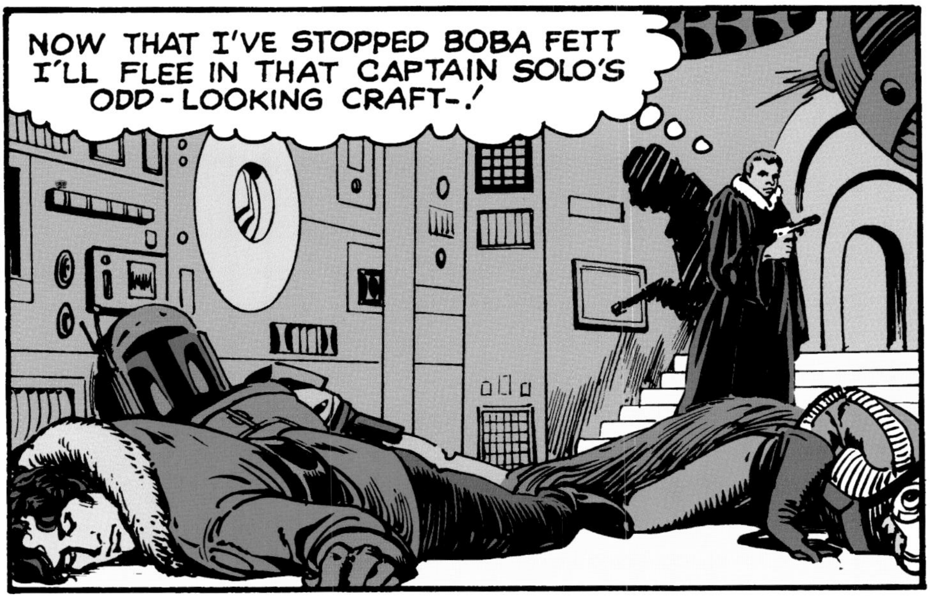
NOW THAT I'VE STOPPED BOBA FETT I'LL FLEE IN THAT CAPTAIN SOLO'S ODD-LOOKING CRAFT-!

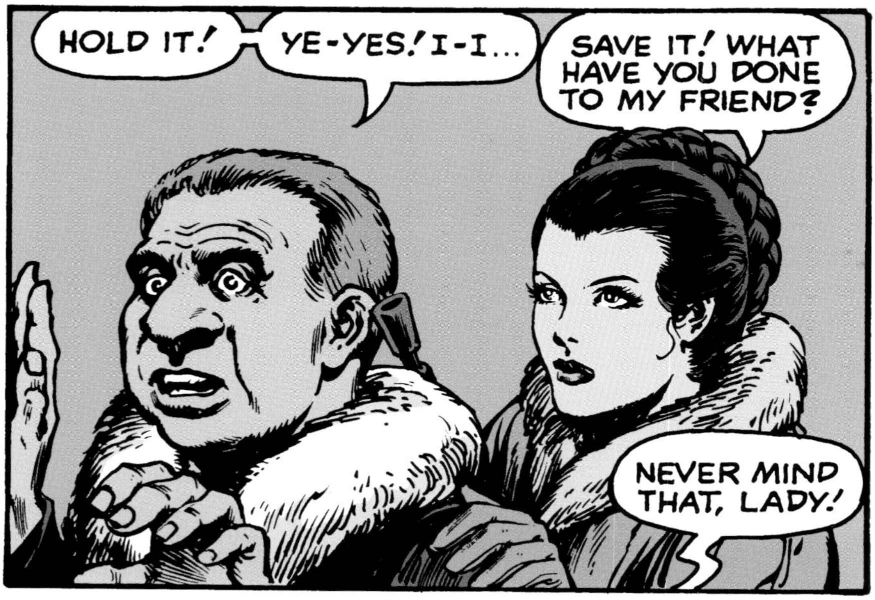
HOLD IT!
YE-YES! I-I...
SAVE IT! WHAT HAVE YOU DONE TO MY FRIEND?
NEVER MIND THAT, LADY!

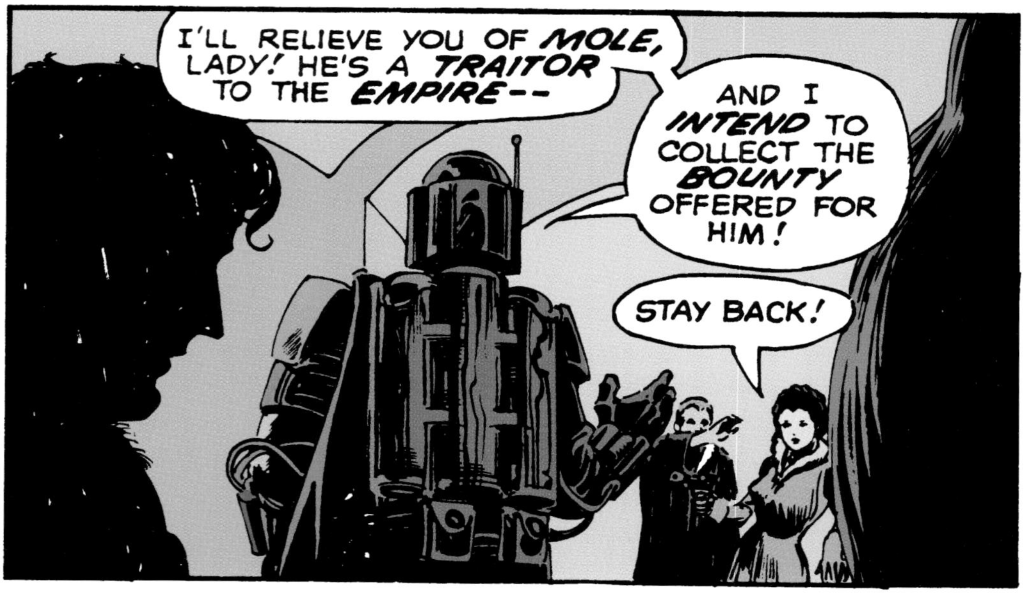
I'LL RELIEVE YOU OF MOLE, LADY! HE'S A TRAITOR TO THE EMPIRE--
AND I INTEND TO COLLECT THE BOUNTY OFFERED FOR HIM!
STAY BACK!

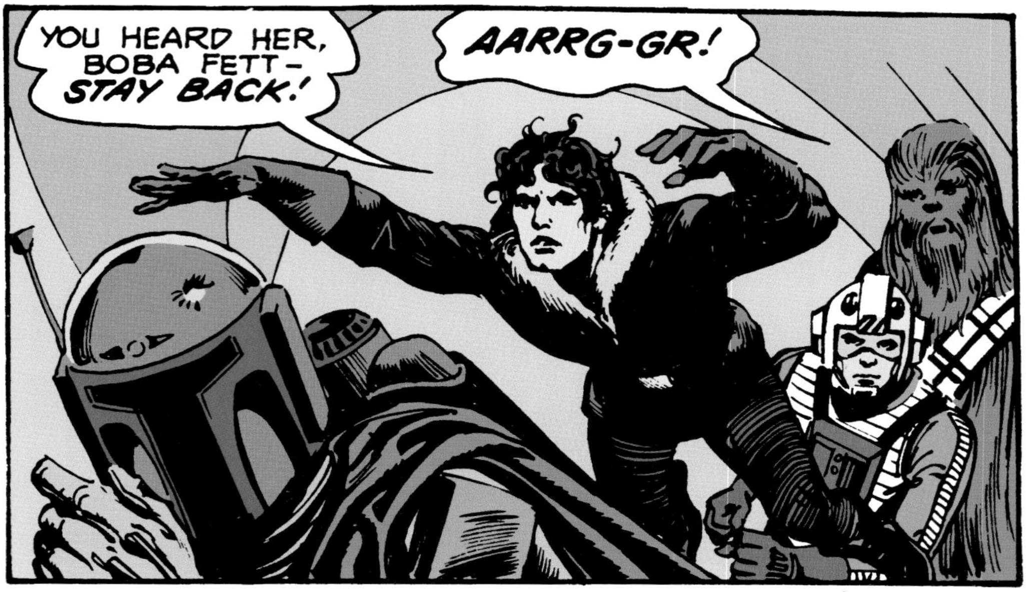
YOU HEARD HER, BOBA FETT- STAY BACK!
AARRG-GR!

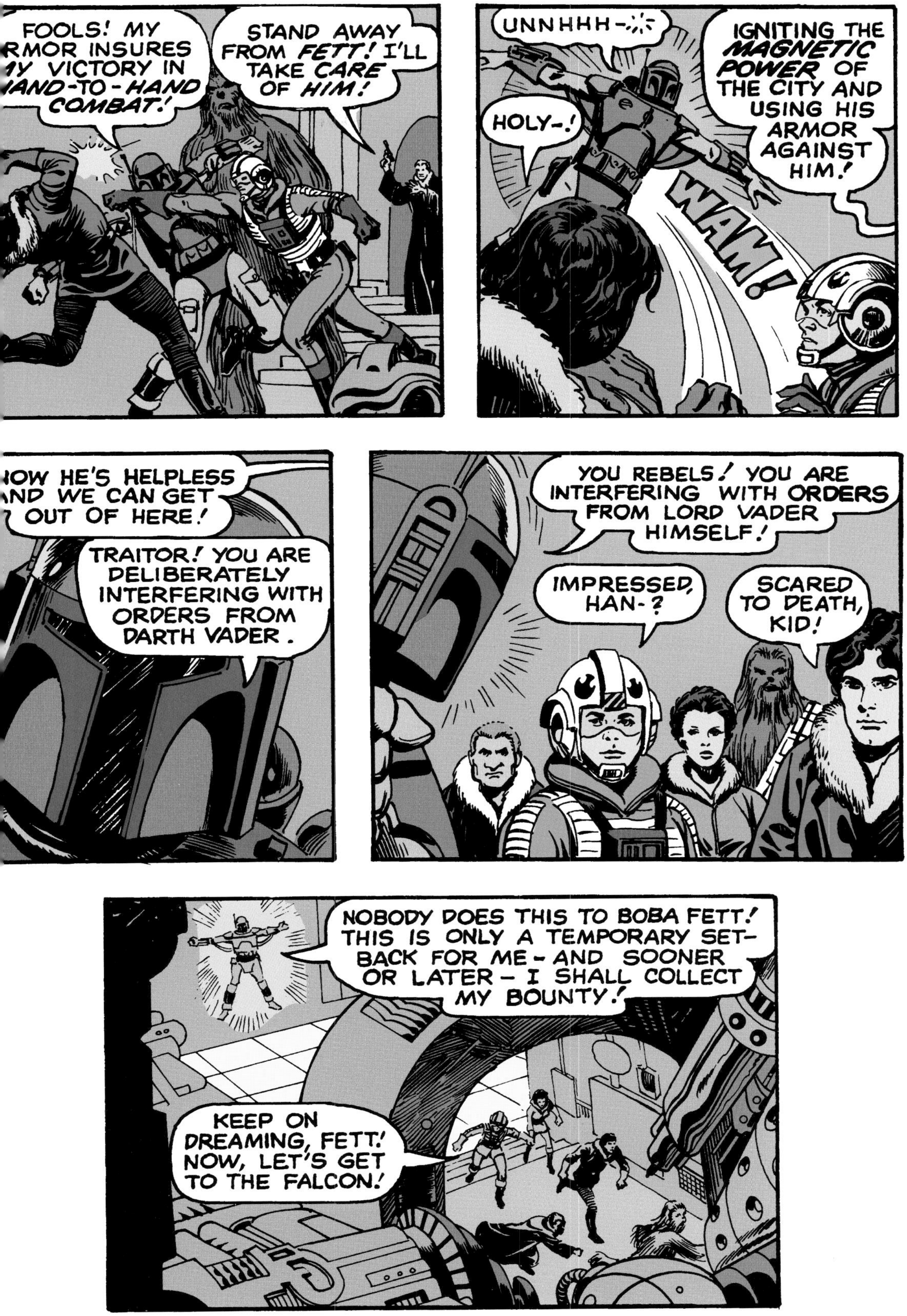
FOOLS! MY RMOR INSURES Y VICTORY IN AND-TO-HAND COMBAT!
STAND AWAY FROM FETT! I'LL TAKE CARE OF HIM!
UNNHHH-
HOLY-!
IGNITING THE MAGNETIC POWER OF THE CITY AND USING HIS ARMOR AGAINST HIM!
WAM!
OW HE'S HELPLESS ND WE CAN GET OUT OF HERE!
TRAITOR! YOU ARE DELIBERATELY INTERFERING WITH ORDERS FROM DARTH VADER.
YOU REBELS! YOU ARE INTERFERING WITH ORDERS FROM LORD VADER HIMSELF!
IMPRESSED, HAN-?
SCARED TO DEATH, KID!
NOBODY DOES THIS TO BOBA FETT! THIS IS ONLY A TEMPORARY SET-BACK FOR ME - AND SOONER OR LATER - I SHALL COLLECT MY BOUNTY!
KEEP ON DREAMING, FETT! NOW, LET'S GET TO THE FALCON!

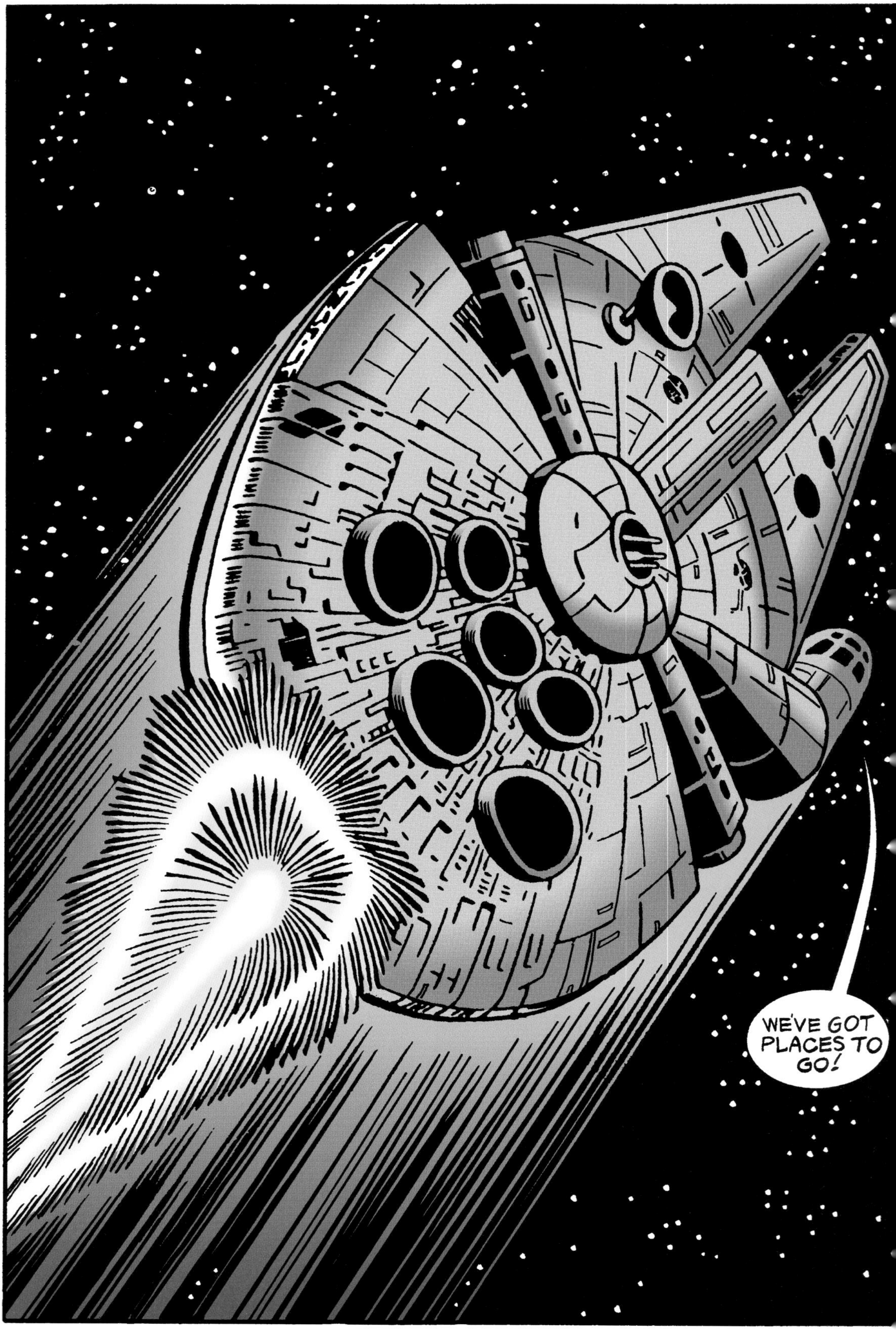
WE'VE GOT PLACES TO GO!

CLASSIC STAR WARS® COVER GALLERY

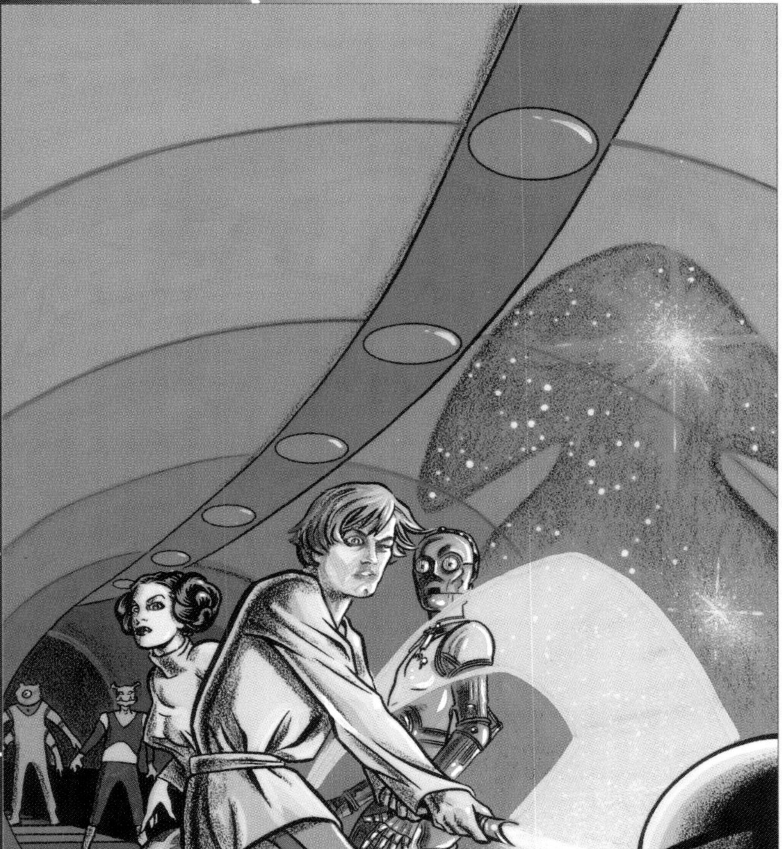
ALL RED 1994

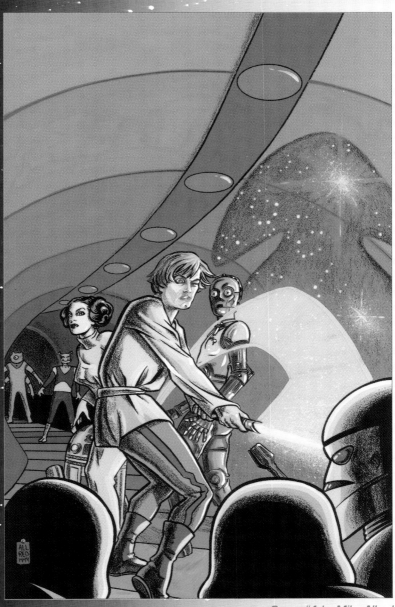

Cover #1 by Mike Allred

Cover #2 pencils by Rick Hoberg, inks by Mike Grell, colors by Matthew Hollingsworth

Cover #3 by Eric Shanower, colors by Matthew Hollingsworth

*Cover #4 by Rick Hoberg,
colors by Matthew Hollingsworth*

*Cover #5 pencils by Rick Hoberg,
inks by Jimmy Palmiotti,
colors by Matthew Hollingsworth*

Cover #6 by Eric Shanower,
colors by Matthew Hollingsworth

Cover #7, pencils by Rick Hoberg,
inks by Mischa McDowell,
colors by Matthew Hollingsworth

Cover #8 by Kilian Plunkett,
colors by Matthew Hollingsworth

Cover #9 by Kilian Plunkett,
colors by Matthew Hollingsworth

CLASSIC STAR WARS
Based on the classic newspaper strips . . .
VOLUME ONE: IN DEADLY PURSUIT
Goodwin • Williamson
192-page color paperback
ISBN: 1-56971-109-7 $16.95
VOLUME TWO: THE REBEL STORM
Goodwin • Williamson
208-page color paperback
ISBN: 1-56971-106-2 $16.95
VOLUME THREE: ESCAPE TO HOTH
Goodwin • Williamson
192-page color paperback
ISBN: 1-56971-093-7 $16.95
VOLUME FOUR: THE EARLY ADVENTURES
Manning • Hoberg
240-page color paperback
ISBN: 1-56971-178-x $19.95
Based on the movie trilogy . . .
A NEW HOPE
Thomas • Chaykin
104-page color paperback
ISBN: 1-56971-086-4 $9.95
A NEW HOPE
The Special Edition
Jones • Barreto • Williamson
104-page color paperback
ISBN: 1-56971-213-1 $9.95
THE EMPIRE STRIKES BACK
Goodwin • Williamson
104-page color paperback
ISBN: 1-56971-088-0 $9.95
THE EMPIRE STRIKES BACK
The Special Edition
Goodwin • Williamson
104-page color paperback
ISBN: 1-56971-234-4 $9.95
RETURN OF THE JEDI
Goodwin • Williamson
104-page color paperback
ISBN: 1-56971-087-2 $9.95
RETURN OF THE JEDI
The Special Edition
Goodwin • Williamson
104-page color paperback
ISBN: 1-56971-235-2 $9.95

DARK EMPIRE
Veitch • Kennedy
184-page color paperback
ISBN: 1-56971-073-2 $17.95

DARK EMPIRE II
Veitch • Kennedy
168-page color paperback
ISBN: 1-56971-119-4 $17.95

DARK FORCES
SOLDIER FOR THE EMPIRE
Dietz • Williams
128-page color hardcover
ISBN: 1-56971-155-0 $24.95

DROIDS
THE KALARBA ADVENTURES
Thorsland • Windham • Gibson
200-page color paperback
ISBN: 1-56971-064-3 $17.95
REBELLION
Windham • Gibson
112-page color paperback
ISBN: 1-56971-224-7 $14.95

HEIR TO THE EMPIRE
Baron • Vatine • Blanchard
160-page color paperback
ISBN: 1-56971-202-6 $19.95

SHADOWS OF THE EMPIRE
Wagner • Plunkett • Russell
160-page color paperback
ISBN: 1-56971-183-6 $17.95

SPLINTER OF THE MIND'S EYE
Austin • Sprouse
112-page color paperback
ISBN: 1-56971-223-9 $14.95

TALES OF THE JEDI
DARK LORDS OF THE SITH
Veitch • Anderson • Gossett
160-page color paperback
ISBN: 1-56971-095-3 $17.95
KNIGHTS OF THE OLD REPUBLIC
Veitch • Gossett
136-page color paperback
ISBN: 1-56971-020-1 $14.95
THE SITH WAR
Anderson • Carrasco
152-page color paperback
ISBN: 1-56971-173-9 $17.95